DB2®:
The Complete Reference

About the Authors

Roman B. Melnyk, Ph.D., is a senior member of the DB2 Information Development team, specializing in database administration and DB2 utilities. During more than seven years at IBM, Roman has written numerous DB2 books and other related materials. Roman recently coauthored *DB2 for Dummies* (IDG Books, 2000), and *DB2 Fundamentals Certification for Dummies* (Hungry Minds, 2001). Roman wrote chapters about SQL. You can reach him at roman_b_melnyk@hotmail.com.

Paul C. Zikopoulos, B.A., M.B.A., is a Database Specialist with the IBM Global Sales Support team. He has more than six years of experience with DB2 and has written numerous magazine articles and books about DB2. He has written articles for such magazines as *DB2 Magazine, Linux Journal, DB2 Update, IDUG Solutions Journal*, and more. Recently, Paul coauthored *DBA's Guide to Databases on Linux* (Syngress, 2000), *DB2 for Dummies* (IDG Books, 2000) and *DB2 Fundamentals Certification for Dummies* (Hungry Minds, 2001). Paul is a DB2 Certified Advanced Technical Expert (DRDA and Cluster/EEE) and a DB2 Certified Solutions Expert (Business Intelligence and Database Administration). Paul wrote chapters about installation and connectivity. You can reach him at paulz_ibm@yahoo.com.

DB2®:
The Complete Reference

Roman B. Melnyk
Paul C. Zikopoulos

Osborne/**McGraw-Hill**

New York   Chicago   San Francisco
Lisbon   London   Madrid   Mexico City
Milan   New Delhi   San Juan
Seoul   Singapore   Sydney   Toronto

Osborne/**McGraw-Hill**
2600 Tenth Street
Berkeley, California 94710
U.S.A.

To arrange bulk purchase discounts for sales promotions, premiums, or fund-raisers, please contact Osborne/**McGraw-Hill** at the above address. For information on translations or book distributors outside the U.S.A., please see the International Contact Information page immediately following the index of this book.

DB2: The Complete Reference

234567890 DOC DOC 0198765432

ISBN 0-07-213344-9

Publisher
   Brandon A. Nordin

Vice President & Associate Publisher
   Scott Rogers

Acquisitions Editor
   Michael Sprague

Project Editor
   Lisa Wolters-Broder

Acquisitions Coordinator
   Paulina Pobocha

Developmental Editor
   Andy Carroll

Copy Editor
   Chrisa Hotchkiss

Proofreaders
   Brian Galloway
   Susie Elkind

Indexer
   Valerie Perry

Computer Designers
   Carie Abrew
   Roberta Steele

Illustrators
   Michael Mueller
   Lyssa Wald

Series Design
   Peter F. Hancik

This book was composed with Corel VENTURA™ Publisher.

Dedicated to the memory of Pierre Troie.
The Shaman was a wonderful colleague, a great mentor, and a friend
who didn't take most things in life too seriously,
but who unfailingly honored his commitments to others.
— R.B.M. and P.C.Z.

Contents at a Glance

Contents

Part I

Relational Database Concepts

Part II

Getting Started with DB2

Part III

Maintaining Data

Part IV

Performance

Part V

SQL

Part VI

Business Intelligence

Part VIII

Reference

Foreword

D B2: *The Complete Reference* is a book about creating, developing applications for, and managing databases using DB2 on UNIX and Windows platforms, but DB2, of course, is by itself no means "complete"! In fact, today it has a large team of creative and talented architects, researchers, developers, testers, technical writers, and service engineers at IBM working energetically on even higher performance, new capabilities and more ease of use and management features. What this book offers is a comprehensive picture of what DB2 provides today.

Back in the early 1970s, a handful of us in IBM Research were working on this new concept called the "relational model." We took that idea and designed and implemented a language, now called SQL, and a research prototype, System R, to test whether this new way of modeling and storing data would be practical and useful. Little did we know that that work was building the foundation of not only an industry but the DB2 dynasty for IBM.

So, in retrospect, IBM's relational database work founded a multi-billion-dollar relational database industry. Moreover, it established some long-lasting fundamental principles:

- Relating data items to one another by their values
- Data independence for application programmers

- Simplicity of database design
- Data integrity enforced by the database engine
- Atomic transactions
- Set-oriented querying of data
- Cost-based optimization to do access path selection for queries

Each of these principles has subsequently been adopted by the entire relational database industry, and have influenced more than a generation of database developers and database application programmers. These principles are covered and reinforced by the sections in this book. You will see the whole picture for yourself, from how these principles are applied, to the concept of the relational model and the principles behind application and database design, all the way through to details of programming, managing, and tuning DB2.

IBM has offered database products for more than 30 years. I have personally been privileged to be a part of this exciting field at IBM for more than 26 years. The authors of this book are experts from IBM DB2's Development and Service team. In writing this book, they share with you some of the accumulated expertise of well over fifteen thousand person-years of IBM database experience. It is a pleasure to see this considerable accumulated expertise captured in this book.

But don't think for a moment that we are resting on our laurels. This heritage built a solid advanced technology foundation that is now in its third generation, and it is accelerating, not slowing down. In all of my years working in the database industry, this is the most exciting time yet, so enjoy this snapshot of what is there today in DB2. In the meantime, all of us in IBM's research and development labs are hard at work and passionately committed to accelerating even more technology and ease of use into DB2's future. Stay tuned; the best is yet to come!

Dr. Pat Selinger
IBM Fellow
Director of Database Integration

Acknowledgments

A big hug and thank you to my wife, Teresa, and to my darling little girls, Rosemary and Joanna, for supporting my efforts to complete this project. — R.B.M.

Most importantly, I want to thank Kelly Doyle (my future wife) for her support and understanding while I worked on this book. I could not have done it without her. I also want to thank Lise Allin (President, Money Concepts, Belleville, Ontario) for a 15-minute conversation almost two years ago that changed the direction of my writing career. — P.C.Z.

This work would not have been possible without the efforts of many people. Many thanks to the talented editorial team at Osborne/McGraw-Hill, including Michael Sprague, Paulina Pobocha, Lisa Wolters-Broder, Andy Carroll, and Chrisa Hotchkiss. Thanks to Carole McClendon of Waterside Productions for the opportunity. We also want to thank two other IBMers: John Botsford, who masterfully cuts through red tape, and Arnold Rosen, who provides comprehensible legal advice. Last, but certainly not least, we would especially like to thank the team of dedicated writers at IBM whose profiles appear here.

Blair Adamache, M.A., is a 17-year veteran of the IBM Toronto Lab. He has a Master's degree in Rhetoric, but promises to use his powers only in the service of good.

His first SQL statement (written in 1986 using 10base, the predecessor to FoxPro) led to a full-time job in relational database technology at IBM, beginning in 1987. In his current role, Blair manages the DB2 Service Team, with the responsibility of ensuring that DB2 customers continue to enjoy the best software support in the database industry. Blair has many years of experience with customers through stints in marketing, service, development, and management. He is the technical editor of *DB2 Fundamentals Certification for Dummies* (Hungry Minds, 2001) and has written many articles for IBM's DB2 Developer's domain, http://www7b.boulder.ibm.com/dmdd/. Blair wrote chapters about DB2 commands. The best way to reach Blair for technical questions is to post to comp.database.ibm-db2.

Scott Bailey is a senior member of the DB2 Information Development team, specializing in parallel and mobile database administration. During more than seven years at IBM, Scott has written numerous DB2 books and other related materials. Scott wrote the chapter about data recovery. You can reach him at scottba@sympatico.ca.

Brad Cassells is the Lead Writer on the *DB2 Universal Database Administration Guide*. He is a senior member of the Information Development group in the IBM Toronto Software Development Laboratory. For the past eight years, he has worked on DB2 Universal Database (UDB) information as team leader, planner, and writer. He is an IBM Certified Solutions Expert (DB2 UDB Database Administration). In addition, he has five years of DB2 for VM and VSE experience, and has worked at IBM for 17 years. Brad wrote chapters about database objects, instances, data storage, creating databases, tables, configuration tuning, and environment and registry variables. You can reach him at cassells@sympatico.ca.

Trisha Causley, Ph.D., is a new member of IBM's DB2 Information Development team. During her time at IBM, she has coauthored a user's guide for the DB2 Administration Tools, contributed articles for the *DB2 Newsletter*, and served as the translation coordinator for IBM's DB2 publications. Trisha wrote chapters about database design and controlling data access. You can reach her at causleybennett@sympatico.ca.

Dirk J. deRoos is a member of the DB2 Information Development team, specializing in database monitoring and DB2 application development. Dirk is a DB2 Certified Solutions Expert (Business Intelligence). Dirk wrote chapters about database monitoring and business intelligence. You can reach him at dderoos_ibm@yahoo.ca.

Chris J. Fender, B.Sc. (EE), P.Eng., is the Team Leader for the DB2 UDB High Availability Service team, specializing in DB2 recovery and data protection. Chris is also a recognized technical expert in all other areas of the DB2 engine, and is a DB2 Certified Solutions Expert. Chris wrote the chapter about problem determination. You can reach him at cjfender@yahoo.com.

Miro Flasza is a software developer with the IBM Toronto Software Laboratory, where he works on the DB2 Universal Database engine development team. During the past four years, Miro has participated in the design and implementation of new features for DB2, and worked closely with a number of DB2 customers. He shares his knowledge of the product's internals by frequently presenting at DB2 users conferences. Miro wrote the chapter about data movement. You can reach him at miro.flasza@sympatico.ca.

Sherri L. Pritchett, B.A., A.I.T., is a new member of the DB2 Information Development team. She has been a DBA with a number of database products on numerous platforms. Sherri wrote the chapter about data replication. You can reach her at sherri_pritchett@hotmail.com.

Dan Scott, M.I.St., is an Information Architect with the DB2 Information Development team. In over three years at IBM, Dan has written a number of DB2 application development books, sample applications, and articles. An avid Linux user, Dan maintains the DB2 for Linux HOWTO for the Linux Documentation Project. Dan is a DB2 Certified Solutions Expert (Application Development and Database Administration). Dan wrote chapters about application development. You can reach him at dbs_ibm@yahoo.ca.

Introduction

Database management software has evolved into the core of enterprise computing. As companies move forward into an Internet age of broadband communications and pervasive markets, database management systems (DBMS) must be able to store and to serve huge multimedia files, manage ever-increasing volumes of data, deliver continually improving performance, and support the next generation of applications that will be required to run on the most constrained devices (such as cellular phones, personal digital assistants, and so on). With its virtually unlimited ability to scale, its multimedia extensibility, its industry-leading performance and reliability, and its platform openness, DB2 Universal Database (UDB) has helped to drive this evolution–or shall we call it a revolution?–and will continue to lead database computing into the future. From Palmtop to Teraflop, you can find DB2 power in the most successful businesses.

A growing concern for businesses today is the cost associated with managing technology. DBMSs, including IBM's DB2, play a critical role in the e-infrastructure: they need to be scalable; they need to be reliable; and they need to have the ability to do the heavy lifting necessary in an increasingly data-centric world. DB2 is recognized for its ability to successfully marry powerful computing technologies with total cost of ownership (TCP).

DB2 Universal Database was the first multimedia, Web-ready relational database management system (RDBMS), strong enough to meet the demands of large corporations and flexible enough to serve medium and small-sized businesses. With each release of DB2 Universal Database, IBM continues in its role as the database innovator.

DB2 Universal Database powers the most demanding e-business applications, such as electronic commerce, enterprise resource planning, customer relationship management (CRM), supply-chain management (SCM), and Web self-service. DB2 UDB is all about an available and scalable, industrial-strength database that should be the foundation of your e-business data management strategy. DB2 includes free support for leading edge Internet technologies, such as storage and manipulation of eXtensible Markup Language (XML)-based documents, high speed in-memory database techniques for "speed of thought" response times over the Web, Simple Object Access Protocol (SOAP), and more.

Business Intelligence with DB2 Universal Database means using data assets to make better business decisions. It's about data access, data analysis, and decisions that help control costs, uncover new opportunities, and increase customer loyalty. A free built-in foundation for creating, populating, storing, and maintaining OnLine Analytical Processing (OLAP) cubes and Data Warehouses/Data Marts helps users to build small repositories of information and grow their most valuable resource–their data–into virtually unlimited data stores. This data can then be leveraged by the enterprise to make faster better decisions that grow the top line. Today's business success means placing the right products into the hands of the right people, at the right time. It doesn't matter if your product is an internal service to your company, or a book sold over the Web: DB2's Business Intelligence tools can help you understand your landscape and make better decisions.

DB2 UDB data management is more than simply running queries and applications. It's about where to store data, how to access it quickly, how to protect it against loss, and how to administer your databases for optimum performance on your hardware and with your mix of applications. DB2 empowers you to work with traditional and non-traditional types of data using the DB2 Structured Query Language (SQL) Application Programming Interface (API). It's a heterogeneous world, and you need a database server that can integrate fully with a multi-platform environment, so your enterprise can enjoy the full benefits of data warehousing, business intelligence, and e-business. Whether you are working with spatial and image data within a database, empowering DB2 to control files on a file system, or accessing data stored in an Oracle, SQL Server, or Sybase database–you can get there with DB2.

Universal Database is a grand name. It implies a product that is designed to be used for all types of purposes and in all kinds of environments, and *that* is a good description of DB2 Universal Database.

This book will serve as your most valuable DB2 resource for DB2 on Windows, Linux, UNIX, and OS/2. This book was written with the most up-to-date information as of DB2 Version 7.2, but can be used for previous versions of DB2 as well. Whether you are new to DB2 and still trying not to look at your manager's shoes when she asks you about "footprint," or you are that back-office shaman who people flock to when things go wrong—you can benefit from this book.

Calling this book "The Complete Reference" is pretty bold. Obviously, this book does not contain *everything* there is to know about DB2. (The DB2 product library spans well over 10,000 pages!) However, what we *did* try to do was to cover the most essential information, the things that you need to know most of the time, and would find incredibly handy if they could all be packaged in one book. This is such a book. It is a valuable desk reference, the most comprehensive book ever written about DB2. If there is information about DB2 that would make your life easier, but that you couldn't find in this, the first edition of the book, please let us know!

How This Book Is Organized

This book is packed with useful information that is logically organized into six parts.

Part I introduces you to "Relational Database Concepts." This part contains two chapters, "Database Design" and "Database Objects." Even the most seasoned DB2 experts can benefit from reading about database objects, because objects that are new to DB2 Version 7.2 are covered in this part of the book.

Part II, "Getting Started with DB2," takes you through the basics of DB2. This part includes chapters on "Creating Databases," "Understanding Instances," "Managing Data Storage," "Working with Tables," and "Controlling Data Access." What's more, "Installing DB2 Products Across Your Enterprise" and "Connecting a DB2 Client to a DB2 Server" contain information that has never before been presented in a cohesive, easy-to-understand format.

Part III, "Maintaining Data", contains chapters that give you the most up-to-date information on using the DB2 load, import, and export utilities ("Moving Data"); on using the DB2 DataPropagator product that is integrated with DB2 ("Replicating Data"); and information on the steps and issues associated with maintaining an available DB2 environment ("Recovering Data").

DB2 comes with comprehensive tools that you can use to monitor the health of your DB2 system. Part IV, "Performance," includes a chapter called "Database Monitoring," which reveals all that you need to know when you want to get an accurate feel for how your database is performing. You will also want to read "Configuration Tuning" when you need to address any issues that you may have discovered while looking at your database's performance history. Finally, if you are having problems with DB2, make sure that you read "Problem Determination," a must-read for anyone charged with the responsibility of troubleshooting a DB2 system.

SQL, an easy-to-learn interpretive language, was invented by IBM and is the standard for accessing information from databases. SQL can handle spatial components, XML, image, video, OLAP, and so much more. Part V covers SQL in two chapters ("Basic SQL" and "Advanced SQL"). Whether you are learning SQL for the first time, or can't remember the format of a ROLLUP or SOUNDEX function, this section has you covered.

Part VI, "Business Intelligence," gives you an introduction to this exciting topic. DB2 provides access to heterogeneous data sources. If you need to access DB2 and Oracle tables to complete a transaction, read "Federated Systems." DB2 Universal

Database includes the foundation for creating, populating, storing, and maintaining data warehouses and OLAP cubes. The "Data Warehousing" and "Online Analytical Processing" chapters introduce you to these concepts.

Part VII, "Application Development," is an application developer's dream resource, with chapters covering a wealth of information about AD: "Introduction to Application Development," "Embedded SQL," "Administration Application Programming Interfaces," "Call Level Interface (CLI) and ODBC," "Java Support," and "SQL Procedures."

The book ends with Part VIII, "References." This part alone is worth the price of admission. Imagine a reference book within a book, concisely covering functions and features (with examples) in one location. "SQL Statements" puts at your finger tips essential information about the SQL statements that are available to DB2 users. "Environment and Registry Variables" covers the different configuration and registry settings that you can use to manage your DB2 environment. Need help with DB2 commands? Check out "Introduction to DB2 Commands, Utilities and Tools."

The Complete Reference

DB2

Part I

Relational Database Concepts

Chapter 1

Database Design

This chapter introduces the elements of database design. A well-designed database offers many advantages:

- **Better performance**   Data can be structured to allow for rapid access and optimal resource use.
- **Easier maintenance**   A well-planned structure for your data can permit you to make updates to a value in a single place, with a single operation.
- **Data integrity**   Because a data value needs to be updated in only one place, fewer inconsistencies are allowed to creep in.

Designing a Database

When you design a database, you are modeling a real-world system that contains a set of objects and their characteristics, and the rules or relationships between those objects.

The first step is to describe the real-world system that you want to represent. As an example, let's take the patient record and scheduling system for a veterinarian's office. This system contains several types of *objects*, such as pets, owners, and appointments. For each of these objects, there are certain pieces of information, or *attributes*, that we are interested in recording.

- **Pets**   We want to keep track of name, species, sex, and whether the pet is spayed or neutered (S/N).
- **Owners**   We want to keep track of name, address, and phone number.
- **Appointments**   We want to keep track of date, time, and reason/treatment type.

We need the database to represent not only these three types of objects and their attributes, but we also need a way to relate these objects to each other. For example, we need to represent the relationship between pets and their owners, and the relationship between pets and their appointments.

We can represent three types of relationships between the entities in the database:

- **One-to-one relationship**   In this type of relationship, each instance of an entity relates to exactly one instance of another entity. Currently, no one-to-one relationships exist in the example. However, if we were to include surgical recovery rooms and their patient assignments in the database, we would have a one-to-one relationship: a given recovery room accommodates a single pet, and a pet is assigned to a single recovery room.
- **One-to-many relationship**   In this type of relationship, each instance of an entity relates to one or more instances of another entity. For example, a single owner could have multiple pets, but each pet has one owner. This is the most common type of relationship modeled in relational databases.
- **Many-to-many relationship**   In this type of relationship, many instances of a given entity relate to one or more instances of another entity. For example, if

we were to include billing information in the database, a given invoice could contain many treatment types (if a pet has multiple treatments in one visit), and a given treatment type could appear on many invoices.

Figure 1-1 shows an entity-relationship diagram that represents the entities (in rectangles), their attributes (in ovals), and the relationships between them (in diamonds). The number *1* and the character *n* identify the "one side" and the "many side," respectively, of a one-to-many relationship.

How do we map this representation to a database structure? Because databases consist of tables, we need to construct a set of tables that will best hold this data, with each cell in the table holding a single value. There are many possible ways to perform this task. As the database designer, your job is to come up with the best set of tables possible.

For example, you could create a single table to hold all of the information. This would be a large table with many columns and rows, and each row would contain information for one owner, pet, and appointment, as shown in Table 1-1.

An important flaw in this table will pose difficulties in both its implementation and usage: the degree of repeated information. Because an owner may have several pets, we may have a single owner appearing in several different rows, along with his or her

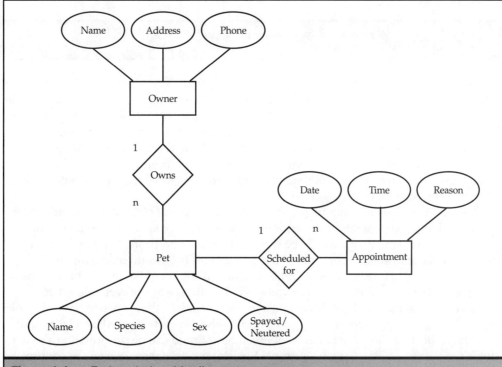

Figure 1-1. *Entity-relationship diagram*

Owner Name	Owner Address	Phone Number	Pet Name	Species	Sex	S/N	Appt. Date	Appt. Time
Lee, Colin	12 Wilson St.	555-1234	Max	Cat	F	Y	02/12	2:15
Short, Mary	421 Cave Rd.	555-5234	Cliff	Dog	M	Y	02/12	3:00
Lee, Colin	12 Wilson St.	555-1234	Bart	Dog	M	Y	02/12	10:00
Jones, Lynn	52 Main St.	555-3503	Tiger	Cat	F	Y	02/13	12:00
March, Joe	742 Key Blvd.	555-9313	Chip	Dog	F	N	02/13	9:00
Dry, Alan	390 Jump St.	555-4921	Will	Cat	M	Y	02/13	11:00

Table 1-1.   *Available Owner, Pet, and Appointment Information*

address and phone number (as is the case for Colin Lee in this example). Also, because this table holds appointment information for each of the pets, we would have to reenter all of this information (owner name, pet name, address, and so on) for each appointment for which a pet is scheduled. (Of course, we could always create additional columns in the table to allow for multiple appointments—perhaps 5 columns, or 10, or 50—but in time, we would run out of appointment slots for some pets, or the table would be so large that it would be unmanageable.)

There are obvious disadvantages to having the degree of redundancy required by Table 1-1. First, it represents a tremendous waste of storage space. Second, both data entry and data maintenance would be time-consuming and prone to error, because every time the information for a pet or owner changes (for example, the owner's address), that value must change in multiple places throughout the table. This increases the possibility that an instance of the value will be mistyped—or even missed entirely.

In contrast to this single-table design, a *relational database* allows you to have multiple simple tables, reducing redundancy and avoiding the difficulties posed by a large and unmanageable table. In a relational database, tables should contain information about a single type of entity. To create the example Veterinarians database, we will need three tables to represent the entities in our system: Owners (Table 1-2), Pets (Table 1-3), and Appointments (Table 1-4).

Name	Address	Phone
Lee, Colin	12 Wilson St.	555-1234
Short, Mary	421 Cave Rd.	555-5234
Jones, Lynn	52 Main St.	555-3503
March, Joe	742 Key Blvd.	555-9313
Dry, Alan	390 Jump St.	555-4921

Table 1-2. *Owners*

Name	Species	Sex	Spayed/Neutered	Owner Name
Max	Cat	F	Y	Lee, Colin
Cliff	Dog	M	Y	Short, Mary
Bart	Dog	M	Y	Lee, Colin
Tiger	Cat	F	Y	Jones, Lynn
Chip	Dog	F	N	March, Joe
Will	Cat	M	Y	Dry, Alan

Table 1-3. *Pets*

Date	Time	Pet Name	Treatment
02/12	2:15	Max	Feline leukemia vaccine
02/12	3:00	Cliff	Annual physical
02/12	10:00	Bart	Dental exam
02/13	12:00	Tiger	Rabies vaccine
02/13	9:00	Chip	Spay
02/13	11:00	Will	Annual physical

Table 1-4. *Appointments*

Notice that these tables are much simpler than Table 1-1 and that individual pieces of information, such as a pet owner's phone number, are entered in only one place. This makes the data simple to enter and simple to maintain.

However, there are still a few problems with the tables as they currently stand. The most striking problem is that the entities in the tables are not linked to one another except through having the same values in some of their columns. For example, there is a column called Name in both the Owners and the Pets tables—how do we know whether these columns refer to the same set of objects in the system? How do we signify that, in fact, the values in the Name column in the Owner table are related to the OwnerName column (rather than the Name column) in the Pets table? We use keys.

Creating Keys and Relating Tables

A *key* is a column or combination of columns that identifies a specific row or set of rows in a table. A *unique key* requires unique data in the key so that the key identifies only a single row. For example, a column that contains customer phone numbers might be identified as a unique key because no two values in this column will be the same (unless, of course, two customers in the table share the same phone).

Because each row in a table with a unique key must be uniquely identifiable by the key value, no NULL values are permitted in unique keys.

A *primary key* is a unique key with a special status in a given table; only one primary key can exist per table, and it—in combination with a corresponding foreign key in another table—is how the data in two tables can be linked. As with other keys, primary keys may be defined on a single column (e.g., customer phone number) or on multiple columns (e.g., last name, first name). Primary keys can be defined at the same time that you create the table or when the table is altered.

Any column or combination of columns that contains unique values is a candidate for a primary key. However, you should carefully consider your choice of primary keys when you design a table. It is more efficient to create a simple primary key on the fewest number of columns possible. It is also important to choose a primary key whose values are stable and subject to only infrequent changes. (To appreciate this point, think about how tedious it can be to inform everyone that your e-mail address or your telephone number has changed.)

It is often a good idea to create an extra column with an arbitrary integer value that is unique for each record, and define the primary key based on this value. This strategy guarantees that you will not run into problems if, by coincidence, the data in your columns would otherwise create identical primary-key values for two different records. A common example of a unique key number is a credit-card number, which identifies

Treatment	Species	Price
Annual physical	Cat	60.00
Annual physical	Dog	75.00
Annual physical	Rabbit	50.00
Rabies vaccine	Cat	40.00
Rabies vaccine	Dog	50.00
Spay	Cat	100.00
Spay	Dog	150.00

Table 1-5.   *Treatment*

transactions against an account regardless of how many customers have the same name, address, or telephone number as the card owner.

In the example, we might want to add a column to the tables in the Veterinarians database to identify the owner, pet, and appointment records by unique integers. We could call these columns OwnerID, PetID, and ApptID.

Instead of creating these unique integers yourself, you can have DB2 automatically generate a unique numeric value for each row by defining an identity column on the table. Values for this column can be provided by default so that your applications can provide their own unique values, but if they fail to provide one, DB2 generates a value. Otherwise, you can have DB2 provide a unique value all of the time. The values provided for the identity column are sequential, but you can specify the units by which DB2 increments each new value.

In some cases, you may need to include more than one column in a primary key. A key consisting of multiple columns is called a *composite key*. For example, if we had another table in the Veterinarians database that contained the prices for different pet treatments, as in Table 1-5, we might want to create a composite primary key on the Treatment and Species columns, because the values in these columns are unique when taken together.

Once you have created your tables and identified primary keys in them, you need to relate the tables to one another. For example, in the Veterinarians database, we want to relate the owners in the Pets table to the owners in the Owners table. This is accomplished by

ID	Name	Address	Phone
01	Lee, Colin	12 Wilson St.	555-1234
02	Short, Mary	421 Cave Rd.	555-5234
03	Jones, Lynn	52 Main St.	555-3503
04	March, Joe	742 Key Blvd.	555-9313
05	Dry, Alan	390 Jump St.	555-4921

Table 1-6.   *Owners*

means of a foreign key in the Pets table. A *foreign key* is a column or combination of columns in one table (the *child table*) that refers to the primary key in another table (the *parent table*).

All the values in a foreign key must exist in the corresponding primary key. For our database, we will define the OwnerID column in the Pets table as the foreign key that corresponds to the primary key ID in the Owners table. This means that we do not expect to see any OwnerIDs in the Pets table that do not exist in the Owners table. (See Tables 1-6 and 1-7.)

ID	Name	Species	Age	Sex	Spayed/ Neutered	OwnerID
0121	Max	Cat	4	F	Y	01
0122	Cliff	Dog	8	M	Y	02
0123	Bart	Dog	9	M	Y	01
0124	Tiger	Cat	1	F	Y	03
0431	Chip	Dog	1	F	N	04
0653	Will	Cat	8	M	Y	05

Table 1-7.   *Pets*

Referential Integrity

Referential integrity is an important aspect of any useful database. After your tables have been created and your database is live, users will be updating the data. What happens if a record is deleted from a parent table, removing a value from the primary key that is referenced by a foreign key in another table? Put more concretely, what happens in the Veterinarians database if the record for an owner is removed from the Owners table, and that owner is referenced in the Pets table? This could lead to us having pets in the Pets table without having any information on the pets' owner.

There are two ways to prevent this situation in DB2 and maintain referential integrity. The first is to prevent deletions or updates of values that serve as the parent key for a column in another table. The other is to allow cascading deletes, cascading updates, or both.

If *cascading deletes* are enabled, deletions in a table are propagated through related tables. For example, if we allowed cascading deletes in the Owners table, the deletion of an owner record would result in the deletion of all pets in the Pets table owned by that owner.

If *cascading updates* are enabled for a table, any changes to primary-key values are propagated through related tables. In our database, enabling cascading updates means that a change in the ID column in the Owners table will be reflected in the Pets table.

The other way to avoid having pet records without owner records is to prevent the deletion of owner records altogether. DB2 allows you to specify that if a table contains records that depend on other records in a parent table, the records in the parent table cannot be deleted. For example, if we have a record for an owner John Smith in the Owners table, we could not delete this record from the table unless no pets in the Pets table are identified as belonging to John Smith. To delete John Smith's record, we would first need to delete all the records in the Pets table that refer to John Smith.

Referential integrity is not the only type of constraint that you can impose on actions taking place in a DB2 database. You can also constrain the values in a column or combination of columns to ensure that they are unique.

You can also require that a particular column have a value for every record. This is a simple case of specifying at creation time or during column alteration that the column is NOT NULL.

You can even specify limits on the values in a column. For example, what would happen if a user tried to schedule an appointment at 6:00 A.M. but the veterinarian's office does not open until 9:00 A.M.? To prevent anyone from scheduling such an appointment, we can define a *table check constraint* on the table that says that the values in the Time column in the Appointments table must be within the operating hours of 9:00 A.M. and 4:45 P.M. When DB2 receives a request to insert a record in the Appointments table, it first checks to make sure that the time requested for the appointment falls within the appropriate range of values specified for the Time column.

Figure 1-2 demonstrates how you can add check constraints quickly through the DB2 Control Center when altering or creating a table. This check constraint makes sure that the only values entered in the Sex column of the Pets table are *M* or *F*.

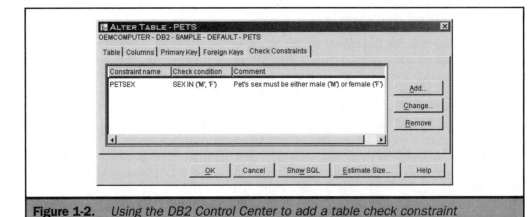

Figure 1-2. *Using the DB2 Control Center to add a table check constraint*

Normalization

Database *normalization* is the process of optimizing the structure of database tables to eliminate redundancy, increase the flexibility of the tables, and avoid potential data inconsistency problems. We took some steps toward normalization of the tables in the Veterinarians database when we separated out the data into three tables.

Normalization basically means ensuring that your tables adhere to a few general rules, or *normal forms.* The first three normal forms are discussed next.

First Normal Form

The requirement of the First Normal Form (often written as 1NF) is that all values in the table be atomic. This means that a single cell should contain a single value. Table 1-8 shows a possible table for the Veterinarians database.

In this table, a single owner record contains the owner name and all of the pets owned by the owner. In the case of the record for Colin Lee, the value for the Pets column contains two pets.

Name	Pets
Lee, Colin	Max, Bart
Short, Mary	Cliff
Jones, Lynn	Tiger
March, Joe	Chip
Dry, Alan	Will

Table 1-8. *A Table That Does Not Meet 1NF Requirements*

Name	Pet
Lee, Colin	Max
Lee, Colin	Bart
Short, Mary	Cliff
Jones, Lynn	Tiger
March, Joe	Chip
Dry, Alan	Will

Table 1-9.   *A Table That Meets 1NF Requirements*

To make this table conform to First Normal Form, we must separate out all the values to ensure that each cell contains only a single item, as shown in Table 1-9.

Second Normal Form

For a table to be in Second Normal Form (2NF), it must fulfill the requirement of 1NF and also meet the requirement that each nonkey attribute be functionally dependent on the entire primary key.

For example, in the "Creating Keys and Relating Tables" section earlier in this chapter, the Treatment table (Table 1-5) has as its primary key a combination of columns: Treatment and Species. Note that this table meets the requirements of 2NF because the nonkey column Price depends on both columns that make up the primary key and not on just one of the columns. That is, you cannot determine the value of Price without having the values for both Treatment and Species.

Third Normal Form

For a table to be in Third Normal Form (3NF), it must fulfill the requirements of both 1NF and 2NF and also meet the requirement that all nonkey attributes be dependent only on the primary key and be independent of other nonkey attributes. For example, Table 1-10 does not meet the requirements of 3NF.

In this table, the ApptID column forms the primary key. Notice that the Date, Time, and PetName columns are all dependent on the ApptID column because each of these attributes is specific to each appointment. The Species column, however, is dependent on the pet, not the appointment. To achieve 3NF, the Species column needs to be moved to a table with information about pets, not appointments. If we need to access both the appointment information and the information about the species of a pet (or other pet-specific information), we would perform a JOIN operation on the Appointments and Pets tables to retrieve information from both tables.

ApptID	Date	Time	PetName	Species
0012345	02/12	2:15	Max	Cat
0012346	02/12	3:00	Cliff	Dog
0012347	02/12	10:00	Bart	Dog
0012348	02/13	12:00	Tiger	Cat

Table 1-10.   *A Table That Does Not Meet 3NF Requirements*

Creating Indexes

Once you have created your tables, you need to consider how rapidly DB2 will be able to retrieve data from them.

Given unconstrained time resources, DB2 could scan an entire table for rows matching the criteria specified in a SELECT statement. Eventually, all applicable rows would be returned to the user. In most situations, however, performance is critical, and users expect their results as quickly as possible.

Creating useful indexes on your tables can significantly improve query performance. Like book indexes, table indexes allow specific information to be located rapidly, with minimal searching. Using an index to retrieve particular rows from a table can reduce the number of expensive input/output operations that the database manager (DB2) needs to perform. This is because an index allows the database manager to locate a row by reading in a relatively small number of data pages, rather than by performing an exhaustive search of all data pages until all matches are found.

When creating indexes, keep in mind that while they may improve read performance, they will negatively impact write performance. This is because for every row DB2 writes to a table, it must also update any affected indexes. Therefore, you should create indexes only when there is a clear overall performance advantage.

When creating indexes, you must also take into account the structure of the tables and the type of queries that are most frequently performed on them. For example, columns appearing in the WHERE clause of a frequently issued query are good candidates for indexes. In less frequently run queries, however, the cost that an index incurs for performance in INSERT and UPDATE statements might outweigh the benefits.

Similarly, columns that figure in a GROUP BY clause of a frequent query might benefit from the creation of an index, particularly if the number of values used to group the rows is small relative to the number of rows being grouped.

The DB2 Create Index Wizard

DB2 provides you with a tool called the Create Index Wizard, which enables you to determine the optimal indexes for your tables given the type of activities you expect on them. The wizard helps you decide which indexes to create in your database based on a specified set of SQL statements known as a *workload*. The relative importance of a particular statement within the workload is determined by the frequency with which it is run against the database.

To use the wizard, right-click the Indexes folder in the object tree in the Control Center. Select Create | Index Using Wizard. You will be asked to specify a workload for the wizard to evaluate. You can create workloads from within this wizard by clicking the Workload tab. You can add SQL statements to a workload by typing them into the window supplied or by importing them from a file. After evaluating the workload, the wizard will present you with recommendations for creating indexes based on the workload you specified.

The
Complete
Reference

Chapter 2

Database Objects

This chapter covers the many objects that are associated with databases. Most of the objects are also found in other relational database products, including those not created or maintained by IBM. The objects may have different names in other products, but the concepts are generally the same. Where they may differ is in the specifics of their implementation.

Several of the objects in this chapter are primarily interesting to system and database administrators. These objects include instances, databases, nodegroups, table spaces, and schemas.

Other objects in this chapter are primarily interesting to application developers and interactive database users. These objects include tables, views, indexes, aliases, and triggers.

Finally, there are objects that are interesting to various degrees to all of the groups mentioned above. These objects tend to be used in specific environments or for specific uses. Some of the objects assist with performance of the database manager and applications. Other objects are part of backup and recovery operations. These objects include user-defined functions and methods, user-defined types, large binary objects, packages, buffer pools, database backup copies, recovery logs, recovery history files, system catalog tables and views, database subdirectories, configuration files, and federated system objects.

All of these objects are introduced in this chapter to give you a sense of the major components of a relational database system. And you will have some understanding of the objects before they are discussed in detail in the remainder of this book.

Instances

An *instance* is also known as the *database manager*. Each instance is a complete environment: it comprises the code that creates all other objects, places data into those objects, manipulates the data in those objects, controls access to data in those objects, maintains the data in those objects, and so on. In a parallel database environment, it contains all defined database partitions.

You can have more than one instance as part of your database environment. While each instance has the code necessary to do those things mentioned above, some of the code is shared so that the large code-base of the entire product is not duplicated each time an instance is created.

A particular type of instance is the *DB2administration server* (DAS). The DAS is a special DB2 administration control point used to assist with the administration tasks only on other DB2 servers. A DAS must be running if you want to use the Client Configuration Assistant to discover or the Control Center remote database. The DAS is described further in Chapter 4.

Chapter 6 has more information about instances: how to create, list, and update them, the different directories that are part of the instance, how to configure instances, and how to remove them.

Databases

A DB2 database is a *relational database*. The *database* stores all data in tables that are related to one another. In Chapter 1, you gathered and placed business data into tables. Instead of repeating data in different tables, relationships are established between tables such that data is shared and duplication is minimized. There are internal DB2 features and functions that establish and maintain these relationships. For example, triggers and referential constraints define how two or more tables work together or are affected by actions occurring in the other tables. This subject is discussed further in Chapter 9.

Each database includes a set of system catalog tables that describe the logical and physical structure of the data. There can be more than one database per instance.

A database is created in the instance that is defined by the DB2INSTANCE environment variable, or in the instance to which you have explicitly attached using the ATTACH command. A *partitioned database* is a relational database in which the data is managed across multiple partitions (also called nodes). A *partition* is a part of the database that consists of its own user data, indexes, configuration files, and transaction logs. The *partitioning,* or splitting, of data is transparent to applications.

Although data is physically divided across many machines or processors within a single machine, logically, the data is worked on and viewed from the user's or application's viewpoint as if it were all together. Only a few data definition SQL statements must take partitioning of the data into consideration, such as CREATE NODEGROUP.

A *federated database* is a relational database whose data is stored in multiple data sources, including other separate relational databases. As in a partitioned database, the data of a federated database appears as if it were all in a single large database. Data in this type of database is accessed through normal SQL queries.

Nodegroups and Database Partitions

A *nodegroup* is a set of one or more database partitions. Each database partition that is part of your database environment must be defined in a *partition configuration file* called db2nodes.cfg. SQL statements allow you to create or alter nodegroups from which you can add or drop one or more database partitions.

Database partitions are important to understand only if your database data is physically divided (or partitioned) across more than one machine. Sometimes, the machine might be grouped with other machines within one physical box, but some form of communication is required to collect the data from all of the physical locations.

From the database manager's perspective, the data is treated as being together and is acted upon as if it were together.

In a DB2 Enterprise Edition environment, only one database partition or one nodegroup exists for each database. In such nonpartitioned databases, no partitioning key or partitioning map is required. There are no user data, indexes, configuration files, or transaction logs to be divided up because there is only one partition. There are no nodegroup design considerations in such a situation. It is the Enterprise-Extended Editions of the DB2 Universal Database product that allow for more than one database partition in a nodegroup. If you are working with a partitioned database, you should read Chapter 8, "Physical Database Design," in the *DB2 Universal Database Administration Guide: Planning* manual.

In a single partition database, you do not need to create and alter nodegroups. By default, the database manager uses three required nodegroups that are created when the database is created. IBMCATGROUP is the default nodegroup for the table space containing the system catalogs. IBMTEMPGROUP is the default nodegroup for system temporary table spaces. IBMDEFAULTGROUP is the default nodegroup for the table spaces containing user-defined tables.

A user temporary table space for a declared temporary table can be created in IBMDEFAULTGROUP or any user-created nodegroups, but not in IBMTEMPGROUP. Table spaces define for the database manager the physical disks where the logical tables will be placed once created. Table spaces are introduced in the next section (and presented more fully in Chapter 7).

When you want to create tables for a database, you first create the nodegroup where one or more table spaces will be stored, or ensure that the default nodegroups exist. Then create a table space where your tables will be stored.

Table Spaces

A *table space* is a place to store tables. The table space defines the relationship between the logical tables and the physical storage of the data associated with those tables. The physical storage locations are known as *containers,* and they may be file locations on disk or the entire disk device. The characteristics of the disks (volume and access speed) help to determine the performance of the database manager.

Table spaces reside in nodegroups. If you do not define which nodegroup will hold the table space when the table space is created, then the table space is placed in a default nodegroup. Information about table spaces is kept in the database system catalog.

When creating a table, you can decide to have certain objects associated with the table—such as indexes and large objects (LOBs)—kept separate from the rest of the table data. Indexes are defined on columns that are part of a table. LOBs generally represent non-traditional data, such as entire books, audio, video, and so on. A column of the table may be defined as containing LONG or LOB data.

You may want to keep these objects separate from the remaining table data for performance reasons: indexes will be accessed more frequently than the rest of the table data because they are used to access the table data; LOBs are accessed less frequently than the rest of the table data because they are so large and difficult to manipulate.

You can control the placement of indexes and LOBs into separate table spaces as part of the CREATE TABLE statement. As a result, table data may be spread over several table spaces.

A table space can be either a system-managed space (SMS) or a database-managed space (DMS):

- **SMS table space**   Each container is a directory in the file space of the operating system. The operating system's file manager controls the storage space. Space is allocated when there is a demand for additional space.

- **DMS table space**   Each container is a fixed-size, preallocated file, or a physical device such as a disk. The database manager controls the storage space.

SMS table spaces are an excellent choice for general purposes. They provide good performance with little administrative cost. DMS table spaces are the best choice when seeking top performance. As previously mentioned, containers may be either file locations or entire disk devices.

Containers that are devices provide the best performance because *double buffering* (data being buffered at the database manager level and then again at the file-system level) can occur when moving data using containers that are file locations or SMS table spaces. Double buffering requires movement of the data twice and is therefore slightly slower than the single buffering that occurs when moving data to containers that are devices.

There are three table space types: regular, long, and temporary.

- **Regular**   Tables containing user data exist in regular table spaces. USERSPACE1 is the default user table space. SYSCATSPACE is the default system catalog table space. Both are regular table spaces. Indexes, when stored separately, are stored in regular table spaces. Only DMS table spaces give administrators the ability to store index data separately from regular data.

- **Long**   Long table spaces are used to store tables containing long field data or LOB data. Multimedia objects are typically stored as LOBs and are placed in long table spaces. Long table spaces can only be DMS table spaces.

- **Temporary**   Two types of temporary table spaces exist: system and user.

    - **System**   The system temporary table spaces are used when the database manager is carrying out SQL operations such as sorting, reorganizing tables, and joining table data. TEMPSPACE1 is the default system temporary table space. There must always be at least one system temporary table space for the database manager to work correctly. You can create any number of system temporary table spaces but it is recommended that you maintain only one system temporary table space.

    - **User**   The user temporary table spaces are used to store declared global temporary tables that store temporary data used by database applications. Declared global temporary tables are discussed in detail in Chapter 9.

Each table space is associated with a specific buffer pool (see the "Buffer Pools" section later in this chapter). The default buffer pool is called IBMDEFAULTBP. If another buffer pool is to be associated with a table space, the buffer pool must first exist. The association between the two objects is defined when the table space is created and can be modified by using the ALTER TABLESPACE statement.

The type and design of your table spaces determine the efficiency of the input and output performed against the table space. Here are three concepts (controlled by configuration parameters) that you should consider while designing table spaces:

- **Big-block reads** A read where several data pages are retrieved in a single request. Instead of moving individual pages, multiple pages are moved together in an *extent*. An extent is the unit of space allocation within a table space and is defined when the table space is created.

- **Prefetching** The reading of data pages in advance of when they are required by a query against the database. The anticipation of needed data causes data pages to be read into the buffer pool to prevent the query from waiting on I/O requests to disk.

- **Page cleaning** The writing of "dirty" or modified data pages from the buffer pool to disk. If the buffer pool is full, or almost full, database agents move modified pages from the buffer pool back to disk, and locations in the buffer pool are made available to needed data. This prevents the performance of the database manager from suffering by waiting for a spot to be cleared from the buffer pool.

For more information on these concepts, see the *DB2 Universal Database Administration Guide: Planning* manual, which is part of the IBM DB2 product library.

Schemas

A *schema* is an identifier, similar to a user ID, used to group tables and other database objects together. The owner of the schema (which can be an individual) controls the access to the data and the objects within the schema. Some of the objects that a schema may contain include tables, views, nicknames, triggers, functions, and packages. Not all objects in the database are part of a schema.

A schema is also an object in the database. The schema can be explicitly created by using the CREATE SCHEMA statement, or it can be created automatically if you have IMPLICIT_SCHEMA privileges and you create the first object in a schema.

The first part of a two-part object name is the schema name. When an object is created, it is assigned to a schema. This can be a specific schema explicitly stated at the time the object is created, or it can be an implicit schema or default schema that is usually the user ID of the person creating the object. The second part of a two-part name is the name of the object. For example, if user Cassells created a table called "staff," the fully qualified name of this object would be Cassells.Staff.

Privileges associated with a schema control which users are allowed to create, alter, and drop objects in the schema. A schema owner is initially given all of the privileges associated with the schema, as well as the ability to grant those privileges to others. An implicitly created schema is owned by the system, and all users are initially allowed to create objects in that schema.

Anyone with DBADM or SYSADM authority can change the privileges held by users on any schema. For more information on authorities and privileges, see Chapter 5.

Tables and Related Objects

Tables are the central objects within the database environment. Database data and user data are kept in tables. The other objects in this section describe how users and applications access some or all of the data within the tables. Also described are the relationships that exist between tables.

Tables

As mentioned previously, data is stored in logical structures called *tables*. A table consists of data logically arranged in a finite number of columns and rows. The maximum number of columns in a table is 1012 for most page sizes, but only 500 when using a 4KB page size. The maximum number of rows in a table is 4 times 10 to the 9th power times the number of partitions in the database. (The maximum partition number is 999, so the number of rows possible for a table is very large.) All system and user data resides in tables, which reside in table spaces, previously described in the "Table Spaces" section of this chapter.

Data is viewed and manipulated based on mathematical principles and operations called *relations*. Access to the data is controlled through SQL or defined authorizations (like SYSADM). A *query* is made up of SQL statements and is used in applications or by users to add, retrieve, or modify database data.

A *base table* is created with the CREATE TABLE statement and is used to hold persistent user data. A *result table* is a set of rows that the database manager selects or generates from one or more base tables to satisfy a query from a user or application.

There are also other types of tables including summary tables, typed tables, and declared global temporary tables. You can read more about them in Chapter 9.

You must name the column, define the type of data, and define the length of the data for each column in the table you are creating. The type of the data (called a *data type*) can be one of the following:

- SMALLINT (A small integer value.)
- INTEGER (or INT) (A large integer value.)
- BIGINT (A big integer value.)

- FLOAT(*integer*) (For a single or double precision floating point number, depending on the value of the *integer*. Integer values of 1 through 24 indicate single precision and the values 25 through 53 indicate double precision. You can also specify REAL for single precision; and DOUBLE, DOUBLE PRECISION, and FLOAT for double precision.)

- DECIMAL(*precision-integer, scale-integer*) or DEC(*precision-integer, scale-integer*) (For a decimal number where the first integer is the total number of digits in the number which can range from 1 to 31; and the second integer is the scale of the number which can range from 0 to the size of the precision of the number. The words NUMERIC and NUM can be used as synonyms for DECIMAL and DEC.)

- CHARACTER(*integer*) or CHAR(*integer*), or CHARACTER or CHAR (For a fixed-length character string of length *integer* in a range from 1 to 254. If no length is specified, a length of 1 character is assumed.)

- VARCHAR(*integer*) or CHARACTER VARYING(*integer*) or CHAR VARYING(*integer*) (For a varying-length character string of maximum length *integer* which can range from 1 to 32,672.)

- LONG VARCHAR (For a varying-length character string with a maximum length of 32,700.)

- FOR BIT DATA (The contents of the column are to be treated as binary data.)

- BLOB(*integer* [*K* | *M* | *G*]) (For a binary large object string of the specified maximum length in bytes. The range is from 1 byte to 2,147,483,647 bytes. You can use K, M, and G to represent kilobytes, megabytes, and gigabytes respectively. If used, the integer value maximum is 2,097,152; or 2,048; or 2 respectively.)

- CLOB(*integer* [*K* | *M* | *G*]) (For a character large object string of the specified maximum length in bytes. The meaning of integers, K, M, and G is the same as for BLOB.)

- DBCLOB(*integer* [*K* | *M* | *G*]) (For a double-byte character large object string of the specified maximum length in double-byte characters. The meaning of the integers K, M, and G is similar to that for BLOB. When working with double-byte characters, the maximum size is 1,073,741,823 double-byte characters.)

- GRAPHIC(*integer*) (For a fixed length graphic string of length *integer* which can range from 1 to 127. If omitted, a length of 1 is assumed.)

- VARGRAPHIC(*integer*) (For a varying-length graphic string of maximum length integer, which can range from 1 to 16,336.)

- LONG VARGRAPHIC(*integer*) (For a varying-length graphic string with a maximum length of 16,350.)

- DATE (For a date.)

- TIME (For a time.)

- TIMESTAMP (For a timestamp.)

- DATALINK or DATALINK(*integer*) (For a link to data stored outside the database. For more information see the *DB2 Universal Database SQL Reference*.)

When a new row is added to a table, the data placed in all of the columns is called a *record*. Each record is placed on disk using table and table space information. The records are organized into pages called *table data pages*. These table data pages are logically grouped together based on the extent size of the table space. The number of records contained within each table data page can vary based on the size of the data page and the size of the records. A maximum of 255 records can fit on one page.

Table data pages do not contain the data for columns defined with LONG VARCHAR, LONG VARGRAPHIC, BLOB, CLOB, or DBCLOB data types. However, the rows in a table data page do contain the descriptors for the columns defined with those data types. The descriptors for these columns include information about the data type so that the database manager can find the actual locations for this data. These data types are very large and can be kept in separate table spaces (and, by implication, on separate disks).

Long field data (LONG VARCHAR, LONG VARGRAPHIC, BLOB, CLOB, or DBCLOB data types) is stored in separate table objects that are structured in such a way as to allow free space to be reclaimed easily. Long field data is stored in 32KB areas. (The supported page sizes include 4KB, 8KB, 16KB, and 32KB.) There will be some amount of unused space in this type of object, and the actual amount depends on the size of the long field data and whether this size is relatively constant across all occurrences of the data. The long field data is divided as evenly as possible into these pages. The last page of the long field data may not take up the full 32KB, so this space is unused.

LOB data is stored in two separate table objects that are structured differently from other data types:

- **LOB data types** Data is stored in 64MB areas that are broken up into segments whose sizes are powers of 2 multiplied by 1024 bytes.

- **LOB allocation objects** Allocation and free space information is stored in 4KB allocation pages that are separated from the actual data. The number of these 4KB pages depends on the amount of data, including unused space, allocated for the large object data.

When determining how to map tables to table spaces, the amount of data for all tables is a primary consideration. For example, if you have many small tables, you might consider placing all of them in a single table space. The table space could be of SMS type rather than DMS type because the advantages of DMS (I/O and space management) are not as important with small tables. If you have a large table requiring fast access, a DMS table space with a small extent size would be a good choice.

The type of data in the table is also a consideration when placing tables in table spaces. For example, data that is infrequently accessed and may not require fast access could be placed in tables and assigned to table spaces having containers on less expensive, slower physical devices. In this case, the table spaces may be SMS or DMS.

Using DMS table spaces, you can also distribute your table data across different table spaces: one for index data, one for LOB and long-field data, and one for regular table data. You specify the table spaces to use for these different types of data when you create the table. For example, you can improve performance in your database by placing your index data on the table space defined with containers on the fastest physical devices.

Administration issues may also determine the placement of tables within table spaces. For example, you can do backups at the table-space level (instead of backing up the entire database). You might want to place tables on different table spaces based on the required backup frequency. Also, if you need to drop and redefine a particular table often, you may want to define the table in its own table space. It is more efficient for the database manager to drop a DMS table space than it is to drop a table.

Finally, working in a partitioned database environment affects the placement of tables in table spaces. You need to ensure that the table space you choose is in a nodegroup that has the partitioning you need. If you are working with a partitioned database, you should read Chapter 8, "Physical Database Design," in the *DB2 Universal Database Administration Guide: Planning* manual.

There are additional considerations for temporary table spaces and the placement of the catalog table spaces. Chapter 7 provides information on these types of table spaces. For more information on tables, see Chapter 9.

Views

Views allow you to view selected data from one or more tables. A view is also known as a *virtual table.* Through a view, you can look at some or all of the columns or rows contained in one or more tables, which also means that views can be used to restrict or limit users' access to data. Depending on how the view is defined, you may be able to update the underlying tables for that view. No permanent storage is associated with a view. A view is simply the named specification of a result table. The specification is a SELECT statement that is run whenever the view is referenced in an SQL statement. For more information on views, see Chapter 9.

Indexes

An *index* is a set of keys used to rapidly search and access data. The index is based on one or more columns of a table. The information in these columns is used to sort the rows of the table into ascending or descending order or to cluster or group related rows together. And it may enforce uniqueness of the column data that makes up the index. Other options may be enforced through the index as well, which are discussed in Chapter 9.

The optimizer of the database manager uses indexes and statistical information to determine the most efficient way to access the data. Mathematical operations on the index provide rapid access to the requested data. The *optimizer* is part of the SQL compiler that generates alternative execution plans to satisfy an application or user request.

It estimates the cost to run each plan using statistics for tables, indexes, columns, and functions, and chooses the plan with the smallest estimated execution cost.

An *index key* is a column or an ordered collection of columns on which an index is defined. Unique indexes can be created to ensure that each value in the index key is unique.

DB2 indexes are an optimized B-tree implementation based on an efficient and high-concurrency index management method using write-ahead logging. A *B-tree* is a hierarchical organization of indexes. *Concurrency* is the ability within the database to access the same data at the same time. The database manager controls concurrency to data through the use of locks. The isolation level of applications accessing table data influences the type of locks used. The *isolation level* is specified as an attribute of a package and applies to the application processes that use that package. The ability to specify isolation levels on a statement-by-statement basis was added in DB2 Version 7.2

Write-ahead logging is the writing of changes in the log buffer to disk before the corresponding changes to the data pages are written to disk. This method can avoid the I/O bottleneck that can occur when both index and data-page changes are written to disk at the time of a COMMIT. For more information on locking, concurrency, and isolation levels, see Part VII, "Application Development."

Aliases

Instead of referencing a database, table, nickname, or view by its name, you can reference it with an *alias* that points to the original object. If you use an alias in a SQL statement, and the original object's name changes, only the definition of the alias must be changed. You don't need to change every SQL statement that uses the alias.

An alias can be used in a view or trigger definition and in any SQL statement in which an existing table or view name can be referenced. There is an exception for table check-constraint definitions where the alias name cannot be used in the check condition. An alias can be created on another alias.

Access to the tables and views referred to by the alias requires the correct privileges on those tables and views as if they were being used directly. Database names can also be represented using a database alias. For example, if a DB2 client needed to access two different databases (both called SAMPLE) residing on a DB2 server, a database alias would have to be used for at least one of the databases. Otherwise, the connection agents would not know which SAMPLE database to connect to.

Triggers

A *trigger* defines a set of actions that are run when an insert, update, or delete operation takes effect on a specified base table or typed table. The set of actions that are "triggered" can be used to support integrity or business rules. There are several benefits of using a trigger:

■ **Faster application development** A trigger is stored in the database. You are not forced to code the trigger actions into every application.

■ **Easier maintenance** A trigger is defined and associated with a table. No further preparation is required to invoke the trigger: it is invoked automatically when the associated table is accessed.

■ **Global enforcement of business rules** When you have business policy changes, only the trigger definitions need to change. You do not need to change each application that accesses the table associated with the trigger.

A trigger can depend on many objects, and all trigger dependencies are recorded in the SYSCAT.TRIGDEP catalog. For more information about triggers, see Chapter 9.

User-Defined Functions and Methods

A *user-defined function* (UDF) is a mechanism with which you can write your own extensions to SQL. *Methods* enable you to write extensions to SQL by defining for structured types the relationship between a set of input data values and a set of result values. There are several reasons to use UDFs and methods, as described in the next sections.

Reuse

Once created, UDFs are treated as extensions to SQL so that other users and programs can use the UDFs and methods. This means different programmers don't have to code the same function each time their applications require it. It also means that if the function changes (and the change is applicable to all the applications using the function), then you need to change the code for the function only once. The function name that is used in all of the applications does not need to change.

Performance

There is a performance advantage to invoking a UDF or method because they are invoked from the database engine and not simply written and run as part of your applications. In addition, you can use the RETURNS TABLE clause of the CREATE FUNCTION statement to define UDFs, called table functions.

A *table function* takes individual scalar values of different types and meanings as its arguments and returns a table to the SQL statement that invokes it (unlike methods, which cannot return tables). Table functions can be written so that only the data you want is generated; unwanted rows and columns are eliminated.

A further performance benefit occurs when working with LOBs. You can create a function to extract information from a LOB right at the database server and pass only the extracted value back to the application. This strategy avoids the passing of the entire LOB value back to the application and then extracting the needed information.

Behavior of Distinct Types

Using a UDF, you can implement the behavior of a user-defined distinct type (UDT; defined more fully in the next section). The process for implementing a UDF or method is to write, compile, link, and then debug it. Finally, you must register the UDF or method with the database manager. Use the CREATE FUNCTION statement to define or register the UDF. Use the CREATE TYPE or ALTER TYPE statement to define a method for a structured type, and then use the CREATE METHOD statement to associate the method body with the method specification.

For more information on UDFs and methods, see Part VII, "Application Development" or the *DB2 Universal Database SQL Reference* manual.

User-Defined Distinct Types

A *user-defined distinct type* (UDT) is a type that is derived from and shares characteristics with existing types called *source types*. Distinct types are a separate and incompatible type for most operations.

Qualified identifiers identify distinct types. Both a schema name and the SQL path may be used to qualify the distinct type name. If the schema name is not used to qualify the distinct type name when used in statements other than the CREATE DISTINCT TYPE, DROP DISTINCT TYPE, or COMMENT ON DISTINCT TYPE statements, the SQL path is searched in sequence for the first schema with a distinct type that matches.

The CURRENT PATH is a special register containing a list of one or more schema names established by you using the SET CURRENT FUNCTION PATH statement. These schema names are used to resolve function references and data-type references that are used in dynamically prepared SQL statements.

Distinct types support strong typing, which means that you cannot directly compare instances of a distinct type with anything other than another instance of that type. This prevents semantically nonsensical operations such as directly adding US_Dollar and Canadian_Dollar distinct types without first going through a conversion process. You define which types of operations can occur for instances of a distinct type. Strong typing ensures that your distinct types will behave appropriately. It guarantees that only functions defined on your distinct type can be applied to instances of the distinct type. A distinct type does not automatically acquire the functions and operators of its source type because these may not be meaningful.

In addition to user-defined distinct types, there are also structured types and reference types. You can read more about these types in the *DB2 Universal Database Application Development Guide*.

Large Binary Objects

LOB data types support multimedia objects such as documents, audio, video, and images. *Binary large objects* (BLOBs) can be photographs, voice, video, and more. *Character large objects* (CLOBs) can be an employee's résumé or a product report. CLOBs can consist of either single- or multibyte characters, or a combination of both. A double-byte CLOB could be a Japanese, Chinese, or Korean employee résumé.

Although any single LOB value may not exceed 2 gigabytes, a single row in a table can contain as much as 24 gigabytes of LOB data. An entire table can contain as much as 4 terabytes of LOB data.

Because LOBs are so large, *locators* are used to identify and manipulate them at the database server. A *LOB locator* is a mechanism that allows an application program to manipulate a LOB value in the database system. A LOB locator is a simple token value that represents a single LOB value. An application program retrieves a LOB locator into a host variable and then can apply SQL functions (including UDFs) to the associated LOB value using the locator.

Locators are also used to extract portions of the LOB value. A file reference variable represents the BLOB, CLOB, and DBCLOB files, just as the LOB locator represents—rather than contains—the LOB bytes. Database queries, updates, and inserts use file reference variables to physically move a LOB value or parts of the LOB to and from a client. File reference variables are defined in all host languages. They are not native data types; therefore, SQL extensions are used and the precompilers generate the host-language constructs necessary to represent each variable.

Changes to the database are logged so that you and the database manager can recover from problems affecting the database. (For more information on logging and recovery, see Chapter 12.) You are not allowed to log changes affecting LOB values greater than 1 gigabyte in size. Even LOB values of several hundred megabytes can tax the capacity of the database log.

The lob-options clause found on the CREATE TABLE and ALTER TABLE statements allows you to turn off logging for specified LOB columns. This affects the values found in LOB columns following a roll-forward recovery.For more information on LOBs, see Chapter 22.

Packages

A *package* is an object stored in the database that includes information needed to run SQL statements in a single source file. A database application uses one package for every precompiled source file used to build the application. Each package is a separate entity and has no relationship to any other packages used by the same or other applications.

Database applications use packages for some of the same reasons applications are compiled: improved performance and compactness. The advantages of precompilation apply only to static SQL statements.

To run applications written in precompiled host languages, you must create the packages needed by the database manager at run time. To do this, you must do the following:

- *Precompile the application.* This converts embedded SQL source statements into a form the database manager can use.
- *Compile and link the application.* This creates the required object modules.
- *Bind the application.* This creates the package to be used by the database manager when the program is run.

The precompiler converts SQL statements found in application source files into comments and creates the DB2 run-time API calls for those statements. The original application source files are then considered to be *modified source files.* The precompiler also creates the information the database manager needs to process the SQL statements against the database. This information is stored with the SQL statements from the application source files and is used later in a package, in a bind file, or in both, depending on the precompiler options selected.

Language compilers convert modified source files into object modules. Then, host-language linkers create executable applications by linking object modules, host-language library APIs, and the database manager library containing the database manager APIs.

Binding is the process that creates the package the database manager needs in order to access the database when the application is run. Binding takes the bind file created by the precompiler and creates a database manager package. There are two ways to create a package through binding:

- Implicitly by specifying the PACKAGE option during precompilation
- Explicitly by using the BIND command against the bind file created during precompilation

Rebinding is the process of recreating a package for an application program that was previously bound. You must rebind packages if they have been marked invalid or inoperative. You may also want to rebind packages to take advantage of a newly created index or to make use of updated statistics.

If a package depends on another database object, and that object is dropped, the package becomes invalid. If the dropped object is a user-defined function, the package becomes inoperative.

Invalid packages are implicitly or automatically rebound when they are next run. The process of rebinding slows the performance of the package. Inoperative packages must be explicitly rebound by running either the BIND or the REBIND command.

Buffer Pools

A *buffer pool* is an amount of main memory allocated to the cache table, index, and catalog data pages on a machine on which the database manager is running. The purpose of the buffer pool is to improve database performance. Data pages are read into the buffer pool from disk and are kept there while they are being modified—data can be accessed much faster from memory than from disk.

A large part of tuning a database involves those configuration parameters that control the movement of data into the buffer pool and the writing of data from the buffer pool out to disk. The fewer times the database manager needs to read from or write to a disk (called disk input and output, or disk I/O), the better the performance of the database. If more of the data needed by applications were present in the buffer pool, then less time would be needed to access this data compared to the time taken to find the data on disk.

Database Backup Copies

A backup copy of the database must be taken for either version recovery or roll-forward recovery methods to be used. There are reasons for using each: version recovery is the simpler of the two, but roll-forward recovery provides a more complete recovery method. Analyzing the data that you must recover to run your business will help you determine which of these two methods is best for your work environment.

Version recovery is the restoration of a previous version of the database. An image of the database is created during a backup operation in anticipation of its possible use sometime in the future when the database is damaged and unusable. In that case, you are able to restore the database to its state when the backup was made.

However, every transaction against the database since the backup operation was carried out is lost. For this reason, the timing of backup operations is critical. If they are too far apart, too many transactions may be lost. If they are too close together, database performance may suffer because of the time and effort required of the database manager to complete the backup operation.

Roll-forward recovery requires a backup operation plus the archiving of the transactions performed against the database after the backup operation completes. These transactions are saved in recovery logs. When the database fails, the backup copy is restored (as in version recovery), and then all the transactions stored in the logs are applied. By applying the logs, you can minimize the loss of transactions that occur after the last backup operation. The database can be restored to the state it was in just before the database failed. Unlike the version-recovery method, no transactions affecting the database are lost.

If the database is set up for forward recovery, it is also possible to back up, restore, and roll table spaces forward. You can back up individual table spaces (in addition to the entire database).

Recovery Logs

Log files are created automatically when a database is created. Even when not using the roll-forward recovery method, log files record the transactions that take place against the tables and other objects in the database over time. The database manager controls the recording of the transactions—you cannot directly modify the information recorded in the logs. If your database becomes damaged, it is important to have these logs so that the database manager and you have an opportunity to apply the recorded changes in the logs. There are two types of logging: circular and archive.

Circular logging is the default for the database when it is first created. With this type of logging, only full, offline backups of the database are valid. Several logs are used in round-robin fashion, in which logs are reused once all the other logs are filled. Eventually, the logs will be overwritten, and transactions recorded there will be lost. The overwritten log records are not recoverable, so there is no ability to roll changes forward on a restored database copy. The logs are used to bring the database to a consistent and usable state (which is what occurs following the abnormal termination of the database and is known as *crash recovery*). Only version recovery is possible.

Archive logging is used specifically for roll-forward recovery. As logs are filled, new logs are started. Once logs are no longer required to move the database to a consistent and usable state when performing crash recovery, the logs can be archived either online or offline. Roll-forward recovery uses both active logs and archived logs to rebuild a database either to the end of the logs or to a specific time.

It is not recommended that you log changes to LOB columns. LOBs are too big and would take up large portions of the logs. LOB column changes are not logged unless the configuration parameter to retain logs (logretain) is used and the LOB column is defined with the logging default when creating a table. Database recovery is discussed in detail in Chapter 12.

Recovery History Files

The *recovery history file* contains a summary of the backup information that can be used in the event that all or part of the database must be recovered. It is used to track recovery-related events such as when backup copies of all or part of the database are taken, when significant changes are made to the database, when load operations take place, and when restoration of all or part of the database takes place. Database recovery is discussed in detail in Chapter 12. The load utility is discussed in Chapter 10.

System Catalog Tables and Views

System catalog tables and *views* are created when a database is created. They contain all the information about the data and database objects under the control of the database manager, and they grow as database objects are added to the database. Statistical information is also contained in the catalog, which is used by the optimizer to determine the fastest way to access data from the database.

The amount of space allocated for the catalog tables depends on the type of table space and the extent size of the table space containing the catalog tables.

Database Subdirectories

When a database is created, the database manager creates a separate subdirectory to store control files and to allocate containers to default table spaces.

The *database subdirectories* are created within the path or drive specified on the CREATE DATABASE command, and the database manager maintains them automatically. If you do not specify the location of the path or drive when creating the database, the default location (which differs by operating system) is used. On OS/2 and Windows, the subdirectories are created under the root directory for a volume that is identified by a drive letter (like C:\). On UNIX-based operating systems, the subdirectories are created in the path where you have created the database.

The subdirectories are created in a directory with the name given to the database manager instance to which you are attached when you create the database. Your directory structure should look something like this:

```
<your directory>/<your instance>/NODE0000/SQL000001/
```

SQL000001 represents the database that is created from the CREATE DATABASE command.

To avoid potential problems, do not create directories that use the same naming scheme as the default path just shown. You should also not rename or move directories that have been created by the database manager.

For more information on database directories, see Chapter 2, "Architecture and Processes Overview," in the *DB2 Universal Database Administration Guide: Performance* manual.

Configuration Files

Configuration files contain the parameter values that define the resources allocated to the DB2 products and to individual databases, and the diagnostic level to be used. Two types of configuration files exist: one for each database manager or instance, and one for each database. You can improve performance or increase the capacity of database-to-server application requests by modifying the values associated with the parameters in these files.

A database manager configuration file is created when a DB2 instance is created. System resources associated with the instance are defined through the parameters in this file. The DAS instance has a special configuration file called the admin configuration file.

There is also one database manager configuration file for each client installation. This file contains information about the client enabler for a specific workstation. A subset of the parameters available to the server is applicable to the client.

A database configuration file is created when a database is created. Resources associated with the database are defined through the parameters in this file. There is one database configuration file for each database created.

Federated Objects

A *federated database system* or *federated system* is a database management system (DBMS) that supports applications and users in a heterogeneous database environment. Applications and users can submit SQL statements referencing two or more database management systems or databases. The database management systems or databases do not have to be from the same company. For example, you can carry out a union operation involving data from a DB2 table and an Oracle view.

A DB2 federated system provides location transparency for database objects. Through the use of *nicknames,* which are references to information in tables or views on other remote database systems, the tables and views on those systems can be moved or changed without requiring changes to local applications requesting information from those systems. All changes can be controlled through the definition of the nickname.

A DB2 federated system also compensates for non-DB2 database management systems that do not support all of the DB2 SQL capabilities. For example, a recursive SQL operation can be run under DB2 that could not be done on certain other database management systems.

A DB2 federated system can also query objects on other database management systems while applications on those systems are accessing the same database objects. A DB2 federated system does not monopolize or restrict access (beyond integrity and locking constraints) to Oracle or other database management system objects.

See Chapter 18 for more information on federated systems.

Wrapper

A *wrapper* identifies the modules used by the federated server to access a particular class or category of data source. To implement a wrapper, the server uses routines stored in a library called a *wrapper module.* These routines allow the server to perform actions like connecting to the data source and retrieving data from that source.

Server

A *server* defines data sources. This is how a heterogeneous database management system is identified to your DB2 federated database manager. In defining a data source to the federated database, you must supply a name for the data source, the type and version of the relational database management system (RDBMS), and the RDBM's name for the data source. The name and all the information that is supplied are collectively called a *server definition.*

Nickname

A *nickname* is an identifier that references a specific data-source object. The reference could be to a table, a view, or an alias object on another database management system. Applications can then use the nickname in the same way they would reference any local or homogeneous database tables or views.

Nicknames are not alternative names for tables and views as aliases are; nicknames are pointers by which the federated server references these objects.

You cannot use a trigger with nicknames.

The Complete Reference

DB2

Part II

Getting Started with DB2

The
Complete
Reference

Chapter 3

Installing DB2 Products Across Your Enterprise

Product installation has become a lot easier over the years with the help of graphical user interfaces (GUIs) and the emergence of user-centered design (UCD) groups that take knowledge about human factors and ease of use and translate that knowledge into installation interfaces. Why has there been such a focus on installation? Many reasons, really. Deployment of code across an enterprise, including maintenance of that code—which is delivered in DB2 through FixPaks—can be an expensive and time-consuming task. This adds to a software's inherent total cost of ownership (TCO).

Suppose a customer is running DB2 on over 185,000 DB2 clients with over 15,000 DB2 servers. Even if this customer reduced these numbers by a scale factor of 1000, a significant TCO would still be associated with the deployment and maintenance of the software. Therefore, it is useful for DB2 experts to understand the various methods and options available for deploying DB2.

Administrators will likely need to deploy hundreds, perhaps thousands, of clients and multiple servers. For example, the task of installing a DB2 client on sales reps' computers cannot be left up to the sales reps. They need to focus on their assignments, marketing mix, and delivery of the right products to the right place at the right time. The responsibility for providing a method of mass deployment lies with the software provider (IBM in the case of DB2) and the IT support staff.

For an installation program to fit into the enterprise, it must meet these two requirements:

- It has to be easy to use.
- It has to be flexible enough to allow for mass deployments.

However, another facet to code installation is sometimes overlooked but can involve just as much expense—*configuration*. If you were to install a DB2 client on an accountant's workstation, it wouldn't help her much if her DB2 client did not know how to connect or which databases to connect to. For example, she may be working with the PeopleSoft Financials package. If the workstation doesn't understand that this database is at a specific node (which contains the IP addressing information required to make the connection and a few other details that don't matter right now), having DB2 isn't going to help.

Just as the code deployment cannot be left up to lines of business, neither can the configuration of the system. This is also the responsibility of IT. What's more, this configuration information may change. If you were to configure database connections for every client in your enterprise and suddenly you had to add a new database (let's say you purchased the Human Resources package), you would have to add that connection to every workstation. If you were using a database that was not designed to be flexible and extendable like DB2, you would have a big headache on your hands!

This adds a couple more potential installation requirements to our software:

- It has to be able to configure performance and database connection information.
- It needs a facility for incremental updates.

This chapter takes you through the installation options that you can use to deploy DB2 software across your enterprise. Most of the examples in the deployment section of this chapter focus on the deployment of clients across your enterprise; however, you can extend most of the information in this chapter to the deployment of servers as well (unless otherwise noted).

Installation Methodologies

You can use one of four installation methodologies to distribute DB2 across your enterprise:

- Interactive installation
- Response file installation
- Citrix installation (also referred to as a Windows Terminal Server installation)
- Code server (Thin-client) installation

Note   *A* distributed *version of DB2 refers to DB2 on the AIX, HP-UX, OS/2, Solaris, Linux, Sequent/PTX, and Windows environments. A* mainframe *version of DB2 often refers to DB2 for iSeries (formerly known as an AS/400 server). And a* host *version of DB2 refers to DB2 for zSeries (formerly known as the OS/390 servers). Only the distributed version of DB2 is covered in this chapter.*

The Interactive Installation

You have surely had many experiences with the *interactive installation*. This installation type derives its name from the one-on-one interaction between the code and the individual charged with the responsibility of performing the installation. This installation interactively asks the user questions about the DB2 installation and configures the installation based on the user's responses.

You will likely perform this installation if you install the copy of DB2 on your own personal workstation. You can insert a CD-ROM into your drive, or mount the CD-ROM on a network drive for access by all users, and install DB2 with the help of the GUI-driven installation windows. Another option is to copy the installation code to a shared drive and perform the installation without reading directly from the CD-ROM device, thereby reducing any CD-ROM I/O performance issues. (This might be a good idea if you are planning to give access to the DB2 image to multiple people for their own personal use so that everyone does not tie up your workstation's CD-ROM device.)

The interactive installation is available on all DB2 platforms in one form or another and for all DB2 products. In the Windows environment, the installation program is called setup.exe and is set to auto-start each time you insert the CD-ROM into the CD-ROM drive. In a UNIX and Linux environment, it is called db2setup (often referred to as the DB2 Installer), and in the OS/2 world, it is called install.exe.

In the UNIX and Linux environments, you can also use each operating system's native installation tools (for example, *rpm* in Linux and *installp* in AIX). When you use the native installation tools for your platform (referred to as a *manual installation*), you cannot take advantage of the intelligence built into the DB2 installation tools to auto-configure your system, set it up for inbound DB2 communications, etc.

Of course, you can write scripts that interact with your operating system's installation commands and distribute code that way, but again, you cannot leverage the intelligence of the DB2 installation tool. For this reason, manual installations are not covered in this book. If you are installing a DB2 product, we strongly recommend that you use the methods outlined in this book—it will save you many hours of work and you will end up at the same place! All of the installation methods are covered in each DB2 product's *Quick Beginnings* guide and in the *DB2 Installation and Configuration Supplement*.

There are advantages and disadvantages to an interactive installation. Although most people are familiar with menu-driven installation programs, each person performing the installation must be somewhat knowledgeable about the product. This means that if you are installing a DB2 server, you should understand what the DB2 Connect component is, and so on. This may not be a steep learning curve and online help is available to guide you through the installation; however, if your workers are focused accountants, they should be concentrating on credits and debits for the Account Receivables ledger, not worrying about the software that enables them.

Tip	*The installation program comes with default selections and settings that are designed to run in a typical DB2 environment. If you are in a position where you must have inexperienced users install DB2 software using this method, they can simply accept the defaults and perform the installation.*

The interactive installation is advantageous because the code is installed locally on each machine (yielding great performance), it is easily customizable for those "in-the-know," and it can be performed by those without vast experience (see the previous tip). This installation type is familiar to most people who own their own personal computer, and the environment will be configured automatically.

However, interactive installation is prone to error when performed by inexperienced users. A user may have to face many decisions, such as setting up user accounts, selecting components, etc. If you give 1000 people the opportunity to install the exact same DB2 product and configuration across your enterprise, you are likely to end up with different outcomes.

If you have mounted the DB2 CD-ROM or created a DB2 code image on the server, performing the installation over a network can give rise to other considerations. Is the network connection suitable for mobile users? Is the LAN fast enough to accommodate local and remote users, or does it introduce a latency factor? Is the LAN robust enough?

Another disadvantage with an interactive installation is that the code is local to the machine where the installation takes place. Any maintenance must be completed on every machine. Each FixPak (released quarterly) must be applied (if needed) to each workstation. Also, if it was determined that a FixPak was not needed, the same cost to deploy the FixPak would be associated with rolling it back.

If your deployment strategy includes plans to ship a CD to various target users who are not local to the brick-and-mortar enterprise, you may need to send a CD shipment for each FixPak as well.

If your shop keeps up its maintenance (which is recommend), a high cost could be associated with an interactive installation.

In conclusion, the interactive installation deployment strategy is not suitable for mass deployments. This method could be suitable for three-tier solutions where only a few copies of the product exist and users have local or dedicated support staff for each system. (For example, a deployment may include thousands of DB2 clients but only five DB2 servers, so it may very well make sense to use an interactive installation to install the DB2 servers and another process to install the DB2 clients.)

When multiple installations of a DB2 product are required, however, an interactive installation is impractical. It is also not suitable to require your business units to install their own software. Finally, if users are remote or spread across the company, you have to ensure that costly support staff is available for installation and support at each location.

Table 3-1 summarizes the advantages and disadvantages of using an interactive installation.

Advantages	Disadvantages
Code is installed locally on the machine, which results in great performance because all code is run locally.	A knowledgeable person must answer questions during the install. (For example, there are implications associated with the choice of Database Administration Server, or DAS, user account.)
During the installation, users can customize the installation to their needs (include/omit documentation, tools, etc.).	Code is local to the machine; therefore, all code maintenance must be applied locally.
Installer can automagically configure the environment, and this saves time compared to a manual configuration.	It is resource- and time-consuming to roll out or roll back a FixPak or code because such maintenance must be performed on each separate workstation.
This installation is a familiar process for even inexperienced users; most users have performed this type of installation before.	This installation is not suitable for mass deployments.

Table 3-1. *Advantages and Disadvantages of Interactive Installation*

The Response File Installation

One solution to the disadvantages associated with an interactive installation is to use a *response file installation* (sometimes called a *silent install* because no one has to do anything or "speak" to the installation program through GUIs). You can use various DB2 utilities to make this option even more powerful and appropriate for mass deployments.

You can use this method on any DB2-distributed platform, and it can be performed with or without system management tools. System management tools give you the ability to PUSH installations to target workstations, without any interaction from the user of that workstation. This is in contrast to a PULL configuration, during which a user on the target workstations "asks" for something to be done (like typing in the setup command to launch the DB2 installation program or double-clicking a .bat file). Response file installations are fully integrated with Microsoft's System Management Server (MS SMS); for more information, refer to the DB2 Connect Installation and Configuration Supplement.

If you are an administrator charged with large-scale code deployments, you should use the response file installation method to install DB2 code in your enterprise for three reasons:

- **Control**   A response file installation gives database administrators (DBAs) *control* over what is installed on a system and how it is configured. Most DB2 environments have multiple DB2 Run-Time clients that are used to provide applications with connections to DB2 databases, and these deployed systems are quite often clones of each other. There are also likely DB2 Administration clients in this DB2 environment that are used for remote administration purposes. These DB2 Administration clients are almost always identical as well. A user may or may not have to invoke the installation program (it can be PUSHED via management tools or scripts or PULLED by a command or e-mail), but they do not need to interact with it.

- **Predictable results**   The number of installation problems is dramatically reduced, and outcomes are guaranteed with this method. Unlike the interactive installation method, users do not have to interpret and answer questions during the installation process, which eliminates errors caused by each individual applying his or her own experiences and interpretations.

- **Increased productivity**   Instead of having thousands of employees install their own copy of DB2 or a team of 15 specialists (local or remote) going to each workstation and installing the code (as required in an interactive installation), one DBA at a central site can work on a perfect DB2 installation, test it, and then roll it out across the enterprise. Because fewer people are involved in the deployment, the TCO is drastically reduced.

A silent installation is controlled by a *response file*, which is an ASCII file that can be edited using any text editor, such as vi, emac, or Notepad. Response files are available for most DB2 products and are located in the following directories:

- **DB2 clients on Windows**   *x*:\db2\windows\common on the DB2 Client Pack CD

- **DB2 servers on Windows** x:\db2\common\
- **DB2 clients on UNIX and Linux**   /cdrom/db2/<*platform*>/install/samples
- **DB2 servers on UNIX and Linux**   /cdrom/db2/install/samples

In each of these paths, the variable x represents a local or remotely mapped drive or device, and the variable <*platform*> represents the platform. UNIX and Linux paths are assumed to mount the CD-ROM in the /cdrom directory.

A response file contains keywords for all the options in an interactive installation, as well as keywords for configuration parameters and DB2 registry variables that you cannot specify during an interactive installation. These features give this installation method more power than traditional methods. Response files are available for all DB2 server and DB2 client installations.

Figure 3-1 shows an excerpt from the db2udbwe.rsp response file for DB2 UDB Workgroup Edition. The entire sample response file is very large and contains keywords

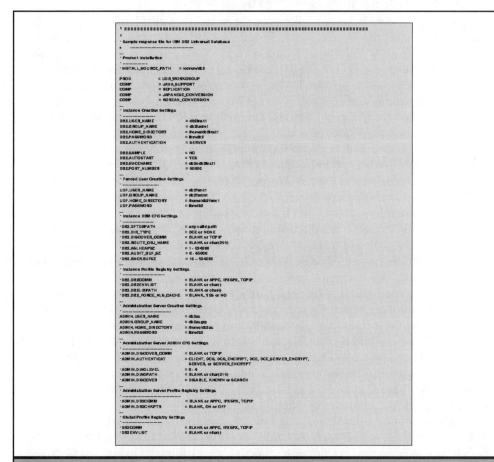

Figure 3-1.   *A response file for DB2 Workgroup Edition*

to set all kinds of parameters and registry variables. To keep things simple, Figure 3-1 includes just enough of the response file for you to get the feel of it. Ellipses (...) indicate where remaining sections have been skipped.

As previously mentioned, you can install base code as well as code maintenance (referred to as maintenance for the remainder of this chapter) when performing a response file installation. Maintenance is delivered in DB2 via FixPaks. When applying maintenance FixPaks using a response file in a Windows environment, you cannot add new components, update database manager configuration (dbm cfg), or change any DB2 registry values. Because you cannot add new components, only the components that are installed on the system before applying the FixPak are maintained. If you are applying maintenance in a UNIX or Linux environment, you must install the FixPak using the operating system's update utilities. (In AIX, use smit update_all; in Solaris, use installallpatch, and in Linux, use installpatch.)

The DB2 Response File Generator

The *response file generator* can be used like a cookie cutter to create identical copies of DB2 code across your enterprise. Basically, you install your DB2 product on a workstation, and when you are happy with the installation and its configuration, you can use this tool to generate a response file for the workstation's existing installation. You can also use this tool to generate profiles for the workstation's configuration settings (its database connections and configuration settings for the database manager, the run-time environment, and Open DataBase Connectivity (ODBC)). This saves the step of recording changes to a system or manually specifying multiple component and configuration parameters in a response file for a complex installation. The response file generator is available only on Windows and OS/2 workstations.

The response file generator creates a response file for the installation and instance profiles for each instance that you specify. The instance profiles contain the instance configuration and database connection information. The response file generator also gives you the option to create just the installation response file, without any instance profiles, if your only goal is to install the code. Response files have the extension .rsp, while instance profiles have the file extension .ins. Figure 3-2 shows an example of an instance profile.

If you are planning to set up and configure identical DB2 products, you need to specify the installation response file with the appropriate installation command only when you perform the installation. The installation response file that was created by the response file generator automatically calls each instance profile. You need to ensure that the instance profiles are located only in the same drive and directory as the installation response file. The response file installation method, especially when used in conjunction with the response file generator (if it is available), is a far more effective and cost-saving solution than the interactive installation solution.

A main benefit of a response file installation is that the requirement for the knowledgeable person to visit each computer has been lifted. Now, you can leverage the skills of one experienced employee to effectively distribute a DB2 product across your enterprise. At the same time, you can still leverage most of the advantages of an interactive installation, like local code for performance, easy customization of the

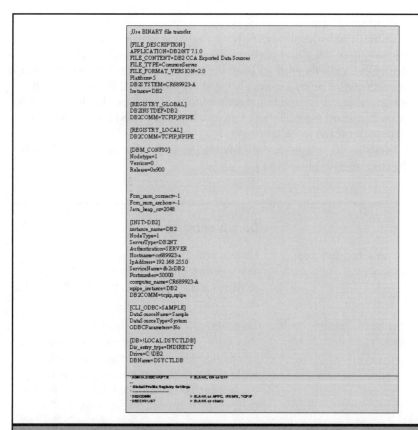

```
;Use BINARY file transfer

[FILE_DESCRIPTION]
APPLICATION=DB2/NT 7.1.0
FILE_CONTENT=DB2 CCA Exported Data Sources
FILE_TYPE=CommonServer
FILE_FORMAT_VERSION=2.0
Platform=5
DB2 SYSTEM=CR689923-A
Instance=DB2

[REGISTRY_GLOBAL]
DB2INSTDEF=DB2
DB2COMM=TCPIP,NPIPE

[REGISTRY_LOCAL]
DB2COMM=TCPIP,NPIPE

[DBM_CONFIG]
Nodetype=1
Version=0
Release=0x900
.
.
.
Fcm_num_connect=-1
Fcm_num_anchors=-1
Java_heap_sz=2048

[INST>DB2]
instance_name=DB2
NodeType=1
ServerType=DB2NT
Authentication=SERVER
Hostname=cr689923-a
IpAddress=192.168.255.0
ServiceName=db2cDB2
Portnumber=50000
computer_name=CR689923-A
npipe_instance=DB2
DB2COMM=tcpip,npipe

[CLI_ODBC>SAMPLE]
DataSourceName=Sample
DataSourceType=System
ODBCParameters=No

[DB>!LOCAL:DSYCTLDB]
Dir_entry_type=INDIRECT
Drive=C:\DB2
DBName=DSYCTLDB

*ADMIN.DESCHKPTn              = BLANK, ON or OFF
--
* Global Profile Registry Settings
--
* DB2COMM                     = BLANK or APPC, IPX SPX, TCP IP
* DB2ENVLIST                  = BLANK or char()
```

Figure 3-2.   *An instance profile that can be used to automate the setup and configuration of DB2 code*

installation (although there is no GUI to dress it up), and the automagic configuration of the installation tool. What's more, you have control over database connection, registry, and configuration settings at the time of installation, as opposed to having to do some separate process afterward. For these reasons, response files are very well suited for mass deployments.

Response file installations can be used with any configuration installation distribution (CID)–compliant installation management program. Specifically, the response file installation method has been integrated into MS SMS. This tight integration gives administrators the ability to PUSH installations out to target workstations. For more information on SMS and DB2 response file installations, refer to the *DB2 Connect Installation and Configuration Supplement.*

With this type of installation, the DB2 code is still local on each machine. While you still have the performance benefits, you also have to contend with the maintenance issues, although you can use a response file for that as well. The maintenance costs are high, but not nearly as high as those associated with an interactive installation.

A potential disadvantage of this method is the learning curve. While this type of installation is not difficult to learn, it does require some experience. Generally, however, companies recognize the value of training one user thoroughly versus training the spectrum of individuals who will use the software on processes unrelated to their jobs (like installations). The end users also still need to PULL the installation, unless, of course, you are using a system management tool. However, this limitation is easily overcome with scripts and e-mails that can launch the required parameters and set up shared drives to kick off the installation.

Table 3-2 summarizes the advantages and disadvantages of a response file installation (with and without the response file generators).

Advantages	Disadvantages
This is an in-the-know created and managed installation.	Unless you are using a system management tool, this method still requires a user to PULL the install or FixPak.
It is relatively easy to customize installation options.	The code is local to the machine; therefore, all code maintenance must be applied locally. Maintenance costs will still be high, but not as high as with the interactive installation because fixes can be applied with a response file.
You can automagically configure the DB2 environment with more power than an interactive installation because you can configure database connection, database manager, and registry settings. What's more, you can use the response file generator on Windows workstations to automatically create a response file.	It is resource- and time-consuming to roll out or roll back a FixPak or code because maintenance must be performed on each separate workstation.
The code is installed locally on the machine, which results in great performance because all code is run locally.	
The installation is integrated with MS SMS for PUSH installations.	

Table 3-2.   *Advantages and Disadvantages of a Response File Installation*

The response file installation method (with or without the response file generator) solves many of the installation problems associated with the interactive installation for large-scale deployments. There are still some maintenance issues that you need to consider, but you will probably be able to live with them.

Citrix Installation

A *Citrix installation* is a special type of DB2 installation that can be used only with Citrix environments. In this environment, the code is installed (and maintained) on the Citrix server. Clients in the Citrix environment (called *dumb terminals*) do not run code locally (hence, their name). Instead, a Citrix client runs its code in cycles allotted to it on the Citrix server. Figure 3-3 shows a typical Citrix environment. This introduces some benefits and some shortcomings to our code deployment dilemma.

First, code is installed and maintained locally on the Citrix server. This is a major benefit because we have found a solution that allows us to leverage the skills of one person for both maintenance and deployments. A Citrix environment creates a "touch one, touch all" environment because all the Citrix clients run programs from the Citrix server.

GETTING STARTED WITH DB2

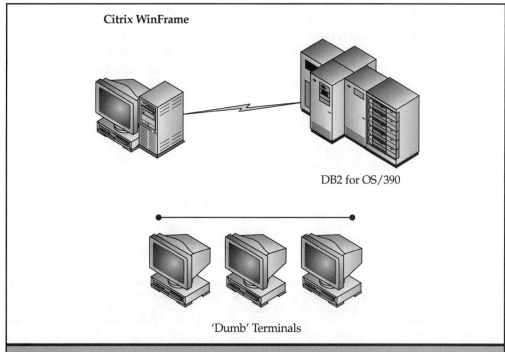

Citrix WinFrame

DB2 for OS/390

'Dumb' Terminals

Figure 3-3. *A typical topology of DB2 deployed in a Citrix environment*

The major drawback of this solution is that it is suitable only for a Citrix environment, and not all DB2 products are supported in this environment (only DB2 clients and DB2 Connect Personal Edition (DB2 Connect PE) servers). You may also suffer from performance problems depending on your network.

Because most people do not run in a Citrix environment, we will not cover this environment in greater detail other than to summarize the advantages and disadvantages in Table 3-3.

If you are running a Citrix environment, you may want to consider using it for DB2 clients or DB2 Connect PE workstations. However, we don't recommend that you go out and implement a Citrix environment to take advantage of the code deployment and maintenance advantages—we have already shown you a better and less expensive way to do this (and we still have one more to show you).

Code Server Installation

In a Windows environment, you can install a DB2 client or DB2 Connect PE on a workstation and have these workstations act as code servers to DB2 Thin-client or DB2 Thin-connect workstations in your enterprise. (The term *Thin-client* is often used

Advantages	Disadvantages
Code needs to be installed only on the Citrix server and therefore only needs to be maintained there as well. You could use an interactive installation method to perform the installation and leverage all the benefits of that installation method because you don't have to be concerned with rolling out the DB2 code to multiple workstations.	Requires a Citrix environment. If you are not currently running a Citrix environment, this could be very expensive and inefficient to implement.
	There are a limited number of DB2 products that can run in this environment.
	Citrix capacity affects the performance of the dumb terminals.

Table 3-3.   *Advantages and Disadvantages of a Citrix Installation*

to represent a DB2 Thin-client or DB2 Thin-connect workstation when discussing this architecture.) Thin workstations load the DB2 client or DB2 Connect PE code across a LAN network connection from their respective code servers.

A *thin workstation* functions like any other DB2 client or DB2 Connect PE workstation; this type of architecture is transparent to the user. The main difference is that the code is installed on a code server, and not individually on each workstation. Each thin workstation needs only a minimal amount of code and configuration to establish links to a code server. This is in contrast to a locally installed DB2 client or DB2 Connect PE workstation, sometimes referred to as *Fat clients,* where all the code is stored and run locally (as in the interactive and response file installations discussed in the previous sections).

Don't confuse this configuration with a Citrix environment. In a Citrix environment, both the code and the processing are handled by the Citrix server. In a thin environment, no processing in done at the code server; the code is simply loaded from the code server.

Figure 3-4 shows a typical DB2 Thin-client and DB2 Thin-connect environment. To install a DB2 Thin-client, you must install a DB2 Administration client with the Thin Client Code Server component. After some configuration, this machine will be known as a DB2 Thin-client code server.

In Figure 3-4, the arrows represent the code that is being loaded on the DB2 Thin-client from the DB2 Thin-client code server. The lighting bolts represent the connection to the database. Once the code is loaded (via the block arrows), all processing and activity is handled on the DB2 Thin-client.

A DB2 Administration client is the only type of client that can act as a code server for Thin-client workstations. The DB2 Thin-client workstations access the code server to dynamically load any code required. Once the code is loaded, all processing is done locally on the DB2 Thin-client workstations. Using local database configuration information (or a central repository like an LDAP (Lightweight Directory Access Protocol) or Active Directory), a connection is made to a target DB2 server and the data can be retrieved for this database. Note that the DB2 code is actually run on the Thin-client or Thin-connect workstations; the code is loaded only from its respective code servers—there is no DB2 code installed on the thin workstations!

This approach offers some definite solutions to the problems raised with the code deployment methods described in "The Interactive Installation" and "The Response File Installation" sections earlier in this chapter. First of all, the code is installed only at one location: the code server. This gives you the benefits of the touch one, touch all maintenance that you get in the Citrix environment, but without needing to change your environment. Another benefit is that you can use a response file installation (including the response file generator) or an interactive installation to set up the environment. Finally, after the initial load of the required dynamic-link libraries (DLLs), there is no need for the thin workstation to communicate with its related code server, so performance is unaffected.

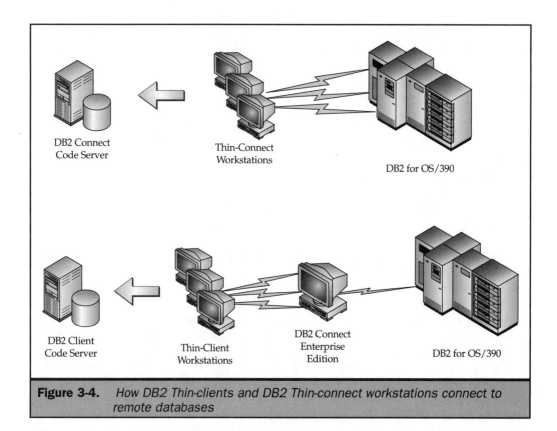

Figure 3-4. *How DB2 Thin-clients and DB2 Thin-connect workstations connect to remote databases*

Although a code server installation solves many of the hurdles that we have identified in an enterprise, it does have some limitations. First, you can only set up DB2 client and DB2 Connect PE workstations using this method. This isn't a big roadblock because you can use this technology for those workstations that carry the highest deployment and maintenance costs (DB2 clients and DB2 Connect PE workstations).

A major drawback of this environment is that it is not suitable for occasional connected users. Mobile users of laptops could not be expected to load code over a telephone line to provide the run-time environment needed for their applications. It may be necessary to use Thin-workstations locally and use the Fat client architecture for mobile users. Another potential drawback of this scenario is the performance loss incurred: the applications are slower to load because DB2 DLLs are loaded from a code server instead of local direct access storage devices (DASD).

Table 3-4 summarizes the strengths and weaknesses of a code server installation.

Advantages

Code needs to be installed in only one location, and therefore needs to be maintained only there as well. You could use an interactive installation method to perform the installation and leverage all the benefits of that installation method because you don't have to be concerned with rolling out the DB2 code to multiple workstations. If you wanted to set up multiple code servers, you could use a response file installation.

After the application loads, performance is unaffected for the rest of the application session.

Disadvantages

The application is slower to load because DB2 DLLs are loaded from a file server instead of local DASD.

Only DB2 clients and DB2 Connect PE workstations support this configuration.

This approach is suitable only for LAN-connected users. It is not suitable for mobile users because application load times can be prohibitive over a wireless connection.

Table 3-4.   *Advantages and Disadvantages of a Code Server Installation*

GETTING STARTED
WITH DB2

Configuration Methodologies

Once your DB2 code is installed on both the server and client workstations, you must consider the configuration of these workstations. In particular, you need to address database connections. You could have successfully installed 2000 clients in a quick and efficient manner using response files, but if they cannot connect to the DB2 server that holds the enterprise information, they are not going to be much use to your business.

The previous section discussed setting up database connections during an installation. This may not be an appropriate solution if the administrator wishes to separate installation and connection procedures or if the database connections require maintenance. However, setting up the database connection information for your clients doesn't have the same maintenance implications as the installation decision does because database connection information does not change often.

Basically, DB2 gives you two options with respect to the location of database connection information: local maintenance and centralized maintenance.

Local Maintenance

In a local maintenance deployment, all database connection information is stored locally on each machine in your enterprise. DB2 offers many methods to set up local database connection information:

- The Client Configuration Assistant (CCA)
- The command line processor (CLP)
- The response file generator
- Client and server profiles
- System management tools

The Client Configuration Assistant

The Client Configuration Assistant (CCA) is a graphical tool that allows you to quickly and efficiently set up remote connections to DB2 severs. The CCA is available on Windows and OS/2 workstations.

The CCA contains a launching point for the Add Database Wizard, shown in Figure 3-5, which helps you easily define database connections to remote DB2 servers

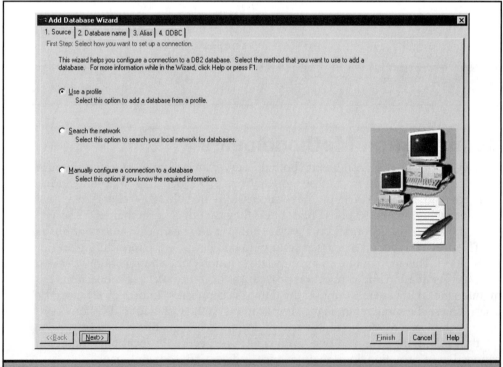

Figure 3-5. *The Client Configuration Assistant*

where your applications can access data. The Add Database Wizard catalogs nodes and databases while shielding you from the inherent complexities of these tasks.

The list of available databases appears in the Client Configuration Assistant's main window. For example, in Figure 3-6, 12 databases are cataloged on the computer called CR689923-A.

Using the CCA, you can use a graphical interface to add database connections to your workstation by using a profile, searching the network, or configuring the connection manually using known configuration information. The CCA is covered in detail in Chapter 4.

Using a Profile The CCA gives you the option of generating or importing profiles that can be used to automatically set up connection and configuration information for your DB2 workstations. Information in a profile can be used to configure clients using the Import function in the CCA. Clients can import all or a subset of the configuration information in a profile. Note that configuration profiles can also be imported using the db2cfimp command, which is discussed in Chapter 4.

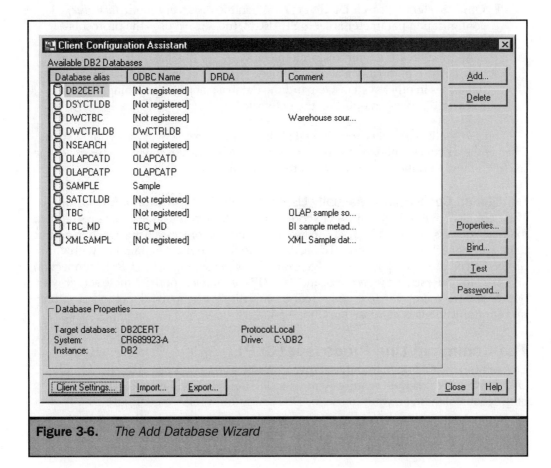

Figure 3-6. *The Add Database Wizard*

Searching the Network   You can search a network to add databases when Discovery is configured and enabled (which is automatically done in a default DB2 installation) on the client and server systems. Discovery is a feature of DB2 that is used to gather information from DB2 servers located on a network. This information can be used by DB2 clients to make automated connections to them using the CCA.

Your database administrator normally provides the names of the DB2 servers where the databases that you need to access reside; this way, you can add that system to the Known Systems list, as shown in Figure 3-7.

You can set your client system to search a network for databases in one of two modes:

- **Known Systems (Directed Discovery)**   When the discovery mode (*discover*) configuration parameter is set to KNOWN, you can specify the connection information to a DAS on the network, and all instance and database information found on that DB2 server system will be returned to the client. To search for databases known to the local machine, you can expand a database object tree until you find the DB2 server and database that you want.

- **Other Systems (Search Discovery)**   When the discovery mode (*discover*) configuration parameter is set to SEARCH, the wizard uses the protocols specified in the Search Discovery Communications Protocols (*discover_comm*) configuration parameter to search the network for databases. In this mode, you can also perform the actions allowed in the KNOWN mode. To search for databases in other systems, expand the database object tree. Doing so initiates a search discovery request on the network.

You can set the discovery mode to DISABLE to disable discovery on your system. Change the discovery mode value by clicking Client Settings in the first window of the CCA. You will find these parameters on the Communications tab.

Configuring Connections Manually Using Known Configuration Information

The CCA also gives you the option to configure database connections using a graphical interface to dress up the manual (using the command line processor) approach to adding database connection information. To use this method, you must be familiar with your protocol's configuration parameters. For example, when setting up a TCP/IP connection, you need to understand the *svcename* and TCP/IP *port_number* of the remote server with which you are attempting to establish communications. The manual method of setting up communications is discussed in Chapter 4.

The Command Line Processor (CLP)

You can use the CLP to manually set up communications between DB2 clients and DB2 servers. This method requires you to understand the configuration parameters of the protocol that you want to use for DB2 communication. To configure DB2 communications using the CLP, you need to catalog directories of information so that

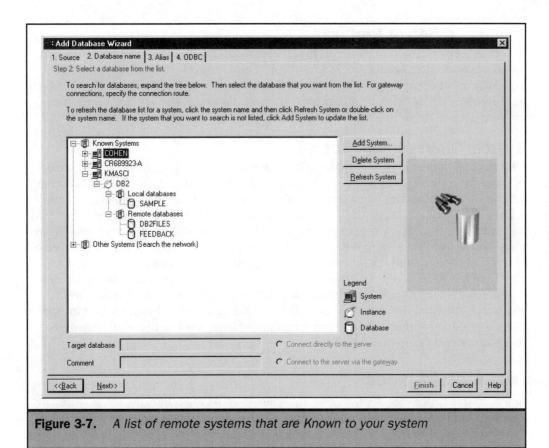

Figure 3-7.   *A list of remote systems that are Known to your system*

the DB2 client knows how to reach the DB2 server. For example, to catalog a remote DB2 server, you need to catalog a node and database directory. If you are attempting to reach a DB2 server that resides on an iSeries or zSeries machine, you also need to catalog the Database Connection Services (DCS) directory. For more information, see Chapter 4.

The Response File Generator

As you have already learned, the response file generator (db2rspgn) allows you to generate an installation response file, as well as instance profiles (which contain connection and instance configuration information). This utility is available on OS/2- and Windows-based workstations. You can use this tool to install and configure DB2 software and database connection information. Installations by this method place local code and connection information on the target workstations. For more information about this utility, refer to the *DB2 Installation and Configuration Supplement* or Chapter 9.

Client and Server Profiles

DB2 provides the option to create profiles that contain database manager configuration, database connection, and ODBC/CLI settings. Using import and export commands, you can import or export this information to and from files. This greatly aids administrators in deploying configuration information across an enterprise. Profiles are discussed in detail in Chapter 4.

System Management Tools

DB2 has a tight integration with MS SMS; therefore, you can use SMS to PUSH script commands to target DB2 clients. Quite simply, this means that the DB2 clients receive scripted instructions that they process without asking for them, in contrast to what is known as a PULL strategy, where instructions are "asked" for. For example, when you replicate your e-mail program to receive incoming e-mail, you are pulling e-mail from your mail server. If you do not have a replication scheme set up for e-mail and receive e-mail when it is sent to you, this e-mail is being pushed to your system.

Using MS SMS, you can distribute database connection information using a push methodology. For example, maybe a new database connection is needed for the workforce. An administrator who uses MS SMS could push out a batch file that imports a client profile or adds a database connection to a target workstation—all transparent to the user of that target workstation.

Central Maintenance

In a central maintenance deployment, all database connection information is stored on a server. A central maintenance configuration deployment is set up using a supported LDAP or an Active Directory server acting as an LDAP server. LDAP servers can be set up on AIX, Solaris, or Windows NT/2000–based workstations.

LDAP is an industry standard access method to directory services. It can also be used for security authentication; however, this support is not in the current release of DB2. A *directory service* is a repository of resource information about multiple systems and services within a distributed environment, and it provides client and server access to these resources. Each database server instance publishes its existence to an LDAP server and provides database information to the LDAP directory when the databases are created. When a client connects to a database, the catalog information for the server can be retrieved from the LDAP directory. Each client is no longer required to store catalog information locally on each machine. Client applications search the LDAP directory for information required to connect to the database.

The easiest way to think of a central maintenance setup is to think of an Internet phone book. In the local maintenance setup, DB2 clients have to maintain their own "personal phone book" with an entry for every database to which they want to connect in the node and database directories. Each client has its own node and database directories that will likely be different from one client to the next. In central maintenance architecture, DB2 clients connect to an LDAP server that has a listing of all the resources in the enterprise (that administrators have chosen to publish), and DB2 clients can use this information on the server to connect to these databases. This is just like looking up someone's phone number on the Internet. You don't have it locally, so you go to a resource.

Administrators who set up this type of environment have to make sure that the LDAP server is highly available. If the LDAP server were not available, DB2 clients would not be able to connect to it to retrieve the database connection information that they need. Similarly, if your Internet connection were down, you would not be able to connect to your online phonebook.

Figure 3-8 shows a typical LDAP implementation.

In DB2, a caching mechanism exists so that the DB2 client searches the LDAP directory only once. Once the information is retrieved, it is stored or cached locally. Subsequent access to the same information is based on the values of the *dir_cache* dbm cfg parameter and the DB2LDAPCACHE registry variable as follows:

- If DB2LDAPCACHE=NO and *dir_cache*= NO, then always read the information from LDAP.

- If DB2LDAPCACHE=NO and *dir_cache*=YES, then read the information from LDAP once and insert it into the DB2 cache.

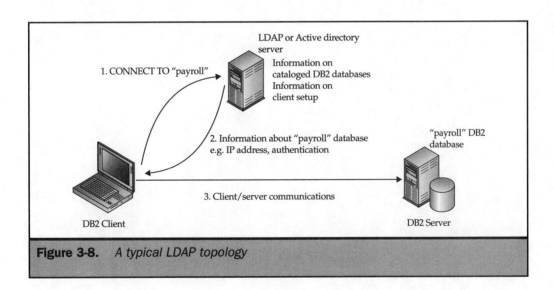

Figure 3-8.   *A typical LDAP topology*

■ If DB2LDAPCACHE=YES or is not set, and if the required information is not found in the local cache, then the information is read from the LDAP directory and the local cache is refreshed.

The benefits of this type of environment are many; however, an inherent complexity comes with any new technology. LDAP allows you to update catalog connection information at one location (the LDAP server), and then all DB2 clients can leverage that information to make their database connections. If you are already using LDAP in your enterprise, this may be a better solution than the local maintenance options. LDAP results in a touch one, touch many database connection architecture.

You can set up a central maintenance environment using the CCA or the CLP, along with the required steps of the LDAP software that you are implementing. The CCA has fields enabled for LDAP servers, and the CATALOG NODE and CATALOG DATABASE commands have LDAP extensions added to their syntax. (See Chapter 30 for more information.)

The
Complete
Reference

DB2

Chapter 4

Connecting a DB2 Client to a DB2 Server

Once you have installed a DB2 client and the DB2 server, you will likely want these machines to be able to talk to one another. If you haven't yet deployed your DB2 clients throughout your enterprise, consider reading Chapter 3, which will give you some tips for the installation of your DB2 clients so that all the configuration information needed to make a database connection is handled during the installation. In many cases, however, database administrators like to separate the installation and configuration processes.

DB2 supports today's most popular communications protocols: TCP/IP, APPC (sometimes called SNA), IPX/SPX, NetBIOS (DB2 uses the NetBEUI part of NetBIOS for communications, so sometimes people may refer to NetBIOS support as NetBEUI), and Named Pipes. The information that is transmitted across these protocols adheres to a DB2 information transfer protocol called DB2RA or the standard database protocol DRDA—depending on which remote DB2 system you are trying to establish communications with.

In the case of communications from a DB2 client on a distributed platform (UNIX, Linux, OS/2, or Windows-based) to a DB2 server on a distributed platform, DB2RA is used. If the connection is from a DB2 Connect gateway or a DB2 Connect Personal Edition (Connect PE) workstation to an iSeries or zSeries server (formerly known as AS/400 and S/390 servers), the DRDA protocol is used. DB2 users need to understand only the basic parameters of the communications protocol that they are using to establish communications between any DB2 clients and DB2 servers.

This chapter discusses the different methods that you can use to connect DB2 clients to DB2 servers. Because most of the world today uses the TCP/IP protocol for communications, this chapter discusses the use of TCP/IP only in a DB2 distributed environment. All supported protocols are summarized in Table 4-1; refer to the *DB2 Installation and Configuration Supplement* for information on protocols other than TCP/IP.

DB2 Clients				DB2 Servers			Windows
	AIX	HP-UX	Linux	OS/2	Numa-Q	Solaris	NT/2000
AIX	APPC TCP/IP	TCP/IP	TCP/IP	APPC TCP/IP	TCP/IP	APPC TCP/IP	APPC TCP/IP
HP-UX	APPC TCP/IP	TCP/IP	TCP/IP	APPC TCP/IP	TCP/IP	APPC TCP/IP	APPC TCP/IP
Linux	TCP/IP	TCP/IP	TCP/IP	TCP/IP	TCP/IP	TCP/IP	TCP/IP

Table 4-1. *Supported DB2 Client–to–DB2-Server Communications Protocols*

DB2 Clients				DB2 Servers			
OS/2	APPC IPX/SPX** TCP/IP	TCP/IP	TCP/IP	APPC IPX/SPX** NetBIOS TCP/IP	TCP/IP	APPC IPX/SPX* TCP/IP	APPC IPX/SPX* NetBIOSTCP/IP
Numa-Q	TCP/IP	TCP/IP	TCP/IP	TCP/IP	TCP/IP	TCP/IP	TCP/IP
SGI/ IRIX	TCP/IP	TCP/IP	TCP/IP	TCP/IP	TCP/IP	TCP/IP	TCP/IP
Solaris	APPC TCP/IP	TCP/IP	TCP/IP	APPC TCP/IP	TCP/IP	APPC TCP/IP	APPC TCP/IP
Windows 9x, Me	TCP/IP IPX/SPXSPX*	TCP/IP	TCP/IP	TCP/IP NetBIOS IPX/ SPXSPX*	TCP/IP	TCP/IP IPX/SPXSPX*	APPC NPIPE IPX/SPX SPX* NetBIOS TCP/IP
Windows NT/2000	APPC IPX/SPX* TCP/IP	TCP/IP	TCP/IP	APPC IPX/SPX* NetBIOS TCP/IP	TCP/IP	APPC IPX/SPX* TCP/IP	APPC IPX/SPX* NetBIOS NPIPE TCP/IP

*Direct addressing
**File server addressing

Table 4-1.   *Supported DB2 Client–to–DB2-Server Communications Protocols* (continued)

Enabling Communications for a DB2 Server

Before a DB2 client can connect to a DB2 server, the DB2 server has to be enabled for inbound communications. In DB2, communications are handled at the DB2 instance level, so each instance on a DB2 server needs to be enabled for communications.

When DB2 is installed using a response file or the automated method for your environment (db2setup for UNIX and Linux workstations and setup for Windows-based systems), most communications protocols on your system are automatically detected and configured.

In a UNIX or Linux environment, many administrators prefer to install DB2 software using the native installation commands such as *installp* in an AIX environment or *rpm* in a Linux shop. However, because the DB2 installation programs automatically detect and configure any supported communications software running on a workstation, we recommend that you use the db2setup program when installing DB2 on a UNIX or Linux-based workstation.

This section of the chapter describes how to use the Control Center and the command line processor (CLP) to configure your DB2 server communications after a manual installation. It also describes how to add support for new communications protocols so that DB2 can use them. Keep in mind that enabling support for a protocol for DB2 doesn't add that protocol to your system. If you enable DB2 to support TCP/IP, but you have not installed TCP/IP services on your workstation (which is installed by default with most of today's operating systems), then you will not be able to get a DB2 client to talk to a DB2 server until you add the required TCP/IP software.

Setting Up Communications Using the Control Center

The Control Center is DB2's central GUI-based administration tool, and it can be used to administer DB2 databases from pervasive devices such as Palm Pilots and cellular phones, to clusters of symmetric multiprocessing (SMP) workstations, to massively parallel processing (MPP) systems like the IBM zSeries servers. The Control Center has a setup communications function that allows you to display the protocols and configuration parameters that a server's instance is configured to use. It also allows you to modify any parameter values of a configured protocol, as well as add or delete supported protocols.

When you add support to the server system for a new protocol, the setup communications function detects and generates server instance parameter values for the new protocol. You can accept or modify these values before use. When you remove from the server system support for an existing protocol, the setup communications function detects the protocol that has been removed and disables its use by the instance.

If you remove protocol support for a server instance, ensure that you take the time to manage the work effort required for each DB2 client that has locally cataloged this server instance's information. For example, if you changed the communications protocol settings on a DB2 server for a particular instance, then all the DB2 clients would need to know about this change. If they didn't, they would not be able to connect to the database. Think about if you moved and neglected to tell anyone your new phone number. Would they be able to call you? Probably not. Same concept here.

If you want to add support for a protocol that was not detected by the DB2 installation program, you must supply all of the parameter values required before you proceed. For example, if you were planning to add APPC to your network, you may need to specify APPC parameters. (Some versions of APPC are undetectable by the DB2 installation program.)

If you have added other DB2 server systems to the main view of the Control Center, and the Database Administration Server (DAS) is running on each of these servers, you can also set up and maintain communications for remote instances as well.

Setting Up Communications for Local Instances

To set up communications for any local instances using the Control Center, perform the following steps:

1. Start the Control Center.

2. Expand the tree view of the DB2 system where the instance for which you want to configure communications resides, right-click, and select the Setup Communications option. The Setup Communications window for the instance that you want to configure appears, as shown in Figure 4-1. Notice that some communications protocols were detected and others were not.

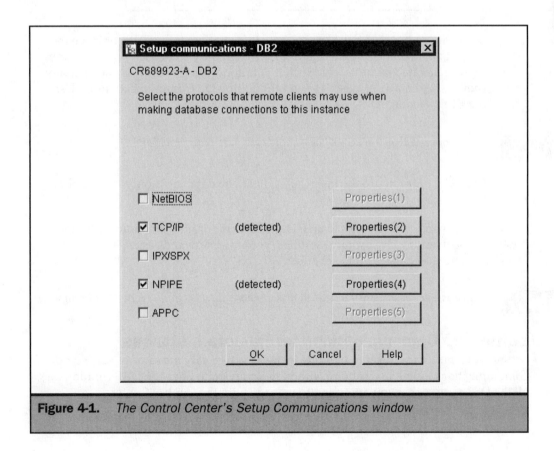

Figure 4-1.   *The Control Center's Setup Communications window*

3. Select the communications protocol that you want to add, remove, or modify, and click the associated Properties button. A protocol-specific parameters dialog box appears. (An example is shown below.)

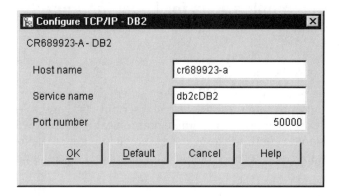

4. In the dialog box, enter the appropriate information in the fields or leave the default value that DB2 generates for each field. If you choose to override any of the generated defaults, ensure that you understand the implications of any changes you make, as described in the "Setting Up Communications by Using the CLP" section.

We recommend that you accept the default values that are provided.

5. Click OK to configure the instance. A dialog box appears notifying you about the progress of your request.

Whenever you make changes to an instance's configuration, including adding, removing, or changing any protocol settings, you must stop and restart the server instance before the changes will take effect.

You can issue the db2start and db2stop commands directly from a command prompt.

Setting Up Communications for Remote Instances

Setting up communications for a remote instance is basically the same as setting up communications for a local instance, although you need to have the DAS running on all the DB2 servers that you are trying to manage with the Control Center.

If the remote server—or in some cases, the remote server instance—does not appear in your view of the Control Center, you need to add it. For example, let's assume that a remote DB2 server (called KMASCI) does not appear in the view of the Control Center. If the instance that you want to configure communications for resides on the KMASCI remote DB2 server, you would need to add it to your view of the Control Center. You can add a remote DB2 server to your view of the Control Center by using the Add function of the Control Center or by using server profiles.

Once you add the remote system and instance, the rest of the steps are the same as if the server and instance were local. To set up communications, just follow the same steps that you would for a local instance.

Adding a Remote Server and Instance by Using the Add Function   The Control Center's Add function allows you to search the network or specify a particular DB2 server that you want to add to your list of systems. If the instance that you want to configure resides on a system that does not appear in your view of the Control Center, perform the following steps to add it:

1. Start the Control Center.

2. Select the Systems folder, right-click, and select the Add option. The Add System window appears.

3. Either click the Refresh button to search the network for other DB2 servers and select a server from the returned list, or enter the hostname of the remote system in the Host Name field and click Retrieve. Refer to online help for more information.

4. When you have selected the system you want to add, click OK. For example, after entering the hostname KMASCI in the Host Name field and clicking Retrieve, the Add System window looks like Figure 4-2.

When you click OK, this system is added to the view of the Control Center, as shown in Figure 4-3.

After you have added a remote DB2 server to the Control Center, you may notice, as in Figure 4-3, that the Instances folder is empty—this does *not* necessarily mean that this DB2 server has no DB2 instances on it. Instances usually do exist on the remote DB2 server; otherwise, it couldn't even have a database on it, and what would be the point of having that workstation act as a DB2 server without databases on it? You just can't see them.

To add the instances you want to configure, perform the following steps.

1. Select the Instances folder underneath the appropriate server icon, right-click, and select Add. The Add Instance dialog box appears.

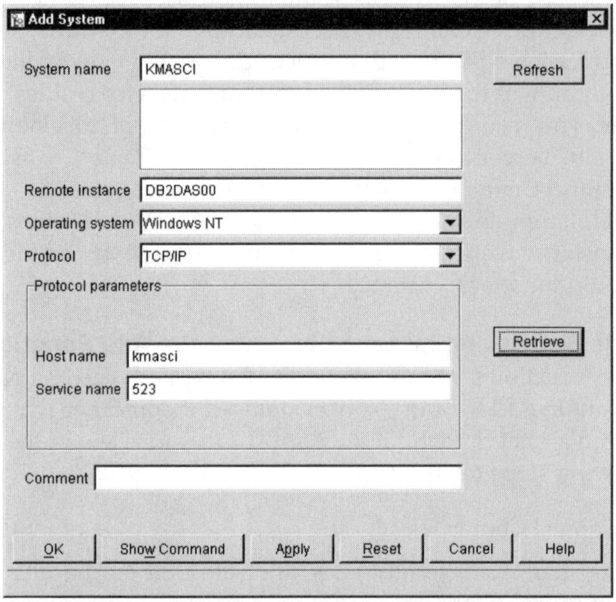

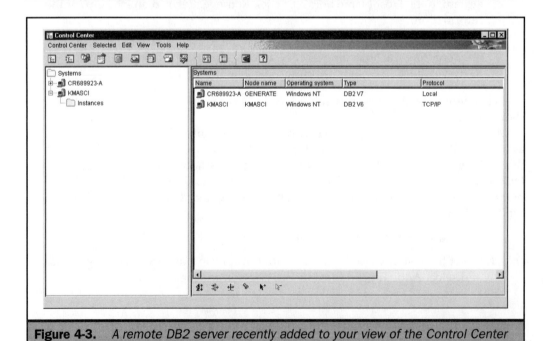

Figure 4-2. Adding a DB2 server to your view of the Control Center

Figure 4-3. A remote DB2 server recently added to your view of the Control Center

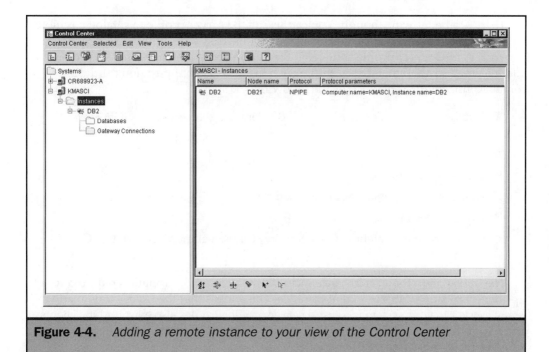

Figure 4-4. *Adding a remote instance to your view of the Control Center*

2. Click the Refresh button. A drop-down list of all the instances available on this DB2 server is displayed.

3. Select the instance that you want to configure (optionally, rename it using the Instance Name field), and click OK.

In Figure 4-4, you can see that a remote instance that resides on the DB2 server called KMASCI was added to the view of the Control Center.

From here on in, you can use the same process that you used to configure the local instance for communications, as explained previously in "Setting Up Communications for Local Instances."

Adding a Remote Server and Instance Using Server Profiles   If you wanted to add multiple servers and instances from a single workstation (which is what the Control Center is for, after all), then the previous process may seem somewhat cumbersome. Having to search the network for all the different servers or knowing their protocol information can be a pain. Notice in Figure 4-4 that no databases exist under the instance DB2. Well, as you may have guessed, you have to add the databases to these instances if you want to manage those as well. (Of course, you don't need to have any databases appear under the instance folder if all you are trying to do is configure communications because communications is handled in DB2 at the instance level.)

There is a better way, though. You can use a DB2 server profile to catalog a remote DB2 server, its instances, and its databases all in one easy step, without searching the network. A DB2 server profile contains information about instances on a server system and information about databases within each instance. A configuration profile may contain connectivity items such as the following:

- Database information (including DB2 Connect gateways and ODBC information)
- Node information
- Protocol information
- Database manager configuration settings
- DB2 registry settings
- Common Open Database Connectivity/Call Level Interface (ODBC/CLI) settings

The information for each instance includes the protocol information required to set up connections to databases in that instance. This means that the fastest way to add a remote server to your system is to use a server profile. Profiles also exist for DB2 clients, and we'll cover those in the "Configuring DB2 Client and Server Communications" section later in this chapter.

Before you can add a server profile to your system, you need to know how to create one. The good news is that this process is very simple. On the DB2 server that you want to profile (in our example, we would do this from the KMASCI workstation), perform the following steps:

1. Start the Control Center on the remote system you want to profile or where the remote server you want to profile is cataloged.
2. Select the name of the server that you want to profile, right-click, and select the Export Server Profile option. A dialog box appears in which you can select the save name and location for this profile.

To add a system, its instances, and databases to your Control Center using a profile, perform the following steps:

1. Start the Client Configuration Assistant (CCA) on the system where you want to import the server profile. The CCA is a graphical tool that allows you to quickly and efficiently set up remote connections to DB2 severs. The CCA is available only on Windows and OS/2 workstations.
2. Click the Import button. The Select Profile box opens.
3. Select the location of the server profile on your workstation or shared directory and click OK. The Import Profile dialog box opens.

4. To customize the information that you want to import, select the Customize radio button, or simply import the profile with all the configuration information using the All radio button. We recommend you just select All and then click OK.

Now refresh your view of the Control Center and expand (if necessary) the tree view of the new system that you just added. Your view will look something like Figure 4-5. As you can see, this is a very fast and efficient way to add remote DB2 servers to your view of the Control Center.

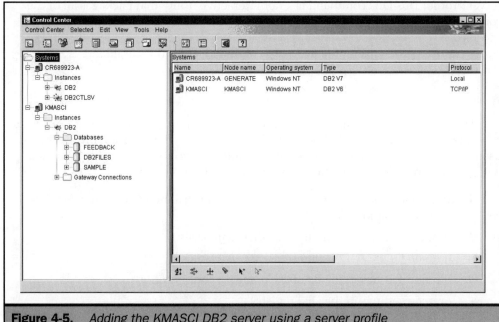

Figure 4-5.   *Adding the KMASCI DB2 server using a server profile*

> **Tip** *You may need to specify a user ID and password when you select the new system or its instances. This is because under the covers, DB2 is attaching to the remote instance and will ask you to authenticate yourself to the remote DB2 server before allowing you to access it. The user ID and password you specify must be defined on the remote DB2 server (or domain, in the case of a Windows environment).*

The CCA allows you to catalog remote databases on a system. To generate client profiles (which you will learn about in the "Adding a Database Connection Using Client Profiles" section later in this chapter) or graphically import server or client profiles, you have to use the CCA.

Currently, the CCA is available only on OS/2 and Windows-based platforms. However, for UNIX and Linux users, the Import and Export features of the CCA are available through the db2cfimp and db2cfexp commands. Any user who has System Administrative (SYSADM) or System Controller (SYSCTRL) authorities can use DB2 system commands to generate and import profiles.

Using the db2cfexp Command to Export a Server Profile   The db2cfexp DB2 system command exports connectivity and configuration information to a configuration profile, which can later be imported on another DB2 workstation. If you run this command on a DB2 server, you can refer to the output of this command as a DB2 server profile. This DB2 command is a noninteractive utility that packages all of the configuration information needed to satisfy the requirements of the export option specified.

To export a profile using the db2cfexp command, enter this command as follows:

```
db2cfexp <filename> TEMPLATE
```

The <filename> is the name and location (full pathname) of the profile you want to export on your system. The TEMPLATE option creates a configuration profile that is used as a template for other instances of the same instance type. A profile generated with this flag includes information about the following:

- All databases, including related ODBC and Distributed Connection Servers (DCS) information
- All nodes associated with the exported databases
- Common ODBC/CLI settings
- Common settings in the database manager configuration
- Common settings in the DB2 registry

You can use two other options with the db2cfexp command instead of the TEMPLATE option: BACKUP and MAINTAIN. The BACKUP option creates a configuration profile of the DB2 instance for local backup purposes. This profile contains all of the instance configuration information, including information specific to the local instance. The MAINTAIN option creates a configuration profile containing database and node-related information only for maintaining or updating other instances. For more information on this command, refer to Chapter 30.

 You would not use the BACKUP option to generate a profile that you wanted to import on a different DB2 server.

Using the db2cfimp Command to Import a Server Profile   The db2cfimp DB2 system command imports connectivity and configuration information from a file known as a *profile*. It is a noninteractive utility that attempts to import all the information found in a configuration profile.

To import a profile using the db2cfimp command, enter this command as follows:

```
db2cfimp <filename>
```

The <filename> parameter represents the name and location (full pathname) of the profile you want to import on your system.

For more information on this command, refer to Chapter 30.

Setting up Communications Using the CLP

If you don't want to use any of the automated tools to configure communications between DB2 servers and clients, you can use the manual method in conjunction with the DB2 command line processor (CLP). This section describes how to use the CLP to configure your server to accept inbound requests from remote clients.

Before you can begin to set up inbound communications on a DB2 server, your DB2 server needs to know which communications protocols it should start DB2 connection managers for. The DB2COMM registry variable tells DB2 which connection managers to start for which communications protocols. (This variable is automatically set during installation when using the DB2 installation tools or when updating an instance's configuration using the Control Center.)

Setting the DB2COMM Registry Variable

A DB2 server can support multiple communications protocols concurrently; however, you need to enable only the protocols that you want to use. To check the value of all the registry variables set on your DB2 server, enter the following command:

```
db2set -all

[i] DB2DBDFT=SAMPLE
[i] DB2COMM=TCPIP,NPIPE
```

```
[g]  DB2SYSTEM=CR689923-A
[g]  DB2PATH=C:\Program Files\SQLLIB
[g]  DB2INSTDEF=DB2
[g]  DB2ADMINSERVER=DB2DAS00
```

If the DB2COMM registry variable (or any registry variable, for that matter) is not set, it will not be returned in the list generated by the db2set –all command. For a complete listing of all the DB2 registry variables, enter the db2set –lr command, and refer to Chapter 29 for details on each variable.

For a DB2 server, the DB2COMM registry variable can be any combination of the following:

- **APPC**   Starts APPC support
- **IPXSPX**   Starts IPX/SPX support
- **TCPIP**   Starts TCP/IP support
- **NPIPE**   Starts Named Pipe support
- **NETBIOS**   Starts NetBIOS support

To set the DB2COMM registry variable, enter the following command:

```
db2set -i <instance_name> DB2COMM=<supported_protocol>
```

The <instance_name> is the name of the instance for which you want to set the DB2COMM registry variable, and the <supported_protocol> is any combination from the preceding list, separated by commas.

For example, if you wanted to enable TCP/IP and APPC support for your DB2 instance, you would enter the following command:

```
db2set -i db2 DB2COMM=tcpip,appc
```

For more information on the db2set command, refer to Chapter 29.

Once you set or change the settings of the DB2COMM registry variable, you will need to stop and restart the instance so that the appropriate connection managers for the communications protocol that you want to use are started. If there are problems starting one of the connection managers when starting the instance, a warning message appears and information is logged in the db2diag.log file.

Setting Up Inbound TCP/IP Communications

Setting up inbound TCP/IP communications for a DB2 server involves two steps: reserving an entry in the local services file, and updating the local database manager configuration (dbm cfg) with the appropriate TCP/IP information. (Of course, to access a remote server through TCP/IP, you must first have installed and configured the TCP/IP communications software for both the client and server workstations.)

Use Table 4-2 to identify the parameters you need to set up communications on your DB2 server.

Parameter	Explanation	Sample Value
Connection service and port number, which is made up of two side-by-side entries:	You will be required to update these parameters in the services file on your DB2 server. The svcename is an arbitrary nickname used to represent the connection service for this port. It must be unique within the services file.	server1 50001/tcp
Connection service name (svcename) Port number/protocol (port_number/tcp)	The connection port is a number that is also arbitrary and must be unique within the services file. This number *must* be followed by a forward slash (/) and the keyword tcp, as shown in the example. The DB2 installation program usually uses ports for default instances from 50,000 and up. Generally, port numbers below 1024 are registered and reserved for well-known applications and should not be used even if available.	

Table 4-2.   *Parameters Required for Setting Up Inbound TCP/IP Communications*

GETTING STARTED WITH DB2

Parameter	Explanation	Sample Value
Service name (svcename)	The name used to update the service name (svcename) parameter in the dbm cfg. This value *must* be the same as the connection service name in the services file, identified previously in this table. Essentially, this parameter maps the service name specified to a port number using the entry in the services file—much as a hostname maps to a machine's IP address.	server1

Table 4-2.   *Parameters Required for Setting Up Inbound TCP/IP Communications (continued)*

To configure your DB2 server for inbound TCP/IP communications, perform the following steps:

1. Log on to your system as a user with SYSADM or SYSCTRL authority.

2. Update the TCP/IP services file and specify the connection service name and port number that the DB2 server should listen on for DB2 client requests for data. In UNIX and Linux environments, the services file is generally located in the /etc directory. In Windows environments, this file is in the \winnt\system32\ drivers\etc directory.

Using a text editor, make an entry in the services file by using the parameters that you identified in Table 4-2. You can optionally add a comment to your entry by using the pound delimiter (#). An example is shown in Figure 4-6.

Tip   *Older versions of DB2 needed to reserve an interrupt port for TCP/IP communications. The service name of this port was often the same as the service name you reserved, with an i tagged on to the end, as seen below the selected line in Figure 4-6. The port number associated with the interrupt is always the next sequential port number. This is no longer required in DB2; however, for backwards compatibility, you will often see the DB2 tools update both entries in the services file.*

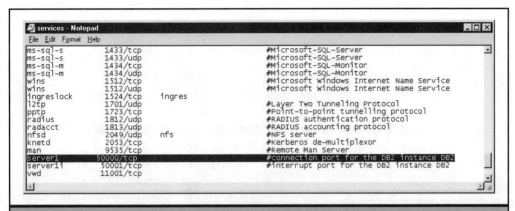

Figure 4-6. *A sample of the contents from a typical TCP/IP services file*

1. Update the dbm cfg file with the service name that you identified in Table 4-2 and added in the services file in the previous step. Use the following command:

   ```
   db2 update dbm cfg using svcename <svcename>
   ```

   For example, if you used the values in Table 4-2, this command would be entered as follows:

   ```
   db2 update dbm cfg using svcename server1
   ```

> **Tip** *The abbreviation dbm stands for "database manager" and cfg stands for "configuration." You can use these abbreviations with any DB2 command that requires the database manager or configuration keyword.*

> **Tip** *You can use the Configure function in the Control Center to update dbm cfg parameters. However, if you are using the Control Center, then you would likely use the setup communications function discussed in the "Setting Up Communications Using the Control Center" section earlier in this chapter.*

2. After you run this command, ensure that your updates ran successfully by entering the following command:

   ```
   db2 get dbm cfg
   ```

   Your output should look similar to Figure 4-7.

3. Enter the db2stop command to stop the instance.

4. Enter the db2start command to restart the instance.

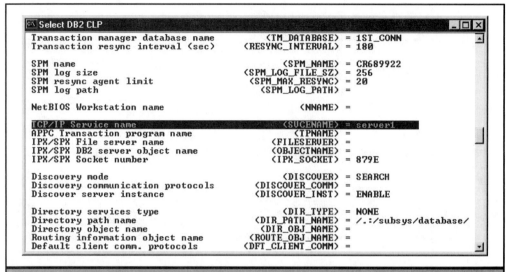

Figure 4-7. *The TCP/IP service name in an instance's dbm configuration file*

Your DB2 server is now ready to accept inbound requests via TCP/IP. For information on how to set up your DB2 server for other supported DB2 protocols, refer to the *DB2 Installation and Configuration Supplement.*

Configuring Communications from a DB2 Client to a DB2 Server

Once a DB2 server has been enabled for communications (which is the default for any DB2 installation performed with a DB2 installation tool), you are ready to set up communications on the DB2 client. There are many ways to do this. In some cases, you can configure the client through the installation by using the response file and instance profiles. For more information on this technique, refer to Chapter 3.

You can also configure a DB2 client to connect to a DB2 server by using the CCA, client profiles, or the command line processor—each of these options also allows you to take advantage of the Lightweight Directory Access Protocol (LDAP) if you are using it in your environment. In a Windows 2000 environment, DB2 also supports the Active Directory protocol.

Before you begin configuring a DB2 client to connect to a DB2 server, ensure that both workstations can talk to each other over the protocol that you selected for communications. Because we are assuming that you are using TCP/IP in this chapter (most people do, so this is a pretty sound assumption), we can test the ability of our DB2 client and DB2 server machines to talk to each other by using the TCP/IP ping command.

We also assume in this chapter that your TCP/IP network supports name resolution via a name server. If a name server does not exist on your network, which would be rare these days, you should specify a hostname that maps to the appropriate machine's IP address in your local hosts file. See your network administrator for more information.

To test TCP/IP communications using the ping command, on each workstation, enter the hostname command to retrieve the hostname of that workstation. When you know each workstation's hostname, you can enter the ping <hostname> command on each workstation to test a TCP/IP connection to the other workstation.

For example, if you entered the hostname command on a DB2 client, you may get a response like the one shown in Figure 4-8. If the hostname command was previously run on the DB2 server and returned the value KMASCI, you would enter the ping KMASCI command on the DB2 client (which is CR689923–a machine shown in Figure 4-10). The hostname of the DB2 clientis the hostname that you would use to test a ping command from the DB2 server to the DB2 client. If both machines can ping each other, then you know that TCP/IP is working fine and you are ready to set up connections from the DB2 client to the remote DB2 server.

The hostname of your workstation is a nickname that represents the IP address of your workstation. In Figure 4-8, you can see that when you ping the DB2 server with the hostname KMASCI, the IP address of that workstation is displayed (in this example, the IP address happens to be 9.21.22.98), so KMASCI really resolves to 9.21.22.98. When you set up communications between DB2 clients and servers using TCP/IP, you have to use either the hostname or the IP address of the remote DB2 server. To retrieve the IP address of the workstation you are working on, you can simply ping that machine. So if you were working on the client in the previous example, you could ping the CR689923-A workstation (the machine you are working on), and it would display the local IP address.

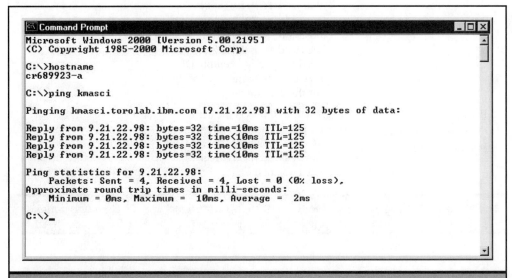

Figure 4-8.   *Pinging a remote workstation*

Configuring Communications Using the CLP

If you plan to use an OS/2 or a Windows-based DB2 client to communicate with a DB2 server, the CCA makes it easy to automate configuration and administration tasks. If you have installed the CCA, we recommended that you use this tool to configure your DB2 client connections. For more information, see the "Configuring Communications using the CCA" section later in this chapter.

However, you can also use the CLP to configure connections from a DB2 client to the DB2 server. You may want to use the CLP method if you are running a DB2 client on a UNIX or Linux-based workstation because the CCA is not available to you. However, we suggest you use the server profile method discussed in the previous section because it minimizes the amount of work you need to do to establish communications. The CLP method is also well suited if you are writing scripts to configure workstations across your enterprise.

Setting up outbound TCP/IP communications for a DB2 client involves several steps, some of which are optional and some of which are not. Table 4-3 can help you to identify and record the parameters you need to set up communications on your DB2 client.

Parameter	Explanation	Sample Value
Hostname <hostname>	The hostname is a nickname used to represent the IP address of a server workstation that uses TCP/IP. In our example, the DB2 server hostname KMASCI represents the IP address 9.21.22.98. You need to specify a remote DB2 server's hostname or IP address for this parameter.	KMASCI 9.21.22.98
or		
IP address <ip_address> (You need to specify one of these parameters.)	The IP address is the actual address of a workstation on a TCP/IP network. This address can be referenced directly or via a hostname.	

Table 4-3.   *Parameters Required for Setting Up Outbound TCP/IP Communications*

Parameter	Explanation	Sample Value
Connection service name <svcename>	The connection service name is an arbitrary local name that represents the connection port number (port_number) on the DB2 server. You need to check the services file on the DB2 server to resolve the port number that was used to configure the DB2 instance on the DB2 server for inbound communications. For more information on the DB2 server's service name and port number, refer to the "Setting Up Communications Using the CLP" section earlier in the chapter.	server1 50001
or		
Port number/protocol <port#>/tcp (You need to specify one of these parameters.)	In our example, we will use the same service name that was used on the DB2 server. If you want to specify a port number, the port number you use must be the one that the <svcename> parameter maps to in the services file on the DB2 server. (The <svcename> parameter is located in the database manager configuration file on the server; see Figure 4-7.) This value must not be in use by any other applications, and it must be unique within each services file on the DB2 client and DB2 server.	

Table 4-3.   *Parameters Required for Setting Up Outbound TCP/IP Communications* (continued)

Parameter	Explanation	Sample Value
Node name <node_name>	The node name is a nickname that represents a DB2 server instance (sometimes referred to as a node) where the database you are trying to connect to resides. You can choose any name you want; however, all node names on your DB2 client must be unique—DB2 will take care of this requirement for you. (For simplicity, if there is only one instance on a machine, we like to use the hostname of the DB2 server as the node name because that is the workstation that this parameter will represent. Of course, if you have multiple instances that you need to connect to, then you need to be a little more creative than this.)	KMASCI
Database name <db_name>	This is the database alias <db_alias> of the remote DB2 database. When you create a database, it is automatically cataloged on the DB2 server with the same database alias and database name, unless otherwise specified. If you created the SAMPLE database on your DB2 server, its default database alias is SAMPLE.	SAMPLE

Table 4-3. *Parameters Required for Setting Up Outbound TCP/IP Communications* (continued)

Parameter	Explanation	Sample Value
Database alias <db_alias>	This is an arbitrary local nickname on the DB2 client that represents the remote DB2 database. If you do not provide a database alias, the database alias name defaults to the same as the database name. You use this database alias name when connecting to the remote database from a DB2 client. In most cases, you can use the same name that you used in the database name parameter. If you were configuring a DB2 server to connect to the SAMPLE database on another DB2 server, and a SAMPLE database already existed on the DB2 server that is acting like a DB2 client, you would need to specify a different name for this parameter.	SAMPLE

Table 4-3.   *Parameters Required for Setting Up Outbound TCP/IP Communications (continued)*

To configure your DB2 client for outbound TCP/IP communications, perform the following steps:

1. Log on to your system as a user with SYSADM or SYSCTRL authority.

2. Update the local services file on the DB2 client.

3. Catalog an entry in the DB2 client's node directory to describe the remote node. (Of course at this point, you want to ensure that the remote database that you are trying to connect to is cataloged on the DB2 server; this is the default.)

4. Catalog an entry in the DB2 client's database directory to describe the remote database.

GETTING STARTED WITH DB2

Once you have finished configuring your DB2 client to connect to a database on a remote DB2 server, we recommend that you test this connection to ensure that everything works. You will learn how to test a connection to a database in the "Testing the Connection to the Remote Database" section that follows.

Updating the Local Services File

You will need to update the local services file on the DB2 client with the connection service name (<svcename>) and port number/protocol (<port#>/tcp). Refer to the earlier "Setting Up Communications Using the CLP" section and Figure 4-6 for more information.

For our example, you would add an entry to the services file on the DB2 client similar to the following:

```
server1 50001/tcp # DB2 connection service port
```

You have the option to configure connections to the remote DB2 server using just the port number of the remote DB2 server. If you want to set up connections using only the port number (which we will show you in the following steps), you do not need to perform this step.

Adding an Entry to the Node Directory

All DB2 instances are known locally to a DB2 client through an entry in a node directory. A node directory may be local or reside on an LDAP or Active Directory server. A node directory contains information about the protocol, address, and name of the instance to which the DB2 client is attempting to establish communications.

You must add an entry to the DB2 client's node directory to describe the remote node. This entry specifies the chosen local alias (node_name), the hostname (or ip_address), and the svcename (or port_number) that the DB2 client uses to access the remote DB2 server.

To catalog a TCP/IP node (which adds an entry to a node directory), enter the following command:

```
db2 catalog tcpip node <node_name> remote <hostname|ip_address> server
<svcename|port_number> ostype
<OS2|AIX|WIN95|NT|HPUX|SUN|MVS|OS400|VM|VSE|SCO|SGI|LINUX|DYNIX>
```

To go back to our continuing example, the following command catalogs an entry in the node directory called KMASCI. This node will be used to connect to the Windows NT DB2 server whose hostname is KMASCI, using the service name server1 (which maps to the same port number used on the remote DB2 server):

```
db2 catalog tcpip node kmasci remote kmasci server server1 ostype NT
```

After entering this command, if you list the contents of the local DB2 node directory, your output would be similar to Figure 4-9.

For more information on the catalog command or to catalog an LDAP directory, refer to Chapter 30.

 If you need to uncatalog an entry in the node directory, use the db2 uncatalog node <node_name> command.

To view the local node directory, enter the following command:

```
db2 list node directory
```

In Figure 4-9, you can see the new entry in the node directory. The node directory entry called KMASCI represents a connection to a machine called KMASCI, uses the TCP/IP protocol for communications, and talks to the remote DB2 server through the port number associated with the service name server1.

You can use any combination or permutation of the optional parameters to catalog the remote connection (for example, using an IP address instead of a server's hostname, the port number instead of the service name, or any combination thereof). For example, the same connection could be cataloged as follows (refer to Table 4-3 for these values):

```
db2 catalog tcpip node kmasci remote 9.21.22.98 server 50000 ostype NT
```

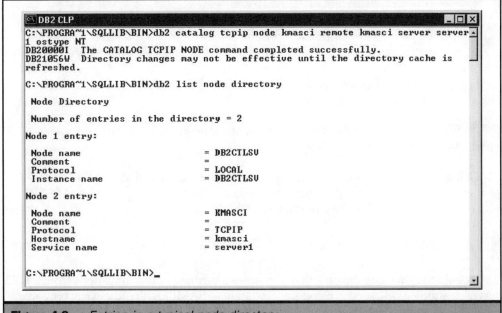

Figure 4-9. *Entries in a typical node directory*

In the earlier example, the service name was specified; therefore, the services file on the DB2 client had to be updated to map this name to the corresponding port number that the remote DB2 server is listening on for inbound requests. In this example, DB2 would bypass the services file because the port number is directly specified, and you would therefore not have to edit the services file to set up communications.

Cataloging the Database

The information in the node directory is not enough to tell DB2 which database to connect to. A DB2 server may have multiple databases in an instance. You tell a DB2 client which DB2 database you want to connect to through a local, Active, or LDAP-enabled database directory. The information in the database and node directories is used by the DB2 client to establish a connection to the remote DB2 database.

However, before a DB2 client application can access a remote DB2 database, the database must be cataloged on the DB2 server *and* on any DB2 clients that will connect to it.

By default, when you create a database, it is automatically cataloged on the DB2 server with the database alias the same as the database name.

To catalog a database, enter the following command:

```
db2 catalog database <db_name> as <db_alias> at node <node_name>
```

You can use the short form db to represent "database" in this command. This abbreviation can be used with any DB2 command that uses the database keyword.

For more information on the catalog command or to catalog an LDAP or Active Directory entry, refer to Chapter 30.

If you need to uncatalog an entry in the database directory, use the db2 uncatalog database <db_name> command.

Going back to our example, to catalog a remote database called SAMPLE that resides on the DB2 server represented by the node directory entry called KMASCI, you would enter the following command:

```
db2 catalog database sample at node kmasci
```

It could very well be the case that you are establishing communications from a DB2 server to another DB2 server. Suppose the database SAMPLE already exists on your local DB2 server with the default database alias SAMPLE. If you tried to catalog the *remote* SAMPLE database on KMASCI, the catalog database command would fail, as shown in Figure 4-10.

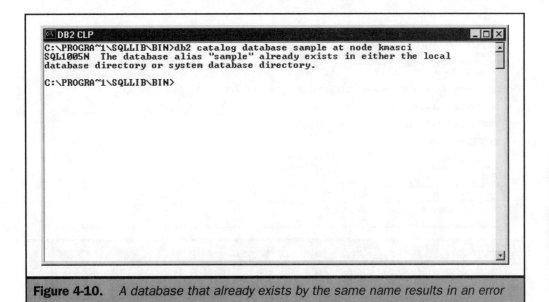

Figure 4-10. *A database that already exists by the same name results in an error*

To view the local database directory, enter the following command:

```
db2 list database directory
```

In this scenario, you would need to enter the catalog database command with a different database alias name. Your command in this case would be similar to the following:

```
db2 catalog database sample as samplekm at node kmasci
```

This command would catalog the remote database SAMPLE, located on the DB2 server KMASCI. However, all applications would have to refer to this database as SAMPLEKM (which is a database alias for the real database called SAMPLE).

Figure 4-11 illustrates a database that needed to be cataloged with a different database name, and shows how it appears in the database directory.

In Figure 4-11, the database SAMPLEKM maps to a remote database called SAMPLE that resides on the computer identified by the node KMASCI. At the bottom of the database directory shown in Figure 4-12, another database called SAMPLE already exists on this system (and you can therefore likely conclude that these examples were done on a DB2 server connecting to another DB2 server).

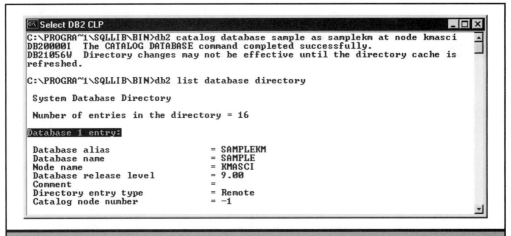

Figure 4-11. *A new entry in the local database directory that uses an alias name*

Tip
Because a DB2 client cannot store and manage a local database, you would not have this exact problem when setting up a client to communicate with a server. However, you may have already cataloged a SAMPLE database on your DB2 client that resides on a different DB2 server called MELNYK, and now you want to catalog a remote database, also called SAMPLE, that resides on a different DB2 server (like KMASCI).

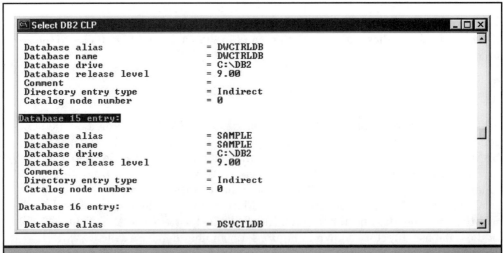

Figure 4-12. *Since a SAMPLE is already cataloged, you must use a database alias name for any other databases that are called SAMPLE*

Testing the Connection to the Remote Database

Now that you have configured a connection from your DB2 client to a remote DB2 database, you should test the connection to verify that your applications will be able to connect to the database.

To test the connection, perform the following steps:

1. Ensure that a database administrator has started the instance where the database that you are trying to connect to resides.

2. Enter the db2 connect command as follows:

```
db2 connect to <db_alias> user <user_id> using <password>
```

In this command, <db_alias> is the local name you selected for the database that you are trying to connect to, <user_id> is a user account that is valid on the DB2 server, and <password> is the password associated with the user account on the DB2 server.

The default authentication method for DB2 is server authentication, which means that all connections are authenticated on the remote DB2 server. Users must be defined on that machine to successfully connect to the remote database. (There are exceptions to this, like in a domain environment for Windows servers.) Ensure that your administrator has set up a user account for you on the DB2 server before entering the preceding command. Other authentication options are available; refer to Chapter 9 for more information on the implications of these settings.

Going back to our example again, to connect to a remote database called SAMPLE that was cataloged with a local database alias name of SAMPLEKM, with the user ID and password db2admin (remember, this has to be valid on the remote DB2 server), enter the following command:

```
db2 connect to samplekm user db2admin using db2admin
```

If your connection is successful, you will receive output similar to that shown in Figure 4-13.

Configuring Communications Using the CCA

The simplest way to establish communications on an OS/2 or Windows-based DB2 client and server is to use the CCA. It gives you the option to use client or server profiles and the ability to "discover" DB2 databases on a network, and it provides users with a graphical interface to the CLP commands.

DB2 has two Discovery methods that it can use to retrieve database connection information: Known and Search Discovery. Known Discovery searches for databases on workstations that are known to your DB2 workstation. For example, when you

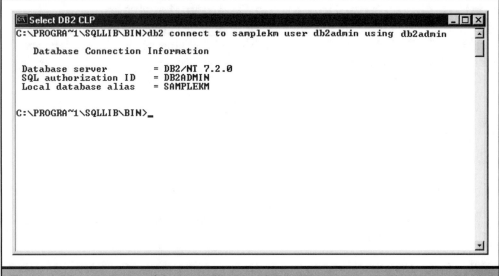

Figure 4-13. *A successful connection to a database*

added the KMASCI machine to your view in the Control Center earlier in this chapter, that machine became known to your workstation. In contrast, Search Discovery is a two-step process. The first step will go out on the network and return a list of servers and their respective databases. (We will talk more about this later.) The second step in a Search Discovery is the same as the Known Discovery process, where a list of instances and their databases is returned to your system. If you want a system to be known to your computer, you have the option to specify its configuration information and make it known as well.

 The DAS must be running on the DB2 server for it to respond to Discovery requests for published instances and databases. There are configuration parameters that also affect whether that DAS will respond to a Discovery request.

No matter which CCA method you use to add a database connection, you need to be logged on to your system as a user with SYSADM or SYSCTRL authority. For more information on authorities, refer to Chapter 5.

Introducing the CCA

The CCA is shown in Figure 4-14. Before we add a database connection, let's look at the different options that are available to you in the main panel of the CCA. All features are detailed in the online help.

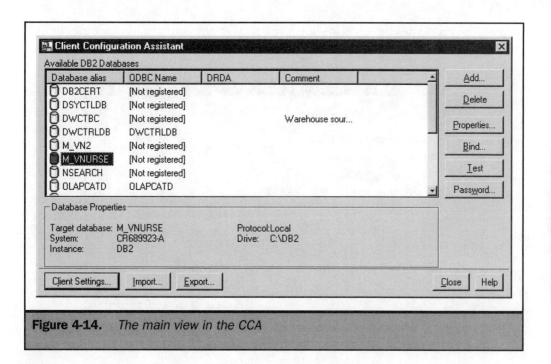

Figure 4-14.   *The main view in the CCA*

> **Tip**   *If you start the CCA for the first time and you do not have any database connections, the Welcome window appears. If the Welcome window appears when you start the CCA on your machine, close it and follow these instructions.*

In the CCA window, clicking the Add button launches a wizard that helps you add a database connection to your DB2 workstation. The Delete button removes a selected database connection from your system. In Figure 4-14, the M_VNURSE database is highlighted, so if you clicked the Delete button, this database would be removed from the database directory and the corresponding node entry from the node directory.

Note that clicking the Delete button does not delete this database. When you configure a connection, you are merely providing the information that DB2 needs to go and find the database. Deleting a connection merely removes that information from your workstation. Think of this as unlisting your phone number. You still have a phone, and it still works; people just don't have your phone number in their phone book, or in the catalog, in DB2's case.

Clicking the Properties button opens the Database Properties dialog box. This dialog box allows you to specify ODBC settings for an existing database connection, and you will have the option to do this whenever you catalog a database using the CCA. You can register a database as a system data source, user data source, or file data source. The Properties button also allows you to alter any configuration settings you have already specified for an existing database connection.

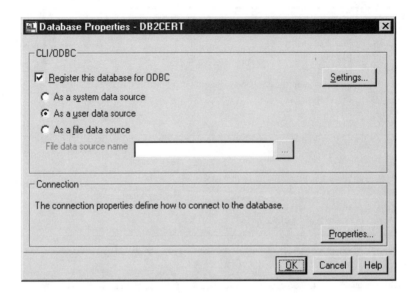

Clicking Bind opens the Bind Database dialog box. This feature gives you the option to bind any DB2 utilities or DB2 applications to a cataloged database. Look in the online help for more information.

The Test button allows you to test a connection to a database that has already been cataloged. You will see how to use this function in the "Testing a Database Connection via CCA" section, where you will learn how to test a connection to a database that you have added by using the CCA.

The Password button allows you to change a user's password on a remote DB2 server.

The Client Settings button launches the Client Settings notebook, a graphical interface for all the DB2 database manager configuration parameters on a DB2 client workstation, as shown in Figure 4-15.

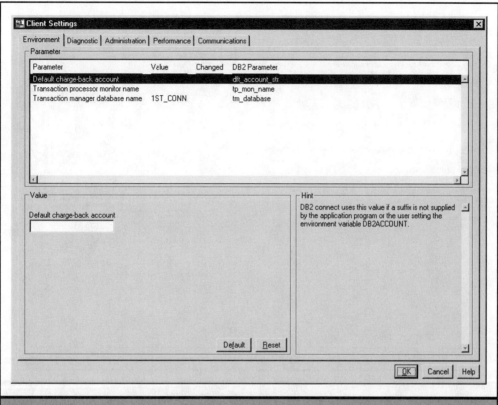

Figure 4-15.   *Working with a DB2 client's database manager configuration file with the CCA*

GETTING STARTED
WITH DB2

The Import and Export buttons allow you to import and export client profiles. Client profiles are much like the server profiles that you learned about in the "Adding a Remote Server and Instance by Using Server Profiles" section earlier in this chapter.

To add a database connection via the CCA, click the Add button in the main window of the CCA. The Add Database Wizard appears, as shown in Figure 4-16.

You are given the option to add a database connection using any of three methods that the CCA supports:

- **Use a Profile**   Adds a database connection by using profiles

- **Search the Network**   Uses Discovery to add a database connection

- **Manually Configure a Connection to a Database**   Uses a graphical interface to the CLP method, described in "Configuring Client to Server Communications Using the CLP." (The CCA does not follow the steps directly in this section because some information that you would specify in separate commands is asked for in the same window.)

Each of these options is described in the following sections.

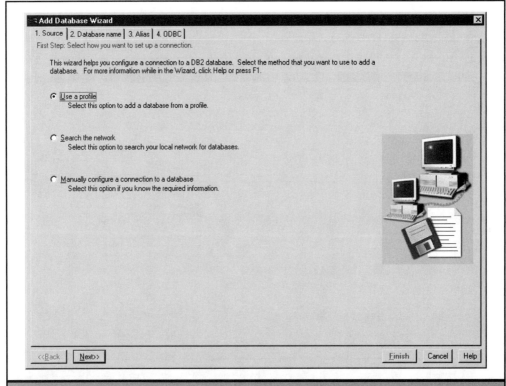

Figure 4-16. *The Source tab of the Add Database Wizard*

Adding a Database Connection Using Client Profiles

A client profile contains information about the DB2 client, its configuration, and the databases that it can connect to. By using a profile, you can literally set up thousands of clients in very minimal time. Chapter 3 discussed some of the benefits of profiles. If you plan to roll out multiple identical copies of DB2 clients, we suggest that you use a client profile.

In this scenario, you would configure a DB2 client to connect to all the databases to which the DB2 client's applications need to connect. Then you would generate a profile that you could distribute to all the DB2 clients across your enterprise. You could have each user import the profile by using the CCA's Import function. Or, if you wanted to automate this process through scripts or use profiles on UNIX or Linux-based workstations, you could import and export the profile with DB2 system commands.

Often, the database connection information needs to be updated. In this case, client profiles are again an excellent choice. If you are planning to update multiple clients with the same database connection information, use client profiles.

Creating a Client Profile Using the CCA   By using the Export option of the CCA, you can customize the client profile that you want to generate to include all or a subset of the following information:

- Database connection information
- Client settings (including dbm cfg parameters and DB2 registry variables)
- CLI or ODBC common parameters

To create a client profile, perform the following steps:

1. Click the Export button in the main window of the CCA (shown in Figure 4-14). The Select Export Option dialog box opens.

2. Select the export option that you want to use for the client profile and click OK. You have three choices:

- **All**   This option exports all database connection, ODBC/CLI, database manager configuration information, and DB2 registry settings on the DB2 client to the client profile.
- **Database connection information**   As this option's name suggests, the client profile generated with this parameter contains only database connection information. No client configuration or ODBC/CLI information is included.
- **Customize**   This option allows you to select a subset of the configuration, connection, or ODBC/CLI information that you want contained in the client profile.

When you select the Customize option when generating a client profile, the Customize Export dialog box opens, as shown in Figure 4-17. Online help is available to assist you through the customization of the profile. Click OK when you have finished specifying all of the information that you want in your profile.

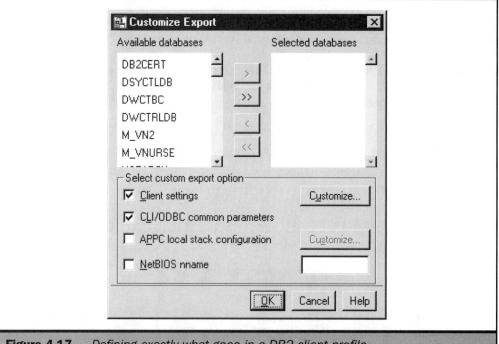

Figure 4-17. *Defining exactly what goes in a DB2 client profile*

Tip *If you click the Customize button associated with the Client Settings check box in the Customize Export dialog box (see Figure 4-17), the configuration parameters you specify will override the configuration parameters detected on the DB2 client to which you are importing. This gives you the option of tailoring a configuration to the target client workstation in the event that the target workstation's environment is not the same as the source workstation. You might be generating a client profile on a DB2 server workstation and may need to set various configuration parameters to different values.*

1. Select the destination filename and location for the client profile, and click OK. You should receive a message that the client profile was exported successfully. Click OK to continue.

In the event that you do not want to use the CCA or it is not available to you, you can use the db2cfexp <filename> command to generate a profile. This command was discussed earlier in the "Using the db2cfexp Command to Export a Server Profile" section.

Importing a Client Profile Using the CCA   You can use various methods to import a client profile on your system. You can import a client profile by selecting the Use a Profile radio button on the Source tab of the Add Database SmartGuide shown in Figure 4-16 (you can add only one database at a time this way), by clicking the Import button on the main panel of the CCA, or by using the db2cfimp command.

Tip	*You can select which information you want to import from a profile.*

Perform the following steps to add a database to your system by using the Use a Profile option of the CCA. (Our example will add a database called SAMPLE to the system.)

1. Enter the location and name of the profile that you want to import in the File field, as shown in Figure 4-18. When the CCA locates and reads the profile you specify, a list of all the instances and databases contained within the profile is shown in the box below the File field.

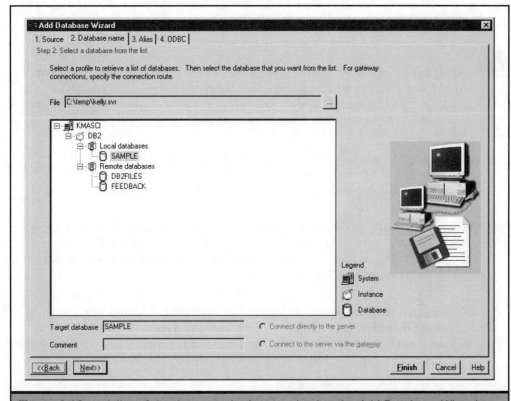

Figure 4-18.   *A list of databases to be imported using the Add Database Wizard*

GETTING STARTED WITH DB2

You can browse your system or any attached network drives from the Database Name tab by clicking the ellipsis (...) to the right of the File field.

2. Select the database that you want to connect to and click Next. For example, in Figure 4-18, we want to add the SAMPLE database that resides on the DB2 server KMASCI in the default instance. Notice that the KMASCI DB2 server also has database connections to other DB2 servers. We could add those databases as well by reimporting the profile and selecting those databases.

   If the database whose connection you are trying to add resides on a zOS (formerly known and OS/390), OS/400, or VM/VSE server, then you can specify how this connection will occur by using the Connect Directly To The Server and Connect To The Server Via The Gateway radio buttons. Refer to the online help for more information.

   Of course, you could use the Import button in the CCA to import all database connection information. The Using a Profile option in the CCA lets you import database connections only one at a time.

Once you have selected a database that you want to add to your system, the Finish button becomes active. At this point, you could add the database connection to your system. However, you may want to specify a different database alias name for this new database (a good reason would be that a database by the same name already exists on your system) or specify ODBC-specific information.

3. Specify a database alias name (as shown in Figure 4-19) and optionally, a comment for the new database connection that you are adding, and click Next. The default is to keep the same name as the database name.

You need an alias if you are adding a database with the same name as one that already exists on your machine. If you were to click the Finish button without specifying a unique database alias name, you would receive an error because a database by that name has already been cataloged on your system.

4. You can use the ODBC tab (see Figure 4-20) in the CCA to indicate how this database should be registered on your system. You need to use this tab only if you are using ODBC. When you have finished specifying your ODBC options for this database connection or if you are not planning to use ODBC, click Finish.

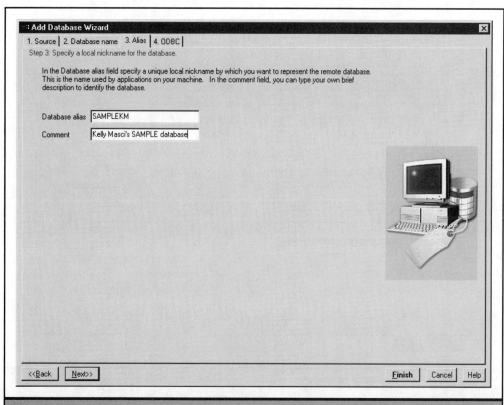

Figure 4-19.   *Specifying a database alias for a new database connection using the CCA*

If the database connection was added successfully, you will be notified by the Confirmation dialog box and given the option to test a connection to that database. The Confirmation dialog box also gives you the option to add another database connection (click Add) or to change any settings you selected.

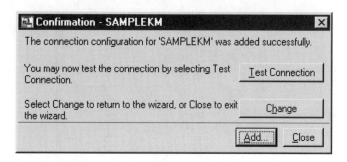

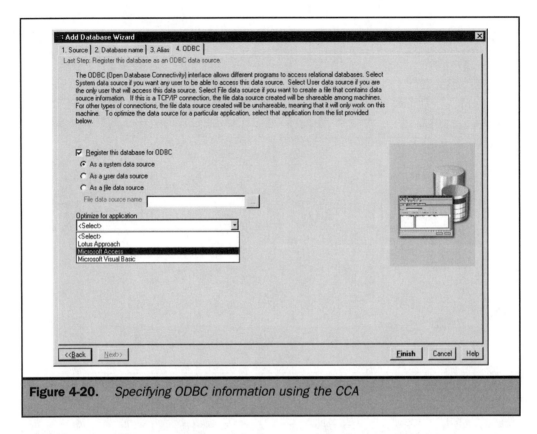

Figure 4-20.   *Specifying ODBC information using the CCA*

Testing a Database Connection via CCA   To test a database connection from the Confirmation dialog box, perform the following steps:

1. Click the Test Connection button. The Connect To DB2 Database dialog box opens.

2. Enter a valid user ID and password on the DB2 server system. You can optionally change your password by selecting the Change Password check box and filling in the appropriate fields. You can also select the mode in which you want to connect to this database: Share or Exclusive.

Tip

By default, when a DB2 client connects to a DB2 server, the user ID and password are always verified on the DB2 server. You can change this option on a DB2 server (see Chapter 9). To connect to a remote database by default, ensure that the user ID and password you specify have been previously defined by an administrator before testing the connection.

If the connection is successful, you will receive a message notifying you that you have successfully connected to the cataloged database.

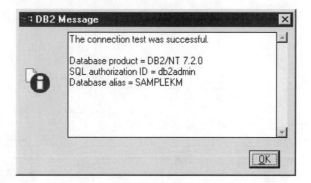

Adding a Database Connection Using Discovery

Another way to add a database connection to your workstation using the CCA is through Discovery. Discovery is really made up of two pieces: Search Discovery and Discovery. Search Discovery is a feature that broadcasts a datagram message over a network segment and asks for all DB2 servers to return their list of published DB2 instances and their respective databases. The Discovery component returns the information. We say "published" because you can set configuration parameters that will hide an instance or one of its databases from Discovery. Chapter 6 discusses how to configure Discovery in more detail. The default is for all instances and databases to respond to Discovery's request for connection information.

To use Discovery to add a database connection to your DB2 client workstation, select the Search the Network radio button in the Add Database Wizard (see Figure 4-16) and click Next. The Database Name tab, shown in Figure 4-21, is a little different in this case than in the previous method.

In Figure 4-21, the machine CR689923-A is already known to the CCA. This is because the machine we are running the CCA on is also a DB2 server. (We see that databases already exist locally and are cataloged on this machine.)

From here, you can use Discovery's two methods: Known and Search.

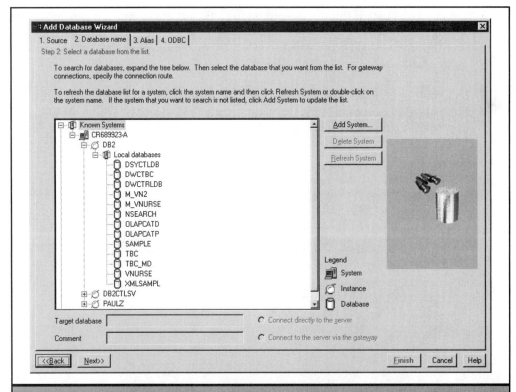

Figure 4-21.   *The Database Name tab when your system knows remote DB2 servers*

    You do not need to catalog local databases on a DB2 server. When you create a database, it is automatically locally cataloged for you.

Using Known Discovery   Known Discovery uses the DAS to request a list of instances and databases cataloged on specific DB2 servers that are known to your workstation. In Figure 4-21, the CCA obviously knows the workstation on which it is running. If you had previously added a remote database connection using the CCA, that DB2 server would appear in the Known Systems list as well.

If you had added a remote database connection using the CLP, the only way that it would show up in the CCA is if you cataloged the DAS. (For more information, refer to the *DB2 Installation and Configuration Supplement*.) To use Known Discovery to add a database connection, you either have to know some protocol specifics (like the hostname of the remote DB2 server where the database that you want to connect to resides), or the remote DAS has to have already been cataloged on your system.

To use Known discovery to add a database connection to your workstation using the CCA, perform the following steps:

1. Click the Add System button. The Add System dialog box opens, as shown in Figure 4-22.

2. You can find a remote DB2 server using a number of different protocols. Because we are assuming that you are using TCP/IP, select TCP/IP from the Protocol drop-down box.

3. Depending on the protocol that you want to use, you will need to know the protocol's related parameters. In the case of TCP/IP, all you need to know is the hostname of the remote DB2 server, so enter it in the Host name field. In our example, we want to add the SAMPLE database (although we will have to rename it using a database alias because a database called SAMPLE already exists on this workstation), which resides on a DB2 server whose hostname is KMASCI. When you have entered all of the protocol-specific parameters, click OK.

Discovery takes the information that you provided, locates the remote DB2 server on the network, and adds an entry for this system under the Known Systems tree with a list of all published instances and databases, as shown in Figure 4-23.

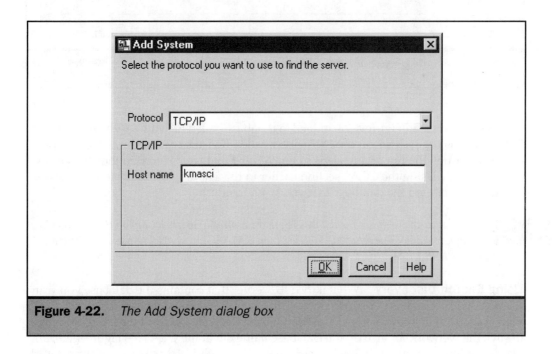

Figure 4-22. *The Add System dialog box*

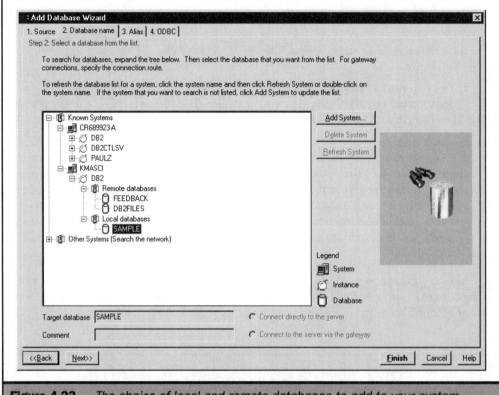

Figure 4-23. *The choice of local and remote databases to add to your system*

As you can see in Figure 4-23, indeed, a database called SAMPLE (which resides in the DB2 instance) exists on the DB2 server called KMASCI. To add it, select it and proceed through the remaining steps of the Wizard that we covered in the "Importing a Client Profile Using the CCA" section earlier in this chapter. (Start at step 3 because you already selected the database that you want to add.)

Don't forget that because the database SAMPLE already exists locally on the CR689923-A system, to catalog the database SAMPLE on KMASCI, you need to use a database alias, like SAMPLEKM.

Using Search Discovery   What if the DB2 server that contains the database you want to add to your system is not known to you (in terms of its protocol parameters) or to your system? In this case, you can use Search Discovery. Just expand the Other Systems (Search the Network) branch on the Database name tab of the CCA (see Figure 4-23), and Discovery sends a request (in the form of a datagram broadcast) out across your network segment asking for all DB2 servers to respond with the instances and databases that are published for cataloging. This information is shown when you click the cross-hatch ([+]) beside the newly added DB2 server, and then a Discovery request is launched that returns this information.

Earlier in this chapter, we talked about Discovery involving a two-step process: one that searches the network (Search Discovery) and the other that returns the information of the discovered DB2 server. You don't need to torture yourself with this level of detail; just know that you can find remote DB2 servers on you network!

 By using the DAS configuration file, you can hide instances and databases from Discovery.

Discovery as a whole returns a list of all DB2 servers, their instances, and their databases in the window of the CCA, as shown in Figure 4-24. From here, you can select the database that you want to add.

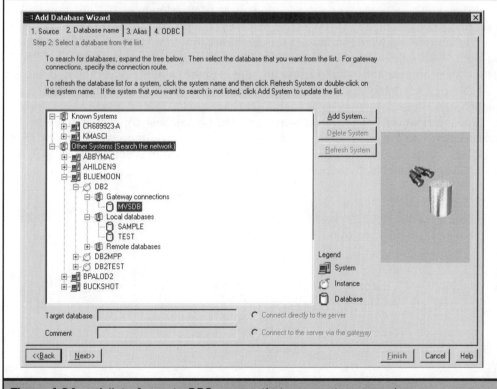

Figure 4-24.   *A list of remote DB2 servers that your system never knew*

GETTING STARTED WITH DB2

You can see that Discovery returned a list of DB2 servers that are on the network. Notice that the DB2 server BLUEMOON has local databases, remote databases, and gateway connections. The MVSDB database actually resides on a zSeries server, and its connection is handled through a DB2 Connect gateway.

From this list, you can select and add any database connection that you want and add it to your system. The remaining steps are the same as with the Known and Profile methods that we talked about in the previous sections. From here, you can go to step 3 in the "Importing a Client Profile Using the CCA" section to finish adding the database you selected to your system.

Adding a Database Connection Using the Manual Method

The CCA allows you to configure database connections in a similar fashion to using the CLP. See the "Configuring Communications Using the CLP" section earlier in the chapter for more information.

To add a database connection manually, select the Manually configure a connection to a database radio button on the Source tab of the Add Database Wizard (see Figure 4-16), and click Next.

When you choose to manually add a database connection over TCP/IP, you will eventually be presented with a window that lists all of the parameters that you would need to know if you were configuring the database connection using the CLP, as shown in Figure 4-25. Of course, using this method kind of defeats the purpose of the CCA, but it does eliminate the need to know the syntax of the catalog node, catalog database, and catalog DCS database commands (if connecting to a host or mainframe DB2 database).

The information that you need to manually add a database connection to your workstation was covered previously in the "Configuring Communications Using the CLP" section earlier this chapter, as well as the steps to test the connection. The CCA's online help is available if you need more information.

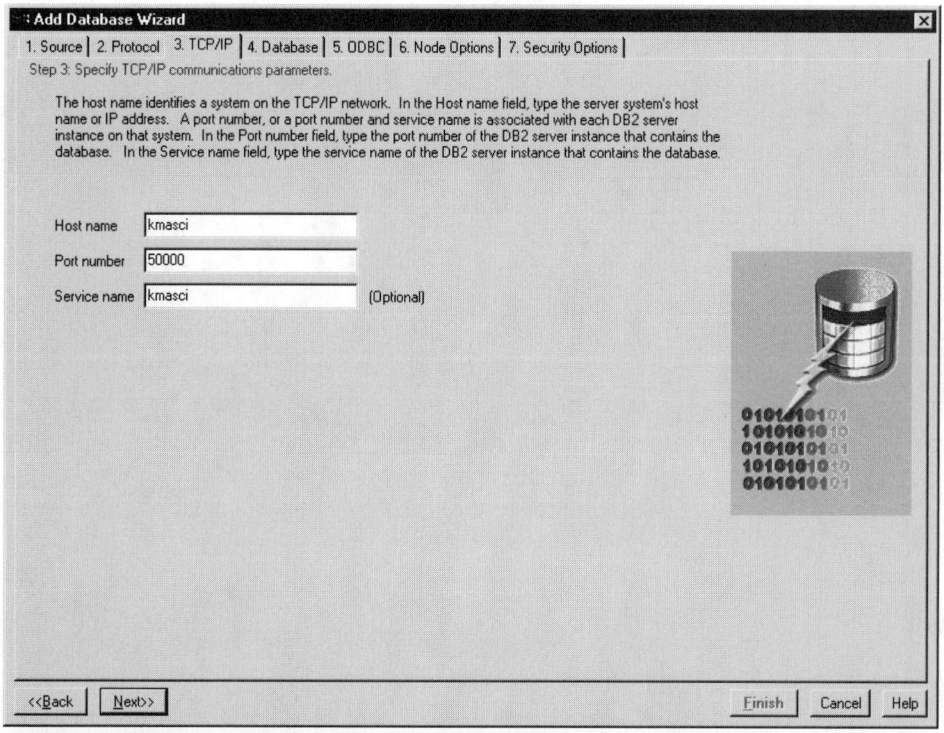

Figure 4-25.   *A way to use the CLP method, but with a nice GUI*

The Complete Reference

DB2

Chapter 5

Controlling Data Access

Security is an important part of any database system. Effective security prevents unauthorized users from accessing confidential data and protects the data from accidental or intentional corruption or loss.

When setting up security for your system, you must consider two important aspects. The first is the list of users who will have access to a particular resource, and the second is the type of access those users will have. Should they be able to create their own databases or tables? Should they be able to make updates and changes to existing data, or will their access be read-only?

DB2 allows you to specify precisely which users may access the objects in your system, and the range of actions that those users may perform. It also provides tools for monitoring system activity so that you can detect any unanticipated data access.

Authentication

Access to a DB2 instance is controlled by a security facility external to DB2. This facility may be part of your operating system or it may be a separate third-party product. Access to databases and database objects *within* a DB2 instance is controlled by DB2 Universal Database (UDB) according to specified database authorities and privileges, discussed in the "Authorities and Privileges" section of this chapter.

Before users can attach to an instance or connect to a database, they must undergo *authentication*: the process of verifying the identity of a user, usually by means of matching a valid user ID and a password.

You can specify whether authentication should take place at the client or at the server when you configure the connection between DB2 UDB clients and servers. This is specified in the authentication type parameter setting in the database manager configuration file.

There are several kinds of authentication types to consider:

- SERVER
- SERVER_ENCRYPT
- CLIENT
- Database Connection Services (DCS)
- DCS_ENCRYPT
- Distributed Computing Environment (DCE)
- DCE_SERVER_ENCRYPT
- KERBEROS
- KRB_SERVER_ENCRYPT

SERVER

This type of authentication specifies that authentication should take place on the server using local operating system security facilities. For authentication to occur, a valid user ID and password combination must be provided to the server.

SERVER_ENCRYPT

This type of authentication specifies that the server accepts encrypted SERVER authentication schemes. Depending on whether there is a specified authentication type for the client, the client may or may not pass an encrypted user ID and password combination to the server for authentication.

Note that if the client authentication type is specified as SERVER_ENCRYPT but the server authentication type is SERVER, an error will be returned because the two authentication types are incompatible.

CLIENT

This authentication type allows the client to perform authentication on behalf of the server. This authentication is performed using local operating system security facilities.

If the CLIENT authentication type is specified at the server, two other parameters in the database manager configuration file are evaluated to determine whether authentication will take place at the client or the server: trust_allclnts and trust_clntauth.

If trust_allclnts is set to YES, then all the clients are assumed to perform adequate authentication on behalf of the server. However, some clients may be running on machines whose operating systems do not have built-in security facilities. These are known as *untrusted clients* and include Windows 95 and Windows 98. Trusted clients are those whose operating environments have built-in security facilities. Such operating systems include Windows NT/2000, OS/2, all supported UNIX operating systems, Multiple Virtual Storage (MVS), OS/390, Virtual Machine (VM), Versatile Storage Server (VSE), and AS/400.

If trust_allclnts is set to NO, then only trusted clients can authenticate the user on behalf of the server. Untrusted clients are authenticated on the server and must pass to the server a valid user ID and password.

To force server authentication of all clients except Distributed Relational Database Architecture (DRDA) clients from DB2 for MVS and OS/390, DB2 for VM and VSE, and DB2 for AS/400, the trust_allclnts parameter should be set to DRDAONLY.

Even when the trust_allclnts parameter is set to YES, this does not guarantee that any clients will perform authentication on behalf of the server. This is instead determined by the setting of the trust_clntauth parameter. If this parameter is set to CLIENT, authentication is done by the client. This is the default setting for this parameter.

If this parameter is set to SERVER, authentication may or may not take place at the server depending on whether a user ID and password are provided in the SQL CONNECT statement or the DB2 ATTACH command. If the user ID and password are provided, then authentication is done at the server. If this information is not provided, authentication is done at the client.

DCS

This authentication type is used to catalog a database accessed through DB2 Connect. It is equivalent to the SERVER authentication type when it is the specified authentication type for a DB2 instance, unless the server is being accessed via DRDA Application Server architecture using the Advanced Program-to-Program Communication (APPC) protocol. In this case, the DCS authentication type specifies that authentication will occur at the server but only in the APPC layer.

DCS_ENCRYPT

This authentication type specifies that DB2 Connect will accept encrypted SERVER authentication schemes. If the client authentication is unspecified, the client is authenticated using the SERVER authentication type specification. If the client authentication type is DCS or SERVER, client authentication is performed by passing the user ID and password to DB2 Connect. If the client authentication type is DCS_ENCRYPT or SERVER_ENCRYPT, the client is authenticated by passing a user ID and an encrypted password. If the client authentication type is DCS_ENCRYPT and the server authentication type is DCS, an error will be returned due to the mismatch in authentication levels.

DCE

This authentication type specifies that the authentication will not be performed by the operating system security facilities on either the client or the server. Instead, DCE security software will be used.

DCE_SERVER_ENCRYPT

This authentication type specifies that the server will accept both DCE authentication or encrypted SERVER authentication schemes.

If client authentication is not specified, the client will be authenticated using DCE security services. If the client authentication specifies SERVER_ENCRYPT or DCS_ENCRYPT, the client will be authenticated by the client after providing a valid user ID and encrypted password combination. The client authentication type cannot be DCE_SERVER_ENCRYPT.

KERBEROS

This authentication type specifies that authentication will not be performed by the operating system security facilities on either the client or the server. Instead, Kerberos security services will be used in authentication. This authentication type is supported only on clients and servers running Windows 2000.

KRB_SERVER_ENCRYPT

This authentication type specifies that the server will accept both KERBEROS authentication or encrypted SERVER authentication schemes. If the client authentication type is specified as KERBEROS, then Kerberos security facilities will be used for authentication. If the client authentication type is specified as something other than KERBEROS, then the authentication type is treated as SERVER_ENCRYPT.

Authorities and Privileges

Once a user has been authenticated, DB2 UDB takes over the responsibility of controlling access to database objects. There are two ways of restricting what users can do with the objects in a database: assigning authorities and granting privileges. Users may be assigned to a group of users with a common authority that comes with the ability to perform a wide range of tasks throughout the database. Or, users may be granted individual privileges, which allows them to perform particular operations on a defined set of database objects.

Authorities

Authorities provide users with the ability to perform administrative and maintenance tasks within an instance or database. DB2 UDB defines several types of authorities:

- System Administration Authority (SYSADM)
- System Control Authority (SYSCTRL)
- System Maintenance Authority (SYSMAINT)
- Database Administration Authority (DBADM)

Users with any one or more of these authorities can perform high-level database management tasks. However, only two authorities, SYSADM and DBADM, allow users to access data in the database. The SYSCTRL and SYSMAINT authorities are appropriate for users who need to administer a database instance, but who should not have access to sensitive data within the instance.

These authorities are related in a hierarchy, with the lowest level having the fewest system abilities, and the highest level having a superset of all the abilities granted to the lower levels (see Figure 5-1).

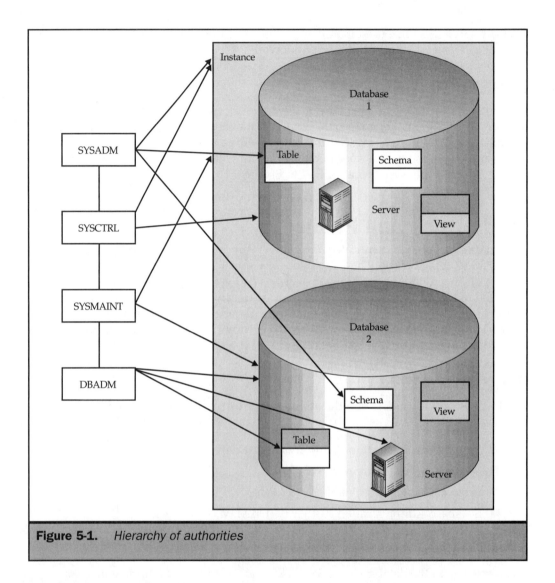

Figure 5-1. *Hierarchy of authorities*

SYSADM Authority

At the top of the hierarchy is the SYSADM authority. This level of authority gives a
user the ability to run utilities, issue database and database manager commands, and
control database objects throughout the database manager instance.

In addition to all of the capabilities granted to the other authorities, users with
SYSADM authority can perform the following functions:

- Migrate a database
- Modify the database manager configuration file
- Grant DBADM authority

To have SYSADM authority, a user must belong to the group specified by the SYSADM _GROUP configuration parameter. On UNIX systems, this parameter is by default set to the primary group of the instance owner. On Windows NT, this group is by default comprised of the set of local administrators on the machine where DB2 UDB is installed. Given the pervasive abilities this authority provides, it is a good idea to revise this parameter setting shortly after installing DB2 Universal Database.

To give a group SYSADM authority, change the SYSADM_GROUP parameter to the name of the intended group.

SYSCTRL Authority

The SYSCTRL authority allows a user to perform all administrative tasks, such as running maintenance and utility operations against the database manager instance and its databases. A user with SYSCTRL authority cannot access data directly unless specifically granted additional privileges.

In addition to the functions of the SYSMAINT authority, a user with SYSCTRL authority or higher can perform the following functions:

- Create or drop a database
- Force applications
- Restore to a new database
- Create, drop, or alter a table space
- Update a database, node, or distributed connection services (DCS) directory

To give a group SYSCTRL authority, change the SYSCTRL_GROUP parameter to the name of the intended group.

SYSMAINT Authority

SYSMAINT authority allows a user to perform maintenance activities without the ability to access data within the database instance.

A user with SYSMAINT or higher system authority can perform the following functions:

- Update database configuration files
- Back up a database or table space
- Restore to an existing database
- Perform roll-forward recovery
- Stop or start a database instance

- Restore a table space
- Run traces
- Take system monitor snapshots of an instance or its databases

To give a group SYSMAINT authority, change the SYSMAINT_GROUP parameter to the name of the intended group.

DBADM Authority

DBADM authority, unlike the other authorities discussed so far, applies to only a single database and not to the entire instance. A user with DBADM authority for a database can perform any administrative task on the database, such as loading data, creating database objects, and monitoring database activity. DBADM authority for a database also comes with the ability to grant and revoke the database privileges of other users.

A user with DBADM authority (or the more powerful SYSADM authority) can perform the following functions:

- Read log files
- Create, activate, and drop event monitors

A user with DBADM, SYSMAINT, or higher authority can perform these functions:

- Query the state of a table space
- Update the log history files
- Quiesce a table space
- Reorganize a table
- Collect catalog statistics using the RUNSTATS utility

The creator of a database will automatically have DBADM authority on that database. This is especially important to remember when databases are created by users in the SYSADM or SYSCTRL groups who later are removed from those groups: they still retain DBADM authority on the databases that they created unless that authority is explicitly revoked.

To give users DBADM authority on a database, a user with SYSADM authority issues a GRANT statement of this form:

```
GRANT DBADM ON DATABASE TO USER Hayward
```

The GRANT statement is discussed in more detail later in the chapter under "Granting Privileges."

DBADM authority can also be granted using the DB2 Control Center, as described in the section "Granting and Revoking Privileges Using the Control Center."

LOAD Authority

There is one special type of authority that provides users with the ability to perform load operations on a particular database. The LOAD authority must be combined with the INSERT privilege on a table to allow a user to load data into a table using the AutoLoader utility. If a user needs to perform loads that replace existing data in the target table, the user also needs to have the DELETE privilege on the table.

A user with this authority for a database can also perform the following commands:

- QUIESCE TABLESPACES FOR TABLE
- RUNSTATS
- LIST TABLESPACES

To give users LOAD authority on a database, a user with SYSADM authority gives authority through the DB2 Control Center, or issues a GRANT statement of this form:

```
GRANT LOAD ON DATABASE TO USER Mackenzie
```

Privileges

A privilege allows a user to perform specific functions on a particular database object. Users can get privileges for an object in three different ways: through ownership of an object, through a specific GRANT statement, or implicitly by having a higher-level privilege that automatically grants other related privileges.

Privileges can be categorized based on their scope of application:

- Database privileges
- Schema privileges
- Table space privileges
- Table privileges
- View privileges
- Nickname privileges
- Server privileges
- Package privileges
- Index privileges

The following sections describe the different privilege categories.

Database Privileges

Database privileges involve actions on the entire database. They include the privileges described in Table 5-1.

Privilege	Allows User To:
CONNECT	Access the database.
BINDADD	Create new packages in the database.
CREATETAB	Create new tables in the database.
CREATE_NOT_FENCED	Create user-defined functions (UDFs) or procedures that are "not fenced." (A UDF or a procedure that is *not fenced* does not run in its own process, and thus, cannot access most DB2 internal control and data areas.)
IMPLICIT_SCHEMA	Create an object and specify a schema name for it that does not already exist. SYSIBM becomes the owner of the new schema, and PUBLIC can create objects in it.

Table 5-1. *Database Privileges*

Only a user with SYSADM or DBADM authority on a particular database can grant these privileges to other users or revoke them from other users.

It is important to note that when a database is created, all users in PUBLIC are automatically granted the following database privileges:

- CREATETAB
- BINDADD
- CONNECT
- IMPLICIT_SCHEMA
- USE privilege on the USERSPACE1 table space
- SELECT privilege on system catalog views

These privileges must be explicitly revoked from PUBLIC, either through a REVOKE statement or through the use of the Control Center. Methods for granting and revoking privileges are discussed in greater detail later in this chapter (see "Granting Privileges" and "Revoking Privileges").

Schema Privileges

Schema privileges involve actions on the objects within schemas, including tables, views, indexes, packages, data types, functions, triggers, procedures, and aliases. There are three different schema privileges that a user may have, as described in Table 5-2.

Privilege	Allows User To:
CREATEIN	Create objects within a schema.
ALTERIN	Alter objects within a schema.
DROPIN	Drop objects within a schema.

Table 5-2.   *Schema Privileges*

The owner of a schema automatically has all of these privileges, in addition to the ability to grant them to or revoke them from other users.

Table Space Privileges

The only table space privilege that users may have is the USE privilege, which allows users to create tables within a table space.

Table Privileges

Table privileges enable users to perform different actions on tables in the database. (See Table 5-3.) To use these privileges, users must also be granted the CONNECT privilege on the database.

Privilege	Allows User To:	Special Notes/Considerations
CONTROL	Drop a table; add columns; create a primary key; delete, retrieve, update, and insert rows; create indexes; create referential constraints; use the export utility; perform table maintenance tasks such as reorganization or updating table statistics; grant other users privileges on table.	Only SYSADM or DBADM can grant the CONTROL privilege on a table. The creator of a table is automatically given the CONTROL privilege.

Table 5-3.   *Table Privileges*

Privilege	Allows User To:	Special Notes/Considerations
ALTER	Add columns; add or change comments on a table or its columns; add primary key/unique constraints; create or drop a table check constraint.	To drop a primary key, a user must have the ALTER privilege on all of the dependent tables.
DELETE	Delete rows from a table.	
UPDATE	Change a row in a table.	This privilege may be held for a specific column in the table.
INDEX	Create indexes on a table.	
INSERT	Insert rows into a table; run the import utility using table as target for importing.	
SELECT	Retrieve rows from a table, create a view on a table, and run the export utility.	
REFERENCES	Create or drop a foreign key.	This privilege may be held for a specific column in the table.

Table 5-3. *Table Privileges* (continued)

View Privileges

To use privileges on a view, users must have the CONNECT privilege on a database. To create a view, the user must have the SELECT privilege on the tables or views involved. Table 5-4 describes the different view privileges.

Privilege	Allows User To:	Special Notes/Considerations
CONTROL	Drop a view; add columns; delete, retrieve, update, and insert rows; use the export utility; grant other users privileges on a view.	Only SYSADM or DBADM can grant the CONTROL privilege on a view. The creator of a view is automatically given the CONTROL privilege.

Table 5-4. *View Privileges*

Privilege	Allows User To:	Special Notes/Considerations
DELETE	Delete rows from a view.	
INSERT	Insert rows into a view; run the import utility on a view.	
UPDATE	Change the values in a row.	This privilege can be held for only a specific column in the view (that is, the user is granted the UPDATE privilege on the column).

Table 5-4.   *View Privileges* (continued)

Nickname Privileges

Nickname privileges allow users to perform actions on nicknames in a database. (See Table 5-5.) A user must have the CONNECT privilege on the database to perform any of the actions permitted by nickname privileges.

Privilege	Allows User To:	Special Notes/Considerations
CONTROL	Perform all of the actions permitted by all nickname privileges; drop the nickname; grant others privileges on the nickname.	To access data source data, a user must also have the appropriate privileges on objects at data sources referenced by the nickname.
ALTER	Change column names in the nickname; add or change the DB2 type that a column's data type maps to; set options for nickname columns.	
INDEX	Create an index specification on a nickname.	
REFERENCES	Create and drop a foreign key, specifying the nickname as the parent.	

Table 5-5.   *Nickname Privileges*

Server Privileges

One server privilege may be granted to a user: PASSTHRU. This privilege allows permitted authorization IDs to issue data definition language (DDL) and data manipulation language (DML) statements directly to data sources.

Package Privileges

Package privileges enable users to create and perform actions on packages. These privileges are described in Table 5-6. Note that a user must have the CONNECT privilege on the database to perform the actions permitted by package privileges.

Index Privileges

When a user creates an index, the user is automatically given the CONTROL privilege on that index. This means that the user can drop the index.

Only users with SYSADM or DBADM authority can grant the CONTROL privilege on an index.

Granting Privileges

DB2 users can be explicitly authorized to access database objects through privileges granted to them with a GRANT statement. Users can be identified individually in a GRANT statement, or they may receive privileges as a member of a group that is identified

Privilege	Allows User To:	Special Notes/Considerations
CONTROL	Rebind, drop, and execute a package; grant privileges on the package to other users	The creator of a package automatically receives the CONTROL privilege on the package.
BIND	Rebind existing packages	A user with the CONTROL or EXECUTE privilege on a package containing nicknames does not need additional privileges on the nicknames to execute the package.
EXECUTE	Execute a package	Users of packages must have appropriate privileges on data source objects at any data source referenced in the package.

Table 5-6. *Package Privileges*

in the GRANT statement. Similarly, a privilege may be revoked from a user, or from an entire group of users, through the execution of a REVOKE statement.

The basic format of the GRANT statement is given schematically here:

```
GRANT privilege ON objecttype objectname TO GROUP/USER groupname/username
```

Because some operating systems allow users and groups to have the same name, you may have to specify the keywords GROUP and USER to distinguish the group ALPHA from the user ALPHA.Similarly, you may have a table and a view with the same name in the same database. To distinguish them, you can specify the object type, for example, TABLE WORKSCHEDULES, before the object name.

You can specify more than one privilege and more than one user in a single statement by separating each item with a comma. The following examples demonstrate the use of the GRANT statement:

```
GRANT INSERT, DELETE ON TABLE EXPENSES TO MIKE
```

The preceding statement grants the authorization ID MIKE both INSERT and DELETE privileges on the table EXPENSES. Note that if the name *MIKE* is defined as both a group and a user, an error will be returned. To distinguish these two uses for this name, the keyword GROUP or USER must be added.

```
GRANT UPDATE ON FACILITIES TO GROUP LEADS WITH GRANT OPTION
```

This statement gives the UPDATE privilege on the table FACILITIES to the members of the group LEADS. The final part of the statement, WITH GRANT OPTION, also gives all of the members of the group LEADS the ability to grant the UPDATE privilege to other users. Other users who can issue such a GRANT statement include users with SYSADM or DBADM authority, and users with CONTROL privileges on FACILITIES.

```
GRANT ALL ON FINALMARKS TO USER COATES
```

The preceding statement grants a set of privileges on the table FINALMARKS to the user COATES. Precisely what set of privileges is granted is determined by the privileges held by the authorization ID that issued the statement. If that authorization ID has DBADM authority, SYSADM authority, or the CONTROL privilege on the table, then all privileges applicable to the table are granted (with the notable exception of the CONTROL privilege). Otherwise, only the privileges for which the issuer has granting authority are granted to user COATES.

```
GRANT DBADM ON DATABASE TO USER WONG
```

This statement gives DBADM authority on a database to the authorization ID WONG. Note that the GRANT statement format for granting DBADM and LOAD authorities is parallel to granting object privileges.

Revoking Privileges

Privileges are revoked using the REVOKE statement. This statement is formally very similar to the GRANT statement. The basic syntax is given schematically here:

```
REVOKE privilege ON objecttype objectname FROM USER/GROUP
username/groupname
```

As with the GRANT statement, if a privilege has been granted to a user and a group that share the same name, you must use the USER or GROUP keywords to distinguish them.

To revoke privileges on an object, you must have DBADM authority, SYSADM authority, or the CONTROL privilege on that object. Having the WITH GRANT option on the object does not allow a user to revoke privileges on that object.

The following examples demonstrate the use of the REVOKE statement.

```
REVOKE UPDATE ON TABLE FINALMARKS FROM USER MATTHEW
```

In the preceding statement, the UPDATE privilege on the FINALMARKS table is revoked from the user MATTHEW.

```
REVOKE ALL ON TABLE FACILITIES FROM GROUP PLANNERS
```

This statement revokes all the privileges granted to the group PLANNERS. Note that this does not guarantee that none of the members of this group will have privileges on this table. If any of the users have been granted privileges as either individuals or members of another group, they will retain these privileges unless additional REVOKE statements are issued.

Granting and Revoking Privileges Using the Control Center

You can also grant and revoke privileges on database objects by using the DB2 Control Center.

To change the privileges on a particular object, select the object in the right frame (the contents pane) of the Control Center and right-click. From the menu that appears, select Privileges. This will bring up the Privileges window for the selected object, as shown in Figure 5-2.

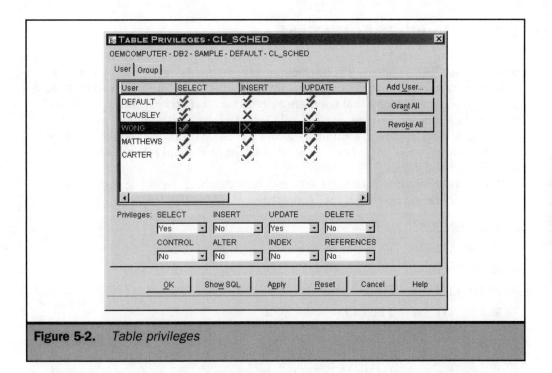

Figure 5-2.   *Table privileges*

On the User tab, each row represents the privileges held by a user for the selected object. Each column identifies a different privilege. A single check mark in a column for a single user indicates that the user has the privilege specified by the column header. A double check mark indicates that the user has that privilege and also the ability to grant that privilege to others. An *X* indicates that the user does not have the specified privilege on the object. You can modify the privileges that a user has on the object by following these steps:

1. Select the user row.

2. Below the display of user privileges, specify the changes to the privileges. For the privileges that you want to change, select YES to grant the privilege, NO to revoke the privilege, and GRANT to grant the privilege with the GRANT option.

3. Click Apply.

To grant a user all of the privileges on the object, click Grant All. To revoke all of a user's privileges on the selected object, click Revoke All.

Granting and revoking group privileges is similar to dealing with user privileges, except that you start from the Group tab of the Privileges window and perform the same steps.

Implicit vs. Explicit Authorization

Privileges can be granted to users implicitly or explicitly. Explicit granting of privileges is done with the GRANT statement or by changing user privileges through the Control Center.

Users may also be granted privileges implicitly. It is important to be aware of these implicit privileges to ensure that users are assigned and retain only those privileges that they are supposed to have. For example, when a user with SYSADM authority creates a database, that user is implicitly granted DBADM authority on the database. If that same user has SYSADM authority revoked, he or she still retains DBADM authority on the database.

When a user is granted DBADM authority on a database, he or she is implicitly granted the following privileges on the database:

- CONNECT
- CREATETAB
- BINDADD
- IMPLICIT_SCHEMA
- CREATE_NOT_FENCED

Even if the user's DBADM authority is later revoked, the user will retain these privileges unless they are explicitly revoked.

When a user is granted the CONTROL privilege on a table, he or she is implicitly granted all other privileges on the table, including the ability to grant others these privileges. Again, all of these implicitly granted privileges are retained, even if the CONTROL privilege is revoked.

A final point to keep in mind when revoking user privileges concerns the WITH GRANT option. Users with CONTROL authority can grant other users privileges on the objects that the grantor controls. Users who have privileges that include the WITH GRANT option also have the ability to grant the same privileges to other users. The privileges granted by a user are unaffected if the grantor later loses the privilege.

Viewing Privilege and Authority Information

Information about which groups are given SYSADM, SYSCTRL, and SYSMAINT authority is contained in the database manager configuration file.

Each DB2 database has a set of system catalog views that contain information about all the privileges held by users and groups, as well as DBADM authority assignments. The system catalog information is updated every time there is a change precipitated by a GRANT, REVOKE, or CREATE statement. Table 5-7 lists privileges-related catalog views and their contents.

You can query these views to retrieve information about the privileges granted on a particular database object, the privileges held by particular users or groups, and the privileges granted by users with granting abilities. For example, the following

System Catalog View	Contents
SYSCAT.DBAUTH	Database privilege assignments
SYSCAT.TBSPACEAUTH	Table space privilege assignments
SYSCAT.TABAUTH	Table and view privilege assignments
SYSCAT.COLAUTH	Column privilege assignments
SYSCAT.INDEXAUTH	Index privilege assignments
SYSCAT.SCHEMAAUTH	Schema privilege assignments
SYSCAT.PACKAGEAUTH	Package privilege assignments
SYSCAT.PASSTHRUAUTH	Server privilege assignments

Table 5-7. *Catalog Views Related to Privileges*

statement retrieves a list of authorization IDs that have been directly granted DBADM authority:

```
SELECT DISTINCT GRANTEE FROM SYSCAT.DBAUTH WHERE DBADMAUTH = 'Y'
```

You can also easily view privilege and authority information through the DB2 Control Center. For any object, you can see which privileges have been granted to different users and groups by doing the following:

1. Right-click the object in the navigation pane (the area of the Control Center window that contains the expandable objects tree).

2. From the menu that appears, select Authorities if you have clicked on a database and Privileges if you have clicked a database object. The window that opens displays all of the user and group privileges granted for the object.

3. To look at all the privileges that a particular user or group holds, right-click the authorization ID of the user or group in the contents pane (the area of the Control Center window to the right of the navigation pane) and select Change. The notebook that opens displays all of the privileges granted to that user or group: the first page shows database privileges, the second page shows schema privileges, the third shows table privileges, and so on.

The system catalog views can also be accessed from within the Control Center. To access one of the views for database object privileges, expand the Views directory in the navigation pane, and select the desired view from the contents pane.

Controlling Access to Data Using Views

In addition to controlling data access by using authorities and privileges, you can do so through the use of views. Views allow you to do the following:

- Restrict access to particular columns in a table
- Restrict access to particular rows in a table
- Restrict access to particular rows or columns in data source tables or views

To create a view, you must have SYSADM authority, DBADM authority, or CONTROL or SELECT privileges on all of the tables or views referenced in the view definition. Your intended users must also have the appropriate privileges to access the tables and views referenced in the view definition. If such privileges are not already granted, you must grant them.

For example, the STUDENTINFO table (Table 5-8) contains student names, student IDs, addresses, and final averages for the term. Information in this table needs to be accessed by many different people, including administration personnel and awards committee members. However, not every person should have access to all of the information in the table.

The registrar's administrative assistant needs to mail out details about upcoming course offerings to former students. To do this, the registrar needs to be able to access the students' names and addresses and make updates as address change requests come in. What this person should not be able to see (or update) is confidential information

NAME	STUDNUMBER	ADDRESS	FINALAVERAGE
William Yu	9203301	12 Elm Street...	96
Monica Jennings	9402214	231 Park Drive...	78
Martin Reid	9832378	#32-546 Waters St.	67
Wanda Matthews	2012532	791 Morningside St.	98
Kayla March	9912453	90 Oliver Drive	80

Table 5-8. *The STUDENTINFO Table*

about the students' final averages for the term. To do this, we need to create a view that selects only particular columns from the table.

```
CREATE VIEW STUDENTCONTACT AS
SELECT NAME, ADDRESS FROM STUDENTINFO
GRANT SELECT ON VIEW STUDENTCONTACT TO GROUP ADMINASST
```

On the other hand, the awards committee needs to know which students achieved 95 percent or better this term so that they can notify these students of an award. This set of users needs to access the table to get students' names, addresses, and final averages. However, they do not need to see the final averages for all of the students—only the ones who have averages of 95 or better. To give the committee access to information for only a subset of the students, we can create a view that selects only particular rows from the table, using a WHERE clause:

```
CREATE VIEW AWARDRECIPIENTS AS
     SELECT NAME, STUDENTID, ADDRESS, FINALAVERAGE
          WHERE FINALAVERAGE >=95
GRANT SELECT ON VIEW AWARDRECIPIENTS TO AWARDCTTE
```

Auditing DB2 Activities

The DB2 UDB audit facility allows you to monitor system use. The audit facility records events associated with a particular instance, including activities involving all of the databases within that instance. For each operation performed in an instance, the audit facility may record it in the audit log (db2audit.log), which is stored in the instance's security folder. For each operation, such as an INSERT statement, a record may be generated in the audit log. These records are categorized into the following groups:

- **AUDIT**   Records generated when audit settings are changed or the audit log is accessed
- **CHECKING**   Records generated during authorization checking when DB2 UDB objects are accessed
- **OBJMAINT**   Records generated when objects are created or dropped
- **SECMAINT**   Records generated when changing authorities or when granting or revoking privileges
- **SYSADM**   Records generated when actions are performed that require SYSADM, SYSCTRL, or SYSMAINT authority

The basic syntax of the audit facility command is given schematically here:

```
db2audit <parameter options>
```

Each of the parameters is described with its range of options in Table 5-9.

Parameter	Description	Options		Option Description	Notes
CONFIGURE	Allows modification of the db2audit.cfg file	RESET		Causes configuration file to revert to initial configuration	
		SCOPE	ALL AUDIT CHECKING OBJMAINT SECMAINT SYSADM VALIDATE CONTEXT	Specifies categories of events to be audited	Additional options: 1. Specify whether only successful events, failing events, or both are logged with STATUS SUCCESS, FAILURE, or BOTH 2. Specify whether audit errors are returned to user with ERRORTYPE AUDIT or NORMAL
DESCRIBE	Displays current audit configuration information and status				
EXTRACT	Allows movement of audit records from audit log to a specified destination	FILE		Specifies audit records to be placed in a file (output_file)	

Table 5-9.   *The db2audit Command*

Parameter	Description	Options	Option Description	Notes
		DELASC	Specifies audit records to be placed in a delimited ASCII format	To override default string delimiter, specify DELASC followed by DELIMITER and the new delimiter
		CATEGORY	Specifies category of events to be extracted (default is all)	
		DATABASE	Specifies audit records for a particular database to be extracted	
		STATUS	Specifies audit records for a particular status to be extracted	
FLUSH	Forces pending audit records to be written to audit log			If audit facility is in an error state, resets audit state to Ready to Log
PRUNE	Deletes audit records from the audit log	ALL	Specifies that all records are to be deleted	
		DATE yyyymmddhh	Specifies that all records prior to specified date/time are to be deleted	
START	Starts audit facility			

Table 5-9.   *The db2audit Command* (continued)

As an illustrative example, the following command configures the audit facility to log all unsuccessful events involving the creation or dropping of objects, and unsuccessful events involving the modification of user privileges or authorities:

```
db2audit configure scope objmaint, secmaint status failure
```

Chapter 6

Understanding Instances

The default instance that was created when you installed DB2 may not be the one that you will use to run your business. For that instance, you were given a limited set of choices regarding the instance, the database, and the user that you created. When the default instance was created, the database manager configuration parameters (used to control the instance) were set to default values that were designed for typical DB2 environments. Your business needs may be different, or and you may find that you need several instances on your machine.

For example, you may need a test instance where you can try out different benchmarking tests before you determine the best configuration values for your production instance. You may also want different instances for different users. Those in the payroll department may have a separate instance to ensure that there is no general access by other members of the company or customers. Before you create another instance, database, or user, you should consider the options available to you.

If you do determine that you need more than one instance on your machine, you should consider the resources that will be required by each. These resources include having sufficient virtual storage and disk space to support each instance and their related databases. Having multiple instances also requires additional administration time to manage and maintain the instances.

Creating an Instance

When you installed DB2, you had the option to create the following:

- An instance of the database manager. In a Windows or OS/2 installation, the name of the default instance is DB2; in a Linux or UNIX environment, it is db2inst1.

- A sample database within the instance, which is used to test that the installation of the instance of the database manager was correct. The sample database may include the DB2 Universal Database (UDB) sample database, the Data Warehousing sample database, and the OLAP sample database.

- A user account that is used for various DB2 services. For example, the installation program demands a user account to be associated with the Database Administration Server (DAS). In a Windows or OS/2 installation, the default user account for the DAS instance owner is db2admin. In a Linux or UNIX installation, it is db2as. During the installation, you have the option to use this user account for all DB2 services (for example, the Control Server) or to specify your own for each service you choose to install.

The settings for the default instance may not meet your current or future business needs, or at some point, you may want to create a new instance. When creating a new instance, there are many options to consider, as explained in the following sections.

DB2 program files are physically stored in a single location on your machine at the time of installation, and each additional instance that is created refers to this location. This means the program files are not duplicated for each instance created.

Types of Instances

Different DB2 products support different instance types. For any instance that you create, you should ensure that your machine has sufficient memory and disk storage to support local or remote (or both) applications running against the database. The amount of memory and storage that you will require is part of the logical and physical design phase of your database. See Chapter 1 for more information on database design. You can determine the correct instance type for your environment by considering each of the types available:

- **Client** If you are at a workstation and you are running applications or running queries that access a database located only on another machine, then this is your choice. This is the type of instance that gets created on a DB2 client. A client instance cannot manage or store databases. A client instance merely provides an environment in which administrators control a DB2 client's operating environment (from a DB2 perspective). This instance can be created on any DB2 client or server.

- **Standalone** If you are at a machine that is to have a database that supports local (direct connection) clients, then this is your choice. This type of instance can only created on a DB2 Personal Edition (DB2 PE) workstation. DB2 PE can store and manage local databases, and connect to remote DB2 servers; however, DB2 PE cannot accept inbound requests from remote client applications.

- **Satellite** If you are in an environment in which the database primarily supports dial-up remote clients (which are usually laptop computers), then this is your choice.

- **EE** DB2 satellites are workstations that operate in an occasionally connected environment. A DB2 satellite can be either a DB2 Personal Edition or a DB2 Workgroup Edition (DB2 WE) workstation. DB2 satellites are controlled by DB2 Enterprise Edition or DB2 Enterprise–Extended Edition servers. A satellite instance can only be created on a DB2 PE or DB2 WE workstation. If you are at a machine with a database that supports local clients (direct connection) and remote clients (connections using modems or other communication methods), then this is your choice. This is the instance type that is created in a DB2 server installation (excluding DB2 PE).

- **EEE** If you want to create a partitioned database environment, then this is your choice. Both local and remote clients can use this database environment. This type of instance can only be created on a workstation on which DB2 Enterprise–Extended Edition is installed. DB2 EEE supports the partitioning of a database across a cluster of nodes.

The db2icrt Command

You can create an instance by using the db2icrt command. The parameters for the command differ for the various operating systems.

When using the db2icrt command to add another instance of DB2, you must provide the login name of the instance owner (if not yourself) and optionally specify the authentication type of the instance. To add an instance, do the following:

1. Log on with a user account that has local Administrator authority (in Windows OS/2 environments) or root access (in UNIX environments).

2. Add an instance using the command line by entering **db2icrt <instance name> <...parameters>.**

With Windows-based operating systems and OS/2, the command parameters you need to know and will use are the following:

-s <inst type>   With this parameter, you specify the type of instance you want to create. The instance type can be Client, Standalone, Satellite, Enterprise Edition (EE), or Enterprise–Extended Edition (EEE):

- Client is used to create an instance for a client.

- Standalone is used to create an instance for a database server with local clients.

- Satellite is used to create an instance for a satellite database server.

- EE is used to create an instance for a database server with local and remote clients.

- EEE is used to create an instance for a partitioned database server.

-p <instance profile path>   This parameter is the instance profile path that is required when creating a partitioned database instance.

-r <port range>   This parameter specifies a range of TCP/IP ports to be used by the partitioned database instance when EEE is the instance type chosen. This parameter is equivalent to the -p <port name> parameter found under the UNIX-based operating systems discussion that follows. -? This parameter indicates that you want additional help or usage information.

With UNIX-based operating systems, the db2icrt command parameters you need to know and will use are the following:

-a <auth type>   With this parameter, you specify the authentication type, which determines how and where a user will be verified or authenticated. Once a user is authenticated, the user is permitted to access the instance. If a user ID and password are specified during a connection or attachment attempt, they are compared to the valid user ID and password combinations at the location specified by this parameter. There is only one authentication type per instance, which covers access to that database server and all the databases under its control. The authentication type can be SERVER, CLIENT, DCS, DCE, or KERBEROS for the instance (the default is SERVER), and there are also encrypted variations on each type. Encryption means that the user ID and password are passed between client and server in encrypted form, which prevents others from reading the user ID and password in the clear.

-s <inst type>   With this parameter, you specify the type of instance you want to create. The instance type can be EEE, EE, or Client.

- Client is used to create an instance for a client.
- EE is used to create an instance for a database server with local and remote clients.
- EEE is used to create an instance for a partitioned database server.

-p <port name>   With this parameter, you specify the port name or number used by the instance.

<instance name>   You must also specify the name of the instance you are creating.
   Other less important command parameters may or may not be used on your operating system:

-h or -?   This parameter indicates that you want additional help or usage information.

-h <host name>   This parameter overrides the default TCP/IP host name when EEE is the instance type chosen. This parameter is only used when DB2 EEE is installed.

-d   This parameter indicates that you want debug mode to be run with this command.

-u <fenced ID>   This parameter is used to specify the user ID under which fenced user-defined functions and fenced stored procedures will run. This is not required if you install the DB2 client or the DB2 Software Developer's Kit. For other DB2 products, this is a required parameter. Note that the <fenced ID> cannot be root or bin. Fenced user-defined functions and fenced stored procedures are defined in such a way as to protect the database manager from modifications by the functions or procedures. A barrier, or "fence," separates the functions or procedures from the database manager.

-u <user name, password>   This parameter is used to specify the account name and password for the database service name needed when EEE is the instance type chosen.

-c <cluster name>   This parameter is used to specify the Microsoft Cluster Server (MSCS) cluster name.
   After you have created an instance, you can work within it by using commands from the command line processor (CLP). Or you can use the Control Center—a graphical interface where you can work with database objects. If you decide to work within the

instance using the Control Center, you will need to determine if you are going to run the Control Center as an application or as an applet. For more information on how to do this, see the chapter on Control Center installation and configuration in the *DB2 Universal Database Quick Beginnings* book appropriate to your environment.

The Instance Directory

The *instance directory* is the location in which all information (code and files) that relates to that instance is stored. Once this directory is created, its location cannot be changed. In a UNIX environment, the instance directory is located in the INSTHOME/sqllib directory, where INSTHOME is the home directory of the instance owner. In a Windows or OS/2 environment, the instance directory is located in the x:\<installation path>\ sqllib\<instance name> directory, where x: is the drive where you installed DB2, <installation path> is the path where the code was installed, and <instance name> is the instance name. For example, in a typical Windows installation, the DB2 instance that is created during the installation is located in the c:\Program Files\SQLLIB\DB2 directory.

Within the instance directory, you will find the following directories and files:

- The database manager configuration file (db2systm). This file contains the database manager configuration parameters.
- The system database directory. This directory contains database location information. The locations of the databases may be local or remote.
- The node directory (SQLNODIR).
- In a DB2 EEE node configuration file (db2nodes.cfg).
- The DB2 diagnostic file (db2diag.log).

There may also be files containing debugging information, such as the exception or register dump, or the call stack for DB2 processes.

Establishing Client-to-Server Communications

You will also need to establish client-to-server communications. A *client* is any program (or workstation on which it is running) that communicates with and accesses a database server that communicates with and accesses a database server. Each DB2 server comes with a DB2 client already installed. For the purposes of this chapter, a client application can be an application running on a DB2 client or an application that runs on a DB2 server that uses the integrated DB2 client components to talk to a DB2 server. A client can be locally or remotely connected to a database server. Typically, applications run on a workstation on which a DB2 client has been installed with the intent of accessing and using data found at the server, and it is the server that responds to requests from the client applications. For the client-to-server environment to work, you need to define the type of communications allowed between the client and the database server. This can be done by using the Client Configuration Assistant (CCA) that comes as part of the DB2 Universal Database product, or the DB2 command line processor. The CCA is only available on Windows- and OS/2-based workstations.

Before starting the CCA at the client, you need to ensure that the remote servers with which the client wants to communicate are configured to accept inbound client requests. The CCA determines which servers the client can communicate with. By default, the server installation program automatically detects and configures most protocols on the server for inbound client connections.

You should install and configure the communications protocols such as TCP/IP on the server machine according to the instructions for your operating system before installing DB2 Universal Database. You can have more than one communications protocol supported by the database server. It is likely the case that communications protocols will be in place before the installation of DB2 UDB because other products and applications on your server machine require them.

There are three possible methods within the CCA to configure your workstation to access a database on a remote server:

- Adding a database by using a server profile. A *server profile* contains information about server instances on a system and databases within each server instance.

- Adding a database by using Discovery. The system being contacted by Discovery must have a DB2 Administration Server (DAS) running.

- Adding a database manually. To do this, you must have the information for the database to which you want to connect and the server on which it resides. This method is much like entering commands via the command line processor.

For more information on these configuration methods, see Chapter 4.

Directory Information

Once you have an instance and the first database or node is created, the files and directories for that object are also created. These files and directories will be frequently used because they contain important information about the instance and the databases that exist inside it. Because these files and directories are used frequently, it is helpful if they are kept in a cache. When directory caching is enabled via the *dir_cache* database manager configuration parameter, the database, node, and DCS directory files are cached in memory.

The directory cache is allocated and has content added to it during the first directory lookup by an application or user. The cache is refreshed only when an application or user modifies any of the directory files. For example, a new database is added to the database directory. To take advantage of any modifications to the cache, already started applications must terminate and re-establish their connection to the database.

Finally, to refresh the cache that is shared between instances of DB2, you must first stop the database manager, by using the db2stop command, and then restart the database manager by using the db2start command.

The TERMINATE Command

The TERMINATE command explicitly terminates the DB2 back-end process. If an application is connected to a database or a process is in the middle of a unit of work, this command causes the database connection to be dropped. An internal commit is performed to complete any inflight transactions. Although the TERMINATE and the CONNECT RESET commands both break the connection to a database, only the TERMINATE command results in the termination of the DB2 back-end process.

You should issue the TERMINATE command if db2start and db2stop were run while the DB2 back-end process was active. The TERMINATE command prevents any application (including the DB2 command line processor) from maintaining an attachment to the database manager instance when this instance is no longer available.

You should also issue the TERMINATE command if you are working in a massively parallel processing (MPP) environment and the DB2NODE environment variable is updated in the session. The DB2NODE environment variable is used to specify the coordinator node number within an MPP multiple logical partition configuration.

To terminate the command line processor's back-end process, use this command:

```
terminate
```

The Node Directory

A *node directory* is created and maintained for any DB2 workstation that needs to establish communications with a DB2 server. Each entry in the directory file has the information about one local or remote computer that has a database that an application can access. When a DB2 client requests access to a database (or a DB2 server through its integrated client component), this directory is used to provide the communication protocol endpoint information. Once this information is available, it is used to establish a database connection or instance attachment.

Cataloging Nodes

The database manager creates a node entry in the node directory from the supplied information in the CATALOG ... NODE command. A new entry is created each time a CATALOG...NODE command is successfully processed. There is a separate CATALOG...NODE command for each type of communications protocol. A detailed example of cataloging a TCP/IP node is shown in Chapter 4. For detailed information on all the CATALOG...NODE commands, see Chapter 30.

For example, the CATALOG LOCAL NODE command creates a local alias for an instance that resides on the same server. This is especially important when there is more than one instance on the same server to be accessed from the user's client.

In another example, you could use the following command to catalog a TCP/IP node on a DB2 workstation:

```
catalog tcpip node <node name> remote <host name> server <svce name>
```

The <node name> is the local alias for the node to be cataloged. This is a name chosen by you and used to identify the node. You should make this a meaningful name so that you can remember it. The name must conform to the database manager naming conventions and must be unique within the directories.

The <host name> is the host name of the node where the target database resides. In this case, the host name is the name of the node that is known to the TCP/IP network. The maximum number of characters that can be used in this name is 255.

The <svce name> specifies the service name or the port number of the server's database manager instance. The value specified is used as a key when searching the local *services* file for an associated port number. If a matching entry is not found, and the value specified is numeric, then the value is interpreted as the port number. The maximum number of characters that can be used in this name is 14. Note that this parameter must not be used when cataloging an ADMIN node for the DAS. In that case, there is a default port number value of 523.

There are other optional parameters on this command:

- You can specify that the node will be SOCKS-enabled.

- You can specify the name of the server instance to which an attachment is being made.

- You can specify the DB2 system name that is used to identify the server machine.

- You can specify the operating system type of the server machine.

- You can specify a comment that describes the node entry so that when the directory contents are listed, you will have an easy way to identify the node associated with that entry in the directory.

When cataloging nodes, be sure that you also catalog administration server nodes.

Listing Nodes

You use the LIST NODE DIRECTORY command to list the contents of the node directory:

```
list node directory
```

The common fields displayed when this command is used include the following:

- **Node name**   This is the name of the remote node and corresponds to the name entered for the <node name> parameter when the node was cataloged.

- **Comment**   This is typically a description of the node. It is entered when the node was cataloged.

- **Protocol**   This is the communications protocol cataloged for the node. The protocol is APPC, APPCLU, APPN, IPX/SPX, local, Named Pipe, NetBIOS, or TCP/IP.

Uncataloging Nodes

To delete an entry from the node directory, use this command:

```
uncatalog node <node name>
```

The <node name> is the node entry to be uncataloged.

This command is used to uncatalog an entry in a node directory. Uncatloging a node removes location information for a specific database that was cataloged at that node, but the database on the remote server still exists.

Use the LIST NODE DIRECTORY command before you remove a node entry from the node directory. You can use the UNCATALOG NODE command once you know the node entry you want to remove.

The Database Directory

Each entry in the database directory has the information about one database that specifies the location of the database: either local or remote. If local, the database is on your server; if remote, the database is on another server that is connected via communications protocols. The database manager automatically catalogs databases when they are created, putting one entry in the local database directory and another entry in the system database directory.

The information about each database in the directory includes the name (and alias) of the database, the local drive or path location or the remote node name, and the authentication type (only for remote databases).

When you create a database, information about it is automatically cataloged in the system database directory. You can use the CATALOG DATABASE command to catalog a database with a different alias name. You can also use this command to catalog databases that were previously uncataloged.

The location of the database is recorded in one of the following ways:

- **Remote**   The database resides on another node.

- **Indirect**   The database resides locally. Databases that reside on the same node as the system database directory indirectly reference the home entry of the local database directory.

- **Home**   The database resides locally. The database directory is on the same path as the local database directory.
- **An LDAP entry**   Database location information is stored in an LDAP directory.

To list the contents of the system database directory, use the LIST DATABASE DIRECTORY command. If the command is issued without the ON <path> parameter, the system database directory is listed. If the command is issued with the ON <path> parameter, the local database directory on the path given is returned.

See the CATALOG DATABASE command in Chapter 30 for specific syntax and command parameter information.

Use the LIST DATABASE DIRECTORY command to list any databases that have been cataloged on your workstation. You can use the UNCATALOG DATABASE command once you know which database entry you want to remove. Use the DROP DATABASE command to remove a database entry from the local database directory. (Or you can use the db2idrop utility if all of the databases in that instance can be dropped. The db2idrop utility is discussed later in this chapter; see "Removing Instances".)

The DCS Directory

The Database Connection Services (DCS) directory contains information about remote host database names that can be accessed from a local system if DRDA Application Request (DRDA AR) support has been installed, DB2 Connect provides DRDA AR support to DB2 workstations that allows them to connect to mainframe- and host-based DB2 servers like DB2 for ZOS. The DCS directory is created the first time the CATALOG DCS DATABASE command is issued. The DCS directory is located on the path and drive where the DB2 database manager was installed. The DCS directory is maintained outside the database.

The DCS directory is needed because you can install DB2 Connect without installing DB2 UDB. In this way, you can have DB2 application through connections pass a DB2 Connect gateway to a remote host database server. The location of the remote host database server is kept in the DCS directory.

Configuring the Database Manager

You can use the GET DATABASE MANAGER CONFIGURATION command to list the database manager configuration parameters and their current values. Then you should review each and determine which of the parameters you want to modify.

Once you know what you want to change, you can use the UPDATE DATABASE MANAGER CONFIGURATION command to specify a change to one or more configuration parameters. Not all of the database manager configuration parameters can be updated. Some, for example, are information-only configuration parameters. The values that may be allowed for each parameter vary by the type of the instance (SERVER, CLIENT, etc.) and by operating system. (See the "Configuration Parameters" section in Chapter 14.)

Changes made to an instances database manager configuration take effect after the instance is stopped and started again. This moves the new values into memory. If you are updating a client configuration parameter, it will become effective after you disconect your application. In most cases, after updating one or more configuration parameters, you should run db2stop and then db2start to have the changes take effect.

If an error occurs during the update of the configuration, the database manager configuration file is reinstated as it was before the changes were made.

A checksum error will result if the database manager configuration file is modified without using the appropriate command. If this happens, you will have to reinstall the database manager. This will reset the database manager configuration file.

After you have made changes to the database manager configuration parameters, the RESET DATABASE MANAGER CONFIGURATION command will reset the parameter values in the database manager configuration file to the system defaults. For those parameter values where different defaults may exist based on the database type, the assumption when using this command is that the database type is a server with remote clients (Enterprise Edition).

To reset the database manager configuration for a remote instance, you will first have to attach to that instance by using the ATTACH command.

The ATTACH Command

If the ATTACH command has not been run, any instance-level commands are run against the current instance as specified by the contents of the DB2INSTANCE environment variable. To determine the current instance, use the command:

```
get instance
```

To have instance-level commands run against an instance other than the current instance, you must specify an ATTACH to the alias of the desired instance. The desired instance may be another instance on the same workstation or an instance on a remote workstation. Once you have successfully attached to the other instance, you can run instance-level commands on that instance.

In most cases, you will be working in a secure environment, so you will want to have authentication take place when you attach to another instance. The ATTACH command has parameters that allow this. You have the ability to specify a user name and a password when attaching to the other instance.

After running the instance-level commands, you must detach from the instance by using the DETACH command.

Configuring the Database Administration Server (DAS)

The GET ADMIN CONFIGURATION command is like the GET DATABASE MANAGER CONFIGURATION command, but it lists only a subset of the database manager configuration file entries. The subset consists of those entries that are relevant to the DB2 Administration Server (DAS). The DAS is a special DB2 instance that enables remote administration of DB2 servers.

The database manager configuration parameters displayed by the GET ADMIN CONFIGURATION command are the following:

- **AGENT_STACK_SZ** (for OS/2 only) Specifies the amount of memory allocated and committed by the database manager for each agent. The size is in number of pages. (The page size varies depending on the choices made for the instance.)

- **AUTHENTICATION** Specifies how and where user authentication happens.

- **DIAGLEVEL** Specifies the severity of diagnostic error messages that are recorded in db2diag.log.

- **DIAGPATH** Specifies the fully qualified path for all instance diagnostic information.

- **DISCOVER** Specifies the type of discovery request supported. The types supported are SEARCH, which supports the search of the network, KNOWN, which supports discovery requests, and DISABLE, which does not support discovery requests.

- **DISCOVER_COMM** Specifies the communication protocols that clients use to issue search discovery requests. The two supported protocols are TCP/IP and NetBIOS.

- **FILESERVER** Specifies the IPX/SPX file server name.

- **IPX_SOCKET** Specifies the IPX/SPX socket number. It must always be socket number 879A.

- **NNAME** (for OS/2 only) Specifies the node name or workstation name. The name is used by clients to access database server workstations using the NetBIOS communications protocol.

- **OBJECTNAME** Specifies the IPX/SPX name that represents this database manager instance at the file server.

- **QUERY_HEAP_SZ** Specifies the maximum memory (in pages) allocated for the query heap. The query heap is used to store each query in the agent's private memory.

- **SVCENAME** Specifies the name used to update the database manager configuration file at the server. This parameter cannot be modified. It must always be TCP/IP port (523).

- **SYSADM_GROUP** Specifies the group name having SYSADM authority on this instance.

- **SYSCTRL_GROUP** Specifies the group name having SYSCTRL authority on this instance.

- **SYSMAINT_GROUP** Specifies the group name having SYSMAINT authority on this instance.

- **TPNAME** Specifies the name of the remote transaction program that the database client must use when it issues an allocate request to the database manager instance using the Advanced Program-to-Program Communication (APPC) protocol.

- **TRUST_ALLCLNTS** Specifies whether all clients are to be trusted and therefore do not require validation in this database environment. The default is to trust all clients. This parameter works with the TRUST_CLNTAUTH configuration parameter.

- **TRUST_CLNTAUTH** Specifies whether all users of trusted clients are validated at the client. The default is that validation takes place at the client. This parameter works with the TRUST_ALLCLNTS configuration parameter.

You can use the UPDATE ADMIN MANAGER CONFIGURATION command to modify the values for these parameters. If you need to undo your changes, you can use the RESET ADMIN MANAGER CONFIGURATION command to reestablish the original default values for these parameters. See Chapter 14 for more information.

Maintaining Instances

The update instances utility (db2iupdt) updates a specified DB2 UDB instance to enable the acquisition of a new system configuration or access to functions associated with the installation or removal of certain product options.

On Windows NT and Windows 2000 operating systems, this command is only used in a DB2 EEE environment. The command updates single partition instances for use in a partitioned database system. This utility is not available on OS/2. You must run the db2iupdt command in a UNIX environment whenever you apply maintenance (through FixPaks) or upgrade your version of DB2.

Listing Instances

To get a list of all the instances that are available on a system, enter the following command on the command line:

```
db2ilist
```

To determine which instance applies to the current session, use this command:

```
get instance
```

Updating Instance Configurations

Running the db2iupdt command updates the specified instance by performing two operations:

- Files in the sqllib subdirectory under the instance owner's home directory are replaced. Replacement of files occurs only when the files being applied by the db2iupdt command are newer than those currently in that location.

- A new database manager configuration file is created if the node type is changed. This is done by merging relevant values from the existing database manager configuration file with the default values from the default database manager configuration file for the new node type. If a new database manager configuration file is created, the old database manger configuration file is placed in the backup subdirectory of the sqllib subdirectory under the instance owner's home directory.

The db2iupdt command is located in the instance subdirectory in the version and release subdirectory. (The name of the version and release subdirectory is different on each operating system.)

The command is used as shown:

```
db2iupdt <inst name> (parameter options…)
```

The <inst name> is the login name of the instance owner. This is determined during the first installation of the product or when the instance is created.

The other optional parameters associated with this command include the following:

-e   This parameter allows you to update each instance that exists. Those that exist can be shown using db2ilist.

-k   This parameter preserves the current instance type. If you do not specify this parameter, the current instance is upgraded to the highest instance type available in the following order:

- Partitioned database server with local and remote clients (DB2 Universal Database Enterprise–Extended Edition default instance type)
- Database server with local and remote clients (DB2 Universal Database Enterprise Edition default instance type)
- Client (DB2 client default instance type)

The -a, -d, -?, and -u parameters that are discussed in "The db2icrt Command" section earlier in this chapter apply to this command as well.

Removing Instances

To remove an instance, use the following command:

```
db2idrop <instance name>
```

However, before removing an instance, you should ensure that the instance is stopped "gracefully" and that appropriate backups have been taken. Follow these steps:

1. Stop all applications on the instance.
2. Stop the command line processor by running db2 terminate commands in each open command line processor window.
3. Stop the instance by running the db2stop command.
4. Back up the instance directory indicated by the DB2INSTPROF registry variable. On UNIX operating systems, consider backing up the files in the sqllib subdirectory of the home directory of the instance owner.
5. (On UNIX operating systems only) Log off as the instance owner.
6. (On UNIX operating systems only) Log on as a user with root authority.
7. Issue the db2idrop command using the instance name that you want to drop.
8. (On UNIX operating systems only) Optionally, as a user with root authority, remove the instance owner's user ID and group (if used only for that instance). Do not remove these if you are planning to recreate the instance. This step is optional because the instance owner and the instance owner group may be used for other purposes.

The db2idrop command removes the instance entry from the list of instances and removes the sqllib subdirectory from under the instance owner's home directory.

The License Management Tool

If you have changed your DB2 installation in any way, you will need to update the license information stored as part of the system. The way to do that is through the license management tool shipped with the product.

The license management tool performs basic license functions, including adding, removing, listing, and modifying licenses and policies on your local system. To use this tool on UNIX-based operating systems, you require root authority. To use this tool on Windows-based operating systems or OS/2, no authentication is required.

To list all the products on your local system having licensed information, use this command:

```
db2licm -l
```

After you have listed all the products on your local system, as part of the list, you will see the product passwords associated with each product. This password is used in several of the commands that follow.

To add a license for a product, use this command:

```
db2licm -a <file name>
```

The file name must contain valid license information about the product added to your local system.

To remove a license for a product, use this command:

```
db2licm -r <product password>
```

After the product license is removed, the product is still present on your system but the operations of the product are in try-and-buy mode.

To update the number of user licenses you have purchased, use this command:

```
db2licm -u <product password> <number of users>
```

When considering the number of user licenses you have purchased, you may want to ensure that you are using only the number of licenses you have purchased. To enforce your use of only the number of licenses you have purchased, use this command:

```
db2licm -e hard
```

The valid values for the -e parameter are "hard" and "soft." Hard specifies that unlicensed requests from users at your system will not be allowed. This means that when users working with the database have exceeded the number of user licenses, no new requests will be allowed. Soft specifies that new requests to work with the database will be logged but not restricted. By monitoring these requests beyond the number of user licenses that you have, you will be able to determine the number you will need in the future based on current usage trends.

To update the license policy type to use on your system, use this command:

```
db2licm -p <product password> REGISTERED CONCURRENT
```

The keywords REGISTERED and CONCURRENT can be used separately or together when updating the license policy type.

A *concurrent user* is a person, application, or device that has established a connection to one or more databases on one server. A user with multiple connections to a single server counts as only one concurrent user. The one exception occurs when a multiplexing program, application server, or another program makes multiple connections to DB2 providing access on behalf of other users. When these configurations are in use, you need to consider each concurrent user of that program as a concurrent DB2 user. In the concurrent user model, the customer must ensure that each server is licensed for the maximum number of users that will use that server at any one time.

The concurrent user-licensing model is the only choice in situations where the identity of the users is unknown. The concurrent user model is also appropriate when users require only occasional access to a particular server.

A *registered user* is a person, application, or device entitled to establish one or more connections to any authorized server installation of a DB2 Universal Database or DB2 Connect product in your enterprise, either directly or through a multiplexing program or application server. Registered users of DB2 Workgroup Edition are counted separately, and DB2 user entitlements are not transferable between products. You should compare the total number of users requiring access to the DB2 server product with the sum of the user entitlements provided with each installation license, and obtain additional user entitlements if required.

Registered users may be the appropriate choice when there are many users (for example, at client workstations) who need to access databases on multiple database servers, or who connect to databases for long periods of time. Determining required licensing and monitoring the licensing requirements is your responsibility.

If your system has multiple processors, you must update the number of processors you are licensed to use. Use this command:

```
db2licm -n <product password> <number of processors>
```

If you need to see the version information recorded in your license file, use this command:

```
db2licm -v
```

If you need to see help information about this command, use this:

```
db2licm -h
```

You could also use -? instead of the -h option. By using either of these options, all other options used with the command are ignored, and only the help information is displayed.

The
Complete
Reference

Chapter 7

Managing Data Storage

Before creating a database (which is described in the next chapter), you need to know something about the logical and physical locations where the data to be stored in the database will be kept. In this chapter, you will learn how to define and use nodegroups (logical), and then you will learn how to create and use table spaces (physical).

Nodegroups

A *database partition* is a part of a database that consists of its own data, indexes, configuration files, and transaction logs. A database partition is sometimes called a *node* or a *database node*. In most cases, you will be creating and working with a *single-partition database*—a database with only one database partition. DB2 Personal Edition, DB2 Enterprise Edition, and DB2 Enterprise–Extended Edition can all store and manage single-partition databases. DB2 Enterprise–Extended Edition can be used to work with multi-partition databases. This book focuses on single-partition databases. You can find detailed information about multi-partitioned databases in the documentation that comes with DB2.

You can define named subsets of one or more database partitions in a database, and each subset you define is known as a *nodegroup*. Each subset that contains more than one database partition is known as a *multipartition nodegroup*. This type of nodegroup can be defined only with database partitions that belong to the same instance.

When you are working in a single-partition database, you will be working with a single nodegroup.

Designing Table Spaces

Table spaces are DB2 objects that are used to logically map data to physical storage locations (files, raw devices, etc.). A table space may be spread over one or more physical storage devices.

Most table spaces that you will create will hold user table data. Depending on your applications, you may also have the need to create user temporary table spaces (to contain declared temporary tables) or a system temporary table space (to contain system temporary tables).

There is also a relationship between table spaces and nodegroups. Each table space is created into a nodegroup when you use the CREATE TABLESPACE statement. Once in a nodegroup, the table space must remain there. You cannot move the table space from one nodegroup to another.

Creating a table space within a database assigns containers to the table space and records the table space definitions and attributes in the database system catalog. Containers are database objects that represent a storage location for DB2 data. Table spaces are made up of containers, which consist of extents, which consist of pages. Once the table space is created, you can create tables in it.

Designing and Choosing Table Spaces

A database must contain at least three table spaces:

- One catalog table space
- One or more user table spaces
- One or more temporary table spaces

In a partitioned database environment, the catalog node contains all three default table spaces, and the other database partitions will each have only TEMPSPACE1 and USERSPACE1.

Table spaces can be divided into two types, depending on what controls the movement of the data to and from the storage space:

- **System-managed space (SMS)**   The operating system's file manager controls the storage space.
- **Database-managed space (DMS)**   The database manager controls the storage space.

Catalog Table Space

The catalog table space contains all of the system catalog tables for the database. When the database is created, a table space called SYSCATSPACE is created. By default, this table space is created as an SMS table space. You can override this default during database creation. This table space cannot be dropped. IBMCATGROUP is the default nodegroup for this table space.

User Table Space

The user table space contains all of the user-defined tables. When the database is created, a table space called USERSPACE1 is created, and IBMDEFAULTGROUP is the default nodegroup for this table space. By default, this table space is created as an SMS table space. You can override this default during database creation. You should explicitly identify a table space name when you create a table—if you do not, the table is placed according to the following rules:

- If one or more user-defined table spaces exist, the one with the smallest page size large enough for the table being created is chosen.
- Otherwise, USERSPACE1 is used if its page size is large enough for the table being created.

If there are no table spaces with a page size large enough, the table is not created and you are notified by an error message.

Temporary Table Space

Temporary tables use temporary table spaces. Two types of temporary table spaces exist: system temporary table spaces and user temporary table spaces.

There must be at least one system temporary table space in the database, and when the database is created, a table space called TEMPSPACE1 is created in the IBMTEMPGROUP nodegroup by default.

There is no user temporary table space created by default when the database is created. User temporary table spaces are explicitly defined by you or by other users. If a database uses more than one user temporary table space, temporary objects are allocated among the temporary table spaces in a round-robin fashion. Any data manipulation language (DML) statement could fail if no temporary table spaces exist with the same page size as the largest page size in the user table space.

You should define a single SMS temporary table space with a page size equal to the page size used in the majority of your user table spaces. This should be adequate for typical environments and workloads.

System-Managed Space Table Space

With this type of table space, you (or other users) decide on the location of the files, the database manager controls their names, and the file system is responsible for managing them. The database manager distributes the data evenly across the table space containers. An SMS table space is the default type of table space.

An SMS table space allows administrators to create file containers that are used to store DB2 data, while the operating system's file system is charged with the responsibility of accommodating storage requests associated with the data size. For this reason, SMS table spaces are inherently easier to manage than are DMS table spaces. The database manager distributes the data evenly across the table space containers. An SMS table space is the default type of table space.

In an SMS table space, a container can only be a file. SMS containers are extended one page at a time as the object grows. You can run the db2empfa utility to enable multipage file allocation to improve insert performance. Once enabled, multipage file allocation cannot be disabled. For more information about this utility, see the *Command Reference.*

You can explicitly define SMS table spaces by using the MANAGED BY SYSTEM clause on the CREATE DATABASE command or on the CREATE TABLESPACE statement. You must consider two factors before you design an SMS table space:

- **The number of containers you wish to specify for the table space** Once an SMS table space is created, you cannot add or delete containers. Each container associated with an SMS table space identifies an absolute or relative directory name. You must use caution when defining containers.

- **The extent size chosen for the table space** The *extent size* is the number of pages the database manager writes to one container before using a different one. The extent size can be specified only when the table space is created. It cannot be changed later. If you do not specify the extent size when the table space is created, the database manager uses the default extent size as defined by the *dft_extent_sz* database configuration parameter. The default for this parameter is 32 pages.

> **Tip**   *The SMS table space is considered to be full as soon as any one of its containers is full. As a result, it's good practice to allocate the same amount of space for each container. Having the same size containers also ensures that the data is distributed evenly across all the containers. This will assist the database's read and write performance.*

Database-Managed Space Table Space

In a DMS table space, the database manager controls the storage space. The storage model consists of a limited number of devices chosen by you, whose space is managed by the database manager. The database manager controls a special-purpose file system implemented to work with the space associated with these devices. The table space definitions include the list of devices belonging to the table space where data can be stored.

A DMS table space contains user-defined tables and data that can be defined as either a *regular* table space for storing normal table and index data, or a *long* table space for storing long field data or large object (LOB) data.

The database manager uses striping to distribute the data evenly across the table space containers. Unlike SMS table spaces, the containers that make up a DMS table space do not need to be the same size; however, suboptimal performance can result if they are not the same size because striping is attempted. To avoid wasted space, the size of the device and the size of the container should be equivalent.

Device containers must use logical volumes with a special character interface, not physical volumes. You can also use files instead of devices with DMS table spaces. No operational differences exist between a file and a device, but a file may be less efficient than a device because of the run-time overhead associated with the file system. Files are useful when devices are not directly supported, when a device is not available, when maximum performance is not required, and when you do not want to set up devices.

If your workload involves LOB or LONG VARCHAR data, you may derive performance benefits from file system caching. Note that LOBs and LONG VARCHARs are not buffered by the database manager's buffer pool.

Some operating systems allow you to have physical devices greater than 2GB in size. You should consider partitioning physical devices into multiple logical partitions when you have physical devices of this size or greater. This way, you can have containers that are always smaller than the size allowed by the operating system.

Choosing an Extent Size for a Table Space

Consider the following three factors when choosing the extent size for the table space:

- **The size and type of tables in the table space**   Space in DMS table spaces is allocated to tables one extent at a time. The initial allocation of space for a table is two extents for each table object. One extent is for a metadata object called an *extent map* that describes all of the extents in the table space that belong to the table object. The other extent is for the table data itself. If you have many small tables in a table space, you may have a relatively large amount of space allocated to store a relatively small amount of data. If this is the case, you should specify a small extent size or use an SMS table space that allocates pages one at a time. If you have a very large table that has a high growth rate, and it is associated with a DMS table space with a small extent size, you will have unnecessary overhead because of the frequent allocation of additional extents. A balance must be reached between the size of the extent and the frequency with which extents are allocated.

- **The type of access to the tables in the table space**   If you are expecting many queries or transactions that process large quantities of data, prefetching data from the tables may provide significant performance benefits. *Prefetching* is the process of reading data pages before those pages are referenced by a query to reduce response time. (Prefetching is discussed in detail in Chapter 14.)

- **The minimum number of extents required**   If there is not enough space in the containers for five extents of the table space, the table space is not created.

Recommendations for Temporary Table Spaces

As discussed earlier in the "Temporary Table Space" section, you should define a single SMS temporary table space with a page size equal to the page size used in the majority of your regular table spaces.

If you expect to be reorganizing tables with different page sizes, you should ensure that temporary table spaces are defined for each different page size. If you do not do this, you can still reorganize without the temporary table space—you reorganize within the table. If this occurs, you must have sufficient extra space in the table for the reorganization process.

Recommendations for Catalog Table Spaces

You should define a single SMS table space for the database catalogs. If you will need to enlarge the catalog table space later, consider using a DMS table space because it is easier to add new containers with this type of table space.

Recommendations for User Data

An online transaction processing (OLTP) workload is characterized by transactions that need random access to data, and those usually return small sets of data. Given that the access is random and involves one or a few pages, prefetching is not possible. DMS table spaces using device containers perform best in this situation.

A query workload is characterized by transactions that need sequential or partially sequential access to data, and those usually return large sets of data. A DMS table space using multiple device containers, where each container is on a separate disk, offers the greatest potential for efficient parallel prefetching.

Overall Recommendations for Table Space Types

In general, small personal databases are easiest to manage with SMS table spaces. For large, growing databases, you should use SMS table spaces for temporary table spaces and separate DMS table spaces with multiple containers for each table. You should also store long field data and indexes on their own table spaces.

By choosing DMS table spaces with device containers, you are also choosing to tune your environment. Be sure to read Part IV, "Performance."

Working with Table Spaces

After you have considered your work environment and decided on your database design, you must create the table spaces that best serve your environment. You can create permanent or temporary table spaces, depending on what you want to do with your data. You can use various DB2 commands or SQL statements to monitor your table spaces, or to add containers to them when they begin to fill up with data.

Alternatively, you may want to increase the size of the containers in your table spaces. You can also monitor the status of a table space. Your table space may be in some pending state requiring further action before it can be accessed. (For example, a table space may be put in roll-forward pending state after it is restored, and it must be rolled forward before it can be used again.) You can also rename a table space or drop a table space. The following sections provide details about each of these operations.

Creating a Table Space

You can create a table space using the Control Center or the CREATE TABLESPACE statement. In its simplest form, the CREATE TABLESPACE statement can be used as follows:

```
CREATE TABLESPACE <table space name>
MANAGED BY <table space type>
USING (<container information>)
```

In this simple statement, the assumption is that the table space being created is going to store user data and have a page size of 4096 bytes.

If you were to create a table space to store different data and have a different page size, you would use the following form of the statement:

```
CREATE <storage type> TABLESPACE <table space name>
```

```
PAGESIZE <integer value in kilobytes>
MANAGED BY <table space type>
USING (<container information>)
```

The assumption in this example is that the table space being created is not associated with a specific nodegroup. The default nodegroup, IBMDEFAULTGROUP, is used when the IN clause is not specified in the statement.

If you were to associate a table space with a specific nodegroup, you would use the CREATE NODEGROUP statement to create the nodegroup (see Chapter 27), and then use the following statement:

```
CREATE TABLESPACE <table space name>
IN <nodegroup name>

MANAGED BY <table space type>
USING (<container information>)
```

Other clauses are used to control the size of extents to be used, the size of the prefetch quantity to be used, the buffer pool to be used, the speed of the I/O controller (including disk seek and latency time), and the transfer rate specifying the time taken to read one page from disk into memory. Each of these clauses is concerned with performance issues relating to the containers. These issues are discussed in more detail in Part IV, "Performance."

Creating a Temporary Table Space

You can create two types of temporary table spaces: a system temporary table space or a user temporary table space. The database manager uses system temporary table spaces to store temporary tables or work areas used by the database manager to perform operations such as sorts or joins. You use user temporary table spaces to store declared global temporary tables.

Creating a System Temporary Table Space

The following is the general case for declaring a system temporary table space:

```
CREATE SYSTEM TEMPORARY TABLESPACE <table space name>
MANAGED BY <table space type>
USING <container information>
IN IBMTEMPGROUP
```

For detailed information about this statement, see Chapter 27.

Creating a User Temporary Table Space

The following is the general case for declaring a user temporary table space:

```
CREATE USER TEMPORARY TABLESPACE <table space name>
MANAGED BY <table space type>
USING <container information>
```

The default nodegroup is IBMDEFAULTGROUP.

The user temporary table space is where you would place declared global temporary tables as defined by the DECLARE GLOBAL TEMPORARY TABLE statement. This type of temporary table is used to share temporary data within an application. The data in these tables exists for use only while the application is running. Chapter 9 discusses this statement in detail.

Modifying a Table Space

You can check how full the containers for a table space are by using the LIST TABLESPACE CONTAINERS or LIST TABLESPACES command. You can also work with table spaces using the Control Center. You should add new containers before the existing containers are full.

The ALTER TABLESPACE statement allows you to add a container to an existing table space. The new space across all containers is not available until rebalancing is complete, and rebalancing occurs automatically once the new container is identified to the database manager. Access to the table space is not restricted during the rebalancing of the data.

If you need to add more than one container, you should add them at the same time. You can do this by using one ALTER TABLESPACE statement or within the same transaction. This prevents the database manager from having to rebalance the same containers two or more times in a row (as you add new containers).

Adding a container that is smaller than existing containers results in an uneven distribution of data. This problem can cause parallel I/O operations to perform less efficiently than they otherwise could on containers of equal size.

There are two ways to increase the size of a table space by modifying containers:

■ You can add one or more containers. To do this, use the ADD clause on the ALTER TABLESPACE statement.

■ You can change the size of one or more containers. To do this, use either the RESIZE clause or the EXTEND clause on the ALTER TABLESPACE statement. You use one or the other depending on whether you know the upper limit of the container you are modifying. If you know the upper limit of the container's new size, you would use RESIZE. With EXTEND, you do not need to know the current size of the container you wish to modify.

Note *You cannot reduce the size of a container.*

When you use the ADD clause, the statement appears as follows:

```
ALTER TABLESPACE <table space name>
ADD (DEVICE '<device path>' <device size>)
```

In this case, a new device with its own size is added to the existing device or devices associated with the table space. The contents of the table space are rebalanced across the new and existing containers that make up the table space.

When you use the RESIZE clause, the statement appears as follows:

```
ALTER TABLESPACE <table space name>
RESIZE (DEVICE '<device path>' <device size>)
```

In this case, the original size of the device is overridden by the new size given as the device size. The contents of the table space are rebalanced across the new size of the containers in the table space.

When you use the EXTEND clause, the statement appears as follows:

```
ALTER TABLESPACE <table space name>
EXTEND (DEVICE '<device path>' <device size>)
```

In this case, the device is increased in size by the device size given. You do not need to know the original size of the container, only the size by which you are going to increase the container. The contents of the table space are rebalanced across the new size of the containers in the table space.

Tip *If you have to change the size of more than one container, you should change all of the containers within a single statement. This strategy is the best way to make these changes because rebalancing takes time, and it is more efficient to make all the changes at once.*

Renaming a Table Space

The RENAME TABLESPACE statement renames an existing table space. The statement appears as follows:

```
RENAME TABLESPACE <old table space name> TO <new table space name>
```

The <old table space name> must identify a table space that already exists in the catalog. <New table space name> must be a unique name that is not already used within the catalog.

The SYSCATSPACE table space cannot be renamed, nor can any table spaces with roll forward or roll forward in progress states be renamed.

Renaming a table space updates the minimum recovery time of a table space to the point in time when the rename takes place. Therefore, a roll forward at the table space level must be to at least this point in time.

The new table space name must be used when restoring a table space from a backup image if the table space was renamed after the backup image was created. For more information on restoring backup images, see Chapter 12.

Dropping a Table Space

The DROP TABLESPACE statement drops the identified table spaces, along with all objects defined in the table spaces. All other database objects with dependencies on the table space being dropped, such as packages and referential constraints, are dropped or invalidated. Dependent views and triggers are also made inoperative. Containers are not deleted, but any directories in the path of the container name are deleted. All containers below the database directory are deleted.

The statement appears as follows:

```
DROP TABLESPACE <table space name>[, <table space name>,…]
```

TABLESPACE may also be TABLESPACES in the previous statement. The <table space name> must identify a table space that is described in the catalog.

The table space is not dropped in the following circumstances:

- If a table in the table space has one or more of its parts in another table space that is not being dropped. Unless you are dropping the other table space at the same time you wish to drop this one, you must drop the parts of the table in the other table space before this table space can be dropped.

- If it is a system table space.

- If it is the only SYSTEM TEMPORARY table space.

- If there is a declared temporary table in a USER TEMPORARY table space. Even if a declared temporary table has been dropped, the USER TEMPORARY table space is still considered to be in use until the unit of work containing the DROP TABLE statement is committed.

For SMS table spaces, the deletions occur after all connections are disconnected or after the DEACTIVATE DATABASE command is issued.

Getting the Table Space State

The db2tbst utility accepts a hexadecimal table space state value and returns the state of the table space. The state value is part of the output from the LIST TABLESPACES command.

The utility is used in the following way:

```
db2tbst <table space state>
```

The <table space state> is a hexadecimal table space state value.
For example,

```
db2tbst 0x0000
```

produces the following output:

```
State = Normal
```

In another example,

```
db2tbst 0x000c
```

produces the following output:

    State = Quiesced: EXCLUSIVE
        Load pending

The
Complete
Reference

Chapter 8

Creating Databases

As you begin this chapter, it is assumed that you now know how to create an instance, nodegroups, and table spaces. A database is created within an instance, is part of one or more nodegroups, and uses three or more table spaces. In many cases, if you have completed the installation of the DB2 product and followed all of the instructions, you will have already created these database objects. Many are created by default when you install the product for the first time. You may have also created your first database, the SAMPLE database, as part of the installation procedure.

Before creating tables or any of the related objects that will hold your data, you need to create a database. A database provides a working environment for all of your data.

In this chapter, you will learn about the database environment, database defaults, and database options. In addition, you will learn how to catalog a database, how to drop a database, and how to use other commands and statements that are associated with a database.

Creating a Database

The easiest way to create a database using the DB2 command line proessor is to enter the following command:

```
CREATE DATABASE <database name>
```

When you use this form of the CREATE DATABASE command, you are accepting the defaults associated with the many clauses that are part of the creation of the database. The clauses associated with the CREATE DATABASE command allow you to specify the following:

- Whether the database should be created only on the node or database partition that issues the CREATE DATABASE command or across all the partitions in the system

- The path on which to create the database (for UNIX-based operating systems) or the letter of the drive on which to create the database (for OS/2 or Windows-based operating systems)

- An alias for the database name

- The code set to be used for the data entered into this database, which is important when communicating with other client or server machines in a multilingual environment

- The type of collating sequence used to order data within the database

- The number of segment directories that will be used to store the data, index, log files, and other files associated with any default database managed space (DMS) table spaces

- The default extent size of the table spaces in the database
- The explicit definition of the system table space that will hold the catalog tables
- The explicit definition of the initial user table space that will hold the user tables
- The explicit definition of the initial system temporary table space
- A comment describing the database within the database directory

Each of the three table spaces mentioned in the preceding points (catalog table space, user table space, and system temporary table space) has defaults, so the explicit definitions are not required. For more information about table spaces, see the "Creating a Table Space" section in Chapter 7.

After a database has been created with the CREATE DATABASE command, the system catalog and the recovery log are created. The system or local database directories are also created if they do not already exist. The specified code set, territory, and collating sequence are all stored. The default table spaces are all created.

There are also privileges and authorities associated with the creation of the database:

- The DBADM authority is granted to the database creator.
- The CONNECT, CREATETAB, BINDADD, and CREATE SYSCATSPACE privileges are granted to the database creator.
- The CONNECT, CREATETAB, BINDADD, and IMPLICIT_SCHEMA privileges are granted to PUBLIC.
- The USE privilege on the USERSPACE1 table space is granted to PUBLIC.
- The SELECT privilege on each system catalog is granted to PUBLIC.
- The BIND and EXECUTE privileges are granted to PUBLIC for each successfully bound utility.

These authorities and privileges are used to ensure that only qualified users carry out actions against the database and the database data. Each authority and privilege empowers a user to carry out specific actions. Authorities and privileges control access to the data and what actions users can perform within the database. For more information on these authorities and privileges, see Chapter 5.

Clauses Used with the CREATE DATABASE Command

In some cases, when creating a database, you will not accept all of the defaults. In this section, we will consider the different clauses that are available and what they are used for when creating the database. Based on the requirements and use of your database,

GETTING STARTED
WITH DB2

you will then be able to choose the clauses that are most appropriate for your needs. The clauses are the following:

<database name>   A name to be assigned to the new database. This must be a unique name that differentiates the database from any other database in either the local or the system database directory.

ON <path or drive>   This clause of the CREATE DATABASE command is used to specify where you would like the database to be created. On UNIX-based operating systems, this clause specifies the path on which to create the database. The default database path is specified in the database manager configuration parameter dftdbpath. The maximum size of the path is 205 characters. On OS/2 or Windows-based operating systems, this clause specifies the letter of the drive on which to create the database.

ALIAS <database alias name>   This clause specifies the name to be used for the database in the system database directory. The default is to use the database name itself.

USING CODESET <code set> TERRITORY <territory>   These clauses specify the national or regional language information used for data entered into the database. These two clauses must be used together when they are used, and they must be in this order.

COLLATE USING SYSTEM/COMPATIBILITY/IDENTITY   This clause specifies the type of collating sequence to be used for the database. The default is SYSTEM, which uses a collating sequence based on the current territory. If you choose COMPATIBILITY with this clause, you are requesting the DB2 Version 2 collating sequence. Some of the collation tables have been enhanced since Version 2. If you are creating a database that requires the Version 2 collating sequence, you must use this option. If you choose IDENTITY with this clause, you are requesting that collation be done on a byte-for-byte basis. The collating sequence is declared as the database is created and cannot be modified. For more information on the collating sequence, see the *IBM DB2 Universal Database SQL Reference.*

NUMSEGS <number of segments>   This clause specifies the number of segment directories created and used to store DAT, IDX, LF, LB, and LBA files for any default system managed space (SMS) table spaces. Other SMS table spaces (both created explicitly now and later) are not affected by this clause, nor are any DMS table spaces.

DFT_EXTENT_SZ <default extent size>   This clause specifies the default extent size of the table spaces in the database. The extent size is important when you consider prefetching data as part of your performance planning. It is good practice to explicitly set the value of the PREFETCH clause on the CREATE or ALTER TABLESPACE statements as a multiple of the value of the EXTENTSIZE clause, or the DFT_EXTENT_SZ clause (whichever is used), and the number of the table space containers.

CATALOG TABLESPACE <table space definition>   This clause defines the SYSCATSPACE table space that will hold the catalog tables. The default when this clause is not used is to create an SMS table space.

USER TABLESPACE <table space definition>   This clause defines the USERSPACE1 table space that is the initial user table space to hold user data. The default when this clause is not used is to create an SMS table space.

TEMPORARY TABLESPACE <table space definition>   This clause defines the TEMPSPACE1 table space that is the initial system temporary table space. If not used, an SMS table space is created. Later, other system temporary table spaces can be created.

WITH "comment string"   This clause is used to describe this database within the database directory. Any comment of up to 30 characters can be used to describe the database. (You cannot use a carriage return or a line feed character as part of the description.) You can use single or double quotation marks to enclose the comment text.

Defining the Database Environment

When you create a database, a database configuration file named SQLDBCON is also created by default. This file contains values that control the resources associated with the database. These values that control the resources are defined through various configuration parameters.

In this section, we will consider some of the information you may need to define your database environment. Chapter 14 discusses detailed database performance tuning.

Recall that when you create an instance, a database manager configuration file (called DB2SYSTM) is created. This file contains parameters that control the system resources allocated to the instance. (See Chapter 6 for more information about instances.) A database configuration file (called SQLDBCON) works similarly to the database manager configuration file except that it defines the environment for the database within an instance. The commands used are similar, along with the procedure of updating the individual configuration parameters, as shown in the descriptions of the commands that follow.

You may have more than one database on your system. Use this command to list the contents of the system database directory:

```
LIST DATABASE DIRECTORY
```

The output of the command shows information about the databases that are known to your system. You can use the database alias name for the database that you want to run the commands that follow. You can use the output from the LIST DATABASE

DIRECTORY command to confirm the database you want to work with. To see the contents of your current database configuration file, use the following command:

```
GET DATABASE CONFIGURATION FOR <database alias name>
```

This command returns the values of individual entries in a specific database configuration file identified by the <database alias name>. There are no other clauses to this command.

To reset the configuration parameters of a specific database to the system defaults, use this command:

```
RESET DATABASE CONFIGURATION FOR <database alias name>
```

Tip   *If you use this command, consider saving the current values of the configuration parameters before they are reset to the default values. Many of this command's configuration parameters will have been modified to get your database to the point where you are comfortable with its performance and operation.*

You can change one or more of the configuration parameters that are identified as changeable. Those that are not changeable are called informational configuration parameters. To change database configuration parameters, use this command:

```
UPDATE DATABASE CONFIGURATION FOR <database alias name>
USING <configuration parameter name> <new value> [,…]
```

Caution   *The SQLDBCON file that holds the database configuration parameters and their values must not be edited directly. If you use a method other than what DB2 supports, you might make the database unusable. Other methods could damage the file and make it unreadable to the database manager.*

Besides using the UPDATE DATABASE CONFIGURATION command from the command line processor (CLP), you can also use the DB2 Control Center or the application programming interface (API). The Control Center provides both the Configure Database notebook and the Performance Configuration Wizard, which allow you to alter the values of database and database manager configuration parameters.

Most changes to the database configuration file become effective only after they are loaded into memory. All applications must disconnect from the database before the database configuration file parameter values are loaded into memory. If the database was activated when the changes were made, it must be deactivated and reactivated. Then, when the next connection to the database occurs, the changes take effect. If an error occurs, the database configuration file does not change.

Note   *The database configuration file cannot be updated if the checksum for the file is invalid. This problem might occur if the database configuration file is changed without using the appropriate command or tool. If this happens, the database must be restored to reset the database configuration file.*

Cataloging a Database

When you create a new database, the database is automatically cataloged in the system database directory. A system database directory exists for each instance of the database manager, and it contains one entry for each database within that instance.

You can also use the CATALOG DATABASE command to explicitly catalog a database in a system database directory. You might need to do this if you want to catalog a database using a different alias name, or to catalog a database entry that was previously deleted using the UNCATALOG DATABASE command. You can also catalog a database on an instance other than the one you are currently using. The CATALOG DATABASE command is also used when setting up connections from a DB2 client to a DB2 server (for more information, see Chapter 4).

The command is used as follows:

```
CATALOG DATABASE <database name> AS <alias name>
AUTHENTICATION <authentication type>
WITH "<comment string>"
```

The AS <alias name> clause identifies a new alias name for the database. The new alias name can then be used by applications and users to refer to the database.

The <authentication type> parameter defines where and how users attempting to connect to the database will be authenticated. The default is SERVER, which means users are authenticated at the database server. You can choose from several authentication types:

- **SERVER**   The authentication takes place on the server (or partition in a DB2 environment) containing the target database. This is the default.

- **CLIENT**   The authentication takes place on the node or partition where the application is invoked.

- **DCS**   This authentication is primarily used to catalog databases accessed through DB2 Connect. DB2 Connect provides Distributed Relational Database Architecture (DRDA) application requester (AR) functionality to DB2. DRDA AR allows DB2 workstations to connect to and work with host or mainframe DB2-based databases. If DCS authentication is used outside of a DB2 Connect environment, it behaves the same as SERVER authentication. When used in a

DB2 Connect environment, authentication is performed on the DRDA application server (AR).

■ **SERVER ENCRYPT** The encrypted authentication scheme is validated on the server (or partition in a DB2 EEE enviornment) containing the target database. To use this authentication mode, you must ensure that both the client and the server are using the same authentication mode. For example, if a DB2 client was using SERVER authentication, but the server was using SERVER_ENCRYPT authentication, the client application would receive an error when trying to establish a database connection.

■ **DCS_ENCRYPT** The DB2 Connect server accepts encrypted SERVER authentication schemes.

■ **KERBEROS** The authentication takes place using Kerberos Security Mechanism. Kerberos authentication also has an optional clause to identify the TARGET PRINCIPAL. This is the Kerberos principal name for the target server, that is, the logon account of the DB2 server service in the form of *userid@xxx.xxx.xxx.com* or *domain\userid.* The Kerberos authentication type is valid only on Windows 2000 clients.

■ **KRB_SERVER_ENCRYPT** The server accepts Kerberos authentication or encrypted SERVER authentication schemes. If the client authentication is KERBEROS, the client is authenticated using the Kerberos security system. If the client authentication is not KERBEROS, the system authentication type is equivalent to SERVER_ENCRYPT.

■ **DCE** The authentication takes place using DCE Security Services.

■ **DCE_SERVER_ENCRYPT** The server accepts DCE authentication or encrypted SERVER authentication schemes.

For more information on authentication and data access, see the corresponding authentication types in Chapter 5.

The WITH "<comment string>" clause is used to describe the database within the entry in the system database directory. For more information about this clause, see "Clauses Used with the CREATE DATABASE Command."

Uncataloging a Database

Use the UNCATALOG DATABASE command to remove a database entry from the system database directory. Only the local directory is affected by this command. Only entries in the system database directory can be uncataloged. It is important to note that when you issue the UNCATALOG DATABASE command, the database still exists—you just can no longer access it. Entries in the local database directory can be deleted using the DROP DATABASE command, but will delete the database.

When communicating with a downlevel server, you may need to change the authentication type of a database. Do this by first uncataloging the database and then cataloging it again with a different authentication type. For more information on the authentication types that can be used by the database, see the "Cataloging a Database" section earlier in this chapter.

To allow faster access to directory information, you can place database, node, and DCS directory files into a cache in memory. An application's directory is created during the first directory lookup. Because the cache is refreshed only when the application modifies any part of the directory files, directory changes made by other applications may not be effective until the application is restarted. You can enable directory caching by setting the dir_cache database manager configuration parameter.

Working with a Database

Once a database is created, you can work with it. However, before you can create any objects in the database or work with data in tables within that database, you must know how to activate and deactivate the database, and how to restart the database following an abnormal termination of the database.

Restarting a Database

When a database has been abnormally terminated and left in an inconsistent state, you need to run the RESTART DATABASE command. Or, if you attempt to connect to a database and an error message is returned indicating that the database must be restarted, then you would use this command. This might happen if there were a power failure.

The command is used as follows:

```
RESTART DATABASE <database alias name>
```

This command affects only the server (or partition in a DB2 EEE environment) on which it is run. If it completes successfully and you have the CONNECT privilege, a database connection is also established to the database identified by the <database alias name> parameter. The database is then in a useable state.

However, warnings may be issued if there are any indoubt transactions. Use the LIST INDOUBT TRANSACTIONS command to generate a list of indoubt transactions for this database. If you use the WITH PROMPTING clause of the LIST INDOUBT TRANSACTIONS command, you can heuristically commit, roll back, or forget each indoubt transaction listed. If all indoubt transactions are not resolved before the last connection to the database is dropped, another RESTART DATABASE must be issued before the database can be used again.

For more information about recovering a database following an abnormal termination, see Chapter 12.

Activating a Database

When a database has not been started, and a CONNECT TO or an implicit connect is issued in an application, the application must wait while the database manager starts the identified database. This first application incurs the entire overhead of waiting for the database manager to perform the startup activity for the database.

You can use the ACTIVATE DATABASE command to start up specific databases. This will eliminate the first application's time spent waiting for the database to be initialized.

To activate a specific database and start up all the associated database services, use this command:

```
ACTIVATE DATABASE <database alias name>
```

There are also clauses to this command that allow you to specify a user and that user's password to start the database. You may need to do this for security reasons such as when you want a database administrator to use this command to start up selected databases on behalf of other users.

If the application issuing the ACTIVATE DATABASE command already has an active database connection to any database, an error message is returned.

If a database requiring a restart receives an ACTIVATE DATABASE command, the ACTIVATE DATABASE command behaves like a CONNECT TO or an implicit connect. If the database is configured with AUTORESTART ON, then the database is restarted before it is initialized by the ACTIVATE DATABASE command.

Deactivating a Database

Databases initialized by the ACTIVATE DATABASE command can be shut down by the DEACTIVATE DATABASE command or by stopping the database manager by using the STOP DATABASE MANAGER (or the db2stop) command.

If a database was initialized by the ACTIVATE DATABASE command, the last application disconnecting from the database will not shut down the database, and DEACTIVATE DATABASE must be used. (In this case, the STOP DATABASE MANAGER command will also shut down the database. The STOP DATABASE MANAGER command stops the instance. It is discussed in Chapter 6.)

If a database was started by a CONNECT TO or an implied connect, and subsequently, an ACTIVATE DATABASE command was issued by another application for the same database, then DEACTIVATE DATABASE must be used to shut down that database. If ACTIVATE DATABASE was not used to start the database, the database will shut down when the last application disconnects from the database.

To stop a database, use this command:

```
DEACTIVATE DATABASE <database alias name>
```

There are also clauses to this command that allow you to specify a user and that user's password to stop the database. You may need to do this for security reasons.

Dropping a Database

You cannot alter a database. You can alter objects within the database and the environment and configuration values associated with the database, but the database itself cannot be altered. You must drop and recreate the database if you want to make complete changes to all aspects of the database.

Caution   *You should not drop a database without carefully considering the consequences. Dropping a database deletes all of the database objects, container definitions, and associated files, including all log files. The dropped database is also removed or uncataloged from the database directories, and the database subdirectory is deleted.*

To drop a database, use the following command:

```
DROP DATABASE <database alias name>
```

The <database alias name> parameter specifies the alias of the database to be dropped. The database must be cataloged in the system database directory.

GETTING STARTED WITH DB2

The
Complete
Reference

Chapter 9

Working with Tables

T*ables* are logical structures maintained by the database manager. The design of the database is determined by the content of individual tables and the relationships that exist between the tables.

As an example, imagine that you have a business that sells products. You create a table that has all the information about each product, in which the columns of each row represent a different quality about the product. The qualities might include a product identifier, manufacturing cost, wholesale cost, retail cost, description, weight, and so on. Because you are selling products, you store information about your customers in a table. The qualities for each customer might include a unique identifier for each customer, the customer address, the name of the chief buyer of that company, the name of the head of that company, and so on.

You also want to record the sales of the products to customers, so you have a table that records all sales for a particular period of time. The columns in this table include a sales identifier, the product identifier, the number of products sold, the selling price (whether wholesale or retail), the taxes charged, the total cost, any payment received, and so on.

The individual tables have information related to clearly defined items. But it is easy to see that you might want information from more than one of these tables. You might also want to change the information in more than one table at the same time. That is where the interrelationships between tables become important. This chapter looks at how to create tables and how to define the interrelationships between tables.

Before you can begin working with tables, you need to create an instance of the database manager. Chapter 1 explained how to design your database tables, and this chapter shows you how to create those tables. After creating one or more tables in this chapter, you will learn how to move data into the tables in the next chapter.

Organizing Objects with Schemas

To help you organize your database objects, including tables, you should use a schema. A *schema* provides a logical classification of objects in the database. For example, two different users could create a table with the same name. However, the schema for each would be different, making the combination of schema name and table name unique within the database. A schema is like a locker that you might have at a camp: everyone has the same items but there is a need to associate each item with the correct camper. Tom's toothbrush is kept separate from Andy's toothbrush by the names that are on the toothbrushes and the fact that each is kept in a separate locker. Tom's toothbrush (object) is kept in his locker (schema), and Andy's toothbrush (object) is kept in his locker (schema).

The schema is itself an object within the database. It is explicitly created using the CREATE SCHEMA statement (or using the Control Center), with one user being identified as the schema's owner. It can also be implicitly created when another object is created, provided the user has IMPLICIT_SCHEMA authority. Note that when a database is created, all users within that database are given IMPLICIT_SCHEMA authority.

A *schema name* is used as the high-order part of a two-part object name. When an object is created, it is assigned and contained within a schema. The schema to which it is assigned is determined by the name of the object, if it was specifically qualified with a schema name, or by the default schema name if it wasn't qualified. The default schema name is the authorization ID of the person creating the object. For more information about authorization IDs (or authorization names), see Chapter 5.

All object names have these schema and object parts, but the two parts are not always shown. An explicit two-part object name is considered *fully qualified*, and a one-part object name is *implicitly qualified* by a schema name. You will see both of these types of qualifications in the examples provided throughout this book.

Implicit qualification of an object occurs when an explicit schema is not provided with a database object. In that case, implicit qualification by the database manager occurs by using the authorization ID of the user creating the object as the schema name.

When a database is created, PUBLIC (that is, all users known to the database) is given IMPLICIT_SCHEMA database authority. With this authority, any users can create a schema when they create an object. They simply specify a schema name that does not already exist. However, SYSIBM becomes the owner of the schema and PUBLIC is given the privilege to create objects in this schema. The IMPLICIT_SCHEMA authority is taken away from PUBLIC so that there is greater control over the creation and ownership of schemas.

Chapter 5 discusses issues related to qualifying names to identify objects.

Creating a Schema

An authorization ID that holds SYSADM or DBADM authority can create a schema that does not already exist, and it can optionally make another user the owner of that schema. A user who does not hold either of these two authorities can still create a schema with his or her own authorization ID.

To create a schema, use this statement:

```
CREATE SCHEMA <schema name>
```

The <schema name> is the name of the schema. This name must be unique within the schemas already recorded in the catalog, and the name cannot begin with *SYS*. In the statement shown, an AUTHORIZATION clause is not specified, so the authorization ID that issued this statement becomes the owner of the schema.

The CREATE SCHEMA statement is used from within an application or through the use of dynamic SQL statements, and it explicitly defines a schema.

For example, to create a schema for user SANDRA, you must have SYSADM or DBADM authority. The statement would appear as follows:

```
CREATE SCHEMA SANDRA
```

You should note that the user that issues this command becomes the owner of this schema (and are likely not SANDRA).

If you were SANDRA and had IMPLICIT_SCHEMA authority, you could create a schema called SANDRA (as long as it was not already created).

You can also specify the AUTHORIZATION <authorization name> clause to create a scheme for a different user.

This clause allows you to identify the user who will be the owner of the schema. The specified authorization name is the schema owner.

For example, if you are not the user SANDRA, and you wanted to create a schema for user SANDRA, then you would use the following statement:

```
CREATE SCHEMA SANDRA AUTHORIZATION SANDRA
```

You must use either AUTHORIZATION <authorization name> or <schema name> AUTHORIZATION <authorization name> to identify the name and owner of the new schema.

An optional schema SQL statement clause may also be part of the statement. One or more of these statements are run as part of the creation of the schema. The schema name being defined becomes the schema name for each of the objects created as part of the CREATE SCHEMA statement. The SQL statements that can be included as part of the CREATE SCHEMA statement are the following:

- **CREATE TABLE**   Creates a table, excluding summary tables and typed tables. It is a complete statement with all of the complexity of a separate CREATE TABLE statement.

- **CREATE VIEW**   Creates a view, excluding typed views. It is a complete statement with all of the complexity of a separate CREATE VIEW statement.

- **CREATE INDEX**   Creates an index on a table and creates metadata indicating to the optimizer that a data source has an index. It is a complete statement with all of the complexity of a separate CREATE INDEX statement.

- **COMMENT ON**   Adds or replaces comments in the catalog descriptions of various objects.

- **GRANT**   Grants privileges on the tables or views created using the CREATE TABLE or CREATE VIEW statements that are included as part of the CREATE SCHEMA statement. In this case, you might have created a table and then granted to a user privileges on that table.

> **Tip**   *Avoid using "SESSION" as a schema name. Declared temporary tables are qualified by SESSION as the schema, so if you or another user on your system also uses SESSION as a schema name, an application may declare a temporary table with a name identical to that of a persistent user table. To handle such a difficulty, any SQL statement that references a table—where both the temporary table and the user table use SESSION as a schema name—resolves to the declared temporary table.*

Setting a Schema

A default schema is needed by unqualified object references in dynamic SQL statements. You can set a default schema for a specific DB2 connection. You do this by setting the CURRENT SCHEMA special register to the schema you want as the default. No designated authorization is required to set this special register, so any user can set the CURRENT SCHEMA.

The syntax of the SET SCHEMA statement follows:

```
SET SCHEMA = <schema name>
```

The statement can be issued interactively by a user or from within an application. The initial value of the CURRENT SCHEMA special register is equal to the authorization ID of the current session user. For more information about the SET SCHEMA statement, see Chapter 27.

Understanding Table Basics

Depending on the design decisions you made in Chapter 1, you will create one or more tables in your database that work together to hold the data you determine should be there. When you create the table, you name it, specify the types of content in each of the columns in the table, and define its other characteristics, such as the primary key and check constraints for the enforcement of business rules. Tables are made up of columns and rows, in which you store the database's data.

The *columns* of a table define the type of data to be stored and the scope of the data in the table. When you define a column, you assign it a data type—all values in that column must be of the same type or one of its subtypes. As a result, data types must encompass all the different possible types of data that may be stored in the database tables. The data types must account for character strings, numbers, dates, and many other kinds of data. All database managers have some built-in data types, and you can build your own data types by using data definition language (DDL) to create a *user-defined data type* (UDT).

One or more values make up a row of data to be placed in a table. A *row* is a sequence of values such that the nth value in the row is a value of the nth column of the table. In many cases, you will have sufficient values in each row of data being inserted into the table to correspond to each of the columns in the table definition. That is, you will have a name value (John Smith) to place in the NAME column, an address value (123 Anywhere Road) to place in the ADDRESS column, and so on.

At the intersection of every column and row is a specific data item called a *value*.

Types of Tables

The different types of tables in a database are presented here:

- **Base table**   A base table is created with the CREATE TABLE statement and is used to hold persistent user data.

- **Result table**   A result table is a set of rows that the database manager selects or generates from one or more base tables to satisfy a query. It is the data in this table that is returned to the application or user requesting it,or that is used for further processing by the database manager. You do not have direct access or control of the contents of this table.

- **Summary table**   A summary table is based on the result set of a query. Summary tables can be used to improve the performance of queries. If the DB2 optimizer determines that a portion of a query could be resolved using a summary table, then the optimizer may rewrite the query so that it uses the summary table instead of a base table. This decision is based on certain special register settings, such as for CURRENT REFRESH AGE and CURRENT QUERY OPTIMIZATION. The CURRENT REFRESH AGE special register specifies a timestamp duration value showing the maximum duration since a REFRESH TABLE statement has been processed on a REFRESH DEFERRED summary table. The CURRENT QUERY OPTIMIZATION special register specifies an integer value controlling the class of query optimization performed by the database manager when binding dynamic SQL statements. If CURRENT REFRESH AGE has a value of ANY and QUERY OPIMIZATION class has a value of 5 or more, REFRESH DEFFERED summary tables are considered to optimize the processing of a dynamic SQL query.

- **Typed table**   A typed table has the data type of each column based on the attributes of a *user-defined structured type*. A user-defined structured type may be part of a *type hierarchy*. Once you have defined attributes of a structured type table, they can be reused in the creation of other tables (typed tables). Within a typed table hierarchy, terms are used to describe the relationship between the attributes of the tables and the tables themselves. Such terms include the following:

- **Subtype**   Inherits attributes from its *supertype*. The term "subtype" applies to a user-defined structured type and all user-defined structured types that are below it in the type hierarchy. Similarly, a typed table can be part of a *table hierarchy*.

- **Subtable**   Inherits columns from its *supertable*.

A proper subtype of a structured type T is a structured type below T in the type hierarchy. Similarly, the term "subtable" applies to a typed table and all typed tables that are below it in the table hierarchy. A *proper subtable* of a table T is a table below T in the table hierarchy.

- **Declared temporary table**   A declared temporary table is created with a DECLARE GLOBAL TEMPORARY TABLE statement and is used to hold temporary data on behalf of a single application. This table is dropped implicitly when the application disconnects from the database.

- **System temporary table**   A system temporary table is created during database processing and can be used only by the database manager. Typically, it is used to sort or merge result tables.

Creating Tables

Tables are created through data definition language (DDL) requests to the database manager. The database manager controls changes and access to the data stored in the tables. You request a change to the content of the table through the database manager by using a data manipulation language (DML) statement. Both the DDL and the DML are subset languages of structured query language (SQL).

The table object is central to the functioning of a database. Complex statements can be used to define all the attributes and qualities of tables. However, if all of the defaults on the definition are used, the statement to create a table can be quite simple.

To create a simple table, use this statement:

```
CREATE TABLE <table name> (<column name> <data type> <column
options>, <column name> <data type> <column options>,…)
```

The <table name> is the name of the table given by the user, and it may or may not include a qualifier. The name must be unique when compared to all table, view, and alias names in the catalog of the database. The name must also not be SYSIBM, SYSCAT, SYSFUN, or SYSSTAT.

The <column name> gives a name of a column in the table. This name cannot be qualified and must be unique within the other columns of the table.

The <data type> must be one of the supported data types for the database.

Any <column options> that exist for a column further define the attributes of the column. The options include NOT NULL to prevent the column from containing null values, specific options for LOB data types, specific options for DATALINK data types, the SCOPE of the reference type columns, any constraints on the columns, any defaults for the columns, and INLINE LENGTH values for columns defined as structured types. For more details on data types, see Chapter 16.

The <column name>, <data type>, and <column options> parameters repeat so that you can create additional columns. The number of columns in a table cannot exceed 1012. For typed tables, the total number of attributes of the types of all of the subtables in the table hierarchy cannot exceed 1010.

Consider the following CREATE TABLE definition for the ADVISE_WORKLOAD explain table that is included as part of the EXPLAIN.DDL script in the misc subdirectory of the sqllib directory:

```
CREATE TABLE ADVISE_WORKLOAD
(WORKLOAD_NAME CHAR(128) NOT NULL WITH DEFAULT 'WK0',
STATEMENT_NO INTEGER NOT NULL WITH DEFAULT 1,
STATEMENT_TEXT CLOB(1M) NOT NULL NOT LOGGED,
STATEMENT_TAG VARCHAR(256) NOT NULL WITH DEFAULT '',
FREQUENCY INTEGER NOT NULL WITH DEFAULT 1,
IMPORTANCE DOUBLE NOT NULL WITH DEFAULT 1,
COST_BEFORE DOUBLE,
COST_AFTER DOUBLE)
```

Note   *The ADVISE_WORKLOAD explain table is used as part of the Index Advisor management tool assisting in the design and definition of indexes on your tables. Other explain tables are used to record information about access plans selected by the DB2 optimizer when evaluating the execution performance of SQL statements.*

There are eight columns shown, each with its own data type. Some have the clause NOT NULL to prevent the column from containing null values. Others have the WITH DEFAULT clause to convey the default to be used if no value is provided for the column when a new row is added. There is a single NOT LOGGED clause associated with the column containing the CLOB data type. Because the data for this column can be up to 1MB in size, logging new rows or changes to existing rows could mean that the log files would fill quickly, with 1MB being added for each change to the table.

Defining a Generated Column

When creating a table in which you know that certain expressions or predicates will be used frequently, you can add one or more generated columns to that table. A *generated*

column is defined in a base table in which the stored value automatically is computed using an expression. Using a generated column can result in performance improvements
when querying table data.

Here are two examples of when it may be costly to evaluate expressions:

■ The evaluation of the expression must be done many times during a query.

■ The computation is complex.

To improve the performance of the query, define a generated column that would contain the results of the expression. Then, when you or an application runs a query that includes the expression within the generated column, the column can be used directly. The query rewrite component of the DB2 optimizer can replace the expression with the generated column.

When queries involve joining data from two or more tables, the addition of a generated column can allow the optimizer a choice of possibly better join predicates.

Defining an Identity Column

An *identity column* allows the database manager to automatically generate a unique numeric value for each row that is added to the table. If you are creating a table and you know you will need to uniquely identify each row that is added to that table, then you can add an identity column to the table definition.

Once created, you cannot alter the table description to include an identity column.

The syntax to create an identity column is found as part of the CREATE TABLE statement:

```
CREATE TABLE <table name>
(<column name 1> INT, <column name 2> DOUBLE, <column name 3> INT NOT NULL
GENERATED ALWAYS AS IDENTITY (START WITH <value 1>, INCREMENT BY <value 2>))
```

In this example, the third column identifies the identity column. One of the attributes that you can define is the value used in the column to uniquely define each row when a row is added. The value following the INCREMENT BY clause shows by how much subsequent values of the identity column contents will be increased for every row added to the table.

Defining a Sequence Object

DB2 Version 7.2 introduces a new database object called a sequence. A *sequence* is a database object that allows the automatic generation of values. Sequences are ideally suited to the task of generating unique key values. Applications can use sequences to avoid possible concurrency and performance problems resulting from the generation of a unique counter outside the database. Unlike an identity column, a sequence is not tied to a particular table column, nor is it bound to a unique table column and only accessible through that table column.

A sequence object can be created, or altered, so that it generates values by incrementing or decrementing values either without a limit; to a user-defined limit, and then stopping; or to a user-defined limit, then cycling back to the beginning and starting again. Sequences are only supported in single partition databases. The following example shows how to create a sequence object:

```
CREATE SEQUENCE orderseq START WITH 1 INCREMENT BY 1 NOMAXVALUE
NOCYCLE    CACHE 24
```

In this example, the sequence is called order_seq. It will start at 1 and increase by 1 with no upper limit. There is no reason to cycle back to the beginning and restart from 1 because there is no assigned upper limit. The CACHE parameter specifies the maximum number of sequence values that the database manager preallocates and keeps in memory.

Working with Data in Tables

Once a table is created, you can move any existing data into the table by using one of the utilities provided with DB2. These utilities, and the methods of moving large amounts of data into a table, are presented in Chapter 10. The utilities include IMPORT, EXPORT, LOAD, AutoLoader, and Data Replication.

The normal day-to-day activity in your business will have applications working with the table data on a row-by-row basis, inserting new data, updating existing data, or deleting data from the table. This activity is controlled through three SQL statements: INSERT, UPDATE, and DELETE.

The INSERT statement inserts rows into a table or view. (Inserting a row into a view actually inserts the row into the table on which the view is based.

The UPDATE statement allows you to update values of specified columns in rows of a table or view. Updating the values of a view updates the values of the corresponding columns in the base table.

The DELETE statement deletes rows from a table or view. Deleting a row from a view deletes the row from the base table of that view.

For more information about these statements, see Chapter 16 and Chapter 27.

Modifying Tables

It is possible to work change the definition of a table, renaming a table, or to drop a table. These actions against a table are presented in this section.

Changing Tables

The ALTER TABLE statement allows you to modify existing tables. You can change a table in almost every area that you considered when creating the table. For example, you can do any of the following:

- Add one or more columns.
- Add or drop a primary key.
- Add or drop one or more unique or referential constraints.
- Add or drop one or more check constraint definitions.
- Alter the length of a VARCHAR column.
- Alter the reference type column to add a scope.
- Alter the generation expression of a generated column.
- Add or drop a partitioning key.
- Change table attributes, such as the data capture option, the append mode, etc.
- Set the table to the not logged initially state.

While this is not a complete list, you get the idea of some of the actions you can perform when altering a table. For more information, see Chapter 27.

When you use the ALTER TABLE statement to add a column to a table, the columns are logically placed to the right of the rightmost existing column definition. When a new column is added to an existing table, only the table description in the system catalog is modified. Therefore, access time to the table is not immediately affected. Existing records are not physically altered until they are modified using an UPDATE statement. If required, a null or default value is provided for the new column when retrieving an existing row from the table. Columns added after a table is created cannot be defined as NOT NULL: they must be defined as either NOT NULL WITH DEFAULT or as nullable.

To alter a table, use this statement:

```
ALTER TABLE <table name> <alter option> <alter option> …
```

The table name identifies the table you are changing. The table must exist in the catalog and not be a view or a catalog table. The table name must not be a nickname. If the table name identifies a summary table, a limited number of options can be used.

One of the common alter options of this statement is to add a <column definition>. This adds a column to the table, but the table must not be a typed table. For tables that have existing rows, adding this column causes each row to take the default value of the data type for the column. This type of change to the table is processed before all other changes. Other changes are processed in the order in which they are specified in the ALTER TABLE statement.

Here is an example of an ALTER statement used to add a column to the DEPARTMENT table—the column is for a contact phone number, including the area code:

```
ALTER TABLE DEPARTMENT
ADD CONTACT CHAR(10) DEFAULT '4165551234'
```

Notice that this example has a default value for the new column. In this case, the phone number provided as a default could be a head office contact phone number.

There are a few points to note when adding a column to a table:

- If there are views based on the table, adding columns to the table does not mean that the column will be added to the views.

- Adding a column to a table invalidates all packages with INSERT usage on the altered table. If the added column is the first user-defined structured type column in the table, packages with DELETE usage on the altered table will also be invalidated.

- A table cannot have more than 500 columns if the table space is using a 4KB page size, and 1012 columns if it is using any other page size. When adding a new column, you must not make the total byte count of all columns exceed the maximum record size. For more information on these upper limits, see the "SQL Limits" section in Chapter 17.

You can also define the attributes of an added column in the same way as when you created the table, such as specifying the data type, specifying whether it is a unique key, and specifying whether there is a constraint on the column. See the Creating Tables discussion earlier in this chapter for more information on defining columns when creating tables.

The PCTFREE option indicates which percentage of each page to leave as free space during the loading or reorganization of table data. The percentage value can be an integer ranging from 0 to 99. The first row is added to each new data page without any restrictions. As additional rows are added, the percentage value used in this option indicates the percentage of free space left on each data page.

The LOCKSIZE option indicates the granularity of the locks used when this table is accessed. The default granularity of the locks is a ROW lock. The other option is a TABLE lock. Using the TABLE value may improve the performance of queries because the number of locks needed is reduced. However, concurrency is also reduced because all locks are held over the complete table. Changing the LOCKSIZE option for a table results in the invalidation of all packages that depend on the altered table.

Defining a Generated Column on an Existing Table   A *generated column* is defined on a base table where the stored value is computed using an expression, rather than being specified through an insert or update operation.

You must do the following to define a generated column on an existing table:

1. Place the table in check pending state:

   ```
   SET INTEGRITY FOR <table name> OFF
   ```

2. Alter the table to add one or more generated columns:

   ```
   ALTER TABLE <table name> ADD COLUMN <column name 3> DOUBLE GENERATED
   ALWAYS AS (<column name 1> + <column name 2>),
   ADD COLUMN <column name 4> GENERATED ALWAYS AS (CASE WHEN <column
   name 1> > <column name 3> THEN 1 ELSE NULL END)
   ```

3. There are several ways to complete this task based on the work to be done against the table:

   1. The table is very large and you are not confident that you have sufficient log space to complete the task. After loading the data but before you turn on integrity checking, you need to COMMIT the work. Then you need to use the db2gncol utility to establish the values for the generated columns. The table is locked for the entire process even though it is in check pending state. There may be other utilities that could access tables in check pending state: the lock prevents this from happening. For more information on the db2gncol utility, see the *IBM DB2 Universal Database Command Reference*.

   2. You anticipate that the log space for updating the generated columns is sufficient for SET INTEGRITY, which will normally be the case. You would use the following statement:

      ```
      SET INTEGRITY FOR <table name 1> IMMEDIATE CHECKED FORCE GENERATED
      ```

4. The table is very large, you are not confident you will have sufficient log space to complete the task, and you do not choose the first method just presented. After loading the data but before you turn integrity checking back on, you need to do the following:

   1. Get an exclusive lock on the table. This prevents all but uncommitted read transactions from accessing the table. Use this statement:

      ```
      LOCK TABLE <table name 1> in <exclusive|share> mode
      ```

   2. Move the table to the online state with the data unchecked:

      ```
      SET INTEGRITY FOR <table name 1> ALL IMMEDIATE UNCHECKED
      ```

   3. Update the generated columns using intermittent commits and predicates to keep the logs from filling up:

      ```
      UPDATE <table name 1> SET (<column name 3>, <column name 4>) =
      (DEFAULT, DEFAULT) WHERE <predicate>
      ```

4. Bring up the table online and check the integrity:

```
SET INTEGRITY FOR <table name 1> OFF
SET INTEGRITY FOR <table name 1> IMMEDIATE CHECKED
```

5. Unlock the table by completing the transaction using a COMMIT statement:

```
COMMIT
```

6. By using the NOT LOGGED INITIALLY option, logging for the table is turned off (with the usual implications and risks) while working with the generated column values.

7. Activate the NOT LOGGED INITIALLY option:

```
ALTER TABLE <table name 1> ACTIVATE NOT LOGGED INITIALLY
```

8. Generate the values:

```
SET INTEGRITY FOR <table name 1> IMMEDIATE CHECKED FORCE GENERATED
```

9. Turn the NOT LOGGED INITIALLY option off again by committing the transaction:

```
COMMIT
```

Applying the expression as if it is an equality check constraint can also simply check the values for generated columns:

```
SET INTEGRITY FOR <table name 1> IMMEDIATE CHECKED
```

Generated columns may be defined only on data types for which an equal comparison is defined. Such data types include the LONG data types as well as the many types of large objects (LOBs, CLOBs, and DBCLOBs). Generated columns cannot be used in constraints, unique indexes, referential constraints, primary keys, and global temporary tables.

Modifying an Identity Column Definition   If you are recreating a table followed by an import or a load operation, and if you have an IDENTITY column in the table, then it will be reset to start generating the IDENTITY value from 1 following the recreation of the contents of the table. When inserting new rows into this recreated table, you do not want the IDENTITY column to begin from 1 again. You do not want duplicate values in the IDENTITY column. To prevent this, follow these steps:

1. Recreate the table.

2. Load data into the table using the MODIFIED BY IDENTITYOVERRIDE clause. The data is loaded into the table but no identity values are generated for the rows.

3. Run a query to get the last counter value for the IDENTITY column:

```
SELECT MAX(<identity column name>)
```

This will return with the equivalent value of what would have been the IDENTITY column value of the table.

4. Use the RESTART clause of the ALTER TABLE statement:

```
ALTER TABLE <table name> ALTER COLUMN <identity column name>
RESTART WITH <last counter value>
```

5. Insert a new row into the table. The IDENTITY column value will be generated based on the value specified in the RESTART WITH clause.

Dropping Tables

The DROP TABLE statement deletes the specified table. Any other objects that are directly or indirectly dependent on that object are either deleted or made inoperative. Whenever a table is deleted, its description is deleted from the catalog, and any packages that reference the table are invalidated. This includes packages dependent on any supertables above the subtable in the hierarchy.

The authorization ID using the DROP TABLE statement must have one of the following privileges or authorities, or the DROP operation will fail:

- SYSADM or DBADM authority
- DROPIN privilege on the schema for the table
- CONTROL privilege on the table
- The authorization ID is recorded as the definer of the table as recorded in the DEFINER column of the catalog view for tables

To delete a table, use this statement:

```
DROP <table name>
```

The table name can identify the base table, declared temporary table, or summary table that is to be deleted. All indexes, primary keys, foreign keys, check constraints, and summary tables referencing the table are made inoperative. Dropping a declared temporary table causes the data in the table to be destroyed, regardless of whether the operation is committed or rolled back.

Renaming Tables

You can rename an existing table, but you must have SYSADM authority, DBADM authority, or the CONTROL privilege on the table being renamed. If you are going to rename a table, the old name must not

- Be referenced in any existing view definitions or summary table definitions
- Be referenced in any triggered SQL statements in existing triggers or be the subject table of an existing trigger

- Be referenced in an SQL function
- Have any check constraints
- Have any generated columns other than an identity column
- Be a parent or dependent table in any referential integrity constraints
- Be the scope of any existing reference column

The violation of any of these conditions will result in an error message. To rename a table, use this statement:

```
RENAME <source table name> TO <target identifier>
```

The source table name is the name of the existing table being renamed. This name, when fully qualified by a schema name, must identify a table that exists in the database. It can also be an alias identifying a table. The source table name cannot be the name of a catalog table, a summary table, a typed table, a nickname, or an object that is not a table or an alias. If an alias is used for the source table name, it must resolve to a valid table name. The table is renamed within the schema of this table. The alias is not changed by this statement and continues to refer to the old table name.

The target identifier specifies the new name for the table. There is no schema name for the new name—the schema name of the source table name is used to qualify the new name for the table. The qualified name must not identify a table, view, or alias that already exists in the database.

As an example, consider renaming the DEPARTMENT table. To do this, use this statement:

```
RENAME DEPARTMENT TO CURRENT_DEPT
```

After renaming a table, all catalog entries referring to the old name are updated to reflect the new name. All authorizations associated with the source table name are transferred to the new table name. Indexes defined over the source table are transferred to the new table. Any packages dependent on the source table are invalidated.

A table with primary key or unique constraints may be renamed if a foreign key references none of the primary key or unique constraints.

Viewing Table Data

So far, we have discussed how to work with tables directly. There are other specialized versions of tables that you can use to improve performance of queries against table data, to share data across applications, to customize a view of part of the data from one or more tables, or to give other names to tables for use within applications.

Summary Tables

A summary table is used by the optimizer to optimize a query if the isolation level of the summary table is equal to, or higher than, the isolation level of the query. The summary table typically contains precomputed results based on the data existing in the table or tables on which its definition is based. If the optimizer determines that a query will run more efficiently against a summary table than against the base table, the query will run against the summary table. Using this method, you can obtain the results from the query faster than you would otherwise.

To create a defined summary table, use a variation on the CREATE TABLE statement:

```
CREATE SUMMARY TABLE <table name> AS (<fullselect>) DEFINITION ONLY
```

A summary table definition is based on the result of a query as shown by the fullselect in the previous statement. When DEFINITION ONLY is used, any valid fullselect that does not reference a typed table or typed view can be specified. The query here is used only to define the table—the table is not populated using the results of the query. The REFRESH TABLE statement cannot refer to this table.

The columns of the table are defined based on the columns that result from the fullselect. If the fullselect references a single table in the FROM clause, select-list items that are columns of that table are defined using the column name, data type, and any null characteristic of the referenced column.

To define a summary table that is to have the contents refreshed, use this statement:

```
CREATE SUMMARY TABLE <table name> AS (<fullselect>) DATA INITIALLY
DEFERRED REFRESH DEFERRED
```

The DATA INITIALLY DEFERRED clause specifies that the data is not to be inserted into the table as part of the CREATE TABLE statement. A later REFRESH TABLE statement specifying this summary table name is used to insert data into the table.

If you specify REFRESH DEFERRED, the data in the table can be refreshed at any time using the REFRESH TABLE statement. The data in the table reflects the result of the query only as a snapshot at the time the REFRESH TABLE statement is processed. Summary tables defined with this attribute do not allow INSERT, UPDATE, or DELETE statements.

If instead of REFRESH DEFERRED, the REFRESH IMMEDIATE clause were used, then changes made to the underlying tables as part of an INSERT, UPDATE, or DELETE statement are cascaded to the summary table. In this case, the content of the summary table, at any time, is the same as if the specified fullselect were processed. Summary tables defined with this attribute do not allow INSERT, UPDATE, or DELETE statements directed against the table.

As an example, consider creating a summary table for employee number 000030 showing the projects for which that employee is responsible. The statement would be as follows:

```
CREATE SUMMARY TABLE SUM_000030 AS
(SELECT PROJNO, PROJNAME, DEPTNO, MAJPROJ
FROM PROJECT
WHERE RESPEMP = 000030)
DATA INITIALLY DEFERRED
REFRESH DEFERRED
```

This summary table would be defined but initially empty of data. A later REFRESH TABLE statement could be used to update the table with a current snapshot of the data in PROJECT that applies to employee 000030.

To refresh the summary table called SUM_000030, use this statement:

```
REFRESH TABLE SUM_000030
```

Altering Summary Tables

You can change a summary table to a regular table or a regular table to a summary table with some restrictions. You cannot change other table types—only regular and summary tables are interchangeable. Once a regular table has been altered to a summary table, the table is placed in check pending state. When altering a regular table in this way, the fullselect in the summary table definition must match the original table definition.

If the summary table is defined on an original table, then the original table cannot itself be altered into a summary table. If the original table has triggers, check constraints, referential constraints, or a defined unique index, then it cannot be altered into a summary table. If you are altering the table properties to define a summary table, you are not allowed to alter the table in any other way in the same ALTER TABLE statement.

When altering a regular table into a summary table, the fullselect of the summary table definition cannot reference the original table directly or indirectly through views, aliases, or summary tables.

See Chapter 27 for more information on the ALTER TABLE statement.

Global Temporary Tables

The syntax used to create global temporary tables is the following:

```
DECLARE GLOBAL TEMPORARY TABLE <table name>
```

```
AS (<fullselect>) DEFINITION ONLY
EXCLUDING IDENTITY COLUMN ATTRIBUTES
ON COMMIT DELETE ROWS
NOT LOGGED
```

The first line of the syntax shows the declaration or creation of the global temporary table, giving it a specific name.

The next line specifies that the table definition be based on the column definitions that result from a query expression. The columns resulting from the fullselect define the columns of the new table. The implicit definition includes the column name, the data type, and the ability to place a NULL value in the column characteristic of each of the result columns of the fullselect.

The third line states that identity column attributes are not copied from the source result table definition.

The fourth line specifies that all rows of the table will be deleted if no WITH HOLD cursor is open on the table. This is the default.

The final line of the syntax specifies that the changes not be logged, including the creation of the table.

When using this syntax to create your own global temporary tables, you should note that every select-list element must have a unique name. The AS clause can be used in the SELECT clause to provide one or more unique names for every element in the select list.

Referencing a Declared Global Temporary Table

To reference a declared global temporary table in an SQL statement, the table must be explicitly or implicitly qualified by the schema name SESSION. If <table name> is not qualified by the schema SESSION, no declared global temporary tables are considered when resolving the reference. Other persistent objects in the catalog are considered when resolving SESSION.<table name>, but if no object with a qualified name of SESSION.<table name> exists, an error is returned.

When binding a package that has static statements referring to tables implicitly or explicitly qualified by the schema name SESSION, those statements are not bound statically. Regardless of the VALIDATE option chosen while binding the package, when these statements are invoked, they are incrementally bound. At run time, each table reference is resolved to a declared global temporary table, if it exists, or to a permanent table. If neither exists, an error is returned.

When a declared global temporary table is defined, everyone who is part of the PUBLIC group, along with the definer of the table, is granted all table privileges on the table. None of the privileges are granted with the GRANT option.

Views

A *view* provides an alternative way of working with the data in one or more tables. A view is the named result set of columns and rows taken or returned from one or more base tables—it is the result of a SELECT statement that is run whenever the view is referenced in an SQL statement. A view is like a base table and can be used like a base table.

Whether a view can be used in an insert, update, or delete operation depends on how the view was defined.

Creating Views

Here is the syntax used to create a view:

```
CREATE VIEW <view name> AS <fullselect>
```

The view name in this syntax must be unique. The schema name must not be SYSIBM, SYSCAT, SYSFUN, or SYSSTAT. It may, however, be the name of an inoperative view, in which case, the inoperative view is replaced following the running of this statement.

The <fullselect> defines the view. The rows of the result set, if the fullselect statement were run, become the result set for this view. There must not be any references to host variables, parameter markers, or declared temporary tables in the fullselect.

Here is an example of the CREATE VIEW statement:

```
CREATE VIEW PROJ_LEAD
AS SELECT PROJNO, PROJNAME, DEPTNO, RESPEMP, LASTNAME, PHONENO
FROM PROJECT, EMPLOYEE
WHERE RESPEMP = EMPNO
```

This example creates a view that can be used as a project leader contact list. This view has six columns. The first four columns of the view are taken from the PROJECT table, and the fifth and sixth columns come from the EMPLOYEE table. This view can be used by you and by other applications.

Here are a few more details about views:

- Creating a view with a schema name that does not already exist implicitly creates that schema, provided the authorization ID of the statement has IMPLICIT_SCHEMA authority. The schema owner is SYSIBM, and the CREATEIN privilege on the schema is granted to PUBLIC.

- View columns inherit the NOT NULL WITH DEFAULT attribute from the base table or view except when columns are derived from an expression.

- When the column of a view is directly derived from a column of a base table, it inherits any constraints that apply to the column of the base table. (Constraints are explained in the "Constraints" section later in this chapter.)

- When a row is inserted or updated into a view that can be updated, it is checked against any constraints defined on the base table.

- You cannot create a view based on declared temporary tables.

- A typed view is a view that has the data type of each column derived from the result table, or that has the types for the columns based on the attributes of a user-defined structured type.

- A typed view can be part of a view hierarchy.

- A subview inherits columns from its superview. A subview applies to a typed view and all typed views below it in the view hierarchy.

- A proper subview of a view V is a view below V in the typed view hierarchy.

Inoperative Views

An *inoperative view* is one in which the view definition has been dropped. For example, when an alias is dropped, any view defined using that alias is made inoperative. All dependent views also become inoperative, and packages dependent on the view are no longer valid.

Until the inoperative view is explicitly recreated or dropped, a statement using that inoperative view cannot be compiled, with the exception of the CREATE ALIAS, CREATE VIEW, DROP VIEW, and COMMENT ON TABLE statements. Until the inoperative view has been explicitly dropped, its qualified name cannot be used to create another table or alias.

You can recreate an inoperative view as a view by issuing a CREATE VIEW statement using the definition text of the inoperative view. This view definition text is stored in the TEXT column of the SYSCAT.VIEWS catalog. When recreating an inoperative view, it is necessary to explicitly grant any privileges required on that view by others, because all authorization records on a view are deleted if the view is marked inoperative. Note that there is no need to explicitly drop the inoperative view to recreate it. Issuing a CREATE VIEW statement using the name of an inoperative view will cause that inoperative view to be replaced, and the CREATE VIEW statement will return a warning.

Inoperative views are indicated by an X in the VALID column of the SYSCAT.VIEWS catalog view and an X in the STATUS column of the SYSCAT.TABLES catalog view.

Aliases

An *alias* is an alternative name for a table or a view, and it can be used whenever a table or view name can be used. The effect of using an alias in an SQL statement is similar to that of text substitution. An alias is an indirect method of referencing a table, nickname, or view, so that an SQL statement can be independent of the qualified name of that table, nickname, or view. As a result, only the alias definition must be changed if the table, nickname, or view name changes. This would be of great benefit when writing applications.

An alias can refer to a table, view, or alias only within the same database, and a new unqualified alias cannot have the same fully qualified name as an existing table, view, or alias. Similarly, an alias name should not be used when a new table or view will use that name. When a CREATE TABLE or CREATE VIEW statement is run using an existing alias name, an error will result.

An alias can be created for a nickname. Nicknames are used to identify disparate date sources in a federated database environment. Federated databases are explained in Chapter 18.

An alias can also be created even though the object it refers to does not exist. In this case, though, the object being referred to must exist by the time any SQL statement using the alias is compiled.

An alias can be created, dropped, and have comments associated with it. In this way, an alias is much like a table or a view. An alias can also refer to another alias in a process called *chaining,* the only restriction being that no circular or repetitive references can be made along the chain of aliases. Tables are not able to chain together in this way.

An alias can be used without requiring a special authority or privilege—an alias is considered to be a publicly referenced name. Access to the tables and views referred to by the corresponding alias, however, still requires authorization.

Note that aliases cannot be used in the check condition of a check constraint, nor can they reference declared temporary tables. Check constraints are explained in the "Constraints" section later in this chapter. Declared temporary tables were described earlier in the "Global Temporary Tables" section.

This is the syntax used to create an alias:

```
CREATE ALIAS <alias name> FOR <table, view, nickname, or another alias name>
```

You can use the CREATE ALIAS or the CREATE SYNONYM statement to associate a new name with the name of a table, view, nickname, or another alias name. If a new name is being associated with another alias name, both names must be unique when fully qualified.

The following is an example of the CREATE ALIAS statement:

```
CREATE ALIAS PROJ_CONTACTS FOR PROJ_LEAD
```

This statement creates an alias called PROJ_CONTACTS that is associated with the PROJ_LEAD view.

Keys and Indexes

If you have a table that is very large both in the complexity of the columns defined and in the number of rows held by the table, then you will need ways to get to the right information quickly. For the database manager to move row by row down an unsorted table to find particular pieces of data can be very expensive from a performance perspective. Keys and indexes are used to identify specific columns in every row and to speed up the access to particular rows within a very large table.

Keys

A *key* is one or more columns used to identify, or access, a particular row or rows in a table. When creating a table, index, or referential constraint, a key must be identified. A given column can be part of more than one key.

There are several different types of keys:

- **Composite key**   A *composite key* is made up of more than one column. The ordering of the columns within the composite key is not constrained by their order within the table.

- **Unique key**   A *unique key* is constrained so that no two of its values are equal, and as a result, the columns of a unique key cannot contain null values. The mechanism used to enforce the constraint is called a *unique index,* and it is the database manager that enforces the constraint. (Indexes are discussed in the next section.) Database operations can change the values in the columns of a unique key, and when that happens, the database manager checks to see whether any constraints have been violated. An error results if the operation violates the constraint.

- **Primary key**   A *primary key* is a special case of a unique key. There is only one primary key for each table.

- **Foreign key**   A *foreign key* is a key that is specified in the definition of a referential constraint. (The different types of constraints are explained later in this chapter in the "Constraints" section.)

Creating a Sequence

A *sequence* is a database object that allows the automatic generation of unique key values. Applications can use sequences to avoid possible concurrency and performance problems resulting from the generation of a unique counter outside the database.

Unlike an identity column attribute, a sequence is not tied to a particular table column nor is it bound to a unique table column and accessible only through that table column.

The sequence can be created, or altered, such that it generates values that increment or decrement with the following possible boundaries:

- Without bound
- To a user-defined limit and stop
- To a user-defined limit and cycle back to the beginning and start again

Use the following syntax to create this object:

```
CREATE SEQUENCE <sequence name>
START WITH <start number>
INCREMENT BY <value 1>
NOMAXVALUE
NOCYCLE
CACHE <maximum number of sequence values>
```

There is no upper limit specified for the sequence when NOMAXVALUE is used. There is also no reason to cycle back to the beginning and restart from the start number (as indicated by NOCYCLE) because there is no assigned upper limit to the sequence. The number associated with the CACHE parameter specifies the maximum number of sequence values that the database manager preallocates and keeps in memory.

If a database that contains one or more sequences is recovered to a prior point in time, then this could cause the generation of duplicate values for some sequences. To avoid this possibility, a database with sequences should not be recovered in this way.

Two expressions are used with a sequence:

- The PREVVAL expression returns the most recently generated value for the specified sequence for a previous statement within the current session.
- The NEXTVAL expression returns the next value for the specified sequence.

The same sequence number can be used as a unique key value in two or more tables by referencing the sequence number with a NEXTVAL expression for the first table and a PREVVAL expression for any additional tables.

Altering a Sequence

Modify the attributes of an existing sequence with the ALTER SEQUENCE statement. The attributes of the sequence that can be modified include the following:

- Changing the increment between future values
- Establishing new minimum or maximum values
- Changing the number of cached sequence numbers
- Changing whether the sequence will cycle

- Changing whether sequence numbers must be generated in order of request
- Restarting the sequence

For more information on this statement, see Chapter 27.

Dropping a Sequence
To delete a sequence, use the DROP statement as you would with any other database object.

Indexes
An *index* is an ordered set of pointers to rows of a base table. It is separate from the table. Each index is based on the values of data in one or more table columns.

Once created, an index is built and maintained by the database manager. The database manager uses indexes to do the following:

- **Improve performance**   In most cases, indexes improve the speed of access to data. An index cannot be created for a view, but indexes created on the underlying tables on which the view is based may improve the performance of operations on the view.

- **Ensure uniqueness**   A table that has a unique index cannot have rows with identical keys. A unique index is composed of unique keys and is said to have the UNIQUE attribute. This prevents the entry of duplicate values in the columns defined this way and guarantees that no two rows of a table are exactly the same.

The following syntax is used to create an index:

```
CREATE INDEX <index name> ON <table name> (<column name>)
```

The table must be a base table or a summary table described in the catalog. The column name must be an unqualified name that exists as part of the referenced table. The defaults associated with this syntax include the following:

- Index entries are kept in ascending order.
- Ten percent of each index page is to be left as free space when building the index.
- Reverse scans are not allowed—only forward scans or scanning based on the order defined (ASC or DESC) at the time the index is created.
- Duplicate indexes are not allowed.

For more information on the CREATE INDEX statement, see Chapter 27.

Indexes can be created on tables that already contain data. Indexes that are "created" on tables that contain no data are really only described. The index entries are actually created, in both cases, when data is inserted into the table.

To take full advantage of any new index, issue the RUNSTATS command once your data is entered and the index is created. The RUNSTATS command updates statistics collected on database tables, columns, and indexes, and the optimizer then uses the statistics to determine the optimal access paths to the table data requested by applications. If you do not issue the RUNSTATS command following the creation of an index, the optimizer will not be able to use any of the advantages provided by the creation of the new index.

Here is an example of the CREATE INDEX statement:

```
CREATE UNIQUE INDEX EMPLOYEELOOKUP
ON EMPLOYEE (EMPNO)
```

This example creates a unique index called EMPLOYEESLOOKUP on the EMPLOYEE table. The index entries are arranged in ascending order by employee number within each department (WORKDEPT). If you required rapid access to the EMPLOYEE table because you had applications requiring this type of information, this index, or one like it, would be beneficial.

The Catalog and Catalog Views

The information about the data under the control of the database manager is found in a set of views and base tables collectively known as the *catalog*. The catalog information concerns the objects that make up the database, such as tables, views, indexes, packages, and functions. The catalog views can be used like any other database views.

The set of catalog views that can be updated can be used to modify certain values in the catalog. These views contain statistical information used by the optimizer. Some columns in these views may be changed to investigate the performance of hypothetical environments.

An object (table, column, function, or index) will appear in the updateable catalog view for a given user only if that user created the object, holds the CONTROL privilege on the object, or holds explicit DBADM privileges. These views are found in the SYSSTAT schema. They are defined on top of the system catalog base tables.

Statistical information is also contained in the catalog. The statistical information is updated by utilities run by an administrator, or through update statements by appropriately authorized users.

Limiting Character Conversion in a Complex System

A *string* is a sequence of bytes that may represent characters, and within a string, all the characters are represented by a common coding representation. Because there are several of these coding representations, in some cases, it might be necessary to convert characters from one coding representation to another. The process of conversion is known as *character conversion*.

When character conversion is required, it is automatic and transparent to the application when the conversion is successful. You require no knowledge of how character conversion works when all of the strings that are part of the running of a statement are represented in the same way. When you are working in a standalone environment or in a network where the same language is used, there is no need to be concerned about character conversion.

However, character conversion can occur when you are running an SQL statement remotely. There are two likely scenarios that could result in character conversion:

- When the values of host variables are sent from the application requestor to the application server
- When the values of the result columns are sent from the application server to the application requestor

In either of these scenarios, the coding representation is different for both requestor and server. Character conversion can occur at either the sending system or the receiving system.

The following terms are used when discussing character conversions:

- **Character set** A defined set of characters.
- **Code page** An attribute of the database. The code page has a set of assignments of characters to code points. Within a code page, each code point has only one specific meaning.
- **Code point** A unique bit pattern that represents character data.
- **Single-byte character set (SBCS)** A character set in which each character is represented by a one-byte code.
- **Double-byte character set (DBCS)** A character set in which each character is represented by a two-byte code.

Many different code pages exist even within the same encoding scheme. The same code point can represent different characters in different code pages.

A byte in a character string does not necessarily represent a character from a single-byte character set. Character strings are also used for mixed and bit data. *Mixed data* is a mixture of single-byte, double-byte, or multibyte characters. *Bit data* are columns defined as FOR BIT DATA, binary large objects (BLOBs), or binary strings, and they are not associated with any character set.

Code Page Attributes

Three general attributes are associated with code pages:

- **The database code page** This code page is stored in the database configuration files. The database code page is determined when the database is created. Once it has been selected for the database, it cannot be altered.

- **The application code page** An application is run using this code page, and it may or may not be the same as the database code page. It is the code page used when the application is bound. For more information on the application code page and binding, see the *IBM DB2 Universal Database Application Development Guide*.

- **Code page 0** This represents a string that is derived from an expression that contains a FOR BIT DATA or BLOB value.

Columns defined as part of a table will be used in the database code page, or code page 0 (if defined as character FOR BIT DATA or BLOB). Constants and special registers are in the database code page. Note, though, that constants in the application are converted to the database code page when an SQL statement is bound to the database. Input host variables are in the application code page.

String Code Page Attributes

A set of rules is used to determine the code page attributes for operations that combine string objects. Some examples of this type of operation include the results of scalar operations, concatenation, or set operations. When operations that combine string objects are run, code page attributes are used to determine any requirements for code page conversions of strings.

Conversion Rules for String Assignments

A character string or graphic string assigned to a column or host variable is first converted, if necessary, to the code page of the target. Character conversion is necessary only if all of the following are true:

- The code pages are different.
- The string is neither null nor empty.
- Neither string has a code page value of 0 (as with FOR BIT DATA).
- The code page conversion selection table indicates that a conversion is necessary.

When the database server is acting as a DRDA application server (AS), input host variables are converted to the code page of the application server, even if they are being assigned, compared, or combined with a FOR BIT DATA column. The input host variables are first associated with the code page of the remote DRDA application requester (AR). Then, as the request for action is sent to the DRDA AS, the data part of the input host variables is converted (if the data page at the DRDA AS is different from the data page of the application as the DRDA AR). If the SQLDA has been modified to identify the input host variable as FOR BIT DATA, conversion is not performed.

Conversion Rules for String Conversions

When moving data between applications and the database server, there must be some rules to convert the character string from the data page of the application to the data page of the database. The code page used to perform an operation is determined by rules that are applied to the operands in that operation.

These rules apply to the following:

- Corresponding string columns in fullselects with set operations (UNION, INTERSECT, and EXCEPT)
- Operands of concatenation
- Operands of predicates (with the exception of LIKE)
- Result expressions of a CASE expression
- Arguments of the scalar function COALESCE (and VALUE)
- Expression values of the in list of an IN predicate
- Corresponding expressions of a multiple row VALUES clause

In each case, the code page of the result is determined at bind time, and running the operation may involve conversion of strings to the code page identified by the code page of the result. A character having no valid conversion is mapped to the substitution character for the character set, and SQLWARN10 is set to W in the SQLCA.

The code page of the operands determines the code page of the result. If there are more than two operands, the code pages of the first two operands determine an intermediate result code page. The intermediate result code page and the code page of the next operand determine the next intermediate result code page. This process repeats until the last intermediate result code page and the code page of the final operand determine the code page of the result string or column.

View columns are considered to have the operand type of the object on which they are ultimately based.

Enforcing Business Rules in the Database

There are business policies and practices that can be enforced from within the database without having to write application programs to do that checking. When the business policies and practices are defined to the database manager, the database manager can apply them to the data and to actions against the tables within the database.

Constraints are restrictions applied to specific data types or columns within the tables. Triggers are actions to be carried out based on actions affecting the data within a table. The application of business policies and procedures is presented in the discussion of constraints and triggers that follows.

Constraints

A *constraint* is a rule that the database manager enforces. Three types of constraints exist:

- A *unique constraint* is a rule that forbids duplicate values in one or more columns within a table. Unique keys and primary keys are the supported unique constraints.

- A *referential constraint* is a logical rule about values in one or more columns in one or more tables. This constraint defines and maintains relationships between tables in a database.

- A *table check constraint* sets restrictions on data added to a specific table. It may not be possible or practical to check data within an application before moving the data into the database or updating a data value in the database. With the rules provided by table check constraints, the database manager can enforce the rules instead of having the application do it.

Referential and table check constraints can be turned on or off, and when you need to load a lot of data into a database, you should consider turning off the enforcement of these types of constraints. The SET INTEGRITY statement is used to turn off integrity checking for one or more tables. The next section explains how to define constraints, followed by the use of the SET INTEGRITY statement.

Unique Constraints

A *unique constraint* is the rule used by the database manager to enforce uniqueness in the values of a key. Any key values that would duplicate existing key values within the table are invalid. Unique constraints are optional: they are not required when defining your tables. The columns specified in a unique constraint must be defined as NOT NULL. A unique index is used by the database manager to enforce the uniqueness of the key during changes to the columns specified in the unique constraint.

You use the CREATE TABLE or ALTER TABLE statements with the PRIMARY KEY clause or the UNIQUE clause to define the unique constraint. A *unique key* is a key that is constrained so that no two of its values are equal. A *primary key* is a special case of a unique key. A table cannot have more than one primary key. A table may have one or more unique keys. The syntax to add a PRIMARY KEY appears like this:

```
ALTER TABLE <table name>
ADD PRIMARY KEY (<column name>)
```

The table must not already have a primary key, and the <column name> must be defined as NOT NULL. No LOB, LONG VARCHAR, LONG VARGRAPHIC, DATALINK, distinct type on any of these types, or structured type column may be used as the primary key. A check is also done to see if an existing index matches the primary key definition.

Only one unique constraint can be defined as a primary key. However, a table can have any number of unique constraints defined, except that a table cannot be defined with more than one unique constraint on the same set of columns.

When a unique constraint is defined in a CREATE TABLE or ALTER TABLE statement, a unique index is automatically created. If the constraint is created using a CREATE TABLE statement, the resulting index is designated as a primary or unique system-required index. If the constraint is created using an ALTER TABLE statement and an index exists on the same columns, the resulting index is designated as a unique system-required index. If the index does not exist, a unique index is automatically created, and it is designated as a primary or unique system-required index.

A unique constraint that is referenced by the foreign key of a referential constraint is called the *parent key*.

Note *There is a distinction between defining a unique constraint and creating a unique index. Although both enforce uniqueness, a unique index allows nullable columns and generally cannot be used as a parent key.*

Referential Constraints

A *foreign key* is a column or set of columns in a table whose values are required to match at least one primary key or unique key value of a row of its parent table. The table containing the parent key is called the parent table of the referential constraint. The table containing the foreign key is said to be a dependent of that table.

Referential integrity is the state of a database in which all values of all foreign keys are valid. A *referential constraint* is the rule that the non-null values of the foreign key are valid only if they also appear as values of a parent key.

Referential constraints are optional. If used, they are defined in the CREATE TABLE and ALTER TABLE statements. An example definition of a constraint appears as follows:

```
CREATE TABLE <table name> …
FOREIGN KEY (<column name>)
REFERENCES <parent table name> (<column name>) ON DELETE SET NULL
```

In this case, a new table is being created and a relationship is being defined with the table identified as <parent table name>. The table being created will have one or more columns defined at the point in the syntax where the ellipsis (…) is shown. The FOREIGN KEY clause is where you define the referential constraint. The column name (there may be more than one) of the FOREIGN KEY must also be defined at the point where the ellipsis is shown. The column name (again, there may be more than one) of the REFERENCES <parent table name> must match the set of columns in the FOREIGN KEY clause. The data types of the columns must also match.

ON DELETE SET NULL is the rules clause that defines the action that will take place on the dependent table when there is an action against a row of the parent table. In this case, when a row of the parent table is deleted, each nullable column of the foreign key is set to null. Other options are NO ACTION (the default), RESTRICT (both of which prevent the deletion action), CASCADE (where the delete action is propagated to the dependent rows in this table), and SET NULL (where each nullable column of the foreign key is set to null). The other rules clause besides ON DELETE is the ON UPDATE rules clause where the options are NO ACTION and RESTRICT. (Both operate in the same fashion as the ON DELETE rules clause.) The rules clause and options are presented in detail in the next few pages.

The database manager carries out the enforcement of the referential constraints at the completion of the INSERT, UPDATE, DELETE, ALTER TABLE ADD CONSTRAINT, and SET INTEGRITY statements.

Referential constraints with a delete or update rule of RESTRICT are enforced before all other referential constraints. Referential constraints with a delete or update rule of NOACTION behave like RESTRICT in most cases, although with certain SQL statements, there can be a difference. These differences are described in the *IBM DB2 Universal Database SQL Reference*.

The *insert rule* is that a non-null insert value of the foreign key must match some value of the parent key of the parent table. When working with a composite foreign key, if any component of the value is null, then the entire key is considered null. The insert rule is implicit when a foreign key is specified.

The *update rule* is specified when the referential constraint is defined with one of two choices: NO ACTION and RESTRICT. Two possible row types could cause this rule to be enforced: updating a row of the parent table, or updating a row of the dependent table.

In the case of a parent row, when updating a value in a column of the parent key, the following conditions apply:

- If the update rule is RESTRICT, if any row in the dependent table matches the original value of the key, then the update is rejected.

- If the update rule is NO ACTION, if any row in the dependent table does not have a corresponding parent key when the update statement is "completed" (excluding AFTER triggers), then the update is rejected. In this case, when the update statement is completed, it means that it is ready to be committed—but it is not, because there is at least one row in the dependent table that does not have a corresponding parent key. Instead of being committed, the update is rolled back.

- If the update rule is neither RESTRICT nor NO ACTION, the update takes effect.

In the case of a dependent row, the update rule that is implicit when the columns of a foreign key are updated is NO ACTION. NO ACTION means that a non-null update value in the columns of a foreign key must match one of the values of the parent key of the parent table when the update statement is completed.

The *delete rule* is specified when the referential constraint is defined. The choices are NO ACTION, RESTRICT, CASCADE, or SET NULL. SET NULL can be specified only if one of the columns of the foreign key allows null values. Recall that the value of a composite foreign key is null if any component of the value is null.

The delete rule of a referential constraint applies when a row of the parent table is deleted:

- If the delete rule is RESTRICT or NO ACTION, an error occurs and no rows are deleted.

- If the delete rule is CASCADE, the delete operation is propagated to the dependents of a parent row that is the object of a delete or propagated delete operation in a dependent table.

- If the delete rule is SET NULL, each nullable column of the foreign key in the matching rows of the dependent table is set to null.

Each referential constraint in which a table is a parent has its own delete rule, and all applicable delete rules are used to determine the result of a delete operation. Therefore, a row cannot be deleted if it has dependents in a referential constraint with a delete rule of RESTRICT or NO ACTION. Nor can the row be deleted if the deletion cascades to any of its descendents that are themselves in the same referential constraint.

Table Check Constraints

A *table check constraint* is a rule that specifies the values allowed in one or more columns of every row of a table. Table check constraints are defined using the CREATE TABLE and ALTER TABLE statements. For example,

```
ALTER TABLE <table name>
ADD CONSTRAINT <constraint name>
CHECK (<check condition>)
```

The third line of this example is where the check constraint is defined. A check condition might be that an employee's base pay may not be less than a certain amount (CHECK(basepay > 20000)) or that the hire date is not before a certain year. Details about what can be included as part of the constraint are discussed in the "Constraints" section.

A table can have any number of table check constraints. The constraints are enforced when a row is inserted into the table or when a row of the table is updated. A check constraint defined on a table automatically applies to all subtables of that table.

A table check constraint is a restricted form of a search condition. A search condition specifies a condition that is true, false, or unknown about a given row. The result of a search condition is derived by applying the specified logical operators (AND, OR, NOT) to the result of each specified predicate; if logical operators are not specified, the result of the search condition is the result of the specified predicate.

Similarly, a table check constraint is enforced by applying its search condition to each row that is inserted or updated. An error occurs if the result of the search condition is false for any row.

When one or more table check constraints are defined in the ALTER TABLE statement for a table with existing data, the existing data is checked against the new condition before the ALTER TABLE statement succeeds. Alternatively, the table can be placed in check pending state by using the SET INTEGRITY statement, which allows the ALTER TABLE statement to succeed without checking the data. The SET INTEGRITY statement is also used to resume the checking of each row against the constraint.

A check constraint specified as part of a column definition applies only to that column. A check constraint specified as part of a table definition can have column references identifying columns previously defined in the same CREATE TABLE statement. Check constraints are not checked for inconsistencies, duplicate conditions, or equivalent conditions. Therefore, contradictory or redundant check constraints can be defined, resulting in possible errors at run time.

The check condition "IS NOT NULL" can be specified; however, it is recommended that nullability be enforced directly using the NOT NULL attribute of a column.

Turning Constraints Off and On

The syntax used to turn off constraints on tables is the following:

```
SET INTEGRITY FOR <table name> OFF
```

This will turn the integrity checking for one or more tables off. This includes the following:

- Check constraint checking
- Referential constraint checking
- Datalink integrity checking

The generation of values for generated columns is also turned off. Moreover, the immediate refreshing of data is turned off for summary tables that are defined REFRESH IMMEDIATE.

Tables that have integrity checking turned off are placed in a check pending state. Primary key and unique constraints continue to be checked.

One version of the syntax used to check for constraints on tables is the following:

```
SET INTEGRITY FOR <table name> ALL IMMEDIATE UNCHECKED
```

The ALL clause in the statement specifies that all integrity options are to be turned on. You have the choice of turning them all on in this way, or you can list each integrity option that you wish to have enforced. One or more can be selected in a single statement.

The table in this example is not checked for integrity violations. If the table is a summary table, immediate refreshing is turned on.

If the ALL clause is not used, one or more integrity options can be chosen for each table. The choices include FOREIGN KEY, CHECK, DATALINK RECONCILE PENDING, SUMMARY, and GENERATED COLUMN. The table is left in check pending state when at least one of the five possible integrity options is off for that table.

If the parent of a dependent table is in check pending state, the foreign key constraints of a dependent table cannot be marked to bypass checking. Check constraints checking can be bypassed.

Here is an example of the use of the SET INTEGRITY statement:

```
SET INTEGRITY FOR EMP_ACT OFF;
ALTER TABLE EMP_ACT ADD CHECK (EMSTDATE <= EMENDATE);
ALTER TABLE EMP_ACT ADD FOREIGN KEY (EMPNO) REFERENCES EMPLOYEE;
SET INTEGRITY FOR EMP_ACT IMMEDIATE CHECKED
```

First, this example shows how constraint checking on the EMP_ACT table is turned off. Then, two changes are made to the table. The first adds a check constraint involving the values found in two columns, EMSTDATE and EMENDATE. This is a simple check to ensure that the start date is earlier than the end date for the employee. The second change adds a foreign key to the table using the EMPNO column and referring to the EMPLOYEE table. Finally, to perform the constraint checking in a single pass through the EMP_ACT table, the IMMEDIATE CHECKED clause is used when the constraint checking is turned back on.

At any time when integrity is being checked, an exclusive lock is held on each table specified in the SET INTEGRITY statement. A shared lock is acquired on each table that is not listed in the SET INTEGRITY statement but that is a parent table of one of the dependent tables being checked.

The following syntax shows another method of establishing constraints:

```
SET INTEGRITY FOR <table name> IMMEDIATE CHECKED
INCREMENTAL
FORCE GENERATED
FOR EXCEPTION IN <table name> USE <table name>
```

The IMMEDIATE CHECKED clause specifies that integrity checking is to be turned on and any integrity checking that was deferred for whatever reason is to be done. If the table having its integrity checking turned on is a summary table, then the data is checked against the query and refreshed as necessary. The IMMEDIATE CHECKED phrase has three check options that are possible: INCREMENTAL, FORCE GENERATED, and FOR EXCEPTION.

The INCREMENTAL clause specifies that deferred integrity checking will be done on the appended portion (if any) of the table. If this phrase is not specified, the system determines whether incremental processing is possible; if not, the whole table will be checked.

The FORCE GENERATED clause specifies that if the table includes generated columns, the values will be computed based on the expression and stored in the column. If this phrase is not specified, the current values are compared to the computed value of the expression as if an equality check constraint existed.

The FOR EXCEPTION clause uses two table names. The first is the table from which rows that violate constraints are to be copied. There must be one exception table specified for each table being checked. The second table name specifies the exception table. This clause cannot be specified if the table having its integrity checking turned on (by the IMMEDIATE CHECKED clause) is a summary table.

If a SET INTEGRITY statement with a FORCE GENERATED clause fails because of a lack of log space, and log space cannot be sufficiently increased, use the db2gncol command to generate the values by using intermittent commits. The SET INTEGRITY statement can be rerun following invocation of the db2gncol command, without the FORCE GENERATED clause.

If an error occurs during integrity checking, all the effects of the checking, including deleting from the original and inserting into the exception tables, will be rolled back.

Triggers

A *trigger* defines a set of actions that are carried out, or triggered, by a delete, insert, or update operation on a specified table. When such an SQL operation is carried out, the trigger is activated.

Triggers can be used, along with referential constraints and check constraints, to enforce data integrity rules. Triggers can also be used to cause updates to other tables, automatically generate or transform values for inserted or updated rows, or invoke functions to perform tasks such as issuing alerts. Triggers are a useful mechanism for defining and enforcing transitional business rules. Transitional business rules involve different states of the data.

Using triggers places the logic that enforces business rules in the database. This relieves applications from having to enforce the rules. Centralized logic enforced on all tables means easier maintenance because no application program changes are required when the logic changes.

Triggers are optional, and they are defined using the CREATE TRIGGER statement. There are several criteria, defined when creating a trigger, that determine when a trigger should be activated:

- The *subject table* specifies the table for which the trigger is defined.

- The *trigger event* specifies the exact SQL operation that activates the trigger. The operation could be a delete, an insert, or an update operation.

- The *trigger activation time* specifies when the trigger should be activated; that is, either before or after the trigger event is performed on the subject table.

The activation of a trigger is caused by an SQL statement whose scope includes a set of *affected rows*. These are the rows of the subject table affected by the triggered event. The *trigger granularity* defines whether the actions of the trigger will be performed once for the statement, or once for each of the rows in the set of affected rows.

The *triggered action* consists of an optional search condition and a set of SQL statements that are executed whenever the trigger is activated. The triggered action may refer to the values in the set of affected rows.

Multiple triggers can be specified for a combination of table, event, or activation time. The order in which the triggers are activated is the same as the order in which they were created—the most recently created trigger will be the last trigger activated.

Activating a trigger may cause the activation of one or more other triggers, which is called *trigger cascading*. There may also be updates to other tables, or other actions as a result of referential integrity delete rules. Depending on how you have established your triggers and your referential integrity delete rules, a significant change to many tables across the database may result from a single DELETE, INSERT, or UPDATE statement.

This is the syntax used to create a trigger:

```
CREATE TRIGGER <trigger name> AFTER
INSERT ON <table name> FOR EACH ROW
MODE DB2SQL
<triggered SQL statement>
```

The trigger name is a unique implicitly or explicitly qualified name. AFTER could also have been NO CASCADE BEFORE: these are the two choices of when to apply the triggered action.

INSERT could also have been DELETE or UPDATE: these are the three choices of triggering action. The table name is a base table or an alias resolving to a base table. It cannot be a catalog table, summary table, declared temporary table, or a nickname.

FOR EACH ROW could also have been FOR EACH STATEMENT: these are the two choices to define the scope of the triggered action.

MODE DB2SQL is the only supported mode of the trigger.

The <triggered SQL statement> could also have been BEGIN ATOMIC <triggered SQL statement> END: these are the two choices of how to define the triggered action. See Chapter 27 for additional details on the CREATE TRIGGER statement.

The following is an example of the CREATE TRIGGER statement:

```
CREATE TRIGGER RAISE_LIMIT
AFTER UPDATE OF SALARY ON EMPLOYEE
REFERENCING NEW AS N OLD AS O
FOR EACH ROW MODE DB2SQL
WHEN (N.SALARY > 1.1 * O.SALARY)
SIGNAL SQLSTATE '7500' ('Salary increase > 10%')
```

This trigger causes an error when an update occurs that results in a salary increase greater than 10 percent of the current salary for an employee. This is an effective way to monitor specific, sensitive updates to tables in the database.

Keep these points in mind when creating triggers:

- Adding a trigger to a table that already has rows in it will not cause any trigger actions to be activated. Only changes to the table contents following the creation of the trigger may cause the trigger actions to be activated.

- Creating a trigger may cause some packages to be marked invalid. The package remains invalid until the application is explicitly bound or rebound, or it is run and the database manager automatically rebinds the package.

- Creating a trigger with a schema name that does not already exist will result in the implicit creation of that schema, provided the authorization ID of the statement has IMPLICIT_SCHEMA authority. The schema owner is SYSIBM. The CREATEIN privilege on the schema is granted to PUBLIC.

An *inoperative trigger* is a trigger that is no longer available and therefore is never activated. In most cases, an inoperative trigger is one in which a trigger definition has been dropped as a result of cascading rules for DROP or REVOKE statements.

When a trigger is made inoperative, each package with statements performing operations that were activating the trigger will be marked invalid. When such a package is rebound (either implicitly or explicitly), the inoperative trigger is completely ignored. Similarly, applications with dynamic SQL statements performing operations that were activating the trigger will also completely ignore any inoperative triggers.

An *X* in the VALID column of the SYSCAT.TRIGGERS catalog view identifies inoperative triggers.

The Complete Reference

Part III

Maintaining Data

The
Complete
Reference

Chapter 10

Moving Data

arely in today's complex business environments will you find a data processing system that operates fully independently. In most cases, the business processes of an enterprise require the exchange of data between several software products. Even agreeing on a common format of data interchange can pose a challenge. Despite the recent progress toward fully automated exchange of business information, usually a fair amount of manual intervention is required. This chapter provides a thorough overview of the data-sharing tools available in DB2.

You can move data directly between tables in the same database by issuing an SQL INSERT statement into the target table while executing an SQL SELECT statement on the source. DB2 federated database technology enables you to execute the same type of INSERT from a SELECT across tables belonging to different databases. For the details about this fascinating technology, see Chapter 18. The built-in replication capabilities of DB2 can also be used to enable data sharing between databases. Please see Chapter 11 for an introduction to the concepts of data replication.

This chapter is devoted to the following topics: moving data between database tables, moving data between different databases, and moving entire databases between separate hardware systems. Here, we will focus on more traditional utilities that enable data transfer into and out of the database: the Import, Export, and Load utilities. We will discuss the basic use and some of the more advanced options of each utility. We will compare the utilities and make it easier for you to decide which tools to use for a particular job. Import offers simplicity and ease of use. Load, on the other hand, is slightly harder to master but rewards you with superior performance in the end.

IMPORT, EXPORT, and LOAD are DB2 command line processor (CLP) commands. They are not SQL statements, and they can be invoked only through the CLP or through a call to their respective APIs from within a user's application. When working with the Control Center, you can perform Import, Export, and Load operations on a table by selecting the appropriate action from the Tables view (Systems | Instances | Databases | Tables). Figure 10-1 illustrates the invocation of the Import notebook using the Control Center.

Most of the examples in this chapter reference tables from the SAMPLE database that can be optionally created during DB2 installation. If you chose not to create the SAMPLE database during installation, you can still do it now by entering the db2sampl command at your operating system's command prompt. The examples in this chapter assume the use of the DB2 CLP for Import, Export, and Load invocation.

File Formats Supported by DB2 Utilities

DB2 Import, Export, and Load utilities support a number of text and binary file formats. In this section, we will examine the structure of each of the file formats in greater detail and provide examples of their use.

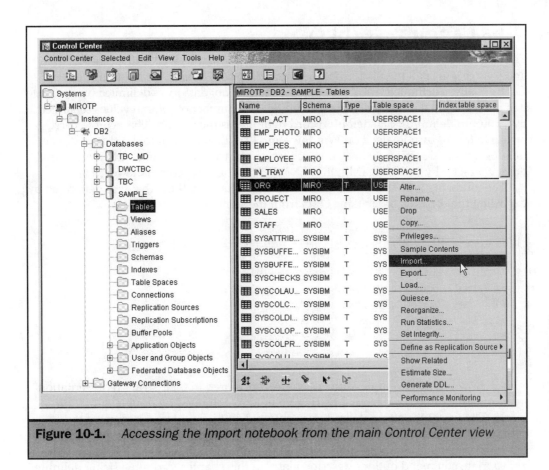

Figure 10-1.   *Accessing the Import notebook from the main Control Center view*

The following table provides a quick overview of file formats supported by each of the DB2 utilities covered in this chapter:

	Import	Export	Load	db2atld	db2move
DEL	Yes	Yes	Yes	Yes	No
ASC	Yes	No	Yes	Yes	No
IXF	Yes	Yes	Yes	No	Yes
WSF	Yes	Yes	No	No	No

Table 10-1.   *File Formats Supported by DB2 Utilities*

MAINTAINING DATA

Delimited ASCII Text (DEL)

The delimited ASCII file format is likely the most popular as well as the most flexible and easy to use of all the file formats supported by DB2 data movement utilities. Conceptually, a delimited ASCII file contains a number of data rows delimited by a record delimiter. Each of the data rows, in turn, consists of a number of column values separated by a column delimiter. The default record delimiter is the newline character (a carriage return followed by a linefeed on Windows and OS/2), and it cannot be changed. The default column delimiter is the comma character, but you can change it to almost any other character by using the IMPORT, EXPORT, and LOAD command options.

The following is an example of a comma-delimited ASCII file that was generated by exporting the contents of the table ORG from the sample database:

```
10,"Head Office",160,"Corporate","New York"
15,"New England",50,"Eastern","Boston"
20,"Mid Atlantic",10,"Eastern","Washington"
38,"South Atlantic",30,"Eastern","Atlanta"
42,"Great Lakes",100,"Midwest","Chicago"
51,"Plains",140,"Midwest","Dallas"
66,"Pacific",270,"Western","San Francisco"
84,"Mountain",290,"Western","Denver"
```

As shown in this example, numeric values are stored in their string representation in an ASCII text file. The character string values are delimited by double quotation marks. The use of the string delimiters is optional, but it could be necessary if the column delimiter character could occur inside a string value. The string delimiter can be changed to a character different than the double quotation marks by using the appropriate command options described later in this chapter. A double string delimiter character can be used to denote the occurrence of the string delimiter character within the string value itself; for example, "M""uller" would be interpreted as M"uller.

There is no limit on the maximum length of the data rows in a delimited ASCII file; however, the maximum length of an individual column value is 32KB.

Although delimited ASCII can be used to transfer almost any type of table data, it is not recommended for use with binary data values.

Nondelimited ASCII Text (ASC)

Another popular data interchange format is the nondelimited ASCII file format, also known as positional ASCII. DB2 supports two variations of this file format: fixed record length and variable record length positional ASCII.

The fixed record length positional ASCII file format uses fixed byte offsets instead of record delimiters to determine individual record boundaries. With this format, each record in the file has the same fixed length. The start of the nth record is determined by multiplying *n* by the fixed record length and using the resulting number as the byte offset from the beginning of the file.

Similarly, the start and the end position of each column value within a data row are also constant and are represented by the byte offset from the start of the record. The following example includes the first three rows of data from the previous example in the fixed record length positional ASCII format. Note that the first row is not part of the data file; it is included for the purpose of demonstrating the column offset calculation.

```
12345678901234567890123456789012345678901234567890123456789012345678901234567890

10          Head Office        160      Corporate    New York
15          New England        50       Eastern      Boston
20          Mid Atlantic       10       Eastern      Washington
```

In this example, each data row is 70 characters long, the data does not contain newline characters, values for column 1 start at offset 1 and end at offset 10, values for column 2 start at offset 11 and end at offset 30, and so on. When used with the IMPORT or LOAD command, the description of the file format in this example should be provided using the following command options:

```
MODIFIED BY RECLEN=70 METHOD L (1 10, 11 30, 31 40, 41 55,
56 70)
```

In the variable length positional ASCII file format, the length of each data row in the input file doesn't need to be constant. A newline character is used to delimit individual data rows. The start and stop position of each column value is constant throughout the entire file and corresponds to the byte offset from the start of the record.

The nondelimited ASCII file format is widely used for exchanging data with the mainframe version of DB2. The Load utility provides support for packed decimal, zoned decimal, and binary numeric values contained in positional ASCII files. The maximum length of a data row in the nondelimited ASCII file format is 32KB.

As of version 7 of DB2 for UNIX, Windows, and OS/2, the Export utility lacks the support for positional ASCII as the output file format.

Integrated Exchange Format, PC Version, Binary (IXF)

Integrated Exchange Format (IXF), PC Version, is a binary file format used primarily for transferring data between DB2 for UNIX, Windows, and OS/2 database tables. The IXF file format has been specifically designed to allow the storage of the table definition together with the table data. As you will see in the section "Copying Entire Databases with db2move" later in this chapter, the db2move utility takes advantage of this capability when performing a copy of the entire database contents.

You can create a copy of a single table by exporting it to IXF and importing it into a new table by using the CREATE option of the Import utility. Numeric column values are stored within IXF files in their binary representation. For a complete description of the structure of the PC/IXF file format, refer to the *DB2 Data Movement Guide and Reference Manual*.

The PC/IXF file format is not compatible with the IXF file format used by DB2 on the mainframe.

Worksheet Format, Binary (WSF)

The worksheet (WSF) file format is a proprietary binary file format used to exchange data between DB2 and the Lotus 1-2-3 and Symphony products. Only the Import and Export utilities support WSF.

Populating Tables Using Import

You can use the SQL INSERT statement to insert data rows into a database table. Quite often, the data to be inserted is stored as text in operating system files. We could, of course, write an application that would parse the file, and for each row, extract the individual column values, convert them from a string value into the desired representation, and issue an INSERT statement to store the row in the database table. However, such an application would have to be modified each time we had to deal with a different table definition.

Fortunately, DB2 provides a flexible, general-purpose utility with this functionality, called Import. It can deal with arbitrary target table definitions without any modification, and it supports a number of different file formats. This section discusses the basic use and some of the more advanced features of the IMPORT command.

To insert data into a table with the help of Import, you need at least SELECT and INSERT privileges on the table. When using Import to replace the table's contents with the data contained in the input file, you need the DELETE privilege on the table in addition to SELECT and INSERT privileges. If you are planning to use Import to create tables from an IXF input file, be sure you have the CREATETAB privilege for the database you are connected to. Users with DBADM or SYSADM authority can perform any type of IMPORT operations. See Chapter 5 for details on the different authority levels and how to grant or revoke them.

Because Import populates its target table by issuing SQL INSERT statements against it, the INSERT processing takes care of verifying all table constraints, firing appropriate triggers, propagating changes to summary tables, etc. In other words, Import behaves in most respects just like any other regular SQL application. This differentiates it from the Load utility, described in the section "Using the High-Speed Bulk Loader" later in this chapter, which interfaces directly with the DB2 storage manager and does not perform regular SQL processing.

You need to be connected to a database before invoking Import. After successfully processing the input file, Import will perform a commit.

IMPORT Syntax and Basic Usage

The following is the basic syntax of the IMPORT command:

```
IMPORT FROM <file name> OF <file type> <mode> INTO <table name>
```

The *table name* should refer to an existing table, an updateable view, or an alias thereof. When creating a new table with IMPORT from an IXF file, the *table name* will be used for the name of the new table. The *table name* can be followed by an optional target column list if a particular mapping of the columns in the input file to the table columns is desired. If not specified, Import assumes the default mapping of the first column in the file to the first column specified in the table definition, and so on.

The *file name* parameter refers to the fully qualified or relative path to the input file. The value of the *file type* parameter can be DEL, ASC, IXF, or WSF, and it provides the information about the format of the input file. The *mode* parameter refers to the mode of execution of the Import utility and can have one of the following values:

- **INSERT**   Import adds data contained in the input file into the target table.
- **INSERT_UPDATE**   For each row of the input, if a row with a matching primary key value is found, Import updates the columns not contained in the primary key definition with the values of the input row. If no matching row is found, Import inserts the input row into the table. This is supported only for tables with a primary key.
- **REPLACE**   When executed with this option, Import truncates the table prior to inserting new data into it, effectively replacing the old contents of the table with the data contained in the input file.
- **REPLACE_CREATE**   Similar to REPLACE, but if the target table does not exist, Import attempts to create it. This option is supported only with files in the IXF format previously created by Export with a SELECT * FROM <table name>.
- **CREATE**   Import creates the table and populates it with data from an IXF file containing the table definition.

 Table truncation is performed at the start of the IMPORT REPLACE processing and cannot be undone. Use this mode with caution.

Several other optional clauses can be included with an IMPORT command—refer to Chapter 30 for the complete syntax.

MAINTAINING DATA

Consider the following simple IMPORT command example, which inserts the data contained in the comma-delimited text file org.del into the table ORG:

```
IMPORT FROM org.del OF DEL INSERT INTO org
```

An example of an Import of a nondelimited positional text file follows next. Note that the METHOD L clause must be included when performing an Import from a positional file to provide Import with the information about the start and end position of the data values for each column in the input file. The position is calculated as the byte offset from the beginning of a data row in the input file:

```
IMPORT FROM org1.asc OF ASC
METHOD L(1 6, 8 23, 25 31, 33 48, 50 65)
INSERT INTO org
```

If the input file doesn't contain newline characters but uses a fixed record length instead, the MODIFIED BY RECLEN clause must be used, as shown next:

```
IMPORT FROM org2.asc OF ASC
MODIFIED BY RECLEN=70 METHOD L(1 6, 8 23, 25 31, 33 48, 50 65)
INSERT INTO org
```

The next and final example demonstrates how you can create a copy of a table by using Import in the REPLACE_CREATE mode with an IXF file:

```
IMPORT FROM org.ixf OF IXF REPLACE_CREATE INTO new_org
```

Note *The table definition information required for successful table creation with Import will be contained in the IXF file only if the file was created during an Export using a SELECT statement of the form SELECT * FROM <table name>.*

Concurrency with Other Applications

Import acquires and holds an exclusive (X) lock on the table it is inserting data into for the entire duration of its execution. This prevents updates to the table by other applications. Only applications using the uncommitted read (UR) isolation level are allowed to read the table while Import is running. When issued in REPLACE mode, Import prevents all access to the table for its entire duration.

Tip *If you need uncommitted read access to the table while IMPORT REPLACE is executing, substitute your original IMPORT command with an IMPORT REPLACE of an empty file followed by an IMPORT INSERT of the original input file.*

Import places no restrictions on concurrent access to other tables.

Advanced Import Options

A selected subset of advanced topics and additional Import options are discussed in this section. For a complete listing of Import options and their meaning, please refer to Chapter 30.

Default Values

Import attempts to substitute a NULL value for a missing column in a delimited text file, regardless of whether the column was defined WITH DEFAULT or not. By specifying the USEDEFAULTS clause on the IMPORT command, you can request the default value to be substituted for a missing value instead of a NULL value if the column was defined WITH DEFAULT.

For columns defined WITH DEFAULT that are missing from the target column list following the table name, Import inserts the default values for every row inserted as part of the Import operation. If you don't want the default values to be used under those circumstances, you can specify the NODEFAULTS clause on the IMPORT command. This will cause Import to attempt to insert NULL values instead of default values in all rows for columns missing from the target list.

Active Log Space Considerations for Large Imports

The fact that Import uses SQL INSERT statements for moving data records into the target table also means that the database engine will perform regular logging of the table updates on behalf of the Import operation. Large Imports can thus potentially hold up the current active log for a long time and eventually cause the database manager to run out of log space. To prevent such situations from occurring, Import can perform commits at regular intervals. The commits are requested by specifying the COMMITCOUNT <n> clause with the IMPORT command. It causes Import to issue a commit every time n records are inserted into the table.

Import prints informational messages about the number of rows committed at each commit point. Should the Import operation fail, all changes performed since the last commit are undone during the transaction rollback processing. Given the information about the last commit point, you can restart (reissue) the IMPORT command and direct it to skip the number of rows in the input file that was previously reported as successfully committed. You can achieve this by providing the RESTARTCOUNT <n> clause when reissuing the IMPORT command, where n corresponds to the number of rows that should be skipped before resuming inserting rows into the target table.

Formatting Options

Input text files generated by other software packages often don't adhere to the strict formatting rules expected by DB2 utilities. In many cases, Import does allow a slight variation of the expected file format through the use of formatting options, the so-called file-type modifiers.

Changing Default Delimiters and Their Precedence

Only single character delimiters are supported by the DB2 data movement utilities. The delimiters must be mutually exclusive, and some characters cannot be used as delimiters: the carriage-return character, the linefeed character, the blank (space) character, and binary zero.

You can provide the new delimiter in its character representation or as a hexadecimal value of its code point. Import provides the following modifiers for use with delimited text files, to be used inside the MODIFIED BY clause:

- **COLDELx**   Use the character x as the column delimiter; the default is a comma.

- **CHARDELx**   Use the character x as the character string delimiter; the default is double quotes.

- **DECPTx**   Use the character x as the decimal point; the default is a period.

The default record delimiter (carriage return) cannot be changed.

The default precedence of delimiters used by Import is record delimiter, string delimiter, column delimiter. This means that if a newline character is encountered inside a string, by default, it will be treated as the end of the record. If you want Import to ignore record delimiters contained inside character strings, use the MODIFIED BY DELPRIORITYCHAR option. This changes the delimiter precedence to string delimiter, record delimiter, column delimiter.

For example, to import a semicolon-delimited file, allowing newline characters to be contained inside string values, you would issue the following:

```
IMPORT FROM data.del of DEL
MODIFIED BY COLDEL; DELPRIORITYCHAR
INSERT INTO mytable
```

Or alternatively, using the hexadecimal representation of a semicolon:

```
IMPORT FROM data.del of DEL
MODIFIED BY COLDEL0x3B DELPRIORITYCHAR
INSERT INTO mytable
```

User-Defined Date, Time, and Timestamp Representation

Import expects date values to be represented by strings containing a date value in the ISO format or strings of form YYYYMMDD, where Y corresponds to digits of the year part, M to digits of the month part, and D to digits of the day part. Because the data files come from various sources and enforcing exact format rules is not always possible, the Import utility allows its users to provide user-defined templates for the expected format of the date, time, and timestamp values contained in the input file. This can be achieved by including the following file-type modifiers inside the MODIFIED BY clause:

- DATEFORMAT=<template>
- TIMEFORMAT=<template>
- TIMESTAMPFORMAT=<template>

The *template* is constructed from characters corresponding to individual digits of the year (*Y*), month (*M*), day (*D*), hour (*H*), minute (*M*), second (*S*), microsecond (*U*), meridian indicator (*T*) values, and other arbitrary characters used as delimiters. A sample format template for the American date format could be represented as MMDDYYYY, or perhaps as MM/DD/YYYY. Because the letter *M* can represent both month and minute, Import uses the surrounding context information when parsing the template.

Identity and Generated Columns Support

Import can add data to tables with identity or generated columns. The following modifiers are supported by Import when processing tables with identity or generated columns:

- **IDENTITYMISSING and GENERATEDMISSING**   Forces the generation of values by Import for columns defined as GENERATED ALWAYS.
- **IDENTITYIGNORE and GENERATEDIGNORE**   Tells Import to ignore the values for the identity and generated columns contained in the input file and to generate new values instead.

If, for example, the target table was defined with a GENERATED ALWAYS identity column and all the rows in the input file contained a value for that column, the Import would fail unless the identity column was explicitly excluded from the target column list, or the MODIFIED BY IDENTITYIGNORE clause was used.

After populating a GENERATED BY DEFAULT identity column with values from an input file using Import, the user can reset the starting value of the identity column to the next higher value by issuing the following:

```
ALTER TABLE <table name> ALTER <column name> RESTART WITH <value>
```

Working with LOB Data

Import restricts the maximum allowed length of a single column value in the input file to 32KB. This includes large object (LOB) values, which usually exceed 32KB. The solution is to export and import LOBs greater than 32KB to and from separate files referenced by name from the main input file. The Import option associated with this behavior is MODIFIED BY LOBSINFILE. In addition to that option, the clause LOBS FROM <directory list> can be used to provide a search path for the LOB file references (filenames) stored in the main input file as LOB column values.

Consider the following example. Let's assume that the main input data file (data.del) contains these three rows:

```
10023, "John Green", "jpeg", "john.jpg"
17250, "Mark Grey", "jpeg", "mark.jpg"
22010, "Cheryl Brown", "tiff", "cheryl.tif"
```

Assuming that the fourth column in the target table BADGE_DATA is indeed a LOB, the following IMPORT command would search for the separate LOB files in the /tmp/data directory, and having found them, place them in the LOB column of the corresponding data rows to be inserted:

```
IMPORT FROM data.del of DEL
LOBS FROM /tmp/data/ MODIFIED BY LOBSINFILE
INSERT INTO badge_data
```

 Note *All LOB source directory names in the LOBS FROM clause need to be terminated by a path separator (a slash (/) on UNIX, a backslash (\) on Windows).*

Import Performance Considerations

Besides following general performance tuning guidelines for update-intensive applications, little can be done to significantly improve Import's performance. Generally speaking, if a significantly higher data throughput rate is required, perhaps because of a limited maintenance window on the system, the Load utility might be a better choice to use than Import.

You can slightly improve the insert performance on a large table by turning the APPEND mode on for the target table with

```
ALTER TABLE <table name> APPEND ON
```

An additional performance boost can be realized by making use of the COMPOUND <n> clause of the IMPORT command. Through the deployment of compound SQL, *n* insert requests will be grouped together and sent in a single request to the server. Besides cutting down on client/server communication costs, it also positively affects server-side insert processing.

When used in partitioned database environments, Import takes advantage of an INSERT statement optimization technique called buffered inserts to minimize interpartition communication costs.

Exporting Table Contents to a File

While Import reads data from an input file into the database, the Export utility performs the reverse function—it writes data from the database into an external output file. Export provides a very flexible selection mechanism for generating the output to be written out to a file: it lets the user access the data via an SQL SELECT statement. The query results constitute the contents of the output file. Through the declarative power of SQL, it allows you to export an entire table as easily as arbitrary horizontal and/or vertical slices of a table, or even a result of a multitable join.

Like Import, Export is basically an SQL application. It opens a cursor for a given SELECT statement, fetches its results, performs any necessary type conversion, and dumps the converted result to a file.

Export requires a database connection to be established prior to its invocation. Also, you need at least the SELECT privilege on all objects referenced in the SELECT statement of the EXPORT command. Export acquires no additional locks beyond those required to process its SELECT statement. By default, the Export package is bound to the database using the repeatable read isolation level. Therefore, Export holds a shared table lock during the execution of the SELECT statement, just like any other application using the repeatable read isolation level.

EXPORT Syntax and Basic Usage

The basic EXPORT syntax is shown next. (For the complete EXPORT syntax, including all optional parameters and their descriptions, refer to Chapter 30.)

```
EXPORT TO <output file> OF <file type> <select statement>
```

The output of the EXPORT command is written to the *output file*. Note that if the file already exists, its current contents will be overwritten. The *file type* parameter can be DEL, IXF, or WSF, and this determines the format of the output file generated by Export. Finally, Export accepts any valid SELECT statement as its data selection criteria.

When Export is used with the IXF file format and when the SELECT statement is of the form of SELECT * FROM <table name>, Export stores the table definition in the IXF file in addition to the table's contents, so the table can be later recreated by using the IMPORT command in the CREATE mode.

For example, the following command dumps the entire contents of the ORG table (part of the SAMPLE database) and the table's definition to an IXF file:

```
EXPORT TO org.ixf OF IXF SELECT * FROM org
```

A copy of the ORG table can then be easily created using the following Import command:

```
IMPORT FROM org.ixf of IXF CREATE INTO org2
```

The following export example also uses the ORG table, this time with the delimited ASCII file format:

```
EXPORT TO org.del OF DEL SELECT * FROM org WHERE DEPTNUMB <= 20
```

The preceding EXPORT command produces the org.del file in its current working directory containing the following data:

```
15,"New England",50,"Eastern","Boston"
10,"Head Office",160,"Corporate","New York"
20,"Mid Atlantic",10,"Eastern","Washington"
```

Advanced Export Options

This section discusses several options that allow you to modify the format of the output files generated by Export. You will also see the use of the EXPORT command with tables containing LOB data.

Export has a number of optional parameters and file-type modifiers that are not discussed in this chapter, for example, the ability to export typed table hierarchies, file-type modifiers related to the DATALINK data type, etc. The complete Export syntax can be found in Chapter 30.

Changing Default Delimiters in the Output

Export offers a number of file-type modifiers for use with the delimited ASCII file format that can assist with generating the output file with nonstandard delimiters.

Only single character delimiters are supported by the DB2 data movement utilities. The delimiters must be mutually exclusive, and some characters cannot be used as delimiters: the carriage-return character, the linefeed character, the blank (space) character, and binary zero.

The following file-type modifiers (i.e., options to be used with the MODIFIED BY clause) can assist you with changing the default delimiters in the Export-delimited ASCII output:

- **COLDELx** Use x as the column delimiter in the output; the default is a comma.
- **CHARDELx** Use x as the character string delimiter in the output; the default is the double quotes character.
- **DECPTx** Use x as the default decimal point; the default is the period.

Like the corresponding Import options, the character used as a delimiter can be specified either in character or hexadecimal code point value representation. For example, to create a semicolon-delimited file, you could issue an EXPORT command similar to the following:

```
EXPORT TO org.del OF DEL MODIFIED BY COLDEL; SELECT * FROM org
```

Similarly, to create a tab-delimited file with Export, you could type the following:

```
EXPORT TO org.del OF DEL MODIFIED BY COLDEL0x09 SELECT * FROM org
```

Exporting LOB Data

As with Import, Export stores LOB values larger than 32KB individually in separate files; the LOB columns of the output file contain filename references to only those LOB files. When exporting LOBs to separate files, you must include the clause MODIFIED BY LOBSINFILE in your EXPORT command.

Two additional Export options are related to LOB processing that are worth mentioning here: LOBS TO <directory list> and LOBFILE <list of base names>. The former can be used to designate a comma-separated list of directories to contain the LOB files; the default is the current directory. LOBFILE is used to provide a comma-separated list of base names from which the LOB filenames will be generated. Export uses each of the base names to generate up to 1000 LOB filenames by appending it with a three-digit extension (from 000 to 999). If LOBFILE is missing, the default base name Export uses is db2exp.

The following example exports LOBs to separate files; the filenames will be stored in the main delimited ASCII output file photo.del:

```
EXPORT TO photo.del OF DEL
LOBS TO /u/miro/lobdata1/, /u/miro/lobdata2/,
/u/miro/lobdata3/, /u/miro/lobdata4/, /u/miro/lobdata5/
LOBFILE pic1, pic2, pic3, pic4, pic5 MODIFIED BY LOBSINFILE
SELECT * FROM emp_photo
```

Note that in this example, we have provided a list of five target directories and five base filenames. This gives us a maximum of up to $5 \times 5 \times 1000 = 25,000$ unique LOB filenames. Should the table contain more than 25,000 LOBs, the export would fail due to Export's inability to generate enough unique filenames for LOB output files.

To work around this problem, we would have to increase the number of LOB directory targets and/or LOB base filenames to enable Export to generate enough unique filenames for all LOBs contained in the result set of the SELECT statement.

Note *Export requires all LOB target directory names (the LOBS TO list) to be terminated by the path separator.*

Using the High-Speed Bulk Loader

In the previous sections of this chapter, we looked at the Import and Export utilities. Both of them access the database manager via the SQL interface, like any regular user application. This section is devoted to the Load utility, which operates on an entirely different principle. It is tightly integrated into the database engine and interfaces directly with its storage manager. In simple terms, Load formats data records in their native storage format, packs them on page buffers, and writes entire extents of data directly to table space containers, all of which happens in parallel.

There are basically three main benefits of using Load versus using Import: performance, performance, and performance. Also, Load performs next to no logging, except for the delete phase (described later in this section). On the other hand, there are quite a few disadvantages of using Load: restricted table space access, lack of triggers support, and somewhat cumbersome error recovery, to name just a few. In many cases, however, the performance difference of several orders of magnitude and the savings in log space makes Load a popular choice with database administrators.

A higher level of authority is required to execute Load than to execute Import. You will need at least LOAD authority for the database and the INSERT privilege for the table to be loaded. Additionally, the DELETE privilege for the table is required for loads invoked with the REPLACE option. If you are using an exception table during load to store data rows violating a unique constraint, you should have the INSERT privilege on the exception table. Users with DBADM or SYSADM authority can also perform loads. Refer to Chapter 5 for details about the different authority levels and how to grant or revoke them.

You need to be connected to a database before invoking Load. After successfully processing the input file, Load will perform a commit.

Load does not verify constraints on the data rows it adds to the table. Instead, it simply puts the target table into check pending state and requires you to execute the SET INTEGRITY statement on the target table following the completion of Load, to verify the validity of table constraints in the data appended by Load. Load does not fire triggers.

Besides populating the table with data rows contained in the input file, Load also updates the table's indexes. Depending on the amount of data added to the table, Load will either fully rebuild all indexes on the table or simply insert the newly loaded keys into the existing indexes. Load employs a heuristic-based costing algorithm to determine the appropriate maintenance option at run time.

During load in REPLACE mode, you can request that table, index, and column statistics be collected as part of the load process.

Load requires exclusive access to all table spaces containing parts of the table being loaded. It uses the QUIESCE command to lock the table spaces in EXCLUSIVE mode and additional administrative table space states (load pending, delete pending). To avoid the concurrency restrictions Load places on other transactions, you can use the two-step staging tables approach. In the first step, load the data into a staging table residing in a separate, dedicated table space. In the second step, use SQL INSERT to move the data from the staging table into the target table.

Due in part to the fact that Load does not log the updates to the table and in part to its long-running transaction characteristics, the error recovery in Load differs from the automatic undo of the changes on rollback that regular transactions take advantage of. Similarly, you should carefully consider the roll-forward recovery planning of table spaces involved in Load. The recovery implications of using Load are discussed in detail in "Implications for Roll-Forward Recovery" later in this chapter.

LOAD Syntax and Basic Usage

Basic LOAD syntax follows. (For the complete syntax, including the description of all options and parameters, refer to Chapter 30.)

```
LOAD FROM <input file> OF <file type> <mode> INTO <table name>
```

The *file type* parameter can be DEL, ASC, or IXF, and it determines the file format of the input file. The *mode* parameter can be INSERT, REPLACE, RESTART, or TERMINATE, and it refers to the utility's mode of execution. In the INSERT mode, Load appends the data contained in the input file to the end of the table; in the REPLACE mode, the target table is truncated and then appended with the data contained in the input. The RESTART and TERMINATE modes of execution perform Load error recovery and are described in greater detail in "Monitoring Load's Progress and Basic Troubleshooting" later in this chapter. The *table name* parameter must refer to a regular table or an alias thereof. Unlike Import, Load does not support loading into updateable views.

Here is a simple Load example with a delimited ASCII file:

```
LOAD FROM org.del OF DEL REPLACE INTO org2
```

The following is another Load example, this time with nondelimited, fixed record length ASCII input and LOBs to be read in from separate files:

```
LOAD FROM photo.asc OF ASC
MODIFIED BY LOBSINFILE RECLEN=70 METHOD L(1 8, 11 18, 21 31)
REPLACE INTO emp_photo
```

Phases of Load Processing

There are three main phases of Load processing: the load phase, the build phase, and the delete phase. Load writes informational messages to its message file every time a phase starts and finishes.

During the load phase, data rows are read from the input, formatted into pages and extents, and sent directly to disk. If indexes are present on the table, then during the load phase, index keys are extracted from the formatted records and inserted into a sort.

The build phase occurs only if the table has indexes. In that case, index keys are retrieved in the sorted order and the index is rebuilt or maintained incrementally. If any of the indexes are unique, duplicate detection is performed as part of the index maintenance.

The last phase of Load processing, the delete phase, occurs only if the table has unique indexes and duplicates were detected during the build phase. If this happened, the duplicates are deleted from the table and the other indexes. Those deletions are performed on individual table rows and are fully logged.

Advanced Load Options

The LOAD command has so many different options and file-type modifiers that it would probably take several pages just to list them all here with a brief description. We had to pick and choose, and we thought it best to cover in greater detail the Load options and parameters related to performance, physical page layout, partitioned environments, and recovery.

The way Load deals with default values, formatting options, identity and generated columns support, and LOB support is very similar and in some cases identical to the way Import deals with these issues. You can refer to the corresponding Import sections and apply similar principles when using Load.

Parameters Influencing Load Performance

A number of explicit LOAD command parameters can affect Load's performance, but performance can also depend on the values of certain database manager and database parameters, as well as decisions made during the physical database design.

The performance of Load greatly depends on the number of CPUs used by the database server as well as the physical layout of the table spaces involved in the Load operation. Load cannot execute in parallel when adding data to a table containing long field or LOB columns. Loads with LOBs and long fields generally don't perform well.

One potential bottleneck is the index key sorting and index rebuild processing during the load and build phases of Load. We recommend reading about sort performance tuning in the *DB2 Administration Guide* to alleviate any potential problems in this area.

The following Load options affect performance:

■ **CPU_PARALLELISM**   The number of Load symmetric multiprocessing (SMP) subagents formatting the input data. Formatting data values is a computational bottleneck in Load, and the higher the SMP degree of the server on which it executes, typically, the better the performance of Load. The default is set to the number of CPUs on the machine.

■ **DISK_PARALLELISM**   The number of asynchronous I/O subagents used to write data extents to table space containers. By default, Load starts as many asynchronous I/O subagents as there are containers in the target table spaces, because it assumes that each container resides on a separate disk device. The value of this parameter needs to be manually increased for setups with a redundant array of independent disks (RAID) subsystem behind a single table space container.

■ **DATA BUFFER**   The number of pages of shared memory available to the Load utility for data communication between subagents. By default, this is set to 25 percent of available memory in the utility heap. If it is set too low, this parameter could prevent Load from reaching the optimal level of SMP parallelism.

- **INDEXING MODE**   The choice of whether Load should rebuild or extend the index. In most cases, the automatic selection algorithm is adequate.

- **ANYORDER**   This option specifies that a user doesn't care about preserving the ordering of the data in the input stream. If this is the case, less synchronization is required, and the potential for SMP scalability is higher.

- **FASTPARSE**   This option causes less error checking to be performed during the formatting of column values in Load. This is recommended only if you are confident that the input data is clean. It reduces the formatting overhead.

If index maintenance is performed during Load, the following parameters could affect the amount of time spent in the load and build phase processing: the SORTHEAP database configuration parameter, the SHEAPTHRES database manager configuration parameter, the physical layout of the temporary table space used for spilling sort data, the size of the buffer pool associated with the temporary table space used for sort spilling, and others.

Page Formatting Options

If substantial insert and update activity is expected on a table following a Load, it can be advantageous to direct Load to leave a certain fraction of page space unused to accommodate future growth without having to allocate new pages.

Because Load formats the data pages directly in its private memory buffers, it is in the ideal position to decide how tightly the data will be packed on each page. Several parameters influence this behavior, some of which are implicit table and index object properties, and others are explicit LOAD command options.

An implicit parameter is the PCTFREE property of the table and index objects. For table objects, PCTFREE is set and updated with the ALTER TABLE statement; for indexes, it is set during the execution of the CREATE INDEX statement and applies to index leaf pages. This property accepts a value between 0 and 99 and determines how much free space will be left on the pages belonging to the object. It is not enforced for the first record on the page. The default PCTFREE value for table objects is 0, and for index objects, it is 10.

The following are some explicit LOAD command options:

- **PAGEFREESPACE file-type modifier**   If specified, this modifier overrides the PCTFREE property of the table object. Supported values are from 0 to 99.

- **INDEXFREESPACE file-type modifier**   If specified, this modifier overrides the PCTFREE property of the index object. Supported values are from 0 to 99.

- **TOTALFREESPACE file-type modifier**   This specifies the percentage of empty pages to be appended to the end of the table. This is based on the size of the table at the end of Load, and the supported values are between 0 and the largest positive integer in 32-bit representation (in excess of 2 billion).

The following is an example of the use of the page free space modifiers in Load. Let's assume that the table's PCTFREE property is set at 20 and the index PCTFREE property is set at 30.

```
LOAD FROM data.del OF DEL
MODIFIED BY PAGEFREESPACE=30 TOTALFREESPACE=100
REPLACE INTO t1 DISK_PARALLELISM 8 INDEXING MODE REBUILD
```

In this example, we have directed Load to leave approximately 30 percent free space on data pages and to append the same number of empty pages to the end of the table as the final table size. Note that because we didn't explicitly specify the INDEXFREESPACE modifier, Load will look up the value of the PCTFREE index object property and use it as a guideline; in this case, it would leave 30 percent empty space on all index leaf pages.

Loading Partitioned Tables

This section contains information specific to the Enterprise—Extended Edition (EEE) version of DB2; you can skip it if you are not using DB2 EEE.

In a partitioned database environment, table rows are distributed among individual nodes based on the value of their partitioning key. While Import, through the use of SQL INSERTs, distributes the table rows to the appropriate partitions in a manner fully transparent to its users, the Load utility accesses the table space containers directly and operates on a single database partition at a time. Load expects the data contained in the input file to have been prepartitioned and destined to reside at the partition on which it currently operates. When loading data into a partitioned table, load verifies that the current partition is the data's correct destination by evaluating information contained in the input file's header. The header is generated by the DB2 data partitioning utility db2split.

While not recommended due to its complexity, you can manually partition the input file into several output files, each containing a proper header and the data destined for an individual partition, by directly invoking the db2split executable. You can then use the files generated by db2split as inputs for loads on the individual partitions.

Instead, we recommend using the AutoLoader utility. It fully automates and parallelizes the task of loading into partitioned tables. During its execution, the AutoLoader utility starts one or more partitioning subagents and initiates Load sessions on the target database partitions. AutoLoader then reads the input file and pipelines the data stream through the partitioning subagents, ultimately sending data rows to be loaded at their correct destination. See Figure 10-2 for a high-level AutoLoader architecture overview.

The AutoLoader utility is invoked through the db2atld executable:

```
db2atld -c <configuration file>
```

You must provide AutoLoader with a configuration file that contains its input parameters. A well-documented sample of an AutoLoader configuration file,

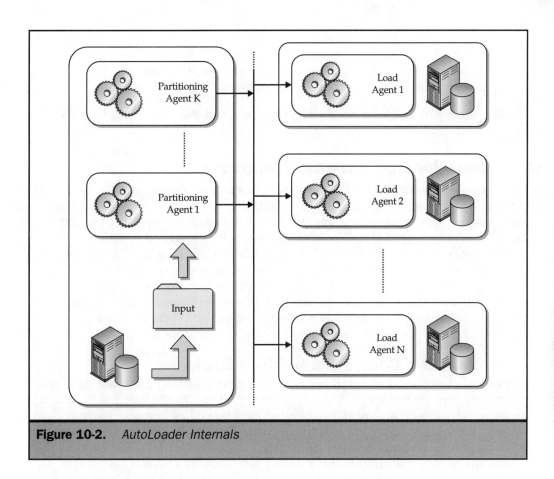

Figure 10-2. *AutoLoader Internals*

autoloader.cfg, can be found in the samples/autoloader directory located in your instance directory. Before using AutoLoader for the first time, simply copy the sample configuration file, edit it, and change the LOAD command and the database name parameter values to match your environment.

Important AutoLoader configuration parameters include the following:

- **LOAD command**   The LOAD command that will be executed on the target partitions. It contains both the name of the input file and the name of the target table. The input file has to be accessible on the partition executing AutoLoader.

- **DATABASE**   The name of the database in which the target table resides.

- **MODE AutoLoader execution mode**   The possible values are SPLIT_AND_ LOAD, SPLIT_ONLY, LOAD_ONLY, and ANALYZE. The SPLIT_AND_LOAD mode is by far the most commonly used because it allows data to be loaded into the correct target partitions in a single step. If you wanted to separate the process of partitioning the data from the actual load, you would invoke AutoLoader in the SPLIT_ONLY mode, followed by a second invocation using the LOAD_ONLY mode. The ANALYZE mode can be used to generate a custom optimal partitioning map for a table, given a representative sample of the table data.

Most other AutoLoader parameters are optional, and their default values are well documented.

Implications for Roll-Forward Recovery

Load writes entire extents of data directly to table space containers, which means that it does not perform regular row-level logging of table updates. Because its changes are not contained in the database log, another method is required of applying the updates during roll-forward recovery of the table spaces involved in a Load operation.

This section discusses three alternative approaches for including Load in your overall recovery strategy. Refer to Chapter 12 for a detailed discussion of recovery concepts. The following information is applicable only if you are planning to archive your database logs and retain them for future use with roll-forward database or table space recovery. It does not apply to nonrecoverable databases set up with circular logging, where only version recovery (i.e., restore from a backup) without rolling forward is used.

Load Without a Copy, Followed by a Backup

By default, when Load is executed in a database with log archiving enabled, Load will not create a copy of its changes. Instead, it places all affected table spaces in the backup pending state. No updates are allowed against objects residing in a table space in backup pending state, except by subsequent loads. The state will be removed only after a backup of the table space has been taken. The backup image provides the means of recovering the data inserted into the table by Load in case of a system failure.

During roll-forward recovery, processing a Load without a copy log record causes the table space to be placed in restore pending state. The table space will then need to be restored from the backup taken after the Load, and only then is the roll-forward operation allowed to continue.

Load with Copy Image

Load can create an incremental backup image of the pages that were updated during its execution. This special type of backup image is referred to as *load copy*. It cannot be used by the RESTORE command directly; rather, the changes contained in it will be automatically reapplied during the processing of the Load commit log record during a roll-forward operation. You should archive the Load copy image because it will be required during roll-forward recovery.

To create a Load copy, you should include this clause on the Load command:

```
COPY YES TO <target> [, <target>]
```

Here, target should be a fully qualified directory path to place the Load copy image in. If you are planning on using the Tivoli Storage Manager (TSM) to archive the Load copy on tape or other media, use the following COPY clause:

```
COPY YES USE TSM
```

Nonrecoverable Load

This option is used frequently for read-mostly tables that are populated mainly by Load. If all the input data files necessary to recreate the table contents can be easily generated or restored from a backup, then after the completion of the roll-forward operation, any tables that are marked as *unavailable* are simply dropped and reloaded. Roll-forward recovery marks the table as unavailable during the processing of a nonrecoverable Load log record. To achieve this behavior, include the keyword NONRECOVERABLE in your LOAD command.

 No access is allowed to a table that is marked as unavailable; it can only be dropped. Insert, update, or delete activity following a nonrecoverable Load on a table will not be redone *during roll-forward recovery.*

Monitoring Load's Progress and Basic Troubleshooting

Load is a resource-intensive and typically a long-running operation. Because it doesn't use the common buffer pool or log its changes, it needs to restrict access to the table spaces on which it operates. A failure in Load leaves the table space inaccessible until the Load operation is either cancelled or successfully restarted and completed.

Monitoring Load's Progress with LOAD QUERY

Load does not print any messages to the console or to its message file until the successful completion of the load and build phases. During a long-running Load operation, you can monitor its progress using the LOAD QUERY command:

```
LOAD QUERY TABLE <SchemaName.TableName>
```

This command returns any messages generated by Load so far and reports the current phase of Load processing.

How to Cancel or Restart an Interrupted Load

Typical causes of Load failure include the following:

■ Insufficient disk space in the target table space

■ Insufficient log space during a Load with a large delete phase caused by a large number of unique constraint violations

- User interrupt
- Too many rows rejected because of invalid data format
- System or power failure

In most cases, the error message returned by Load will clearly indicate the cause of failure. On rare occasions, you might need to examine the DB2 diagnostics and error logs to determine the exact circumstances of the Load failure. See Chapter 15 for details on DB2 problem determination.

Once a failure occurs, Load leaves all affected table spaces inaccessible. The table spaces will be in load or delete pending state and potentially also in the quiesce exclusive state.

After the cause of the failure has been identified and the problem is fixed, you can restart a failed Load by issuing the LOAD RESTART command:

```
LOAD FROM <file name> OF <file type> … RESTART INTO <table name> …
```

During restart, the values of all Load command parameters should be exactly the same as those used by the failed Load operation, except for the INSERT or REPLACE keywords, which should be replaced with the RESTART keyword.

Load restart automatically detects in which phase of Load processing the most recent failure occurred and initiates the restart processing from that phase on. In addition, you can request that consistency points be taken at regular intervals during the load phase. In case of a failure, a subsequent Load restart automatically continues the work from the last *successful* consistency point. Use the SAVECOUNT <n> clause to establish consistency points after each *n* rows have been processed.

> **Tip**   *Given that Load is a high-speed utility, we recommend that you do not request consistency points too frequently because it could adversely affect Load performance while providing minimal benefit during restart; 100,000 is a sufficient value for SAVECOUNT in most cases.*

To cancel a previously failed Load operation, issue the LOAD TERMINATE command:

```
LOAD FROM <file name> OF <file type> TERMINATE INTO <table name>
```

Canceling a Load INSERT operation restores the table to a state prior to the start of the load, while canceling a Load REPLACE leaves the table empty. In both cases, the table space will become accessible and its state will be restored to normal. The filename and file type parameters are meaningless during a terminate operation; the table name parameter should refer to the same table as the previously failed Load did.

Tip   *If you no longer know the name of the table, the LIST TABLESPACES SHOW DETAILS command can help you determine its table space and table ID. That information can then be used to obtain the fully qualified name of the table by querying the SYSCAT.TABLES catalog table.*

In certain circumstances, the quiesce exclusive state of the table space might prevent you from canceling or restarting a Load. In that case, you will need to explicitly reacquire the quiesce:

```
QUIESCE TABLESPACES FOR TABLE <fully qualified table name> EXCLUSIVE
```

Reacquiring the quiesce succeeds only when it is performed by the same user who originally quiesced the table space (possibly implicitly by issuing a Load command) and when the connection under which the original quiesce was acquired has been terminated.

Comparing Load and Import

The following table summarizes the main differences between the Load and Import utilities:

Import Utility	Load Utility
Performs SQL INSERTs. Slow for large input files, but easier to use than Load.	Writes full pages of data directly to table space containers. Significantly faster than Import for large input files.
Restricts write access to the table being loaded. Uncommitted read access to the table allowed when executing in INSERT mode. Other tables can be accessed without restrictions.	Restricts all access to all table spaces containing parts of the target table.
Fully logged.	Performs only minimal logging.
Automatically performs rollback on error.	Failure in Load leaves table spaces inaccessible. Error recovery requires issuing a RESTART or TERMINATE.
No special considerations for roll-forward recovery.	Provides three different options for roll-forward recovery: COPY YES, COPY NO, and NONRECOVERABLE.

Table 10-2.   *Functionality Comparison Between Load and Import*

MAINTAINING DATA

Import Utility	Load Utility
Fires triggers; validates all constraints.	Doesn't fire triggers; doesn't verify constraints (with the exception of the uniqueness constraint).
	Requires prepartitioned input in a partitioned database environment. Use the AutoLoader utility when loading data into a partitioned table.

Table 10-2.   *Functionality Comparison Between Load and Import* (continued)

Copying Entire Databases with db2move

The db2move tool is provided with DB2. It performs a copy of a group of tables by exporting them to IXF and then recreates them in a different database using the IMPORT CREATE mode. The default group of tables contains all user tables in the database, effectively allowing the copy of an entire database with a single command.

Backup and restore also allow you to create a copy of the entire database and then restore it to a different machine. However, DB2 does not support cross-platform backup and restore, except between Solaris and HP-UX.

The db2move tool is basically an application that connects to a database, queries its catalogs for a full list of user tables, and invokes the Export API to individually unload all user tables to IXF. When used in the reverse direction, that is, with the IMPORT option, it simply connects to a database and recreates all the previously exported tables from its internal list of IXF files. Note that the IXF format does not store all of the information about the table definition; for example, no trigger definition or referential integrity information is maintained. Thus, it might be necessary to use the db2look tool when exporting the database via db2move, to ensure that all pertinent information is preserved and can be recreated if necessary.

Basic db2move Syntax and Usage Examples

The basic db2move syntax is as follows:

```
db2move <database name> <action> <additional options>
```

The *action* parameter can be EXPORT, IMPORT, or LOAD, and it determines the mode in which the utility executes.

Here is an example of using db2move with the EXPORT option:

```
db2move SAMPLE EXPORT
```

Once executed, the preceding command exports all the user tables' data and definitions to IXF files in the current working directory numbered in ascending order. It also creates the db2move.lst control file, which contains information about all the tables exported and the names of their corresponding output files:

```
!"MIRO     "."ORG"!tab1.ixf!tab1.msg!
!"MIRO     "."STAFF"!tab2.ixf!tab2.msg!
!"MIRO     "."DEPARTMENT"!tab3.ixf!tab3.msg!
!"MIRO     "."EMPLOYEE"!tab4.ixf!tab4.msg!
!"MIRO     "."EMP_ACT"!tab5.ixf!tab5.msg!
!"MIRO     "."PROJECT"!tab6.ixf!tab6.msg!
!"MIRO     "."EMP_PHOTO"!tab7.ixf!tab7.msg!
!"MIRO     "."EMP_RESUME"!tab8.ixf!tab8.msg!
!"MIRO     "."SALES"!tab9.ixf!tab9.msg!
!"MIRO     "."CL_SCHED"!tab10.ixf!tab10.msg!
!"MIRO     "."IN_TRAY"!tab11.ixf!tab11.msg!
!"MIRO     "."T"!tab12.ixf!tab12.msg!
!"MIRO     "."B"!tab13.ixf!tab13.msg!
```

The current directory and all of its contents can than be moved to a different machine, where a newly created database can be populated with the data generated during Export:

```
db2move NEW_SAMPLE IMPORT
```

After the preceding command has finished executing, all of the user tables from the SAMPLE database, including their contents, will have been copied to the new NEW_SAMPLE database. When using db2move with the LOAD option, you must create the target tables in the new database prior to invoking db2move.

Chapter 11

Replicating Data

With the evolving needs of database users, the ability to maintain duplicate sets of data in more than one central location has increased. For example, as technology continues to evolve, so does the number of mobile users with laptop computers who need to access data from a base source. And there is not only a need to access existing data, but also to manipulate and update it. This process of creating and maintaining duplicate versions of a database is known as *data replication.*

Data replication supports flexibility in database environments by enabling you to maintain your data from more than one place. It enables you to work with a local copy of a database, but also to manipulate it as if you were updating one centralized database. Because data is rarely static, it is often necessary for you to synchronize all sets of data so that changes made to one data set are reflected in the others. Data replication allows you to keep the local database copy (the *target*) in synch with the master database copy (the *source*). Data replication is the most efficient method of database access for database applications whose users are geographically distributed.

This chapter introduces you to the concepts, components, and processes of data replication. For more information on replication, refer to the *IBM DB2 Data Replication Guide and Reference* that is available through the DB2 Information Center, if installed, or from the DB2 Technical Library web site at www-4.ibm.com/software/data/db2/library.

Data Replication Concepts

To fully understand data replication and its potential benefits, it is important to understand the underlying concepts associated with the process. A number of key concepts are associated with database replication that you should be familiar with:

- Data replication source
- Registration
- Subscription sets
- Subscription set members
- Data replication target
- Capture program
- Apply program
- Apply qualifier
- Control tables
- Logical servers
- Before- and after-image data
- Data manipulation

Data Replication Source

A *data replication source* is one of the basic elements of the data replication scenario. In simple terms, it is the table or view from which you want to copy data. The source is available to you from any database located on the network, and you must define it as a replication source only once.

Registration

Registration is the process of defining a table or view as a replication source. By defining the replication source, you determine how your replication environment will act. A source table or view is registered only once, and a particular registration can be associated with only one database.

Subscription Sets

To replicate data from the source, you must create a relationship between the replication source and the replication target. The attributes of this association are defined by using *subscription sets*. The following attributes are defined when you create a subscription set:

- Subscription set name
- Source and target servers
- Apply qualifier
- Replication start times, frequency, and whether to use interval, event timing, or both
- Data blocking

By using subscription sets, you ensure that all of the subscription set members have equal attributes. They also preserve referential integrity by allowing you to copy changes that have occurred to multiple related source tables and then apply these changes to the target in a single transaction.

Subscription Set Members

By simple definition, a *subscription set member* is a table or view that is associated with a particular subscription set. A subscription set must have at least one subscription set member for each replication target table or view.

The following attributes are defined when you create a subscription set member:

- Source and target table or view
- Structure of the target table or view
- Columns that you want to replicate
- Rows that you want to replicate

MAINTAINING DATA

Data Replication Target

A *data replication target* is another basic element of the data replication scenario. In simple terms, the target is where you want to copy the data to, and it is always in the form of a table. Many different targets can share the same replication source. You can define a target table and its structure when you define a subscription set member.

Capture Program

After you have used an administration interface, such as the Control Center, to set up your data replication environment, you must use the *Capture program* to synchronize your data. By running the Capture program, any updates that you have made to your source data are identified, collected, and stored temporarily in DB2 tables until the Apply program is executed.

Apply Program

Following the Capture program, you must use the *Apply program* to complete the data synchronization process. When you run the Apply program, the changes to the data source that were temporarily stored by the Capture program are applied to the target. Note that the Apply program can also copy data directly from a source to a target.

Apply Qualifier

The *Apply qualifier* associates one or more subscription sets with an Apply program. You specify a case-sensitive string as the value for the Apply qualifier when you define a subscription set. By using more than one Apply qualifier, you can run more than one instance of the Apply program from a single user ID.

Control Tables

The replication components use *control tables* to communicate with each other and to manage replication tasks, such as managing replication sources and targets. Control tables are used to determine how the replication is to be performed and also to monitor the replication performance.

You use the DB2 UDB Control Center to create the control tables. The tables are created automatically for you at all servers in your replication environment, so you must be able to connect to all of the necessary databases (control, source, and target) from the Control Center where you are performing the replication administration.

The following are some of the control tables that the Capture program uses in the replication process:

- Register table
- Pruning control table
- Subscription set table

The following are some of the control tables that the Apply program uses in the replication process:

- Unit-of-work table
- Tuning parameters table
- Register table

Logical Servers

All of the replication components (administration interface, Apply program, and Capture program) reside on a *logical server*. In the context of data replication, logical servers refer to *databases*, not to servers in the typical client/server scenario.

There are three types of logical servers: source, target, and control.

Source Server

The *source server* is the home of the Capture program, the source tables that you want to replicate, and the control tables for the Capture program that are also used by the Apply program.

Target Server

The *target server* is the home of the target tables.

Control Server

The *control server* is the home of the control tables for the Apply program. Note that the Apply program can reside on any of the logical servers in the network. It can connect to the source, target, and control servers by using DB2 distributed technology.

Before- and After-Image Data

The data that exists at the target before updates or changes are applied is known as the *before-image data*. Subsequently, the updated target data is the *after-image data*. When you replicate data, you have the option of keeping an image (copy) of the data from before the changes were applied. This is obviously a benefit for rollback and auditing purposes.

Data Manipulation

Even though you are using the data replication process to copy data from a source to a target, you can *manipulate* how your data is presented in the target by customizing the data replication process. For example, you can replicate a subset of a source table, create a simple view of the source data and have the view replicated to the target, or use joins and unions to alter the presentation of your target data.

Data Replication Components

Three primary components are involved in the data replication process:

- An administration interface: either DB2 Control Center or DataJoiner Replication Administration (DJRA)
- Capture mechanisms
- Apply program

The Administration Interface

One of the primary components of the data replication process is the *administration interface*. It is a focal point for creating replication components and for administering replication tasks.

There are two principal tools that can be used as an administration interface:

- DB2 Control Center
- DataJoiner Replication Administration Tool (DJRA)

Although both of these tools are available for data replication administration, DJRA must be used if you have a replication environment that contains non-IBM databases.

The DB2 Control Center

The *DB2 Control Center* is the primary database administration tool for DB2, as well as the primary interface for you to administer data replication. You can use the DB2 Control Center to complete replication tasks such as the following:

- Define data replication sources (tables and views)
- Define data replication targets
- Define or remove subscription sets
- Remove subscription-set members from existing subscription sets

DataJoiner Replication Administration Tool

The *DataJoiner Replication Administration (DJRA)* tool can be used for DB2-to-DB2 replication; however, you *must* use DJRA if your replication environment contains non-IBM databases.

Capture Mechanisms

The following mechanisms are available to synchronize data in the replication process:

- Capture program
- Capture triggers

The Capture Program

After you have used the Control Center to set up your data replication environment, you must use the *Capture program* to synchronize your data. The Capture program is used if the source is a DB2 table and runs at the source server. By running the Capture program, any updates that you have made to your source data are identified, collected, and stored temporarily in DB2 tables.

The Capture program normally runs continuously; however, you can stop it when modifying replication sources or running utilities.

Capture Triggers

Capture triggers promote changes that you make to the source when the source table is a non-IBM database (except for Teradata, Microsoft Access, and Microsoft Jet). Capture triggers are fired when either an UPDATE, INSERT, or DELETE event occurs.

Apply Program

Following the Capture program, you must use the *Apply program* to complete the data synchronization process. When you run the Apply program, the data source updates and changes that were temporarily stored by the Capture program are applied to the target. If the source tables are non-IBM databases, the Apply program reads the data from a nickname. The Apply program can also copy data directly from a source to a target.

The Apply program generally runs at the target server; however, you can run it at any server in your network that can connect to the source, control, and target servers.

Planning Replication

As with any technical operating environment, you must first determine the appropriate replication environment to suit your needs before you can move forward with your task of performing data replication. To aid in your planning, ask yourself the following questions:

- Where will the source data come from?
- How many copies (or targets) do I need and where will they be located?
- Do I want all or only part of the information copied, or do I want only changes copied?
- How synchronized do I want my copies (or targets) to be?
- Who needs to access the data and how frequently do they need to access it?
- What resources are available to me for optimum performance?

MAINTAINING DATA

Once you have determined your application data requirements, you can begin to plan an environment that best suits your replication needs. You can customize the replication scenario based on your answers to the preceding questions.

Design Decisions

The configuration of your replication environment should be a direct result of your operating needs. You can make a number of design decisions to determine the parameters of your data replication environment. The following are a few of these design decisions:

- Replication configurations
- Control server
- Target table types
- Constraint levels
- Use of joins

Replication Configurations

Although a number of data replication configurations are available, four primary configurations are used most often: data distribution, data consolidation, update anywhere, and occasionally connected. These configurations are explained in Table 11-1.

Based on your data requirements, you must define your replication configuration by determining which one, or combination, of these configurations to use.

Control Server

You will experience improved performance in your data replication environment if your control tables are on the same server as the Apply program, as opposed to having the control tables locally. This increased performance occurs because the Apply program frequently reads the control tables at the control server; thus, it makes sense to have them at the control server too.

Configuration Type	Description
Data distribution	Source data resides on a source server.
Data consolidation	A central database server acts as a repository for data that comes from several data sources.
Update anywhere	Replication targets are read-write tables.
Occasionally connected	Users can connect to and transfer data as required.

Table 11-1. *Data Replication Configuration Types and Descriptions*

Target Table Types

The *target table type* that you choose depends on whether you want the target table type to be read-only or read-write. "Read-only" in this context means that only the Apply program has the ability to change the target table. The target table type is set through the DB2 Control Center.

Table 11-2 describes each of the target table types.

Constraint Levels

If you have target tables that are replica tables, you must use *referential constraints* to enforce referential integrity. As previously noted, the definition of the subscription sets ensures the referential integrity of the other target table types if the sets are defined properly.

Use of Joins

Joins can be used in the replication process to allow you to replicate data from more than one source to a single target or to structure your target data in a manner different from the source table.

A Data Replication Example

There are numerous possible data replication scenarios that could be implemented in your operating environment. These scenarios range in complexity depending on your operating needs. The following is a basic example to provide an overview of the data replication process.

Table Type	Description
User copy	Most commonly used type. A read-only copy of the replication source. No columns are added during the replication process.
Point-in-time	Same as user copy table, except that a time stamp column is added to indicate when the update occurred.
Aggregate tables	Read-only tables that use SQL column functions to compute summaries of the contents of the source tables or of the changes made to the source tables.
Replica	The only read-write target table type. You can change the target data and replicate the changes back to the source.

Table 11-2. *Target Table Types and Descriptions*

Preliminary Steps

First, you must ensure that your system is set up correctly to perform the data replication example:

1. Ensure that DB2 for Windows NT is installed on your computer.

2. Ensure that your DB2 Control Center uses the default settings; otherwise, some of the steps in this scenario will not exactly match what you see as your output.

3. Use the DB2 Control Center to create a new database called COPYDB to use as the target and control server. To create the database, right-click the Database folder and use the wizard with default options.

Creating the Replication Source

Once you have determined that your system has been set up properly, the next step is to create a *replication source* by following these steps:

1. In the Control Center, right-click the Tables folder for the database that you want to use as your source. Select it to display the database's tables in the Control Center contents pane (the pane on the right-hand side).

2. Right-click the table that you want to define as your replication source and select Define as a Replication Source | Custom.

3. In the Define as Replication Source window, ensure that all of the table's columns are selected. Also ensure that no before images are captured for any of the columns.

4. Ensure that the Data Capture is Full Refresh Only option and the options available at the bottom of the window are not selected.

5. Click OK. The Run Now or Save SQL window will open.

6. Click Run Now and then click OK. A message will appear, indicating that the replication source was successfully defined.

Creating the Replication Subscription and Setting the Replication Target

Once the replication source has been defined, the *replication subscription* must be created. Follow these steps:

1. To view the replication source that you created, right-click the Replication Sources folder in the left pane of the Control Center window. Select Refresh.

2. In the right-pane of the Control Center, right-click the table that you defined as the source and select Define Subscription. The Define Subscription window will open.

3. Type a name for the subscription in the Subscription Name text box. (You can provide any name.)

4. In the Target Server drop-down list box, select the name of the target database that you created. For this example, the target database is the COPYDB database that was created in the "Preliminary Steps" section.

5. Type a name for the Apply qualifier in the Apply Qualifier text box. (You can provide any name.)

6. Select the Create Table check box.

7. Click the Advanced button. The Advanced Subscription Definition window will open.

8. Click the Target Type tab and select both the Target Table Is Read-Only and the User Copy options.

9. Click the Target Columns tab. Ensure that all of the columns are selected under the Subscribe column.

Note   *For this example, we are not setting any of the options available from the Rows tab.*

MAINTAINING DATA

10. Accept the default value for all other options, and click OK. You will be returned to the Define Replication Subscription window.

11. Click the Timing button. The Subscription Timing window will open.

12. On the Source to Target tab, set the relative timing interval to every two minutes. This indicates the replication frequency.

13. Click OK to close the Subscription Timing window, and then click OK in the Define Replication Subscription window. The Run Now or Save SQL window will open.

14. From the drop-down box, select the name of the target database that will act as the Control Server. For this example, the target database is the COPYDB database that was created in the "Preliminary Steps" section. Select the Run Now option and click OK To Create The Subscription. A message will appear indicating that the replication subscription was successfully defined.

Using the Capture Program to Replicate the Data

Once the replication source and subscription have been created, the data can be replicated. To do this, run the Capture program by following these steps:

1. Open a DB2 command window.

2. Type **asnccp** *<source database name>*, where *<source database name>* is the name of the database from which you are copying. Press Enter.

If the command prompt returns no error messages, the Capture program has run successfully.

Using the Apply Program to Complete Replication

After the Capture program has completed, you must run the Apply program to complete the data replication process. As previously discussed, the Apply program takes the temporarily stored data and applies (copies) it to the replication target. To run the Apply program, follow these steps:

1. Open a DB2 command window.

2. Type **asnapply** *<apply qualifier name> <target database name>*, where *<apply qualifier name>* is the name that you gave to the Apply qualifier in Step 5 of the "Creating the Replication Subscription and Setting the Replication Target" section, and *<target database name>* is the name of the target database to which you are copying the data. Press Enter.

If the program begins to run and no command prompt appears, the Apply program is running successfully. Once the Apply program has finished processing, the data replication process has been completed.

The Complete Reference

Chapter 12

Recovering Data

A database can become unusable because of hardware or software failure (or both), and different failure scenarios may require different recovery actions. You should have a rehearsed strategy in place to protect your database against the possibility of failure.

This chapter describes different recovery methods that you can use if you experience a problem with a database, and it shows you how to determine which recovery method is best suited to your business environment. Each recovery method is described, along with the associated concepts and commands to support these methods.

One type of problem that requires point-in-time roll-forward recovery is the corruption of data caused by errant logic or incorrect input in an application. You can use roll-forward recovery to recover the database to a point in time that is close to when the application began working with the database. Or you can attempt to back out the effects of the application on the database by executing the transactions in reverse. You must exercise caution if you decide to follow the second approach. This chapter does not provide information about recovering from application errors.

This chapter also does not discuss recovery strategies or considerations for partitioned databases, nor for databases that contain DATALINK columns. It doesn't describe how to use Tivoli Storage Manager (TSM) for managing database and table space backups, nor how to use a user exit when implementing a recovery solution. For information about these topics, see the *IBM DB2 Universal Database Data Recovery and High Availability Guide and Reference.*

Overview of Recovery

You need to know the strategies available to you when you have database problems, including difficulties with media and storage, power interruptions, and application failures. You can back up your database or individual table spaces and then rebuild them should they be damaged or corrupted in some way.

A *database backup* is the same as any other data backup: it involves taking a copy of the database's data and storing it on a different medium in case of failure or damage to the original. The simplest type of database backup involves shutting down the database to ensure that no further transactions occur and then simply copying it.

The rebuilding of the database is called *recovery*. In *crash recovery*, DB2 automatically attempts to recover the database after a failure. If the database is damaged, there are two ways to recover it: version recovery and roll-forward recovery.

Crash Recovery Basics

Crash recovery protects a database from being left in an inconsistent, or unusable, state. *Transactions* (or units of work) against the database can be interrupted unexpectedly, and if a failure occurs before all of the changes that are part of the unit of work are completed and committed, the database is left in an inconsistent and unusable state.

When this happens, the database needs to be moved to a consistent and usable state by rolling back incomplete transactions and completing committed transactions that were still in memory when the crash occurred.

When a database is in a consistent and usable state, it has attained what is known as a *point of consistency*—all transactions are resolved and the data is available to other users or applications. An offline database backup represents a point of consistency.

You can move to a point of consistency following a crash by invoking the RESTART DATABASE command. If you want this done in every case of a failure, consider using the automatic restart enable (*autorestart*) configuration parameter. The default behavior for this database configuration parameter is to invoke the RESTART DATABASE command whenever it is needed. When the *autorestart* configuration parameter is enabled, the next connect request to the database after a failure causes the RESTART DATABASE command to be invoked.

Crash recovery moves the database to a consistent and usable state. However, what if crash recovery is applied to a database that is enabled for forward recovery (that is, the *logretain* configuration parameter is set to RECOVERY or the *userexit* configuration parameter is enabled), and an error occurs during crash recovery that is attributable to an individual table space? That table space must be taken offline and cannot be accessed until it is repaired. Crash recovery continues. At the completion of crash recovery, the other table spaces in the database are still usable, and connections to the database can be established. (There are exceptions involving the table spaces that have temporary tables or the system catalog tables. These issues are described in "Roll-Forward Recovery Basics" later in this chapter.)

Version Recovery Basics

Version recovery is performed on *nonrecoverable databases*: those that have both the *logretain* and the *userexit* database configuration parameters disabled. This means that the only logs that are kept are those required for crash recovery—these logs are known as *active logs,* and they contain current transaction data. Version recovery from an offline backup of the database is the only means of recovery for a nonrecoverable database. (An *offline backup* means that no other application can use the database when the backup operation is in progress.) Such a database can only be restored offline. It is restored to the state it was in when the backup image was taken. Every unit of work from the time of the backup to the time of the failure is lost.

If you use the version recovery method, you must schedule and perform full backups of the database regularly.

Roll-Forward Recovery Basics

To use the roll-forward recovery method, you must have taken a backup of the database and archived the logs (by enabling either the *logretain* or the *userexit* database configuration parameters, or both). Active logs are still available for crash recovery, but you also have the archived logs, which contain committed transaction data.

A nonrecoverable database can only be restored offline from a backup of the database, and it is restored to the state it was in when the backup image was taken. However, with a recoverable database, you can restore it and roll the database forward (that is, past the time when the backup image was taken) by using the active and archived logs either to a specific point in time or to the end of the active logs.

Restoring the database and specifying the WITHOUT ROLLING FORWARD option is equivalent to using the version recovery method—the database is restored to a state identical to the one at the time that the offline backup image was made. If you restore the database and do not specify the WITHOUT ROLLING FORWARD option for the restore database operation, the database will be in roll-forward pending state at the end of the restore operation. This allows roll-forward recovery to take place.

Recoverable database backup operations can be performed either offline or *online* (that is, other applications can connect to the database during the backup operation). However, database-wide restore and roll-forward operations must always be performed offline. During an online backup operation, the logs record the ongoing transactions, and roll-forward recovery ensures that all table changes are captured and reapplied if that backup is restored.

The two types of roll-forward recovery to consider are the following:

- **Database roll-forward recovery** In this type of roll-forward recovery, transactions recorded in database logs are applied following the database restore operation. The database logs record all changes made to the database. This method completes the recovery of the database to its state at a particular point in time, or to its state immediately before the failure (that is, to the end of the active logs).

- **Table space restore and roll forward** If the database is enabled for forward recovery, it is also possible to back up, restore, and roll forward table spaces. To perform a table space restore and roll-forward operation, you need a backup image of either the entire database (that is, all of the table spaces), or one or more individual table spaces. You also need the log records that affect the table spaces that are to be recovered. You can roll forward through the logs to one of two points:

  - The end of the logs
  - A particular point in time (called *point-in-time recovery*)

When using the roll-forward recovery method with table spaces, you must identify key table spaces in the database to be recovered, as well as schedule and perform a backup of the database (or the key table spaces) regularly.

Note   *Table spaces that are not selected at the time of the backup operation will not be in the same state as those that were restored.*

Table space roll-forward recovery can be used in the following two situations:

■ After a table space restore operation, the table space is always in roll-forward pending state, and it must be rolled forward. Invoking the ROLLFORWARD DATABASE command will apply the logs against the table spaces to either a point in time or to the end of the logs.

■ If one or more table spaces are in roll-forward pending state after crash recovery, the problem with the table space must first be corrected. In some cases, correcting the problem with the table space does not involve performing a restore database operation. For example, a power loss could leave the table space in roll-forward pending state. If the problem is corrected before crash recovery, crash recovery may be sufficient to take the database to a consistent, usable state, and a restore database operation will not be required in this case. Once the problem with the table space is corrected, you can use the ROLLFORWARD DATABASE command to apply the logs against the table spaces to either a point in time or to the end of the logs.

 If the table space in error contains the system catalog tables, you will not be able to start the database. You must restore the SYSCATSPACE table space and perform roll-forward recovery to the end of the logs.

Factors Affecting Recovery

To decide which database recovery method to use, you must consider the following key factors:

■ Will the database be recoverable or nonrecoverable?

■ How near to the time of failure will you need to recover the database (the point of recovery)?

■ How much time can be spent recovering the database? This includes the following:

■ **Time between backups**   With a nonrecoverable database, the greater the time between backups, the greater the potential loss of data. With a recoverable database, a longer time between backups means that the logs will contain more changes to be reapplied to the database during the roll-forward operation.

■ **Time the database is usable or accessible**   With an online backup, data is available to users. With an offline backup, users cannot access the data.

■ How much storage space can be allocated for backup copies and archived logs?

■ Will you be using table space–level or full database-level backups?

In general, a database maintenance and recovery strategy should ensure that all information is available when it is required for database recovery. The strategy should include a regular schedule for taking database backups, as well as scheduled backups when a database is created. In addition to these basic requirements, a good strategy includes elements that reduce the likelihood and impact of database failure.

While the general focus of this section is on recovering the database, your overall recovery planning should also include recovering the following:

- The operating system and DB2 executables

- Applications, user-defined functions (UDFs), and stored procedure code in operating system libraries

- Commands for creating DB2 instances and non-DB2 resources

- Operating system security

- Load copies from a load operation (if you specify COPY YES on the LOAD command)

General Database Considerations

The following sections describe basic information that you should be familiar with before deciding on a recovery strategy for your database. Topics include recoverable and nonrecoverable databases, the implications for recovery that arise when using one strategy over the other, and the different types of log strategies that you can use with your database. Information is also provided on different ways of managing logs and work tables.

Recoverable and Nonrecoverable Databases

If you can easily recreate the data, consider making the database holding that data a nonrecoverable database. For example, the following should be considered for placement within a nonrecoverable database:

- Tables that hold data from an outside source, and those tables that are used for read-only applications (their data is not mixed with existing data).

- Tables with small amounts of data. Here, recovery is not a problem. Not enough logging is done for the data to justify the added complexity of managing log files and rolling forward after a restore.

- Large tables in which small numbers of rows are periodically added. Again, there is not enough volatility to justify managing log files and rolling forward after a restore operation.

If you cannot easily recreate the data, make the database holding that data a recoverable database. The following are examples of data that should be part of a recoverable database:

- Data that you cannot recreate. This includes data whose source is destroyed after the data is loaded and data that is manually entered into tables.

■ Data that is modified by applications or workstation users after it is loaded into the database.

Point of Recovery

The version and roll-forward recovery methods provide different points of recovery. The version method involves making an offline, full database backup copy of the database at scheduled times, which results in a recovered database that is only as current as the backup copy that was restored. For instance, if you make a backup copy at the end of each day and you lose the database midway through the next day, you will lose half a day of changes.

In the roll-forward recovery method, changes made to the database are retained in logs. With this method, you first restore the database or table spaces using a backup copy; then you use the logs to reapply changes that were made to the database since the backup copy was created.

With roll-forward recovery enabled, you can also take advantage of online backup and table space backups. Full database and table space roll-forward recovery allow you to recover to the end of the logs or to a specified point in time. For instance, if an application corrupted the database, you could start with a restored copy of the database and roll forward changes up to just before that application started. No units of work written to the logs after the time specified are reapplied.

Logging Strategies

All databases have logs associated with them. These logs keep records of database changes. If a database needs to be restored to a point beyond the last full offline backup, then logs are required to roll the data forward to the point of failure.

You can use two types of log strategies: circular and archive. Each provides a different level of recovery capability.

Circular logging is the default behavior when a new database is created. As the name suggests, circular logging uses a ring of logs to provide recovery from transaction failures and system crashes. The logs are used and retained only to the point of ensuring the integrity of current transactions, so circular logging does not allow you to roll forward a database through prior transactions from the last full backup. With this type of logging, only full offline backups of the database can be used to restore the database. Recovery from media failures and disasters must be done by restoring from a full offline backup, and all changes since the last backup are lost. Because this type of restore recovers your data to the specific point in time of the full backup, it is called *version recovery*.

The active logs in circular logging are used during crash recovery to prevent a failure (system power or application error) from leaving a database in an inconsistent state. The RESTART DATABASE command uses the active logs, if needed, to move the database to a consistent and usable state. During crash recovery, changes recorded in these logs that were not committed because of the failure are rolled back. Changes that were committed but that were not physically written from memory (the buffer pool) to disk (the database containers) are redone. These actions ensure the integrity of the database. The ROLLFORWARD DATABASE command may also use the active logs, if needed, during a point-in-time recovery or during a recovery to the end of the logs. With circular logging, all logs are located in the database log path directory (which is specified by the *logpath* configuration parameter).

Use *archive logging* if you want to be able to perform roll-forward recovery on the database. Archived logs can be of two types:

- **Online archived logs**   When changes in the active log are no longer needed for normal processing, the log is closed and it becomes an archived log. An archived log is said to be online when it is stored in the database log path directory.

- **Offline archived logs**   An archived log is said to be offline when it is no longer found in the database log path directory. You can also store archived logs in a location other than the database log path directory by using a user exit program. (For additional information, see the description of user exits in the *IBM DB2 Universal Database Data Recovery and High Availability Guide and Reference*.)

Roll-forward recovery can use both archived logs and active logs to rebuild a database either to the end of the logs or to a specific point in time. The roll-forward function achieves this by reapplying committed changes found in the archived and active logs to the restored database.

Roll-forward recovery can also use logs to rebuild a table space by reapplying committed changes in both archived and active logs. You can recover a table space to the end of the logs or to a specific point in time.

Archiving Database Logs for Roll-Forward Recovery

During an online backup, all changes that occur to data while the online backup is running are logged. When an online backup is restored, you must roll forward the database at least to the point in time at which the backup was completed. This ensures that the data in the database is consistent. To be able to roll forward, you must archive the logs and make them available when the database is to be restored.

Two database configuration parameters also allow you to change where archived logs are stored: the newlogpath parameter and the userexit parameter. Changing the *newlogpath* parameter also affects where active logs are stored.

To determine which log extents in the database log path directory are archived logs, check the value of the *loghead* database configuration parameter. This parameter indicates the lowest numbered log that is active. Those logs with sequence numbers less than *loghead* are archived logs and can be moved. You can check the value of this parameter by using the Control Center. You can also use the command line processor to enter the GET DATABASE CONFIGURATION command. See the First Active Log File field in the output returned by this command for the value of *loghead*.

If you erase an active log, the database becomes unusable and must be restored before it can be used again. You will be able to roll forward only up to the first log that was erased.

Log Placement

You can improve performance for databases that are frequently updated by placing the logs on a separate device. In the case of an online transaction processing (OLTP) environment, often, more I/O is needed to write data to the logs than to store a row of data. Placing the logs on a separate device minimizes the disk arm movement that is required to move between a log and the database files.

You should also consider which other files are on the disk. For example, moving the logs to the disk used for system paging in a system that has insufficient real memory will defeat your tuning efforts.

On Demand Log Archive

DB2 also supports the closing (and, if the user exit option is enabled, the archiving) of the active log for a recoverable database at any time. This allows you to collect a complete set of log files up to a known point and then use these log files to update a standby database.

 On demand log archiving does not guarantee that the log files will be archived immediately; it truncates the log file and issues an archive request, but the request is still subject to delays associated with the user exit program.

You can initiate on demand log archiving by invoking the DB2 ARCHIVE LOG command or by calling the db2ArchiveLog API.

Log Mirroring

DB2 supports log mirroring at the database level. Mirroring log files helps protect a database from two types of loss:

- Accidental deletion of an active log
- Data corruption caused by hardware failure

If you are concerned that your active logs may be damaged (as a result of a disk crash), consider using the DB2 registry variable DB2_NEWLOGPATH2.This registry variable specifies the secondary path where the database will write an identical, secondary copy of the log files. You should place the secondary log path on a physically separate disk (preferably one that is also on a different disk controller). That way, the disk controller cannot be a single point of failure.

 Because Windows NT and OS/2 do not allow mounting a device under an arbitrary path name, it is not possible (on these platforms) to specify a secondary path on a separate device.

MAINTAINING DATA

DB2_NEWLOGPATH2 can be enabled (set to 1) or disabled (set to 0). The default value is 0. If this variable is set to 1, the secondary path name is the current value of the logpath parameter concatenated with the character 2. For example, in a symmetric multiprocessing (SMP) environment, if logpath is /u/dbuser/sqllogdir/logpath, the secondary log path will be /u/dbuser/sqllogdir/logpath2.

When DB2_NEWLOGPATH2 is first enabled, it will not be used until the current log file is completed on the next database startup. This is similar to how the newlogpath parameter is used.

If there is an error writing to either the primary or secondary log path, the database will mark the failing path as bad, write a message to the db2diag.log file, and write subsequent log records only to the remaining good log path. DB2 will not attempt to use the bad path again until the current log file is completed. When DB2 needs to open the next log file, it will verify that this path is valid, and if so, will begin to use it. If not, DB2 will not attempt to use the path again until the next log file is accessed for the first time. There is no attempt to synchronize the logs, but DB2 keeps information about access errors so that the correct paths are used when log files are archived. If a failure occurs while writing to the remaining good log path, the database ends abnormally.

Reducing Logging on Work Tables

If your application creates and populates work tables from master tables, and you are not concerned about the recoverability of these work tables because they can be easily recreated from the master tables, you may want to create the work tables specifying the NOT LOGGED INITIALLY parameter on the CREATE TABLE statement. The advantage of using the NOT LOGGED INITIALLY parameter is that any changes made on the table (including insert, delete, update, or create index operations) in the same unit of work that creates the table will not be logged. This not only reduces the logging that is done, but it may also increase your application's performance. If the table persists after the unit of work, changes that occur to it in subsequent units of work are logged.

You can achieve the same result for existing tables by using the ALTER TABLE statement with the NOT LOGGED INITIALLY parameter. You can also create more than one table with the NOT LOGGED INITIALLY parameter in the same unit of work.

Note	*Changes to the catalog tables and other user tables that occur in the unit of work are still logged.*

Because changes to the table that occur in the same unit of work that that creates the table are not logged, consider the following when deciding to use the NOT LOGGED INITIALLY parameter:

- All changes to the table must be flushed to disk at commit time. This means that the commit may take longer.

- An error returned for any operation in a unit of work in which the table is created will result in the rollback of the entire unit of work (the error returned is SQLCODE -1476, SQLSTATE 40506).

You cannot recover tables that are NOT LOGGED INITIALLY when rolling forward the database. If the roll-forward operation encounters a table that was created with the NOT LOGGED INITIALLY option, the table is marked as unavailable. After the database is recovered, any attempt to access the table returns SQL1477N.

Note | *When a table is created, row-level locks are held on the catalog tables until a COMMIT is done. To take advantage of the no logging behavior, you must populate the table in the same unit of work in which it is created. The locking that occurs on the catalog tables has implications for concurrency. For more information, refer to the description of concurrency in the IBM DB2 Universal Database Administration Guide: Performance.*

Using Declared Temporary Tables

If you plan to use declared temporary tables as work tables, note the following:

- Declared temporary tables are not created in the catalog tables; therefore, locks are not held on the catalog tables.
- Logging is not performed against declared temporary tables, even after the first COMMIT.
- Use the ON COMMIT PRESERVE option to keep the rows in the table after a COMMIT; otherwise, all rows will be deleted.
- Only the application that creates the declared temporary table can access that instance of the table.
- The table is implicitly dropped when the application connection to the database is dropped.

Errors in operation during a unit of work using a declared temporary table do not cause the unit of work to be completely rolled back. However, an error in operation in a statement changing the contents of a declared temporary table will delete all the rows in that table. A rollback of the unit of work (or a savepoint) will delete all rows in declared temporary tables that were modified in that unit of work (or savepoint).

For more information about declared temporary tables and their limitations, refer to the DECLARE GLOBAL TEMPORARY TABLE statement in the *IBM DB2 Universal Database SQL Reference*.

General Backup Considerations

The sections that follow provide general information that you should consider when deciding on a backup strategy for your database. Topics include how to identify backup images and information about them, how to use suspended I/O to work with split mirror images of your database, how often you should perform backups, and how long it takes to do them. Other sections describe incremental backups, storage space requirements, and how the relationships that exist among tables in the database should affect your recovery strategy. The final sections cover restrictions and capabilities that are operating system–specific.

Backup Images Created by BACKUP

Backup images are created at the target specified when you call the BACKUP command:

- In the directory for disk backups
- At the device specified for tape backups
- At a TSM server
- At another vendor's server

The recovery history file is updated automatically with summary information whenever you carry out a backup or restore of a full database. This file can be a useful tracking mechanism for restore activity within a database. This file is created in the same directory as the database configuration file. For more information about the recovery history file, see the "Recovery History File Information" section later in this chapter.

In UNIX-based environments, the filenames created on disk consist of a concatenation of the following information, separated by periods; on other platforms, a four-level subdirectory tree is used:

- **Database alias**   A one-to-eight-character database alias name that was supplied when the backup command was invoked.
- **Type**   The type of backup taken, where 0 is for full database, 3 is for a table space backup, and 4 is for a backup generated by the LOAD...COPY TO command.
- **Instance name**   A one-to-eight-character name of the current instance of the database manager that is taken from the DB2INSTANCE environment variable.
- **Node number**   The node number.
- **Catalog node number**   The node number of the database's catalog node.
- **Time stamp**   A fourteen-character representation of the date and time the backup was performed. The timestamp is in the format *yyyymmddhhnnss,* where
  - *yyyy* is the year (1995 to 9999)
  - *mm* is the month (01 to 12)
  - *dd* is the day of the month (01 to 31)
  - *hh* is the hour (00 to 23)
  - *nn* is the minutes (00 to 59)
  - *ss* is the seconds (00 to 59)
- **Sequence number**   A three-digit sequence number used as a file extension.

In UNIX-based operating systems, the format appears as follows:

```
Database alias.Type.Instance name.NODEnnnn
.CATNnnnn.timestamp.number
```

On other operating systems, the format looks like this:

```
Database alias.Type\Instance name.NODEnnn
\CATNnnn\yyyymmdd\hhmmss.number
```

For example, in UNIX-based environments, a database named STAFF on the DB201 instance may be backed up on disk to a file named

```
STAFF.0.DB201.NODE0000.CATN0000.19950922120112.001
```

For tape-directed output, filenames are not created; however, the preceding information is stored in the backup header for later verification purposes.

 Note   *If you want to use tape media for database backup and restore operations, a tape device must be available through the standard operating system interface.*

Displaying Backup Information

The db2ckbkp backup utility is used to display information about existing backup images. It allows you to do the following:

■ Test the integrity of a backup image and determine whether it can be restored.

■ Display the information about the backup that is stored in the backup header.

You must have read permissions on the backup images you specify when using this utility.

To simply verify the existence of a backup image, you can use the utility as follows:

```
db2ckbkp STAFF.0.DB201.NODE0000.CATNOOOO.19950922120112.001
```

The output from this utility is similar to this:

```
[1] Buffers processed:  ##
Image Verification Complete - successful.
```

Using Online Split Mirror and Suspended I/O Support

Suspended I/O supports continuous system availability by providing a full implementation for online split mirror handling; that is, splitting a mirror without shutting down the database. A *split mirror* is an instantaneous copy of the database that can be made by mirroring the disks containing the data and splitting the mirror when a copy is required. *Disk mirroring* is the process of writing all of your data to two separate hard disks; one is the mirror of the other. *Splitting a mirror* is the process of making a backup copy of the mirror.

If you would rather not back up a large database using the DB2 backup utility, you can make copies from a mirrored image by using suspended I/O and the split mirror function. This approach also provides the following advantages:

- Eliminates backup operation overhead from the production machine.

- Represents a fast way to clone systems.

- Represents a fast implementation of idle standby failover. There is no initial restore operation, and if a roll-forward operation proves to be too slow or encounters errors, reinitialization is very fast. For information about failover, see the *IBM DB2 Universal Database Data Recovery and High Availability Guide and Reference*.

The db2inidb command initializes the split mirror so that it can be used for these purposes:

- For making a clone database. A read-only clone of the primary database can be used, for example, to create reports.

- As a standby database.

- As a backup image.

The db2inidb command can be issued only against the split-off mirror, and the split-off mirror must first run db2inidb before it can be used.

Making a Clone Database   A database clone can represent an offline backup of the primary production database. You cannot, however, back up the cloned database, restore this image on the original system, and roll forward through log files produced on the original system. To clone a database, follow these steps:

- Suspend I/O on the primary database:

```
db2 set write suspend for database
```

- Use an appropriate operating system–level command to split the mirror from the primary database.

- Resume I/O on the primary database:

```
db2 set write resume for database
```

- Attach to the mirrored database from another machine.

- Start the database instance:

```
db2start
```

- Initialize the mirrored database as a clone of the primary database:

```
db2inidb database_alias as snapshot
```

Note   *This command will roll back transactions that are not committed when the split occurs.*

Using the Split Mirror as a Standby Database   As the mirrored (standby) database continually rolls forward through the logs, new logs that are being created by the primary database are continually fetched from the primary system. To use the split mirror as a standby database, follow these steps:

- Suspend I/O on the primary database:

```
db2 set write suspend for database
```

- Use an appropriate operating system–level command to split the mirror from the primary database.
- Resume I/O on the primary database:

```
db2 set write resume for database
```

- Attach the mirrored database to another instance.
- Put the mirrored database in roll-forward pending state:

```
db2inidb database_alias as standby
```

  If you have DMS table spaces (database managed space), you can take a full database backup to offload the overhead of taking a backup on the production database.

- Set up a user exit program to retrieve the most recent log files from the primary system.
- Roll the database forward to the end of the logs.
- Continue retrieving log files and rolling the database forward to the end of the logs until the primary database goes down.

Using the Split Mirror as a Backup Image   To use the split mirror as a backup image, follow these steps:

- Suspend I/O on the primary database:

```
db2 set write suspend for database
```

- Use an appropriate operating system–level command to split the mirror from the primary database.

- Resume I/O on the primary database:

  ```
  db2 set write resume for database
  ```

- Use operating system–level commands to copy the mirrored data and logs over the primary system.

- Start the database instance:

  ```
  db2start
  ```

- Initialize the mirrored database as a backup image that can be used to copy the data on split-off disks back to the disks on the original system. (Do not bring back the file system that contains the log files because the logs will be needed during the roll-forward process.)

  ```
  db2inidb database_alias as mirror
  ```

- Roll forward the database (on the original system) to the end of the logs.

Frequency of Backups

Your recovery plan should allow for regularly scheduled backups because backing up a database requires time and system resources. You should try to ensure that the backup schedule does not interfere with other business activities.

You should take full database backups regularly, even if you archive the logs (which allows for roll-forward recovery). If your recovery strategy includes roll-forward recovery, a recent full database backup means that there are fewer archived logs to apply to the database, which reduces the amount of time required by the ROLLFORWARD utility to recover the database.

Time Required for Backups

If you are concerned about the amount of time needed to apply archived logs when recovering and rolling forward a very active database, consider the cost of backing up the database more frequently. Having more frequent backups reduces the number of archived logs you need to apply when rolling forward.

If the database is recoverable, you can perform a backup while the database is either online or offline. If it is online, other applications or processes can continue to connect to the database, as well as read and modify data while the backup operation is running. If the backup is performed offline, however, only the backup operation can be connected to the database; the rest of your organization cannot connect to the database while the backup task is running.

To reduce the amount of time that the database is not available, consider using online backups. Online backups are supported only if roll-forward recovery is enabled for the database. If roll-forward recovery is enabled and you have a complete set of logs, you can rebuild the database to either a specific point in time or to the end of the logs.

Also consider the following when deciding whether to use online or offline backups:

- You can use an online backup only if you have the database log (or logs) that span the time taken for the backup operation.

- Offline backups are faster than online backups.

If a database contains large amounts of long field and large object (LOB) data, backing up the database could be very time-consuming. Fortunately, the BACKUP command provides the capability of backing up selected table spaces. If you use database-managed space (DMS) table spaces, you can store different types of data in their own table spaces to reduce the time required for backup operations. You can keep table data in one table space, long field and LOB data in another table space, and indexes in another table space. By storing long field and LOB data in separate table spaces, the time required to complete the backup can be reduced by choosing not to back up the table spaces containing the long field and LOB data.

If the long field and LOB data is critical to your business, compare the time it takes to back up these table spaces against the time required to complete the restore operation for these table spaces. If the LOB data can be reproduced from a separate source, choose the NOT LOGGED option when creating or altering a table to include LOB columns.

Incremental Backup and Recovery

As the size of databases, and particularly warehouses, continues to expand into the terabyte and petabyte range, the time and hardware resources required to back up and recover these databases are also growing substantially. Full database and table space backups are not always the best approach when dealing with large databases because the storage requirements for multiple copies of such databases are enormous. Consider the following issues:

- When a small percentage of the data in a warehouse changes, it's not necessary to back up the entire database.

- Appending table spaces to existing databases and then taking only table space backups is risky because data outside of the backed up table spaces may change.

DB2 now supports incremental backup and recovery (but not of long field or LOB data). An *incremental backup* is a backup image that contains pages that have been updated only since the previous backup was taken. In addition to updated data and index pages, each incremental backup image also contains all of the initial database metadata (such as database configuration, table space definitions, database history, and so on) that is normally stored in full backup images.

Two types of incremental backup are supported:

- **Incremental**   An *incremental backup image* is a copy of all database data that has changed since the most recent successful full backup operation. This is also known as a cumulative backup image because a series of incremental backups taken over time will each have the contents of the previous incremental backup images. The predecessor of an incremental backup image is always the most recent successful full backup of the same object.

- **Delta**   A *delta,* or *incremental delta, backup image* is a copy of all database data that has changed since the last successful backup (full, incremental, or delta) of the table space in question. This is also known as a *differential,* or *noncumulative, backup image.* The predecessor of a delta backup image is the most recent successful backup containing a copy of each of the table spaces in the delta backup image.

The key difference between incremental and delta backup images is their behavior when successive backups are taken of an object that is continually changing over time. Each successive incremental image contains the entire contents of the previous incremental image, plus any data that has changed or is new since the previous backup was produced. Delta backup images contain only the pages that have changed since the previous image was produced. Combinations of database and table space incremental backups are permitted in both online and offline modes of operation.

Caution   *Be careful when planning your backup strategy. Combining database and table space incremental backups implies that the predecessor of a database backup (or a table space backup of multiple table spaces) is not necessarily a single image, but could be a unique set of previous database and table space backups taken at different times.*

To rebuild the database or the table space to a consistent state, the recovery process must begin with a consistent image of the entire object (database or table space) to be restored, and it must then apply each of the appropriate incremental backup images in the order described in the "Restoring from Incremental Backup Images" section that follows.

To enable the tracking of database updates, DB2 provides the database configuration parameter trackmod, which can have one of two accepted values:

- **NO**   Incremental backup is not permitted with this configuration. Database page updates are not tracked or recorded in any way.

- **YES**   Incremental backup is permitted with this configuration. When update tracking is enabled, the change becomes effective at the first successful connection to any database in the instance. A full database backup is necessary before an incremental backup can be taken.

The default trackmod setting for existing databases is NO; for new databases, it is YES.

The granularity of the tracking is at the table space level for both system-managed space (SMS) and DMS table spaces. The tracking of updates to the database can have a minimal impact on the run-time performance of transactions that update or insert data.

Restoring from Incremental Backup Images   A restore operation from incremental backup images always consists of the following steps:

1. *Identify the incremental target image.* You must first determine the final image to be restored and request an incremental restore operation from the DB2 restore utility. This image is known as the target image of the incremental restore because it will be the last image to be restored. An incremental restore command against this image may initiate the creation of a new database with the configuration and table space definitions from this target image. You specify the incremental target image by using the TAKEN AT parameter in the RESTORE DATABASE command.

2. *Restore the most recent full database or table space image.* This establishes a baseline against which each of the subsequent incremental backup images can be applied.

3. *Restore each of the required full or table space incremental backup images.* This must be done in the order in which they were produced, on top of the baseline image restored in Step 2.

4. *Repeat Step 3 until the target image from Step 1 is read a second time.* The target image is accessed twice during a complete incremental restore operation. During the first access, only initial data is read from the image; none of the user data is read. The complete image is read and processed only during the second access.

The target image of the incremental restore operation must be accessed twice to ensure that the database is initially configured with the correct history, database configuration, and table space definitions for the database that will be created during the restore operation. When a table space has been dropped since the initial full database backup image was taken, the table space data for that image will be read from the backup images but ignored during incremental restore processing.

The following commands show the different ways in which you can restore a database from an incremental backup:

- db2 restore database sample incremental taken at *ts*

  Where *ts* points to the last incremental backup image to be restored.

- db2 restore database sample incremental taken at *ts1*

  Where *ts1* points to the initial full database (or table space) image.

- db2 restore database sample incremental taken at *tsX*

  Where *tsX* points to each incremental backup image in creation sequence.

Storage Space Required

When deciding which recovery method to use, consider the storage space required. The version recovery method requires space to hold the backup copy of the database and the restored database. The roll-forward recovery method requires space to hold the backup copy of the database or table spaces, the restored database, and the archived database logs.

If a table contains long field or LOB columns, you should consider placing this data into a separate table space. These types of columns will affect your storage space considerations as well as your plan for recovery. With a separate table space for long field and LOB data, and knowing the time required to back up long field and LOB data, you may decide to use a recovery plan that only occasionally saves a backup of this table space. You may also choose, when creating or altering a table that includes LOB columns, not to log changes to those columns. This will reduce the size of the required log space and the corresponding log archive space.

The backup of an SMS table space that contains LOBs can be as much as 40 percent larger than the original table space, depending on the LOB data size in the table space. For example, if you take a backup of a 1GB SMS table space (with LOBs), you will need more than 1GB of disk space when you restore it. This occurs only on file systems that support sparse allocation (for example, on UNIX-based operating systems).

The database logs can use up a large amount of storage. If you plan to use the roll-forward recovery method, you must decide how to manage the archived logs. Your choices are the following:

- Dedicate enough space in the database log path directory to retain the logs.

- Manually copy the logs to a storage device or directory other than the database log path directory after they are no longer in the active set of logs.

- Use a user exit program to copy these logs to another storage device in your environment. See the *IBM DB2 Universal Database Data Recovery and High Availability Guide and Reference* for more information about user exits.

Note   *On OS/2, DB2 supports a user exit program to handle the storage of both database backup images and database logs on standard and nonstandard devices.*

You should consider not overwriting backups and logs, saving more than one full database backup and its associated logs as an extra precaution against the possible loss of the data. This will also affect the amount of storage space required to implement your recovery strategy.

Keeping Related Data Together

You should know the relationships that exist between your database tables. These relationships can be expressed at the application level, when transactions update more than one table, or at the database level, where referential integrity exists between tables, or where triggers on one table affect another table. Consider these relationships when developing a recovery plan, and back up related sets of data together. Such sets can be established at either the table space or the database level. By keeping related sets of data together, you can recover to a point where all of the data is consistent. This is especially important if you want to be able to perform point-in-time roll-forward recovery on table spaces.

Restrictions on Using Different Operating Systems

When working in an environment that has more than one operating system, you must consider that the backup and recovery plans cannot be integrated. That is, you cannot use the BACKUP DATABASE command on one operating system and the RESTORE DATABASE command on another operating system, except as described in "Cross-Platform Backup and Restore Support on Sun Solaris and HP" later in this chapter. Ordinarily, you should keep the recovery plans for each operating system separate and independent.

If you must move tables from one operating system to another, use the db2move command, or use the EXPORT with the IMPORT or LOAD commands.

Backing Up to Named Pipes

You can perform a database backup to (and a database restore from) local named pipes on UNIX-based systems. Both the writer and the reader of the named pipe must be on the same machine, and the pipe must exist and be located on a local file system. Because the named pipe is treated as a local device, there is no need to specify that the target is a named pipe.

Following is an AIX example:

- Create the named pipe:

  ```
  mkfifo /u/dbuser/mypipe
  ```

- Use this pipe as the target for database backup operation:

  ```
  db2 backup db sample to /u/dbuser/mypipe
  ```

- Restore the database:

  ```
  db2 restore db sample into mynewdb from /u/dbuser/mypipe
  ```

Cross-Platform Backup and Restore Support on Sun Solaris and HP   With DB2 Universal Database version 7.2, you can perform cross-platform backup and restore between Sun Solaris and HP. When you transfer the backup image between systems, you must transfer it in binary mode. On the target system, the database must be created with the same code page/territory as the system on which the original database was created.

General Recovery Considerations

The following sections provide general information that you should be familiar with when planning your recovery strategy. The topics include recovery time and performance, DB2's use of multiple agents for parallel recovery, recovery of damaged table spaces, and disaster recovery.

Recovery Time Required

The time required to recover a database consists of two parts: the time required to complete the restoration of the backup, and, if the database is enabled for forward recovery, the time required to apply the logs during the roll-forward operation. When formulating a recovery plan, you should take into account these recovery costs and their impact on your business operations.

Testing your overall recovery plan will assist you in determining whether the time required to recover the database is reasonable given your business requirements. Following each test, you may want to increase the frequency with which you take a backup. If roll-forward recovery is part of your strategy, this will reduce the number of logs that are archived between backups, and, as a result, reduce the time required to roll forward the database after a restore operation.

Note *The setting of the enable intra-partition parallelism (intra_parallel) database manager configuration parameter does not affect the performance of either backup or restore operations. Multiple processes will be used for each of these operations, regardless of the setting of the* intra_parallel *parameter.*

Recovery Performance

To reduce the amount of time required to complete a restore operation, perform these actions:

- Adjust the restore buffer size. The buffer size must be a multiple of the buffer size that was used during the backup operation.

- Increase the number of buffers. If you use multiple buffers and I/O channels, you should use at least twice as many buffers as channels to ensure that the channels do not have to wait for data. The minimum recommended number of buffers is the number of media devices or containers plus the number specified for the PARALLELISM option.

- Adjust the size of the buffers. The size of the buffers also contributes to the performance of the restore operation. The ideal restore buffer size is a multiple of the extent size for the table spaces. If you have multiple table spaces with different extent sizes, specify a value that is a multiple of the largest extent size.

- Use multiple source devices.

- Set the PARALLELISM option for the restore operation to be at least one (1) greater than the number of source devices.

- Decide how essential it is to restore tables that contain large amounts of long field and LOB data, because restoring it can be very time-consuming. If the database is enabled for roll-forward recovery, the RESTORE command provides the capability to restore selected table spaces, so you should consider the need to restore long field and LOB data table spaces against the time required to complete the backup task for these table spaces. By storing long field and LOB data in separate table spaces, the time required to complete the restore operation can be reduced by choosing not to restore these table spaces. If the LOB data can be reproduced from a separate source, choose the NOT LOGGED option when creating or altering a table to include LOB columns. If you choose not to restore the table spaces that contain long field and LOB data, but you need to restore the table spaces that contain the table, you must roll forward to the end of the logs so that all table spaces that contain table data are consistent.

> **Note** *If you back up a table space that contains table data without the associated long or LOB fields, you cannot perform point-in-time roll-forward recovery on that table space. All the table spaces for a table must be rolled forward simultaneously to the same point in time.*

The following points apply for both backup and restore operations:

- Use multiple I/O buffers and devices.

- Allocate at least twice as many buffers as devices being used.

- Do not overload the I/O device controller bandwidth.

- Use more and smaller buffers rather than a few large buffers.

- Tune the number and the size of the buffers according to the system resources.

Parallel Recovery

DB2 uses multiple agents to perform both crash recovery and database roll-forward recovery. You can expect better performance during these operations, particularly on SMP machines; using multiple agents during database recovery takes advantage of the extra CPUs that are available on SMP machines.

The agent type introduced by this enhancement is db2agnsc. DB2 chooses the number of agents to be used for database recovery based on the number of CPUs on the machine. For SMP machines, the number of agents used is (number of CPUs + 1). On a machine with a single CPU, three agents are used for more efficient reading of logs, processing of log records, and prefetching of data pages.

DB2 distributes log records to these agents so that they can be reapplied concurrently, where appropriate. The processing of log records is parallelized at the page level. (Log records on the same data page are processed by the same agent.) Therefore, performance is enhanced, even if all the work was done on one table.

Damaged Table Space Recovery

A damaged table space has one or more containers that cannot be accessed. This is often caused by media problems that are either permanent (for example, a bad disk) or temporary (for example, an offline disk or an unmounted file system).

If the damaged table space is the system catalog table space, the database cannot be restarted. If the container problems cannot be fixed leaving the original data intact, the only available options are the following:

- Restore the database.
- Restore the catalog table space.

 Table space restore is valid only for recoverable databases because the database must be rolled forward.

If the damaged table space is not the system catalog table space, DB2 attempts to make as much of the database available as possible; success in this case depends on the logging strategy.

If the damaged table space is a sole temporary table space, you should create a new temporary table space as soon as a connection to the database is made. Once created, the new temporary table space can be used, and normal database operations requiring the temporary table space can resume. If you want, you can drop the offline temporary table space. There are special considerations for table reorganization using a system temporary table space:

- If the database or database manager configuration parameter indexrec is set to RESTART, all invalid indexes must be rebuilt during database activation; this includes indexes from reorganization that crashed during the build phase.
- If there are incomplete reorganization requests in a damaged temporary table space, you may have to set the *indexrec* configuration parameter to ACCESS to avoid restart failures.

Damaged Table Space Recovery for Recoverable Databases

If you are restoring a recoverable database and the restore operation determines that a table space is damaged, the damaged table space is put in the offline and not accessible state and in the roll-forward pending state because crash recovery is necessary. The restart operation will succeed if there is no additional problem. The damaged table space can be used again once you do either of the following:

- Fix the damaged containers without losing the original data, and then complete a table space roll-forward operation. (The roll-forward operation will first attempt to bring the table space from the offline to the normal state.)
- Perform a table space restore operation after fixing the damaged containers (with or without losing the original data), and then roll forward the table space.

Damaged Table Space Recovery for Nonrecoverable Databases

Because crash recovery is necessary and logs are not kept indefinitely, the restart operation for a nonrecoverable database can succeed only if you are willing to drop the damaged table spaces. (Successful completion of recovery means that the log records necessary to recover the damaged table spaces to a consistent state will be gone; therefore, the only valid action against such table spaces is to drop them.)

You can find the damaged table spaces by invoking an unqualified restart database operation. The operation will succeed if there are no damaged table spaces. If the operation fails (SQL0290N), you can look in the db2diag.log file for a complete list of table spaces that are currently damaged.

If you are willing to drop all of these table spaces after the restart database operation is complete, you can initiate another restart database operation, listing all of the damaged table spaces under the DROP PENDING TABLESPACES option. If a damaged table space is included in the DROP PENDING TABLESPACES list, the table space is put into the drop pending state, and your only option after recovery is to drop the table space. The restart operation continues without recovering this table space. If a damaged table space is not included in the DROP PENDING TABLESPACES list, the restart database operation fails with SQL0290N.

If you are unwilling to drop (and thus lose the data in) these table spaces, you have these options:

- Wait and fix the damaged containers (without losing the original data), and then try the restart database operation again.
- Perform a database restore operation.

Note *Putting a table space name into the DROP PENDING TABLESPACES list does not mean that the table space will be in the drop pending state. This event occurs only if the restart operation determines that the table space is damaged. When the restart operation is successful, you should issue DROP TABLESPACE statements to drop each of the table spaces that are in drop pending state. (Invoke the LIST TABLESPACES command to find out which table spaces are in this state.) This way, the space can be reclaimed or the table spaces can be recreated.*

Disaster Recovery

The term *disaster recovery* is used to describe the activities that need to be done to restore the database in the event of a fire, earthquake, vandalism, or other catastrophic events. A plan for disaster recovery can include one or more of the following:

- A site to be used in the event of an emergency
- A different machine on which to recover the database
- Offsite storage of database backups and archived logs

If your plan for disaster recovery is to recover the entire database on another machine, you require at least one full database backup and all the archived logs for the database. You may choose to keep a standby database up to date by applying the logs to it as they are archived. Or you may choose to keep the database backup and log archives in the standby site and perform restore and roll-forward operations only after a disaster has occurred. (In this case, a recent database backup is clearly desirable.) With a disaster, however, it is generally not possible to recover all of the transactions up to the time of the disaster.

The usefulness of a table space backup for disaster recovery depends on the scope of the failure. Typically, disaster recovery requires that you restore the entire database; therefore, a full database backup should be kept at a standby site. Even if you have a separate backup image of every table space, you cannot use them to recover the database. If the disaster is a damaged disk, a table space backup of each table space on that disk can be used to recover. If you have lost access to a container because of a disk failure (or for any other reason), you can restore the container to a different location.

Both table space backups and full database backups can play a role in any disaster recovery plan. The DB2 facilities available for backing up, restoring, and rolling forward data provide a foundation for a disaster recovery plan. You should ensure that you have tested your recovery procedures to protect your business.

Reducing the Impact of Failure

The sections that follow provide information about reducing the impact of media and transaction failure.

Reducing the Impact of Media Failure

To reduce the probability of media failure and to simplify recovery from this type of failure, mirror or duplicate the disks that hold the data and logs for important databases.

To prevent media failure from destroying a database and your ability to rebuild it, keep the database backup, the database logs, and the database itself on different devices. It is highly recommended that you use the newlogpath configuration parameter to put database logs on a separate device once the database is created.

Protecting Against Disk Failure   If you are concerned about the possibility of damaged data or logs due to a disk crash, consider using some form of disk fault tolerance. Generally, you accomplish this by using a disk array. A *disk array* consists of a collection of disk drives that appear to an application as a single large disk drive. Disk arrays involve *disk striping,* which is the distribution of a file across multiple disks, the mirroring of disks, and data parity checks.

Disk arrays are sometimes referred to simply as redundant arrays of independent disks (RAID), although the specific term *RAID* generally applies only to hardware disk arrays. Disk arrays can also be provided through software at the operating system or application level. The distinction between hardware and software disk arrays is how

CPU processing of I/O requests is handled. For hardware disk arrays, disk controllers manage I/O activity; for software disk arrays, this is done by the operating system or an application.

Hardware Disk Arrays   In a RAID disk array, multiple disks are used and managed by a disk controller, complete with its own CPU. All of the logic required to manage the disks forming this array is contained on the disk controller; therefore, this implementation is operating system–independent.

Five types of RAID architecture exist, RAID-1 through RAID-5, and each provides disk fault tolerance. Each varies in function and performance. In general, RAID refers to a redundant array. RAID-0, which provides only data striping (and not fault-tolerant redundancy), is excluded from this discussion. Although the RAID specification defines five architectures, only RAID-1 and RAID-5 are typically used today.

RAID-1 is also known as disk mirroring, or duplexing. *Disk mirroring* duplicates data (a complete file) from one disk onto a second disk, using a single disk controller. *Disk duplexing* is the same as disk mirroring, except that disks are attached to a second disk controller (like two SCSI adapters). With this type of data protection, either disk can fail, and data is still accessible from the other disk. With duplexing, a disk controller can also fail without compromising data protection. Performance is also good with RAID-1, but the trade-off in this implementation is that the required disk capacity is twice that of the actual amount of data because data is duplicated on pairs of drives.

RAID-5 involves data and parity striping by sectors, across all disks. Parity is interleaved with data information, rather than stored on a dedicated drive. Data protection is good—if any disk fails, the data can still be accessed by using the information from the other disks, along with the striped parity information. Read performance is good, although write performance is considerably worse than RAID-1 or normal disk. A RAID-5 configuration requires a minimum of three identical disks. The amount of extra disk space required for overhead varies with the number of disks in the array. In the case of a RAID-5 configuration of five disks, the space overhead is 20 percent.

When using a RAID (but not RAID-0) disk array, a failed disk will not prevent you from accessing data on the array. When hot-pluggable or hot-swappable disks are used in the array, a replacement disk can be swapped with the failed disk while the array is in use. With RAID-5, if two disks fail at the same time, all data is lost (but the probability of simultaneous disk failures is very small).

You might consider using RAID-1 or software-mirrored disks for your logs because this provides for recoverability to the point of failure, and it offers good write performance, which is important for logs. In cases where reliability is critical (time cannot be lost recovering data following a disk failure) and write performance is not so critical, consider using RAID-5 disks. Alternatively, if write performance is critical and you are willing to achieve this despite the cost of additional disk space, consider RAID-1 for your data, as well as for the logs.

Software Disk Arrays   A software disk array accomplishes much the same objectives as a hardware disk array, but disk traffic is managed by either an operating system task or an application running on the server. Like other programs, the software array must contend for CPU and system resources. This is not a good option for a CPU-constrained system. Remember that overall disk array performance depends on the server's CPU load and capacity.

A typical software disk array provides disk mirroring. Although redundant disks are required, a software disk array is comparatively inexpensive to implement because costly RAID disk controllers are not required.

Having the operating system boot drive in the disk array prevents your system from starting if that drive fails. If the drive fails before the disk array is running, the disk array cannot allow access to the drive. A boot drive should be separate from the disk array.

Reducing the Impact of Transaction Failure

To reduce the impact of a transaction failure, try to ensure the following:

- An uninterrupted power supply
- Adequate disk space for database logs

Crash Recovery

Crash recovery using the RESTART DATABASE command or the automatic restart enable configuration parameter (autorestart) protects a database from being left in an inconsistent, or unusable, state.

A transaction failure is not the failure of a database action that is caused by an incorrect parameter, a limit being exceeded, or a rollback caused by a deadlock. Rather, a *transaction failure* is a severe error or condition that causes the database or database manager to end abnormally, and it requires that the database be recovered. Examples include a power failure on a machine (causing the database manager and databases on it to crash), or a full disk containing the database log, which means no additional log files can be allocated for writing the COMMIT/ROLLBACK record, causing a COMMIT/ROLLBACK failure.

An interruption in power or the failure of an application may cause the immediate cessation of all activity within the database. One or more of the applications or commands may have started working with the data in the database but were not complete. Some committed units of work may not have been flushed to disk, and these partially completed (or nonflushed) units of work leave the database in an inconsistent, or unusable, state. When the database is in this state, it must be restored.

Automatic Restart

Only use automatic restart if you want the database manager to automatically roll back the incomplete units of work that result from a failure. To achieve this behavior, enable the automatic restart (*autorestart*) configuration parameter by setting it to ON. (This is the default.) If you do not have the automatic restart enabled, be prepared to issue the RESTART DATABASE command when a database failure occurs.

If you have enabled the automatic restart, a restart will begin following a database failure. The restart may take some time, so don't think that the database is hanging or not responding. The db2diag.log file records when a database restart begins. If you want to know what is happening at all times and not be worried that the database is not responding, consider disabling the automatic restart.

Version Recovery

Version recovery, using the BACKUP command in conjunction with the RESTORE command, puts the database in a state that has been previously saved. You use this recovery method with nonrecoverable databases (that is, databases for which you do not have archived logs). You can also use this method with recoverable databases by using the WITHOUT ROLLING FORWARD option.

This section reviews planning considerations and discusses how to invoke the specific utilities or commands to carry out the version recovery method. It also presents related issues that allow effective use of this method.

Backing Up a Database

To make a backup copy of the database, use the BACKUP command or the DB2 Control Center. Within the DB2 Control Center, select the database to be backed up and then select the backup action.

In a distributed request system, the BACKUP and RESTORE commands apply to the distributed request database and the metadata stored within that database catalog (wrappers, servers, nicknames, and so on). Data source objects (tables and views) are not backed up or restored unless those objects are stored in the distributed request database.

This section and following sections describe pages. In the recovery context, pages refer to the pages of the backup and restore utilities. These pages are always 4KB in size and should not be confused with the multiple page sizes allowed for database data.

When you are planning to use the BACKUP command, consider the following:

- You must have SYSADM, SYSCTRL, or SYSMAINT authority to use the BACKUP command.
- The database may be local or remote. The backup remains on the database server unless a storage management product such as TSM is used.
- You can back up a database to a fixed disk, a tape, or a location managed by TSM or another vendor storage management product. Under OS/2, you can also back up to disk or to a user exit.

- Under supported Windows operating systems, you can back up to disk.

- When creating a backup image (or restoring a backup image), the buffer size is 1024 pages (of 4KB size). This is important if you are using tape as your backup device. If you are using variable block sizes, you must lower your buffer size to a range that your tape drive uses.

- Under most versions of Linux, using DB2's default buffer sizes for backup and restore to a SCSI tape device results in this error message: SQL2025N, reason code 75. To prevent the overflow of Linux internal SCSI buffers, use this formula: bufferpages <= ST_MAX_BUFFERS * ST_BUFFER_BLOCKS / 4, where bufferpages is the value of either the *backbufsz* or the *restbufsz* configuration parameter. ST_MAX_BUFFERS and ST_BUFFER_BLOCKS are defined in the Linux kernel under drivers/scsi directory.

- Under OS/2, a user exit is used when backing up to tape because the operating system has no native tape support. Under UNIX-based operating systems and Windows NT, native tape support is available.

> **Note**
> *If you use a variable block size with your tape devices, ensure that the DB2 buffer size is either less than or equal to the maximum variable block size for which the device is configured. Otherwise, the backup will succeed but the resulting image is not guaranteed to be recoverable.*

- Multiple files may be created to contain the backed up data from the database.

- At the completion of an online backup, the active log is closed and written to disk.

- To use tape devices, DB2 users on SCO UnixWare 7 must specify BUFFER to be 16. The default value of BUFFER is 1024 pages. If BUFFER is set to 0, the database manager configuration parameter backbufsz must be set to 16.

Planning to Use Tapes When Backing Up

When you back up your table space or database to tape, you must correctly set your block size and your buffer size. This is particularly true when you are using a variable block size (for example, on AIX when the block size has been set to 0).

There is a restriction on the number of fixed block sizes that can be used when backing up to tape. This restriction exists because DB2 writes out the backup image header as a 4KB block. The only fixed block sizes DB2 supports are 512, 1024, 2048, and 4096 bytes. If you are using a fixed block size, you can specify any buffer size for the backup. However, you may find that your backup will not complete successfully if the fixed block size is not one of those mentioned here.

If your database data is large, using these fixed block sizes means your backup will take a long time. You may want to consider using a variable block size.

When you are using a variable block size, you must also specify a buffer size in the BACKUP command that is less than or equal to the maximum limit for the tape device you are using. The buffer size must be equal to the maximum block size limit of the device being used if you would like the best performance.

Be aware that restoring from a backup image where the block size is variable might return an error. If this happens, you might need to rewrite the image using an appropriate block size. An example of doing this in AIX follows:

```
tcl -b 0 -Bn -f /dev/rmt0 read > backup_filename.file
dd if=backup_filename.file of=/dev/rmt0/ obs=4096 conv=sync
```

This example dumps the backup image to a file called backup_filenam.file. The dd command then dumps the image back onto the tape using a block size of 4096.

The complication with this method of correction occurs if the image is too large to dump to a file. One possible solution with such a large image is to use the dd command to dump the image from one tape device to another. This will work as long as the image does not span more than one tape. When using two tape devices, the dd command is as follows:

```
dd if=/dev/rmt1 of=/dev/rmt0 obs=4096
```

If using two tape devices is not possible, you may be able to dump the image to a raw device by using the dd command, and then dump the image from the raw device to tape. The difficulty of using this method is that the dd command must keep track of the number of blocks dumped to the raw device because the number of blocks dumped needs to be specified when the image is moved back to tape. When the dd command is used to dump the image from the raw device to tape, the command dumps the entire size of the raw device to tape. The dd command cannot tell how much of the raw device is used to hold the image.

When using the BACKUP command, you will need to know the maximum block size limit for the tape device you are using. Table 12-1 provides some examples.

Device	Attachment	Block Size Limit	DB2 Buffer Size Limit (in 4KB pages)
8mm	scsi	131,072	32
3420	s370	65,536	16
3480	s370	65,536	16

Table 12-1. *Maximum Block Size for Tape Device Types*

Device	Attachment	Block Size Limit	DB2 Buffer Size Limit (in 4KB pages)
3490	s370	65,536	16
3490E	S370	65,536	16
7332 (4mm)*	scsi	262,144	64
3490e	scsi	262,144	64
3590**	scsi	2,097,152	512
3570 (magstar MP)		262,144	

* The 7332 device does not implement a block size limit. 256KB is simply a suggested value. The parent adapter imposes the block size limit.

** While the 3590 device supports a 2MB block size, you might experiment with lower values (like 256KB), provided the performance is adequate for your needs. Check your device limit in the device documentation and/or with the device vendor.

Table 12-1.   *Maximum Block Size for Tape Device Types* (continued)

Invoking the BACKUP Command

The following considerations are useful when running the BACKUP command. For a description of this command, see Chapter 30.

- You must start the database manager (DB2START) before running the BACKUP command or API. When using the DB2 Control Center, you do not need to explicitly start the database manager.

- When using the command, API, or task under DB2 Control Center, you must specify a database alias name, not the database name itself.

- To reduce the amount of time required to complete a backup, do the following:
  - Increase the value of the PARALLELISM parameter. Using this parameter can dramatically reduce the amount of time required to complete the backup. The PARALLELISM parameter defines the number of processes or threads that are started to read data from the database. Each process or thread is assigned to back up a specific table space. When it completes backing up the table space, it requests another. Note, however, that each process or thread requires both memory and CPU overhead: for a heavily loaded system, leave the PARALLELISM parameter at its default value of 1.

- Increase the backup buffer size.

- Increase the number of buffers. If you use multiple buffers and I/O channels, you should use at least twice as many buffers as channels to ensure that the channels do not have to wait for data. The size of the buffers used also contributes to the performance of the backup operation. The ideal backup buffer size should be a multiple of the extent size for the table space(s); if you have multiple table spaces with different extent sizes, specify a value that is a multiple of the largest extent size. You may specify the number of pages to use for each backup buffer when you invoke the BACKUP command. The minimum number of pages is 16. If you do not specify the number of pages, each buffer will be allocated based on the database manager configuration parameter *backbufsz*. If not enough memory is available to allocate the buffer, an error will be returned.

- Use multiple target devices. In OS/2, when backing up a database to removable media such as tape, the database manager writes information to media volume 1. Once the first media is in the drive, do not remove the media unless the operating system backup facility prompts you for media 2.

- You cannot back up a database that is not in a usable state except for a database in the backup pending state:

  - If a database is in a partially restored state due to a system crash during any stage of restoring the database, you must successfully restore the database before you can back it up.

  - If a database was created with a previous release of the database manager and the database has not been migrated, you must migrate the database before you can back it up. See the *DB2 Universal Database Administration Guide: Planning* for information about migrating a database.

  - If any of the table spaces in a database is in an abnormal state, you cannot back up the database unless it is in the backup pending state.

  - If a system crash occurs during a critical stage of backing up a database, you cannot successfully connect to the database until you reissue the BACKUP command.

The BACKUP command provides a concurrency control for multiple processes that are making backup copies of different databases. The control keeps the backup target device open until the entire backup process has ended. If an error occurs during a backup process and the open container cannot be closed, other backup processes to the same target drive may receive access errors. To correct any access errors, you must completely exit the backup process that caused the error and disconnect from the target device.

If you are using the BACKUP command for concurrent backup processes to tape, ensure that the processes do not target the same tape.

Restoring a Database

You must have SYSADM, SYSCTRL, or SYSMAINT authority to restore to an existing database from a full database backup. To restore to a new database, you must have SYSADM or SYSCTRL authority. For a description of this command, see Chapter 30.

You can use the RESTORE command only if the database has been previously backed up with the BACKUP command. If you use the DB2 Control Center, you cannot restore backups that were taken previous to the current version of DB2.

At the time of the restore, you can choose which type of restore is to be carried out. You can select from the following types:

- A full restore of everything from the backup
- A restore of only the recovery history file
- A subset of the table spaces in the backup

A database restore requires an exclusive connection; that is, no applications can be running against the database when the task is started. Once the restore starts, it prevents other applications from accessing the database until the restore is completed. A table space restore can be done online, and the database may be local or remote.

The RESTORE command can use the TSM utility, and any restrictions of that utility should also be considered. (See the *IBM DB2 Universal Database Data Recovery and High Availability Guide and Reference* for more information about the TSM utility.) Another vendor storage management product may also be used if that product was used to store the original backup.

To use tape devices, DB2 users on SCO UnixWare 7 must specify BUFFER to be 16. The default value of BUFFER is 1024 pages. If BUFFER is set to 0, the database manager configuration parameter *backbufsz* must be set to 16.

Invoking the RESTORE Command

The database to which you restore the data can be the same as the one the data was originally backed up from, or it can be different. You can restore the data to a new or an existing database. In either case, the database manager must be started before you can issue the RESTORE DATABASE command.

During the restore procedure, you can optionally select to use multiple buffers to improve the performance of the restore procedure. The multiple internal buffers might be filled with data from the backup media.

You can specify the number of pages to use for each restore buffer when you invoke the RESTORE command. The value you specify must be a multiple of the number of pages that you specified for the backup buffer, and the minimum number of pages is 16. If you do not specify the number of pages, each buffer will be allocated based on the database manager configuration parameter *restbufsz*. If there is not enough memory available to allocate the buffer, an error will be returned.

The TAKEN AT parameter of the RESTORE DATABASE command requires the timestamp for the backup. The timestamp can be exactly as it was displayed after the completion of a successful BACKUP command, that is, in the format *yyyymmddhhnnss*. You can also specify a partial timestamp. For example, assume that you have two different backups with the timestamps 19971001010101 and 19971002010101. If you specify 19971002 for TAKEN AT, the 19971002010101 backup image is used. If TAKEN AT is not specified, there must be only one backup on the source media.

The backup copy of the database to be used by the RESTORE command can be located on a fixed disk, a tape, or a location managed by the TSM utility or another vendor storage management product. Under OS/2, the backup copy of the database could also be located on disk. Under supported Windows operating systems, the backup copy of the database could also be located on disk. On Windows operating systems and on OS/2, you must specify only the device letter when using the TO target-directory clause. If a longer path is specified, an error is returned.

Once the RESTORE command starts, the database is not usable until the RESTORE command completes successfully. If a system failure occurs during any stage of restoring a database, you cannot connect to the database until you reuse the RESTORE command and successfully complete the restore.

If the code page of the database being restored does not match a code page available to an application, or if the database manager does not support code page conversions from the database code page to a code page that is available to an application, the restored database will not be usable.

Redefining Table Space Containers During a Restore

During a backup of a database, a record is kept of all the table space containers in use by the table spaces that are backed up. During a restore, all containers listed in the backup are checked to see if they currently exist and are accessible. If one or more of the containers is inaccessible because of a media failure (or for any other reason), the restore will fail. To allow a restore in such a case, table space containers can be redirected during the restore. This includes adding, changing, or removing table space containers.

Similarly, sometimes you will want to restore even though the containers listed in the backup do not exist on the system. For example, maybe you need to recover from a disaster on a different system from that from which the backup was taken, and the new system may not have the necessary containers defined. To allow a restore in this case, redirecting table space containers at the time of the restore to alternate containers is supported.

In both situations, this type of restore is commonly referred to as a *redirected restore*.

Note   *The ability to perform container redirection on any restore provides considerable flexibility in managing table space containers. For example, even though DB2 does not directly support adding containers to SMS table spaces, you could accomplish this task by simply specifying an additional container on a redirected restore. Similarly, you could move a DMS table space from file containers to device containers.*

MAINTAINING DATA

You can redefine table space containers through the restore task from within the DB2 Control Center. You can also use the REDIRECT parameter of the RESTORE command to specify the redirection. If you are using the DB2 Control Center, one way to perform a redirected restore is to use the Containers page of the Restore Database notebook, which allows you to add new containers, change the path of an existing container, or remove a container. If, during the process of the restore database operation, an invalid container path is detected, the DB2 Control Center will prompt you to either change the container path or remove the container.

 Directory and file containers are automatically created if they do not exist. No redirection is necessary unless the containers are inaccessible for some other reason. The database manager does not automatically create device containers.

Redirected restore is also supported through a number of APIs. Although you could write a program to perform redirected restore for a specific case, these APIs are primarily intended for developers who want to produce a general-purpose utility.

Restoring to an Existing Database

You can restore a backup copy of a full database backup to an existing database. To restore to an existing database, you must have SYSADM, SYSCTRL, or SYSMAINT authority. The backup image may differ from the existing database in its alias name, its database name, or its database seed.

A database *seed* is a unique identifier of a database that remains constant for the life of the database. The database manager assigns this seed when the database is first created. The seed is unchanged following a restore of a backup, even if the backup has a different database seed. For example, if you restore a database backup to a new database, the new database will still have the seed assigned to it by the database manager, instead of the seed of the database from which the backup image was taken.

When restoring to an existing database, the restore operation performs the following functions:

- Deletes table, index, and long field contents for the existing database and replaces them with the contents from the backup.
- Replaces table space table entries for each table space being restored.
- Retains the recovery history file unless the one on disk is damaged. If the file on the disk is damaged, the database manager will copy the file from the backup.
- Retains the authentication for the existing database.
- Retains the database directories for the existing database that define where the database resides and how it is cataloged.

When the database seeds are different, the restore operation performs the following functions:

- Deletes the logs associated with the existing database.
- Copies the database configuration file from the backup. If newlogpath is specified on the RESTORE command, the restore operation sets the value of newlogpath to the log path (which is specified by the *logpath* parameter) in the database configuration file.

When the database seeds are the same, the restore task performs the following functions:

- Retains the current database configuration file unless the file is corrupted, in which case, this file will be copied from the backup.
- Deletes the logs if the image is of a nonrecoverable database.
- If newlogpath is specified on the RESTORE command, sets this parameter to the value of the logpath database configuration parameter. Otherwise, copies the current log path to the database configuration file.
- Validates the log path: if it cannot be used by the database, changes the database configuration to use the default log path.

Restoring to a New Database

As an alternative to restoring a database to a database that already exists, you may create a new database and then restore the backup of the data. To restore to a new database, you must have SYSADM or SYSCTRL authority.

Note *The code pages of the backup and the target database must match. If they do not, first create the new database specifying the correct code page and then restore it.*

When you restore to a new database, the RESTORE command performs the following functions:

- Creates a new database, using the database name and database alias name that were specified by the target database alias parameter. (If this target database alias was not specified, the RESTORE command creates a database with the name and alias the same as the source database alias parameter.)
- Restores the database configuration file from the backup. If newlogpath is specified on the RESTORE command, sets this parameter to the value of the *logpath* parameter in the database configuration file.
- Validates the log path. If it cannot be used by the database, changes the database configuration to use the default log path.
- Restores the authentication type from the backup.

- Restores the database comments from the backup for the database directories.
- Restores the recovery history file for the database.

Roll-Forward Recovery

Roll-forward recovery using the BACKUP command in conjunction with the RESTORE and ROLLFORWARD commands allows you to recover the database or table space to its state at a specified point in time.

When you first create a database, only circular logging is enabled for it. This means that logs are reused (in a circular fashion), and they are not saved or archived. With circular logging, roll-forward recovery is not possible: only crash recovery or version recovery is enabled. When log archiving is performed, however, roll-forward recovery is possible because the logs record changes to the database after the time at which the backup was taken. You perform log archiving by having either the *logretain* database configuration parameter set to RECOVERY, the *userexit* database configuration parameter enabled, or both. When either of these parameters is so configured, the database is enabled for roll-forward recovery.

When the database is recoverable, you can perform backup, restore, and roll-forward recovery at both the database and the table space level. The backups of the database and table space can be completed online. Online restore and roll forward are also available at the table space level.

Roll-forward recovery reapplies the completed units of work recorded in the logs to the restored database, table space, or table spaces. Roll-forward recovery can follow the completion of a full database restore. It can also be done with table spaces that are in a roll-forward pending state. You can specify roll-forward recovery to the end of the logs or to a particular point in time.

For more information about the database configuration parameters associated with logging, see the "Configuration Parameters for Database Logging" section later in this chapter.

Backup Considerations

Roll-forward recovery is disabled by the default setting (NO) of the *logretain* and *userexit* configuration parameters. Both parameters are initially set to NO because no backup has yet been taken. Initially, the database cannot be recovered, so you cannot perform forward recovery on it.

To enable a new database for roll-forward recovery, you must enable at least one of the *logretain* and *userexit* configuration parameters before taking the first backup of the database. When you change the value of one or both parameters, the database will be put into the backup pending state, which requires that you take an offline backup of the database. After the backup operation completes successfully, the database can be used.

Before you can back up a database, it must be in a usable state, or it can be in the backup pending state if either of the following conditions apply:

- If a database or a table space is in a partially restored state due to a system crash during any stage of restoring the database, you must successfully restore the database or the table space before you can back it up.

- If any of the table spaces in a database is in an abnormal state, you cannot back up the database or that table space unless it is in the backup pending state.

The recovery history file is updated automatically with summary information whenever you carry out a backup or restore of a full database or table space. This file can be a useful mechanism for tracking restore activity within a database. This file is created in the same directory as the database configuration file.

Backup Destinations

You can back up a database or table space to a fixed disk, a tape, or a location managed by TSM or another vendor storage management product. Under OS/2, you can also back up to disk or to a user exit.

If your database is enabled for roll-forward recovery and you are using a tape system that does not support the ability to uniquely reference a backup, you should not keep multiple backup copies of the same database on the same tape.

The backup operation may create multiple files to contain the backed up data from the database or table space.

In OS/2, when you restore from a user exit and roll forward the database, the path to the database is the only reference used to locate the containers. Therefore, all the containers for that database that are on the backup tape are restored.

Time Required for Backups

To reduce the amount of time required to perform the backup, perform these actions:

- Use table space backups. You can back up (and subsequently recover) part of a database by using the TABLESPACE option of the BACKUP command. This makes it easier to administer data, indexes, and long fields and LOBs in separate table spaces.

- Increase the value of the PARALLELISM parameter so that it reflects the number of table spaces that are being backed up.

Table Space Backups

The considerations for backing up table spaces are as follows:

- A table space backup and a table space restore cannot be run at the same time, even if the backup and restore are working on different table spaces.

- If you have tables that span more than one table space, you should back up (and restore) the set of table spaces together.

MAINTAINING DATA

■ If each table space is on a different disk, a media error affects only a particular table space, not the entire database. The table space with the error is placed in a roll-forward pending state. You can still use the other table spaces in the database unless the table space in this state has the system catalog tables—in this situation, you cannot connect to the database.

■ The system catalog table space can be restored independently of the rest of the database if a table space–level backup containing the system catalog table space is available.

■ The backup will fail if a list of the table spaces to be backed up contains a temporary table space.

■ If you reorganize a table, you should back up the affected table spaces after the operation completes. If you have to restore the table spaces, doing the backup means you will not have to roll forward through the data reorganization.

If you back up a table space that does not contain all of the table data, you cannot perform point-in-time roll-forward recovery on that table space. You must simultaneously roll forward to the same point in time all the table spaces that contain any type of data for a table.

Restore Considerations

To restore to an existing database, you must have SYSADM, SYSCTRL, or SYSMAINT authority. The backup image may differ from the existing database in its alias name, its database name, or its database seed. When you restore to an existing database and the database seeds are the same, the logs are retained.

You can restore the database or table space only if it was previously backed up using either the BACKUP command or the Control Center.

After a database enabled for roll-forward recovery is restored, it is in the roll-forward pending state. The database is unusable until it is rolled forward. The exception occurs when a restore WITHOUT ROLLING FORWARD is specified. However, you cannot turn roll forward off if an online database backup was restored or only selected table space backups were restored.

Backup Copy Locations

The backup copy of the database or table space to be used by the RESTORE command can be located on a fixed disk, a tape, or a location managed by the TSM utility or another vendor storage management product.

Under OS/2, the backup copy of the database or table space can also be located on disk or through a user exit.

Under Windows 95 and Windows NT, the backup copy of the database or table space can be located on disk.

The Roll-Forward Pending State

While restore and roll-forward are independent operations, your recovery strategy may have restore as the first phase of a complete roll-forward recovery of a database. After a successful restore, a database that was configured for roll-forward recovery at the time the backup was taken enters a roll-forward pending state, and it is not usable until the ROLLFORWARD command is successfully run:

■ If the database is in the roll-forward pending state, the ROLLFORWARD command rolls the database forward.

■ If the database is not in the roll-forward pending state, but table spaces in the database are, when you issue the ROLLFORWARD command and specify a list of table spaces, only those table spaces are rolled forward. If you do not specify a list, all table spaces that are in the roll-forward pending state are rolled forward.

 If you have renamed a table space following your most recent backup, when rolling forward the table space, ensure that you use the new name. The previous table space name will not be recognized.

If you are restoring from a full database backup that was created using the offline option of the BACKUP command, you can bypass this roll-forward pending state during the restore process. Using the WITHOUT ROLLING FORWARD option allows you to use the restored database immediately without rolling forward the database.

However, if you are restoring from a backup that was created using the online option of the BACKUP command, you cannot bypass this roll-forward pending state.

 You cannot run another database restore when the roll-forward process is running.

Restoring Table Spaces

The considerations for restoring table spaces are as follows:

■ You can restore a table space only if the table space currently exists and the table space was not dropped and recreated between taking the backup image and attempting to restore the table space.

■ If you have renamed a table space following your most recent backup, when rolling forward the table space, ensure that you use the new name. The previous table space name will not be recognized.

■ You cannot restore a table space backup to a new database.

■ If you backed up tables that spanned more than one table space, you should restore the set of table spaces together.

■ Once the RESTORE command starts for a table space backup, the table space is not usable until the RESTORE command followed by a roll-forward recovery completes successfully.

■ A table space restore can be online or offline.

■ If a system failure occurs during the restoring of a table space backup, only the table space being restored is unusable. The other table spaces in the database can still be used.

■ You cannot perform an online table space restore of the system catalog tables.

■ When performing a partial or subset restore, you can use either a table space backup or a full database backup and choose one or more table spaces from that image. All the log files associated with the table space (or table spaces) must exist from the time the backup was created.

■ In OS/2, a partial or subset restore is not possible when restoring from a user exit.

Performing Redirected Restores

During a backup of a database or one or more table spaces, a record is kept of all the table space containers in use by the table spaces that are backed up. During a restore, all containers listed in the backup are checked to see if they currently exist and are accessible. If one or more of the containers is inaccessible because of a media failure (or for any other reason), the restore will fail. To allow a restore in such a case, you can *redirect* table space containers during the restore. This includes adding, changing, or removing table space containers.

A restore is often followed by a roll forward to reapply changes recorded in the database logs after the point in time when the backup was taken. During a roll-forward operation, you may re-execute or rerun a transaction that carries out an ALTER TABLESPACE statement with the ADD option (to add a container). For the roll forward to be successful, the container to be added must be accessible. If the container is not accessible, then the roll forward for the table space is suspended, and the table space is left in a roll-forward pending state.

You may or may not want to redo the add container operations in the database logs. In fact, you may not know which containers have been added since the backup was taken. Therefore, you cannot anticipate which containers are needed. Alternatively, depending on why you are performing a redirected restore, you may simply prefer the list of containers you specified at the time of the restore and not want any other containers added. To control this behavior, you can indicate at the time of the restore whether you want the roll forward to recreate the containers during the roll-forward recovery. (You can edit the list of table space containers in the CONTAINERS - CHANGE window of the Restore Database or Restore Table Space notebook in the DB2 Control Center.)

Rolling Forward Changes in a Database

Roll-forward recovery builds on a restored database and allows you to restore a database to a particular time that is after the time that the database backup was taken. This point can be either the end of the logs or a point between the time of the database backup and the end of the logs.

Note   *When a restore and roll forward is carried out to the end of the logs, the backup ID shown following a LIST HISTORY command represents the end of time. That is, the backup ID value is 99991231235959. The backup ID is transformed this way only when a roll forward is carried out.*

You might use point-in-time recovery if an active or an archived log is not available. In this situation, you could roll forward to the point where the log is missing. You might also roll forward to a point in time if a bad transaction were run against the database. In this situation, you would restore the database and then roll forward to just before the time when the bad transaction was run.

To use this method, the database must be configured to enable roll-forward recovery. Considerations for the database configuration file and database logs are presented in the following sections.

Configuration Parameters for Database Logging

The database configuration file contains parameters related to roll-forward recovery. The default parameters do not support this recovery, so if you plan to use it, you need to change some of these defaults.

Primary Logs (*logprimary*)

The primary logs (*logprimary*) configuration parameter specifies the number of primary logs that will be created. A primary log, whether empty or full, requires the same amount of disk space. Thus, if you configure more logs than you need, you use disk space unnecessarily. If you configure too few logs, you can encounter a log-full condition. As you select the number of logs to configure, you must consider the size you make each log and whether your application can handle a log-full condition.

If you are enabling an existing database for roll-forward recovery, change the number of primary logs to the sum of the number of primary and secondary logs, plus 1. The extra log is required for the additional information that is logged for LONG VARCHAR and LOB fields in the database.

The total log file size limit is 32GB. That is, the number of log files (*logprimary* +*logsecond*) multiplied by the size of each log file in bytes (*logfilsiz* * 4096) must be less than 32GB.

Secondary Logs (*logsecond*)

The secondary logs (*logsecond*) configuration parameter specifies the number of secondary log files that are created and used for recovery log files (only as needed).

When the primary log files become full, the secondary log files (of size *logfilsiz*) are allocated one at a time as needed, up to a maximum number as controlled by this parameter. An error code will be returned to the application, and activity against the database will be stopped if more secondary log files are required than are allowed by this parameter.

MAINTAINING DATA

Log Size (*logfilsiz*)

The log size (*logfilsiz*) parameter determines the number of pages for each of the configured logs. A log page is 4096 bytes (4KB) in size.

> **Note** *The total log file size limit is 32GB; that is,* (logfilsiz + logprimary) *x* logfilsiz < *32GB/4096.*

The size of each primary log has a direct bearing on performance. When the database is configured to retain logs, each time a log is filled, a request is issued for allocation and initialization of a new log. Increasing the size of the log reduces the number of requests required to allocate and initialize new logs. (Keep in mind, however, that with a larger log size, it takes more time to format each new log.) The formatting of new logs is transparent to applications connected to the database so that database performance is unaffected by formatting.

Assuming that you have an application that keeps the database open to minimize the processing time to open a database, the value for the log size should be determined by the amount of time it takes to make offline archived log copies.

Also, the data transfer speed of the device you use to store offline archived logs and the software used to make the copies must at a minimum match the average rate at which the database manager writes data in the logs. If the transfer speed cannot keep up with new log data being generated, you may run out of disk space if logging activity continues for a sufficiently long period of time. If this happens, database processing will stop.

The data transfer speed is most significant when using tape or some optical media. Some tape devices require the same amount of time to copy a file, regardless of its size. You must determine the capability of your archiving device.

Additionally, tape devices have some unique considerations. The frequency of the archiving request is important. If the time for any copy operation is five minutes, the log size should be large enough to hold five minutes of log data during your peak workload. Also, the tape device may have design limits that restrict the number of operations per day. These factors must be considered when you determine the log size.

Minimizing log file loss is also an important consideration in setting the log size. Archiving takes an entire log, so if you use a single large log, you increase the time between archiving. If the medium containing the log fails, some transaction information will probably be lost. Decreasing the log size increases the frequency of archiving but can reduce the amount of information lost in the case of a media failure because the smaller logs before the lost log can be used.

Log Buffer (*logbufsz*)

The log buffer (*logbufsz*) parameter allows you to specify the amount of database shared memory to use as a buffer for log records before writing these records to disk. The log records are written to disk when one of the following occurs:

- A transaction commits.
- The log buffer is full.
- Some other internal database manager event occurs.

Buffering the log records results in more efficient logging file I/O because the log records will be written to disk less frequently and more log records will be written at each time.

Number of Commits to Group (*mincommit*)

The number of commits to group (*mincommit*) configuration parameter allows you to delay the writing of log records to disk until a minimum number of commits have been performed. This delay can help reduce the database manager overhead associated with writing log records and, as a result, improve performance when you have multiple applications running against a database and many commits are requested by the applications within a very short time frame.

This grouping of commits occurs only when the value of this parameter is greater than 1, and when the number of applications connected to the database is greater than the value of this parameter. When commit grouping is being performed, application commit requests are held until one of the following events occurs:

- One second elapses.
- The number of commit requests equals the value of this parameter.

New Log Path (*newlogpath*)

The new log path (*newlogpath*) configuration parameter allows you to store database logs in a location of your choosing. The database logs are initially created in SQLOGDIR, which is a subdirectory of the database directory. You can change the location where active logs and future archive logs are placed by changing the value for this configuration parameter to point either to a different directory or to a device. Archive logs that are currently stored in the database log path directory are not moved to the new location if the database is configured for roll-forward recovery.

Because you can change the log path location, the logs needed for roll-forward recovery may exist in different directories or on different devices. You can change this configuration parameter during the roll-forward process to access logs in multiple locations.

The change to the value of newlogpath will not be applied until the database is in a consistent state. An informational database configuration parameter, *database_consistent*, indicates the status of the database.

Log Retain (*logretain*)

The log retain (*logretain*) configuration parameter causes archived logs to be kept in the database log path directory. Enabling it by setting it to RECOVERY allows the database manager to use the roll-forward recovery method. You do not require *userexit* to be enabled when the *logretain* configuration parameter is enabled. Either one of the two parameters is sufficient to allow the roll-forward recovery method.

Using this parameter means that the circular logging, which is the default, is being overridden.

User Exit (*userexit*)

The user exit (*userexit*) configuration parameter causes the database manager to call a user exit program for archiving and retrieving logs. With the user exit enabled, roll-forward recovery is allowed. You do not require logretain to be enabled when the userexit configuration parameter is enabled—either of the two parameters is sufficient to allow the roll-forward recovery method.

Using this parameter means that the circular logging, which is the default, is being overridden. The *userexit* parameter implies logretain, but the reverse is not true.

The active log path is important when using either the *userexit* configuration parameter or the logretain configuration parameter to allow roll-forward recovery. When the *userexit* configuration parameter is enabled, the user exit is called to archive log files away from the active log path. When the *logretain* configuration parameter is set to RECOVERY, this ensures that the log files remain in the active log path. The active log path is determined by either the path to log files (*logpath*) or the changed path to log files (*newlogpath*) parameter.

See the *IBM DB2 Universal Database Data Recovery and High Availability Guide and Reference* for information about the user exit program.

Rolling Forward Changes in a Table Space

If the database is enabled for forward recovery, you have the option of backing up, restoring, and rolling forward table spaces instead of using the entire database. You may want to implement a recovery strategy for individual table spaces because doing so can save time: it takes less time to recover a portion of the database than it does to recover the entire database. For example, if a disk is bad and it contains only one table space, the table space can be restored and rolled forward, and you won't need to recover the entire database. (This also won't affect user access to the rest of the database.) Also, table space–level backups allow you to back up critical portions of the database more frequently than other portions, and they require less time than backing up the entire database.

If you have renamed a table space following your most recent backup, ensure that you use the new name when rolling forward the table space. The previous table space name will not be recognized. You must also roll forward to at least the point in time when you renamed the table space.

If the data and long objects of a table are in separate table spaces and the table has been reorganized, the table spaces for both the data and long objects must be restored and rolled forward together. You should take a backup of the affected table spaces after the table is reorganized.

It is possible to recover the data from tables that have been accidentally dropped, given certain conditions. See "Recovering a Dropped Table" later in this chapter for more information.

Table Space States

Different states are associated with a table space to indicate its current status:

- **Roll-forward pending**   A table space will be placed in the *roll-forward pending* state after it is restored, or following an I/O error. When the I/O error is corrected, the table space must be rolled forward to remove the roll-forward pending state. If the table space has been restored, it must be rolled forward.

- **Roll-forward-in-progress**   A table space will be placed in the roll-forward-in-progress state when a roll-forward operation is in progress on that table space. The table space will be removed from the roll-forward-in-progress state when the ROLLFORWARD command completes successfully. The table space could also be in the roll-forward-in-progress state if the backup image were taken online and the roll-forward operation did not complete.

- **Restore pending**   A table space will be placed in the restore pending state after a ROLLFORWARD CANCEL command or a roll-forward operation in which an unrecoverable error occurs on that table space. The table space must be restored and rolled forward again.

  - **Backup pending**   A table space will be placed in the backup pending state after a roll-forward operation to a point in time, or after a LOAD NO COPY command. The table space must be backed up before it can be used.

After a table space is restored, it is always in the roll-forward pending state. (That is, if you restore a table space and specify the WITHOUT ROLLING FORWARD parameter, the parameter is ignored.) To make the table space usable, you must perform roll-forward recovery on it.

Rolling Forward Table Spaces to Different Points

You have the option of rolling forward to the end of the logs or rolling forward to a point in time. If you want to roll forward a table space to a point in time, you should be aware of the following:

- You cannot roll forward system catalog tables to a point in time. These must be rolled forward to the end of the logs to ensure that all table spaces in the database remain consistent.

- A table space that is to be rolled forward to a point in time must have been restored from a backup that is earlier than the point in time specified for the roll forward.

If you do not want to roll the table space forward, you can specify the ROLLFORWARD STOP command, which is the same as rolling the table space forward to the time that the backup was started. Note that you cannot do this if the backup image was taken online. In this situation, you must roll forward to at least the end of the backup to ensure that the table data is consistent.

There are a number of other considerations when rolling forward table spaces:

- **Tables in multiple table spaces** If you are rolling forward to a point in time and a table is contained in multiple table spaces, all table spaces that contain the table must be rolled forward simultaneously. If, for example, the table data is contained in one table space and the index for the table is contained in another table space, you must roll forward both table spaces simultaneously to the same point in time.

- **Minimum recover time** Before rolling forward a table space, use the LIST TABLESPACES SHOW DETAIL command. This command returns information on the *minimum recover time*: the earliest point in time to which the table space can be rolled forward. The minimum recovery time is updated when data definition language (DDL) statements are executed against the table space or against tables in the table space. The table space must be rolled forward to at least the minimum recovery time so that it is synchronized with the information in the system catalog tables.

- **Renamed table spaces** If you have renamed the table space, you must roll forward to at least the point in time when the table space was renamed.

- **Tables containing identity columns** If you recover a table space that contains a table with an identity column to a point in time that is before the end of the logs, a gap in the sequence of generated values may result. This situation could cause DB2 to generate duplicate values for some identity columns. These values would be duplicates in fact, but looking only at the content of the database, they would not appear to be duplicates.

- **Quiescing table spaces** You can issue the QUIESCE TABLESPACES FOR TABLE command to create a transaction-consistent point in time that you can use for rolling forward table spaces. When you quiesce table spaces for a table (in share, intent to update, or exclusive), the request will wait (through locking) for all running transactions that are accessing objects in the table spaces to complete while blocking new requests against the table spaces. When the quiesce request is granted, all outstanding transactions are already completed (committed or rolled back), and the table spaces are in a consistent state. You can look in the recovery history file to find quiesce points and check whether they are past the minimum recovery time to determine a desirable time to stop the roll forward.

- **Tables with referential integrity relationships** If you want to roll forward a table space to a point in time, and a table in the table space participates in a referential integrity relationship with another table that is contained in another table space, you should roll forward both table spaces simultaneously to the same point in time. If you do not, both table spaces will be in the check pending state at the end of the point-in-time roll-forward operation. If you roll forward both table spaces at the same time, the constraint will remain active at the end of the point-in-time roll-forward operation.

- **Summary tables**   If you want to roll forward a table space to a point in time, and a table in the table space is either an underlying table for a summary table that is in another table space, or it is a summary table for a table in another table space, you should roll forward both table spaces to the same point in time. If you do not, the summary table is placed in the check pending state at the end of the roll-forward operation.

- **Rolling back and committing transactions**   You should be careful that a point-in-time table space roll-forward operation does not cause a transaction to be rolled back in some table spaces and committed in others. You should find a point in time to stop rolling forward that will prevent this problem from happening. This problem can occur when either of the following occurs:

  - A point-in-time roll forward is performed on a subset of the table spaces that were updated by a transaction, and the point in time is before the time that the transaction committed.

  - Any table contained in the table space being rolled forward to a point in time has an associated trigger, or it is updated by a trigger that affects table spaces other than the one that is being rolled forward.

Backing Up After Rolling Forward

After a table space point-in-time roll-forward operation completes, the table space (or table spaces) is placed in the backup pending state. You must take a backup of the table space because all updates made to it between the point in time to which you rolled forward and the current time have been removed. You can no longer roll forward the table space to the current time from a previous database or table space backup. (The following example shows why the table space backup is required and how it is used.) To make the table space available, you can either back up the entire database, the table space that is in the backup pending state, or a set of table spaces that includes the table space that is in the backup pending state.

In this example, you back up the database at time T1. Then, at time T3, you roll forward table space TABSP1 to the point in time T2, then take a backup of the table space after T3. (Because the table space is in the backup pending state, you must take a backup of it. The timestamp of the table space backup is after T3, but the table space is at time T2. Because TABSP1 is rolled forward to T2, the roll-forward operation does not apply log records to TABSP1 from T2 to T3.)

At time T4, you restore the database with the backup you took at T1 and roll forward to the end of the logs. The table space TABSP1 will be placed into the restore pending state when time T3 is reached.

Table Space Backup Requirement

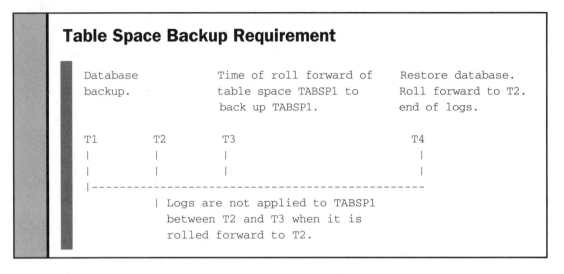

```
Database              Time of roll forward of    Restore database.
backup.               table space TABSP1 to      Roll forward to T2.
                      back up TABSP1.            end of logs.


T1          T2        T3                                   T4
|           |         |                                    |

|           |         |                                    |
|-------------------------------------------------------------
            | Logs are not applied to TABSP1
              between T2 and T3 when it is
              rolled forward to T2.
```

The table space is put into the restore pending state at T3 because the database manager assumes that operations were performed on TABSP1 between T3 and T4 without the log changes between T2 and T3 having been applied to the table space. (If the log changes between T2 and T3 were reapplied as part of the ROLLFORWARD on the database, this assumption would be violated.) The required backup of a table space that must be taken after it is rolled forward to a point in time allows you to roll that table space forward past a previous point-in-time roll forward (T3 in the example).

Assuming that you want to recover table space TABSP1 to T4, you would restore the table space from a backup that was taken after T3 (either the required backup or a later one), and then roll forward TABSP1 to the end of the logs.

In the preceding example, the most efficient way of restoring the database to time T4 would be to perform the following steps:

1. Restore the database.

2. Restore the table space.

3. Roll forward the database.

4. Roll forward the table space.

Because you restore the table space before rolling forward the database, log records are not applied to the table space when the database is rolled forward, which would happen if you rolled forward the database before you restored the table space.

If you cannot find the backup image of TABSP1 from after time T3, or you want to restore TABSP1 to T3 or before, you can do one of the following:

- Roll forward the table space to the T3 point in time. You do not need to restore the table space again because it was restored from the database backup.

- Restore the table space again from the backup of the database that you took at time T1, and then roll forward the table space to a time that precedes time T3.

- Drop the table space.

Recovering a Dropped Table

If a table is accidentally dropped from a REGULAR table space, you can recover the table by restoring and rolling forward the table space or database that contained it. In either situation, the DROPPED TABLE RECOVERY attribute must have been on for the table space before the table was dropped. You can activate this attribute for a table space by using the ALTER TABLESPACE statement for an existing table space or by using the CREATE TABLESPACE statement when you create a table space.

Activating the DROPPED TABLE RECOVERY attribute for a table space increases the amount of I/O for log files and history files when tables are dropped. This can affect the performance of the database system if large numbers of tables are dropped regularly.

To recover a dropped table, follow these steps:

1. Obtain the ID that you use to identify the dropped table to the ROLLFORWARD command.

2. Obtain the DDL statement that was originally used to create the table. To obtain this information, use the LIST DROPPED TABLES command. This command displays the list of tables that have been dropped, their names, when they were dropped, the ID that you use to identify them for roll-forward processing, and the DDL that was used to create them.

3. Restore the table space that contained the dropped table from a backup image that was taken before the table was dropped. The backup image can be for either the table space or its database.

4. Roll forward the table space to the end of the logs using the RECOVER DROPPED TABLE *dropped_table_id* TO *export_directory* option. The *dropped_table_id* is the ID obtained from the LIST DROPPED TABLES command, and the *export_directory* is the directory where you want the output files to be written.

During the roll-forward processing, data files are written that you must later import into the recreated table to populate it. These files are written in the PC/IXF format. If an error such as a disk-full condition occurs during the roll-forward processing, the operation will terminate.

To obtain the fastest recovery time and keep the database online, you should restore and roll forward at the table space level. This allows you to keep the database online, and it minimizes the number of log entries that the database manager must process.

5. Recreate the table by using the DDL statement that you obtained from the LIST DROPPED TABLES command.

6. Import or load the data that was exported by the Rollforward utility into the table. The table data that was exported during the roll-forward processing is in a file called data.000. This file is located in the NODE*nnnn* subdirectory of the specified export directory (or directories), where *nnnn* identifies the node number.

You can recover only one dropped table at a time. If you have more than one table that you want to recover, you must repeat the procedure for each table.

Planning to Use the ROLLFORWARD Command

To use the ROLLFORWARD command, you must have SYSADM, SYSCTRL, or SYSMAINT authority. The database must already be configured for roll-forward recovery. (That is, either logretain, userexit, or both configuration parameters must be enabled.) When a database is first configured for the roll-forward function, you must make a backup copy of it. The database to be rolled forward can be local or remote. For a description of the ROLLFORWARD command, see Chapter 30.

A database must be restored successfully (using the RESTORE command) before it can be rolled forward, but a table space does not have to be restored before being rolled forward. A table space may be temporarily put into the roll-forward pending state, but it does not require a restore to fix it (for example, if a power interruption occurs).

A database roll forward runs offline. The database is not available for use until the roll forward completes (either by reaching the end of the logs during a table space roll forward, or by specifying STOP on the ROLLFORWARD command). You can, however, perform an online roll forward of table spaces as long as SYSCATSPACE is not included. When you perform an online roll-forward operation on a table space, it is not available for use, but the other table spaces in the database are.

When rolling forward, do the following:

■ Issue ROLLFORWARD (without the STOP option).

■ Issue ROLLFORWARD QUERY STATUS. If you perform end-of-log forward recovery, the QUERY STATUS can indicate that a log file (or files) is missing if the point in time returned by QUERY STATUS is earlier than you expect. If you perform point-in-time forward recovery, the QUERY STATUS will help you ensure that the roll forward is to the correct point.

■ Issue ROLLFORWARD STOP. After a ROLLFORWARD STOP, it is not possible to roll forward additional changes.

If you need to cancel a roll-forward operation to start it over again (that is, if ROLLFORWARD STOP was not specified or the ROLLFORWARD command failed), you can use ROLLFORWARD CANCEL to cancel the operation. If you use ROLLFORWARD CANCEL against a database, this places the database into the restore pending state, whether or not a roll forward is in progress against the database.

ROLLFORWARD CANCEL behavior for table spaces is as follows:

■ If you issue ROLLFORWARD CANCEL and you specify a list of table spaces that are in the roll-forward pending state, they are put in the restore pending state. In this situation, there is no roll forward command in progress.

Note   *If no table space list is specified for ROLLFORWARD CANCEL, SQL4906 is issued.*

■ If multiple table spaces are being rolled forward to the end of the logs and you specify ROLLFORWARD CANCEL with a list, only the table spaces that are in the list are put in the restore pending state. The table spaces that are not in the list remain in the roll-forward-in-progress state. If you specify ROLLFORWARD CANCEL without a list, all table spaces that are in the roll-forward-in-progress state are put in the restore pending state and the ROLLFORWARD command is no longer in progress.

■ If you issue ROLLFORWARD CANCEL and one or more table spaces are being rolled forward to a point in time, they are all put in the restore pending state, whether or not you specify a list. Even if you specify a list, the list is ignored and all table spaces that are in the roll-forward-in-progress state are put in the restore pending state, and the ROLLFORWARD command is no longer in progress.

Note   *You cannot use ROLLFORWARD CANCEL to cancel a roll-forward operation that is running. You can use it to cancel only a roll-forward operation that completed but did not have ROLLFORWARD STOP issued for it, or for a roll-forward operation that failed before completing.*

■ You can perform a partial or subset restore of a backup created using the current version of DB2. This cannot be done with earlier versions of DB2.

■ A table space requires roll-forward recovery if it is in a roll-forward pending state. It is in this state following a table space–level restore or being taken offline because of a media error.

■ You do not have to recover your database with the latest backup copy of the database: you can start with any backup, as long as you have the logs associated with and following that backup.

■ You should continue to make periodic backups of a database to reduce recovery time.

Invoking the ROLLFORWARD Command

When you invoke the ROLLFORWARD command, you can specify a time to limit the transactions that will be recovered from the database logs. If you are restoring from a backup that was created using the online option of the BACKUP command, the time on the ROLLFORWARD command must be later than the online backup end time.

MAINTAINING DATA

If you are rolling forward a table space (or table spaces) to a point in time, you must roll forward at least to the minimum recovery time, which is the last update to the system catalogs for this table space or its tables. You can get the minimum recovery time for a table space by using the LIST TABLESPACES SHOW DETAIL command.

A log uses a timestamp associated with the completion of a unit of work. The timestamp in the logs uses the Coordinated Universal Time (UTC), which helps to avoid having the same timestamp associated with different logs (because of a change in time associated with daylight saving time, for example). The timestamp used on the backup is based on the local time that the BACKUP started. As a result, when you call the ROLLFORWARD command, you must specify the time in Coordinated Universal Time.

 The special register CURRENT TIMEZONE holds the difference between UTC and the local time at the application server database. Local time is the UTC plus the current time zone contents.

If you stop the roll-forward operation before it passes the point where the online backup ended, the database is left in a roll-forward pending state. If a table space is being rolled forward, it is left in the roll-forward-in-progress state.

Using the Load Copy Location File

The DB2LOADREC registry variable is used to identify the file with the load copy location information. This file is used during roll-forward recovery to locate the load copy. It has information on the following:

- Media type
- Number of media devices to be used
- Location of the load copy generated during table load
- Filename of the load copy, if applicable

If the location file does not exist or no matching entry is found in the file, the information from the log record is used. The information in the file may be overwritten before the roll-forward recovery takes place.

 If an entry in the file identified by the DB2LOADREC registry variable is not valid, then the old load copy location file will be used to provide information to replace the invalid entry.

The following information is provided in the location file. The first five parameters must have valid values and are used to identify the load copy. The entire structure is repeated for each load copy recorded.

```
TIMestamp        19950725182542        * Timestamp generated at load time
SCHema           PAYROLL               * Schema of table loaded
TABlename        EMPLOYEES             * Table name
DATabasename     DBT                   * Database name
DB2instance      TORONTO               * DB2INSTANCE
BUFfernumber     NULL           * Number of buffers to be used for recovery
SESsionnumber    NULL           * Number of sessions to be used for recovery
TYPeofmedia      L              * Type of media - L for local device.
                                                  A for TSM
                                                  O for other vendors

LOCationnumber 3               * Number of locations
     ENTry       /u/toronto/dbt.payroll.employes.001
     ENT         /u/toronto/dbt.payroll.employes.002
     ENT         /dev/rmt0
TIM              19950725192054
SCH              PAYROLL
TAB              DEPT
DAT              DBT
DB2              TORONTO
SES              NULL
BUF              NULL
TYP              A
TIM              19940325192054
SCH              PAYROLL
TAB              DEPT
DAT              DBT
DB2              TORONTO
SES              NULL
BUF              NULL
TYP              O
SHRlib           /@sys/lib/backup_vendor.a
```

In the preceding example:

■ The first three characters for each keyword are significant. All keywords are required in the specified order. No blank lines will be accepted.

■ The timestamp is in the format *yyyymmddhhnnss*.

■ All fields are mandatory except for BUF and SES, which may be NULL. If SES is NULL, the value specified by configuration parameter NUMLOADRECSES will be used. If BUF is NULL, the default is SES+2.

■ If even one of the entries in the location file is not valid, the previous load copy location file is used to provide those entries.

■ The type of media may be local device (L, for tape, disk, or diskettes), TSM (A), or other vendor (O). If the type is L, the number of locations followed by the location entries is required. If the type is A, no further input is required. If the type is O, the shared library name is required. For details about using TSM and other vendor products as backup media, see the *IBM DB2 Universal Database Administration Guide: Planning.*

■ The SHRlib parameter points to a library that can store the LOAD COPY data.

If you run LOAD COPY NO and do not take a backup copy of the database or affected table spaces after running LOAD, you cannot restore the database or table spaces to a point in time after the LOAD was performed. That is, you cannot use roll-forward recovery to rebuild the database or table spaces to a state after the LOAD. You can restore the database or table spaces only to a point in time that precedes the LOAD.

If you want to use a particular load copy, the LOAD timestamps are recorded in the recovery history file for the database.

Recovering Dropped Tables

Sometimes you may have accidentally dropped one or more tables whose data you still need. If you have such tables where the data must not be lost, even accidentally, consider making that table recoverable following a drop.

You can recover the table's data by performing a database restore followed by a database roll forward. This may be time-consuming if the database is large, and it will make your data unavailable during the recovery. Alternatively, by using the dropped table recovery, you can recover your dropped table's data using table space–level restore and roll forward. This will be faster than a database-level recovery and will allow your database to remain available to the users.

For a dropped table to be recoverable, the table space in which the table resides must have its DROPPED TABLE RECOVERY option turned on. To do so, use the ALTER TABLESPACE statement or the CREATE TABLESPACE statement.

The DROPPED TABLE RECOVERY option is table space–specific and can be specified only for a regular table space. To determine if a table space has this characteristic, you can query the DROP_RECOVERY column of the table space name in the SYSCAT.TABLESPACES catalog table.

When a DROP TABLE statement is run against a table in a table space that has the DROPPED TABLE RECOVERY option ON, an additional log entry is made in the log files. The log entry has information identifying the dropped table. An entry is also made in the recovery history file and contains information that can be used to recreate the table.

You can recover a dropped table by doing the following:

■ Obtain the identification of the dropped table. This identification can be found in the recovery history file by using the LIST HISTORY DROPPED TABLE command. A list of tables that have been dropped is displayed, as well as the information needed to recreate the table. (The dropped table ID is listed in the LIST HISTORY output under the Backup ID column.)

■ Restore a database or table space backup taken before the table was dropped.

■ Roll forward to a point in time after the drop using the RECOVER DROPPED TABLE option on the ROLLFORWARD command. Other information that is required when using this option includes the dropped table identification and the directory path where the output files will be written.

■ Recreate the table using the CREATE TABLE statement from the recovery history file.

■ Import the data exported by the ROLLFORWARD command into the table.

The exported data is written to files using the following naming convention. Under the *export_directory* specified in the ROLLFORWARD command, a subdirectory is created by the database manager. You can create the subdirectory before the roll-forward request is issued, and you can use this subdirectory to export the data to a particular drive or machine. The subdirectory is named NODE*nnnn,* where *nnnn* is the node number. In the subdirectory, a data file is exported under the name "data," containing the dropped table's data.

There are some restrictions on the type of data that is recoverable from the dropped table. Only a single dropped table can be recovered at a time. To recover several dropped tables, the recovery sequence presented previously must be carried out each time another table is to be recovered. It is not possible to recover the following:

■ **LOB or LONG data**   The DROPPED TABLE RECOVERY option is not supported for LONG table spaces. Attempts to use it for a LONG table space will return error SQL628N. In an attempt to recover a dropped table that contains LOB or LONG VARCHAR columns, these columns will be set to NULL in the generated export file. The DROPPED TABLE RECOVERY option should be turned ON only for regular table spaces and not for temporary or long table spaces.

■ **The meta information associated with row types**   (The data is recovered, but not the metadata.) The data in the hierarchy table of the typed table will be recovered. This data may contain more information than appeared in the typed table that was dropped.

Considerations for Managing Log Files

The numbering scheme for archived logs starts with S0000000.LOG and goes through S9999999.LOG (10,000,000 logs). The database manager restarts using S0000000.LOG under these conditions:

■ When a database configuration file is changed to enable the roll-forward function

■ When a database configuration file is changed to disable the roll-forward function

■ When the logs wrap; that is, after log S9999999.LOG is used

When the roll-forward recovery method completes successfully, the last log that was used by roll-forward is truncated, and logging begins with the next sequential log. The practical effect is that any log in the log path directory with a sequence number greater than the last log used for roll-forward recovery is reused. Be sure to make a copy of the logs before executing the ROLLFORWARD command. (You can use a user exit program to copy the logs to another location.)

You can have duplicate names for different logs because

- The database manager starts renaming logs with S0000000.LOG (as described previously).

- The database manager reuses log names after restoring a database (with or without roll-forward recovery).

The database manager ensures that an incorrect log is not applied during roll-forward recovery, but it cannot detect the location of the required log. You must ensure that the correct logs are available for roll-forward recovery.

If you moved log files to a location other than that specified by the *logpath* database configuration parameter, use the OVERFLOW LOG PATH parameter of the ROLLFORWARD command to specify the additional path to them. If you are rolling forward changes in a database or table space and the roll-forward operation cannot find the next log, the log name is returned in the SQLCA, indicating the next log file needed, and roll-forward recovery stops. At this time, if there are no more logs available, you can use the ROLLFORWARD command to stop processing.

Archived logs are placed in the log path. The log path defaults to the SQLOGDIR subdirectory but can be changed with the *newlogpath* configuration parameter. To place them elsewhere, enable the database for user exit, or change the log path with *newlogpath*. In this case, you may need to use the OVERFLOW LOG PATH parameter of the ROLLFORWARD command to point to them when you roll forward.

If you enable a user exit by changing the database configuration file, the archived logs can be redirected to a user-defined storage device such as a tape drive. Also, you can use a user exit program to manage the storage of archived logs. If you change the *newlogpath* parameter, any existing archived logs are unaffected. You must keep track of the location of the logs.

If you terminate the roll-forward recovery (by specifying the STOP option on the ROLLFORWARD command) and the log containing the completion of a transaction has not been applied to the database or table space, the incomplete transaction will be rolled back to ensure that the database or table space is left in a consistent state.

If a database enabled for roll-forward recovery is restored either without being rolled forward or without being rolled forward to a specific time, an archived log may be associated with two or more different log sequences of a database because log names are reused. Before discarding an archived log, you must ensure that you do not need it. (Figure 12-1 provides an illustration of the logs that are created.)

If, during a full database recovery, you have rolled forward to a point in time and stopped in the middle of the logs (as shown in Figure 12-1), you have created a new log sequence. The two log sequences cannot be combined. If you have an online backup that spans through the first log sequence, you must use the first log sequence to complete the roll-forward recovery.

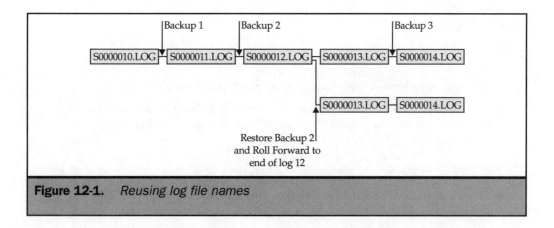

Figure 12-1. *Reusing log file names*

If you have created a new log sequence after recovery, any table space backups taken in the old log sequence are invalidated. Restore rejects the table space backups in this case. There may be times when restore fails to recognize that the backup is no longer valid (particularly for online backups) and the restore is successful. However, roll forward for the table space will fail, and the table space will be left in a roll-forward pending state.

In Figure 12-1, assume that a table space backup, Backup 3, is completed between S0000013.LOG and S0000014.LOG in the top log sequence. If you restored and rolled forward using database Backup 2, you would have to roll forward through S0000012.LOG. After this, you could continue to roll forward through either the top log sequence or the newer bottom log sequence. If you rolled forward through the bottom sequence, you would not be able to use the table space Backup 3 to do a table space restore and roll-forward recovery.

If you wanted to restore the database and roll forward a table space to the end of the logs using the table space Backup 3, you would have to restore using database Backup 2 and then roll forward using the top log sequence. After the table space Backup 3 has been restored, you can then request a roll forward to end of logs.

A log uses a timestamp associated with the completion of a unit of work. The timestamp in the logs uses the Coordinated Universal Time (UTC), which helps to avoid having the same timestamp associated with different logs (because of a change in time associated with daylight saving time, for example). The timestamp used on the backup is based on the local time. As a result, when you call the ROLLFORWARD command, you must specify the time in Coordinated Universal Time.

Note *The special register CURRENT TIMEZONE holds the difference between UTC and the local time at the application server database. Local time is the UTC plus the current time zone contents.*

Using Raw Logs

You can use a raw device for your database log. There are advantages and disadvantages in doing so. The advantages are the following:

- You can attach more than 26 physical drives to a system.
- The file I/O path length is shorter. This may improve performance on your system. You should conduct benchmarks to evaluate whether there are measurable benefits for your workload.

The disadvantages are the following:

- The device cannot be shared by other applications; the entire device *must* be assigned to DB2.
- The device cannot be operated on by any operating system utility or third-party tool that would back up or copy from the device.
- You can easily wipe out the file system on an existing drive if you specify the wrong physical drive number.

Note *If you use the sqlurlog API, you should not use a raw device for logging.*

You can configure a raw log with the *newlogpath* database configuration parameter. See the *IBM DB2 Universal Database Administration Guide: Implementation* for an example of the syntax to use to specify a raw device during table space creation. Before doing so, however, consider the advantages and disadvantages just listed and the additional considerations listed next:

- Only one device is allowed. You can define the device over multiple disks at the operating system level. DB2 will make an operating system call to determine the size of the device in 4KB pages. If you use multiple disks, this will provide a larger device, and the striping that results can improve performance by faster I/O throughput.
- DB2 will attempt to write to the last 4KB page of the device. If the device size is greater than 2GB, the attempt to write to the last page will fail on operating systems that do not provide support for devices larger than 2GB. In this situation, DB2 will attempt to use all pages, up to the supported limit. Information about the size of the device is used to indicate the size of the device (in 4KB pages) available to DB2 under the support of the operating system. The amount of disk space that DB2 can write to is referred to as the device-size-available. The first 4KB page of the device is not used by DB2. (This space is generally used by operating systems for other purposes.) This means that the total space available to DB2 is device-size = device-size-available –1.

- The logsecond parameter is not used. DB2 will not allocate secondary logs. The size of active log space is the number of 4KB pages that result from logprimary × logfilsiz.

- Log records are still grouped into log extents, each with a log file size (logfilsiz) of 4KB pages. Log extents are placed in the raw device, one after another. Each extent also consists of an extra two pages for the extent header. This means that the number of available log extents the device can support is device-size/ (logfilsiz + 2).

- The device must be large enough to support the active log space. That is, the number of available log extents must be greater than (or equal to) the value specified for the *logprimary* configuration parameter.

- If you are using circular logging, the *logprimary* configuration parameter will determine the number of log extents that are written to the device. This may result in unused space on the device.

- If you are using log retention (*logretain*) without a user exit, after the number of available log extents are all used up, all operations that result in an update will receive a log-full error. At this time, you must shut down the database and take an offline backup of it to ensure recoverability. After the database backup, the log records written to the device are lost, which means that you cannot use an earlier database backup to restore the database and roll it forward. If you take a database backup before the number of available log extents are all used up, you can restore and roll forward the database.

- If you are using log retention (logretain) with a user exit, the user exit program is called for each log extent as it is filled with log records. The user exit program must be able to read the device and to store the archived log as a file. DB2 will not call a user exit to retrieve log files to a raw device. Instead, during roll-forward recovery, DB2 will read the extent headers to determine if the raw device contains the log file to be used. If the required log file is not found in the raw device, DB2 will search the overflow log path. If the log file is still not found, DB2 will call the user exit to retrieve the log file into the overflow log path. If you do not specify an overflow log path for the ROLLFORWARD command, DB2 will not call the user exit to retrieve the log during the roll-forward operations.

- If you are using DPropR and writing logs to a raw device, the read log API will not call the user exit to retrieve log files. Requested log records, however, will still be returned if they are available on the device. If you request logs that predate the oldest ones on the device, they will not be returned. (The behavior is similar to DB2 not being able to find the log file that contains the requested log records.)

Note   *It is recommended that you do not use DPropR when you use a raw device for logging.*

MAINTAINING DATA

Losing Logs

Dropping a database erases all logs in the current database log path directory. Before dropping a database, you may need to make copies of the logs.

If you are rolling forward a database to a point in time, the last log used in the roll-forward recovery and all existing logs following it are reused. You lose the ability to recover past that particular point in time. Therefore, you should copy all the logs in the current database log path directory before beginning a point-in-time recovery. When the roll-forward processing completes, the log file with the last committed transaction is truncated, and logging begins with the next sequential log. If you do not have a copy of the log before it was truncated and those with higher sequence numbers, you cannot recover the database past the specified point in time. (Once normal database activity occurs following the roll forward, new logs are created that can then be used in any subsequent recovery.)

If you change the log path directory and then remove the subdirectory or erase any logs in that subdirectory called for in the log path, the database manager will look for the logs in the default log path, SQLOGDIR, when the database is opened. If the logs are not found, the database will enter a backup pending state, and you must back up the database before it is usable. This backup must be made even if the subdirectory contained empty logs.

If you lose the log containing the point in time of the end of the online backup and you are rolling forward the corresponding restored image, the database will not be usable. To make the database usable, you must restore the database from a different backup and all associated logs.

You may encounter a situation similar to the following: you would like to do a point-in-time recovery on a full database, but you are concerned that you might lose a log during the recovery process. (This scenario could occur if you have an extended number of archived logs between the time of the last backup database image and the point in time when you would like to have the database recovered.) To solve this problem, you should first copy all of the applicable logs to a safe location. Then you can run the RESTORE command and use the roll-forward recovery method to the point in time you want for the database. If any of the logs you need are damaged or lost during this process, you have a backup copy of all of the logs elsewhere.

Recovery History File Information

A recovery history file is created with each database and is automatically updated whenever there is any of the following:

- Backup of a database or table space
- Restore of a database or table space
- Roll forward of a database or table space

- Alter of a table space
- Quiesce of a table space
- Rename of a table space
- Load of a table
- Drop of a table
- Reorganization of a table
- Update of table statistics

You can use the summarized backup information in this file to recover all or part of the database to a given point in time. The information in the file includes the following:

- An identification (ID) field associated with each entry to uniquely identify that entry
- The part of the database that was copied and how it was copied
- The time the copy was made
- The location of the copy (stating both the device information and the logical way to access the copy)
- The last time a restore was done
- The time a table space was renamed showing the previous and the current name of the table space
- The status of the backup: active, inactive, expired, or deleted
- The last log sequence number saved by the database backup or by a roll-forward recovery

To see the entries in the recovery history file, use the LIST HISTORY command.

Note   *When a restore and roll forward is carried out to the end of all the logs, the backup ID shown following a LIST HISTORY command represents the end of time. That is, the backup ID value is 99991231235959. The backup ID is transformed this way only when a roll forward is carried out.*

Every backup operation (both table space and full database) includes a copy of the recovery history file. The recovery history file is linked to the database, so dropping a database deletes the recovery history file. Restoring a database to a new location restores the recovery history file to the new location. Restoring an existing database does not overwrite the existing recovery history file for the database.

If the current database is unusable or not available and the associated recovery history file is damaged or deleted, an option on the RESTORE command allows only the recovery history file to be restored. The recovery history file can then be reviewed to provide information on which backup to use to restore the database.

MAINTAINING DATA

The size of the file is controlled by the *rec_his_retentn* configuration parameter that specifies a retention period (in days) for the entries in the file. Even if the number for this parameter is set to 0, the most recent full database backup plus its restore set is kept. (The only way to remove this copy is to use the PRUNE with FORCE option.) The retention period has a default of 366 days. The period can be set to an indefinite number of days by setting it to –1. In this case, explicit pruning of the file is required.

You can query and run commands against the recovery history file by using an API function call, the command line processor, or the DB2 Control Center. The five basic queries and commands are OPEN, CLOSE, GET NEXT, UPDATE, and PRUNE. Detailed information about the history file is recorded in the SQLUHINFO structure. For more information about this structure, refer to the *IBM DB2 Universal Database Administrative API Reference.*

Garbage Collection

The number of DB2 database backups documented in the recovery history file is monitored automatically by something called DB2 Garbage Collection. The configuration parameter *num_db_backups* defines how many active backups are kept. An *active backup* is one that can be restored and rolled forward by using the current logs to reach the current state of the database. An *inactive backup* cannot be restored and rolled forward to reach the current state of the database because it requires a different set of log files.

DB2 Garbage Collection is also responsible for marking the history file entries for a DB2 database or table space backup as inactive, if that backup does not correspond to the current log sequence (also called the *current log chain*). The current log sequence is determined by the DB2 database backup that has been restored and the log files that have been processed. After a database backup is restored, all database backups that were taken after the backup that was restored become inactive because the restored backup begins a new log chain. A table space backup becomes inactive when, after restoring it, the current state of the DB2 database cannot be reached by applying the current sequence of logs.

DB2 Garbage Collection is invoked after completing a DB2 database backup. The value of the *num_db2_backups* configuration parameter is used to scan the current history file starting with the last entry. DB2 Garbage Collection is also invoked after completing a restore of a database backup with or without rolling forward the logs.

If an active database backup is restored, but it is not the most recent database backup recorded in the history file, any subsequent database backups belonging to the same log sequence are marked as inactive. If an inactive database backup is restored, any inactive database backups belonging to the current log sequence are marked as active again. As with restoring an active database backup, all active database backups that are no longer in the current log sequence are marked as inactive.

After every full database backup, the *rec_his_retentn* configuration parameter is used to prune expired entries from the history file. All expired backups are removed.

You can use the PRUNE HISTORY command at any time to prune only backups that are marked as expired from the history file (unless you use the WITH FORCE option).

The Complete Reference

Part IV

Performance

The Complete Reference

DB2

Chapter 13

Database Monitoring

Database monitoring serves an important function in maintaining the performance and health of your database management system (DBMS). To facilitate monitoring, DB2 collects information from the database manager (DBM), its databases, and any connected applications. In this chapter, we will look at how you can access this information.

Introducing the System Monitor

There are two components to the database system monitor, each serving a different purpose: the snapshot monitor and the event monitor. The *snapshot monitor* returns a snapshot of database activity at a point in time. The *event monitor* logs data as events occur. While these approaches differ in their presentation of monitor data, they use a common model of data organization.

Data Organization in the System Monitor

The system monitor stores information it collects in entities called *data elements.* Each data element has a unique name, and it stores information only of a certain type. For example, the Deadlocks Detected data element has an element name of *deadlocks* and stores data of type *counter*.

Data Element Types

The following are the available data element types, along with their characteristics.

- **Counter**   counts the number of times an activity occurs. Counter values increase during monitoring. Most are resettable.

- **Gauge**   indicates the current value for an item. Gauge values can go up and down depending on database activity (for example, the number of locks held).

- **Water mark**   indicates the highest (maximum) or lowest (minimum) value an element has reached since monitoring was started. These are not resettable.

- **Information**   provides reference-type details of your monitoring activities. This can include items such as node names, aliases, and path details.

- **Timestamp**   indicates the date and time that an activity took place by providing the number of seconds and microseconds that have elapsed since January 1, 1970.

- **Time**   returns the number of seconds and microseconds spent on an activity.

Logical Data Groups

Data elements return data for one or more logical data groups. Each *logical data group* represents a specific scope of database activity and is composed of data elements that collect data at that scope (or level). The snapshot monitor and event monitor each have their own set of logical data groups because the scopes of activity for each differ. For example, some of the levels from which the snapshot monitor collects data are the database manager and the buffer pool; the corresponding logical data groups are *db2* and *bufferpool*. The event monitor, for example, collects deadlock and statement data (among other types of data); the corresponding logical data groups are *deadlock_event* and *stmt_event*. Data elements are organized by the logical data groups for which they return data.

In Chapter 31, all the logical data groups for both the snapshot and event monitor are presented, along with their data elements.

Initialization of Counters

The data collected by the database manager includes several accumulating counters. These counters are incremented during the operation of the database, for example, every time an application commits a transaction.

Counters are initialized when their applicable object becomes active. For instance, the number of buffer pool pages read for a database is set to zero when the database is activated.

Counters under switch control are reset to zero when their associated switch is turned on. Counters returned by event monitors are reset to zero when the event monitor is activated.

Memory Requirements

The memory required for maintaining the private views of the database system monitor data is allocated from the monitor heap. Its size is controlled by the *mon_heap_sz* configuration parameter. The amount of memory required for monitoring activity varies widely, depending on the following: the number of monitoring applications, the event monitors, the settings of monitor switches (see the "Snapshot Monitor Switches" section later in this chapter), and the level of database activity.

The following formula provides an approximation of the number of pages required for the monitor heap:

```
(number of monitoring applications + 1) *
(number of databases * (800 + (number of tables accessed * 20) +
  ( (number of applications connected + 1) *
      (200 + (number of table spaces * 100) ) ) ) )
/ 4096
```

You may need to experiment with this value, increasing it if monitor commands occasionally fail with an SQLCODE of –973.

Using the Snapshot Monitor

You use the snapshot monitor to capture DBMS information at a specific time. Administrators take snapshots to evaluate the status of a database. Snapshots taken at regular intervals are useful for observing trends and foreseeing potential problems.

Preparing to Use the Snapshot Monitor

To perform any of the snapshot monitoring tasks, you must have SYSMAINT, SYSCTRL, or SYSADM authority on the database manager instance you want to monitor.

The application (the command line processor (CLP), the performance monitor, or the C application) that will issue snapshot tasks must be attached to the instance to be monitored. If there is no attachment to an instance, a default instance attachment is created.

All snapshot monitor requests invoked by the application are directed to its attached instance. This allows a client to monitor a remote server by simply attaching to an instance on it. To explicitly attach to an instance from the CLP, use the ATTACH command, which is discussed further in Chapter 30. Chapter 23 explains how to make an explicit instance attachment from a C application.

Snapshot Monitor Switches

Collecting information for the system monitor demands system resources and therefore affects database performance. Because of this, *monitor switches* must be activated to collect information for the more expensive data elements. Information for basic data elements is always collected.

Table 13-1 lists the nonbasic types of data returned by the snapshot monitor and the corresponding monitor switches.

Monitor Switch	DBM Parameter	Information Provided
BUFFERPOOL	DFT_MON_BUFPOOL	Number of reads and writes, time taken
LOCK	DFT_MON_LOCK	Number of locks held, deadlocks
SORT	DFT_MON_SORT	Number of heaps used, sort performance
STATEMENT	DFT_MON_STMT	Start/stop time, statement identification
TABLE	DFT_MON_TABLE	Measure of activity (rows read/written)
UOW	DFT_MON_UOW	Start/end times, completion status

Table 13-1.   *Snapshot Monitor Information*

You can set monitor switches at the database manager level or at the application level. When applications are started, they automatically inherit the monitor settings of the database manger. Refer to the upcoming section "Visibility of Snapshot Monitor Data" for a discussion on the scope of monitor switches.

Using the CLP to Set Monitor Switches

You set monitor switches at the database manager level within the database manager configuration file. (The DBM parameters for each monitor switch are listed in Table 13-1.) By default, all monitor switches at the database manager and application level are turned off.

The following CLP command issued from a DB2 command line turns on the LOCK monitor switch at the database manager level:

```
update dbm cfg using DFT_MON_LOCK on
```

We can then use the GET DATABASE MONITOR SWITCHES command to check the status of monitor switches at the database manager level:

```
get database manager monitor switches
```

The results are as follows:

```
      DBM System Monitor Information Collected

Switch list for node 0
Buffer Pool Activity Information   (BUFFERPOOL) = OFF
Lock Information                         (LOCK) = ON   06-10-2001 20:46:08.528
Sorting Information                      (SORT) = OFF
SQL Statement Information           (STATEMENT) = OFF
Table Activity Information              (TABLE) = OFF
Unit of Work Information                  (UOW) = OFF
```

We see that LOCK is listed as being ON, and a date and time are provided, indicating when the switch was turned on. Based on the preceding information, we can deduce that the database manager is collecting information for basic data elements and all data elements controlled by the LOCK switch.

To activate any changes made to database manager monitor switches while an application is running, you must issue the TERMINATE command:

```
terminate
```

PERFORMANCE

At the application level, you update monitor switches by using the UPDATE MONITOR SWITCHES command. The following command turns on the TABLE switch:

```
update monitor switches using TABLE on
```

The GET MONITOR SWITCHES command shows the status of monitor switches at the application level:

```
get monitor switches
```

The results are as follows:

```
            Monitor Recording Switches

Switch list for node 0
Buffer Pool Activity Information   (BUFFERPOOL) = OFF
Lock Information                         (LOCK) = ON  06-10-2001 20:46:08.528
Sorting Information                      (SORT) = OFF
SQL Statement Information          (STATEMENT) = OFF
Table Activity Information              (TABLE) = ON  06-10-2001 20:58:52.108
Unit of Work Information                 (UOW) = OFF
```

In the preceding output, both the LOCK switch and the TABLE switch have been enabled. Also note that the date and time information given for the LOCK switch is the same as in the earlier example in which the status for monitor switches at the database manager level was displayed.

Using the db2MonitorSwitches API to Set Monitor Switches

You can set monitor switches in C applications by using the db2MonitorSwitches API. In the following code sample, the function TurnOnAllSwitches() will do as its name suggests and activate all of the monitor switches. An instance connection is required for the db2MonitorSwitches API, and hence, for this function to work.

```c
#include <sqlutil.h>
#include <db2ApiDf.h>

int TurnOnAllSwitches(void) {
  int rc = 0;
  struct sqlca sqlca;
  db2MonitorSwitchesData switchesData;
  struct sqlm_recording_group switchesList[SQLM_NUM_GROUPS];
  sqluint32 outputFormat;
```

```
switchesList[SQLM_UOW_SW].input_state = SQLM_ON;
switchesList[SQLM_STATEMENT_SW].input_state = SQLM_ON;
switchesList[SQLM_TABLE_SW].input_state = SQLM_ON;
switchesList[SQLM_BUFFER_POOL_SW].input_state = SQLM_ON;
switchesList[SQLM_LOCK_SW].input_state = SQLM_ON;
switchesList[SQLM_SORT_SW].input_state = SQLM_ON;
switchesData.piGroupStates = switchesList;
switchesData.poBuffer = NULL;
switchesData.iVersion = SQLM_DBMON_VERSION7;
switchesData.iBufferSize = 0;
switchesData.iReturnData = 0;
switchesData.iNodeNumber = SQLM_CURRENT_NODE;
switchesData.poOutputFormat = &outputFormat;
db2MonitorSwitches(db2Version710, &switchesData, &sqlca);
return 0;
}
```

In the preceding function, there are two main steps. First, the *sqlm_recording_group* structure's elements are altered to indicate the desired status of individual switches. Second, the db2MonitorSwitches() function is called and the alterations of the individual switches are submitted. This is done by passing the db2MonitorSwitchesData structure, which contains the *sqlm_recording_group* structure as a parameter.

Visibility of Snapshot Monitor Data

Each application has its own private logical view of monitor switches and data elements. This is hinted at in the previous examples of CLP commands that alter monitor switches at the database manager level and application level. Changes to switch settings made at the database manager level are global, and they will affect every application started after the change is made (and every active application after the TERMINATE command is issued). Changes made to switch settings at the application level, however, are local—they are felt only by the application that issued the change. In the previous CLP example, the system monitor collects TABLE information only for the application that activated the TABLE switch.

The information in data elements also depends on the application accessing it. An application taking snapshots can reset its view of counters at any time by using the RESET MONITOR ALL command. Only the application issuing this command is affected; all other applications will still see the original counter values (plus any new additions).

Availability of Snapshot Monitor Data

System monitor information for a database is available only while the database is active. The information disappears when the database is deactivated.

CLP Access to Snapshot Monitor Information

DB2 has a number of CLP commands that provide access to snapshot monitor information. Table 13-2 lists these commands, ordered by the level of database monitoring information they return. Included are listings of the logical data groups whose data elements may be returned by the given command. See Chapter 31 to determine whether desired data elements are under monitor switch control.

In previous examples in this chapter, we set the TABLE switch on at the application level. Therefore, any data elements in the table and table_list logical data groups will

Monitoring Level	CLP Command	Logical Data Groups Called
Database manager	get snapshot for dbm	db2, fcm, fcm_node
Database	get snapshot for database on *dbname*	dbase, rollforward, tablespace
Database	get snapshot for all databases	dbase, rollforward, tablespace
Database	get snapshot for a federated system database	dbase_remote
Database	get snapshot for all federated system databases	dbase_remote
Application	get snapshot for application applid *appl-id*	appl, agent, appl_info, lock_wait, stmt, subsection
Application	get snapshot for application agentid *appl-handle*	appl, agent, appl_info, lock_wait, stmt, subsection
Application	get snapshot for applications on *dbname*	appl, agent, appl_info, lock_wait, stmt, subsection
Application	get snapshot for all applications	appl, agent, appl_info, lock_wait, stmt, subsection

Table 13-2. *Snapshot Monitor CLP Commands*

Monitoring Level	CLP Command	Logical Data Groups Called
Application	`get snapshot for federated system applications on dbname`	dbase_appl
Application	`get snapshot for all federated system applications`	dbase_appl
Table	`get snapshot for tables on dbname`	table_list, table
Lock	`get snapshot for locks for application applid applid`	appl_lock_list, lock_wait, lock
Lock	`get snapshot for locks for application agentid appl-handle`	appl_lock_list, lock_wait, lock
Lock	`get snapshot for locks on dbname`	appl_lock_list, lock_wait, lock, db_lock_list
Table space	`get snapshot for tablespace on dbname`	tablespace_list, tablespace
Buffer pool	`get snapshot for all bufferpools`	bufferpool
Buffer pool	`get snapshot for bufferpools on dbname`	bufferpool
Dynamic SQL	`get snapshot for dynamic sql on dbname`	dysql_list, dysql

Table 13-2.   *Snapshot Monitor CLP Commands* (continued)

PERFORMANCE

be collected. After connecting to the SAMPLE database provided with DB2 UDB, let's issue an SQL statement against the STAFF table:

```
CONNECT TO sample

UPDATE staff SET salary = salary*1.10 WHERE years = 7
```

In its original form, the STAFF table in the SAMPLE database has 35 records. Six of these records will be altered by the UPDATE statement.

Now, let's take a snapshot of table activity from the current application (the application that issued the preceding SQL statement):

```
GET SNAPSHOT FOR TABLES ON sample
```

This command returns the following:

```
                Table Snapshot

First database connect timestamp       = 06-11-2001 19:40:20.957113

Last reset timestamp                   = 06-11-2001 20:06:52.388666
Snapshot timestamp                     = 06-11-2001 20:07:13.272448
Database name                          = SAMPLE
Database path                          = C:\DB2\NODE0000\SQL00002\
Input database alias                   = SAMPLE
Number of accessed tables              = 1

Table List
  Table Schema        = DB2ADMIN
  Table Name          = STAFF
  Table Type          = User
  Rows Read           = 41
  Rows Written        = 6
  Overflows           = 0
  Page Reorgs         = 0
```

From this snapshot, we can see that six rows have been written, which is as expected given that the same number of records met the condition in the UPDATE statement.

API Access to Snapshot Monitor Information

You can use the snapshot APIs to build customized C language applications to access snapshot monitor data. The snapshot APIs are listed in Table 13-3.

Snapshot Monitor API	Description
db2MonitorSwitches()	Set or query monitor switch settings
db2GetSnapshot()	Take a snapshot
db2ResetMonitor()	Reset system monitor counters
db2GetSnapshotSize()	Estimate the size of the data that would be returned for a particular invocation of db2GetSnapshot()

Table 13-3. *Snapshot Monitor APIs*

The db2MonitorSwitches API was already discussed in the earlier section, "Using the db2MonitorSwitches API to Set Monitor Switches." Once the desired switch settings have been established, the db2GetSnapshot API is ready for use.

For more information on the snapshot monitor API calls, see the sqlmon.h include file. It contains data structures that map directly to the snapshot monitor data stream, and it also contains identifiers for the snapshot monitor logical data groups and their corresponding data elements. You can find this file in the include subdirectory (SQLLIB\Include in Windows environments, and /sqllib/include in UNIX environments). The include subdirectory is present only if the DB2 Application Development Client is installed.

Depending on the snapshot information desired, a number of request types correspond to different types of monitor data. Table 13-4 lists these request types, along with the logical data groups whose data elements may be returned. See Chapter 31 to determine whether desired data elements are under monitor switch control.

Monitoring Level	API Request Type	Logical Data Groups Called
Connections List	SQLMA_APPLINFO_ALL	appl_id_info
Connections List	SQLMA_DBASE_APPLINFO	appl_id_info
Database Manager	SQLMA_DB2	db2, fcm, fcm_node
Database	SQLMA_DBASE	dbase, rollforward, tablespace

Table 13-4. *Snapshot Monitor API Request Types*

Monitoring Level	API Request Type	Logical Data Groups Called
Database	SQLMA_DBASE_ALL	dbase, rollforward, tablespace
Database	SQLMA_DBASE_REMOTE	dbase_remote
Database	SQLMA_DBASE_REMOTE_ALL	dbase_remote
Application	SQLMA_APPL	appl, agent, appl_info, lock_wait, stmt, subsection
Application	SQLMA_AGENT_ID	appl, agent, appl_info, lock_wait, stmt, subsection
Application	SQLMA_DBASE_APPLS	appl, agent, appl_info, lock_wait, stmt, subsection
Application	SQLMA_APPL_ALL	appl, agent, appl_info, lock_wait, stmt, subsection
Application	SQLMA_DBASE_APPLS_REMOTE	dbase_appl
Application	SQLMA_APPL_REMOTE_ALL	dbase_appl
Table	SQLMA_DBASE_TABLES	table_list, table
Lock	SQLMA_APPL_LOCKS	appl_lock_list, lock_wait, lock
Lock	SQLMA_APPL_LOCKS_AGENT_ID	appl_lock_list, lock_wait, lock
Lock	SQLMA_DBASE_LOCKS	appl_lock_list, lock_wait, lock, db_lock_list
Table space	SQLMA_DBASE_TABLESPACES	tablespace_list, tablespace
Buffer pool	SQLMA_BUFFERPOOLS_ALL	bufferpool

Table 13-4. *Snapshot Monitor API Request Types* (continued)

Monitoring Level	API Request Type	Logical Data Groups Called
Buffer pool	SQLMA_DBASE_BUFFERPOOLS	bufferpool
Dynamic SQL	SQLMA_DYNAMIC_SQL	dysql_list, dysql

Table 13-4. *Snapshot Monitor API Request Types* (continued)

Making a Snapshot Request

The following code demonstrates how to implement the snapshot monitor API. In this sample, the supporting structures required by db2GetSnapshot() are initialized, and they are set up to capture database manager–level information. This is indicated by the passing of the API request type, SQLMA_DB2 to db2GetSnapShot(). The API request types and the values they return are described in Table 13-4.

```
#include <stdio.h>
#include <sqlmon.h>
#include <db2ApiDf.h>
#define SNAPSHOT_BUFFER_UNIT_SZ 1024

typedef struct SnapshotData
{ char *buffer;
  struct sqlma *pRequestedDataGroups;
  sqluint32 bufferSize;
  char *curGroup;
  sqlint32 serverTimeZoneDisp;
} SnapshotData;

int SnapshotGet()
{ int rc = 0;
  struct sqlma *pRequestedDataGroups;
  SnapshotData snapshotData;
  struct sqlca sqlca;
  static sqluint32 snapshotBufferSize = SNAPSHOT_BUFFER_UNIT_SZ;
  char *snapshotBuffer;
  db2GetSnapshotData getSnapshotParam;
  struct sqlm_collected collectedData;
```

PERFORMANCE

```
  sqluint32 outputFormat;

  pRequestedDataGroups = (struct sqlma *)malloc(SQLMASIZE(1));
  pRequestedDataGroups->obj_num = 1;
// The next line determines the API request type.
  pRequestedDataGroups->obj_var[0].obj_type = SQLMA_DB2;
  snapshotBuffer = (char *)malloc(snapshotBufferSize);
  if (snapshotBuffer == NULL)
  { printf("\nMemory allocation error.\n");
    return 1;
  }
  getSnapshotParam.piSqlmaData = pRequestedDataGroups;
  getSnapshotParam.poCollectedData = &collectedData;
  getSnapshotParam.iBufferSize = snapshotBufferSize;
  getSnapshotParam.poBuffer = snapshotBuffer;
  getSnapshotParam.iVersion = SQLM_DBMON_VERSION7;
  getSnapshotParam.iStoreResult = 0;
  getSnapshotParam.iNodeNumber = SQLM_CURRENT_NODE;
  getSnapshotParam.poOutputFormat = &outputFormat;
  db2GetSnapshot(db2Version710, &getSnapshotParam, &sqlca);
  while (sqlca.sqlcode == 1606)
  { free(snapshotBuffer);
    snapshotBufferSize = snapshotBufferSize + SNAPSHOT_BUFFER_UNIT_SZ;
    snapshotBuffer = (char *)malloc(snapshotBufferSize);
    if (snapshotBuffer == NULL)
    { printf("\nMemory allocation error.\n");
      return 1;
    }
    getSnapshotParam.iBufferSize = snapshotBufferSize;
    getSnapshotParam.poBuffer = snapshotBuffer;
    db2GetSnapshot(db2Version710, &getSnapshotParam, &sqlca);
  }
// Before the snapshot buffer is cleared, process the snapshot data stream.
  free(snapshotBuffer);
  free(pRequestedDataGroups);
  return 0;
} /* SnapshotGet */
```

Once a snapshot is taken, db2GetSnapshot() returns the snapshot monitor output to a string of characters (the snapshotBuffer variable in the preceding code).

The Snapshot Monitor Self-Describing Data Stream

The data returned by db2GetSnapshot() is in a self-describing format. (This format bears some similarities to the self-describing format used for event monitor output.) In its raw form, the snapshot monitor buffer is simply a continuous string of alphanumeric data. This data is arranged in a nested fashion to enable processing. Hence, the buffer is divided into sections based on the logical data groups present.

The collected logical data group is the first logical data group to appear in the snapshot buffer. Its data elements collect snapshot metadata, for instance, the state of monitor switches and the time a snapshot was taken. It contains the following pieces of information:

- **Size** The size in bytes of the entire snapshot buffer.
- **Type** The type of data in an element. For logical data group headings, including collected, this data will always be the character string "header."
- **Element** The name of this logical data group: collected.

The subsequent logical data groups presented in the data stream contain the following pieces of information:

- **Size** The number of bytes of data stored in the logical data group. This value includes space used by the data elements and any nested logical data groups.
- **Type** The type of data in an element. For logical data group headings, this data will always be the character string "header."
- **Element** The name of the logical data group.

Each data element presented in the data stream contains the following information:

- **Size** The number of bytes used in the data section of this data element.
- **Type** The type of data in the element. For example, counter information is typically stored as type u16bit (unsigned 16-bit integer).
- **Element** The name of the data element.
- **Data** The collected value for the element. Corresponds to the data type specified previously.

Reading the Snapshot Monitor Data Stream   To effectively use the self-describing snapshot monitor output, parse the buffer byte by byte according to the structure outlined previously in the section "The Snapshot Monitor Self-Describing Data Stream". Write your applications based on the values you expect to encounter as you parse the buffer.

All logical data groups and their data elements contain a size element. When reading the buffer, you can use the size element to skip over logical data groups or elements you do not want to examine. The size element of strings for snapshot monitor data represents the actual size of data for the string element. This size does not include a null terminator because the strings are not null terminated.

Table 13-5 shows a sample snapshot monitor buffer, formatted based on the previous descriptions of the buffer components.

Using the Performance Monitor

Snapshot monitor information can also be accessed from the Control Center via the performance monitor. The *performance monitor* is a graphical tool that captures snapshots of selected monitor information at regular time intervals and converts the results into continuous graphs. Furthermore, it is possible to set thresholds for particular variables which, when approached and reached, will alert the database administrator. These features enable administrators to detect trends and problems in the use of their DBMS, making the performance monitor an excellent diagnostic tool.

Logical Data Group	Information Type	Buffer Content
collected	Size	1000
	Type	header
	Element	collected
	Size	4
	Type	u32bit
	Element	server_db2_type
	Data	sqlf_nt_server
. . .	. . .	. . .
db2	Size	200
	Type	header
	Element	db2
	Size	4
	Type	u32bit
	Element	sort_heap_allocated
	Data	16
	Size	4
	Type	u32bit
	Element	local_cons
	Data	3

Table 13-5. *Snapshot Monitor Buffer Content*

A more thorough explanation of the performance monitor and its use can be found in the online help. (Select Help from the Performance Monitor window menu bar.)

Using the Event Monitor

The event monitor is used to collect information about aspects of the database and any attached applications when specified events occur. *Events* represent transitions in database activity, for instance, deadlocks, statements, connections, and transactions. You can define an event monitor by the type of event you want it to monitor. For example, a deadlock event monitor waits for a deadlock to occur; when one does, it collects information about the applications involved and the locks in contention.

Whereas the snapshot monitor is typically used for preventative maintenance, the event monitor is used to alert administrators to immediate or impending problems.

Preparing to Use the Event Monitor

To define and use an event monitor on a database, you must have at least DBADM authority on that database.

Each event monitor has its own private logical view of information in data elements. If a particular event monitor is deactivated and then reactivated, its view of counters is reset. Only the newly activated event monitor is affected; all other event monitors will still see the original counter values (plus any new additions).

Creating and Activating an Event Monitor

Event monitors are database objects, and as such, they are created using SQL data definition language (DDL) statements. When creating an event monitor with the CREATE EVENT MONITOR statement, the *event type* to be monitored must be specified. An event monitor can be specified to monitor more than one event type.

Table 13-6 lists supported event types, definitions of the events (the point at which data is collected), and the information returned by the event monitor.

Before an event monitor is created, you must decide whether output will be directed to a file or a named pipe. Both means of directing output are discussed later in the sections, "File Output" and "Pipe Output," but for the purposes of the following example, we will use file output.

First, we will create an event monitor to log table updates:

```
CREATE EVENT MONITOR tblmon FOR TABLES WRITE TO FILE 'c:\temp'
```

The event monitor tblmon now exists, but it still needs to be activated. This is done with the SET EVENT MONITOR statement:

```
SET EVENT MONITOR tblmon STATE 1
```

PERFORMANCE

Event Type	Event Definition	Information Returned
Deadlocks	Detection of a deadlock	Applications involved and locks in contention
Statements	End of SQL statement	Statement start/stop time, CPU used, text of dynamic SQL, SQLCA (return code of SQL statement), and other metrics
Transactions	End of unit of work	UOW start/stop time, previous UOW time, CPU consumed, locking and logging metrics
Connections	End of connection	All application-level counters
Database	Database deactivation or last connect reset	All database-level counters
Bufferpools	Database deactivation or last connect reset	Counters for buffer pools, prefetchers, page cleaners, and direct I/O for each buffer pool
Tablespaces	Database deactivation or last connect reset	Counters for buffer pools, prefetchers, page cleaners, and direct I/O for each table space
Tables	Database deactivation or last connect reset	Rows read/written for each table

Table 13-6. *Event Types*

To provide tblmon with events to monitor, let's issue the following statement, altering the STAFF table in the SAMPLE database:

```
UPDATE staff SET salary = salary*1.10 WHERE years = 7
```

As in the previous snapshot-monitoring example, the STAFF table has 35 records, 6 of which meet the condition in this statement.

According to Table 13-6, the TABLES event is recorded either when the database is deactivated or when the last connected application disconnects.

```
DISCONNECT sample
```

Disconnecting from the SAMPLE database also causes the tblmon event monitor to be deactivated, and its buffer is then automatically flushed to file. For event types that are recorded while the database is active, use the FLUSH EVENT MONITOR statement to write the buffer to a file for examination.

The DB2EVMON system command (see Chapter 29) is used to convert the files written by event monitors into meaningful results:

```
db2evmon -path c:\temp
```

The results are as follows:

```
    Reading c:\temp\00000000.EVT ...
----------------------------------------------------------------
                        EVENT LOG HEADER
  Event Monitor name: TBLMON
  Server Product ID: SQL07010
  Version of event monitor data: 6
  Byte order: LITTLE ENDIAN
  Number of nodes in db2 instance: 1
  Codepage of database: 1252
  Country code of database: 1
  Server instance name: DB2
----------------------------------------------------------------


----------------------------------------------------------------
  Database Name: SAMPLE
  Database Path: C:\DB2\NODE0000\SQL00002\
  First connection timestamp: 06-11-2001 22:55:43.022550
  Event Monitor Start time:   06-11-2001 23:06:13.696286
----------------------------------------------------------------

3) Table Event ...
  Table schema: DB2ADMIN
  Table name: STAFF

  Record is the result of a flush: FALSE
  Table type: User
  Rows read: 41
  Rows written: 6
  Overflow Accesses: 0
  Page reorgs: 0
  Table event timestamp: 06-11-2001 23:06:43.668877
```

```
4) Table Event ...
   Table schema: SYSIBM
   Table name: SYSTABLES

   Record is the result of a flush: FALSE
   Table type: Catalog
   Rows read: 1
   Rows written: 0
   Overflow Accesses: 0
   Page reorgs: 0
   Table event timestamp: 06-11-2001 23:06:43.668928
```

This event monitor trace shows that two tables were accessed: DB2ADMIN.STAFF and SYSIBM.SYSTABLES. In the db2admin.staff table event, we see that six rows are written, as was expected, given that the same number of records met the condition in the UPDATE statement.

Deactivating an Event Monitor

To deactivate, or turn off, an event monitor, use the SET EVENT MONITOR statement:

```
SET EVENT MONITOR tblmon STATE 0
```

Deactivating an event monitor does not result in its deletion. It simply exists as a dormant database object.

Deactivating an event monitor flushes all its contents. Hence, if you reactivate a deactivated event monitor, it will contain information collected only since its reactivation.

Querying the State of an Event Monitor

You can determine whether an event monitor is active by using the SQL function EVENT_MON_STATE in a query against the table SYSCAT.EVENTMONITORS.

```
SELECT evmonname, EVENT_MON_STATE(evmonname) FROM
syscat.eventmonitors
```

All existing event monitors will be listed, along with their status. A returned value of 0 indicates that the specified event monitor is inactive, and 1 indicates that it is active.

Dropping an Event Monitor

To eliminate an event monitor object, use the DROP EVENT MONITOR statement. You can do this only if the event monitor to be dropped is inactive.

```
DROP EVENT MONITOR tblmon
```

File Output

A *file event monitor* allows you to store event records in files. In the example in the previous section, "Creating and Activating an Event Monitor," a file event monitor was created with the CREATE EVENT MONITOR statement:

```
CREATE EVENT MONITOR tblmon FOR TABLES WRITE TO FILE 'c:\temp'
```

File Buffering

The event monitor output thread buffers records, using two internal buffers, before writing them to disk. Records are written to the trace only when a buffer is full. To force an event monitor to flush its buffers, you must either deactivate it or empty the buffers by using the FLUSH EVENT MONITOR statement.

The size of these buffers can be specified on the CREATE EVENT MONITOR statement with the BUFFERSIZE argument. Specifying larger buffers reduces the number of disk accesses and improves monitoring performance for event monitors with high amounts of throughput.

Blocked Event Monitors

A blocked event monitor suspends the database process that is sending monitor data when both of its buffers are full. This is to ensure that no event records are discarded while the blocked event monitor is active. The suspended database process and consequently, any dependent database processes cannot run until a buffer has been written. This can introduce a significant performance overhead, depending on the type of workload and the speed of the I/O device.

Event monitors are blocked by default.

Nonblocked Event Monitors

A nonblocked event monitor simply discards monitor data coming from the agents when the data is coming faster than the event monitor can write the data. This allows event monitoring to have less impact on other database activities. The following DDL creates a nonblocked event monitor:

```
CREATE EVENT MONITOR stmon FOR STATEMENTS WRITE TO FILE 'c:\temp'
NONBLOCKED
```

An event monitor that has discarded event records generates an *overflow event*. It specifies the start and stop time during which the monitor was discarding events and the number of events that were discarded during that period.

It is possible for an event monitor to terminate or be deactivated with a pending overflow to report. If this occurs, the following message is written to the following db2diag.log.

> `DIA1603I Event Monitor` *monitor-name* `had a pending overflow record`
> `when it was deactivated.`

Event File Management

All the output of the event monitor goes in the directory supplied in the FILE argument for the CREATE EVENT MONITOR statement. This directory will not be created by DB2 if it does not exist. Before the monitor is activated, the directory must exist, or the SET EVENT MONITOR statement will return an error.

When a file event monitor is first activated, a control file named db2event.ctl is created in this directory. Do not remove or modify this file.

Limiting Trace Size   By default, an event monitor writes its trace to a single file, called 00000000.evt. This file keeps growing as long as there is space on the file system. You can limit the maximum size of a trace by using the MAXFILESIZE and MAXFILES arguments for the CREATE EVENT MONITOR statement.

Running out of Disk Space   When a file event monitor runs out of disk space, it shuts itself down after logging a system-error-level message in the error logs, db2diag.log and db2err.log.

Restarting a File Event Monitor   When a file event monitor is restarted, it can either erase any existing data or append new data to it. This option is specified in the CREATE EVENT MONITOR statement, where either an APPEND monitor or a REPLACE monitor can be created. APPEND is the default option.

An APPEND event monitor starts writing at the end of the file it was last using. If you have removed that file, the next file number in sequence is used. When an append event monitor is restarted, only a start_event is generated. The event log header and database header are generated only for the first activation.

A REPLACE event monitor always deletes existing event files and starts writing at 00000000.evt.

Pipe Output

A *pipe event monitor* allows you to process event records in real time. This enables an event monitor application to ignore unwanted data as it is read off the pipe, thus considerably reducing storage requirements. It also allows an application to store event monitor data in real time into an SQL database.

When you direct data to a pipe, I/O is always blocked, and the only buffering is that performed by the pipe. The monitoring application reads the data from the pipe as the event monitor writes the event data. If the event monitor is unable to write the data to the pipe (for example, because the pipe is full), monitor data will be lost.

Creating Pipe Event Monitors on UNIX and Windows NT/2000

The steps for using pipe event monitors are essentially the same on most operating systems; however, the implementation details differ. The following are the basic steps for creating named pipes for the UNIX and Windows NT/2000 platforms.

Step 1: Define the event monitor

UNIX:

```
CONNECT TO sample
CREATE EVENT MONITOR stmt2 FOR STATEMENTS WRITE TO PIPE '/tmp/evmpipe1'
```

Windows NT/2000:

```
CONNECT TO sample
CREATE EVENT MONITOR stmt2 FOR STATEMENTS WRITE TO PIPE '\\.\pipe\evmpipe1'
```

Step 2: Create the named pipe   In UNIX (this includes AIX environments), use the mkfifo() function or MKFIFO command. In Windows NT, use the CreateNamedPipe() function. The pipe name must be the same as the target path specified on the CREATE EVENT MONITOR statement.

Step 3: Open the named pipe   In UNIX, use the open() function. In Windows NT, use the ConnectNamedPipe() function. You can also use the DB2EVMON command, specifying the database and pipe name. For example,

```
db2evmon -db sample -evm stmt2
```

This will open the named pipe and wait for the event monitor to write to it.

Step 4: Activate the event monitor   If the event monitor is started automatically, you do not need to take any specific action to start it unless the database is already active. (However, the pipe must already be open.)

```
SET EVENT MONITOR stmt2 STATE 1
```

Step 5: Read data from the named pipe   In UNIX, use the read() function. In Windows NT, use the ReadFile() function. Your application may stop reading data from the pipe at any time. When it reads an EOF, there is no further monitor data.

Step 6: Deactivate the event monitor

```
SET EVENT MONITOR stmt2 STATE 0
```

PERFORMANCE

You can use this statement to stop an event monitor. If you do not explicitly stop an event monitor, it will be stopped when either of the following occur:

- The last application disconnects from the database.

- It experiences an error while writing to the named pipe. For example, the monitoring application closes the pipe before deactivating the event monitor. In this case, the event monitor will turn itself off and log a system-error-level message in the diagnostic log, db2diag.log.

Step 7: Close the named pipe   In UNIX, use the close() function. In Windows NT/2000, use the DisconnectNamedPipe() function.

Step 8: Delete the named pipe   In UNIX, use the unlink() function. In Windows NT/2000, use the CloseHandle() function.

For UNIX-based operating systems, named pipes are like files, so you are not required to delete them and create them again before each use.

Pipe Overflows

There must be enough space in the named pipe to handle incoming event monitor information. If the application does not read the data fast enough from the named pipe, the pipe will fill up and overflow. The smaller the pipe buffer, the greater the chance of an overflow.

When a pipe overflow occurs, the monitor creates overflow event records indicating that an overflow has occurred. The event monitor is not turned off, but monitor data is lost. If there are outstanding overflow event records when the monitor is deactivated, a diagnostic message will be logged. Otherwise, the overflow event records will be written to the pipe when possible.

If your operating system allows you to define the size of the pipe buffer, use a pipe buffer of at least 32KB. For high-volume event monitors, you should set the monitoring application's process priority equal to or higher than the database process priority.

Reading Event Monitor Output

Due to its streaming nature, event monitor output is not as convenient to handle as snapshot monitor output. Information from event monitors is encoded either in files or comes from pipes, and it requires interpretation. Two utilities are provided to aid users in interpreting the encoded output: DB2EVMON and DB2EVA. A third option is to build a custom C language application to decode the output. Before we explore the various means to format event monitor data, let's explore the output records themselves.

Event Monitor Output Records

Event monitor output is composed of logical data groups presented in a fixed order. Regardless of the event type, the output records always contain the same opening and closing logical data groups. These frame the logical data group(s) called by the event type.

Table 13-7 presents a breakdown of event monitor output and the corresponding event types and logical data groups. For a listing of the data elements belonging to each logical data group, see Table 31-2 in Chapter 31.

As was suggested previously, the Monitor, Prolog, and Epilog sections are seen in every event monitor output stream. It is in the Contents level that the information specific to the event type is presented.

Events recorded in the Contents level contain references to the application that spawned them (an application handle or an application ID). If you are tracking events from multiple applications, use the application identifiers to keep track of the various events.

The overflow event, unlike all the others in the Contents level, does not correspond to a specific event type. It tracks the number of records lost: those generated when the system cannot keep up with a nonblocked event monitor.

Output Level	Event Type	Logical Data Group
Monitor	Monitor level	event_log_stream_header
Prolog	Log header	log_header_event
Prolog	Database header	db_header_event
Prolog	Event monitor start	start_event
Prolog	Connection header	connheader_event
Contents	Statement event	stmt_event
Contents	Subsection event	subsection_event
Contents	Transaction event	xaction_event
Contents	Connection event	conn_event
Contents	Deadlock event	deadlock_event
Contents	Deadlocked connection event	dlconn_event
Contents	Overflow	overflow_event
Epilog	Database event	db_event
Epilog	Buffer pool event	bufferpool_event
Epilog	Table space event	tablespace_event
Epilog	Table event	table_event

Table 13-7.   *Event Monitor Output Records*

PERFORMANCE

Using the DB2EVMON Tool

DB2EVMON is a utility that formats file event monitor and pipe event monitor output. An example of its use was presented earlier in the "Creating and Activating an Event Monitor" section.

```
db2evmon -path c:\temp
```

In the preceding example, the directory specified by the tblmon file event monitor is given as a parameter, and the formatted monitor output is written to the screen.

Alternatively, it is also possible to provide the database name and event monitor name as parameters:

```
db2evmon -db sample -evm tblmon
```

Event Analyzer

The DB2EVA command spawns the *event analyzer*, a GUI tool for formatting file event monitor output. For more information on its use, see Chapter 29 or the Event Analyzer online help.

Developing an Application to Format Event Monitor Output

If the DB2EVMON and DB2EVA tools do not meet your requirements for formatting event monitor output, you can develop your own application. If you are developing your application in C (or C++), be sure to make use of the sqlmon.h include file. It contains data structures that map directly to the event monitor data stream (both file output and pipe output share the same format), and it also contains identifiers for the event monitor logical data groups and their corresponding data elements. This file is located in the include subdirectory (SQLLIB\Include in Windows environments, and /sqllib/include in UNIX environments). The include subdirectory is present only if the DB2 Application Development Client is installed.

Some possibilities for event monitor output applications are as follows:

- Highlight events from certain applications.
- Create a printed report of event records, sorted by application or event type.
- Process the data stream from a pipe event monitor and save only the desired event records to file.

The Event Monitor Self-Describing Data Stream

Both pipe and file event monitors return their data in a self-describing format. (This format bears some similarities to the self-describing format used for snapshot monitor output.) In its raw form, the event monitor data stream is simply a continuous string of alphanumeric data arranged in a nested fashion to enable processing. Hence, the data stream is divided into sections based on the logical data groups present.

The order in which the logical data groups appear follows the model presented previously in Table 13-7:

- *event_log_stream_header*
- Logical data groups in the prolog output level
- Logical data groups in the contents output level (these depend on the types of events collected by an event monitor)
- Logical data groups in the epilog output level

The *event_log_stream_header* logical data group contains the following pieces of information:

- **Byte order**   The byte order of information in the data stream. The possible values are 'sqlm_little_endian' or 'sqlm_big_endian.' See the upcoming section "Transferring Event Monitor Data Between Operating Systems" for more information on this.
- **Size**   Although a value is present, it is not meaningful. The value exists to ensure compatibility with previous versions of DB2.
- **Version**   The version of the database manager that returned the data. Only version 6 and 7 event monitors write data in the self-describing format. The possible values are "sqlm_dbmon_version6" and "sqlm_dbmon_version7."

The subsequent logical data groups presented in the data stream contain the following pieces of information:

- **Size**   The number of bytes of data stored in the logical data group. This value includes space used by the data elements.
- **Type**   The type of data in the element. For logical data group headings, this data will always be the character string, "header."
- **Element**   The name of the logical data group.

Each data element presented in the data stream contains the following pieces of information:

- **Size**   The number of bytes used in the data section of this data element.
- **Type**   The type of data returned by the data element. For example, counter information is typically stored as type u16bit (unsigned 16-bit integer).
- **Element**   The name of the data element.
- **Data**   The collected value for the element. Corresponds to the data type specified previously.

PERFORMANCE

Reading the Event Monitor Data Stream   To effectively use the self-describing event monitor output, parse the data stream byte by byte according to the structure outlined previously, in the section, "The Event Monitor Self-Describing Data Stream." Write your applications based on the values you expect to encounter as you parse the data stream.

The logical data group *event_log_stream_header* is the first to be processed in the data stream. If the byte order indicated in the data stream is not consistent with that of the current system, then byte reversal is required for numeric data. Another critical piece of information is the version of the database manager that wrote the event monitor output. Only versions 6 and 7 database managers write monitor data in the self-describing format.

All logical data groups and their data elements contain a size element. When reading the data stream, you can use the size element to skip over logical data groups or elements you do not wish to examine. There is one important exception: you should not use the size element for the *event_log_stream_header* logical data group because it does not contain a meaningful value.

All timestamps in event monitor records are returned in two unsigned 4-byte data elements (seconds and microseconds). These represent the number of seconds at Greenwich Mean Time that have elapsed since January 1, 1970.

The size element of strings for event monitor data represents the actual size of data for the string element. This size does not include a null terminator because the strings are not null terminated.

Table 13-8 shows a sample event monitor data stream, formatted based on the previous descriptions of the data stream components.

Logical Data Group	Information Type	Data Stream Content
event_log_stream_header	Byte order	sqlm_little_endian
	Size	1000
	Version	sqlm_dbmon_version7
log_header_event	Size	100
	Type	header
	Element	sqlm_event_log_header
	Size	4
	Type	u32bit
	Element	byte_order
	Data	little_endian

Table 13-8.   *Event Monitor Data Stream Content*

Logical Data Group	Information Type	Data Stream Content
	Size	2
	Type	u16bit
	Element	codepage_id
	Data	850
...	...	...
db_event	Size	100
	Type	header
	Element	event_db_header
	Size	4
	Type	u32bit
	Element	lock_waits
	Data	2

Table 13-8.   *Event Monitor Data Stream Content* (continued)

Transferring Event Monitor Data Between Operating Systems

When transferring event monitor information between systems using different conventions for storing numerical values, conversions must be made. Information on UNIX platforms is stored in little endian byte order, and information on OS/2 and Windows platforms is stored in big endian byte order. If event monitor data from a little endian source is to be read on a big endian platform or vice versa, byte conversion is necessary.

The following segment of C language code contains functions that convert the numeric values in logical data group headers and data elements.

```
#include sqlmon.h
#define SWAP2(s) (((((s) >> 8) & 0xFF) | (((s) << 8) & 0xFF00))
#define SWAP4(l) (((((l) >> 24) & 0xFF) | ((((l) & 0xFF0000) >> 8) & 0xFF00)
               | (((l) & 0xFF00) << 8) | ((l) << 24))
#define SWAP8( where )
  {  sqluint32 temp;
     temp = SWAP4(*(sqluint32 *) (where));
     * (sqluint32 *) (where) = SWAP4(* (((sqluint32 *) (where)) + 1));
     * (((sqluint32 *) (where)) + 1) = temp;
  }
int HeaderByteReverse( sqlm_header_info * pHeader)
```

```
{  int rc = 0;
   pHeader->size = SWAP4(pHeader->size);
   pHeader->type = SWAP2(pHeader->type);
   pHeader->element = SWAP2(pHeader->element);
   return rc;
}
int DataByteReverse( char * dataBuf, sqluint32 dataSize)
{  int rc = 0;
   sqlm_header_info * pElemHeader = NULL;
   char * pElemData = NULL;
   sqluint32 dataOffset = 0;
   sqluint32 elemDataSize  = 0;
   sqluint32 elemHeaderSize = sizeof( sqlm_header_info);
   while( dataOffset < dataSize)
   {  /* byte reverse the element header */
      pElemHeader = (sqlm_header_info *) (dataBuf + dataOffset);
      rc = HeaderByteReverse( pElemHeader);
      if( rc != 0) return rc;
      elemDataSize = pElemHeader->size;
      pElemData = (char *)( dataBuf + dataOffset + elemHeaderSize);
      if(pElemHeader->type == SQLM_TYPE_HEADER)
      {   rc = DataByteReverse( pElemData, pElemHeader->size);
          if( rc != 0) return rc;
      }
      else
   { switch( pElemHeader->type)
         {  case SQLM_TYPE_16BIT:
            case SQLM_TYPE_U16BIT:
               *(sqluint16 *)(pElemData) =  SWAP2(*(short *)(pElemData));
               break;
            case SQLM_TYPE_32BIT:
            case SQLM_TYPE_U32BIT:
              *(sqluint32 *)(pElemData) = SWAP4(*(sqluint32 *)(pElemData));
               break;
            case SQLM_TYPE_64BIT:
            case SQLM_TYPE_U64BIT:
               SWAP8(pElemData);
               break;
            default:
               break;   // Not a numeric type. Do nothing.
         }
      }
      dataOffset = dataOffset + elemHeaderSize + elemDataSize;
   }
   return 0;
} /*  end of DataByteReverse */
```

The
Complete
Reference

DB2

Chapter 14

Configuration Tuning

In the previous chapter, you saw how to work with the database system monitor. The *database system monitor* is used to monitor and tune database activity and performance. It can collect data to help diagnose the cause of the performance problems and to analyze the performance of individual applications or SQL queries. You can also use the monitor to assemble the information needed to evaluate and tune your database manager and database configuration. Some of those activities can be useful when used in conjunction with the configuration tuning explained in this chapter.

You can configure several parameters to improve performance. *Database manager configuration parameters* help you control how your instance is set up; *database configuration parameters* help you control how your databases are set up. Some of these parameters significantly affect the performance of the instance and each database, so they are the most important parameters to consider. *Buffer pools* are areas of memory in which pages of database data are temporarily stored—they improve performance because it is quicker to read data pages from memory than from disk.

Several database manager configuration parameters have less of an effect on your instance performance. And several database configuration parameters have less of an effect on your database performance but are still worth looking at once the more important tuning is done. Finally, there are a few other performance factors to consider, such as how tables are organized and how data is moved into buffer pools. All of these topics are discussed in this chapter.

Configuration Parameters

Database manager configuration parameters are stored in a file named db2systm—only one configuration file exists for the instance of the database manager. The database manager configuration parameters either affect the amount of system resources that will be allocated to a single database instance of the database manager, or they configure the setup of the database manager and the different communications subsystems based on environmental considerations. Some of the configuration parameters provide information only about the instance and cannot be changed. The values for these parameters are assigned during installation and are applied across all databases stored under the instance of the database manager.

Parameters for an individual database are stored in a configuration file named sqldbcon. Each database has its own configuration file. The database configuration parameters specify the amount of resources allocated to a specific database. Some of the parameters provide information only about the database and some act as flags indicating the status of the database.

Neither the database manager configuration file nor the database configuration file can be directly edited. Instead, tools and application programming interfaces (APIs) are supplied that allow you to edit the files. The tools are similar for both the database manager configuration file and the database configuration file. You can use the following:

- **The DB2 Control Center**   From the Control Center, you can use the Configure Instance notebook or the Configure Database notebook. There is also a Performance Configuration Wizard that alters the values of the configuration parameters based on your responses to questions asked by the wizard.

- **The command line processor (CLP)**   By using the command line processor commands, you can get, update, and reset the database manager or database configuration parameters.

- **The application programming interfaces (APIs)**   Refer to the *IBM DB2 Universal Database Administration API Reference* for more information about the APIs that can be called from a host-language program.

In most cases, after the database manager parameters are changed, you must stop and start the database manager using db2stop and db2start, respectively. This causes the changes to the configuration parameters to take effect. For clients, changes in the database manager configuration parameters take effect the next time the client connects to the server. After the database configuration parameters are changed, you must have all applications disconnect from the database. Then, when the first new connection takes place, the changes will take effect.

The next two sections present the key parameters for both the database manager configuration and the database configuration. Those parameters that have the greatest effect on the performance of your database manager and each database are presented in sufficient detail for you to make reasonable decisions regarding the values you should use.

Key Database Manager Configuration Parameters

To see the current values of configuration parameters in the database manager configuration file, use the following command:

```
GET DATABASE MANAGER CONFIGURATION
```

To update the values for individual configuration parameters in the database manager configuration file, use the following command:

```
UPDATE DATABASE MANAGER CONFIGURATION
USING <parameter name> <new value>, <next parameter name> <next value>, …
```

PERFORMANCE

To reset the values of all the configuration parameters in the database manager configuration file, use the following command:

```
RESET DATABASE MANAGER CONFIGURATION
```

 Be careful when resetting the configuration parameters because you will lose all of the values that were there. Some configuration parameters might be reset to NULL values, which can prevent certain functions from working in the instance. Sometimes, however, you will want to use this command, like when you are working with a test machine and environment.

You can also use the DB2 Control Center or application programming interfaces to view, update, or reset database manager configuration parameters.

The following are the key database manager configuration parameters.

agentpri   The default value for the Priority of Agents database manager configuration parameter is –1 (minus 1). This parameter controls the priority given to all agents, other database manager instance processes, and threads by the operating system scheduler. When set to –1, no special action is taken. You can use this parameter to increase database manager throughput. The values you can use for setting this parameter depend on the operating system on which the database manager is running.

Recommendation: Use the default value to start. Use benchmark techniques to determine the optimum setting for this parameter.

Special considerations: If you set this parameter on UNIX-based platforms, you cannot use the governor to alter agent priorities.

aslheapsz   The default value for the Application Support Layer Heap Size database manager configuration parameter is 15 pages (4KB each). This parameter represents a communication buffer between the local application and its associated agent. The parameter is also used to determine the I/O block size when a blocking cursor is opened. This parameter is used to determine the initial size of the query heap for both local and remote clients.

Recommendation: On a memory-constrained system with small application requests, reduce the number of pages. On a system that is not memory constrained and that has large application requests, increase the number of pages.

Related parameters: The maximum size of the query heap is defined by the *query_heap_sz* database manager configuration parameter.

Special considerations: This parameter affects the number and potential size of the block cursors. See the details in Chapter 13, "Configuring DB2" of the *IBM DB2 Universal Database Administration Guide: Performance* volume.

audit_buf_sz   The default value for the Audit Buffer Size database manager configuration parameter is 0 pages (4KB each). This parameter specifies the size of the buffer used when auditing the database. If you change the value of this parameter to be greater than 0, the audit facility will use the buffer to store records before writing them asynchronously to disk.

Recommendation: If you are not auditing, leave this parameter at the default value (0). If you are auditing and are concerned about performance, make the value of this parameter greater than 0. Then stop and start the database manager before issuing db2audit start. Asynchronous writing of audit records, which happens when the value for the parameter is greater than 0, provides better performance than synchronous writing, which happens when the value for this parameter is 0.

dos_rqrioblk The default value for the DOS Requester I/O Block Size database manager configuration parameter is 4096 bytes. This parameter specifies the size of the communication buffer between DOS/Windows 3.1 applications and their database agents on the database server. This parameter is also used to determine the I/O block size at the database client when a blocking cursor is opened.

Recommendation: For nonblocking cursors, increase the value if the data being transmitted by a single SQL statement is large. For blocking cursors, large row blocks may yield better performance if the number or size of rows being transferred is large.

Special considerations: Large record blocks may cause more fetch requests than the application actually requires. See the details in Chapter 13, "Configuring DB2" , of the *IBM DB2 Universal Database Administration Guide: Performance* volume.

fcm_num_anchors The default value for the Number of FCM Message Anchors database manager configuration parameter is –1, or 75 percent of the value specified for *fcm_num_rqb,* and the range is from 128 to the value of *fcm_num_rqb.* This parameter specifies the number of Fast Communication Manager (FCM) message anchors for the instance. Agents use the message anchors to send messages among themselves.

Related parameters: On single-partition database systems, the *intra_parallel* parameter must be active before this parameter can be used.

fcm_num_buffers This parameter specifies the number of 4KB buffers used for internal messages both among and within database servers. The default value for the Number of FCM Buffers database manager configuration parameter is 512, 1024, or 4096 4KB buffers depending on the type of the instance, and the range is from 128 to the value of *fcm_num_rqb.ng* and within database servers.

Related parameters: On single-partition database systems, the *intra_parallel* parameter must be active before this parameter can be used.

fcm_num_connect The default value for the Number of FCM Connection Entries database manager configuration parameter is –1, or 75 percent of the value specified for *fcm_num_rqb,* and the range is from 128 to the value of *fcm_num_rqb.* This parameter specifies the number of FCM connection entries. Agents use connection anchors to pass data among themselves.

Related parameters: On single-partition database systems, the *intra_parallel* parameter must be active before this parameter can be used.

fcm_num_rqb   The default value and range limits for the Number of FCM Request Blocks database manager configuration parameter vary by platform and by the type of instance. *Request blocks* are the media through which information is passed between the FCM daemon and an agent, or between agents.

Recommendations: Use the default to start, and then modify the number based on results from the system monitor.

Related parameters: On single-partition database systems, the *intra_parallel* parameter must be active before this parameter can be used.

intra_parallel   The default value for the Enable Intra-Partition Parallelism database manager configuration parameter is No and the acceptable values are No, Yes, and System. Some operations, including database queries and index creation, can take advantage of parallel performance improvements when this parameter is Yes. After changing the value for this parameter, it is recommended that packages be rebound to the databases within this instance.

java_heap_sz   The default value for the Maximum Java Interpreter Heap Size database manager configuration parameter is 512 pages and the range is from 0 to 4096 pages. There is one heap for each DB2 process, and there is one heap for each fenced user-defined function (UDF) and fenced stored procedure process. Only agents or processes that run Java UDFs or stored procedures ever allocate this memory.

max_querydegree   The default value for the Maximum Query Degree of Parallelism database manager configuration parameter is Any, which means system determined, and the range is from 1 to 32,767. This parameter specifies the maximum degree of intrapartition parallelism used for any SQL statement running on this instance. The *intra_parallel* parameter must be set to Yes for intrapartition parallelism to be used.

You can modify the maximum query degree of parallelism for an active application by using the SET RUNTIME DEGREE command. The actual run-time degree used is the lower of the value for this parameter, the application run-time degree, and the SQL statement compilation degree.

An exception exists when indexes are created—if *intra_parallel* is Yes and the table is large enough to benefit from the use of multiple processors, then creating an index uses the number of online processors to a maximum of 6 + 1. In that case, there is no effect from the other parameter, bind option, or RUNTIME DEGREE special register.

Related parameters: Both *dft_degree* and *intra_parallel* should be considered when modifying this parameter.

num_poolagents   The default value for the Agent Pool Size database manager configuration parameter is –1, which provides a value appropriate to the environment you have set up for your machine. The range of possible values for this parameter is from 0 to the value for *maxagents*. This parameter is a guideline for how large you want the agent pool to grow. (This parameter replaces the *max_idleagents* parameter that was used in DB2 version 2.) If the value is 0, agents will be created as needed and may be terminated when they finish running their current request.

Recommendation: When running a decision-support environment, you can set this parameter to a small value. When running a transaction-processing environment, you can set this parameter to a larger value.

Related parameters: *num_initagents, maxagents, max_querydegree,* and *max_coordagents.*

rqrioblk   The default value for the Client I/O Block Size database manager configuration parameter is 32,767 bytes. This parameter specifies the size of the communication buffer between remote applications and their database agents on the database server. This parameter is also used to determine the I/O block size at the database client when a blocking cursor is opened.

This memory for blocked cursors is allocated out of the application's private address space. As a result, you should determine the optimal amount of private memory to allocate for each application. If the database client cannot allocate space for a blocking cursor out of an application's private memory, then a nonblocking cursor will be used.

Recommendation: For nonblocking cursors, a reason for increasing the value of this parameter would be if the data to be transmitted by a single SQL statement were so large (for example, a LOB) that the default value is insufficient. You should also consider the effect of this parameter on the number and potential size of the blocking cursors. Large row blocks may yield better performance if the number or size of rows being transferred is large.

sheapthres   The default value and range for the Sort Heap Threshold database manager configuration parameter varies by platform. On OS/2 and Windows, the default is 10,000 pages (4KB each); the other operating systems have a default of 20,000 pages (4KB each). This parameter specifies the limit on sort memory per partition. Examples of operations that use the sort heap include sorts, hash joins, dynamic bitmaps (used for index ANDing and star joins), and operations where a table is in memory. Explicit definition of the threshold prevents the database manager from using excessive amounts of memory for large numbers of sorts.

Recommendation: Set this parameter to a reasonable multiple (at least two times) of the largest *sortheap* parameter you have in the instance.

Related parameters: *sortheap.*

Special considerations: Private and shared sorts use memory from two different memory sources. The shared sort memory area is statically predetermined at the time of the first connection to a database based on the value of *sheapthres.* The size of the private sort memory is unrestricted. When this parameter is used with private sorts, it is a soft limit on the total amount of memory that can be consumed by private sorts at any given time. When this parameter is used with shared sorts, it is a hard limit on the total amount of memory that can be consumed by shared sorts at any given time.

Key Database Configuration Parameters

To see the current values of configuration parameters in the database configuration file, use this command:

```
GET DATABASE CONFIGURATION
```

To update the values for individual configuration parameters in the database manager configuration file, use this command:

```
UPDATE DATABASE CONFIGURATION
USING <parameter name> <new value>, <next parameter name> <next value>, …
```

To reset the values of all the configuration parameters in the database configuration file, use this command:

```
RESET DATABASE CONFIGURATION
```

Caution   *Be careful when resetting the configuration parameters because you will lose all of the values that were there. Some configuration parameters might be reset to NULL values, which can prevent certain functions from working in the instance. Sometimes, however, you will want to use this command, like when you are working with a test machine and environment.*

You can also use the DB2 Control Center or application programming interfaces to view, update, or reset database configuration parameters.

The following are key database configuration parameters.

avg_appls   The default value for the Average Number of Active Applications database configuration parameter is 1. The range is from 1 to *maxappls*. This parameter specifies the average number of active applications that are running against the database at any one time. The SQL optimizer uses this value to help estimate buffer pool usage when the application is run.

Recommendation: Estimate the value for this parameter based on the number of complex query applications that use the database. If you have difficulty estimating, you should use the database system monitor and a sampling technique to determine an estimate of the number of applications running against the database; remember not to count less-complex online transaction processing (OLTP) applications. You should adjust this parameter in small increments. After adjusting the value, you should consider rebinding your applications using the REBIND PACKAGE command.

Related parameters: When modifying this parameter, also consider changing *maxappls*.

buffpage   The default value for the Buffer Pool Size database configuration parameter on UNIX 32-bit operating systems is 1000 with a range from 2 to 524,288; the default on UNIX 64-bit operating systems is 1000 with a range from 2 to 2,147,483,647; and the default on OS/2 and Windows NT is 250 with a range from 2 to 524,288. The unit of measure is pages. This parameter specifies the size of the buffer pool when the CREATE BUFFERPOOL or ALTER BUFFERPOOL statements are run with the clause NPAGES –1. Otherwise, this parameter is ignored. The SQL optimizer uses the size of the buffer pool to determine access plans. To determine whether the *buffpage* parameter is active for a buffer pool, use this command:

```
SELECT * FROM SYSCAT.BUFFERPOOLS
```

Each buffer pool showing NPAGES with a value of –1 uses the value of the *buffpage* parameter when creating the buffer pool.

Recommendation: Use the CREATE BUFFERPOOL or ALTER BUFFERPOOL statements to explicitly create and change buffer pools and their sizes. Do not rely on the default associated with this parameter. After adjusting the value of this parameter, and when you know that some of your buffer pools will rely on its value, consider rebinding your applications by using the REBIND PACKAGE command.

chngpgs_thresh   The default value for the Changed Pages Threshold database configuration parameter is 60 percent with a range of 5 to 99 percent. The percentage given for this parameter is used to specify the threshold at which asynchronous page cleaners are started. The asynchronous page cleaners keep track of the pages of the buffer pool to write to disk.

Recommendation: If your database has a large number of updates, you will want to ensure that there are enough clean pages in the buffer pool by setting this parameter value equal to or less than the default value. You would use a larger percentage value if your database had a lower number of updates or a small number of very large tables that are active.

Related parameters: When modifying this parameter, you should also consider the number of asynchronous page cleaners (*num_iocleaners*).

dft_degree   The default value for the Default Degree database configuration parameter is 1 and the range is from 1 to 32,767 or –1. This parameter specifies the default value for the CURRENT DEGREE special register and the DEGREE bind option. It is useful only if you are working in an *intrapartition parallelism environment*: an environment where you have more than one processor that can work on SQL queries against the database.

This parameter is one of the factors used to determine whether SQL queries from applications will take advantage of the multiple processors to handle the queries. A value of 1 for this parameter means you have only one processor and there is no intrapartition parallelism environment. A value of –1 means the optimizer determines the degree of intrapartition parallelism based on the number of processors and the type of query requested.

PERFORMANCE

Related parameters: When modifying this parameter, you should also consider the database manager configuration parameter maximum query degree of parallelism (*max_querydegree*).

locklist   The default value for the Maximum Storage for Lock List database configuration parameter varies from 25 to 100 pages, based on operating system and environment. The value for this parameter is in pages and indicates the amount of storage allocated to the lock list. There is one lock list per database, and it contains the locks held by all applications concurrently connected to the database. Each lock takes up space in the lock list: 72 bytes for the first lock on an object and 36 bytes for subsequent locks on the same object. Lock escalation occurs when one application reaches the value of *maxlocks.*

Recommendation: Perform frequent COMMITs within your applications to release held locks. Also consider using the SQL LOCK TABLE statement to lock an entire table: this will reduce concurrency but will keep other applications from interfering with table update operations. Finally, consider using the cursor stability isolation level to decrease the number of share locks held. These actions should reduce the time when the lock list is full and performance degrades because of lock escalation.

Related parameters: When modifying this parameter, you should also consider modifying the *maxlocks* and *maxappls* parameters.

logbufsz   The default value for the Log Buffer Size database configuration parameter is 8 pages and the range is from 4 to an upper limit of 4096 or 65,535 pages (depending on the operating system involved). Just as there is a buffer location to hold data pages to speed up performance of applications working against the database, there is a buffer for the database logs. Every action against the database is recorded in a log record. The log buffer holds these log records before writing them to disk. The value of this parameter must be less than or equal to the *dbheap* database configuration parameter.

Recommendation: Increase the size of this buffer area if there is high read activity on a dedicated log disk, or if there is high disk use. You should use the system monitor to determine how much of the log buffer space is used for complex transactions or units of work.

Related parameters: If you modify this parameter, you should also consider modifying the following parameters: *catalogcache_sz, dbheap,* and *mincommit.*

maxappls   The default value for the Maximum Number of Active Applications database configuration parameter on UNIX-based operating systems is 40; on OS/2 and Windows NT servers with local and remote clients, it is 20; on OS/2 and Windows NT servers with local clients, it is 10. The range for all operating systems is from 1 to 60,000. This parameter specifies the maximum number of concurrent applications that can be connected (both local and remote) to a database. Each application attaching to the database causes some private memory to be allocated. As a result, allowing more active applications uses more memory.

Recommendation: The value of this parameter must be equal to or greater than the sum of all connected applications plus the number of these same applications that may be involved in completing a two-phase commit or rollback. Add to this sum the anticipated number of indoubt transactions that might exist at any one time. When increasing the value of this parameter, you should lower the value of the *maxlocks* parameter or increase the value of the *locklist* parameter. If you do not do either of these, you could reach the database limit on locks (controlled by the *locklist* parameter) before reaching the number of applications limit. This could cause pervasive lock escalation problems. Those parameters controlling the type and number of agents could also prevent new applications from connecting to the database.

maxlocks   The default value for the Maximum Percent of Lock List Before Escalation database configuration parameter on UNIX platforms is 10 percent, and on all others, it is 22 percent. The value of this parameter is the percentage of the lock list that must be held by a single application before the database manager performs lock escalation for the locks held by that application. Lock escalation also occurs if the lock list runs out of space. The database manager finds the table with the most row locks and replaces the locks with a single table lock. The database manager proceeds with the next table having the new highest number of row locks and replaces the locks with a single table lock. This process continues until the *maxlocks* value is no longer exceeded.

Recommendation: Use the following formula to limit any application to holding twice the average number of locks: $maxlocks = 2 * 100 / maxappls$. If few applications run concurrently, you can change the formula, replacing *maxappls* with the average number of applications that may run concurrently.

Related parameters: When modifying this parameter, you should also consider modifying the *locklist* and *maxappls* parameters.

mincommit   The default value for the Number of Commits to Group database configuration parameter is 1 and the range is from 1 to 25 commits that must be performed before the log records in the log buffer are written to disk. Having the log records not written out for more than one commit reduces the database manager overhead associated with writing log records. Reducing this overhead is significant to the overall performance of the database, especially when you have multiple applications with potentially many commits requested over a short period of time.

Recommendation: Increase the value of this parameter if multiple read/write applications request concurrent database commits. This will lower the I/O overhead delay because more log records will be written in large groups rather than individually or in small groups. You could use the system monitor to sample the number of transactions per second. Accommodating peak activity minimizes the overhead of writing log records during transaction-intensive periods. The *logbufsz* database configuration parameter value may need to be increased to avoid having a full log buffer force a write during these transaction-intensive periods.

Related parameters: If you modify this parameter, you should also consider the *logbufsz* configuration parameter.

PERFORMANCE

num_iocleaners The default value for the Number of Asynchronous Page Cleaners database configuration parameter is 1 and the range is from 0 to 255. This parameter specifies the number of page cleaner agents that will write data pages from the buffer pool to disk before the space in the buffer pool is required by another database agent. By ensuring that there are always free pages within the buffer pool, there will be better performance for all the applications running against the database.

Recommendation: If your buffer pool is very large, you will want to increase the value of this parameter. If your applications do a lot of updates to data in the database, you will want to increase the value of this parameter. If you have more than one container (physical storage device) as part of your system, you should increase the value of this parameter to between 1 and the number of containers. If the database is not going to be updated at all or only very infrequently, then you will not need to modify this parameter from the default value. If you are unsure of the best value to give to this parameter, you should consider using the system monitor to track and tune this parameter.

num_ioservers The default value for the Number of I/O Servers database configuration parameter is 3 and the range is from 1 to 255. I/O servers are used on behalf of other database agents to perform prefetch I/O and asynchronous I/O by utilities such as backup and restore. Prefetching anticipated data pages from disk and placing those pages into the buffer pool is a key method of keeping the processing of queries against the database moving quickly.

Recommendation: You should set the value of this parameter to one or two more than the number of physical devices on which the database resides. It is better to configure more than enough I/O servers because there is only minimal overhead associated with each I/O server. Unused I/O servers remain idle and do not take any of the database manager's processing time.

Related parameters: When modifying this parameter, you should also consider the default prefetch size (*dft_prefetch_sz*) and the sequential detection flag (*seqdetect*).

pckcachesz The default value for the Package Cache Size database configuration parameter is –1 and the range is from 32 to 128,000 pages or to 524,288 pages, depending on the operating system. The default value (–1) means that the page allocation is eight times the value specified by the *maxappls* database configuration parameter. There is an exception when eight times *maxappls* is less than 32. In this case, the *pckcachesz* is set to 32 pages. The package cache size is the space used to cache static and dynamic SQL statements for the database. By caching packages, there is less database manager overhead—reloading of packages used more than once is reduced if the package can be kept in the package cache.

Recommendation: You should consider using benchmarking techniques to determine whether the memory space allocated for the package cache could be better used as part of the buffer pool for the database. If this cache is made too large, then memory is wasted holding copies of packages that may never be used again. If the cache is too small, additional time is required by the database manager to reload needed packages. You should use the system monitor and some database system monitor elements to assist you in determining whether you should adjust the value of this database configuration parameter.

seqdetect   The default value for the Sequential Detection Flag database configuration parameter is Yes. By having this parameter enabled, you are allowing the database manager to be able to detect sequential page reading during I/O activity. If detected, the database manager activates sequential prefetching of data pages from disk into the buffer pool. Again, having the data pages in the buffer pool before they are needed speeds up the performance of the database.

Recommendation: Leave the default value as is. You should consider turning this parameter off only if other tuning efforts are not correcting serious query performance problems.

Related parameters: You should consider modifying the *dft_prefetch_sz* database configuration parameter if you modify the current parameter.

sortheap   The default value for the Sort Heap Size database configuration parameter is 256 pages (4KB each). This parameter specifies the maximum number of private memory pages and shared memory pages. Private memory pages are used for private sorts affecting agent private memory. Shared memory pages are used for shared sorts affecting database-shared memory. Each sort is allocated to a separate sort heap as needed by the database manger. The sort heap is where the data is sorted.

Recommendation: Having the right indexes on your table can minimize the use of the sort heap. When you are anticipating frequent large sorts, increase the value associated with this parameter. Increasing this value may require you to change the *sheapthres* value. The optimizer uses the sort heap size to determine access paths. Rebind your applications after modifying this parameter by using the REBIND PACKAGE command.

Related parameters: If you modify this parameter, you should also consider modifying the *sheapthres* database manager configuration parameter.

Buffer Pool Importance to Performance

A buffer pool is an area of memory into which database pages are temporarily read and perhaps updated. Data can be accessed much faster from memory than from a disk, so the fewer times the database manager has to read from a disk or write to a disk, the better the overall performance of the database manager and any databases.

Many of the configuration parameters in the previous section are either directly or indirectly related to the buffer pool and how it is used to improve overall database performance. We saw that, in addition to the actual definition of the buffer pool, the configuration parameters can be used to affect data moving out of the buffer pool and data being moved into the buffer pool. The speed with which the data is moved into and out of the buffer pool can affect the speed of the query processing by the database manager.

Pages stay in the buffer pool until the database is shut down or until the space occupied by the page is required by another page. Database agents can be assigned the responsibility of moving out old, unneeded pages and replacing them with new and needed pages. There are actually two general categories of pages in the buffer pool: *in-use pages,* which are currently being read or updated, and *dirty pages,* where data has been changed on the page but the page has not been written to disk. After being written to disk, the page is considered clean and remains in the buffer pool. If not needed by a recent agent, the page space can be used for new page requests from new applications.

The sizes of all buffer pools can have a major impact on the performance of your database. Consider the following factors to ensure that excessive page swapping does not occur:

- The amount of installed memory on your machine
- The memory required by other applications running concurrently with the database manager on the same machine

Page swapping occurs when there is insufficient memory to hold all the pages being accessed. The result is that some pages are written or swapped to temporary disk storage to make room for other pages. When the page on temporary disk storage is needed, it is swapped back into main memory.

You may wish to allocate up to 75 percent of the machine's memory to the database buffer pools when you have the following circumstances on the machine:

- Multiple users
- A machine used only as a database server
- A significant amount of repeated access to the same data and index pages
- One database on the machine

For every buffer pool page allocated, some space is used in the database heap for internal control structures. If the total size of the buffer pool (or buffer pools) is increased, you may also need to increase the *dbheap* database configuration parameter.

If the data source collating sequence matches the database manager collating sequence, ensure that the server option collating_sequence is set to this.

You can use the database system monitor to calculate the buffer pool hit ratio, which can help you tune your buffer pools. For more information, see Chapter 13.

The CREATE BUFFERPOOL Statement

The CREATE BUFFERPOOL statement defines a new buffer pool to be used by the database manager. When this statement is committed, the buffer pool is reflected in the system catalog tables, but the buffer pool does not become active until the next time the database is started.

The statement is used as follows:

```
CREATE BUFFERPOOL <buffer pool name> SIZE <number of pages>
PAGESIZE 4096
NOT EXTENDED STORAGE
```

The <buffer pool name> is a one-part name that identifies a buffer pool in the system catalogs.

The <number of pages> could be the number of pages to be allocated to this specific buffer pool. You can also use a value of <–1>, which indicates that the size of the buffer pool should be the value found in the *buffpage* database configuration parameter.

The PAGESIZE clause defines the size of the pages used for the buffer pool. The valid values when not using the K suffix are 4096 (which is also the default), 8192, 16,384, and 32,768. The valid values when using the K suffix are 4, 8, 16, or 32.

The statement may also have a NOT EXTENDED STORAGE clause (the default) or an EXTENDED STORAGE clause that works in conjunction with extended storage configuration. Setting the database configuration parameters *num_estore_segs* and *estore_seg_sz* to nonzero values turns on extended storage configuration.

When the EXTENDED STORAGE clause is present in this statement, and if the extended storage configuration is turned on, pages that are being migrated out of this buffer pool are cached in the extended storage for this buffer pool.

When the NOT EXTENDED STORAGE clause is present in this statement, and if the extended storage configuration is turned on, pages that are being migrated out of this buffer pool are *not* cached in the extended storage.

You can also define the buffer pool to be created differently on specified partitions or nodes in a partitioned database. The size of the buffer pool can be different on these partitions.

There should be enough real memory on the machine for the total of all the buffer pools that you have created and for any extended storage cache that you want to use. There also needs to be sufficient real memory for the rest of the database manager and for your applications.

More on Extended Storage

Extended storage acts as a side buffer or cache for the main buffer pool. The extended storage cache is defined in terms of memory segments. The following database configuration parameters influence the amount and size of the memory available for extended storage:

- *num_estore_segs* defines the number of extended storage memory segments.
- *estore_seg_sz* defines the size of each extended memory segment.

If you decide to use some of the real addressable memory as an extended storage cache, this memory can no longer be used for other purposes such as for a journaled filesystem cache (jfs-cache) or as a process private address space. Higher system paging can result from assigning additional real addressable memory to the extended storage cache.

Extended storage support and Windows 2000 Address Windowing Extensions (AWE) support are mutually exclusive. When using one type of support, you cannot use the other.

For more information on extended storage support, see the *IBM DB2 Universal Database Administration Guide: Performance* volume.

Microsoft Address Windowing Extensions

On Windows 2000, DB2 Universal Database supports buffer pool sizes of up to 64GB in size (minus the size of DB2 and the operating system). Although AWE can be used with buffer pools of any size, you should consider using Windows 2000 Advanced Server, which provides support for up to 8GB of memory. Or you should consider using Windows 2000 Data Center Server, which provides support for up to 64GB of memory.

To have a 3GB user space allocated, use the /3GB Windows 2000 boot option. This allows a larger AWE window size to be used. To enable access to more than 4GB of memory, use the /PAE Windows 2000 boot option. To verify that you have the correct boot option, select Control | System | Startup and Recovery. From the drop-down list, you can see the available boot options and those that are selected.

You must also set the DB2_AWE profile registry variable. To set this registry variable correctly, you will need to know the buffer pool ID of the buffer pool that will use AWE support. You can find the buffer pool ID in the SYSCAT.

Windows 2000 AWE support and extended storage support are mutually exclusive. When using one type of support, you cannot use the other.

For more information on Windows AWE support, see the *IBM DB2 Universal Database Administration Guide: Performance* volume.

The ALTER BUFFERPOOL Statement

The ALTER BUFFERPOOL statement is used for the following tasks:

- To modify the size of the buffer pool
- To turn the extended storage on or off
- To add the buffer pool definition to a new nodegroup

The statement is run embedded as part of an application or run interactively. The statement appears as follows:

```
ALTER BUFFERPOOL <buffer pool name> SIZE <number of pages>
```

The <buffer pool name> is a one-part name that identifies a buffer pool described in the system catalogs.

The <number of pages> could be the new number of pages to be allocated to this specific buffer pool. You can also use a value of <–1>, which indicates that the size of the buffer pool should be the value found in the *buffpage* database configuration parameter.

The statement may also have a NOT EXTENDED STORAGE clause or an EXTENDED STORAGE clause that works in conjunction with extended storage configuration. The information about extended storage presented in "The CREATE BUFFERPOOL Statement" section also applies here.

The statement may also have an ADD NODEGROUP <nodegroup name> clause, which adds the specified nodegroup to the list of nodegroups for which this buffer pool definition is applicable.

Changes to the buffer pool as a result of this statement are reflected in the system catalog tables when the statement is committed. However, no changes to the actual buffer pool take effect until the next time the database is started.

There should be enough real memory on the machine for the total of all the buffer pools that you have created, and for any extended storage cache that you want to use. There also needs to be sufficient real memory for the rest of the database manager and for your applications.

The DROP BUFFERPOOL Statement

The DROP statement for buffer pools is similar to those for dropping other objects. You need to ensure that no table spaces are assigned to the buffer pool, and you cannot drop the IBMDEFAULTBP buffer pool. The storage from the buffer pool is not actually released until the database is stopped.

The statement can appear as follows:

```
DROP BUFFERPOOL <buffer pool name>
```

Other Database Manager Configuration Parameters

Table 14-1 summarizes those database manager configuration parameters that have a lesser effect on the overall performance of the instance. Those at the end of the table are informational database manager configuration parameters with information established when the instance was created. The informational parameters cannot be modified.

Configuration Parameter Name	Comments
agent_stack_sz	This parameter specifies the virtual memory allocated for each agent. The default stack size should be sufficient. If the size is too small, an error is logged and you will need to increase the size and restart the database instance. This parameter does not apply to UNIX-based operating systems.
authentication	This parameter determines how and where authentication of users takes place. The default of SERVER is sufficient in most cases. If you have incoming requests that are handled by Kerberos, DB2 Connect, or DCE, refer to Chapter 5, "Controlling Database Access, in the *IBM DB2 Universal Database Administration Guide: Implementation* volume.
backbufsz	This parameter specifies the size of the buffer used when backing up the database when a value is not explicitly specified in the backup utility. This provides some performance improvement for the backup utility.
catalog_noauth	This parameter specifies whether users are able to catalog and uncatalog databases and nodes without SYSADM authority. It also controls cataloging and uncataloging of DCS and ODBC directories without SYSADM authority. When this parameter is set to Yes, SYSADM authority is not required.
comm_bandwidth	This parameter specifies the value calculated for the communications bandwidth, in megabytes per second, used by the SQL optimizer to estimate the cost of performing operations between the database partition servers of a partitioned database system. The default value is calculated based on the presence of a high-speed switch as part of your system environment. The range allowed is from .1 to 100,000MB per second. Adjust this parameter only if you want to model a different environment.
conn_elapse	This parameter specifies the number of seconds that limit the time to connect two database servers using TCP/IP. The default is ten seconds. A related parameter is *max_connretries*.

Table 14-1. *Database Manager Configuration Parameters Having a Lesser Performance Impact*

Configuration Parameter Name	Comments
cpuspeed	The SQL optimizer uses CPU speed in milliseconds per instruction to estimate the cost of performing certain operations. The default is calculated automatically when you install the database manager. Adjust this parameter only if you want to model a different environment.
datalinks	This parameter specifies whether Data Links support is enabled. The default is No.
dft_account_str	This parameter is applicable only to DB2 Connect. It specifies the suffix used with a DB2 Connect–generated prefix to create a unique accounting identifier for each application connect request. The default is a null string.
dft_client_adpt	This parameter defines the default client adapter number for the NetBIOS communications protocol whose server *nname* is extracted from DCE Cell Directory Services (CDS). The default is 0. It is applicable only to OS/2 and can be used only with DCE.
dft_client_comm	This parameter indicates the communications protocols (note that there are more than one) that the client applications on this instance can use for remote connections. The default is Null. This parameter can be temporarily overridden by setting the DB2CLIENTCOMM registry variable. The most often used protocol should be listed first.
dft_monswitches *dft_mon_bufpool* *dft_mon_lock* *dft_mon_sort* *dft_mon_stmt* *dft_mon_table*	These switches control the collection of monitor data related to each switch. The default is for all of the switches to be turned off. Depending on the interface used to update the database manager configuration, you may be able to update this parameter directly. Or you may be able to update each of the switches independently using the individual parameters. Unless you are collecting additional monitor data, you should not turn these switches on because each increases the database manager overhead and impacts system performance. For more information on these switches and the database monitor, see Chapter 13.

Table 14-1.   *Database Manager Configuration Parameters Having a Lesser Performance Impact* (continued)

PERFORMANCE

Configuration Parameter Name	Comments
dftdbpath	This parameter specifies the default file path used to create databases under the database manager. If no path is specified when the database is created, the file path in this parameter is used. You should use different paths for each database for management and security reasons. Your own physical resources will also influence the placement of databases in your environment.
diaglevel	This parameter indicates the type of diagnostic errors recorded in the db2diag.log file. The default is 3 and the range can be from 0 to 4. The *diagpath* parameter specifies the location of the db2diag.log. You should increase the value for this parameter when gathering additional problem determination to help resolve a problem.
diagpath	This parameter specifies the fully qualified path for the location of DB2 diagnostic information. The default is Null. Trap files, core dump files, an error log, and an alert log are all placed at that location (depending on your platform).
dir_cache	This parameter specifies whether the database, node, and DCS directory files are cached in memory. The use of the directory cache reduces connect costs by eliminating directory file I/O and minimizing the directory searches required to retrieve directory information. Use this parameter if your directory files do not change frequently and performance is critical. Use should be considered for remote clients and when taking database system monitor snapshots. (There are snapshot exception conditions.)
dir_obj_name	This is the object name representing your instance (or database) in the directory. The default is Null. This parameter is meaningful only if the *dir_path_name* parameter is specified.
dir_path_name	The unique name of the instance in the global namespace is made up of this value and the value in the *dir_obj_name* parameter. It can be overridden by the value of the DB2DIRPATHNAME registry variable. The default is /.:/subsys/database/.

Table 14-1. *Database Manager Configuration Parameters Having a Lesser Performance Impact* (continued)

Configuration Parameter Name	Comments
dir_type	The default for this parameter is None, meaning that DCE directory services are not used. Only local directory files are searched for the target of all CONNECT or ATTACH requests.
discover	The default discovery mode is SEARCH. The administration server, when DB2ADMIN starts, handles SEARCH and KNOWN discovery requests from clients. The client can issue SEARCH or KNOWN discovery requests. What is discovered are other network servers that have the protocols specified in *discover_comm*. The acceptable values for this parameter are SEARCH, KNOWN, and DISABLE. See the complete description of each value shown in Chapter 13, "Configuring DB2," of the *IBM DB2 Universal Database Administration Guide: Performance* volume.
discover_comm	This parameter defines the search discovery managers that are started when DB2ADMIN starts on an administration server. It defines the protocols clients use to issue search discovery requests. Protocols defined here must also be specified in the DB2COMM registry variable. The default is None.
discover_inst	The default is Enable, which enables the detection of this instance by DB2 discovery. When specified as disable, the instance may not be discovered.
drda_heap_sz	This parameter specifies the number of pages for the memory used by DB2 Connect and the Distributed Relational Database Architecture (DRDA) Application Server Support feature. Use the default value for this parameter unless you receive a DRDA heap memory error, in which case, you should increase the value.
federated	This parameter enables or disables support for applications submitting distributed requests for data managed by data sources (such as other members of the DB2 family and Oracle). The default is No (disabled).

Table 14-1.   *Database Manager Configuration Parameters Having a Lesser Performance Impact* (continued)

PERFORMANCE

Configuration Parameter Name	Comments
fileserver	This parameter specifies the name of the NetWare file server where the internetwork address of the database manager is registered. The default is Null.
indexrec	This parameter specifies when the database manager will attempt to rebuild invalid indexes. There are three choices: SYSTEM, ACCESS, and RESTART. You should review the three choices in the complete descriptions shown in Chapter 13, "Configuring DB2," of the *IBM DB2 Universal Database Administration Guide: Performance* volume and consider your own environment to determine the best choice for your situation. The default varies by operating system and is acceptable at first.
initdari_jvm	The default is No, which specifies that each fenced DARI process will not load the Java Virtual Machine (JVM) when started.
ipx_socket	The default is 879E and the range is 879E to 87A2. This specifies a well-known socket number and represents the connection end point in a DB2 server's internetwork address. It must be unique for each DB2 server instance.
jdk11_path	This parameter specifies the directory under which the Java Development Kit 1.1 is installed. The CLASSPATH and other environment variables used by the Java interpreter are computed from the value of this parameter. The default is a null string.
keep_dari	The default is Yes to keep a DARI process after a DARI call is completed. Although additional system resources are used as a result, subsequent DARI process requests are processed quicker.
maxagents	The value for this parameter should be at least the sum of the values for *maxappls* in each database allowing concurrent access. Each additional agent requires additional memory, so total memory usage is limited by this parameter.

Table 14-1. *Database Manager Configuration Parameters Having a Lesser Performance Impact* (continued)

Configuration Parameter Name	Comments
maxcagents	The default value (equivalent to *max_coordagents*) is likely to be a sufficient number of concurrent agents for your instance. If not sufficient, you should use benchmark testing to optimize the performance of the database.
max_connretries	This parameter specifies the number of connection retries attempted to another instance. If the value specified for the parameter is exceeded, an error message is returned. This parameter is used in conjunction with *conn_elapse*. The default is five attempts. The parameter is applicable only to partitioned database environments.
max_coordagents	This parameter determines the maximum number of coordinating agents that can exist at one time on a server in a partitioned or nonpartitioned environment.
maxdari	This parameter specifies the maximum number of DARI processes that may be kept active by the database manager. The default value (equivalent to *max_coordagents*) is a reasonable upper limit.
max_logicagents	The default value (equivalent to *max_coordagents*) is likely to be a sufficient maximum number of applications that can connect to the instance at any one time. The concentrator feature is activated when the value is greater than the default (–1).
max_time_diff	Each instance has its own system clock. This parameter specifies the maximum time difference allowed, in minutes, among the instances listed in the node configuration file. Coordinated Universal Time (UTC) is used, so differences in time zones are not a factor. This parameter is applicable only to partitioned database environments.
maxtotfilop	This parameter specifies the number of file handles used for each database in the instance, based on the calculation *maxappls * maxfilop*. The resulting value must be less than the parameter maximum of 32,768. The default value is 16,000.

Table 14-1. *Database Manager Configuration Parameters Having a Lesser Performance Impact* (continued)

Configuration Parameter Name	Comments
min_priv_mem	Use the default value. This is the number of pages the database server process will reserve as private virtual memory. Do not set it too high because it will affect the performance of non-DB2 applications.
mon_heap_sz	Use the following formula to determine an estimated number of pages for this parameter: (monitoring applications + 1) * (databases * (800 + (tables accessed * 20) + ((applications connected + 1) * (200 + (table spaces * 100)))))) / 4096.
nname	Use this parameter to assign a unique name to the database instance on a workstation in the NetBIOS local area network environment. Client applications must know this name to access databases in that instance.
notifylevel	The default is 2 and the range is from 0 to 4. At the default level, all errors are written to a file. You should increase the value for this parameter when you want to gather additional problem determination data to help solve a problem.
numdb	This parameter specifies the number of local databases that can be active concurrently. The default is either 3 or 8 depending on the operating system and database environment. The range can be from 1 to 256 local databases. Set this value to the actual number of databases already defined, and then add several to account for future growth. Changing this parameter may impact the total amount of memory allocated, so do not change its value frequently.
num_initagents	This parameter determines the initial number of idle agents created in the agent pool when the database is started. The default is 0.
num_initdaris	This parameter indicates the number of idle fenced DARI processes created in the DARI pool when the database is started. The default is 0.

Table 14-1. *Database Manager Configuration Parameters Having a Lesser Performance Impact* (continued)

Configuration Parameter Name	Comments
objectname	This is the name of the database manager instance in an IPX/SPX network. The default is Null.
priv_mem_thresh	This parameter specifies the amount of unused agent private memory that is kept allocated, ready for use by new agents. If set too high, this parameter prevents unused memory from being used by other processes that require memory.
query_heap_sz	This parameter specifies the maximum amount of memory that can be allocated for the query heap. In most cases, the default value is sufficient. It should be set five times larger than *aslheapsz*. The value also needs to be large enough for large objects (LOBs).
restbufsz	This parameter specifies the size of the buffer used when restoring the database when a value is not explicitly specified in the restore utility. This can provide some performance improvement for the restore utility.
resync_interval	This parameter specifies the time interval in seconds to retry to synchronize any outstanding indoubt transactions. This parameter is important in a distributed unit of work (DUOW) environment.
route_obj_name	This parameter specifies the name of the default routing information object entry used by all client applications attempting to access a DRDA server. The default is Null. This parameter is meaningful only if the *dir_type* parameter is set to DCE.
spm_log_file_sz	This parameter specifies the sync point manager (SPM) log file size in pages. The default is 256 pages. The size you should use depends on the number of transactions issuing protected conversations and how often COMMIT or ROLLBACK statements are issued. Note that there is a specific process to change the size.
spm_log_path	This parameter specifies the directory location where SPM logs are written. The default is the sqllib/spmlog directory.

Table 14-1. *Database Manager Configuration Parameters Having a Lesser Performance Impact* (continued)

PERFORMANCE

Configuration Parameter Name	Comments
spm_max_resync	This parameter specifies the number of agents that can simultaneously perform resynchronization operations. The default is 20 agents. The range is from 10 to 256.
spm_name	This parameter identifies the name of the SPM instance to the database manager.
ss_logon	This parameter is applicable only to the OS/2 environment. The default is Yes, which means that a logon user ID and password is required before issuing a START DATABASE MANAGER or STOP DATABASE MANAGER command.
start_stop_time	This parameter specifies the time, in minutes, within which all partitioned database instances must respond to a START DATABASE MANAGER or a STOP DATABASE MANAGER command. It is also used as the timeout value during an ADDNODE operation. It is applicable only to partitioned database environments.
svcename	This parameter is used to assign a unique port name to the database instance on a workstation in a TCP/IP environment. Client applications must know this name to access databases in that instance. The interrupt port number typically follows the first port number by one.
sysadm_group	This parameter defines the group name with SYSADM authority within this instance of the database manager.
sysctrl_group	This parameter defines the group name with SYSCTRL authority within this instance of the database manager.
sysmaint_group	This parameter defines the group name with SYSMAINT authority within this instance of the database manager.
tm_database	This parameter identifies the name of the transaction manager for each instance. The default is 1ST_CONN. The TM database is then the first database to which a user connects.

Table 14-1.   *Database Manager Configuration Parameters Having a Lesser Performance Impact* (continued)

Configuration Parameter Name	Comments
tp_mon_name	This parameter identifies the name of the transaction processing (TP) monitor product being used. See the complete description for each of the TP monitors supported in the *IBM DB2 Universal Database Administration Guide: Performance* volume.
tpname	This parameter defines the remote transaction program used by a database client in an environment where the Advanced Program-to-Program Communications (APPC) communications protocol is used.
trust_allclnts	This parameter is active only when the *authentication* parameter is set to CLIENT. It is used with the *trust_clntauth* parameter to determine where users are validated to the database environment. For more information on using this parameter, refer to the "Selecting an Authentication Method for Your Server" section in Chapter 5, "Controlling Database Access," of the *IBM DB2 Universal Database Administration Guide: Implementation* volume.
trust_clntauth	This parameter is active only when the *authentication* parameter is set to CLIENT. It is used with the *trust_allclnts* parameter to determine where users are validated to the database environment. For more information on using this parameter, refer to the "Selecting an Authentication Method for Your Server" section in Chapter 5, "Controlling Database Access," of the *IBM DB2 Universal Database Administration Guide: Implementation* volume.
udf_mem_sz	This parameter specifies the size of memory used to pass data to a UDF. The default is sufficient unless you are passing LOB data to the UDF. Increase the memory, if LOB data is used, to two pages larger than the size of the UDF input arguments.
nodetype	This parameter provides information about the DB2 products installed on your machine.
release	This parameter provides information about the release level of the configuration file.

Table 14-1.   *Database Manager Configuration Parameters Having a Lesser Performance Impact* (continued)

PERFORMANCE

Other Database Configuration Parameters

Table 14-2 summarizes those database configuration parameters that have a lesser effect on the overall performance of the database. Those at the end of the table are informational database configuration parameters with information established when the database was created. The informational parameters cannot be modified.

Other Performance Considerations

If you have tables that are updated and changed frequently, you will need to use utilities to keep the tables organized so that the optimizer can take full advantage of the relational

Configuration Parameter Name	Comments
app_ctl_heap_sz	For partitioned databases and nonpartitioned databases with intrapartition parallelism enabled, this parameter is the size of the shared memory area allocated for the application control heap. For nonpartitioned databases when intrapartition parallelism is disabled, this is the maximum private memory area allocated for the application control heap. There is one application control heap per connection per partition. The default size varies by operating system and database environment.
applheapsz	This parameter specifies the number of private memory pages available for use by the database manger on behalf of a specific agent or subagent. Increase the value of this parameter if your applications receive an insufficient storage error.
autorestart	This parameter specifies whether crash recovery is to be performed following an abnormal termination of the database. The default is On, which means that the database manager automatically calls the restart database utility, if needed, when an application connects to a database. The goal of the operation is to get the database to a consistent state. Committed transactions in the buffer pool are written to disk, and uncommitted transactions are backed out.

Table 14-2. *Database Configuration Parameters Having a Lesser Performance Impact*

Configuration Parameter Name	Comments
catalogcache_sz	This parameter specifies the maximum space in pages that the catalog cache can use from the database heap (*dbheap*). Table descriptor information is stored in this cache. The default size varies by operating system and database environment. Use the database system monitor to determine when to adjust this parameter's value.
copyprotect	This parameter enables the copy-protect attribute and is disabled by default (the default is No). The backup and restore database utilities are not affected by this parameter. Attention: Remove copy protection from all databases before reinstalling either the database manager or the operating system.
dbheap	This parameter specifies the size in pages of the database heap. There is only one database heap per database. The size of the heap depends on the number of control blocks stored in the heap at any given time. Other parameters (*catalogcache_sz* and *logbufsz*) are allocated from this cache. The default size varies by operating system and database environment.
dft_extent_sz	This parameter specifies the number of extended storage memory segments. The default is 0 segments. A related parameter is *estore_seg_sz*. This parameter is used only if your environment has more memory than the maximum address space and you wish to use that memory.
dft_loadrec_ses	This parameter specifies the default number of sessions used during the recovery of a table load. This parameter is applicable only if roll forward recovery is enabled. You can override this parameter through entries in the copy location file specified by the DB2LOADREC environment variable.
dft_prefetch_sz	When a table space is created, PREFETCHSIZE n can be optionally specified. If not specified, the value of this parameter is used. This is a parameter for all table spaces in the database—for this reason, you should explicitly set the prefetch size for each table space.

Table 14-2.   *Database Configuration Parameters Having a Lesser Performance Impact* (continued)

PERFORMANCE

Configuration Parameter Name	Comments
dft_queryopt	This parameter sets the default query optimization class when the class is not set in the application or when the application is being bound. The default is 5 and the range is from 0 to 9. See the *Administration Guide: Performance* volume for more information on query optimization classes.
dft_refresh_age	This parameter specifies the maximum time duration after a REFRESH TABLE statement has been processed on a specific REFRESH DEFERRED summary table during which that summary table can be used to optimize the processing of a query. The default is 0.
dft_sqlmathwarn	This parameter sets the default value that determines the handling of arithmetic errors and retrieval conversion errors or warnings during SQL statement compilation. The default is No. Attention: By changing the value of this parameter, other database behaviors (check constraints, triggers, and views using arithmetic expressions) may change. See the complete description shown Chapter 13, "Configuring DB2," of the *IBM DB2 Universal Database Administration Guide: Performance* volume.
dir_obj_name	This parameter is the object name representing your instance (or database) in the directory. The default is Null. This parameter is meaningful only if the *dir_path_name* parameter is specified.
discover_db	This parameter is used to prevent information about a database from being returned to a client when a discovery request is received at the server. The default is Enable. You may want to change this parameter value to Disable to hide any databases you have that contain sensitive data.

Table 14-2.   *Database Configuration Parameters Having a Lesser Performance Impact* (continued)

Configuration Parameter Name	Comments
dlchktime	This parameter defines the length of time in milliseconds between checks for deadlocks by the database manager. If the deadlock interval is too small, run-time performance is decreased. If the value is set lower to improve concurrency, ensure that *maxlocks* and *locklist* are set appropriately to avoid unnecessary lock escalation. The default is 10,000 (ten seconds).
dl_expint	This parameter specifies the interval time for which the generated file access control token is valid. The default is 60 seconds and the range is from 1 to 31,536,000 seconds. Minus one (–1) is also an option that implies that the token will not expire. The Data Links Filesystem Filter checks validity.
dl_num_copies	This parameter specifies the number of additional copies of a file to be made in the archive server when a file is linked to the database. This parameter applies to the DATALINK columns that specify "Recovery=Yes." The default is 0 copies with the range between 0 and 15 copies. Note that this specifies the number of *additional* copies.
dl_time_drop	This parameter specifies the number of days a file is retained on an archive server after a DROP DATABASE is issued. The default is 1 day and the range is from 0 to 365 days. A value of 0 means delete the files immediately. The file is not deleted unless the ON UNLINK DELETE parameter was specified for the DATALINK column. This parameter applies to the DATALINK columns that specify "Recovery=Yes."
dl_token	This parameter specifies the algorithm used in the generation of DATALINK file access control tokens. The default is MAC0 with the only other option being MAC1. This parameter applies to the DATALINK columns that specify "READ PERMISSION DB." MAC1 is more secure and more costly.

Table 14-2. *Database Configuration Parameters Having a Lesser Performance Impact* (continued)

PERFORMANCE

Configuration Parameter Name	Comments
dl_upper	This parameter indicates whether the file access control tokens use uppercase letters. The default is No, which means that both upper- and lowercase letters are allowed in the token. This parameter applies to the DATALINK columns that specify "READ PERMISSION DB."
dyn_query_mgmt	This parameter is relevant only when DB2 Query Patroller is installed. With this parameter enabled, and when the cost of the dynamic query exceeds a threshold for the user or group (as set in the DB2 Query Patroller user profile table), then the query will be caught and processed by DB2 Query Patroller. By default, this parameter is disabled.
estore_seg_sz	This parameter specifies the number of pages in each of the extended memory segments in the database. The default is 16,000 pages and the range is from 0 to 1,048,575 pages. A related parameter is *dft_extent_sz*. This is used only if your environment has more memory than the maximum address space and you wish to use that memory.
indexrec	This parameter specifies when the database manager will attempt to rebuild invalid indexes. There are three choices: SYSTEM, ACCESS, and RESTART. You should review the three choices in the complete descriptions shown in Chapter 13, "Configuring DB2, "of the *IBM DB2 Universal Database Administration Guide: Performance* volume and consider your own environment to determine the best choice for your situation. The default is acceptable at first.
indexsort	This parameter specifies whether sorting of index keys will occur during index creation. Use the default for this parameter (Yes) unless you do not have enough disk space. Index creation performance is improved by performing a sort first.

Table 14-2. *Database Configuration Parameters Having a Lesser Performance Impact* (continued)

Configuration Parameter Name	Comments
locktimeout	This parameter specifies the number of seconds an application will wait to obtain a lock. The default is –1, which means lock timeout detection is turned off. In an online transaction processing (OLTP) environment, use an initial starting value of 30 seconds. In a query-only environment, a higher initial starting value could be used.
logfilsz	This parameter defines the size in pages of each primary and secondary log file. You should balance the size of the log files with the number of primary log files. The size should be increased if the log file becomes full quickly due to a high transaction rate. If disk space is scarce, the primary log file size should be decreased.
logprimary	This is the number of primary log files. This value and the size of the primary logs (*logfilsz*) determine the disk requirements for logging database changes. The default is 3 because there is an assumption of circular logging. If archival logging is used, you may want to change the value of this parameter.
logretain	The default for this parameter is No, which indicates that logs are not retained. (See also *userexit*.) A value of Recovery indicates that logs are retained; and, if you are using data replication, the Capture program can write the updates recorded in the log to the change table. A value of Capture indicates that the logs are retained only so that the Capture program can write the updates recorded in the log to the change table. In this last case, the logs can be used for forward recovery if they have not been pruned following their use by the Capture program.
logsecond	This parameter specifies the number of secondary logs that are created and used for recovery log files (only as needed). Use these logs for databases that have periodic needs for large amounts of log space. The default is 2. Logs are allocated only as needed.

Table 14-2. *Database Configuration Parameters Having a Lesser Performance Impact* (continued)

PERFORMANCE

Configuration Parameter Name	Comments
maxfilop	This parameter specifies the maximum number of file handles that can be opened for each database agent. The default is 64. If this parameter is set too small, the overhead of opening and closing files to avoid exceeding this limit becomes excessive and may degrade performance.
min_dec_div_3	This parameter changes the resulting scale of decimal arithmetic operations involving division. The default is No. Attention: Changing the value of this parameter may cause changes to applications for existing databases.
newlogpath	This parameter is a string of up to 242 bytes that can be used to change the location where the log files are stored. The string can specify a pathname or a raw device. Consider placing the log files on a disk that does not have a high rate of activity resulting from other objects being accessed on that disk.
num_db_backups	This parameter specifies the number of database backups to be retained for a database. The default is 12. Following the specified number of backups, the oldest backup is marked expired in the recovery history file. Once marked as expired, physical backups can be removed from where they are stored. The *rec_his_retentn* database configuration parameter should be set to a value compatible with the value in this parameter.
num_estore_segs	Use this parameter to establish the use of extended storage memory segments only if your platform environment has more memory than the maximum address space and you wish to use this memory. The default is 0 extended storage memory segments and the range is from 0 to 2,147,483,647.

Table 14-2. *Database Configuration Parameters Having a Lesser Performance Impact* (continued)

Configuration Parameter Name	Comments
num_freqvalues	This parameter specifies the number of most frequent values that will be collected when the WITH DISTRIBUTION option is specified on the RUNSTATS command. The default is 10 values to be retained; the range is from 0 to 32,767. Updating this parameter can help the optimizer obtain better selectivity estimates for some predicates over data that is nonuniformly distributed. More accurate selectivity calculations may result in the choice of more efficient access plans. Attention: Collecting frequent value statistics requires significant CPU and memory.
num_quantiles	This parameter specifies the number of quantiles that will be collected when the WITH DISTRIBUTION option is specified on the RUNSTATS command. The default is 20 values to be retained; the range is from 0 to 32,767. Updating this parameter can help the optimizer obtain better selectivity estimates for range predicates over data that is nonuniformly distributed. This information has a strong influence on whether an index scan or a table scan will be chosen.
rec_his_retentn	This parameter specifies the number of days that historical information on backups should be retained. If the recovery history file is not needed, this parameter can be set to a small number. The default is 366 days and the range is from 0 to 30,000 days. If set to −1, the recovery history file can be pruned explicitly using only the available commands or APIs.
softmax	The default is 100 percent of the size of one primary log file. If you specify 300 as the value, the database manager attempts to keep the number of logs that need to be recovered to three. The value is also used to determine the frequency of soft checkpoints. Your acceptable recovery window significantly influences your decision regarding the value for this parameter.

Table 14-2. *Database Configuration Parameters Having a Lesser Performance Impact* (continued)

PERFORMANCE

Configuration Parameter Name	Comments
stat_heap_sz	This parameter specifies the maximum size in pages of the heap used in collecting statistics with the RUNSTATS command. You should adjust the value for this parameter based on the number of columns for which statistics are being collected. (Many columns require significantly more memory.)
stmtheap	This parameter specifies the workspace dynamically allocated for the SQL compiler during the compilation of an SQL statement. The default is 2048 pages.
trackmod	This parameter allows the backup utility to determine which pages should be part of an incremental backup. The default is No. When this parameter is Yes, the database manager tracks those pages in the database that have changed since the most recent full backup. After changing this parameter to Yes, take a full database backup to give a baseline for the future incremental backups.
tsm_mgmtclass	The Tivoli Storage Manager (TSM) management class states how the TSM server should manage the backup versions of the objects being backed up. The default is that there is no TSM management class.
tsm_nodename	This parameter is used to override the default setting for the node name associated with the TSM product. The node name is needed to allow you to restore a database that was backed up to TSM from another node.
tsm_owner	This parameter is used to override the default setting for the owner associated with the TSM product. The owner name is needed to allow you to restore a database that was backed up to TSM from another node. Note that the owner name is case-sensitive.
tsm_password	This parameter is used to override the default settings for the password associated with TSM. The default is that you can restore a database from TSM only on the same node from which you did the backup. The *tsm_nodename* can be overridden. If it is, this parameter may also have to be set.

Table 14-2.   *Database Configuration Parameters Having a Lesser Performance Impact* (continued)

Configuration Parameter Name	Comments
userexit	The default is No, which means there is no ability to move logs to a program outside the database to archive them. If this parameter is set to Yes, log retention logging is performed regardless of how *logretain* is set. Both *logretain* and this parameter must be cleared if no logging is to be used for a roll-forward recovery operation.
util_heap_sz	This parameter specifies the maximum amount of memory that can be used simultaneously by the backup, restore, and load utilities (including load recovery). The default is 5000 pages. This should be sufficient. If it is not large enough, consider not running the utilities concurrently, and then increase the value of the parameter.
numsegs	This is an informational parameter applying only to SMS table spaces, indicating the number of containers created within the default table spaces. This is only a record: the CREATE TABLESPACE statement does not use this parameter in any way.
logpath	This is an informational parameter containing the current path being used for logging purposes. You cannot change this parameter directly. The database manager sets this parameter.
loghead	This is an informational parameter containing the name of the log file that is currently active.
release	This is an informational parameter providing information about the release level of the configuration file.
database level	This is an informational parameter indicating the release level of the database. If there is an incomplete or failed migration, this value will be different from the value for *release*. With a successful migration, both parameters will be identical.

Table 14-2. *Database Configuration Parameters Having a Lesser Performance Impact* (continued)

PERFORMANCE

Configuration Parameter Name	Comments
territory	This is an informational parameter showing the territory used to create the database. It is used to determine *country* parameter values. See Appendix E, "National Language Support, " in the *IBM DB2 Universal Database Administration Guide: Planning* volume.
codeset	This is an informational parameter showing the codeset that was used to create the database. It is used to determine *codepage* parameter values. See Appendix E, "National Language Support, " in the *IBM DB2 Universal Database Administration Guide: Planning* volume.
codepage	This is an informational parameter showing the code page that was used to create the database. It is derived from the *codepage* parameter value. See Appendix E, "National Language Support," in the *IBM DB2 Universal Database Administration Guide: Planning* volume.
collate_info	This is an informational parameter that can be displayed only by using the GET DATABASE CONFIGURATION API. It provides 260 bytes of database collating information. The first 256 bytes specify the database collating sequence. The last 4 bytes contain internal information about the type of the collating sequence.
backup_pending	This is an informational parameter that indicates that a full backup of the database is required before accessing the database. Typically, the database has moved from being nonrecoverable to recoverable, leaving the database in this state.
database_consistent	This is an informational parameter that indicates whether the database is in a consistent state. If consistent, no RESTART DATABASE command is needed to make the database usable.

Table 14-2. *Database Configuration Parameters Having a Lesser Performance Impact* (continued)

Configuration Parameter Name	Comments
rollfwd_pending	This is an informational parameter that can be one of the following: DATABASE A roll-forward recovery procedure is required for this database. TABLESPACE One or more table spaces must be rolled forward. NO The database is usable and no other action is required.
log_retain_status	This is an informational parameter that, if set, indicates that log files are being retained for use in roll-forward recovery. This parameter is set when the *logretain* parameter is given a value of "Recovery."
user_exit_status	This is an informational parameter that, if set to Yes, indicates that the database manager is enabled for roll-forward recovery and that the user exit program will be used to archive and retrieve log files.
restore_pending	This is an informational parameter that states whether a RESTORE PENDING status exists in the database.
multipage_alloc	This is an informational parameter that states whether multipage file allocation is used to improve insert performance. This applies only to SMS table spaces. All SMS table spaces are affected; no other selection is possible for individual SMS table spaces. The default value for the parameter is No, meaning that multipage file allocation is not enabled. The db2empfa tool can enable multipage file allocation, but once enabled, it cannot be disabled. See the *IBM DB2 Universal Database Command Reference*.

Table 14-2.   *Database Configuration Parameters Having a Lesser Performance Impact* (continued)

operations to access the data. You can also define the relationship between table spaces and the database manager buffer pool so that movement of data to the buffer pool happens efficiently. Both of these topics are presented in the following sections.

There are also environment and profile registry variables that can impact the performance and operation of your database and environment. These variables are presented in Chapter 28.

Table Organization and Optimizer Performance

The performance of SQL statements that use indexes can be slowed down after many updates, deletes, or inserts. This activity makes the information in the indexes spread out across the index. As a result, logically sequential data may not be placed physically close to related data because, over time, the intermediate data locations have been filled with other data. Additional read operations are required when the database manager needs to access the data sequentially. Table and index data should be reorganized periodically to ensure that performance does not deteriorate too much.

Reorganizing a table takes time. You should also consider updating your database statistics, which takes less time. With the most recent database and table statistics, the optimizer knows the most efficient route to the data.

The REORGCHK command returns information about the physical characteristics of a table and whether it would be beneficial to reorganize the table.

The REORGANIZE TABLE command optionally rearranges data into a physical sequence according to a specified index. If you do not request the reorganization of the table according to a specified index, the records in the table are reorganized without regard to an order. (The REORGANIZE TABLE command cannot use an index that is based on an index extension.) The REORGANIZE TABLE command clusters the table data according to the index, and this improves the statistics associated with the reorganized table. The optimizer takes advantage of the new statistics once you use the RUNSTATS command.

The RUNSTATS Command

The RUNSTATS command updates the statistics about the physical characteristics of a table and the associated indexes. These characteristics include the number of records, the number of pages, and the average record length. The optimizer uses these statistics to determine the best access paths to the data in the table. You should run this command periodically after a table has received many updates including deletions and inserts. You should also run this command following the reorganization of a table.

The command can be used as follows:

```
RUNSTATS ON TABLE <table name>
```

The <table name> must be a fully qualified name or alias in the form <schema.table-name>, where the schema is the user name under which the table was created. If no options are specified, as in this example, only table statistics are updated.

The options that may be used with this command request other types of statistics, including distribution statistics that have to do with frequency of values and quantiles collected. You can also request the updating of statistics on indexes. Additionally, you can control the type of access to the table that is having its statistics updated. See the *IBM DB2 Universal Database Command Reference* for more information on these options.

There are some restrictions on the use of this command with tables: the command does not support declared temporary tables or the use of nicknames.

You should rebind all packages that use the table following the updating of the statistics. The packages can then take advantage of the latest and best ways the optimizer has to access the data.

The REORGCHK Command

The REORGCHK command calculates statistics on the database to determine whether tables need to be reorganized. The command can be used as follows:

```
REORGCHK ON TABLE <table name>
```

The REORGCHK command calculates statistics obtained from six different formulas to determine whether performance has deteriorated or can be improved by reorganizing a table. Some of the formulas concern themselves with analyzing the physical location of rows and the size of the table, and others analyze the relationship of the indexes to the table data.

Because the REORGCHK command uses statistics to complete the analysis of the table to see if reorganization is necessary, the command allows you to request a RUNSTATS request as part of the procedure. The command appears as follows:

```
REORGCHK UPDATE STATISTICS ON TABLE <table name>
```

The phrase UPDATE STATISTICS calls the RUNSTATS routine to update table statistics and then uses the updated statistics to determine if table reorganization is necessary.

The REORGANIZE TABLE Command

The REORGANIZE TABLE command reorganizes a table by moving the rows around so that the rows are not separated, but rather, are placed in order according to an index. Fragmented data is eliminated and rows are physically moved together. The command appears as follows:

```
REORG TABLE <table name> INDEX <index name> USE <table space name>
```

The <table name> is the table to be reorganized. The table can be at a local or remote database. The <table name> must be a fully qualified name or alias in the form <schema.table-name>, where the schema is the user name under which the table was created.

The <index name> specifies the index to be used when reorganizing the table. The <index name> must also be a fully qualified name. If there is more than one index on the table to be reorganized, you should specify the index that is most often used in the SQL queries that access the table. This has the effect of improving the performance of the database when accessing this table. If <index name> is not specified, the records of the table are reorganized without regard to order. Also, if the <index name> is not specified and if a clustering index exists on the table, the data will be ordered according to the clustering index.

The <table space name> is the name of a system temporary table space where the database manager can temporarily store the table being reorganized. If not specified, a working copy of the table is placed in the same table space as the table being reorganized.

The REORG TABLE command is not supported for declared temporary tables or for nicknames. The command cannot be used on views.

An online reorganization is possible—you need to provide a user-defined threshold for the maximum amount of free space on an index leaf page. When an index key is deleted from a leaf page and the threshold is crossed, the neighboring index leaf pages are checked to determine if two leaf pages can be merged. If there is sufficient space on a page for a merge to take place, the merge of the two index leaf pages occurs without needing to take the database offline. Online reorganization is possible only with indexes created in version 6 and later.

To turn on online index reorganization for a particular index, specify a MINPCTUSED value when the index is created. The value given to this parameter becomes the threshold value that must be reached before attempting a merge of two index leaf pages. The recommended value for MINPCTUSED is a value less than 50 percent. (Both index leaf pages must be less than 50 percent before it is possible to consider merging two of the pages together.) A value of 0 percent for MINPCTUSED, which is the default, disables online reorganization.

The REBIND Command

The REBIND command allows the user to recreate a package stored in the database without the need for a bind file. This command provides a quick way to recreate a package. It also provides a method to recreate inoperative packages. Finally, with this command, users are given control over the explicit rebinding of invalid packages without the packages being automatically or implicitly rebound by the database manager when they are next run. In this case, the automatic or implicit rebinding may result in a noticeable delay in the running of the first SQL request for the invalid package.

The command is as follows:

```
REBIND <package name> /RESOLVE ANY
```

The <package name> is a name that may be either qualified or unqualified but that designates the package to be rebound. An unqualified package name is implicitly qualified by the current authorization ID.

The RESOLVE option specifies whether the rebinding of the package is to be performed with or without conservative binding semantics. The binding semantics affect whether new functions and data types are considered during function resolution and type resolution on static DML statements in the package. This option is not supported by DRDA. The valid values are the following: ANY, where any of the functions and types in the SQL path are considered for function and type resolution (the default); and CONSERVATIVE, where only functions and types in the SQL path that were defined before the last explicit bind timestamp are considered for function and type resolution.

Note that REBIND does not automatically commit the transaction following a successful rebind. You must explicitly commit the transaction. The only exception is if autocommit is enabled; in this case, the REBIND command commits the transaction.

Limiting the Need to Reorganize Tables

You can perform some tasks after you create a table to delay the need for reorganizing it:

1. Alter the table to add PCTFREE.
2. Create a clustering index with PCTFREE on the index.
3. Sort the data to be loaded into the table.
4. Load the table.

The clustering index on the table, in conjunction with PCTFREE on the table, preserves the original sorted order. Over time, as more data is inserted into the table, the pages become full and records have to be appended to the end of the table. As a result, the table gradually becomes unclustered.

Prefetching and Performance

In conjunction with the creation of table spaces and the buffer pool, you can set up appropriate sizes for the information that will be moved into the buffer pool (as determined by the table space definition).

Chapter 7 presented information on how to create a table space and how to select an extent size for the table space. One of the influences on the decision regarding the size of the extents for the table space has to do with prefetching. One of the influences is the type of access to the tables in the table space. If you are expecting many queries or transactions that process large quantities of data, prefetching data from the tables may provide significant performance benefits. *Prefetching* is the reading of data pages in advance of those pages being referenced by a query, to reduce response time.

The CREATE TABLESPACE statement (and ALTER TABLESPACE statement) has parameters that influence performance as related to prefetching. A typical CREATE TABLESPACE statement may have the following parameters:

```
CREATE TABLESPACE <table space name>
```

```
MANAGED BY DATABASE USING (DEVICE '<container string>' <number of pages>)
EXTENTSIZE <number of pages>
PREFETCHSIZE <number of pages>
BUFFERPOOL <buffer pool name>
OVERHEAD <number of milliseconds>
TRANSFERRATE <number of milliseconds>
```

The EXTENTSIZE parameter specifies the number of PAGESIZE pages (which have a default size of 4096 bytes) that will be written to a container before skipping to the next container. The default value is provided by the *dft_extent_sz* database configuration parameter. The writing of data occurs when the data is placed into the table.

The PREFETCHSIZE parameter specifies the number of PAGESIZE pages (default of 4096 bytes) that will be read from the table space when data prefetching is being performed. Prefetching reads data needed by a query prior to it being referenced by the query so that the query does not wait for the I/O to be carried out to retrieve the needed data. It is good practice to explicitly set the PREFETCHSIZE value as a multiple of the EXTENTSIZE value and the number of table space containers.

For example, if you have an extent size given as 16 pages and the table space has 4 containers, you should set the prefetch value to 64 pages. To enable prefetching, the database manager starts separate threads of control, known as I/O servers. These are configured with the *num_ioservers* database configuration parameter. The I/O servers use the value of the PREFETCHSIZE parameter when prefetching data.

The BUFFERPOOL parameter specifies the name of the buffer pool used for tables in this table space. If not specified, the default buffer pool is IBMDEFAULTBP. The page size of the buffer pool must match the page size specified (or defaulted) for the table space.

The OVERHEAD parameter specifies the I/O controller overhead and disk seek and latency time in milliseconds. The value given here should be the average for all containers belonging to this table space. This may be a concern only if you have containers of different specifications all being associated with the same table space. The value is used to determine the cost of I/O during query optimization.

The TRANSFERRATE parameter specifies the time to read one page into memory, in milliseconds. The value given here should be the average for all containers belonging to this table space. This may be a concern only if you have containers of different specifications all being associated with the same table space. The value is used to determine the cost of I/O during query optimization.

These last two parameters represent the container characteristics that can affect the I/O cost of running a query. For additional information, see "Table Space Impact on Query Optimization" in Chapter 4 of the *IBM DB2 Universal Database Administration Guide: Performance* volume.

The
Complete
Reference

Chapter 15

Problem Determination

If you're reading this chapter, then you have probably encountered a problem—or problems—with DB2. This chapter outlines how to accurately describe the problem and identify its source. We'll also consider various tools that you can use and references you can review to resolve problems quickly and effectively.

Problem Identification

When identifying problems, it is important to put together a good problem description. You can develop an accurate problem description by answering a few basic questions:

- Where is the problem occurring?
- What are the problem symptoms?
- When does the problem occur?
- Under what conditions does the problem occur?
- Which events led up to the problem?
- Is the problem reproducible?

Where Is the Problem Occurring?

Identifying where the problem is occurring is the first step in determining a good problem description. If you are receiving an error message, then you can usually isolate the location of the failure by determining which layer of connectivity the problem is being encountered in: client, gateway, or server. If the error message is returned to an application, then determine where this application is running at the time of the problem.

For investigating complex problems, you will also need to completely describe the environment in which the error condition is encountered. Start by recording the following general information:

- Operating system platforms and levels
- DB2 versions and levels (via db2level)
- Network protocols
- Hardware
- Third-party software

Compare this information against supported DB2 environments to ensure that the problem is not due to an unsupported configuration. Often, problems are simply due to untested configurations that are not supported by DB2. For example, DB2 may require that a certain level of Tivoli Storage Manager (TSM) client and APIs be used with specific versions and FixPak levels of DB2. (DB2 has TSM APIs embedded within many of its utilities.)

You should also note whether there have been any recent changes in the environment that might be causing the problem. In almost every problem case, the root cause is due to some recent adjustment in system configuration.

For DB2 Universal Database Enterprise—Extended Edition (EEE) environments, it is very important to identify on which partition, or partitions, the problem occurred so that you know where to concentrate your investigation.

What Are the Problem Symptoms?

The next step in developing a good problem description is to determine what the problem symptoms are. Symptoms can range from returned error messages and operation hangs or slowdowns to entire database or DB2 instance crashes.

Error Message Symptoms

If the symptom is an error message, then you will need to obtain more details about exactly what that error message means. DB2 error messages are of the form *XXXnnnnnL*, which can be broken down as follows:

- **XXX** An identifier of the DB2 component returning the error
- **nnnnn** A four to five digit numeric representation of the error code
- **L** A severity indicator

The following are the most common error message prefixes that DB2 returns:

- **ASN** replication messages, such as Apply and Capture
- **CCA** Client Configuration Assistant messages
- **CLI** Call Level Interface messages
- **DB2** command line processor messages
- **DBA** Control Center and Database Administration Utility messages
- **DBI** installation or configuration messages
- **DWC** Data Warehouse Center messages
- **FLG** Information Catalog Manager messages
- **SAT** satellite messages
- **SPM** Synch Point Manager messages
- **SQJ** embedded SQLJ in Java messages
- **SQL** database manager messages

Note *Some error messages are returned in combination with other reason codes or return codes that should be recorded with the error message itself.*

To collect more information on which error was returned, you can type the following command on any machine where DB2 is installed:

```
db2 "? XXXnnnnnL"
```

Note that you may leave out the trailing single-digit letter at the end of the error message; it is optional and does not change the meaning of the message.

For example, a sample error message returned from the database manager is SQL0104N. Using this message with the preceding command yields the following output:

```
db2 "? sql0104"

SQL0104N An unexpected token "<token>" was found following
        "<text>".  Expected tokens may include:
        "<token-list>".

Explanation:  A syntax error in the SQL statement was detected at
the specified token following the text "<text>".  The "<text>"
field indicates the 20 characters of the SQL statement that
preceded the token that is not valid.

As an aid to the programmer, a partial list of valid tokens is
provided in the SQLERRM field of the SQLCA as "<token-list>".
This list assumes the statement is correct to that point.

The statement cannot be processed.

User Response:  Examine and correct the statement in the area of
the specified token.

sqlcode:  -104

sqlstate:  42601
```

The resulting information combines the original error message returned to the application with a detailed explanation of that message, suggested actions for the user, the sqlcode, and the sqlstate. Note that the suggested actions cannot always be directly applied to the operation you are performing because several different operations could result in the same error message.

The *sqlcode* is the internal DB2 representation of the error message, and the *sqlstate* is a platform-consistent representation of the error condition. We are usually most interested in the sqlcode for problem identification. Note that in the previous example, there would have been much more information returned with the actual error in the form of tokens and text, so it is important to record those tokens and text along with the sqlcode.

In most situations, the information returned from the previous command is all you need to determine what the error is and how to remedy the problem. In this sample case, the information is very useful. It indicates that the error returned was simply due to a syntax error. If we had the additional tokens and text, we would have easily been able to identify where the syntax problem was in our command.

If the information returned from the previous procedure is inadequate to determine the problem cause, then you will need to investigate information logged by DB2 or consider using some of the DB2 Problem Determination and Problem Source Identification (PD/PSI) utilities to collect more information. We will discuss this in more detail in the "Problem Determination and Problem Source Identification" section later in this chapter.

For a complete listing of all DB2 messages and sqlstates, refer to the *DB2 Message Reference,* available online at the DB2 Customer Service web site: http://www.ibm.com/software/data/db2/udb/winos2unix/support.

Hang and Performance Symptoms

Some of the most difficult types of problems to debug are hangs, slowdowns, or looping symptoms. The most important detail to determine is whether the operation is actually hanging or if it is just moving very slowly. Very slow operations are often mistaken for hang situations.

By monitoring the resources that the operation is using, through either DB2 or operating system monitoring tools, you can usually determine which one is the problem. For example, when taking a backup, you would monitor the disks that are being read (the source, where the database resides) for activity. You would also monitor the disks or tapes that are being written to (the target, where the backup image is being backed up to) through normal operating system directory listing commands showing disk space consumption.

At the same time, you could monitor DB2 to ensure that the application is still connected and actively performing work by using the LIST APPLICATIONS SHOW DETAIL command. By reviewing the output of that command, you can see which db2agent is associated with the backup, and you can monitor the CPU usage of that and other agents and processes and/or threads concurrently (depending on the operating system being used for the backup).

It is also important to determine whether it is only a single operation that is hanging or slow, or if the hang or slowdown is actually on a much larger scale—at a database, instance, or system level.

Only by investigating all aspects of the situation and by answering all of the other questions in this "Problem Identification" section can you paint an accurate picture of what the problem really is.

For more details on which information you need to collect in a hang situation, refer to the "Problem Determination and Problem Source Identification" section of this chapter.

PERFORMANCE

Database Shutdown Symptoms

A database shutdown indicates that all applications and connections are forcibly removed from the database. This type of problem is also typically referred to as "marking the database bad." These situations are usually due to critical problems, such as a disk failure, in which case DB2 cannot safely guarantee the integrity of your data if it is to continue operation. In these cases, the database is marked "bad" and is brought down immediately. This allows the database and system administrators to remedy the immediate concern so that the database can go through crash recovery and ensure the consistency of the data.

To determine the root cause of a database shutdown, much information will probably need to be collected and investigated. DB2 dumps out a significant amount of information in these situations, usually in the form of db2diag.log messages, and dump, trap, and core files. Often, the operating system dumps out information in these situations as well, depending on the problem, of course. Refer to the "Problem Determination and Problem Source Identification" section of this chapter for more details on these DB2 files, the operating system information, and how you can use them to aid root cause analysis.

Instance Crash Symptoms

A DB2 instance crash indicates that the entire DB2 instance has come down, such that another db2start would be necessary to bring the instance up. It is important to distinguish between an instance crash and a database being marked bad because the availability of resources is quite different in each case. In an instance crash, all databases within the instance are affected; however, in a database shutdown, the problem is isolated to a single database. Instance crashes, or traps, occur when a DB2 process (for example, a db2agent) receives a signal or raises an exception as a result of an instruction that cannot be executed.

Symptoms that indicate you may have had an instance crash include the following:

- Connections receive SQL1224N, SQL1229N, SQL0900N, or SQL1032N messages.
- A pop-up window opens on Windows (for example, exception C0000005 in db2syscs.exe) and OS/2 (SYS3175).
- The database manager is no longer active or responsive. (On Intel platforms, the machine may require a reboot.)
- The DIAGPATH file system fills from a large core dump.
- Applications fail or hang.
- Crash recovery is necessary, and it takes a long time. (This may seem like a hang.)
- An SQL1072C occurs on db2stop and db2start. (This indicates an inconsistent state of resources, in which case, the resources need to be cleaned up.)
- A hang or error occurs on db2start, or a message states that the instance is already started, whereas db2stop states that the instance is not started.

Note that these crashes can occur if an installation (either full or FixPak) is bad or incomplete, in which case, DB2 is using mixed code–level libraries. If you receive these crashes several times during any type of operation, and you have recently applied DB2 maintenance, then you should ensure that the installation was performed successfully.

As in database shutdown situations, DB2 dumps out much information to aid the investigation of the root cause of these problems. Often, these problems are due to DB2 code defects. You will learn how to investigate this type of problem in the "Problem Determination and Problem Source Identification" section.

When Does the Problem Occur?

Record the exact timestamp of when the problem occurs (or occurred). This is vital in performing proper problem determination. In this fast-paced world of gigahertz over gigabytes, milliseconds and nanoseconds can make all the difference in determining the root cause of many problems.

This information is important in trying to determine whether a problem is due to a specific sequence of events, or possibly due to some operation external to DB2. For example, a certain batch job may fail at almost exactly 3:00 A.M. every morning. This would lead to the suspicion that some scheduled maintenance starts at exactly that time, which could interfere with DB2 processing and cause the problem that you are encountering.

 As previously mentioned, if any changes have been recently made to the environment reporting a problem, it could be related to the original problem cause.

Under What Conditions Does the Problem Occur?

As hinted at in the previous example relating to scheduled batch jobs, the environment in which the problem occurs is always vital in determining the root cause. It is important to document exactly which DB2 applications, DB2 utilities, operating system utilities, or other possibly invasive applications were running when, or directly before, the problem was reported. Some examples of these operations are processing batch jobs, backing up file systems at the operating system level, and running antivirus software. These types of operations can seriously affect the operation of DB2.

For example, all of DB2's data and index page modification is performed in memory, within the buffer pool. If there are any file system operations being performed on disk (such as file system checking with the option to correct problems, or a file system reorganization) while the pages are being modified in memory, then problems could result; the information in memory may not match what is physically written to disk. This could even cause possible data corruption.

Which Events Led Up to the Problem?

Many problems are due to a certain combination of events. That is why it is imperative to investigate which events led up to the time the problem was reported. For example, if you run a certain script directly before your application reports a problem, then something in that script may be responsible for modifying the expected environment of the application, thus causing it to fail.

These events are best viewed by piecing bits of collected information together. By combining your application's logs with the operating system's error reporting and DB2's message logs, you can usually paint a fairly descriptive picture of which events led up to the problem. Refer to the "Problem Determination and Problem Source Identification" section for more details on which information can be used to complete the picture.

Is the Problem Reproducible?

It is important to note whether this problem happened only once or if the same action (or set of actions) continually causes the problem. A reproducible problem is always easier to diagnose than a single occurrence. It is also important to determine whether the problem can be re-created in another different environment, such as a testing or development environment, so that you can minimize the impact on your production system for performing problem determination.

Once you have identified a problem as being reproducible, then you have the great advantage of being able to use PD/PSI tools or of generating more diagnostics to help investigate the problem's cause. For example, if you have a specific reproducible problem, you can re-create it by setting the database manager configuration diaglevel parameter to 4 so that the most information possible will be dumped out into DB2's db2diag.log file. For more details on which information to collect in a reproducible problem scenario and for which tools to use in such a situation, refer to the "Problem Determination and Problem Source Identification" and "PD/PSI Tools" sections.

Problem Determination and Problem Source Identification

Once you have developed a clear problem description and you have a comprehensive understanding of the environment in which the problem occurred, you need to determine what the problem actually was by identifying the problem source, or root cause. There are three stages to determining the root cause of a DB2 problem:

- DB2 internals interpretation
- First failure data capture (FFDC)
- Data collection and examination

DB2 Internals Interpretation

To completely understand DB2 as a product and how to solve problems with it, you need to first understand how it fits together. This section provides a brief overview of the DB2 internals necessary for performing proper PD/PSI. We will describe how each function within DB2 code can map to a specific operation or how, by looking at the function name, you can get an idea of the responsibilities for that area of code. These area descriptions will aid you in analyzing key files created by DB2 that we will explain in more detail in upcoming sections.

DB2 is broken up into several different areas, called *components*, and it maintains a common naming convention based on functional responsibilities. Most components have the prefix **sql** directly preceding the component area, which is a representation of one or more letters. For example, **sqlo** is the prefix for all operating system services functions, that is, functions that tie directly to DB2's operating system interaction.

These components map directly to the functions they contain, where the functions usually have a decent description of the action they are performing. For example, **sqloread** is the DB2 function that is responsible for reading from a file. There are some component exceptions to this common naming convention, but for the scope of this chapter, we will concentrate on the most common component areas.

The following sections briefly explain the most common DB2 components. Once you understand how the internals of DB2 are functionally represented, we can proceed to investigate the files that DB2 provides for analysis.

Base System Utilities (BSU)—sqle

BSU is the main "engine" component for the DB2 instance. It is responsible for invoking all of the other components at db2start time. Some other operations it performs are memory allocation for the instance and each database, and system interrupt handling.

Communications Layer (CCI)—sqlc

The CCI receives protocol-specific information from client connections, and it retrieves the DB2RA data structure. This structure is the buffer used for communications between client and server. The DB2RA is sent to the Relational Data Services (RDS) component for processing. Once it has been processed and a result set is available, the CCI receives the DB2RA from RDS and sends it back to the client. In EEE, the partition that receives the connect request for the agent will be the coordinator partition for that agent, and all data will flow through this partition back to the application.

Relational Data Services (RDS)—sqlr

RDS is responsible for receiving input DB2RA from the CCI. It then optimizes the statements and works with the DB2 Optimizer (component **sqlno**) to build the necessary access plans, compare them, and prepare them for execution. These plans are then sent to the Data Management Services (DMS) component for data retrieval. Once the result set is available, RDS receives it from DMS, builds the output DB2RA, and passes the output DB2RA to the CCI.

Data Management Services (DMS)—sqld

DMS is responsible for receiving access plans from RDS. Once the plan is obtained, it retrieves the data based on the plan. It may call several other components to complete the plan execution, including the Index Manager (IXM, **sqlx**) component for index scans and the Sort List Services (SLS, **sqls**) component for sorts. Finally, DMS returns the result set to RDS.

DMS is also mainly responsible for reading and moving the data pages during the REORG command.

Bufferpool Services (BPS)—sqlb

BPS performs all operations related to the buffer pool(s). All regular and index data is manipulated in the buffer pool. If the data and/or index pages are not already in the buffer pool, then this component will retrieve them from disk. It will use different storage managers (file or raw) to get the pages from disk depending on whether the table spaces are defined as system-managed space (SMS) or database-managed space (DMS). The calls to read from and write to disk are made through the Operating System Services (OSS, **sqlo**) component.

BPS is also responsible for mapping table space layout and maintaining the table space states.

Data Protection Services (DPS)—sqlp

DPS provides the mechanisms to guarantee data integrity by managing DB2's transactional logging. All transactions must be logged to ensure that they can be rolled back or reapplied if needed. Records being read or changed are also locked to ensure that the changes will not be overwritten. DPS involves both locking and logging, and it is responsible for such operations as roll-forward recovery, crash recovery, and log archival/retrieval via userexit.

Operating System Services (OSS)—sqlo

OSS is responsible for making all operating system calls. It handles all memory management and file I/O. OSS is used within DB2 to latch memory or disk, handle semaphore event processing, and create processes and/or threads. In many cases, the return codes from OSS function calls are from the operating systems themselves, so you can usually interpret the results.

For reference, the return codes for each operating system can be found in the following files. (Note that the Intel platforms required the operating system's software development kit to obtain the files—the OS return codes should also be available on their associated web sites.)

- **UNIX** /usr/include/sys/errno.h
- **Windows NT/2000** Winerror.h (also, net helpmsg <error> will give the same information)
- **OS/2** bseerr.h

Other Common DB2 Component Areas

The following are some other common DB2 component areas (and their corresponding functional prefixes) that may be of interest to you:

- Application Precompilers (various programming languages)—**sqla**
- Database/Database Manager Configuration—**sqlf**
- Distributed Data Services—**sqlj**
- Fast Communication Manager (FCM)—**sqlkf**
- Monitoring—**sqlm**
- Optimizer—**sqlno**
- Tracing—**sqlt**
- Utilities (BACKUP/RESTORE/LOAD/IMPORT/EXPORT/etc.)—**sqlu**

First Failure Data Capture

Whenever a problem is encountered within DB2, certain information is dumped out in various locations to help you determine what the problem actually was. This dumping of information is termed first failure data capture (FFDC). The idea behind FFDC is that all information necessary to determine a problem is dumped on the first occurrence, so problem re-creation need not be necessary.

Usually this information is sufficient, but we have to remember that every problem is different. Because all problems vary in severity and impact, the information dumped out on the first occurrence is often insufficient to determine the actual problem cause due to physical CPU and space limitations. It would be nice to be able to log every single event that any operation performs; however, this is not physically possible, so we have to rely on a comfortable level of logged information that minimally impacts system performance.

The FFDC files available to DB2 are as follows:

- The db2diag.log file
- The db2alert.log file and operating system error reports
- Trap files
- Dump files
- Core files
- Locklist dump files
- Messages files

The next few sections briefly describe the purpose of each of these FFDC files and thoroughly explains how to interpret the information.

The db2diag.log file

This file is the single most important diagnostic file for DB2. It is an ASCII file that gathers information as the problem is occurring, and it has information appended to it over time. Every problem encountered by DB2 should have information logged in the db2diag.log file. However, based on the configuration the file is using, the severity of the problem encountered may not justify a message to be logged. Before we get into the details of how to interpret the data recorded in db2diag.log, we need to review where the file itself is found and how to control the information flowing into it.

Each db2diag.log file is associated with an instance. Therefore, each instance has its own db2diag.log file. The Database Administration Server (DAS) is its own instance, so it has its own db2diag.log file.

The db2diag.log file physically resides on both the client and the server, and its location (like many of the other DB2 FFDC files) is determined by the database manager configuration diagpath parameter. In an EEE environment, this path can be either a shared network mounted path so that all partitions dump their information to the same file, or separate paths so that all partitions dump their information to separate files. The default path is different for UNIX and Intel installations:

- **UNIX** $HOME/sqllib/db2dump, where $HOME is the home directory of the DB2 instance owner
- **Intel** <INSTALL DRIVE/DIR>\SQLLIB\<DB2INSTANCE>

The amount of information that is logged in the db2diag.log file is determined by the database manager configuration diaglevel parameter. The following amount of data is captured for each DIAGLEVEL value:

- **DIAGLEVEL (0)** No diagnostic data (this level is not recommended)
- **DIAGLEVEL (1)** Only severe errors
- **DIAGLEVEL (2)** All errors (severe and not severe)
- **DIAGLEVEL (3)** All errors and warnings (the default value)
- **DIAGLEVEL (4)** All errors, warnings, informational messages, and other internal diagnostic information

The default for DIAGLEVEL is 3, and this is usually sufficient for determining most problems. The value should be changed to 4 only when you are first installing, migrating, or configuring your production system, or when you are experiencing problems. Running with DIAGLEVEL 4 could cause some serious performance problems (especially in EEE, with a network-mounted and shared DIAGPATH), because a significant amount of information is dumped, even during a minimal workload. Use it with caution.

Now that you know how to control what is dumped into the file, you need to know how to read the information that is dumped. It is important to understand that the db2diag.log file is not only appended to when there is a problem, but also during normal operation. There are two types of entries in db2diag.log:

- Administrative events—Information regarding utilities, crash recovery, and other important events during normal database activity. An example of an administrative event is running a LOAD. The information dumped out to the db2diag.log file indicates when the different phases of the LOAD (load phase, build phase, and delete phase) begin and end.

- Error conditions—Information dumped to indicate that a problem has occurred. The information provided aids in problem diagnosis and information gathering. An example of an error condition is when a database crashes. The db2diag.log file would contain key error information, as well as information on other files that may have been created during the error condition, with their locations.

The best way to understand the entries in the db2diag.log file is to investigate an example. The following scenario shows how we issued a command and used db2diag.log to assist in determining the problem cause. The scenario begins with the command, and its SQL error is returned:

```
db2 create tablespace testspace managed by system using ('E:\testspace0')

DB21034E  The command was processed as an SQL statement because it was not a
valid Command Line Processor command.  During SQL processing it returned:
SQL0294N  The container is already in use.  SQLSTATE=42730
```

This SQL code already gives us a good idea of the problem; however, we will investigate the db2diag.log file to see how to analyze errors that are logged. If we did not have the command that was issued and that caused the error to be logged or the returned SQL code, then investigating the db2diag.log file would be necessary to determine the root cause. Figure 15-1 shows the messages that are created in the db2diag.log file when the error occurred.

Using the numbered identifiers in Figure 15-1, the fields from the db2diag.log entries can be broken down as follows:

1. Date and timestamp of the message

2. Instance name

3. Partition number (or node), even for non-EEE

4. Process ID (PID), process name in brackets, and thread ID (TID)

5. Application ID

6. DB2 internal component identifier

7. DB2 internal function identifier

8. Unique error identifier (Probe ID)

9. Database name

10. Error description and/or error code

This information is usually sufficient to determine the reason for the entry; however, sometimes, certain fields may be left out due to the type of entry that is being created. This can make problem investigation more difficult.

The db2diag.log messages returned in our example are fairly straightforward, and they indicate (using the numbers as references) that a local application (5) tried to incorrectly access or alter container E:\testspace0 (10) on 2001-06-17 at around 17:23 (1), which is already in use by table space 3 in database SAMPLE (9) on node 0 (3) within the DB2 instance (2). Using the information we learned in the previous section with the DB2 internal component identifier (6), we can determine that DB2 is using the Bufferpool Services code to perform the create table space operation. The DB2 internal function identifiers sqlbSetupPool and sqlbCreatePool (7) give us a good idea of which operations we were trying to perform during the problem. (Note that "pool" is another term for "table space" within DB2.)

These identifiers would be invaluable if we did not have the original command that was issued to cause the error. It is important to note that the unique error identifiers (8) aren't really useful to general readers of the file. They are much more useful to the DB2 customer service analysts, however, because they indicate message or failure points within the functions, which can be used for debugging the code. Continuing with our example, the second db2diag.log entry's error description (10) is a little bit cryptic, and it will require some investigation to determine the meaning of the message.

Sometimes, as in our example, the information provided in the error description (10) is returned as an internal DB2 return code in a hexadecimal format. These hexadecimal codes are in the form "FFFF xxxx", where "*xxxx*" is the internal DB2

Figure 15-1. *A db2diag.log file Example*

return code. You may need to byte-reverse the value from "xxxx FFFF" for some messages on Intel platforms. For example, "0AE6 FFFF" would become "FFFF E60A", so "E60A" would be the internal DB2 return code.

When one of these return codes is indicated in the db2diag.log file, you need to first determine whether it is an sqlcode or an internal DB2 return code. You can determine whether it is an sqlcode simply by converting the value from hexadecimal to a signed decimal number. In our example, "FFFF 8139" converts to –32455, which is not a valid sqlcode. This must mean that "8139" is an internal DB2 return code.

We have included a list of DB2's internal return codes in Table 15-2 at the end of this chapter, and they are also available within the *DB2 Troubleshooting Guide,* available online at the link provided in the "DB2 Customer Service References" section of this chapter. From that table, we can find the meaning of the "8139" internal DB2 return code shown in Table 15-1.

This indicates that the message returned to the application was an SQL0294N, which is consistent with what we received upon issuing the command, and with the previous message in the db2diag.log file. This error indicates that we cannot create a table space using the container that is already defined by another table space. Using db2 "? SQL0294N" (as outlined previously in the "Problem Identification" section of this chapter) will also reveal a whole list of possible reasons and suggestions for resolving this error. Thus, the solution to our problem is to define the table space container on a different path.

Another type of error condition message that can be dumped out into the db2diag.log file is an SQLCA structure. These messages do not have timestamps, so it is more difficult to pinpoint their exact occurrence. They are much more common to see at DIAGLEVEL 4 because every negative sqlcode returned to an application is logged as an SQLCA structure message in the db2diag.log file. Again, we will use an example to describe the message. With the DIAGLEVEL set to 4, we issued this command:

```
db2 select * from fender.or
SQL0204N  "FENDER.OR" is an undefined name.  SQLSTATE=42704
```

Figure 15-2 shows the resultant SQLCA structure entry in the db2diag.log file.

Internal DB2 Return Code	SQL Code	Reason Code	Description
8139	–294		Container is already being used

Table 15-1. *Internal DB2 Return Code Example*

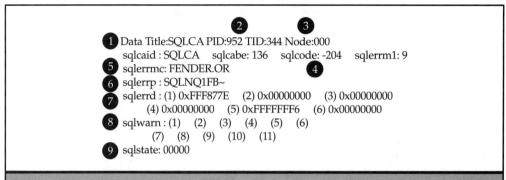

Figure 15-2.   *A db2diag.log file SQLCA structure example*

Using the numbered identifiers in Figure 15-2, the fields from the db2diag.log entries can be broken down as follows:

1. SQLCA entry identifier

2. Process ID (PID) and thread ID (TID)

3. Partition number (or node), even for non-EEE

4. sqlcode

5. sqlerrmc indicates tokens or reason codes associated with the sqlcode

6. sqlerrp indicates the DB2 version, release, and modification identifier if no sqlcode indicated in (4), or DB2 internal function identifier if an sqlcode

7. sqlerrd indicates the DB2 return codes leading to the final sqlcode; field (6) of the sqlerrd indicates the partition number in an EEE environment

8. sqlwarn indicates warning indicators

9. sqlstate indicates the outcome of the most recently executed SQL statement

Again, when we have the actual command issued and the error returned, it makes our investigation much easier. However, if we do not have that information, we need to look to the db2diag.log file for assistance. Assuming that we do not have the command and sqlcode in our example, we can see that field (4) isolates the sqlcode returned to the application as –204, or SQL0204N.

Investigating further into the actual message text using the command db2 "? SQL0204N" indicates that <name> is an undefined name. Because we have the token (5) returned with the SQL code, we know that this <name> is FENDER.OR, which was probably an incorrect or unqualified object name. This is accurate; we intended to select from the FENDER.ORG table in the SAMPLE database.

The DB2 return codes indicated in field (7) could be investigated as we did in the previous example; however, they (as with the rest of the nonidentified fields) are more for use by the DB2 Customer Service analysts.

In an EEE environment, one SQL statement may be executed by a number of agents on different partitions, and each agent may return a different SQLCA for different errors or warnings. In addition, the coordinator agent will return an SQLCA. To provide a consistent view for applications, all SQLCA values are merged into one structure, and SQLCA fields indicate global counts.

You can see the resultant SQLCA from any command (which will also be dumped out to the db2diag.log) by issuing db2 –a <command>.

As you can see, the db2diag.log file is very powerful for problem determination, but it is not always sufficient to solve every problem on its own. Several more types of messages are dumped to the file, as different information is needed to debug each unique problem. However, the messages most useful to you are contained in the two examples we have provided.

The db2alert.log File and Operating System Error Reports

An *alert* is an error notification issued when a severe error occurs. It can be sent to a central machine or to the attention of database, system, or network administrators. If an error is determined to be an alert, then an entry is made in the db2diag.log file, the db2alert.log file, and to the operating system or native logging facility. Unlike entries in db2diag.log, the db2alert.log entries can be easier to identify by administrators because they will be logged only upon severe conditions, and they can be broadcast using the following systemwide error logging facilities:

- **UNIX** The *syslog*: the file location and type of information written is set in the /etc/syslog.conf file
- **Windows NT/2000** System, security, and application event log files, and the Dr. Watson log file in %windir%\drwtsn32.log
- **OS/2** FFST log in <install>:\OS2\SYSTEM\RAS\LOG*.DAT

For convenience, we will refer to all of these operating system error logs as the *syslog*.

The syslog entries have information very similar to that in the db2diag.log file; each entry contains date and time information, the process ID, the internal component and function encountering the error, as well as an error description and/or return code. You can use the same procedures to investigate these files as presented in the previous section for the db2diag.log file.

Regardless of whether anything is logged to the syslog or not, you should always check whether the operating system itself reported any operating system–level problems at the same time as the DB2 problem was reported because this can usually provide very good hints about the actual problem cause. Different platforms record operating system events quite differently, so you need to know where to go to obtain this system-level message information and how to interpret it. The following list identifies where to find the operating system–level report on some common platforms. (Note that for certain platforms, the syslog is in the location for finding operating system–level messages.)

- **AIX** Use the /usr/bin/errpt –a command
- **Solaris** In the files prefixed with "messages" in the /var/adm directory, or use the /usr/bin/dmesg command
- **Linux** In the files prefixed with "messages" in the /var/log directory
- **HP-UX** In the /var/adm/syslog/syslog.log file, or use the /usr/bin/dmesg command
- **Windows NT/2000** In the system, security, and application event log files, and in the Dr. Watson log file, found in %windir%\drwtsn32.log (where *%windir%* is the drive and directory where Windows is installed)
- **OS/2** In the FFST log in the <install>:\OS2\SYSTEM\RAS\LOG*.DAT file (where *<install>* is the drive where OS/2 is installed)

Trap Files

When a database shuts down, an instance crashes, or further diagnostic information is generated for DB2, *trap files* are created. These files are not always generated when an actual database or instance crash occurs, but they are usually related to such an event. They are created in the DIAGPATH whenever a DB2 process receives a signal from the operating system (UNIX) or raises an exception (Intel). Trap files are named in the following format based on the platform on which they are created:

- **UNIX** t<pppppp>.<nnn>, where *<pppppp>* indicates the PID, and *<nnn>* indicates the node where the trap occurred
- **Intel** DB<ppp><ttt>.TRP, where *<ppp>* indicates the PID and *<ttt>* indicates the TID

On the Windows platforms, these files are not as useful (outside of DB2 Customer Service) as those of the other platforms simply because they are written in binary, and they must be formatted by DB2 Customer Service personnel. In those situations, the Dr. Watson log may provide similar information.

For the platforms that have ASCII trap files created, the most important information to note is the signal received or exception raised, and the offending function with its stack calling chain. Note that the trap files are quite different on every platform, but the general information remains the same. Figure 15-3 shows some excerpts from a sample trap file named t750202.000 on AIX.

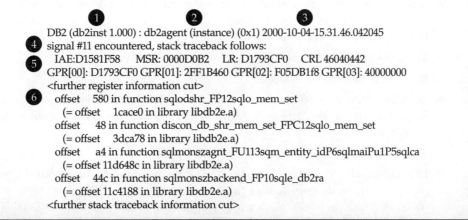

Figure 15-3. *Trap file t750202.000 example*

Using the numbered identifiers from Figure 15-3, the fields from the db2diag.log entries can be broken down as follows:

1. Instance and node (<instance>.<node>) the offending process "belongs" to
2. Process name
3. Date and timestamp of the trap
4. Signal number
5. Register information
6. Stack traceback, with the "trapping" function at the top and the program entry point at the bottom

Intel platform trap files also contain a raw stack dump, an instruction stream dump, and currently loaded DLLs.

First, you need to determine which signal or exception was encountered. The most common types of signals DB2 receives can be described as follows (note that there are others, but these are the most common):

- Illegal instructions occur because of a bad (possibly NULL) function pointer or stack overwrites:
  - UNIX Signal #4—SIGILL
  - Intel Exception C000001C

- Invalid memory addresses occur when memory is not mapped (doesn't exist), or when the process doesn't have permission to perform the desired action (for example, to write to protected memory):
    - UNIX Signal #11—SIGSEGV (segmentation violation)
    - INTEL Exception C0000005
- Stack overflow exceptions occur when the stack is too small or when the stack is used in excess (Windows platforms are the most common to encounter this exception):
    - Windows platforms exception C000001D
- Programming signals are caused by DB2 (or externally) to dump out diagnostic trap files. These diagnostic files can be created by using DB2 tools (such as db2_call_stack on UNIX platforms) or operating system commands (such as kill –36 <pid> on AIX). See the "PD/PSI Tools" section of this chapter for more information on how to generate these diagnostic trap files. Here are the corresponding signals (UNIX) or exceptions (Intel) for programming signals, listed by platform:
    - AIX Signal #36—SIGPRE
    - Solaris and DYNIX/ptx Signal #21—SIGPRE
    - HP Signal #29—SIGPRE
    - Linux Signal #23—SIGPRE
    - Intel Exception C0010002

Note *The database and instance should stay active when programming signals are received because they are purely informational dumps; however, they may be signaled as a result of a more fatal underlying problem, in which case, the database will be shut down, or the instance will crash.*

- Kill signals caused by users or scripts manually killing DB2 processes; note that these signals are not in trap files because they cannot be caught:
    - UNIX Signal #9—SIGKILL
- Abort Signals caused by an intentional abort call. In these cases, the abort itself should not be investigated; rather, what caused DB2 to abort in the first place should be investigated:
    - UNIX Signal #6—SIGABRT

To determine what any of the above signals mean, refer to the following files: (Note that the Intel files require the software development kits.)

- **UNIX** /usr/include/sys/signal.h
- **Windows** Winnt.h
- **OS/2** bsexcpt.h

Aside from the signal or exception encountered by the process, the most important information contained within trap files is the stack traceback; this gives you the history of which function path the process has followed.

Using the trap file example in Figure 15-3 and the corresponding numbered identifiers, we can determine that PID 750202 received a Signal #11 (4), also known as a segmentation violation or SIGSEGV, on node 0 in the db2inst1 instance (1) on 2000-10-04 at 15:31 (3). This was a db2agent process (2), and the trap occurred within the sqlodshr function call (6).

By looking at the first few functions in the stack calling chain, we can conclude that this trap occurred as a result of trying to disconnect from the database shared memory set from within DB2 monitoring code. You can determine this because the failing function was in the **sqlo** component (Operating System Services) called from an **sqlm** component (Monitoring) function.

We don't know the exact details of the functions because we don't have the source code; however, we can safely say that we should begin our investigation with which DB2 monitoring was being performed around the date and time indicated in the trap file. This would include investigating such details as which scripts may have been running the GET SNAPSHOT command, or which monitoring switch may have recently been enabled.

From this information, we may be able to determine the exact operation that caused the trap so that we can possibly prevent that from happening again. This will enable us to perform further research or possibly to re-create the operation within another test environment, while keeping our production system safe from a second occurrence, thus minimizing the impact.

You should always provide these files to DB2 Customer Service if you contact them for assistance.

Dump Files

When a DB2 error occurs for which there is additional internal information that would be useful in problem diagnosis, DB2 creates *dump files.* The information contained within the dump files is mostly IBM confidential information (such as internal control blocks and structures), so they are created in binary format. The primary audience for dump files is DB2 Customer Service personnel, so they are not of much use to users and administrators. However, when they are created in the DIAGPATH, administrators should know to look into the db2diag.log file to try and determine what may have caused them. The types of problems that could cause these files to be created vary quite a bit, but they are usually related to some sort of a severe error, such as the detection of a bad page in the database.

Dump files are named in the following format based on the platform on which they are created:

- **UNIX** <pppppp>.<nnn>, where *<pppppp>* indicates the PID and *<nnn>* indicates the node where the problem occurred
- **Intel** <ppp><ttt>.<nnn>, where *<ppp>* indicates the PID, *<ttt>* indicates the TID, and *<nnn>* indicates the node where the problem occurred

Similar to trap files, you should always supply these files to DB2 Customer Service when you contact them for support because dump files are important for defect investigation.

Core Files

When certain problems are encountered on UNIX-based operating systems, files might be created in core dump directories under the instance home sqllib/db2dump directory (for example, $HOME/sqllib/db2dump), not the DIAGPATH. These files are called *core files*. If a program terminates abnormally, a core file is created by the system to store a memory image of the terminated process. The core files contain the data region, stack, and attached shared segments for the process, as well as additional information about the process. Errors such as memory address violations, illegal instructions, bus errors, and user-generated quit signals cause core files to be dumped. Note that system core files are distinct from DB2 core files.

DB2 core files are each located within a directory for the offending process. The naming convention of the directory is similar to the UNIX trap and dump file, but the core file itself is simply named "core." The directory names start with the letter *c*, followed by the PID of the affected process and the three-digit directory suffix of the failing node. For example, where $HOME indicates the home directory of the instance owner user ID, $HOME/sqllib/db2dump/c71198.010 would be a directory containing a core file for a problematic DB2 process with PID 71198 running on node 10. At the same time, you may discover that trap, dump, and locklist dump files were created in the DIAGPATH for the same PID.

As of version 4.3 of AIX, DB2 core dumps include shared memory segments, so DB2 cores are much larger than they used to be (for example, they include bufferpools). Changing the 'Use pre-430 style CORE dump' setting to "true" using smit or smitty (in the System Environments >> Change / Show Characteristics of Operating System menu) will override this, causing only the data segment to get dumped. You may need more than 2GB available on the file system where the instance home is located to accommodate cores (especially at AIX 4.3 and later, if the registry variable is not used).

To analyze a DB2 core, you can use the UNIX **dbx** command. This aids in determining where the failure occurred within DB2 by providing such information as the stack traceback of the process. The **dbx** command includes a lot more functionality than is described in this section. To find out more, enter **man dbx** at a UNIX-based command prompt. For the HP-UX operating system, the **xdb** command can be used similarly.

Locklist Dump Files

When a database or instance crash occurs, there may still be locks held on objects in the database. When the crash occurs, this database object lock information is dumped out in the form of locklist dump files. Like trap, dump, and core files, *locklist dump files* are created in the DIAGPATH, and they are named in the following format based on the platform on which they are created:

- **UNIX** l<pppppp>.<nnn>, where *pppppp* indicates the PID and *nnn* indicates the node where the problem occurred

- **Intel** l<ppp><ttt>.<nnn>, where *ppp* indicates the PID, *ttt* indicates the TID, and *nnn* indicates the node where the problem occurred

Aside from knowing that these dump files exist, you shouldn't need to worry about them for investigation. The information dumped out into these files is of use primarily for DB2 Customer Service analysts when performing investigation into possible DB2 defects, and should be provided when contacting them.

Messages Files

Certain utilities within DB2 have the option to create *messages files* when they are run. Specifying this option within the command logs activities during its operation to a file that you can review later. For example,

```
db2 load from test.ixf of ixf replace into fender.org messages msg.txt
```

This command creates a file named msg.txt within the directory from which the command was issued. This file contains detailed information about the processing of the LOAD, and it could aid in problem resolution should the LOAD fail.

Some utilities that have this option in DB2 include BIND, LOAD, EXPORT, IMPORT, etc.

Data Collection and Examination

Now that you are aware of the different types of FFDC information DB2 supplies, it is important to collect the correct set of files so that you can determine the problem cause as quickly and effectively as possible. The information you gather is based on the problem you are encountering at the time (as previously identified in the "Problem Identification" section). The following few sections outline the information you should gather in different problem situations.

Investigating Error Messages

The error message is the most common problem users and administrators encounter. In those cases, the actual error message text is usually the most help. If that is not sufficient, then the db2diag.log file is the best second reference; it provides a history of how the error message developed over time.

If, after you have examined the error message and db2diag.log file, you are no closer to resolving the problem, then performing a DB2 trace (via the db2trc utility) or using other DB2 tools may be the next alternative. See the "PD/PSI Tools" section for more information on using this and other utilities and tools.

Investigating Hangs and Performance

Hangs and/or potential performance problems are always difficult to investigate. Only through experience can you understand how to solve these complex problems. First, you should analyze whether there is a bottleneck and if so, where the bottleneck exists.

A bottleneck could exist in any processing layer of the application or DB2. These bottlenecks could include I/O or CPU-bound systems, network delay, third-party application processing, DB2 processing, or others. For each situation, a different set of data needs to be collected. Every problem is unique and uses different layers of connectivity and processing. Because the scope of hang and performance problems requires much experience in debugging, we will only briefly cover some tools and procedures that you can use to help solve those problems.

A hang or performance problem is typically encountered due to bottlenecks at one of the levels described in the following sections.

Query Level   For query-level performance problems, you can use utilities such as DB2 Explain to generate access plans for specific queries, or you can use the db2batch tool to see SQL prepare and execution timings. (See the "PD/PSI Tools" section for more details on the db2batch tool.) You can examine the plans to determine if the optimal access plan is being chosen by the DB2 Optimizer. If not, then specific query tuning will be required to obtain the best results. Because query tuning alone is a very complicated and in-depth topic, it is beyond the scope of this chapter.

Database and Database Manager (Instance) Level   For database- or instance-level hang or performance problems, you can use the DB2 monitoring utilities and stack traceback dumps in conjunction with operating system commands to determine what the problem is. The DB2 monitoring utilities include snapshot and event monitors, and you can use them to analyze a problem over a period of time to narrow down the cause to a specific operation.

If you suspect a hang, then you can use the tools outlined in the "Generating Stack Traceback Files" section of this chapter for investigation. Some examples of these tools on the UNIX platforms include db2_call_stack and db2ncstack. Please refer to the aforementioned section for more details on using these and other DB2 tools. Because these files are generated in the same format as trap files, you can use the same method of analysis as previously described in the "First Failure Data Capture" section to isolate the DB2 problem area.

The operating system commands vary between UNIX and Intel platforms, but they usually contain the same basic information for memory (CPU) analysis, I/O analysis, and swap or paging space analysis. Some examples of UNIX commands that you can use to perform this analysis are vmstat, iostat, ps, and ipcs. Refer to your operating system documentation for more details on which utilities are available and how you can use them to perform this type of investigation.

It is always best to collect this information in a standard interval over a fixed period of time so that you can review all of the information collected in stages. If there is little or no change in any of the information collected, then a database or instance hang has probably been encountered, in which case, you would most likely need to contact DB2 Customer Service for assistance.

System Level   If the entire system appears to be having performance or hang problems, then the problem is usually much larger than just DB2. It may be simply an issue of overallocating available resources, but you should start the investigation at the system level before concentrating on any specific DB2 operation. You can use the previously described operating system commands to get started on the investigation in this area.

Investigating Database Shutdowns

A database shutdown is probably one of the most severe types of problems you can encounter. A shutdown almost always indicates a difficult problem to resolve. In these situations, all of the files previously explained come into play, with the db2diag.log file again being of primary importance.

In these situations, the first piece of information to investigate is the db2diag.log file. You should thoroughly review this file, and you should correlate the problem timestamps with the operating system error logs to ensure that no external factors could have caused the problem.

Corruption   One common type of database shutdown is due to corruption. Corruption is almost always the result of some sort of operating system (file system) or hardware interference with DB2 processing. When corruption is detected (which could surface as a consistency bit, or CBIT error), determining the problem source is usually of secondary importance. You would want to correct the current situation first. Corruption problems can be detected on reads or on writes.

If the corruption is detected on a read (usually from function **sqlbrdpg**), then it is most important to determine if the read error is permanent or not. For nonpermanent errors (which means a subsequent read is possible), the problem is almost always due to the operating system or hardware. You can test whether a corruption is permanent by repeating the same operation that caused the problem originally. Another option is to run db2dart against the problem object (or page, if identified from the db2diag.log file) repeatedly to see if the failure is repeated. (See the "PD/PSI Tools" section for details on the db2dart utility.)

For permanent read errors, the db2dart utility combined with the operating system error logs and hardware diagnostics is the best combination for identifying the problem source. A full database db2dart report is best because you probably would not know the extent of the damage if only one bad page is detected; however, this may not be feasible given the size of the database or the time the database would have to be down. The db2dart utility has the option of running against an individual object or table space to minimize this impact.

After the initial investigation into the cause is complete, the next step is to get rid of the bad page (because DB2 will crash every time it sees the bad page). The possible options for recovering are as follows:

- Drop the table, index, table space, or database.
- Restore and roll forward the database or table space.
- Rebuild the index via db2dart with the /MI option (assuming the corrupted page is an index page).
- Reinitialize the page using db2dart with the /IP option. (This option is risky, and it can be used only with the consultation of DB2 Customer Service due to the implications of use.)

For full correction, the best solution is to restore a recent database or table space backup; however, if you are restoring the backup over an already corrupt file system or a bad disk, then you may still encounter problems.

For reoccurring intermittent or reoccurring permanent errors (meaning the problem happens on the same page again even after fixing the bad page, or it occurs in other locations), it can often be useful to track down in which containers each problem page resides. Once you know the containers, you can attempt to track down which disk (and even controller) they are on.

Often, all occurrences point to one of many disks or to disks of just one controller. This can be a great hint that a single disk or controller card is bad, so replacement can be one option. Again, note that many corruptions are due to file system checks (with the option to fix lost file fragments), file system defragmentation utilities running with the database active (most of the db is modified in memory and is not aware of the operating system making changes under the covers), or hardware failures.

If the corruption is detected on a write (usually in function **sqlbwrpg**), then these are *in memory only* corruptions. That is, these pages will not make it to the disk (because DB2 will prevent the write). These types of corruptions are almost always due to one of two factors:

- Ninety percent memory corruption; the page header was corrupted
- Ten percent buffer pool protocol problems; possible DB2 defect

For either type of corruption issue, it is best to gather the db2diag.log file, a db2dart report of the entire database (if possible), or the problem table or table space, any trap and dump files created at the problem time, and any operating system error logs and hardware diagnostic reports.

If no obvious hardware error was indicated in the files collected, then you may wish to contact DB2 Customer Service for assistance in the investigation.

Crash Recovery Failures   If the database shutdown problem is occurring during crash recovery, which is usually invoked upon first connection to the database after a system restart or failure, then you may wish to investigate the following:

- If the db2diag.log file indicates failures when trying to access a certain index (in the db2diag.log file, an index object type is 0x1, a data object type is 0x0, and a temporary object type is 0x128), try the following:

    - Set the INDEXREC parameter to ACCESS (instead of RESTART) so that the index records will not be replayed during crash recovery, and the index will be rebuilt upon first access once the database is brought up.

    - Mark indexes invalid via db2dart <db> /MI. (See the "PD/PSI Tools" section for more details.)

- If the db2diag.log file indicates failures when trying to access a certain data object, then using filtered recovery may be an option:

    - db2 RESTART DB <db> DROP PENDING TABLESPACES allows you to connect to your database and place certain table spaces into a drop-pending status, thereby skipping the log records used during crash recovery. Upon the connect completion, the offending table space can be dropped.

    - db2dart <db> /MT allows you to mark the table as invalid, which you may need to do if an operation is failing on a specific table every time. (See the "PD/PSI Tools" section for more details, and note that you must contact DB2 Customer Service to perform this operation.)

If you still cannot determine the problem's cause using the information and DB2 tools provided, then you should contact DB2 Customer Service. Provide all of the details of the problem scenario, along with the db2diag.log file and any traps and dumps created at the problem time, with a DB2 trace (if reproducible).

Investigating Instance Crashes

Instance crashes, or traps, are almost always due to a DB2 code defect. The best action you can take in these cases is to search known product defects, termed authorized program analysis reports (APARs), for possible fixes. However, before proceeding with an exhaustive search of known problems, ensure that there is no related db2diag.log entry immediately before the trap (within a few seconds). For the db2diag.log entry to be worth considering, it would have to occur in the same process that trapped.

One such db2diag.log entry is when a kill signal is encountered, as shown below. This message indicates that a SIGKILL (signal #9) was received by a DB2 process. Once a DB2 process receives a kill signal, the entire instance comes down, even though there is no code defect. In this case, simply looking at the db2diag.log file was sufficient to determine the problem cause.

PERFORMANCE

```
2001-06-03-17.04.06.589595    Instance:fender    Node:000
PID:37882(db2ipccm)    Appid:none
oss_2                   sqloEDUCodeTrapHandler    Probe:156

DiagData
0000 0009 <<<< exit status of child process (usually Signal number received)
```

When there is a suspected code defect, the db2diag.log file for instance crashes almost always look like this:

```
2000-10-04-15.31.46.055296    Instance:db2inst1    Node:000
PID:750202 (db2agent (instance))    Appid:none
base_sys_utilities  sqleagnt_sigsegvh    Probe:10


Error in agent servicing application with coor_node:0000            ..


2000-10-04-15.31.46.138919    Instance:db2inst1    Node:000
PID:750202(db2agent (instance))    Appid:none
base_sys_utilities  sqleagnt_sigsegvh    Probe:10


Error in agent servicing application with coor_agent_index:001c      ..

2000-10-04-15.31.46.222742    Instance:db2inst1    Node:000
PID:750202(db2agent (instance))    Appid:none
base_sys_utilities  sqleagnt_sigsegvh    Probe:1


value of ptr to db2ra_as_cb2066 7b78
f{x
```

If you suspect a code defect because of the db2diag.log entries, then you need to review more information. Most importantly, the trap file is of interest because it indicates the function call stack for the process that died. From that, you can search for known APARs at the DB2 Customer Service web site by using the top function in the stack as a keyword.

However, if the top functions are memory functions such as **sqlofmblkEx** and **MemTreePut**, or C programming calls like **memcpy**, try also using the function underneath those calls as a search keyword; usually the caller causes a memory trap. When searching for keywords, always use wildcards before and after the search word to ensure maximum search coverage.

Note that function stacks might appear slightly different on different operating systems, and that there may be more than one path to a trap; that is, the top of the stack might match, but the rest of the stack might not. In these cases, if you had found a similar traceback from another operating system, it is still possible—and even likely— that it is due to the same problem.

When contacting DB2 Customer Service for these types of problems, the db2diag.log, dump files, trap files, and operating system error logs are of most importance. If the problem is reproducible, then a DB2 trace of the recurrence is also suggested.

PD/PSI Tools

DB2 offers a multitude of different tools to be used in a variety of situations. We will first look at how you can generate stack tracebacks within DB2 by using PD/PSI tools, and we'll then proceed to the other standalone tools provided by DB2.

Generating Stack Traceback Files

DB2 automatically generates stack traceback files when problems are detected that warrant this type of diagnostic information. However, when you want to see the function call stack at a particular point in time (usually for investigating hang situations), you need to force these files to be created. The method for doing this varies by platform.

On UNIX, DB2 supplies two utilities to generate stack traceback files:

■ db2_call_stack generates traceback files for all DB2 processes on all nodes.

■ db2ncstack generates traceback files for all DB2 processes on a single node.

These commands are issued at an instance level (which means all databases within the instance may be affected), and all trap files will be created within the DIAGPATH directory. The files will be in the trap file format outlined in the "First Failure Data Capture" section earlier in this chapter. Use the db2_call_stack tool with caution in an EEE environment; it could take a long time to generate all of the required files. The time required depends on the number of nodes in your environment, the amount of agents currently allocated, and the amount of activity within the database manager.

If you do not wish to use the DB2 utilities, then UNIX users can alternatively create stack tracebacks without any special DB2 involvement by using the UNIX kill command with the proper signal and syntax. For a stack traceback, the programming signal, or SIGPRE, is the signal you need to send to the DB2 processes.

For the complete list of signals based on the operating system, again refer to the trap file description in the "First Failure Data Capture" section. The proper usage of this command is simply the following:

```
kill <signal> pid
```

PERFORMANCE

For example, based on the different versions of UNIX, the command would be as follows if we wanted to dump the call stack for PID 29654:

- AIX `kill -36 29654`
- Solaris `kill -21 29654`

To dump the entire DB2 process group, simply issue the same command against the db2sysc PID with a dash (–) directly before the db2sysc PID. For example,

- AIX `kill -36 -<db2sysc_pid>`

This sends the kill signal to all of the db2sysc child processes and creates the desired trap files.

For Intel platforms, DB2 supplies similar utilities as those on UNIX. For Windows, there are two utilities: db2bddbg and db2nstck. For all Intel platforms, there is db2ras, and on OS/2, you can use pstat to view the threads.

   db2, db2bp, db2atld, and other DB2 utilities will dump stacks when programming signals are received.

Standalone Tools

Standalone tools are provided for troubleshooting. You can find these tools in the bin, misc, and adm subdirectories of the sqllib directory. In UNIX-based systems, the sqllib directory is a subdirectory of the instance owner's home directory. On other operating systems, you can specify the directory where you would like the sqllib directory to be placed. Typically, this is under the drive where you install DB2.

The following sections highlight some of the tools available to you and briefly describe their usage.

db2batch

The db2batch tool gives performance information (prepare and execution timings, result set analysis) for SQL statements. For more details on the tool syntax and options, type **db2batch -h** at the command line.

db2bfd

The db2bfd tool provides a detailed description of the contents of a bind file. For more details on the tool syntax and options, type **db2bfd** at the command line.

db2cat

The db2cat tool analyzes the contents of a table's packed descriptor. It has options to validate and dump the contents of packed descriptors so that they can be displayed in a readable form.

A packed descriptor is a column within the system catalog tables that DB2 uses to identify the details of a database object.

For more details on the tool syntax and options, type **db2cat -h** at the command line.

db2ckbkp

The db2ckbkp tool checks a single DB2 backup image or multiple parts of an image. Using one or more of the options displays various information results, including such items as page checking, table space data, media header information, log header information, and object data.

For more details on the tool syntax and options, type **db2ckbkp** at the command line.

db2dart

The db2dart tool verifies that the architectural integrity of a database is correct and has the ability to repair some database damage. For example, this tool confirms the following:

- The control information is correct.
- There are no discrepancies in the format of the data.
- The data pages are the correct size and contain the correct column types.
- Indexes are valid.

The db2dart tool can be run at the table, table space, or database level (default), and also can dump data and index pages. Note that using db2dart with the /DDEL option is a very powerful data recovery tool. It can dump all data for a table into delimited ASCII format without requiring a connection to the database. This is advantageous when, for example, somebody had accidentally deleted all of the active logs for your recoverable database and you don't have any backup images (which should never happen, of course).

The connect will probably receive an SQL1036C trying to access a log file that has been deleted. In this case, you can use db2dart to dump all of the data into delimited ASCII files. There are some disadvantages to this, however, because only certain data types can be dumped (SMALLINT, INTEGER, DECIMAL, FLOAT, CHAR, VARCHAR, DATE, TIME, and TIMESTAMP), and DEL files do not store the object DDL, so you must have that available as well.

These are the repair options available in db2dart:

- **/MI** Marks an index invalid, to be rebuilt according to the INDEXREC database and database manager configuration parameters
- **/MT** Marks a table as drop-pending (unavailable) state; this cannot be run without the consultation of DB2 Customer Service
- **/IP** Initializes a data page of a table as empty; this cannot be run without the consultation of DB2 Customer Service

- **/UBPF** Updates the buffer pool with new specifications
- **/CHST** Changes the database state to turn backup pending OFF or ON

You must run this tool on the DB2 server where the database resides. You must also ensure that there are *no active connections* to the database. (Use the LIST APPLICATIONS FOR DATABASE *database-alias* command and disconnect any applications that are listed.) In an EEE environment, db2dart must be run on each database partition server.

The output of this utility is created in the current working directory as <DBNAME>.RPT, and the previously run file is renamed as <DBNAME>.BAK. One other file named DART.ERR is created on every run, but this file can be safely ignored. It is simply used for tool analysis and development. The file information can be minimized with the /ERR N option.

For more details on the tool syntax and options, type **db2dart** at the command line.

db2drdat

The db2drdat tool traces the DRDA dataflows (send and receive buffers, plus SQLCA structures, with optional timestamps) exchanged between DRDA Application Requestors and DRDA Application Servers. For more details on the tool syntax and options, type **db2drdat** at the command line.

db2flsn

The db2flsn tool returns the name of the log file that contains the log record identified by a specified log sequence number (LSN). The log header control file (SQLOGCTL.LFH, found in the database directory, for example, E:\DB2\NODE0000\SQL00001) must reside in the current directory before using this tool. This tool can be used only with *recoverable* databases—databases that have either LOGRETAIN or USEREXIT enabled.

For more details on the tool syntax and options, type **db2flsn** at the command line.

db2ipxad

The db2ipxad tool returns the DB2 server's IPX/SPX internetwork address. This command *must* be issued locally from the DB2 server machine. Issuing the command from a remote client is not supported.

db2level

The db2level tool displays detailed output about the level of DB2 Universal Database code, including the FixPak level, currently installed.

db2look

The db2look tool extracts the DDL necessary to re-create a database or database objects. For example, this tool allows you to mimic a production database in your testing environment. Using the '-m' option against a production database generates update statements for matching the catalog statistics of a test database with those of the production database. Use the '-e' option to generate the DDL for one or more tables from the database catalogs.

For introductory information on db2look, type **db2look** at the command line. For detailed information, type **db2look -h**.

db2move

The db2move tool performs mass data movement from one database to another. It allows you to specify multiple tables to EXPORT out of, and then IMPORT or LOAD into another database. For more details on the tool syntax and options, type **db2move** at the command line.

db2recri

The db2recri tool re-creates indexes that were marked invalid during restart or from use of the db2dart tool. For more details on the tool syntax and options, type **db2recri** at the command line.

db2tbst

The db2tbst tool provides a text description for a given hexadecimal table space state. For more details on the tool syntax, type **db2tbst** at the command line.

db2trc

The db2trc facility traces all functions within the database manager (per physical node in an EEE environment). Note that the DB2 trace facility is at the instance level, so activity within all databases in the instance will be traced. It is usually sufficient to trace to shared memory (this is the default), rather than to trace directly to a file, because the performance impact is quite drastic when tracing to a file.

The instance activity should always be as minimal as possible when using the DB2 trace, to avoid tracing unnecessary information (and to keep the trace as clean as possible). You should consider the instance activity, combined with the operation you are trying to trace, when determining the size of the trace buffer. Note that when you use the 'on –l' option (which is usually the case), you will capture the last trace records to the size of the buffer. So even if the trace is wrapped when you format it (the buffer is overwritten if it is filled), it may still contain the information you require within the last records of the trace buffer.

The internal component information, combined with the internal DB2 return codes provided in the "Problem Identification" section, should be sufficient to aid you in using the DB2 trace. Here is a brief example of how you can use the DB2 trace facility:

```
E:\>db2trc on -l 5000000
E:\>db2 "connect to sample"
```

```
    Database Connection Information

 Database server         = DB2/NT 7.1.0
 SQL authorization ID     = FENDER
 Local database alias     = SAMPLE


E:\>db2trc clear
E:\>db2 "select * from fender.or"
SQL0204N  "FENDER.OR" is an undefined name.   SQLSTATE=42704


E:\>db2trc dump select.trc
Trace has been dumped to file


E:\>db2trc off
Trace is turned off


E:\>db2trc flw select.trc select.flw
Trace wrapped              : NO
Size of trace              : 232588 bytes
Records in trace           : 4895
Records formatted          : 226    (pid: 1616; tid: 1260; node: 0
<other pids/tids output cut>


E:\db2trc fmt select.trc select.fmt
Trace wrapped              : NO
Size of trace              : 232588 bytes
Records in trace           : 4895
Records formatted          : 4895
```

This example to take the trace followed these steps:

1. Turn the trace on.

2. Connect to the database.

3. Clear the trace buffer.

4. Perform the failing operation.

5. Dump the trace from memory into a file.

6. Turn the trace off.

7. Get the flow (flw) output of the binary trace file.

8. Get the format (fmt) output of the binary trace file.

Once that is done, you can use your favorite editor to search for the following items within the formatted flw/fmt trace files:

- Reference to the returned sqlcode of the form–204 or the hexadecimal equivalent (often the internal DB2 return code equivalent) ffff ff34
- Function calls to whatever is dumping an error in the db2diag.log file at the time of the occurrence (if any)
- Function calls to **sqltfast**, the function that writes to the db2diag.log file (if there were db2diag.log entries)

This example is fairly straightforward, so it may seem like more work than necessary to trace this type of problem. This is completely accurate, and you need to ensure that you are not collecting more information for a problem than is necessary. In our example, quite a large trace file is created and a large function path is traversed, even though it appears to be a simple operation. However, in reviewing the trace output, you can see how the functional flow follows the path outlined in the "DB2 Internals Interpretation" section of this chapter.

Note *Don't forget to turn the trace off via **db2trc off**. Accidentally leaving the trace active has caused many performance problems.*

For basic details on the tool syntax and options, type **db2trc** at the command line. For more in-depth information on each option, type **db2trc <option> -u** at the command line.

db2untag

The db2untag tool removes the DB2 tag from a table space container. The tag is used to prevent DB2 from using a container for more than one table space. If a table space or database is destroyed, this tag may be left behind, preventing future DB2 use of the resource.

Use this tool if a DROP TABLESPACE command does not work. Typically, the SQL0294N message is received.

Note *Use this tool in consultation with DB2 Customer Service, and only if you are an experienced database administrator. You must be completely sure that the container is not used by any other database because this command is equivalent to dropping the container. Running this command on a container that has data will result in the loss of all the data from that container.*

For more details on the tool syntax and options, type **db2untag** at the command line.

PERFORMANCE

DB2 Customer Service References

While you are exhausting all means of investigation by using the information provided in this chapter, you should also be using the information contained within the DB2 Customer Service web site at this address:

http://www.ibm.com/software/data/db2/udb/winos2unix/support

This site contains all of the latest information regarding the following:

- **APARs** Individual DB2 code fix information, including highly pervasive (HIPER) APAR information
- **FixPaks** Downloadable/orderable DB2 code fix deliveries
- **Technotes** Technical documents for known problems
- **Documentation** Manuals, whitepapers, redbooks
- **Contact info** DB2 Customer Support phone numbers
- **Newsgroups** Discussions and advice from colleagues
- **Conferences** International DB2 Users Group (IDUG) information
- **Education** Available DB2 courses, books, and reference material
- **Development forums** IBM's DB2 Developer Domain and developerWorks, IBM's worldwide resource for developers
- **DB2 certifications** Learn about DB2 Certification Programs from IBM
- **DB2 product end of service dates** Knowledge for when to migrate to recent DB2 releases
- **DB2 trial and beta code** For testing upcoming releases
- **DB2 newsletters** Subscriptions to DB2 mailing lists for monthly information and FixPak announcements
- **DB2 case studies** Information on DB2 usage around the world

A wealth of information is available, and it is all easily searchable from this web site. The problem you are encountering has probably already been seen and solved by another person somewhere in the world, so it is worth checking out!

DB2 Internal Return Codes

Table 15-2 will help you interpret some of the hexadecimal return codes you may encounter when analyzing a db2diag.log or a DB2 trace. The list represents a substantial set of the return codes you may encounter. If you encounter a return code that is not in the list, then please contact DB2 Customer Service.

When using Table 15-2, please remember that not every internal return code corresponds to an SQL code, and not every SQL code has associated reason codes.

Internal Return Code	SQL Code	Reason Code	Description
80D3	–4977		Invalid export directory specified
80D4	–4978		Dropped table cannot be accessed
80D5	–4979		Unable to export the dropped table data
80D6	–1620	1	Unable to flush event monitor because it wasn't started
80D7	–1620	2	Unable to flush event monitor because it is running at a preversion 6 output level
80E9	–20086		ADT too large
811E	–996		Invalid user-specified directory
812F	–290		Access not allowed: table space is quiesced
8130	–290		Access not allowed: table space is load-pending
8131	–290		Access not allowed: table space is delete-pending
8132	–290		Access not allowed: table space is backup-pending
8133	–290		Access not allowed: table space is roll-forward-pending
8134	–290		Access not allowed: table space is roll-forward-in-progress
8135	–290		Access not allowed: table space is recovery-pending

Table 15-2. *DB2 Internal Return Codes*

Internal Return Code	SQL Code	Reason Code	Description
8136	−290		Access not allowed: table space is disabled
8137	−290		Access not allowed
8138	−291		Invalid state transition
8139	−294		Container is already being used
813A	−295		Container names are too long
813B	−297		Path name is too long
813C	−298		Bad container path
813D	−299		Duplicate container
813E	−257		Raw device is not allowed
813F	−258		Add containers pending
8146	−1442		Bad container size
8173			No dirty buffers
81A7			Invalid alternate
81EF	−242		Duplicate in ALTER
81F0	−1764		Cannot resize smaller
81F1	−1550		No suspension allowed
81F2	−1551		No resumption allowed
81F3	−1552		Restart failed
81F6	−290		Access not allowed: BACKUPin progress
81F7	−290		Access not allowed: RESTORE in progress
8201	+100		End of file reached
8203	−952		I/O interrupt
8212	−804		Invalid request
82E2	−452		Invalid LOB filename

Table 15-2. *DB2 Internal Return Codes* (continued)

Internal Return Code	SQL Code	Reason Code	Description
82E3	–452		Invalid LOB file mode
82E4	–452		LOB file not found
82E5	–452		LOB file already exists
82E6	–452		Access to LOB file denied
82E7	–452		LOB file in use
82E8	–452		Unexpected LOB end of file
8303	–952		Interrupt
8380			No termination: requests pending
8381			No interrupt: commit pending
8382			No interrupt: abort pending
8383			Incompatible release level
8384			Operation not supported
8385			Server/requester migration level incompatible
8386			ASP protocol error
8387			Bad ASP object OBJDSS
8388			Bad FDOCA object
8389			SNA protocol error
838A			Invalid SQL request
838B			Cursor already open
838C			Cursor not open
838D			Syntax error
838E			Invalid FDOCA descriptor
8390			End of SQLDTAGRP
8394			Parameter error

Table 15-2. *DB2 Internal Return Codes* (continued)

Internal Return Code	SQL Code	Reason Code	Description
8395			Value error
8396			SQLDA too small
8397			Invalid RPYDSS
8398			Parser syntax error
8399			FDOCA error
839A			End of input
839B			Code point not found
839C			SQLCODE set in parse
839D			Data descriptor mismatch
839E			Required parameter not received
839F			Bad format
83A0			Duplicate parameters detected
83A3			Translation substitution
8401	+100		End of file reached
8403	−952		Interrupt
8404	−950		Active cursor
8406	−508		Invalid cursor position
842E	−668		Check-pending state
8443	−804		General-purpose validation error
844B	−1477		Table not available because forward recovery encountered no log operation
8451	−680		Too many columns
8502	−911		Deadlock encountered
8503	−1044		Interrupt

Table 15-2. *DB2 Internal Return Codes* (continued)

Internal Return Code	SQL Code	Reason Code	Description
8507	–998		XID already exists
8544	–911		Lock timeout with transaction rollback
8550	–913		Lock timeout with statement rollback
856D	–902		SQLCA has been built and saved in a component-specific control block
8574	–1035		File open error
8575	–1015		Database needs recovery
8576	–1042		Deadlock start error
8577			Deadlock stop error
8578	–1034		Recovery failed
8579			Conditional conflict
85A1			Backup pending
85A2			Recovery pending
85A4	+993		Invalid new log path
85A5	+995		Invalid current log path
85A6	–1267		Exist file not found
85AA			Table space roll forward stopped
85AB			I/O error encountered
85AC			Duplicate entry
85B3			Missing log extent
85B4			Log extent is of a different size
85B5	–1472		System clock difference exceeds max_time_diff on connect (log synchronization)

Table 15-2.   *DB2 Internal Return Codes* (continued)

Internal Return Code	SQL Code	Reason Code	Description
85B6	–1473		System clock difference exceeds max_time_diff on commit
85B7	+1474		System clock difference exceeds max_time_diff on commit (read-only)
85B8	–276		Restore pending
85B9	–1275		Invalid stop time for roll forward
85BA	–1276		Invalid time to stop roll forward
85BB	–4970		Roll forward is missing log files
85BC	–4971		Roll-forward log is already truncated
85BD	–4972		Roll-forward log path is full
85BE	–4973		Roll forward log mismatch
85BF	–4974		Roll forward query error
85C0	–4975		Roll forward cancelled
85C1	–4976		Roll forward not issued on catalog
85C3	–4906		Table space roll forward has invalid table space set
85C4	–1278		Table space roll forward required for rollback
85C5	–1280		Invalid stop time for table space ROLLFORWARD
85CF			DLFM error
85D0	+4909		Tables in data link ROLLFORWARD pending
85D1			Bad new password
85F4	–20153		Split DB access error

Table 15-2. *DB2 Internal Return Codes* (continued)

Internal Return Code	SQL Code	Reason Code	Description
85F5	+803		Duplicate key (warning only)
8659			Term characters not provided
865A			Conversion table not loaded
865B			No conversion table exists
865C			Invalid target code page
865D			Invalid source code page
865F	−5123		Invalid code page
8660	−5124		Invalid country code
8661	−5125		Incompatible CP and CC
8662			Invalid stored procedure
8663			Invalid name
8664			Expired password
8665			Bad password
8666			User or group description over 8 characters
8667			User or group ID over 8 characters
8668			Password over 8 characters
8669			Bad group ID
866A			Bad user ID
866E			Not a descendant
866F			SMG started in background
8670			Invalid thread ID
867F	−10nn		Dropped current directory
86A8			Range too large
86A9			Invalid username

Table 15-2. *DB2 Internal Return Codes* (continued)

PERFORMANCE

Internal Return Code	SQL Code	Reason Code	Description
86AA			Owner died
86AB			Path error
86AC			Programming error
86AD			Exit list full
86AE			Exit list not found
86AF			Services not initialized
870B	–138		Invalid SUBSTR parameter
8711	–910		Table or table space drop pending
8712	–804		Invalid request
8713	–804		Bad request context
8714	–804		Invalid section number
8719	–811		Nonunique answer
871D	–994		Savepoint error
871E	–996		Invalid directory involving the path length of the REORG directory
874A	–1476		Forced rollback on unit of work because of an error on number of log tables
876B			Authorization error
876C			Authorization with different ID
876D	–902		SQLCA has been built and saved in a component-specific control block
877E			RDS error

Table 15-2.   *DB2 Internal Return Codes* (continued)

Internal Return Code	SQL Code	Reason Code	Description
8803	−1044		Interrupt
8905	−803		Duplicate key
8957	−603		Duplicate key
8971			Index scan incomplete
897A			Index end of file
897B			Index internal error
897D			User ID suspended
8A72			Compilation error
8B07	−302		Output truncated
8B08	−413		Values out of range
8B09	−304		Conversion overflow converting date or time to character string
8B0A	−303		Incompatible types
8B0C	−309		Null input invalid
8B0D	−305		Null output invalid
8B0E	−804		Invalid output type
8B0F	−822		Invalid input address
8B10	−802		Math overflow
8B15	−311		Negative SQLDA length
8B16	−301		Incompatible types (dynamic)
8B17	−180		Time or date syntax error
8B18	−181		Time or date range error
8B1A	−404		String column overflow
8B1B	−406		Numeric column overflow

Table 15-2. *DB2 Internal Return Codes* (continued)

Internal Return Code	SQL Code	Reason Code	Description
8B1C	−407		Non-nullable column
8B1F	−183		Date/time arithmetic result out of range
8B20	−182		Date/time arithmetic duration out of range
8B21	−176		Translate scalar run-time error
8B22	−436		Null term missing on input CSTR
8B47	−304		Conversion overflow (numeric value)
8B48	−302		Numeric value out of range
8B49	−801		Divide by zero operation not allowed
8B4C	−420		Invalid input format
8B4D	−410		Float string too long
8B4E			Null-only truncation
8B4F			Date is truncated
8C03	−952		Interrupt
8C05	−803		Duplicate key
9301			Allocation failure
9302			Conversion failure
9303			Transaction processor (TP) not started
9304			TP limit reached
9305			Remote TP exit normal
9306			Allocation failed: attempting retry

Table 15-2. *DB2 Internal Return Codes* (continued)

Internal Return Code	SQL Code	Reason Code	Description
9307			Allocation failed: no retry attempted
9308			General allocation error
9309			Conversion failed: no retry attempted
930A			TP not started: no retry attempted
930B			Remote TP abend
930C			Communications Manager not loaded
930D			Communications Manager abend
930E			Bad security on conversation
930F			Unknown APPC error
9310			Communications Manager parameter bad
9311			Communications Manager bad request state
9312			External communications error
9313			Remote TP send error
9332			Invalid name or name number
9333			Invalid session ID
9334			Invalid command
9335			Invalid data
9336			Adapter error
9337			Reset error
9338			Other NetBIOS error

Table 15-2.   *DB2 Internal Return Codes* (continued)

Internal Return Code	SQL Code	Reason Code	Description
9364			Node environment is corrupted
960C			Communications Manager not loaded
960F			Generic APPC error
9617			Already connected
9618			Connection in progress
9619			Connection refused
962A			Connection timed out
962B			Address already in use
962C			No connection
962D			Socket is bound already
962E			Socket is not bound yet
962F			Socket not writable/readable yet
9630			Partial message was sent
9631			Partial message was received
9C14			FCM communication error
9C15			FCM node not found
9C16	−1229		Node recovery
A602	−901		Invalid memory address
A603	−901		General memory management error
A604	−901		Memory management error: invalid size
AB01	−901		Internal error

Table 15-2.   *DB2 Internal Return Codes* (continued)

Internal Return Code	SQL Code	Reason Code	Description
AC01	–901		Internal program error
C107	–986		File error
C109	–8100		Segmented tables: page number too high
C119	–995		EMP indirect not found
C11A	–995		EMP map information ended
C11B	–995		EMP map information not found
C11C	–996		Mapping information should exist but cannot be found
C11D	–292		Cannot create file
C11E	–293		Container not accessible
C180			Agent file close error
C201	–970		Access denied
C211	–982		Seek error
C212	–452		Unknown media error
C213	–452		File not found
C214			File already exists
C215			File in use
C216			Invalid filename
C217	–982		Commit failed
C218	–982		Undo failed
C40A	–659		Maximum object size reached
C47E			Index needs to be recreated
C47F			I/O error: file renamed
C57F			I/O error: file renamed

Table 15-2.   *DB2 Internal Return Codes* (continued)

PERFORMANCE

Internal Return Code	SQL Code	Reason Code	Description
C601	–970		Access denied
C602	–972		Change disk
C603	–972		Not a DOS disk
C604	–974		Drive locked
C605	–976		Device not ready
C606	–978		File write-protected
C607	–986		File error
C608	–902		Delete directory error
C67C			Device is busy
C721	–2423		Missing index during offline backup
C90A			Maximum object size reached
CE0B	–1614	1	Encountered an unknown event monitor target type
CE0C	–1614	2	The event monitor target path was not sent
CE0D	–1614	3	Access to event monitor target path was denied
CE0E	–1614	4	Event monitor target path is not the name of a pipe
CE0F	–1614	5	No process has opened the event monitor target pipe for reading
CE10	–1614	6	Encountered an unexpected I/0 error
D085		21	Authentication failed due to no user licenses available

Table 15-2.   *DB2 Internal Return Codes* (continued)

Internal Return Code	SQL Code	Reason Code	Description
D107	–960		No more file tokens
D121	–289		Container full
D122			Exceeded maximum quiescers
D123	–296		Table space limit exceeded
D124	–259		Map too big
D12C	–1218		No more buffer pool pages
D12D	–270		No extend/resize
D20C	–968		Disk full: LOB
D21A	–930		No memory: UNDO heap
D315			No memory on requester
D316			No memory on server
D31D			Vectored I/O request too big (maximum block size reached)
D408	–962		Maximum tables in file
D40D	–912		Too many locks
D411	–902		Maximum long field file size
D505	–930		Memory allocation failure: no memory
D509	–964		Log file full
D50A	–912		Lock list full
D57F	–1004		Disk full: log files
D584	–1762		Not enough space in log path
D600			No memory heap
D601	–954		No memory heap (for application)

Table 15-2.   *DB2 Internal Return Codes* (continued)

PERFORMANCE

Internal Return Code	SQL Code	Reason Code	Description
D602	–956		No memory heap (for database)
D603	–101		No memory heap (for compiler)
D604	–930		Share buffer exceeded
D605	–930		Memory allocation failure: no segment(s)
D606	–958		Too many open files
D607	–960		No more file tokens
D60B	–955		No memory sort heap
D60C	–968		Disk full
D60D	–912		Too many locks
D60E	–973		No memory: application control heap
D610	–902		No memory: BSU heap
D612	–953		No memory: agent heap
D613	–957, –959		No memory: Com heap
D614	–961, –962		No memory: RS heap
D615			No memory: users/groups
D616	–930		No memory: DrIdx heap
D617	–930		No memory: ASP heap
D619	–930		No memory: queue heap
D61A	–930		No memory: undefined heap
D61B	–930		No memory: lock heap
D61C	–930		No memory: system RS heap
D61D	–930		No memory: utility heap

Table 15-2. *DB2 Internal Return Codes* (continued)

Internal Return Code	SQL Code	Reason Code	Description
D61E	−930		No memory: statistics heap
D620	−930		No memory: resync heap
D625	−930		No memory: DBAT heap
D62B	−930		No memory: SQL cache heap
D67D			Shared memory set exists
D67E	−9		No memory for DosLoadMod
D905	−930		Memory allocation failure: memory error
D90F	−990		Index structure problem
DC26	−6042		No FCM MSG_ANCHOR
DC27	−6040		No FCM buffer
DC28	−6041		No FCM connection entry
DC29	−6043		No FCM request block
DC2A	−902		No high priority buffer
E101	−980	1	Bad page
E10A	−980	10	File does not exist
E10E	−982		Bad signature
E119	−1034		Page CHECKSUM error
E11A	−1035		Bad database: won't flush it
E11B	−980	27	Both primary and shadow ORFs are bad
E11C	−980	28	Primary ORF is bad
E11D	−980	29	Secondary ORF is bad
E11E	−980	30	Both primary and shadow SSFs are bad
E11F	−980	31	Primary SSF bad

Table 15-2.   *DB2 Internal Return Codes* (continued)

Internal Return Code	SQL Code	Reason Code	Description
E120	−980	32	Secondary SSF bad
E40B	−980	11	Object does not exist
E50D	−980	13	Bad log file
E510	−5123		Error in log control file
E511	−1258		Log control file not found
E512	−1259		I/O error accessing log control file
E513	−1260		Database not recoverable
E514	−1261		Recovery not pending
E515	−1263		Invalid log extent file
E516	−1264		Log extent file does not belong to the database
E517	−1265		Log extent file is the incorrect version
E518	−1266		Point in time prior to recovery
E521	−1034		Recovery failed
E522	−1268		Error while retrieving file during forward recovery
E57F	−1036		Adjust log file error
E602	−980	2	CRC error
E603	−980	3	Disk error
E604	−980	4	General failure
E605	−980	5	Read fault
E606	−980	6	Seek error
E607	−980	7	Sector not found
E608	−980	8	Unknown media error

Table 15-2. *DB2 Internal Return Codes* (continued)

Internal Return Code	SQL Code	Reason Code	Description
E609	–980	9	Write fault
E60A	–980	10	File does not exist
E60C	–980	12	Cannot open file
E60F	–980	15	Network access denied
E623	–931		Too many open system files
F051	–1042		Invalid log record encountered during redo or undo: unknown component
F102	–902	2	BPS logic error
F103	–902	3	Invalid buffer pointer
F104	–902	4	No buffers
F109	–902	9	Data does not exist
F10A	–902	10	File already exists
F10B	–902	11	Unfixed buffer page
F10C	–902	12	Invalid file token
F10D	–902	13	Invalid file type
F110	–902	16	Invalid mode parameter
F117	–902	23	Invalid reference
F121	–902	33	RAM semaphore error
F124	–902	36	Bad configuration file
F136	–902	54	Bad header
F13B	–902	59	File not found in the reorg linked list
F149	–902	73	Bad database path
F156	–902	86	Page already exists
F176	–902	118	Invalid pool ID

Table 15-2.   *DB2 Internal Return Codes* (continued)

PERFORMANCE

Internal Return Code	SQL Code	Reason Code	Description
F17D			State already off
F210	−902	16	Invalid mode parameter: LOB
F21B	−902	27	Bad transaction ID
F225	−902	37	Invalid file handle
F331	−902	49	Bad selector
F33C	−902	60	Tokenizer stack overflow
F345			The server STARTDBM failed
F34A	−902	74	Node manager thread failed
F34B	−902	75	Database is bad
F34C	−902	76	Parser stack overflow
F34D	−902	77	Token buffer overflow
F34E	−902	78	Bad value in code page table
F34F	−902	79	Configuration mismatch
F401	−902	1	DMS data file error
F418	−902	24	Bad table handle
F419	−902	25	Bad record ID
F42D	−902	45	Reallocation error
F42E	−902	46	Set signal error
F42F	−902	47	Invalid mode
F432	−902	50	Floating-point error
F451	−1042		Invalid log record encountered during redo or undo: bad record length
F455	−902	85	DMS programming error
F47A	−902	122	Record deleted
F47C	−902	124	Missing defaults
F51B	−902	27	Bad transaction ID

Table 15-2. *DB2 Internal Return Codes* (continued)

Internal Return Code	SQL Code	Reason Code	Description
F51C	−902	28	Log file overflow
F51D	−902	29	Fatal logic error
F51E	−902	30	No active transaction
F51F	−902	31	Maximum savepoints
F520	−902	32	No active savepoint
F527	−902	39	Bad record type
F528	−902	40	Transaction ID table overflow
F529	−902	41	Invalid LSN
F52A	−902	42	Transaction already started
F550	−902	80	Database in recovery mode
F605	−1068		Message file not found
F606	−1068		Message not found
F609	−902	9	Data does not exist
F60A	−902	10	File already exists
F60B	−902	11	Unfixed buffer page
F60C	−902	12	Invalid file token
F60D	−902	13	Invalid file type
F60E	−902	14	Lock violation
F60F	−902	15	Directory overflow
F610	−902	16	Invalid mode parameter
F611	−902	17	Invalid path
F612	−902	18	Invalid page number
F613	−902	19	Sector boundary error
F614	−902	20	System internal error
F616	−902	22	File sharing error
F617	−902	23	Invalid reference

Table 15-2.   *DB2 Internal Return Codes* (continued)

Internal Return Code	SQL Code	Reason Code	Description
F61A	–902	26	Invalid selector
F621	–902	33	RAM semaphore error
F622	–902	34	Access error
F624	–902	36	Bad configuration file
F625	–902	37	Invalid file handle
F626	–902	38	No file descriptor
F631	–902	49	Bad selector
F635	–902	53	Conditional failure
F637	–902	55	Infinite retry
F638	–902	56	Stored procedure not found
F639	–902	57	Invalid drive
F63A	–902	58	Bad heap ID
F63D	–902	61	Duplicate queue
F63E	–902	62	Bad queue handle
F63F	–902	63	Queue message too big
F640	–902	64	No message in queue
F641	–902	65	Message not sent
F642	–902	66	Queue does not exist
F643	–902	67	Max queue limit
F644	–902	68	Invalid queue name
F690			DB2NODE environment variable has a bad value
F691			The db2nodes.cfg file contains an error
F730	–902	48	Invalid file
F733	–902	51	Invalid compile request
F85F	–902	95	Generic LOB manager error

Table 15-2.   *DB2 Internal Return Codes* (continued)

Internal Return Code	SQL Code	Reason Code	Description
F860	−902	96	Cannot redo operation
F861	−902	97	Beginning segment (BSEG) already trimmed
F862	−902	98	Insufficient space
F863	−902	99	No minidirectory
F864	−902	100	Invalid LM descriptor
F865	−902	101	Invalid address
F866	−902	102	LF space exhausted
F867	−902	103	BSEG size/address conflict
F868	−902	104	BSEG not free or allocated
F869	−902	105	Incorrect BSEG size
F86A	−902	106	BSEG not free
F86B	−902	107	Bad count array
F86C	−902	108	Lock error
F86D	−902	109	Not found error
F86E	−902	110	Value out of bounds
F86F	−902	111	Unexpected NULL value
F870	−902	112	Encountered fatal error
F871	−902	113	Bad state
F872	−902	114	Request too big
F873			No slots for threads
F874			Thread not waiting
F875			Owner died
F87B			Too many active threads
F912	−902	18	Invalid page number
F915	−902	21	Memory allocation error

Table 15-2.   *DB2 Internal Return Codes* (continued)

PERFORMANCE

Internal Return Code	SQL Code	Reason Code	Description
F92B	−902	43	Index token does not exist
F92C	−902	44	Key not found
F952	−902	82	SMP problems
F953	−902	83	Invalid database release
F954	−902	84	Index programming error
FB2E	−902	46	Set signal error
FC07	−902	7	Severe internal error
FC21	−902	33	RAM semaphore error
FC7E	−902	126	FCM/BQS component interface error
FC7F	−902	127	FCM programming error
FC80	−902	128	FCM daemon not available
FC81	−902	129	FCM node configuration file error
FC88	−902	136	BDS communication error
FC89	−902	137	BDS partner error
FC8F	−1445		No context
FD8A	−902	138	Invalid partition map ID
FD8B	−902	139	Not able to fetch from catalog
FD8C	−902	140	Invalid data type
FD8D			Invalid partition number
FD8E			PMAP is of a one-node nodegroup

Table 15-2. *DB2 Internal Return Codes* (continued)

The Complete Reference

Part V

SQL

The Complete Reference

DB2

Chapter 16

Basic SQL

SQL, or *structured query language,* is a standardized language for defining and manipulating data in a relational database. Let's look at the components of this definition. A *relational database* is a collection of tables, and the relationships among them are represented by data values in those tables. SQL is a *standardized* language, which means that the language is basically the same, no matter which relational database management system (such as DB2) you're using. And, finally, SQL is a *language* that you use to define and manipulate database objects, the most obvious of these objects being a database table. SQL is the language that you use to define a database table, insert data into the table, change the data in the table, and retrieve data from the table. Like all languages, SQL has a defined syntax and set of language elements.

Most of the examples in this chapter are based on the SAMPLE database that comes with DB2.

SQL Language Elements

Most SQL statements contain one or more of the following language elements:

- Characters
- Tokens
- Identifiers
- Data types
- Constants
- Functions
- Expressions
- Predicates

The following sections describe each of these elements.

Characters

The basic symbols of SQL are single-byte *characters* each at which can be a letter, a digit, or a special character:

- A *letter* is any of the 26 uppercase (*A* through *Z*) or 26 lowercase (*a* through *z*) letters, or any of the three characters $, #, and @. A letter can also be a member of an *extended character set,* which contains additional alphabetic characters, such as those with diacritical marks, for example.
- A *digit* is any character from 0 to 9.
- A *special character* is any of the characters in Table 16-1.

Character	Description
	blank
.	period
,	comma
;	semicolon
:	colon
*	asterisk
'	single quotation mark (apostrophe)
"	double quotation mark
−	minus sign
+	plus sign
=	equals
<	less than
>	greater than
%	percent
/	slash
&	ampersand
(	left parenthesis
)	right parenthesis
?	question mark
_	underline (underscore)
|	vertical bar
^	caret
!	exclamation mark

Table 16-1.   *SQL Special Characters*

Tokens

A *token* is a sequence of one or more characters. A token cannot contain blank characters unless it is a delimited identifier or a string constant. A token can be an *ordinary token*: for example, an ordinary identifier, a numeric constant, or a keyword. A token can also be a *delimiter token*: for example, a delimited identifier, a string constant, or an operator symbol. (Identifiers are explained in the following section.)

Any token can include lowercase letters, but a lowercase letter in an ordinary token is usually folded to uppercase. For example,

```
select * from staff where job = 'Mgr'
```

is equivalent, after folding, to the following:

```
SELECT * FROM STAFF WHERE JOB = 'Mgr'
```

Identifiers

An SQL *identifier* is a token that is used to form a name. An identifier can be an *ordinary identifier*: a letter followed by zero or more characters, each of which is an uppercase letter, a digit, or the underscore character, for example, SALES_DATE. An identifier can also be a *delimited identifier*: one or more characters enclosed by double quotation marks, for example, "sales_date".

Data Types

The *data type* of a value determines how DB2 interprets the value. DB2 supports a large number of built-in data types, and you can also create user-defined data types (UDTs) to handle special circumstances. The following sections describe each of the supported built-in data types.

Numeric Data Types

Numeric data types include SMALLINT, INTEGER, BIGINT, DECIMAL(p,s), REAL, and DOUBLE. All numbers have a sign and a precision. The *precision* is the number of bits or digits excluding the sign. The sign is considered positive if the value of a number is zero or more.

Small Integer, SMALLINT   A *small integer* is a two-byte integer with a precision of five digits. The range of small integers is –32,768 to 32,767.

Large Integer, INTEGER, or INT   A *large integer* is a four-byte integer with a precision of ten digits. The range of large integers is –2,147,483,648 to 2,147,483,647.

Big Integer, BIGINT   A *big integer* is an 8-byte integer with a precision of 19 digits. The range of big integers is –9,223,372,036,854,775,808 to 9,223,372,036,854,775,807.

Decimal, DECIMAL(*p,s*), DEC(*p,s*), NUMERIC(*p,s*), or NUM(*p,s*)   A *decimal value* is a packed decimal number with an implicit decimal point. Packed decimal numbers are stored in a variation of binary-coded decimal (BCD) notation, in which each nibble (one half of a byte, or four bits) represents one decimal digit. For example, the binary value 0110 1001 represents the decimal value 69. The position of the decimal point is determined by the precision (*p*) and the scale (*s*) of the number. An example of the following value

```
SALARY DECIMAL(7,2)
```

is 45000.00. The *scale,* which is the number of digits in the fractional part of the number, cannot be negative or greater than the precision. The maximum precision is 31 digits. If precision and scale are not specified, they are assumed to be five and zero, respectively.

All values in a decimal column have the same precision and scale. The maximum range is $-10**31+1$ to $10**31-1$.

Single-Precision Floating-Point, REAL   A *single-precision floating-point number* is a 32-bit approximation of a real number. The number can be zero or can range from –3.402E+38 to –1.175E-37, or from 1.175E-37 to 3.402E+38.

Double-Precision Floating-Point, DOUBLE, DOUBLE PRECISION, or FLOAT   A *double-precision floating-point number* is a 64-bit approximation of a real number. The number can be zero or can range from –1.79769E+308 to –2.225E-307, or from 2.225E-307 to 1.79769E+308.

Character Strings

A *character string* is a sequence of bytes. Character strings include fixed-length character strings of type CHAR(*n*), and varying-length character strings of type VARCHAR(*n*), LONG VARCHAR, or CLOB(*n*). The length of the string is the number of bytes in the sequence. An empty string has a length of zero.

Fixed-Length Character String, CHARACTER(*n*) or CHAR(*n*)   A *fixed-length character string* must be between 1 and 254 bytes long. If a length is not specified, it is assumed to be one. All values in a fixed-length character string column have the same length, which is determined by the length attribute of the column.

Varying-Length Character String, VARCHAR(*n*), CHARACTER VARYING(*n*), or CHAR VARYING(n)   *VARCHAR(n) type strings* are varying-length character strings that can be up to 32,672 bytes long.

LONG VARCHAR   *LONG VARCHAR type strings* are varying-length character strings that can be up to 32,700 bytes long.

Character Large Object String, CLOB(*n*[K|M|G])   A *character large object* is a varying-length character string that can be up to 2,147,483,647 bytes long. If only *n* is specified, the value of *n* is the maximum length. If *n*K is specified, the maximum length is *n**1,024 (with a maximum value for *n* of 2,097,152). If *n*M is specified, the maximum length is *n**1,048,576 (with a maximum value for *n* of 2,048). If *n*G is specified, the maximum length is *n**1,073,741,824 (with a maximum value for *n* of 2). For example,

```
RESUME CLOB(5120)
RESUME CLOB(5k)
```

A CLOB is used to store large single-byte character set (SBCS) character-based data or mixed (multibyte character set (MBCS) and SBCS) character-based data.

Graphic Strings

A *graphic string* is a sequence of bytes that represents double-byte character data. Graphic strings include fixed-length graphic strings of type GRAPHIC(*n*) and varying-length graphic strings of type VARGRAPHIC(*n*), LONG VARGRAPHIC, and DBCLOB(*n*). The length of the string is the number of double-byte characters in the sequence. An empty string has a length of zero.

Fixed-Length Graphic String, GRAPHIC(*n*)   A *fixed-length graphic string* must be between 1 and 127 double-byte characters long. If a length is not specified, it is assumed to be 1. All values in a fixed-length graphic string column have the same length, which is determined by the length attribute of the column.

Varying-length Graphic String, VARGRAPHIC(*n*)   *VARGRAPHIC(n) type strings* are varying-length graphic strings that can be up to 16,336 double-byte characters long.

LONG VARGRAPHIC   *LONG VARGRAPHIC type strings* are varying-length graphic strings that can be up to 16,350 double-byte characters long.

Double-Byte Character Large Object String, DBCLOB(*n*[K|M|G])   A *double-byte character large object* is a varying-length graphic string of double-byte characters that can be up to 1,073,741,823 characters long. If only *n* is specified, the value of *n* is the maximum length. If *n*K is specified, the maximum length is *n**1,024 (with a maximum value for *n* of 1,048,576). If *n*M is specified, the maximum length is *n**1,048,576 (with a maximum value for *n* of 1,024). If *n*G is specified, the maximum length is *n**1,073,741,823 (with a maximum value for *n* of 1).

A DBCLOB is used to store large DBCS (double-byte character set) character-based data.

Binary Large Object, BLOB(n[K|M|G])

A *binary large object (BLOB)* is a varying-length string that can be up to 2,147,483,647 bytes long. If only *n* is specified, the value of *n* is the maximum length. If *n*K is specified, the maximum length is *n**1,024 (with a maximum value for *n* of 2,097,152). If *n*M is specified, the maximum length is *n**1,048,576 (with a maximum value for *n* of 2,048). If *n*G is specified, the maximum length is *n**1,073,741,824 (with a maximum value for *n* of 2). For example:

```
PICTURE BLOB(102400)
PICTURE BLOB(100 K)
```

A BLOB is used to hold nontraditional data, such as pictures, voice, and mixed media, and can also be used to hold structured data for user-defined types and user-defined functions.

Datetime Data Types

Datetime data types include DATE, TIME, and TIMESTAMP. Datetime values can be used in certain arithmetic and string operations, and they are compatible with certain strings, but they are neither strings nor numbers.

DATE A *DATE* is a three-part value (year, month, and day). The range of the year part is 0001 to 9999. The range of the month part is 1 to 12. The range of the day part is 1 to *n*, where the value of *n* depends on the month.

The internal representation of a date is a 4-byte string, each byte consisting of two packed decimal digits: the first two bytes represent the year, the third byte represents the month, and the fourth byte represents the day. The length of a DATE column is ten bytes.

TIME A *TIME* is a three-part value (hour, minute, and second). The range of the hour part is 0 to 24. The range of both the minute part and the second part is 0 to 59. If the hour is 24, the minute value and the second value are both zero.

The internal representation of a time is a 3-byte string, each byte consisting of two packed decimal digits: the first byte represents the hour, the second byte represents the minute, and the third byte represents the second. The length of a TIME column is eight bytes.

TIMESTAMP A *TIMESTAMP* is a seven-part value (year, month, day, hour, minute, second, and microsecond). The range of the year part is 0001 to 9999. The range of the month part is 1 to 12. The range of the day part is 1 to *n*, where the value of *n* depends on the month. The range of the hour part is 0 to 24. The range of both the minute part and the second part is 0 to 59. The range of the microsecond part is 000000 to 999999. If the hour is 24, the minute value, the second value, and the microsecond value are all zero.

The internal representation of a timestamp is a 10-byte string, each byte consisting of two packed decimal digits: the first four bytes represent the date, the next three bytes represent the time, and the last three bytes represent the microseconds. The length of a TIMESTAMP column is 26 bytes.

String Representations of Datetime Values

Internal representations of DATE, TIME, and TIMESTAMP values are transparent to the user. However, dates, times, and timestamps can be represented by character strings, and the CHAR function can be used to create a string representation of a datetime value. For example:

```
SELECT SUBSTR(CHAR(sales_date),7) FROM sales
```

When a valid string representation of a datetime value is used in an operation with an internal datetime value, the string representation is converted to the internal form of the date, time, or timestamp before the operation is performed.

Date Strings   A string representation of a date value is a character string that starts with a digit and has a length of at least eight characters. Trailing blanks may be included, and leading zeros may be omitted from the month and the day parts of the date value.

Table 16-2 shows valid string formats for date values.

Format Name	Abbreviation	Date Format	Example
International Organization for Standardization	ISO	yyyy-mm-dd	2001-03-08
IBM USA Standard	USA	mm/dd/yyyy	03/08/2001
IBM European Standard	EUR	dd.mm.yyyy	08.03.2001
Japanese Industrial Standard (Christian Era)	JIS	yyyy-mm-dd	2001-03-08
Site-defined	LOC	Depends on the country code for the database	—

Table 16-2.   *Valid String Formats for Date Values*

Time Strings   A string representation of a time value is a character string that starts with a digit and has a length of at least four characters. Trailing blanks may be included, and a leading zero may be omitted from the hour part of the time value; seconds may be omitted entirely. If a value for seconds is not specified, it is assumed to be 0. For example, 13.30 is equivalent to 13.30.00.

Table 16-3 shows valid string formats for time values.

Timestamp Strings   A string representation of a timestamp value is a character string that starts with a digit and has a length of at least 16 characters. The complete string representation of a timestamp has the form *yyyy-mm-dd-hh.mm.ss.nnnnnn*. Trailing blanks may be included, and leading zeros may be omitted from the month, day, or hour part of the timestamp value; microseconds may be truncated or omitted entirely. If any trailing zeros are omitted from the microseconds part of the timestamp value, a value of 0 is assumed for the missing digits. For example, 2001-3-8-8.30.00 is equivalent to 2001-03-08-08.30.00.000000.

DATALINK Values

A *DATALINK value* contains a logical reference to a file stored outside of the database. For example, the following statements create a table and insert a DATALINK value

Format Name	Abbreviation	Time Format	Example
International Organization for Standardization	ISO	hh.mm.ss	13.30.05
IBM USA Standard	USA	hh:mm AM or PM	1:30 PM
IBM European Standard	EUR	hh.mm.ss	13.30.05
Japanese Industrial Standard (Christian Era)	JIS	hh:mm:ss	13:30:05
Site-defined	LOC	Depends on the country code for the database	—

Table 16-3.   *Valid String Formats for Time Values*

SQL

into that table. The table is called HOME_PAGES, and it contains one DATALINK column called PAGE:

```
CREATE TABLE home_pages (page DATALINK LINKTYPE url)

INSERT INTO home_pages VALUES (DLVALUE
('http://dlfs.torolab.ibm.com/x/y/a.b','URL','A comment'))
```

A SELECT * statement issued against this table returns the following record:

```
URL  HTTP://DLFS.TOROLAB.IBM.COM/x/y/a.b A comment
```

The DATALINK value has the following components:

- **Link type** The currently supported link type is Uniform Resource Locator (URL). The link type is specified as part of the column definition.
- **Data location** This represents the location of a linked file in the form of a URL. The URL has the following parts:
  - **Scheme name (HTTP or FILE)** The scheme name is always stored in uppercase characters.
  - **File server name** For example, DLFS.TOROLAB.IBM.COM. The file server name is always stored in uppercase characters.
  - **Full pathname on the file server** For example, /x/y/a.b
  - **Comment** This can be descriptive information, such as an alternative identifier for the location of the data. The maximum length of a comment is 254 bytes.

Constants

A *constant* (sometimes called a *literal*) specifies a value. Constants are classified as string constants (character, graphic, or hexadecimal) or numeric constants (integer, decimal, or floating-point).

Character String Constants

A *character string constant* consists of a sequence of characters that is delimited by a pair of single quotation marks, or apostrophes ('). For example,

```
'12/14/1985'
'32'
'DON''T CHANGE'
```

Two consecutive string delimiters denote an apostrophe that is actually part of the string. The maximum length of the character string is 32,672 bytes.

Graphic String Constants

A *graphic string constant* consists of a sequence of double-byte characters that is delimited by a pair of single quotation marks, or apostrophes ('), and is preceded by the character *G* or *N*. For example:

```
G'double-byte character string'
N'double-byte character string'
```

The maximum length of the graphic string is 16,336 bytes.

Hexadecimal String Constants

A *hexadecimal string constant* consists of the character *X* followed by a sequence of characters that is delimited by a pair of single quotation marks, or apostrophes ('). The characters between the apostrophes must be an even number of hexadecimal digits, the number of digits not exceeding 16,336. A *hexadecimal digit* represents four bits and is specified as a digit or any of the uppercase or lowercase letters from *A* to *F*, where *A* represents the bit pattern 1010, *B* represents the bit pattern 1011, and so on. For example,

```
X'FFFF' represents the bit pattern '1111111111111111'
X'4672616E6B' represents the VARCHAR pattern of the ASCII string
'Frank'
```

Integer Constants

An *integer constant* is a signed or unsigned integer with a maximum of 19 digits. For example:

```
64     -15     +100     32767
```

The data type of an integer constant is large integer (INTEGER) if its value is within the range of a large integer. The data type of an integer constant is big integer (BIGINT) if its value is outside the range of a large integer, but within the range of a big integer. A constant that is defined outside of the range of big integer values is considered to be a decimal constant.

Decimal Constants

A *decimal constant* is a signed or unsigned number with a maximum of 31 digits. For example,

```
25.5     1000.     -15.     +37589.3333333333
```

SQL

The number may include a decimal point, or it may be an integer outside of the range of big integer values. It must be within the range of decimal numbers. The precision of a decimal constant is the total number of digits (including leading and trailing zeros); the scale is the number of digits to the right of the decimal point (including trailing zeros).

Floating-Point Constants

A *floating-point constant* is a floating-point number with a maximum of 30 characters. For example,

```
15E1     2.E5     2.2E-1     +5.E+2
```

The data type of a floating-point constant is double-precision floating-point (DOUBLE). The value of the constant is the product of the first number and ten raised to the power of the second number, and must be within the range of floating-point numbers.

Functions

A *function* is a relationship between a set of input data values and a set of result values. Database functions can be either built-in or user-defined:

■ Built-in functions are provided by DB2 and are associated with the SYSIBM schema.

■ User-defined functions can be registered to a database in the SYSCAT.FUNCTIONS catalog table (using the CREATE FUNCTION statement). User-defined functions are not associated with the SYSIBM schema.

Most database functions can be classified as column functions or scalar functions.

The argument of a *column* function is a collection of like values. It returns a single value, and it can be specified in an SQL statement wherever an expression can be used. For example,

```
SELECT AVG(salary) FROM employee
```

In this example, the AVG function is used to return the average salary from the EMPLOYEE table. The function computes the mean of all the values in the SALARY column of this table.

Most of the column functions that are supported by DB2 are presented in Table 16-4.

Function Name	Description	Example(s)	Optional Keywords
AVG	Returns the average of a set of numbers.	`SELECT AVG(salary) FROM employee`	DISTINCT
CORRELATION or CORR	Returns the coefficient of correlation of a set of number pairs.	`SELECT CORRELATION (salary, bonus) FROM employee`	
COUNT	Returns the number of rows or values in a set of rows or values.	`SELECT COUNT(salary) FROM employee` `SELECT COUNT(*) FROM employee`	DISTINCT *
COVARIANCE or COVAR	Returns the (population) covariance of a set of number pairs.	`SELECT COVARIANCE (salary, bonus) FROM employee`	
MAX	Returns the maximum value in a set of values.	`SELECT MAX(salary) FROM employee`	DISTINCT
MIN	Returns the minimum value in a set of values.	`SELECT MIN(salary) FROM employee`	DISTINCT
STDDEV	Returns the standard deviation of a set of numbers	`SELECT STDDEV(salary) FROM employee`	DISTINCT
SUM	Returns the sum of a set of numbers.	`SELECT SUM(salary) FROM employee`	DISTINCT
VARIANCE or VAR	Returns the variance of a set of numbers.	`SELECT VARIANCE(salary) FROM employee`	DISTINCT

Table 16-4. *Column Functions*

SQL

The arguments of a *scalar function* are individual scalar values, which can be of different types and have different meanings. The function returns a single value and can be specified in an SQL statement wherever an expression can be used. For example,

```
SUBSTR('Jennifer Gibbs', 6, 3)
```

In this example, the SUBSTR function is used to return a three-character substring of the string 'Jennifer Gibbs', starting with the sixth character.

Most of the scalar functions that are supported by DB2 are presented in Table 16-5.

Function Name	Description	Example(s)
ABS or ABSVAL	Returns the absolute value of the argument.	`ABS(-3.4)`
ACOS	Returns the arccosine of the argument as an angle expressed in radians.	`ACOS(0.9)`
ASCII	Returns the ASCII code value of the leftmost character of the argument as an integer.	`ASCII('r')`
ASIN	Returns the arcsine of the argument as an angle expressed in radians.	`ASIN(0.9)`
ATAN	Returns the arctangent of the argument as an angle expressed in radians.	`ATAN(0.9)`
ATAN2	Returns the arctangent of x and y coordinates as an angle expressed in radians.	`ATAN2(0.5, 0.9)`
BIGINT	Returns a 64-bit integer representation of a number or character string in the form of an integer constant.	`SELECT BIGINT(empno) FROM employee`
CEILING or CEIL	Returns the smallest integer value greater than or equal to the argument.	`CEILING(3.56)`

Table 16-5. *Scalar Functions*

Function Name	Description	Example(s)
CHAR	Returns a character string representation of a datetime value, a character string, an integer number, a decimal number, or a double-precision floating-point number.	`SELECT CHAR(salary,',') FROM employee`
CHR	Returns the character that has the ASCII code value specified by the argument.	`CHR(156)`
CONCAT	Returns the concatenation of two string arguments. The two arguments must be compatible types.	`SELECT CONCAT(firstnme, lastname) FROM employee`
COS	Returns the cosine of the argument, where the argument is an angle expressed in radians.	`COS(0.451)`
COT	Returns the cotangent of the argument, where the argument is an angle expressed in radians.	`COT(0.451)`
DATE	Returns a date from a value. The argument must be a date, a timestamp, a positive number less than or equal to 3,652,059, a valid character string representation of a date or a timestamp, or a character string of length 7 that represents a valid date in the form *yyyynnn*, where *yyyy* are digits denoting a year, and *nnn* are digits between 001 and 366, denoting a particular day of that year.	`DATE(3652059)`
DAY	Returns the day part of a value. The argument must be a date, a timestamp, a date duration, a timestamp duration, or a valid character string representation of a date or a timestamp.	`DAY('03/01/2001')`

Table 16-5.   *Scalar Functions* (continued)

SQL

Function Name	Description	Example(s)
DAYS	Returns an integer representation of a date. The argument must be a date, a timestamp, or a valid character string representation of a date or a timestamp.	`DAYS('03/01/2001')`
DECIMAL or DEC	Returns a decimal representation of a number, a character string representation of a decimal number, or a character string representation of an integer. You can specify the desired precision and scale of the result.	`DECIMAL('567',9,2)`
DEGREES	Returns the number of degrees converted from the argument expressed in radians.	`DEGREES(3.14159)`
DIFFERENCE	Returns a value from 0 to 4 representing the difference between the sounds of two strings based on applying the SOUNDEX function to the strings. A value of 4 is the best possible sound match.	`DIFFERENCE ('Roman', 'roaming')`
DIGITS	Returns a character string representation of a number.	`DIGITS(567)`
DLCOMMENT	Returns the comment value, if it exists, from a DATALINK value.	`DLCOMMENT(col1)`
DLLINKTYPE	Returns the link type value from a DATALINK value.	`DLLINKTYPE(col1)`
DLURLCOMPLETE	Returns the data location attribute from a DATALINK value with a link type of URL. When appropriate, the value includes a file access token.	`DLURLCOMPLETE (col1)`

Table 16-5.   *Scalar Functions* (continued)

Function Name	Description	Example(s)
DLURLPATH	Returns the path and file name necessary to access a file within a given server from a DATALINK value with a link type of URL. When appropriate, the value includes a file access token.	`DLURLPATH(col1)`
DLURLPATHONLY	Returns the path and file name necessary to access a file within a given server from a DATALINK value with a link type of URL. The value *never* includes a file access token.	`DLURLPATHONLY (col1)`
DLURLSCHEME	Returns the (uppercase) scheme from a DATALINK value with a link type of URL.	`DLURLSCHEME (col1)`
DLURLSERVER	Returns the (uppercase) file server from a DATALINK value with a link type of URL.	`DLURLSERVER (col1)`
DLVALUE	Returns a DATALINK value, and may also create a link to a file (if a data location is specified).	`DLVALUE ('http://dlfs.torola b.ibm.com/x/y/a.b',' URL','A comment')`
DOUBLE	Returns a floating-point number corresponding to a number if the argument is a numeric expression, and a character string representation of a number if the argument is a string expression.	`DOUBLE('567')`
EVENT_MON_ STATE	Returns the current state of an event monitor. The value can be 0 (inactive) or 1 (active).	`SELECT evmonname, EVENT_MON_ STATE(evmonname) FROM syscat.eventmonitors`
EXP	Returns the exponential function of the argument.	`EXP(1)`

Table 16-5.   *Scalar Functions* (continued)

Function Name	Description	Example(s)
FLOAT	Returns a floating-point representation of a number.	`FLOAT(567)`
FLOOR	Returns the largest integer value less than or equal to the argument.	`FLOOR(3.56)`
GENERATE_ UNIQUE	Returns a bit data character string (13 bytes long) that is unique compared to what is returned by any other execution of the same function.	`GENERATE_ UNIQUE()`
HEX	Returns a hexadecimal representation of a value as a character string.	`HEX(16)`
HOUR	Returns the hour part of a value. The argument must be a time, a timestamp, a time duration, a timestamp duration, or a valid character string representation of a time or a timestamp.	`HOUR('16:42:22')`
INSERT	Returns a string where *exp3* bytes have been deleted from *exp1*, beginning at *exp2*, and where *exp4* has been inserted into *exp1*, beginning at *exp2*.	`CHAR(INSERT('hat', 1, 1, 'gn'), 10)`
INTEGER	Returns an integer representation of a number or a character string in the form of an integer constant.	`INTEGER('567')`
LCASE or LOWER	Returns a string in which all the SBCS characters have been converted to lowercase characters.	`SELECT LCASE(job) FROM employee`
LEFT	Returns a string consisting of the leftmost *exp2* bytes in *exp1*.	`CHAR (LEFT ('Zikopoulos', 4), 4)`
LENGTH	Returns the length of a value.	`LENGTH('Tallerico')`
LN or LOG	Returns the natural logarithm of the argument.	`LN(10)`

Table 16-5. *Scalar Functions* (continued)

Function Name	Description	Example(s)
LOCATE	Returns the starting position of the first occurrence of *exp1* within *exp2*. An optional *exp3* indicates the character position in *exp2* at which the search is to begin. If *exp1* is not found within *exp2*, the function returns 0.	`LOCATE('a', 'Roman', 2)`
LOG10	Returns the base 10 logarithm of the argument.	`LOG10(10)`
LONG_VARCHAR	Returns a LONG VARCHAR representation of a character string data type.	`LONG_VARCHAR ('A comment')`
LTRIM	Removes blanks from the beginning of a string expression.	`LTRIM('   A comment')`
MICROSECOND	Returns the microsecond part of a value. The argument must be a timestamp, a timestamp duration, or a valid character string representation of a timestamp.	`MICROSECOND ('2001-03-01-17.12.3 0.123456')`
MIDNIGHT_ SECONDS	Returns an integer value representing the number of seconds between midnight and the time value specified in the argument. The argument must be a time, a timestamp, or a valid character string representation of a time or a timestamp.	`MIDNIGHT_SECONDS ('2001-03-01-17.12.3 0.123456')`
MINUTE	Returns the minute part of a value. The argument must be a time, a timestamp, a time duration, a timestamp duration, or a valid character string representation of a time or a timestamp.	`MINUTE('16:42:22')`
MOD	Returns the remainder of *exp1* divided by *exp2*.	`MOD(20, 3)`

Table 16-5.   *Scalar Functions* (continued)

Function Name	Description	Example(s)
MONTH	Returns the month part of a value. The argument must be a date, a timestamp, a date duration, a timestamp duration, or a valid character string representation of a date or a timestamp.	`MONTH('03/01/2001')`
NODENUMBER	Returns the partition number of the row.	`SELECT NODENUMBER(job) FROM employee`
NULLIF	Returns a NULL value if *exp1* is equal to *exp2*; otherwise, returns the value of *exp1*.	`NULLIF('hello', 'hello')`
PARTITION	Returns the partitioning map index of the row obtained by applying the partitioning function on the partitioning key value of the row.	`SELECT PARTITION(job) FROM employee`
POSSTR	Returns the starting position of the first occurrence of one string within another string.	`POSSTR('See Dick.', 'ick')`
POWER	Returns the value of *exp1* to the power of *exp2*.	`POWER(2, 5)`
RADIANS	Returns the value of the argument in radians, where the argument is an angle expressed in degrees.	`RADIANS(180)`
RAND	Returns a random floating-point value between 0 and 1.	`RAND()` `RAND(9)`
REAL	Returns a single-precision floating-point representation of a number.	`REAL(10)`
REPEAT	Returns a character string composed of *exp1* repeated *exp2* number of times.	`CHAR(REPEAT ('repeat ', 3),21)`
REPLACE	Replaces all occurrences of *exp2* in *exp1* with *exp3*.	`CHAR(REPLACE ('Roman', 'man', 'bert'),10)`

Table 16-5. *Scalar Functions* (continued)

Function Name	Description	Example(s)
RIGHT	Returns a string consisting of the rightmost *exp2* bytes in *exp1*.	`CHAR (RIGHT ('Zikopoulos', 4), 4)`
ROUND	Returns *exp1* rounded to *exp2* places to the right of the decimal point. If *exp2* is negative, *exp1* is rounded to the absolute value of *exp2* places to the left of the decimal point.	`ROUND(345.678, 2)` `ROUND(345.678, -2)`
RTRIM	Removes blank spaces from the end of a string expression.	`RTRIM('A comment   ')`
SECOND	Returns the seconds part of a value. The argument must be a time, a timestamp, a time duration, a timestamp duration, or a valid character string representation of a time or a timestamp.	`SECOND('16:42:22')`
SIGN	Returns an indicator of the sign of the argument. If the argument is less than zero, the function returns –1. If the argument equals zero, the function returns 0. If the argument is greater than zero, the function returns 1.	`SIGN(-567)`
SIN	Returns the sine of the argument, where the argument is an angle expressed in radians.	`SIN(0.451)`
SMALLINT	Returns a small integer representation of a number or a character string in the form of a small integer constant.	`SMALLINT('567')`
SOUNDEX	Returns a four-character code based on the way the string in the argument sounds rather than on how it is spelled. The result can be used to compare this sound to the sound of other strings.	`SOUNDEX('Roman Melnyk')`

Table 16-5.   *Scalar Functions* (continued)

SQL

Function Name	Description	Example(s)
SPACE	Returns a character string consisting of blanks with length specified by the argument.	SPACE(10)
SQRT	Returns the square root of the argument.	SQRT(25)
SUBSTR	Returns a substring of a string (*exp1*), starting at *exp2*, the position of the first byte of the result for a character string or a binary string, or the position of the first character of the result for a graphic string. The length of the result (*exp3*) can also be specified, but it is optional.	SUBSTR('Jennifer Gibbs', 6) SUBSTR('Jennifer Gibbs', 6, 3)
TAN	Returns the tangent of the argument, where the argument is an angle expressed in radians.	TAN(0.451)
TIME	Returns a time from a value. The argument must be a time, a timestamp, or a valid character string representation of a time or a timestamp.	TIME ('2001-03-01-17.12.3 0.123456')

Table 16-5.   *Scalar Functions* (continued)

Function Name	Description	Example(s)
TIMESTAMP	Returns a timestamp from a value or a pair of values. If only one argument is specified, it must be a timestamp, a valid character string representation of a timestamp, or a character string of length 14. The character string of length 14 must be a string of digits that represents a valid date and time in the form *yyyyxxddhhmmss*, where *yyyy* is the year, *xx* is the month, *dd* is the day, *hh* is the hour, *mm* is the minute, and *ss* is the second. If both arguments are specified, the first argument must be a date or a valid character string representation of a date, and the second argument must be a time or a valid string representation of a time.	`TIMESTAMP ('20010301171230')` `TIMESTAMP('03-01-2001', '17.12.30')`
TIMESTAMP_ISO	Returns a timestamp value based on a date, a time, or a timestamp argument. If the argument is a date, the function inserts zero for all the time elements. If the argument is a time, the function inserts the value of the CURRENT DATE special register for the date elements, and zero for the fractional time element. The argument must be a date, a timestamp, or a valid character string representation of a date or a timestamp.	`TIMESTAMP_ISO ('2001-03-01')`

Table 16-5.   *Scalar Functions* (continued)

Function Name	Description	Example(s)
TRUNCATE or TRUNC	Returns *exp1* truncated to *exp2* places to the right of the decimal point. If *exp2* is negative, *exp1* is truncated to the absolute value of *exp2* places to the left of the decimal point.	`TRUNCATE(345.678, 2)` `TRUNC(345.678, -2)`
UCASE or UPPER	Returns a string in which all the SBCS characters have been converted to uppercase characters.	`SELECT UCASE(job)` `FROM employee`

VARCHAR	Returns a varying-length character string representation of a character string, a datetime value, or a graphic string. An optional integer value between 0 and 32,672 specifies the length of the result; if this argument is not specified, the length of the result is the same as the length of the argument.	`SELECT`
		`VARCHAR(lastname,`
		`50) FROM employee`

YEAR	Returns the year part of a value. The argument must be a date, a timestamp, a date duration, a timestamp duration, or a valid character string representation of a date or a timestamp.	`YEAR('03/01/2001')`

Table 16-5. *Scalar Functions* (continued)

Expressions

An *expression* specifies a value. The value can be simple, such as a constant or a column name without any operators, or it can be more complex and include one or more different operator types. There are string expressions, arithmetic expressions, and case expressions. Each of these expression types is described in the sections that follow.

The String Expression

The *concatenation operator* CONCAT links two compatible string operands to form a string expression. For example,

```
SELECT firstnme CONCAT ' ' CONCAT lastname FROM employee
```

The Arithmetic Expression

Arithmetic operators can be applied to numeric or datetime operands. For example, the infix operators +, −, *, and / specify addition, subtraction, multiplication, and division, respectively. The only arithmetic operations that can be performed on datetime values are addition and subtraction. If a datetime value is one operand of an addition, the other operand must be a duration. A datetime duration can be the following:

- A *labeled duration*, such as YEAR (or YEARS), MONTH (or MONTHS), DAY (or DAYS), HOUR (or HOURS), MINUTE (or MINUTES), SECOND (or SECONDS), and MICROSECOND (or MICROSECONDS). For example,

```
SELECT sales_date, sales_date + 1 YEAR + 2 DAYS FROM sales
```

- A *date duration*, which represents a number of years, months, and days, expressed as a DECIMAL(8,0) number. The number must have the format *yyyymmdd*, where *yyyy* represents the number of years, *mm* the number of months, and *dd* the number of days. For example,

```
SELECT sales_date, sales_date + 00010001. FROM sales
```

- A *time duration*, which represents a number of hours, minutes, and seconds, expressed as a DECIMAL(6,0) number. The number must have the format *hhmmss*, where *hh* represents the number of hours, *mm* the number of minutes, and *ss* the number of seconds. For example,

```
TIME('12:23:10') - 011005.
```

- A *timestamp duration*, which represents a number of years, months, days, hours, minutes, seconds, and microseconds, expressed as a DECIMAL(20,6) number. The number must have the format *yyyyxxddhhmmss.nnnnnn*, where *yyyy, xx, dd, hh, xx, ss*, and *nnnnnn* represent the number of years, months, days, hours, minutes, seconds, and microseconds, respectively. For example,

```
TIMESTAMP('20010301171230') - 00000000011005.000022
```

Dates, times, and timestamps can be subtracted, incremented, or decremented. For example,

```
SELECT sales_date, CHAR(sales_date - '04/01/1994') FROM sales
SELECT sales_date, sales_date + 00010101. FROM sales
SELECT sales_date, sales_date - 00010101. FROM sales
TIME('12:34:15') - '01:01:01'
TIME('12:34:15') + 010101.
TIME('12:34:15') - 010101.
CHAR(TIMESTAMP('20010301171230') - '2001-03-01-16.02.24.999978')
TIMESTAMP('20010301171230') + 00000000011005.000022
TIMESTAMP('20010301171230') - 00000000011005.000022
```

The Case Expression

You can use *case expressions* to specify a particular result based on the evaluation of one or more conditions. For example,

```
SELECT firstnme CONCAT ' ' CONCAT lastname AS name,
CASE SUBSTR(workdept,1,1)
WHEN 'A' THEN 'Administration'
WHEN 'B' THEN 'Human Resources'
WHEN 'C' THEN 'Accounting'
WHEN 'D' THEN 'Design'
ELSE 'Operations'
END
AS department FROM employee
```

The value of the case expression is the value of the result expression following the first case that evaluates to true. A *result expression* is an expression following the THEN or the ELSE keyword. If no case evaluates to true and the ELSE keyword is present, the result is the value of the result expression following the ELSE keyword, or a NULL value, if that is what has been specified. If no case evaluates to true and the ELSE keyword is not present, the result is a NULL value.

Predicates

A *predicate* specifies a condition that is true, false, or unknown about a given row or group. Supported predicates are described in the following sections.

The Basic Predicate

A *basic predicate* compares two values. If the value of either operand is NULL, the result of the predicate is unknown. Otherwise, the result is either true or false.

Table 16-6 shows the results for values *x* and *y*.

For example,

```
INTEGER(empno) = 200
lastname <> 'Smith'
salary < 45000
salary > (SELECT AVG(salary) FROM employee)
bonus >= comm
```

Predicate	is true if and only if
x = y	x is equal to y.
x <> y	x is not equal to y.
x < y	x is less than y.
x > y	x is greater than y.
x >= y	x is greater than or equal to y.
x <= y	x is less than or equal to y.

Table 16-6.   *Basic Predicates*

The Quantified Predicate

A *quantified predicate* compares one or more values with a collection of values.
For example,

```
"SELECT salary FROM staff WHERE salary < ALL(SELECT salary FROM employee)"
```

In this example, the result set contains staff salaries that are less than *all* the salaries
in the Employee table.

```
"SELECT salary FROM staff WHERE salary < ANY(SELECT salary FROM employee)"
```

In this and the following example, the result set contains staff salaries that are less
than *any* (that is, at least one) salary in the Employee table. The ANY predicate and the
SOME predicate are equivalent.

```
"SELECT salary FROM staff WHERE salary < SOME(SELECT salary FROM employee)"
```

The BETWEEN Predicate

The *BETWEEN predicate* compares a value with a range of values. For example, the
following BETWEEN predicate

```
salary BETWEEN 20000 AND 40000
```

is equivalent to the following search condition:

```
salary >= 20000 AND salary <= 40000
```

The following NOT BETWEEN predicate

```
salary NOT BETWEEN 20000 AND 40000
```

is equivalent to the following search condition:

```
NOT(salary BETWEEN 20000 AND 40000)
```

or to

```
salary < 20000 OR salary > 40000
```

The EXISTS Predicate

The *EXISTS predicate* tests for the existence of certain rows. The fullselect may specify any number of columns, and:

- ■ The result is true if the number of rows specified by the fullselect is not zero.
- ■ The result is false if the number of rows specified is zero.
- ■ The result cannot be unknown.

For example,

```
"SELECT 'Yes!' AS big_salaries FROM staff WHERE EXISTS
(SELECT salary FROM staff WHERE salary >= 20000)"
```

In this example, the fullselect, which specifies a result table, is the query that is delimited by parentheses. The result table in this case is a column of staff salaries that exceed $20,000. The result set that is returned by the query is a column called Big_Salaries that contains the string Yes! in each row that corresponds to a salary greater than $20,000. A fullselect returns a set of rows that is filtered by the subselect according to the specified predicate. For more information about fullselect and subselect, see the "Queries and Subqueries" section.

The IN Predicate

The *IN predicate* compares one or more values with a collection of values. The fullselect must identify a number of columns that is the same as the number of expressions specified to the left of the IN keyword. The fullselect can return any number of rows. For example,

```
SELECT * FROM staff WHERE dept IN (10, 15)
```

In this example, the result set contains all the rows from the Staff table that are associated with departments 10 and 15.

```
"SELECT * FROM staff WHERE dept IN (SELECT dept FROM staff
WHERE dept < 20)"
```

In this example, the result set contains all the rows from the Staff table that are associated with departments whose IDs are less than 20.

```
"SELECT * FROM staff WHERE dept NOT IN (SELECT dept FROM staff
WHERE dept > 15)"
```

In this example, the result set contains all the rows from the Staff table that are associated with departments whose IDs are less than 16.

The LIKE Predicate

The LIKE predicate searches for strings that have a certain pattern. The pattern is specified by a string in which the underscore character and the percent sign may have special meaning. The underscore character (_) represents any single character. The percent sign (%) represents a string of zero or more characters. Any other character represents itself. Trailing blanks in a pattern are part of the pattern.

ESCAPE is an optional argument that specifies a character to be used to override the special meaning of the underscore character and the percent sign; this allows the LIKE predicate to be used to match values that contain actual underscore and percent signs.

For example, the following statement searches for the string 'PROGRAM' in the PROJNAME column of the PROJECT table:

```
SELECT projname FROM project WHERE projname LIKE '%PROGRAM%'
```

The next example searches for a string that begins with 'O' and that is exactly nine characters long in the PROJNAME column of the PROJECT table:

```
SELECT projname FROM project WHERE projname LIKE 'O_____'
```

The following statement is a search for a string of any length that begins with 'O' in the PROJNAME column of the PROJECT table:

```
SELECT projname FROM project WHERE projname LIKE 'O%'
```

The next statement is a search for a string of any length that does not begin with 'O' in the PROJNAME column of the PROJECT table:

```
SELECT projname FROM project WHERE projname NOT LIKE 'O%'
```

Finally, the following statements retrieve all strings that contain the underscore character in the PROJNAME column of the PROJECT table. You first have to update the PROJECT table to create a string that can be returned by the query:

```
UPDATE project SET projname = 'ADMIN_SERVICES' WHERE projno = 'AD3100'
SELECT projname FROM project WHERE projname LIKE '%\_%' ESCAPE '\'
```

The NULL Predicate

The *NULL predicate* tests for null values:

- The result is true if the value of the expression is NULL.
- The result is false if the value of the expression is not NULL.
- The result cannot be unknown.

For example,

```
SELECT name FROM staff WHERE comm IS NULL
```

In this example, the result set contains the names of staff members who did not receive a commission.

```
SELECT name FROM staff WHERE comm IS NOT NULL
```

In this example, the result set contains the names of staff members who *did* receive a commission.

SQL Language Categories

SQL is divided into three major categories:

- Data control language (DCL) provides access control to database objects.
- Data definition language (DDL) is used to create, modify, or drop database objects.
- Data manipulation language (DML) is used to select, insert, update, or delete data.

Data Control Language

DCL is used to grant database privileges to (or revoke privileges from) users. *Privileges* are specific rights that allow users to create or access specific database objects. Privileges are stored in the system catalog tables for a database. There are three types of privileges:

- **CONTROL privileges**   If you create an object, you usually have full access to that object. You can give access to others, and give others permission to grant privileges on the object. These users can grant or revoke privileges using two SQL statements, GRANT and REVOKE:

  - The GRANT statement gives privileges to a user. For example,

    ```
    GRANT CONTROL ON TABLE employee TO Cerny
    ```

  - The REVOKE statement takes privileges away from a user. For example,

    ```
    REVOKE ALL PRIVILEGES ON TABLE employee FROM Cerny
    ```

- **Individual privileges**   These privileges allow you to perform a specific function on a specific object. They include SELECT, INSERT, DELETE, and UPDATE.

- **Implicit privileges**   These privileges are granted to you automatically when you are explicitly granted certain high-level privileges. These privileges are not revoked when the high-level privileges are explicitly revoked.

To grant privileges on database objects, you must have SYSADM authority, DBADM authority, the CONTROL privilege, or have the WITH GRANT OPTION (a selectable option on the GRANT statement) on those objects. You must have SYSADM or DBADM authority to grant the CONTROL privilege, and you must have SYSADM authority to grant DBADM authority to another user. For more information about privileges, see Chapter 5.

SQL

Data Definition Language

DDL is used to create, modify, and drop database objects; it consists of four general statements:

- CREATE
- DECLARE
- ALTER
- DROP

The CREATE Statement

The CREATE statement is used to create database objects, including tables, views, indexes, schemas, user-defined functions (UDFs), user-defined data types (UDTs), buffer pools, table spaces, stored procedures, and triggers. The syntax and examples of specific CREATE statements can be found in Chapter 27.

The DECLARE Statement

The DECLARE statement is similar to the CREATE statement, except that it is used to create temporary tables that exist only for the duration of a database connection. A table is the only object that can be declared, and it must be located in an existing user temporary table space. Temporary tables are useful when you are working with intermediate results. Declared tables can be altered or dropped, but no other database objects can be derived from or applied against them. Declared tables can be referenced like any other table.

Following is an example of the DECLARE GLOBAL TEMPORARY TABLE statement. The columns in this table will have the same names and definitions as the columns in the EMPLOYEE table. The rows of the temporary table will not be deleted whenever a COMMIT statement is processed, and changes to the temporary table will not be logged. (This is the only option.)

```
DECLARE GLOBAL TEMPORARY TABLE temp1 LIKE employee ON COMMIT PRESERVE ROWS
NOT LOGGED IN mytempspace
```

The ALTER Statement

The ALTER statement lets you change some of the characteristics of an existing database object, such as a table, a view, a buffer pool, or a table space. The syntax and examples of specific ALTER statements can be found in Chapter 27. You cannot alter an index. If you want to change an index, you must drop it and then create a new index with a different definition.

The DROP Statement

You can drop any object that was created through an SQL CREATE or DECLARE statement, including tables, views, indexes, schemas, aliases, functions, buffer pools, table spaces, nodegroups, triggers, and event monitors. The DROP statement removes object definitions from the system catalog tables, and therefore, from the database itself. The syntax and examples of specific DROP statements can be found in Chapter 27.

Data Manipulation Language

DML is used to retrieve or modify table data; it consists of four main SQL statements:

- SELECT
- INSERT
- UPDATE
- DELETE

The SELECT Statement

The SELECT statement retrieves table data.

You can use the SELECT statement to retrieve *all* of the data in a table. For example, to retrieve all of the EMPLOYEE data from the SAMPLE database, issue this statement:

```
SELECT * FROM employee
```

If you specify more than one table in the FROM clause, the intermediate result table consists of all possible combinations of the rows in the specified tables. The number of rows in the result is the product of the number of rows in all the individual tables.

Use the FETCH FIRST clause to restrict the number of rows in a result set. For example,

```
SELECT * FROM employee FETCH FIRST 10 ROWS ONLY
```

You can use the SELECT statement to retrieve specific columns from a table by specifying a *select list* of column names separated by commas. For example, the following statement selects the Name and Salary columns from the STAFF table:

```
SELECT name, salary FROM staff
```

The WHERE Clause   Use the WHERE clause to select specific rows from a table by specifying one or more selection criteria, or search conditions. A *search condition* consists of one or more predicates. For example,

```
"SELECT name, salary FROM staff WHERE salary > 20000"
```

Enclosing the statement within *double* quotation marks prevents the operating system from misinterpreting the greater than symbol as an output redirection request.
    The next example shows that you can specify more than one condition in a single query:

```
"SELECT name, job, salary FROM staff WHERE job <> 'Mgr' AND salary > 20000"
```

Character values must be enclosed within *single* quotation marks.

The GROUP BY Clause   Use the GROUP BY clause to organize rows in a result set. Each group is represented by a single row in the result set. For example,

```
SELECT sales_date, MAX(sales) AS max_sales FROM sales GROUP BY sales_date
```

In this example, the Sales_Date that follows the GROUP BY clause is called a grouping expression. A *grouping expression* is an expression used to define the grouping of the result set; it cannot be more than 255 bytes long. More complex forms of the GROUP BY clause include grouping sets and super groups. For information about these forms, see Chapter 17.

The HAVING Clause   Use the HAVING clause to retrieve results only for groups that satisfy a specific condition. A HAVING clause can contain one or more predicates that compare some property of the group with either another property of the group or a constant.
    For example,

```
"SELECT sales_person, SUM(sales) AS total_sales FROM sales
GROUP BY sales_person HAVING SUM(sales) > 25"
```

In this example, the result set contains the names of salespersons and their sales totals, but *only if their sales totals exceed 25.*

```
"SELECT job, MIN(salary) AS min_salary, MAX(salary) AS max_salary
FROM employee GROUP BY job HAVING COUNT(*) > 1
AND MAX(salary) >= 27000"
```

In this example, the result set contains the minimum and the maximum salary for each job category for which the maximum salary is greater than or equal to $27,000. The query considers only those job categories that are represented by at least two rows in the EMPLOYEE table.

The ORDER BY Clause   Use the ORDER BY clause to sort the result set by values that are returned from one or more columns. For example,

```
"SELECT name, salary FROM staff WHERE salary > 20000 ORDER BY salary DESC"
```

If more than one column is specified in the ORDER BY clause, the rows are sorted by the values in the first specified column, then by the values in the second specified column, and so on. The column names in the ORDER BY clause do not have to be specified in the select list.

The sort key can also be specified by one or more integers that are greater than zero, but not greater than the number of columns in the result table. The integer n identifies the nth column of the result table. You can sort the result set in descending order by specifying DESC in the ORDER BY clause. The default sort order is ascending, or ASC.

The DISTINCT Clause   Use the DISTINCT clause to eliminate duplicate rows in a result set. For example,

```
"SELECT DISTINCT dept, job FROM staff WHERE dept < 30 ORDER BY dept, job"
```

The default behavior is to select *all* rows that satisfy the selection criteria, including duplicates. Although an ALL clause (instead of the DISTINCT clause) can be specified when duplicate rows in a result set are acceptable, it does not have to be explicitly specified; the ALL clause is implied when the DISTINCT clause is absent.

The AS Clause   Use the AS clause to assign a meaningful name to an expression or to any item in the select list. For example,

```
"SELECT name, salary + comm AS pay FROM staff WHERE (salary + comm) < 12000 ORDER BY name"
```

Without the AS clause, the column name would have been "2," meaning that the derived column is the second column in the result set; in this example, it will now be labeled as "Pay." Because the WHERE clause is processed before Salary + Comm is labeled as Pay, Pay cannot be used in the predicate.

Queries and Subqueries   A *query* specifies a result table and is a component of certain SQL statements. The three forms of a query are the fullselect, the subselect, and the SELECT clause.

A *fullselect* specifies a result table; it is a component of the SELECT statement, the INSERT statement, and the CREATE VIEW statement. You can specify a UNION, EXCEPT, or INTERSECT set operator in a fullselect. These set operators process the results of both queries, eliminate duplicates, and return the final result set.

You can combine two or more queries into a single query by using the UNION set operator, which generates a result table by combining two or more result tables. For example,

```
"SELECT sales_person FROM sales WHERE region = 'Ontario-South'
UNION
SELECT sales_person FROM sales WHERE sales > 3"EXCEPT set operator.
```

You can combine two or more queries into a single query by using the EXCEPT set operator, which generates a result table by including all rows that are returned by the first query but not by the second and any subsequent queries. For example,

```
"SELECT sales_person FROM sales WHERE region = 'Ontario-South'
EXCEPT
SELECT sales_person FROM sales WHERE sales > 3"INTERSECT set operator.
```

You can combine two or more queries into a single query by using the INTERSECT set operator, which generates a result table by including only rows that are returned by all the queries. For example,

```
"SELECT sales_person FROM sales WHERE region = 'Ontario-South'
INTERSECT
SELECT sales_person FROM sales WHERE sales > 3"
```

A fullselect that is a component of a predicate is called a subquery. A *subquery* is a SELECT statement that appears within a WHERE clause, and that feeds its result set to that WHERE clause. A subquery can itself include another subquery. A WHERE clause can include different subqueries for more than one search condition. Moreover, a subquery often refers to tables and columns that are different from the ones used in the main query.

For example, the following two SELECT statements both contain subqueries in their WHERE clauses:

```
"SELECT lastname FROM employee WHERE lastname IN (SELECT sales_person FROM
sales WHERE sales_date < '01/01/1996')"

"SELECT lastname FROM employee e WHERE salary <
(SELECT AVG(salary) FROM employee WHERE workdept = e.workdept) ORDER BY lastname"
```

A *scalar fullselect* is a fullselect enclosed in parentheses that returns a single row consisting of a single column value. Scalar fullselects are useful for computing data values from the database for use in an expression. For example, the following query returns the names of employees whose salary is greater than the average salary for all employees; the scalar fullselect is used to calculate the average salary for all employees:

```
"SELECT lastname, firstnme, salary FROM employee WHERE salary > (SELECT
AVG(salary) FROM employee) ORDER BY salary DESC"
```

A *subselect* is a component of a fullselect, and it specifies a result table. It contains a SELECT clause and a FROM clause and, optionally, a WHERE clause, a GROUP BY clause, and a HAVING clause. For example,

```
"SELECT job, MIN(salary) AS min_salary, MAX(salary) AS max_salary FROM
employee WHERE salary >= 27000 GROUP BY job HAVING COUNT(*) > 1"
```

A SELECT clause specifies the columns of the final result table. It contains a *select list* consisting, typically, of a list of column names (or *), one or more AS clauses and, optionally, a DISTINCT (or ALL) clause. Column values are produced by the application of the select list to the result of a subselect.

Correlation Names   A *correlation name* is an identifier that is usually associated with a table and is defined in the FROM clause of a query. You can use a correlation name as a convenient short name for a table. Correlation names also eliminate ambiguous references to identical column names from different tables. For example,

```
"SELECT e.salary FROM employee e WHERE e.salary < (SELECT AVG(s.salary) FROM staff s)"
```

Once you have defined a correlation name (by including the short name after the table name), you can only use this name to qualify the table.

Use correlation names when you need to compare a table with itself. In the following example, the EMPLOYEE table is compared with itself to find the managers of all employees. It returns the names of employees who are not designers, the names of their managers, and the department numbers:

```
"SELECT e2.lastname, e2.job,
e1.lastname AS mgr_lastname, e1.WORKDEPT FROM employee e1,
employee e2
WHERE e1.workdept = e2.workdept
AND e1.job = 'MANAGER'
AND e2.job <> 'MANAGER'
AND e2.job <> 'DESIGNER'"
```

SQL

The INSERT Statement

The INSERT statement is used to add new rows to a table or view. Inserting a row into a view also inserts the row into the table on which the view is based. When preparing an INSERT statement, you can do one of the following:

- Use a VALUES clause to specify column data for one or more rows. For example,

```
INSERT INTO staff VALUES (501,'White',20,'Sales',18,90000.00,10000.00)
INSERT INTO staff (id, name, dept) VALUES (501,'White',66),(502,'Kurtz',38)
```

- Specify a fullselect to identify data contained in other tables or views. This form of the INSERT statement is useful for populating a table with values from rows in other tables. For example,

```
INSERT INTO personnel (id, name, dept, job, years, salary) SELECT id, name,
dept, job, years, salary FROM staff WHERE dept = 20
INSERT INTO personnel SELECT id, name, dept, job, years, salary FROM staff
WHERE dept = 20
```

The UPDATE Statement

The UPDATE statement is used to change the data in a table or view. Updating a row in a view updates a row in its base table. You can change the value of one or more columns for each row that satisfies the conditions specified by a WHERE clause. For example,

```
UPDATE staff SET dept = 51, salary = 55000 WHERE id = 300
UPDATE staff SET (dept, salary) = (51, 55000) WHERE id = 300
```

If the WHERE clause is omitted, DB2 updates each row in the table or view with the values you supply.

The DELETE Statement

The DELETE statement is used to delete entire rows of data from a table or view. Deleting a row from a view deletes the row from the table on which the view is based. You can delete each row that satisfies the conditions specified by a WHERE clause. For example,

```
DELETE FROM staff WHERE id IN (501, 502)
```

If you omit the WHERE clause in a DELETE statement, DB2 *deletes all the rows* in the table or view.

The
Complete
Reference

Chapter 17

Advanced SQL

This chapter covers more advanced topics in SQL, including the following:

- **Correlated subqueries**   Refer to previously identified tables.
- **Recursive queries**   Use result sets to get additional results.
- **Joins**   Join two or more tables so that related information can be selected from them using a single query.
- **Grouping sets, ROLLUP groupings, CUBE groupings**   Extensions of the GROUP BY clause that can be used to analyze data in multiple dimensions—or different levels of data aggregation—in a single pass.
- **OLAP functions**   Additional online analytical processing (OLAP) features that operate over a subset of the data. The subset is defined on the basis of how the data should be partitioned, sorted, or aggregated during processing. OLAP functions that are described include the ranking function, the numbering function, and the aggregation function.

A section on SQL limits provides information on length limits for SQL identifiers, the limits associated with numeric data types, string data types, and datetime data types, plus various database manager limits.

This chapter also describes the *SQL Communications Area* (SQLCA), which is a data structure that is updated following the execution of every SQL statement or DB2 command. The SQLCA is used by the database manager to return error information. (For an introduction to SQL, see Chapter 16.)

Most of the examples in this chapter are based on the SAMPLE database that comes with DB2.

Correlated Subqueries

A *correlated subquery* can refer to a previously identified table; the subquery is said to have a *correlated reference* to a table in the main query.

Suppose you want to list all employees whose salary is greater than the average salary of their department. You can do this with a correlated subquery running once for each row identified in the main query:

```
"SELECT e1.lastname, e1.workdept, e1.salary FROM employee e1
WHERE salary >
(SELECT AVG(salary) FROM employee e2
```

```
WHERE e2.workdept = e1.workdept)
ORDER BY e1.workdept"
```

The subquery (within parentheses) contains column references that are qualified by a correlation name that was defined in the outer query. In this example, E1 is the correlation name, and E1.Workdept refers to the Workdept value of the *current* table row in the outer query. The statement returns the following output:

```
LASTNAME         WORKDEPT SALARY
--------------   -------- -----------
HAAS             A00         52750.00
LUCCHESSI        A00         46500.00
KWAN             C01         38250.00
STERN            D11         32250.00
ADAMSON          D11         25280.00
YOSHIMURA        D11         24680.00
BROWN            D11         27740.00
LUTZ             D11         29840.00
PULASKI          D21         36170.00
MARINO           D21         28760.00
PEREZ            D21         27380.00
HENDERSON        E11         29750.00
SCHNEIDER        E11         26250.00
SPENSER          E21         26150.00
LEE              E21         25370.00
GOUNOT           E21         23840.00
```

Recursive Queries

A *recursive query* uses result sets to get additional results; it contains a common table expression that includes a reference to itself. A *common table expression* is like a temporary view inside of a complex query.

The SAMPLE database contains a table called ORG, which contains information about a corporation's offices in various cities. Suppose you need to know which options are available for traveling between the head office (in New York) and the other offices belonging to the corporation. For example, to get from New York to San Francisco, you could fly direct, or you could transfer at one or more intermediate locations. A recursive query can help you understand your options.

You would begin by creating a new table that contains information about the distances between cities. For example,

```
CREATE TABLE distances (
start VARCHAR(15) NOT NULL,
end VARCHAR(15) NOT NULL,
distance SMALLINT NOT NULL)
IN userspace1
```

You can populate this table with data by using INSERT statements like the following:

```
INSERT INTO distances VALUES('New York','Chicago',719)
```

This record specifies that the distance between New York City and Chicago is 719 miles.

The recursive query generates a list showing the distances between New York City (the head office) and the other cities in which corporate offices are located. In this example, recursive SQL treats each "end" point as a potential "start" point for another distance calculation, and it does this until all the records have been processed:

```
WITH path (start, end, distance) AS
(SELECT d.start, d.end, d.distance FROM distances d
WHERE start = 'New York'
UNION ALL
SELECT p.start, d.end, p.distance + d.distance
FROM distances d, path p
WHERE p.end = d.start)
SELECT DISTINCT start, end, distance FROM path
ORDER BY end, distance;
```

The common table expression in this query has been given the name "path":

```
(SELECT d.start, d.end, d.distance FROM distances d
WHERE start = 'New York'
UNION ALL
SELECT p.start, d.end, p.distance + d.distance
FROM distances d, path p
WHERE p.end = d.start)
```

The first part of this common table expression returns the *direct* distances between New York City and other cities:

```
SELECT d.start, d.end, d.distance FROM distances d
WHERE start = 'New York'
```

The second part of the common table expression references itself:

```
SELECT p.start, d.end, p.distance + d.distance
FROM distances d, path p
WHERE p.end = d.start
```

Here, the common table expression and the base table are joined to create the recursion. Total distances are also calculated. The UNION ALL clause is a required part of recursive queries.

The main query retrieves all the possible routes from New York City:

```
SELECT DISTINCT start, end, distance FROM path
ORDER BY end, distance;
```

Infinite loops can occur when you create recursive common table expressions. Such expressions should include a predicate that prevents infinite loops by enforcing a limit on the number of possible iterations of the fullselect (counter_col < 10, for example). To make this work, you need an integer column counter that is incremented by 1 during each iteration (counter_col+1). The value of the counter is initialized to 1 during the initialization fullselect (the first part of the common table expression).

Here is our example, modified with protection against the possibility of infinite loops:

```
WITH path (counter_col, start, end, distance) AS
(SELECT 1, d.start, d.end, d.distance FROM distances d
WHERE start = 'New York'
UNION ALL
SELECT counter_col+1, p.start, d.end, p.distance + d.distance
FROM distances d, path p
WHERE p.end = d.start AND counter_col < 10)
SELECT DISTINCT start, end, distance FROM path
ORDER BY end, distance;
```

A warning is returned by all recursive queries, whether or not they include protection against the possibility of infinite loops.

Joins

A *join* is a query that combines data from two or more tables. If you want a result set that contains attribute information about several related entities, you need to construct a query that joins several related tables.

The simplest join is one in which no conditions are specified. For example,

```
SELECT * FROM org, staff
```

This statement returns 280 records, representing all combinations of rows from the ORG table and the STAFF table. Such a result set is referred to as the *cross product* of the two tables.

You can also specify a *join condition* to produce a result set with meaningful information. For example,

```
SELECT deptnumb, deptname, id AS manager_id, name AS manager
FROM org, staff WHERE manager = id ORDER BY deptnumb
```

In this example, the join condition is the WHERE clause, which links the two tables by their corresponding columns, Manager and ID. This statement returns the following:

```
DEPTNUMB DEPTNAME        MANAGER_ID MANAGER
-------- --------------- ---------- ---------
      10 Head Office            160 Molinare
      15 New England             50 Hanes
      20 Mid Atlantic            10 Sanders
      38 South Atlantic          30 Marenghi
      42 Great Lakes            100 Plotz
      51 Plains                 140 Fraye
      66 Pacific                270 Lea
      84 Mountain               290 Quill
```

Inner Joins

Inner joins return rows only from the cross product of the two tables that meet the join condition. If a row exists in one table but not the other, it is not included in the result set. To explicitly specify an inner join, the previous query could be rewritten with an INNER JOIN operator in the FROM clause, as follows:

```
SELECT deptnumb, deptname, id AS manager_id, name AS manager FROM org
INNER JOIN staff ON manager = id ORDER BY deptnumb
```

The keyword ON is used to specify the join conditions for the tables being joined. The result set for the inner join consists of rows that have matching values for the Manager and ID columns in the left table (ORG) and the right table (STAFF), respectively.

Outer Joins

Outer joins return the rows that are generated by an inner join operation, plus rows that would not be returned by the inner join operation.

When you perform an outer join on two tables, you arbitrarily designate one table to be the left table and the other one to be the right table. Three types of outer joins exist, as defined in the following sections: a left outer join, a right outer join, and a full outer join.

Left Outer Join

A *left outer join* includes the inner join, plus the rows from the left table that are not returned by the inner join. For example,

```
SELECT deptnumb, deptname, id AS manager_id, name AS manager FROM org
LEFT OUTER JOIN staff ON manager = id ORDER BY deptnumb
```

The LEFT OUTER JOIN (or LEFT JOIN) operator specifies that a left outer join operation should be used when processing the statement. The keyword ON is used to specify the join conditions for the tables being joined.

Right Outer Join

A *right outer join* includes the inner join, plus the rows from the right table that are not returned by the inner join. For example,

```
SELECT deptnumb, deptname, id AS manager_id, name AS manager FROM org
RIGHT OUTER JOIN staff ON manager = id ORDER BY deptnumb
```

This statement returns the following:

```
DEPTNUMB DEPTNAME        MANAGER_ID MANAGER
-------- --------------- ---------- ---------
      10 Head Office            160 Molinare
      15 New England             50 Hanes
      20 Mid Atlantic            10 Sanders
      38 South Atlantic          30 Marenghi
      42 Great Lakes            100 Plotz
      51 Plains                 140 Fraye
      66 Pacific                270 Lea
      84 Mountain               290 Quill
       - -                       20 Pernal
       - -                       40 O'Brien
       - -                       60 Quigley
```

```
    - -                         70 Rothman
    - -                         80 James
    - -                         90 Koonitz
    - -                        110 Ngan
    - -                        120 Naughton
    - -                        130 Yamaguchi
    - -                        150 Williams
    - -                        170 Kermisch
    - -                        180 Abrahams
    - -                        190 Sneider
    - -                        200 Scoutten
    - -                        210 Lu
    - -                        220 Smith
    - -                        230 Lundquist
    - -                        240 Daniels
    - -                        250 Wheeler
    - -                        260 Jones
    - -                        280 Wilson
    - -                        300 Davis
    - -                        310 Graham
    - -                        320 Gonzales
    - -                        330 Burke
    - -                        340 Edwards
    - -                        350 Gafney
```

The RIGHT OUTER JOIN (or RIGHT JOIN) operator specifies that a right outer join operation should be used when processing the statement. The keyword ON is used to specify the join conditions for the tables being joined.

Full Outer Join

A *full outer join* includes the inner join, plus the rows from both the left table and the right table that are not returned by the inner join. For example,

```
SELECT deptnumb, deptname, id AS manager_id, name AS manager FROM org
FULL OUTER JOIN staff ON manager = id ORDER BY deptnumb
```

This statement returns the same result set that was returned by the right outer join, because the right outer join in this example already accounts for all the records in both tables. The FULL OUTER JOIN (or FULL JOIN) operator specifies that a full outer join operation should be used when processing the statement. The keyword ON is used to specify the join conditions for the tables being joined.

Combining Outer Joins

The following statement combines two outer joins in a single query:

```
SELECT empno, deptname, projname FROM (employee LEFT OUTER JOIN project
ON respemp = empno) LEFT OUTER JOIN department ON mgrno = empno
```

The first outer join returns the name of the project for which an employee is responsible. If an employee is responsible for two projects, the employee is represented by two records in the result set. If an employee is not responsible for any project, a NULL value appears in the Projname column. The first outer join is enclosed by parentheses and is resolved first.

The second outer join returns the name of the employee's department if that employee is a manager. Because these are both outer join operations, all employees are represented in the result set. Records with values in all columns are the result of the inner join operation. Records in which the join condition is not satisfied contain the NULL value in columns representing the right table. All rows from the left table are included in the result set.

Star Joins

Star joins are typically used in queries against databases with a star schema design. (See Chapter 20.) A star join contains *local predicates* referencing values in dimension tables and *join predicates* connecting the dimension tables to a fact table. For example,

```
SELECT empno, firstnme, lastname, SUM(sales) AS tot_sales,
(salary + bonus + comm) AS compensation
FROM employee, sales
WHERE sex = 'M' AND
YEAR(sales_date) = 1996 AND
employee.lastname = sales.sales_person
GROUP BY empno, firstnme, lastname, (salary + bonus + comm)
```

The fact table in this case is the SALES table, and there is one relevant dimension table, EMPLOYEE. There are two local predicates:

```
WHERE sex = 'M' AND YEAR(sales_date) = 1996
```

and one join predicate:

```
WHERE lastname = sales_person
```

Grouping Sets

You can use *grouping sets* to analyze data in multiple dimensions—or different levels of data aggregation—in a single pass. To do this, use the GROUPING SETS specification in the GROUP BY clause.

A simple GROUP BY clause specifying a single column is really a grouping set with one element. For example,

```
GROUP BY region
```

is equivalent to

```
GROUP BY GROUPING SETS (region)
```

Similarly,

```
GROUP BY YEAR (sales_date), region, sales_person
```

is equivalent to

```
GROUP BY GROUPING SETS (YEAR(sales_date), region, sales_person)
```

To get a grand total in your result set, add the grand total group—represented by the empty parentheses ()—to the grouping sets list. For example,

```
SELECT YEAR(sales_date) AS year, region, sales_person, COUNT(*) AS tot_sales
FROM sales
GROUP BY GROUPING SETS (YEAR(sales_date), region, sales_person, ())
```

The statement returns the following:

```
YEAR          REGION            SALES_PERSON      TOT_SALES
-----------   ---------------   ---------------   -----------
       - -                      -                          41
       - -                      GOUNOT                     13
       - -                      LEE                        19
       - -                      LUCCHESSI                   9
       - Manitoba               -                          11
```

```
              - Ontario-North   -                          5
              - Ontario-South   -                         13
              - Quebec          -                         12
      1995 -                    -                          5
      1996 -                    -                         36
```

You can also modify the granularity of the summaries by specifying multiple columns enclosed by parentheses in the GROUPING SETS list. For example,

```
SELECT YEAR(sales_date) AS year, region, sales_person,
COUNT(*) AS tot_sales
FROM sales
GROUP BY GROUPING SETS (YEAR(sales_date), region, sales_person,
(YEAR(sales_date), region, sales_person), ())
ORDER BY YEAR(sales_date), region, sales_person
```

The result set for this query includes subtotals for each possible aggregation, and a grand total at the bottom of the list.

You can also include a super group specification in the GROUPING SETS list. Super groups use either the ROLLUP operator or the CUBE operator to achieve even greater levels of data aggregation.

ROLLUP Groupings

The ROLLUP operator generates a result set that shows different aggregates, or data groupings, in a single pass. A *ROLLUP grouping* is a series of grouping sets. The result set from a ROLLUP operation includes subtotal rows, giving you the opportunity to analyze the results from a general to a more specific perspective.

The order in which the grouping expressions are specified is significant. For example,

```
GROUP BY ROLLUP (YEAR(sales_date), region)
```

is *not* equivalent to

```
GROUP BY ROLLUP (region, YEAR(sales_date))
```

The ORDER BY clause is the only way to guarantee the order of the rows in the result set.

SQL

Following is a simple example, based on the SALES table in the SAMPLE database. Suppose you want to see the total number of sales by year:

```
SELECT YEAR(sales_date) AS year, COUNT(*) AS tot_sales FROM sales
GROUP BY ROLLUP (YEAR(sales_date))
```

The statement returns the following:

```
YEAR          TOT_SALES
-----------   -----------
          -            41
       1995             5
       1996            36
```

The result set shows the grand total number of sales (41), followed by the totals for each year.

Suppose you want to see the results broken down by sales region. The following statement is identical to the previous one, except for the specification of the Region column in two places:

```
SELECT YEAR(sales_date) AS year, region, COUNT(*) AS tot_sales
FROM sales GROUP BY ROLLUP (YEAR(sales_date), region)
```

The statement returns these results:

```
YEAR          REGION            TOT_SALES
-----------   ----------------  -----------
          -   -                          41
       1995   -                           5
       1996   -                          36
       1995   Manitoba                    1
       1995   Ontario-South               2
       1995   Quebec                      2
       1996   Manitoba                   10
       1996   Ontario-North               5
       1996   Ontario-South              11
       1996   Quebec                     10
```

This result set is more complex. In addition to the previous totals, there are now regional totals for each year.

Suppose you want to see these results broken down by salesperson:

```
SELECT YEAR(sales_date) AS year, region, sales_person, COUNT(*) AS tot_sales
FROM sales GROUP BY ROLLUP (YEAR(sales_date), region, sales_person)
```

You now have totals for each salesperson by region by year.

CUBE Groupings

The CUBE operator also generates a result set that shows different aggregates, or data groupings, in a single pass; it extends the output from the ROLLUP operator by generating cross-tabulation rows. A *CUBE grouping* is a series of grouping sets.

The order in which the grouping expressions are specified is *not* significant. For example,

```
GROUP BY CUBE (YEAR(sales_date), region)
```

is equivalent to

```
GROUP BY CUBE (region, YEAR(sales_date))
```

The ORDER BY clause is the only way to guarantee the order of the rows in the result set.

The following example shows that, in comparison to the ROLLUP operator, the CUBE operator can return considerably more information. You now have data groupings that represent every possible permutation of Year, Region, and Sales_Person.

```
SELECT YEAR(sales_date) AS year, region, sales_person, COUNT(*) AS tot_sales
FROM sales GROUP BY CUBE (YEAR(sales_date), region, sales_person)
```

The statement returns these results:

```
YEAR          REGION            SALES_PERSON      TOT_SALES
-----------   ---------------   ---------------   -----------
     -        Manitoba          GOUNOT                     3
     -        Manitoba          LEE                        5
     -        Manitoba          LUCCHESSI                  3
     -        Manitoba          -                         11
     -        Ontario-North     GOUNOT                     1
     -        Ontario-North     LEE                        4
     -        Ontario-North     -                          5
     -        Ontario-South     GOUNOT                     4
     -        Ontario-South     LEE                        5
     -        Ontario-South     LUCCHESSI                  4
     -        Ontario-South     -                         13
     -        Quebec            GOUNOT                     5
     -        Quebec            LEE                        5
     -        Quebec            LUCCHESSI                  2
     -        Quebec            -                         12
```

– –		GOUNOT	13
– –		LEE	19
– –		LUCCHESSI	9
– –		–	41
1995	Manitoba	–	1
1996	Manitoba	–	10
1996	Ontario-North	–	5
1995	Ontario-South	–	2
1996	Ontario-South	–	11
1995	Quebec	–	2
1996	Quebec	–	10
1995	–	–	5
1996	–	–	36
1995	–	GOUNOT	1
1996	–	GOUNOT	12
1995	–	LEE	3
1996	–	LEE	16
1995	–	LUCCHESSI	1
1996	–	LUCCHESSI	8
1995	Quebec	GOUNOT	1
1996	Manitoba	GOUNOT	3
1996	Ontario-North	GOUNOT	1
1996	Ontario-South	GOUNOT	4
1996	Quebec	GOUNOT	4
1995	Manitoba	LEE	1
1995	Ontario-South	LEE	1
1995	Quebec	LEE	1
1996	Manitoba	LEE	4
1996	Ontario-North	LEE	4
1996	Ontario-South	LEE	4
1996	Quebec	LEE	4
1995	Ontario-South	LUCCHESSI	1
1996	Manitoba	LUCCHESSI	3
1996	Ontario-South	LUCCHESSI	3
1996	Quebec	LUCCHESSI	2

OLAP Functions

SQL has other useful OLAP features, in addition to star joins and ROLLUP or CUBE operators. *OLAP functions* operate over a *window* (or subset) of the data. A window can be defined on the basis of how the data should be partitioned, sorted, or aggregated during calculations. OLAP functions include the ranking function, the numbering function, and the aggregation function.

The Ranking Function

The *ranking function* returns the ordinal rank of a row within the data window. For example, to see a table of staff salaries ranked by department, use a statement like this:

```
SELECT name, dept, salary, RANK() OVER
(PARTITION BY dept ORDER BY salary DESC) AS salary_rank FROM staff
ORDER BY dept, salary_rank
```

The window in this case is defined on the basis of a partition by department, in which staff salaries are sorted in descending order.

The result set for Department 10 is as follows:

NAME	DEPT	SALARY	SALARY_RANK
Molinare	10	22959.20	1
Jones	10	21234.00	2
Lu	10	20010.00	3
Daniels	10	19260.25	4

What if Daniels had the same salary as Molinare? We can use the UPDATE statement to change Daniels' salary to match that of Molinare:

```
UPDATE staff SET salary = 22959.20 WHERE name = 'Daniels'
```

The RANK() function now returns the following:

NAME	DEPT	SALARY	SALARY_RANK
Molinare	10	22959.20	1
Daniels	10	22959.20	1
Jones	10	21234.00	3
Lu	10	20010.00	4

Rows that are not distinct with respect to other values in the window are assigned the same rank. If RANK() is specified, the rank of a row is defined as 1 plus the number of rows that precede the row, so if two or more rows are not distinct with respect to other values in the window, there will be one or more gaps in the number sequence. If DENSE_RANK(), or DENSERANK(), is specified, the rank of a row is defined as 1 plus the number of preceding rows that are distinct, with respect to other values in the window. There are no gaps in the number sequence. For the preceding example, the DENSERANK() sequence for Department 10 would be 1, 1, 2, 3.

The Numbering Function

The *numbering function* ROW_NUMBER(), or ROWNUMBER(), returns the sequential row number of each row in the window, starting with 1 for the first row. If the ORDER BY clause is not specified in the window, the row numbers are assigned to the rows as they are returned by the subselect. The statement looks like this:

```
SELECT name, dept, salary, ROW_NUMBER() OVER (PARTITION BY dept)
AS row_number FROM staff
```

The Aggregation Function

When a column function, such as AVG, is to be applied to the window, the applicable rows can be further specified, relative to the current row, as a number of rows preceding and a number of rows following the current row. For example, an *aggregation function* can be used to calculate moving (or smoothed) averages.

Suppose the SALES table in the SAMPLE database had ten additional sales records associated with sales person Lee, covering ten consecutive days from April 2 to April 11, 1996. The following example query uses an aggregation function to calculate moving averages on Lee's sales data:

```
"SELECT sales_date, AVG(sales) OVER
(ORDER BY sales_date ROWS BETWEEN 1 PRECEDING AND 1 FOLLOWING)
AS smoothed_sales
FROM sales
WHERE sales_date > '03/28/1996' AND sales_person = 'LEE'
AND region = 'Ontario-South'"
```

Description	Limit in Bytes
Longest authorization name (single-byte characters only)	30
Longest constraint name	18
Longest correlation name	128

Table 17-1. *Length Limits for SQL Identifiers*

Description	Limit in Bytes
Longest condition name	64
Longest cursor name	18
Longest data source column name	128
Longest data source index name	128
Longest data source name	128
Longest data source table name (remote-table-name)	128
Longest external program name	8
Longest host identifier [a]	255
Longest identifier of a data source user (remote-authorization-name)	30
Longest label name	64
Longest method name	18
Longest parameter name [b]	128
Longest password to access a data source	32
Longest savepoint name	128
Longest schema name [c]	30
Longest server (database alias) name	8
Longest SQL variable name	64
Longest statement name	18
Longest transform group name	18
Longest unqualified column name	30
Longest unqualified package name	8
Longest unqualified user-defined type, user-defined function, buffer pool, table space, nodegroup, trigger, index, or index specification name	18
Longest unqualified table name, view name, stored procedure name, nickname, or alias	128

Table 17-1.   *Length Limits for SQL Identifiers* (continued)

SQL

Description	Limit in Bytes
Longest wrapper name	128

[a] Individual host language compilers may have a more restrictive limit on variable names.

[b] Parameter names in an SQL procedure are limited to 64 bytes.

[c] The schema name for a user-defined structured type is limited to eight bytes.

Table 17-1.   *Length Limits for SQL Identifiers* (continued)

The *window aggregation group clause* in this example includes the keyword ROWS to specify that the aggregation group is to be defined by counting rows; *n* PRECEDING to specify the number of rows *preceding* the current row that are to be included in the

Description	Limit
Smallest INTEGER value	–2,147,483,648
Largest INTEGER value	2,147,483,647
Smallest BIGINT value	–9,223,372,036,854,775,808
Largest BIGINT value	9,223,372,036,854,775,807
Smallest SMALLINT value	–32,768
Largest SMALLINT value	32,767
Largest decimal precision	31
Smallest DOUBLE value	–1.79769E+308
Largest DOUBLE value	1.79769E+308
Smallest positive DOUBLE value	2.225E-307
Largest negative DOUBLE value	–2.225E-307
Smallest REAL value	–3.402E+38
Largest REAL value	3.402E+38
Smallest positive REAL value	1.175E-37
Largest negative REAL value	–1.175E-37

Table 17-2.   *Numeric Limits*

Description	Limit
Maximum length of CHAR (in bytes)	254
Maximum length of VARCHAR (in bytes)	32,672
Maximum length of LONG VARCHAR (in bytes)	32,700
Maximum length of CLOB (in bytes)	2,147,483,647
Maximum length of GRAPHIC (in characters)	127
Maximum length of VARGRAPHIC (in characters)	16,336
Maximum length of LONG VARGRAPHIC (in characters)	16,350
Maximum length of DBCLOB (in characters)	1,073,741,823
Maximum length of BLOB (in bytes)	2,147,483,647
Maximum length of a character constant (in bytes)	32,672
Maximum length of a graphic constant (in bytes)	16,336
Maximum length of a concatenated character string (in bytes)	2,147,483,647
Maximum length of a concatenated graphic string (in characters)	1,073,741,823
Maximum length of a concatenated binary string (in bytes)	2,147,483,647
Maximum number of hexadecimal constant digits	16,336
Maximum length of a catalog comment (in bytes)	254
Largest instance of a structured type column object at run time (in gigabytes)	1

Table 17-3.   *String Limits*

Description	Limit
Smallest DATE value	0001-01-01
Largest DATE value	9999-12-31
Smallest TIME value	00:00:00

Table 17-4.   *Datetime Limits*

Description	Limit
Largest TIME value	24:00:00
Smallest TIMESTAMP value	0001-01-01-00.00.00.000000
Largest TIMESTAMP value	9999-12-31-24.00.00.000000

Table 17-4. *Datetime Limits* (continued)

Description	Limit
Maximum number of columns in a table [a]	1012
Maximum number of columns in a view [b]	5000
Maximum length of a row, including all overhead (in bytes) [c][a]	32,677
Maximum size of a table, per partition (in gigabytes) [d][a]	512
Maximum size of an index, per partition (in gigabytes)	512
Maximum number of rows in a table, per partition	4×10^9
Longest index key, including all overhead (in bytes)	1024
Maximum number of columns in an index key	16
Maximum number of indexes on a table	32,767 or storage
Maximum number of tables referenced in an SQL statement or a view	storage
Maximum number of host variable declarations in a precompiled program [d]	storage
Maximum number of host variable references in an SQL statement	32,767
Longest host variable value used for insert or update (in bytes)	2,147,483,647
Longest SQL statement (in bytes)	65,535

Table 17-5. *Database Manager Limits*

Description	Limit
Maximum number of elements in a select list [a]	1012
Maximum number of predicates in a WHERE or HAVING clause	storage
Maximum number of columns in a GROUP BY clause [a]	1012
Maximum total length of columns in a GROUP BY clause (in bytes) [a]	32,677
Maximum number of columns in an ORDER BY clause [a]	1012
Maximum total length of columns in an ORDER BY clause (in bytes) [a]	32,677
Maximum size of an SQLDA (in bytes)	storage
Maximum number of prepared statements	storage
Maximum number of declared cursors in a program	storage
Maximum number of cursors opened at one time	storage
Maximum number of tables in an SMS table space	65,534
Maximum number of constraints on a table	storage
Maximum level of subquery nesting	storage
Maximum number of subqueries in a single statement	storage
Maximum number of values in an INSERT statement [a]	1012
Maximum number of SET clauses in a single UPDATE statement [a]	1012
Maximum number of columns in a unique constraint, supported by a unique index	16
Maximum total length of columns in a unique constraint, supported by a unique index (in bytes)	1024
Maximum number of referencing columns in a foreign key	16
Maximum total length of referencing columns in a foreign key (in bytes)	1024

Table 17-5.   *Database Manager Limits* (continued)

SQL

Description	Limit
Maximum length of a check constraint specification (in bytes)	65,535
Maximum number of columns in a partitioning key [f]	500
Maximum number of rows changed in a unit of work	storage
Maximum number of packages	storage
Maximum number of constants in a statement	storage
Maximum number of concurrent users of a server [e]	64,000
Maximum number of parameters in a stored procedure	32,767
Maximum number of parameters in a user-defined function	90
Maximum run-time depth of cascading triggers	16
Maximum number of simultaneously active event monitors	32
Maximum size of a regular DMS table space (in gigabytes) [da]	512
Maximum size of a long DMS table space (in terabytes) [d]	2
Maximum size of a temporary DMS table space (in terabytes) [d]	2
Maximum number of databases concurrently in use, per instance	256
Maximum number of concurrent users, per instance	64,000
Maximum number of concurrent applications, per database	1000
Maximum partition number	999
Maximum number of table objects in a DMS table space [g]	51,000
Longest variable index key part (in bytes)	255
Maximum number of columns in a data source table or view that is referenced by a nickname	5000
Maximum number of pages in a buffer pool (32-bit releases)	524,288
Maximum number of pages in a buffer pool (64-bit releases)	2,147,483,647
Maximum number of nested levels in a stored procedure	16

Table 17-5. *Database Manager Limits* (continued)

Description	Limit
Maximum number of table spaces in a database	4096
Maximum number of attributes in a structured type	4082

[a] For page size–specific values, see Table 17-6.

[b] This maximum can be achieved by using a join operation in a CREATE VIEW statement. Note that the maximum number of elements in a select list is 1012.

[c] The actual data in BLOB, CLOB, LONG VARCHAR, DBCLOB, or LONG VARGRAPHIC columns is not included in this limit; however, information about the location of that data does take up space in a row.

[d] The value shown is a theoretical limit; the actual limit may be less.

[e] The actual limit will be the value of the *maxagents* database manager configuration parameter. For detailed information about *maxagents,* see the *DB2 Administration Guide: Performance* (Version 7.1).

[f] The value shown is a theoretical limit; use the maximum number of columns in an index key (16) as the practical limit.

[g] Table objects include data, indexes, LONG VARCHAR or LONG VARGRAPHIC columns, and LOB columns.

Table 17-5.   *Database Manager Limits* (continued)

Description	4KB page size limit	8KB page size limit	16KB page size limit	32KB page size limit
Maximum number of columns in a table	500	1012	1012	1012
Maximum length of a row, including all overhead	4005	8101	16,293	32,677
Maximum size of a table, per partition (in gigabytes)	64	128	256	512
Maximum size of an index, per partition (in gigabytes)	64	128	256	512

Table 17-6.   *Database Manager Page Size–Specific Limits*

Description	4KB page size limit	8KB page size limit	16KB page size limit	32KB page size limit
Maximum number of elements in a select list	500	1012	1012	1012
Maximum number of columns in a GROUP BY clause	500	1012	1012	1012
Maximum total length of columns in a GROUP BY clause (in bytes)	4005	8101	16,293	32,677
Maximum number of columns in an ORDER BY clause	500	1012	1012	1012
Maximum total length of columns in an ORDER BY clause (in bytes)	4005	8101	16,293	32,677
Maximum number of values in an INSERT statement	500	1012	1012	1012
Maximum number of SET clauses in a single UPDATE statement	500	1012	1012	1012
Maximum size of a regular DMS table space (in gigabytes)	64	128	256	512

Table 17-6. *Database Manager Page Size–Specific Limits* (continued)

window; and *n* FOLLOWING to specify the number of rows *following* the current row that are to be included in the window. If the keyword UNBOUNDED were specified instead of a positive integer *n*, the window would include all of the rows preceding or following the current row.

SQL Limits

The following tables provide information on some of SQL's limits. Table 17-1 lists the length limits (in bytes) for SQL identifiers. Table 17-2 identifies the limits associated with numeric data types, Table 17-3 identifies the limits for string data types, and Table 17-4 identifies the limits for datetime data types. Table 17-5 lists the database manager limits, and Table 17-6 identifies the database manager page size limits.

Field Name[a]	Data Type	Description
sqlcaid	CHAR(8)	An eye catcher for storage dumps, sqlcaid is usually SQLCA. The sixth byte is L if line number information is returned from parsing an SQL procedure body.
sqlcabc	INTEGER	Length of the SQLCA (136 bytes).
sqlcode	INTEGER	The SQL return code. For detailed information about specific SQL return codes, see the *DB2 Message Reference*. A value of 0 indicates successful execution (although one or more sqlwarn indicators may have been set). A positive value indicates successful execution, but with a warning condition. A negative value indicates an error condition.
sqlerrml	SMALLINT	Length indicator for sqlerrmc, with values ranging from 0 to 70. Zero means that sqlerrmc is not relevant.
sqlerrmc	VARCHAR (70)	Contains one or more tokens (separated by X'FF') that are substituted for variables in the descriptions of error conditions. This field is also used when a successful connection is completed. For a NOT ATOMIC compound SQL statement, sqlerrmc may contain information on up to seven errors. For detailed information about specific SQL return codes, see the *DB2 Message Reference*.

Table 17-7. *Fields of the SQLCA*

Field Name[a]	Data Type	Description
sqlerrp	CHAR(8)	A three-letter product identifier, followed by five digits corresponding to the version, release, and modification level of the product. For example, SQL07010 means DB2 Universal Database version 7, release 1, modification level 0. If sqlcode indicates an error condition, this field identifies the module that returned the error. This field is also used when a successful connection is completed.
sqlerrd	ARRAY	Six INTEGER variables that provide diagnostic information. These values are usually 0 if there are no errors.
sqlerrd(1)	INTEGER	After a successful connection, contains the maximum expected difference in length of mixed-character data (CHAR data types) when converted to the database code page from the application code page. A value of 0 or 1 indicates no expansion; a value greater than 1 indicates a possible expansion in length; a negative value indicates a possible contraction.[b] Upon successful return from an SQL procedure, contains the return status value.
sqlerrd(2)	INTEGER	After a successful connection, contains the maximum expected difference in length of mixed-character data (CHAR data types) when converted to the application code page from the database code page. A value of 0 or 1 indicates no expansion; a value greater than 1 indicates a possible expansion in length; a negative value indicates a possible contraction.[b] If the SQLCA is associated with a NOT ATOMIC compound SQL statement that encountered one or more errors, the value is set to the number of statements that failed.

Table 17-7. *Fields of the SQLCA (continued)*

Field Name[a]	Data Type	Description
sqlerrd(3)	INTEGER	After a successful PREPARE operation, contains an estimate of the number of rows that will be returned. After INSERT, UPDATE, or DELETE operations, contains the actual number of rows affected. If compound SQL is invoked, contains an accumulation of all substatement rows. If CONNECT is invoked, contains 1 if the database can be updated, or 2 if the database is read-only. If CREATE PROCEDURE for an SQL procedure is invoked and an error is encountered while parsing the SQL procedure body, contains the line number where the error was encountered. The sixth byte of sqlcaid must be L for this to be a valid line number.
sqlerrd(4)	INTEGER	After a successful PREPARE operation, contains a relative cost estimate of the resources required to process the statement. If compound SQL is invoked, contains a count of the number of successful substatements. If CONNECT is invoked, contains 0 for a one-phase commit from a down-level client, 1 for a one-phase commit, 2 for a one-phase read-only commit, and 3 for a two-phase commit.
sqlerrd(5)	INTEGER	Contains the total number of rows deleted, inserted, or updated as a result of both the enforcement of constraints after a successful delete operation and the processing of triggered SQL statements from activated triggers. If compound SQL is invoked, contains an accumulation of the number of such rows for all substatements. In some cases when an error is encountered, this field contains a negative value that is an internal error pointer. If CONNECT is invoked, contains an authentication type value of 0 for server authentication, 1 for client authentication, 2 for authentication using DB2 Connect, 3 for DCE security services authentication, or 255 for unspecified authentication.

Table 17-7.   *Fields of the SQLCA (continued)*

SQL

Field Name[a]	Data Type	Description
sqlerrd(6)	INTEGER	For a partitioned database, contains the partition number of the partition that encountered the error or warning. If no errors or warnings were encountered, this field contains the partition number of the coordinator node. The number in this field is the same as that specified for the partition in the db2nodes.cfg file.
sqlwarn	Array	A set of warning indicators, each containing a blank space or W. If compound SQL is invoked, contains an accumulation of the warning indicators set for all substatements.
sqlwarn0	CHAR(1)	Blank if all other indicators are blank; contains W if at least one other indicator is not blank.
sqlwarn1	CHAR(1)	Contains W if the value of a string column was truncated when assigned to a host variable. Contains N if the null terminator was truncated. Contains A if the CONNECT or ATTACH operation is successful and the *authID* for the connection is longer than eight bytes.
sqlwarn2	CHAR(1)	Contains W if NULL values were eliminated from the argument of a function.[c]
sqlwarn3	CHAR(1)	Contains W if the number of columns is not equal to the number of host variables.
sqlwarn4	CHAR(1)	Contains W if a prepared UPDATE or DELETE statement does not include a WHERE clause.
sqlwarn5	CHAR(1)	Reserved for future use.
sqlwarn6	CHAR(1)	Contains W if the result of a date calculation was adjusted to avoid an impossible date.
sqlwarn7	CHAR(1)	After a successful connection, contains E if the dyn_query_mgmt database configuration parameter is enabled.
sqlwarn8	CHAR(1)	Contains W if a character that could not be converted was replaced with a substitution character.

Table 17-7.   *Fields of the SQLCA (continued)*

Field Name[a]	Data Type	Description
sqlwarn9	CHAR(1)	Contains W if arithmetic expressions with errors were ignored during column function processing.
sqlwarn10	CHAR(1)	Contains W if there was a conversion error when converting a character data value in one of the fields of the SQLCA.
sqlstate	CHAR(5)	A return code that indicates the outcome of the most recently executed SQL statement.

[a] The field names shown are those present in an SQLCA that is returned by an INCLUDE statement.

[b] For details, see the "Character Conversion Expansion Factor" section of the "Programming in Complex Environments" chapter in the *DB2 Application Development Guide*.

[c] Some functions may not set sqlwarn2 to W, even though NULL values were eliminated, because the result was not dependent on the elimination of NULL values.

Table 17-7. *Fields of the SQLCA* (continued)

SQL Communications Area

The *SQL Communications Area* (SQLCA) is a collection of variables (a data structure) that is updated at the end of the execution of every SQL statement or DB2 command. The database manager uses the SQLCA structure to return error information to an application. To display the SQLCA when using the command line processor, issue this command from a DB2 command window:

```
db2 -a
```

Table 17-7 describes each field in the SQLCA data structure.

The Complete Reference

Part VI

Business Intelligence

The Complete Reference

Chapter 18

Federated Systems

A *federated database* is a relational database whose data is stored in multiple data sources, including other separate relational databases. Federated systems provide an environment for the seamless integration of data from different database management systems. This chapter examines the various components of a federated system, provides the steps for creating a federated environment, covers the issues involved in submitting federated queries, and explores means of optimizing a federated system's performance.

Introducing Federated Database Systems

A federated system enables users and applications to reference tables or views from multiple database management systems (DBMSs) within a single SQL statement. Statements such as this are known as *distributed requests.* For example, you can join data from a local DB2 table, a Sybase table, and an Oracle view to form a distributed request.

A federated system allows data from various sources to be accessed as if it all existed in one local database. If any tables cataloged in the federated database were to be moved, their references, known as nicknames, would be updated so that applications or users referring to them would be unaffected.

Supported Environments

A DB2 federated system supports distributed requests to DB2 family, Oracle, Microsoft SQL Server, and Sybase DBMSs. Table 18-1 lists the supported versions of each system. The second column contains keywords required in the CREATE

Data Source	Wrapper Type	Server Type
IBM DB2 Universal Database	DRDA	DB2/UDB
IBM DB2 DataJoiner V2.1 and V2.1.1	DRDA	DataJoiner
IBM DB2 for AIX	DRDA	DB2/6000
IBM DB2 for HP-UX V1.2	DRDA	DB2/HPUX
IBM DB2 for Windows NT	DRDA	DB2/NT
IBM DB2 Enterprise— Extended Edition	DRDA	DB2/EEE
IBM DB2 for Solaris V1 and V1.2	DRDA	DB2/SUN

Table 18-1. *Supported Database Environments*

BUSINESS INTELLIGENCE

IBM DB2 for OS/2	DRDA	DB2/2
IBM DB2 for Linux	DRDA	DB2/LINUX
IBM DB2 for NUMA-Q	DRDA	DB2/PTX
IBM DB2 for SCO Unixware	DRDA	DB2/SCO
IBM DB2 for AS/400	DRDA	DB2/400
IBM DB2 for OS/390	DRDA	DB2/390
IBM DB2 for MVS	DRDA	DB2/MVS
IBM DB2 for VM	DRDA	DB2/VM
IBM DB2 for VSE	DRDA	DB2/VSE
IBM SQL/DS	DRDA	SQL/DS
Oracle V7.0.13 (or later)	SQLNET or NET8	ORACLE
Sybase V10.0 (or later)	CTLIB or DBLIB	SYBSERVER
Microsoft SQL Server V6.5 and V7.5	DJXMSSQL3 or MSSQLODBC3	MSSQLSERVER
Any OLE database	OLEDB	—

Table 18-1.   *Supported Database Environments (continued)*

WRAPPER statement, while the third column contains keywords required in the CREATE SERVER statement.

For a more complete discussion about the CREATE SERVER statement or any of the other SQL statements referred to in this chapter, see Chapter 27.

Components

A DB2 federated system, depicted in Figure 18-1, consists of a DB2 Universal Database (UDB) instance, a database on this instance that will serve as the federated database, and one or more data sources. The server occupied by the instance owning the federated database is known as the *federated server*. The federated database contains catalog entries identifying data sources and their characteristics. Each data source consists of an instance of a relational database management system (RDBMS) plus the database or databases that the instance supports.

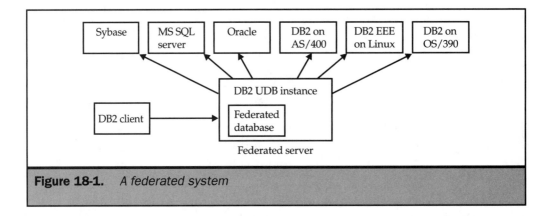

Figure 18-1.   *A federated system*

To end users and client applications, the data sources appear as a single collective database. In actuality, users and applications interface with the federated database, which, in turn, interfaces with the data sources. To obtain data from data sources, the users and applications submit queries in DB2 SQL to the federated server, which then distributes those queries to the appropriate data sources. DB2 also provides access plans for optimizing the queries. (In some cases, these plans call for processing the queries at the federated server rather than at the data source.) Finally, DB2 collects the requested data and passes it to the users and applications.

Inside the federated database are catalog entries, which identify data sources and their characteristics. Each catalog entry is composed of a set of database objects, for which a wrapper, server, and nickname are required. The following sections describe each of the various data source objects.

Wrapper

A *wrapper* is the mechanism the federated server uses to communicate with a data source and retrieve data from it. The CREATE WRAPPER statement registers a wrapper for a certain category of data source to the federated database. Use Table 18-1 to determine the appropriate wrapper type for the data source in question.

Server Definition

A *server definition* describes a given data source. Included in this definition are the wrapper name, server name, server type, server version, authorization information, and server options. It also includes the type and version of the specified RDBMS and the metadata that is specific to it.

The SQL statements for creating and modifying a persistent server definition are CREATE SERVER and ALTER SERVER. For the definition to function properly, the authorization ID in the statement must have SYSADM or DBADM authority on the federated database. The identifier provided for the server name parameter must be unique: no other data sources or table spaces in the federated database can share this identifier.

You can figure out the server type parameter from Table 18-1 by determining the data source and the corresponding server type. The wrapper name parameter is also found in Table 18-1, and must have already been initialized by the CREATE WRAPPER statement (discussed in the "Creating a Wrapper Definition" section later in the chapter).

The term server, as it is used in this context, refers only to data sources. According to the client/server model of computing, the federated server, when submitting queries to a data source, is acting as a client, and the data source is acting as a server.

Nickname

A *nickname* is a pointer to a table or view belonging to a data source. Nicknames and their associated metadata hide the details involved in accessing external data from end users, ensuring location transparency.

To define nicknames, use the CREATE NICKNAME statement, and to modify them, use the ALTER NICKNAME statement. When creating a nickname, you need to provide a unique identifier and a remote object name, which is composed of the data source name (the server definition name), remote schema name, and remote table or view name. Once you have created the nickname, you can use the unique identifier in queries to refer to the specified table or view in the data source.

User Mappings

The federated server can send the distributed request of an authorized user or application to a data source under either of these conditions:

- The user or application uses the same user name and password for both the federated database and the data source.

- The user or application uses a different authorization to access the federated database than the data source, but a user mapping exists, enabling the federated server to pass the correct authorization to the data source.

In the latter case, a user mapping was defined with the authorization information of the specified data source. To define and modify user mappings, use the CREATE USER MAPPING and ALTER USER MAPPING statements.

Data Type Mappings

For a federated server to retrieve data from columns of data source tables and views, the columns' data types at the data source must map to corresponding data types already defined in the federated database. DB2 supplies default mappings for most foreign data types. For example, the Oracle type FLOAT maps by default to the DB2 type DOUBLE. No mappings exist for the data types that DB2 federated servers do not support: LONG VARCHAR, LONG VARGRAPHIC, DATALINK, large object (LOB) types, and user-defined types.

When values from a data source column are returned, they conform fully to the DB2 type in the type mapping that applies to the column. Meanwhile, from the perspective of the data source, the column in question remains unchanged.

Use the CREATE TYPE MAPPING statement to override default mappings to modify the length or format of column data coming from one or more data sources. To modify a data type mapping for a specific column of a specific table, use the ALTER NICKNAME statement.

Function Mappings

For a federated server to recognize a data source function, a mapping needs to exist between it and a corresponding DB2 function. DB2 provides default mappings between common built-in data source functions and built-in DB2 functions. If, however, you want to use a data source function that the federated server does not recognize (for example, a new built-in function or a user-defined function), then you must create a mapping between this function and its counterpart at the federated database.

If a counterpart does not exist, you must create one that meets the following requirements: the counterpart and the data source function must have the same number of input parameters, and the counterpart's data types for input parameters and returned values must be compatible with the data source function's corresponding data types. The counterpart can be either a complete function or a function template— a partial function with no executable code. The latter cannot be invoked independently because its only purpose is invoking a data source function from the federated server.

You create function mappings by using the CREATE FUNCTION MAPPING statement. The optimizer examines parameters entered in this statement to evaluate various execution options. Optimization is discussed further in the section titled "Optimizing Federated System Performance."

Index Specifications

When a nickname is created for a data source table, the federated server supplies the catalog with information about any indexes for the data source table. The optimizer uses this information to facilitate retrieval of the table's data.

If the table has no indexes, you can still supply information that an index definition typically contains: for instance, which table column to search to find information quickly. To do this, issue a CREATE INDEX statement with the appropriate information, and reference the table's nickname.

You can also supply the optimizer with information for tables that have indexes of which the federated server is unaware. Typical scenarios include a table that doesn't have an index when assigned a nickname but that acquires one later, or a nickname being created for a view of a table with an index.

The information provided in the CREATE INDEX statement is cataloged as a set of metadata called an *index specification*. Note that when CREATE INDEX references a nickname, it produces only an index specification, not an actual index.

Creating a Federated System

Before distributed queries can be issued, some setup is necessary. First, federated functionality must be enabled. Second, nicknames representing the desired data sources must be configured. And third, the transmission of authentication information to data sources must be controlled.

The steps involved in creating a federated system are presented in sequential order, with subsections containing explanations for specific platforms. Because each step involved in creating a federated system builds on the previous steps, the examples for each platform likewise refer to previous examples.

Enabling Federated Database Functionality

Both DB2 Enterprise Edition (EE) and DB2 Enterprise—Extended Edition (EEE) support federated databases. For a DB2 EE or EEE DBMS to function as a federated server, federated system support must be enabled during installation. The process is different for UNIX and Windows systems.

UNIX Systems

During the installation of DB2 Universal Database on UNIX systems, select the Distributed Join setting for DB2 Data Sources and optionally create an instance to use with this setting. If you choose to create an instance, the *federated* parameter will be set to YES by default. If you choose to create an instance later, you must manually set the *federated* parameter to YES for that instance.

This is necessary only if you are creating an instance using DB2ICRT. If you go back to using DB2SETUP to either create or set up an existing instance, then the *federated* parameter will be set to YES again.

Windows Systems

Federated database functionality is enabled by default on Windows systems as a part of DB2 installation.

Adding a Data Source

Depending on the type of DBMS being configured as a data source, the steps involved in enabling the federated server to recognize external databases vary. In spite of the differences, these steps can be generalized as follows:

■ Establish communication with the data source DBMS.

- Create a wrapper definition.
- Create a server definition.
- Create a user mapping.
- Create a nickname.

Establishing Communications

Before you can add a data source, you must first establish communications with the DBMS on which the data source resides. This usually means installing the applicable client software (for example, an Oracle client if connecting to an Oracle data source) and configuring it to connect to the data source's DBMS.

The Oracle, Sybase, and SQL Server wrappers are not available in DB2 UDB version 7.2. These are contained in DB2 Relational Connect version 7.2, which you must purchase and install separately.

DB2 Family   To establish communications with a DB2 family database, catalog an entry in the federated server's node directory that points to the location of the DB2 data source. The federated server determines the access method to use based on the type of node being cataloged and the type of DB2 family database being accessed.

For example, if you are using TCP/IP as a communications protocol, issue the following command to catalog the database you wish to use as a data source:

```
CATALOG TCPIP NODE DB2Node REMOTE SalesDB SERVER DB2TCPSALES
```

The following list describes the elements of this statement:

- **DB2Node**   The name assigned to the node being cataloged
- **SalesDB**   The host name of the system where the data source resides
- **DB2TCPSALES**   The primary port name that is defined by the data source for use by data source clients

Oracle   To establish communications with an Oracle database, install and configure the Oracle client software on the DB2 federated server.

Sybase   To establish communications with a Sybase database, install and configure the Sybase Open Client software on the DB2 federated server. Ensure that the catalog stored procedures and the Sybase Open Client libraries are included in this install.

Microsoft SQL Server   To establish communications to an instance of Microsoft SQL Server, install and configure the ODBC driver on the DB2 federated server. On DB2 for Windows NT/2000 servers, configure a system DSN, using the ODBC device driver. On DB2 for AIX servers, install the threaded version of the libraries by MERANT:

specify the MERANT library directory as the first entry in the LIBPATH, and set up the .odbc.ini file in the home directory.

OLE DB   To establish communications with an OLE DB database, install and configure OLE DB 2.0 (or later) and an OLE DB provider for a data source.

Setting Environment Variables (Oracle, Sybase, and SQL Server Only)

If you are connecting to an Oracle, Sybase, or SQL Server database, you will need to set data source environment variables for the types of DBMSs you will be using. First, modify the DB2DJ.ini file (found in sqllib/cfg), which contains configuration information about the client software installed on your federated server. Second, issue the DB2SET command to update the DB2 profile registry with your changes.

Following are data source environment variables and related information for different DBMS platforms.

Oracle   SQL*Net and Net8 require that the ORACLE_HOME variable be set prior to starting your federated instance:

```
ORACLE_HOME=<oracle_home_directory>
```

If this variable is changed, the federated instance must be stopped and restarted before the new ORACLE_HOME value takes effect.

If an individual user of the federated instance has the ORACLE_HOME environment variable set, it is not used by the federated instance. The federated instance uses only the value of ORACLE_HOME that you set in the DB2 profile registry.

For federated servers running on versions of UNIX, if you set the ORACLE_BASE variable during the installation of the Oracle client software, you should also set the ORACLE_BASE environment variable on the federated server:

```
ORACLE_BASE=<oracle_home_directory>
```

For federated servers running on versions of UNIX that will be accessing an Oracle 7.2 or later data source, set the ORA_NLS environment variable:

```
ORA_NLS=<oracle_home_directory>/ocommon/nls/admin/data
```

If the SQL*Net or Net8 tnsnames.ora file resides outside the default search path, you must set the TNS_ADMIN environment variable to specify the location of this file:

```
TNS_ADMIN=x:\path\tnsnames.ora
```

For Windows servers, the default location of this file varies depending on the client software that is being used. If you are using SQL*Net, tnsnames.ora is in the %ORACLE_HOME%\Network\Admin directory; if you are using Net8, tnsnames.ora is in the %ORACLE_HOME%\Net8\Admin directory.

For UNIX servers, the default location of this file is $ORACLE_HOME/admin/util/network.

Sybase   The <sybase home directory> is the directory where the Sybase client is installed:

```
SYBASE="<sybase home directory>"
```

After setting the environment variable, update the .profile file of the DB2 instance with the Sybase environment variable. Use these commands:

```
export PATH="$SYBASE/bin:$PATH"
export SYBASE="<sybase home directory>"
```

Then execute the DB2 instance .profile by entering the following:

```
. .profile
```

SQL Server   To be able to connect to a SQL Server data source, you must set the following data source environment variables prior to starting your federated instance:

```
ODBCINI=$HOME/.odbc.ini
DJX_ODBC_LIBRARY_PATH=<path to the Merant driver>/lib
LIBPATH=<path to the Merant driver>/lib
DB2ENVLIST=LIBPATH
```

DB2SET Command Possibilities   If you are using this DB2DJ.ini file in a nonpartitioned database system, or if you want the values in this DB2DJ.ini file to apply only to the current node, issue the following command:

```
db2set DB2_DJ_INI = sqllib/cfg/db2dj.ini
```

If you are using this DB2DJ.ini file in a partitioned database system and you want the values in this DB2DJ.ini file to apply to all nodes within this instance, issue this command:

```
db2set -g DB2_DJ_INI = $INSTHOME/sqllib/cfg/db2dj.ini
```

If you are using this DB2DJ.ini file in a partitioned database system and you want the values in this DB2DJ.ini file to apply to a specific node, issue the following command:

```
db2set -i <instance_name> 3 DB2_DJ_INI = sqllib/cfg/node3.ini
```

In this case, the following applies:

- **3**   The node number as listed in the db2nodes.cfg file
- **node3.ini**   The modified and renamed version of the DB2DJ.ini file

Linking DB2 to Client Software (Oracle, Sybase, and SQL Server Only)

For DB2 federated servers running on UNIX platforms, run the *djxlink* script to link-edit the Oracle SQL*Net, Net 8, CTLIB, DBLIB, DJXMSSQL3, or MSSQLODBC3 libraries to your DB2 federated server. Run the *djxlink* script only after installing the given DBMS' client software on the DB2 federated server. The location of the *djxlink* script depends on your platform:

- **AIX**   /usr/lpp/db2_07_01/bin
- **Solaris**   /opt/IBMdb2/V7.1/bin
- **Linux**   /usr/IBMdb2/V7.1/bin

Updating the tnsnames.ora File (Oracle Only)

You must ensure that the SQL*Net or Net8 tnsnames.ora file is updated for each Oracle server to which communications are configured. Within the tnsnames.ora file, the SID is the name of the Oracle instance, and the HOST is the host name where the Oracle server is located.

Recycling the DB2 Instance (Oracle, Sybase, and SQL Server Only)

To ensure that the environment variables are set, recycle the DB2 instance.

For Windows servers, issue the following commands:

```
NET STOP instance_name
NET START instance_name
```

For UNIX servers, issue these commands:

```
db2stop
db2start
```

Creating an Interface File (Sybase Only)

To create and set up an interfaces file, you must create the file and make the file accessible.

Use the Sybase-supplied utility to create an interfaces file that includes the data for all the Sybase open servers that you want to access. Windows NT/2000 typically names this file sql.ini. Rename the file you just created to "interfaces" to maintain the same name across all platforms. On AIX and Solaris systems, this file is named <instance_ home>/sqllib/interfaces.

You then need to make the interfaces file accessible to DB2. In Windows NT/2000, put the file in the DB2 instance's %DB2PATH% directory. In AIX or Solaris, put the file in the DB2 instance's $HOME/sqllib directory. Use the LN command to link to the file from the DB2 instance's $HOME/sqllib directory.

Creating a Wrapper Definition

Use the CREATE WRAPPER statement to define the wrapper module that will be used to access data sources. Federated servers use wrappers to communicate with and retrieve data from data sources.

DB2 Family   For the DB2 family of servers, use this statement:

```
"CREATE WRAPPER DRDA"
```

DRDA is the default name of the wrapper module used to access DB2 family data sources.

Oracle   Two different Oracle wrapper modules are included with DB2 Relational Connect: one for use with the SQL*Net V1 or V2 client software, and one for use with the Net8 client software. Regardless of the client software that you use, you can access both Oracle version 7 and Oracle version 8 data sources.

Use the following statement to create the wrapper:

```
CREATE WRAPPER SQLNET
```

SQLNET is the default name of the wrapper module used with Oracle's SQL*Net client software. If you are using Oracle's Net8 client software, use NET8 instead.

Sybase   Two different Sybase wrappers are available with DB2 Relational Connect: CTLIB and DBLIB. Ensure that the wrapper you use matches the ctlib or dblib set of libraries used by your Sybase DBMS. Use the following statement to create the wrapper:

```
CREATE WRAPPER CTLIB
```

CTLIB is the default wrapper name used with Sybase Open Client software. Both the
CTLIB and DBLIB wrappers can be used on Windows NT/2000, AIX, and Solaris servers.

SQL Server   Two different SQL Server wrappers are available with DB2 Relational
Connect. DJXMSSQL3 is the default wrapper name used on a DB2 for Windows NT/2000
server using the ODBC 3.0 (or later) driver. MSSQLODBC3 is the default wrapper name
on a DB2 for AIX server using the MERANT DataDirect Connect ODBC 3.6 driver.

Create the wrapper by using the following statement, changing the wrapper name
if you need to use the MSSQLODBC3 wrapper:

```
CREATE WRAPPER DJXMSSQL3
```

OLE DB   OLEDB is the default name of the wrapper module used with OLE DB
providers. Use the following statement to create the wrapper:

```
CREATE WRAPPER OLEDB
```

Improving Wrapper Performance (Optional)

The DB2_DJ_COMM environment variable controls whether a wrapper module is
loaded when the federated server initializes, which can result in improved performance
when the DB2 family data source is first accessed. Set the DB2_DJ_COMM environment
variable to include the wrapper library that corresponds to the wrapper module that
you created in the previous step. For example,

```
db2set DB2_DJ_COMM=libdrda.a
```

Table 18-2 contains the names for wrapper library files, ordered by DBMS and
platform.

When issuing the DB2SET command for the Sybase wrapper, put single quotation
marks around the library file name.

Creating a Server Definition

Use the CREATE SERVER statement to define each DB2 server to which communications
are configured.

DBMS	Operating System	Library File
DB2 family	Windows NT/2000	drda.dll
DB2 family	AIX	libdrda.a
DB2 family	Solaris	libdrda.so
DB2 family	HP-UX	libdrda.sl
DB2 family	Linux	libdrda.a
Oracle	Windows NT/2000	sqlnet.dll
Oracle	AIX	libsqlnet.a
Oracle	Solaris	libsqlnet.so
Oracle	HP-UX	libsqlnet.sl
Oracle	Windows NT/2000	net8.dll
Oracle	AIX	libnet8.a
Oracle	Solaris	libnet8.so
Oracle	HP-UX	libnet8.sl
Sybase	Windows NT/2000	ctlib.dll
Sybase	AIX	libctlib.a
Sybase	Solaris	libctlib.so
SQL Server	Windows NT/2000	djxmssql3.dll
SQL Server	AIX	libmssql3.a
OLE DB	Windows NT/2000	db2oledb.dll

Table 18-2.   *Wrapper Library Files According to DBMS and Platform*

DB2 Family   Use the following statement to create a server definition for a DB2 data source:

```
CREATE SERVER DB2Server TYPE DB2/390 VERSION 6.1 WRAPPER DRDA
OPTIONS (NODE 'db2node', DBNAME 'ibmdb')
```

The following list describes the elements of this statement:

■ **DB2Server**   A name that you assign to the DB2 data source. This name must be unique.

■ **DB2/390**   The type of DB2 data source to which you are configuring access. You can determine this value from Table 18-1.

■ **6.1**   The version of DB2 for OS/390 that you are accessing.

■ **DRDA**   The wrapper name that you defined in the CREATE WRAPPER statement.

■ **db2node**   The name of the node where DB2Server resides. Obtain the node value by issuing the LIST NODE DIRECTORY command at the DB2 data source. This value is case-sensitive.

■ **ibmdb**   The name of a database at DB2Server. This value is case-sensitive.

Although the node and database values are specified as options, they are required for DB2 data sources.

Oracle   Use the following statement to create a server definition for an Oracle data source:

```
CREATE SERVER ORAServer TYPE ORACLE VERSION 7.2 WRAPPER SQLNET
OPTIONS (NODE "oranode")
```

The following list describes the elements of this statement:

■ **ORAServer**   A name that you assign to the Oracle server. This name must be unique.

■ **ORACLE**   The type of data source to which you are configuring access.

■ **7.2**   The version of Oracle that you are accessing.

■ **SQLNET**   The wrapper name that you defined in the CREATE WRAPPER statement.

■ **oranode**   The name of the node where ORAServer resides. Obtain the node value from the tnsnames.ora file. This value is case-sensitive.

Although the node value is specified as an option, it is required for Oracle data sources.

Sybase   Use the following statement to create a server definition for a Sybase data source:

```
CREATE SERVER SYBServer TYPE SYBASE VERSION 12.0 WRAPPER CTLIB
OPTIONS (NODE 'sybnode', DBNAME 'sybdb')
```

The following list describes the elements of this statement:

- **SYBServer** A name that you assign to the Sybase server. This name must be unique.
- **SYBASE** The type of data source to which you are configuring access.
- **12.0** The version of Sybase that you are accessing.
- **CTLIB** The wrapper name that you defined in the CREATE WRAPPER statement.
- **sybnode** The name of the node where SYBServer resides. This value is case-sensitive.
- **sybdb** The name of a database at SYBServer. This value is case-sensitive.

Although the node and database values are specified as options, they are required for Sybase data sources.

SQL Server Use the following statement to create a server definition for a SQL Server data source:

```
CREATE SERVER SQLServer TYPE MSSQLSERVER VERSION 7.0 WRAPPER DJXMSSQL3
OPTIONS (NODE 'sqlsnode', DBNAME 'sqlsdb')
```

The following list describes the elements of this statement:

- **SQLServer** A name that you assign to the SQL Server. This name must be unique.
- **MSSQLSERVER** The type of data source to which you are configuring access.
- **7.0** The version of SQL Server that you are accessing.
- **DJXMSSQL3** The wrapper name that you defined in the CREATE WRAPPER statement.
- **sqlsnode** The name of the node where SQLServer resides. This value is case-sensitive.
- **sqlsdb** The name of a database at SQLServer. This value is case-sensitive.

Although the node and database values are specified as options, they are required for SQL Server data sources.

OLE DB Use the following statement to create a server definition for an OLE DB data source:

```
CREATE SERVER OLEDBServer WRAPPER OLEDB OPTIONS (
CONNECTSTRING 'Provider=Microsoft.Jet.OLEDB.4.0;
Data Source=c:\msdasdk\bin\oledb\oledbserver.mdb', COLLATING_SEQUENCE 'Y')
```

The following list describes the elements of this statement:

- **OLEDBServer** A name that you assign to an OLE DB data source. This name must be unique.
- **OLEDB** The wrapper name.
- **OPTIONS** Lists other parameters.
- **CONNECTSTRING** Provides initialization properties needed to connect to a data source. For the complete syntax and semantics of the CONNECTSTRING option, see the *Microsoft OLE DB 2.0 Programmer's Reference and Data Access SDK,* (Microsoft Press, 1998).
- **COLLATING_SEQUENCE** Specifies whether the data source uses the same collating sequence as DB2 Universal Database. If a COLLATING_SEQUENCE is not specified, the data source is assumed to have a different collating sequence from DB2 Universal Database.

Creating a User Mapping

If a user ID or password at the federated server is different from a user ID or password at a data source, you will need to use the CREATE USER MAPPING statement to map the local user ID to the user ID and password defined at the data source.

DB2 Family Use the following statement to create a user mapping for a DB2 family data source:

```
CREATE USER MAPPING FOR db2user SERVER DB2Server
OPTIONS (REMOTE_AUTHID 'db2admin', REMOTE_PASSWORD 'map1e1eafs')
```

The following list describes the elements of this statement:

- **db2user** The local user ID that you are mapping to a user ID defined at a DB2 family data source.
- **DB2Server** The name of the DB2 family data source that you defined in the CREATE SERVER statement.
- **db2admin** The user ID at the DB2 family data source to which you are mapping db2user. This value is case-sensitive.
- **map1e1eafs** The password associated with db2admin. This value is case-sensitive.

Oracle Use the following statement to create a user mapping for an Oracle data source:

```
CREATE USER MAPPING FOR db2user SERVER ORAServer
OPTIONS (REMOTE_AUTHID 'orauser', REMOTE_PASSWORD 'rapt0rs')
```

The following list describes the elements of this statement:

- **db2user**   The local user ID that you are mapping to a user ID defined at an Oracle data source.
- **ORAServer**   The name of the Oracle data source that you defined in the CREATE SERVER statement.
- **orauser**   The user ID at the Oracle data source to which you are mapping db2user. This value is case-sensitive.
- **rapt0rs**   The password associated with orauser. This value is case-sensitive.

Note	*For the user mapping to work, the Oracle user ID (at the Oracle data source, not at the DB2 federated server) must have been created by using the Oracle CREATE USER command with the IDENTIFIED BY clause, instead of the IDENTIFIED EXTERNALLY clause.*

Sybase   Use the following statement to create a user mapping for a Sybase data source:

```
CREATE USER MAPPING FOR db2user SERVER SYBServer
OPTIONS (REMOTE_AUTHID 'sybuser', REMOTE_PASSWORD 'bluejays')
```

The following list describes the elements of this statement:

- **db2user**   The local user ID that you are mapping to a user ID defined at a Sybase data source.
- **SYBServer**   The name of the Sybase data source that you defined in the CREATE SERVER statement.
- **sybuser**   The user ID at the Sybase data source to which you are mapping db2user. This value is case-sensitive.
- **bluejays**   The password associated with 'sybuser'. This value is case-sensitive.

SQL Server   Use the following statement to create a user mapping for a SQL Server data source:

```
CREATE USER MAPPING FOR db2user SERVER SQLServer
OPTIONS (REMOTE_AUTHID 'sqlsuser', REMOTE_PASSWORD 'arg0s')
```

The following list describes the elements of this statement:

- **db2user**   The local user ID that you are mapping to a user ID defined at a SQL Server data source.
- **SQLServer**   The name of the SQL Server data source that you defined in the CREATE SERVER statement.
- **sqlsuser**   The user ID at the SQL Server data source to which you are mapping db2user. This value is case-sensitive.
- **arg0s**   The password associated with sqlsuser. This value is case-sensitive.

OLE DB   Use the following statement to create a user mapping for an OLE DB data source:

```
CREATE USER MAPPING FOR db2user SERVER OLEDBServer
OPTIONS (REMOTE_AUTHID 'oleuser', REMOTE_PASSWORD 'r0ck')
```

The following list describes the elements of this statement:

- **db2user**   The local user ID that you are mapping to a user ID defined at an OLE DB data source.
- **OLEDBServer**   The name of the OLE DB data source that you defined in the CREATE SERVER statement.
- **oleuser**   The user ID at the OLE DB data source to which you are mapping db2user. This value is case-sensitive.
- **r0ck**   The password associated with oleuser. This value is case-sensitive.

Creating a Function (OLE DB Only)

You can create functions that retrieve table data from OLE DB data source tables. These are known as *external user-defined table functions.* While one of these functions can extract data from an OLE DB data source, it is not a part of the data source. You can use table functions in the FROM clause of a SELECT statement.

Using an existing OLE DB server definition, you can use the CREATE FUNCTION statement:

```
CREATE FUNCTION orders () RETURNS TABLE (orderid INTEGER, ...)
LANGUAGE OLEDB EXTERNAL NAME 'OLEDBServer!orders'
```

This statement registers the OLE DB table function, orders(), which retrieves order information from a Microsoft Access database at the data source, OLEDBServer.

Creating a Nickname

You can use the CREATE NICKNAME statement to assign a nickname to a view or table located at your data source. You will use this nickname when you query the data source.

DB2 Family   To create a nickname for a DB2 family data source, use this statement:

```
CREATE NICKNAME DB2Sales FOR DB2Server.SALESDATA.NAMERICA
```

The following list describes the elements of this statement:

- **DB2Sales**   A unique nickname for the DB2 table or view
- **DB2Server.SALESDATA.NAMERICA**   A three-part identifier that follows this format: data_source_name.remote_schema_name.remote_table_name

Oracle   To create a nickname for an Oracle data source, use this statement:

```
CREATE NICKNAME ORASales FOR ORAServer.SALESDATA.SAMERICA
```

Here are the elements in this statement:

- **ORASales**   A unique nickname for the Oracle table or view
- **ORAServer.SALESDATA.SAMERICA**   A three-part identifier that follows this format: data_source_name.remote_schema_name.remote_table_name

Sybase   To create a nickname for a Sybase data source, use this statement (using double quotation marks around the schema and table names):

```
"CREATE NICKNAME SYBSales FOR SYBServer."SALESDATA"."ASIA""
```

In this statement, these are the elements:

- **SYBSales**   A unique nickname for the Sybase table or view
- **SYBServer.SALESDATA.ASIA**   A three-part identifier that uses quotes around the schema and table names, following this format: data_source_name."remote_schema_name"."remote_table_name"

SQL Server   To create a nickname for a SQL Server data source, use this statement:

```
CREATE NICKNAME SQLSSales FOR SQLServer.SALESDATA.EUROPE
```

These are the elements of this statement:

- **SQLSSales**   A unique nickname for the SQL Server table or view
- **SQLServer.SALESDATA.EUROPE**   A three-part identifier that follows this format: data_source_name.remote_schema_name.remote_table_name

Authentication Processing

In a federated system, you must consider the authentication requirements of your data sources. Data sources are normally set up to require authentication, so you must ensure that IDs and passwords (as required) can flow to data sources. DB2 provides methods for supporting the various authentication requirements of data sources.

There are three ways to control the transmission of authentication information to data sources: DB2 authentication settings, user mappings, and server options.

Authentication Settings

Authentication settings influence global authentication processing in a federated system. For example, if DB2 authentication is set to SERVER or DCS, a user ID and password are required for a connection; therefore, a user ID and password are available for transmission to data sources.

If data source authentication processing requires a password (or perhaps a different user ID and a password), you must create a user mapping. If authentication is set to CLIENT, and the *trust_clntauth* parameter setting is SERVER, it is possible that a password is sent to DB2 and that it is available for transmission to data sources.

User Mappings

DB2 can send either the authorization name used to connect to DB2 or an authorization name defined at DB2. User mappings store authorization names defined at DB2.

User mappings are flexible: you can map an ID to a password or to a different ID and password. You can use them to provide missing information or to change an ID and password to values accepted at the data source.

You must create a user mapping if your authentication setting is DCE and a data source requires authentication processing. DB2 will pass the DCE user ID only to data sources. A password must be mapped to that user ID and then sent to the data source.

If the only difference between the authorization name (or password) at DB2 and the authorization name (or password) at the data source is the case of the passed string, consider using server options (described next) to fold the case to the desired setting instead of creating new IDs and passwords.

See Chapter 5 for more information on authentication.

Server Options

You can use server options to provide overall authentication support. Use them to indicate whether passwords are passed to data sources and whether user IDs and passwords need to be folded to uppercase or lowercase. (User IDs are always sent to or SET SERVER or OPTION statements.

Password Server Option The default setting for the password server option is 'Y'. Leave or set this option to 'Y' for all cases where a data source will perform authentication and is not expecting an encrypted password.

DB2 can transmit encrypted passwords. Set the password server option to 'ENCRYPTION' if passwords should be sent in an encrypted form to DB2 family data sources. It is recommended that you set the password to 'ENCRYPTION' if your authentication setting at DB2 is DCS_ENCRYPT or SERVER_ENCRYPT.

ID and Password Folding Options Data sources can have varying authorization name and password requirements relative to the use of case for IDs and passwords. DB2 provides two server options that can help you resolve naming differences: *fold_id* and *fold_pw*. Their settings are as follows:

- **'U' DB2** Folds the ID or password to uppercase before sending it to the data source.
- **'N' DB2** Does not fold the ID or password.
- **'L' DB2** Folds the ID or password to lowercase before sending it to the data source.
- **null** DB2 first sends the ID or password as uppercase; if that fails, DB2 folds it to lowercase and sends it again.

The null setting might seem attractive because it covers many possibilities. However, from a performance perspective, it is best to set these options so that only one attempt is made for connections. If both the *fold_id* and *fold_pw* options are set to null, DB2 could make up to four attempts to send the authorization name and password.

Issuing Federated Queries

Once a federated system has been enabled and one or more data sources added, federated queries can be issued. These come in the form of distributed requests, issued in the DB2 UDB dialect of SQL, or in passthrough statements in a data source's local SQL dialect.

Distributed Requests

In a federated system, distributed queries appear identical to queries referencing multiple local tables or views. The fundamental difference is that nicknames are used instead of table or view names. To illustrate this, the following is a sample query issued against tables referenced by nicknames created in the "Creating a Federated System" section earlier in this chapter.

```
SELECT * FROM ORASales, SYBSales
```

ORASales and SYBSales are nicknames representing tables on an Oracle and a Sybase DBMS, respectively.

Distributed queries from a federated server that are issued against data sources operate in a semiautonomous manner. For instance, a DB2 query referencing an Oracle table can be issued while Oracle applications are accessing the same server. A DB2 federated system does not restrict access to cataloged data source objects outside of integrity and locking constraints.

A DB2 federated system also provides compensation for DBMSs that do not support all of the DB2 SQL dialect, or certain optimization capabilities. Operations that cannot be performed under such a DBMS are run under DB2. Consider the following example: DB2's SQL includes the clause common-table-expression. In this clause, a name can be specified by which all FROM clauses in a fullselect can reference a result set. The federated server processes a common-table-expression for an Oracle database, even though Oracle's SQL dialect does not include common-table-expression.

Some restrictions apply in the types of statements that can be issued in a DB2 federated system. Distributed requests are restricted to read-only operations. Hence, SQL commands that modify data, such as INSERT, DELETE, and ALTER have no effect on nicknames. Furthermore, the execution of utility operations (for instance, LOAD, IMPORT, REORG, and RUNSTATS) against nicknames is not possible. To issue a write operation or a utility operation, a passthrough statement must be used.

Passthrough Statements

The passthrough facility in DB2 allows Data Manipulation Language (DML) and Data Definition Language (DDL) statements to be submitted to a DBMS in its own SQL dialect. The federated server provides the following SQL statements to manage passthrough sessions:

- **SET PASSTHRU**   Opens and terminates passthrough sessions
- **GRANT (Server Privileges)**   Grants a user, group, list of authorization IDs, or PUBLIC the authority to initiate passthrough sessions to a specific data source
- **REVOKE (Server Privileges)**   Revokes the authority to initiate passthrough sessions

SQL Processing in Passthrough Sessions

If an SQL statement is submitted to a data source for processing in a passthrough session, it must be prepared dynamically in the session and executed while the session is still open. There are a couple of ways of doing this:

- If a SELECT statement is submitted, use the PREPARE statement to prepare it, and then use the OPEN, FETCH, and CLOSE statements to access the results of the query.

■ To prepare and execute supported statements other than SELECT, either use the PREPARE statement, and then use the EXECUTE statement, or use the EXECUTE IMMEDIATE statement.

Considerations and Restrictions

A number of considerations and restrictions apply to passthrough processing. The following passthrough considerations and restrictions apply to all data sources:

■ LOBs are not supported in passthrough mode.

■ Statements prepared within a passthrough session must be executed within the same passthrough session.

■ Users and applications can use passthrough to write to data sources: for example, to insert, update, and delete table rows. Note that a cursor cannot be opened directly against a data source object in a passthrough session.

■ An application can have several SET PASSTHRU statements in effect at the same time to different data sources. Although the application might have issued multiple SET PASSTHRU statements, the passthrough sessions are not truly nested. The federated server accesses each data source directly.

■ If multiple passthrough sessions are open at the same time, each unit of work within each session must be concluded with a COMMIT or ROLLBACK statement. The sessions can then be ended in one operation with the SET PASSTHRU statement and its RESET option.

■ It is not possible to pass through to more than one data source at a time in the same passthrough statement.

■ The passthrough facility does not support stored procedure calls.

■ The passthrough facility does not support the SELECT INTO statement.

The following passthrough considerations and restrictions apply to all Oracle sources:

■ To issue passthrough statements, remote clients must use a DB2 SDK, version 5 or later.

■ Any DDL statement issued against an Oracle server is performed at parse time and is not subject to transaction semantics. The operation, when complete, is automatically committed by Oracle. If a rollback occurs, the DDL is not rolled back.

■ When a SELECT statement is issued from raw data types, the RAWTOHEX function should be invoked to receive the hexadecimal values. When an

INSERT into raw data types is performed, the hexadecimal representation should be provided.

Optimizing Federated System Performance

The DB2 optimizer handles federated queries differently from conventional queries. In addition to generating more efficient SQL statements for both types of queries, the optimizer determines whether it is better to run a federated query at the data source or on the federated server. The optimizer does this in two steps: pushdown analysis, where the possibility of processing the query at the data source is considered; and global optimization, where the costs of all available processing options are weighed and a conclusion is drawn.

Updating Data Source Information

In both pushdown analysis and global optimization, a number of factors affect the decisions made, and hence, the federated system's performance. More important than all of these factors is that accurate and current information about data sources and their objects is stored in the federated database. Without correct information, the DB2 optimizer could not make cost-effective decisions.

Updating the System Catalog

Catalog statistics describe the overall size of nicknames and the range of values in associated columns. They are used by the optimizer when calculating the least-cost path for processing queries containing nicknames. Nickname statistics are stored in the same catalog views as table statistics.

Statistical data related to a nickname is transferred from the data source to the federated database only once: when the CREATE NICKNAME statement is issued. Therefore, changes to the nickname's corresponding table or view at the data source go undetected. DB2 also has no mechanism for handling object definition or structural changes (adding a column) to objects at data sources. If the statistical data or structural data for an object has changed, you should do the following:

- Run the equivalent of RUNSTATS at the data source.
- Drop the current nickname.
- Recreate the nickname.

If the changes are only statistical, you can manually update the statistics in the SYSSTAT.TABLES view without having to drop and recreate the nickname.

Aside from nicknames, it is also common for data sources to change (for instance, if a server is upgraded with a faster processor). The system catalog must be informed of changes to a server with the ALTER SERVER statement.

Pushdown Analysis

The DB2 optimizer uses pushdown analysis to determine whether an operation can be performed at a remote data source. An *operation* can be a function or an SQL operator. If the remote data source can perform the required operation, it is *pushed down*: the optimizer designates the operation to be performed by the remote data source. Operations that cannot be pushed down could significantly impact query performance.

Consider the effect of having an ORDER BY operator sort remote data locally instead of at the data source: DB2 would retrieve the entire table from the remote data source and then sort the rows. If your network is constrained and the table is large, query performance will likely suffer.

Factors affecting the outcome of pushdown analysis fall under three categories: server characteristics, nickname characteristics, and query characteristics.

Server Characteristics Affecting Pushdown Opportunities

Whether server characteristics affect pushdown opportunities depends on the differences between the DB2 UDB SQL dialect and that of the data source in question. DB2 can compensate for the lack or difference of function at a data server, but doing so requires that the operation take place at the federated server.

SQL Capabilities   Each data source supports a variation of the SQL language and different levels of functionality. For example, consider the GROUP BY list. Most data sources support the GROUP BY operator, but some have restrictions on the number of items on the GROUP BY list or restrictions on whether an expression is allowed on the GROUP BY list. If there is a restriction at the remote data source, DB2 might have to perform the GROUP BY operation locally.

SQL Restrictions   Each data source can have different SQL restrictions. For example, some data sources require parameter markers to bind in values to remote SQL statements. Therefore, parameter marker restrictions must be checked to ensure that each data source can support such a bind mechanism. If DB2 cannot determine a good method to bind in a value for a function, this function must be evaluated locally.

SQL Limits   DB2 might allow the use of larger integers than its remote data sources; however, limit-exceeding values cannot be embedded in statements sent to data sources. Therefore, the function or operator that operates on this constant must be evaluated locally.

Collating Sequence   Configuring a federated database to use the same collating sequence that a data source uses and then setting the *collating_sequence* server option to 'Y' allows the optimizer to consider pushing down character range comparison predicates.

In general, you can perform numeric comparisons at either location even if the collating sequence is different. You may get unusual results, however, if the weighting of null characters is different between the federated database and the data source. Likewise, for comparison statements, be careful if you are submitting statements to a case-insensitive data source. The weights assigned to the characters *I* and *i* in a case-insensitive data source are the same. DB2, by default, is case-sensitive and would assign different weights to the characters.

If the collating sequences of the federated database and the data source differ, DB2 retrieves the data to the federated database so that it can do the sorting and comparison locally. The reason for this is that users expect to see the query results ordered according to the collating sequence defined for the federated server; by ordering the data locally, the federated server ensures that this expectation is fulfilled.

If the collating sequences at the federated database and the data source differ, and you need to see the data ordered in the data source's sequence, you can submit your query in passthrough mode or define the query in a data source view.

DB2 Type Mapping and Function Mapping Factors   The default local data type mappings for the supported data source platforms are designed so that sufficient buffer space is given to each data source data type (to avoid loss of data). A user can choose to customize the type mapping for a specific data source to suit specific applications.

DB2 can compensate for functions not supported by a data source. Function compensation occurs in three cases:

■ The function does not exist at the remote data source.

■ The function does exist; however, the characteristics of the operand violate function restrictions: for example, allowing a column name only on the lefthand side of the IS NULL operator.

■ The function, if evaluated remotely, may return a different result.

Nickname Characteristics Affecting Pushdown Opportunities

A couple of nickname-specific factors can affect pushdown opportunities: the local data type of a nickname column and the column options.

You should ensure that the local data type of a column does not prevent a predicate from being evaluated at the data source. As mentioned in "DB2 Type Mapping and Function Mapping Factors," the default data type mappings are provided to avoid any possible overflow. However, a joining predicate between two columns of different lengths might not be considered at the data source whose joining column is shorter, depending on how DB2 binds in the longer column. This situation can affect the number of possibilities in a joining sequence evaluated by the DB2 optimizer.

As for column options, you can use the ALTER NICKNAME SQL statement to add or change column options for nicknames.

One of these options is VARCHAR_NO_TRAILING_BLANKS. You can use it to identify a column that contains no trailing blanks. The compiler pushdown analysis step then takes this information into account when checking all operations performed on columns so indicated. Based on this indication, DB2 may generate a different but equivalent form of a predicate to be used in the remote SQL statement sent to a data source. A user might see a different predicate being evaluated against the data source, but the net result should be equivalent.

Another column option is NUMERIC_STRING. Use this option to indicate whether the values in that column are always numbers without trailing blanks.

Query Characteristics Affecting Pushdown Opportunities

A federated query can reference an SQL operator that involves nicknames from multiple data sources. When DB2 must combine the results from two referenced data sources using one operator, the operation must take place at DB2; it cannot be pushed down.

Global Optimization

The global optimization phase helps produce a globally optimal access strategy to evaluate a query. For a federated database query, the access strategy may involve breaking down the original query into a set of remote query units and then combining the results.

Using the output of pushdown analysis as a recommendation, the optimizer decides whether each operation will be evaluated locally at DB2 or remotely at a data source. The decision is based on the output of its cost model, which includes not only the cost to evaluate the operation but also the cost to transmit the data or messages between DB2 and data sources.

Many factors can affect the output from global optimization and thus affect query performance. The key factors are discussed in two groups: server characteristics and nickname characteristics.

Server Options Affecting Global Optimization

When defining a data source server, a number of options for the CREATE SERVER and ALTER SERVER statements provide the DB2 optimizer with information used in evaluating queries:

- **Relative Ratio of CPU Speed**   Use the CPU_RATIO server option to indicate how much faster or slower the data source CPU speed is compared to the DB2 CPU. A low ratio indicates that the data source workstation CPU is faster than the DB2 workstation CPU. With low ratios, the DB2 optimizer is more likely to consider pushing down CPU-intensive operations to the data source.

- **Relative Ratio of I/O Speed**   Use the IO_RATIO server option to indicate how much faster or slower the data source system I/O speed is compared with the DB2 system. A low ratio indicates that the data source workstation I/O speed is faster than the DB2 workstation I/O speed. With low ratios, the DB2 optimizer will consider pushing down I/O-intensive operations to the data source.

- **Communication Rate Between DB2 and the Data Source**   Use the COMM_RATE server option to indicate network capacity. Low rates (indicating a slow network communication between DB2 and the data source) encourage the DB2 optimizer to reduce the number of messages sent to or from this data source. If the rate is set to 0, the optimizer produces a query requiring minimal network traffic.

- **Data Source Collating Sequence**   Use the COLLATING_SEQUENCE server option to indicate whether a data source collating sequence matches the local DB2 database collating sequence. If this option is not set to 'Y', the optimizer considers the data retrieved from this data source as unordered.

- **Remote Plan Hints**   Use the PLAN_HINTS server option to indicate whether plan hints are supported at a data source. *Plan hints* are statement fragments that provide extra information for data source optimizers. This information can, for certain query types, improve query performance. The plan hints can help the data source optimizer decide whether to use an index, which index to use, or which table join sequence to use.

- **Information in the DB2 Optimizer Knowledge Base**   DB2 has an optimizer knowledge base that contains data about native data sources. The DB2 optimizer does not generate remote access plans that cannot be generated by specific DBMSs. In other words, DB2 avoids generating plans that optimizers at remote data sources cannot understand or accept.

Nickname Characteristics Affecting Global Optimization

DB2 can use information about indexes at data sources to optimize queries. For this reason, it is important that the index information available to DB2 be current. The index information for nicknames is initially acquired at nickname creation time. Index information is not gathered for view nicknames.

Index specifications build an index definition (not an actual index) in the catalog for use by the DB2 optimizer. Consider creating index specifications in the following situations:

- DB2 is unable to retrieve any index information from a data source during nickname creation.

- You want an index for a view nickname.

- You want to urge the DB2 optimizer to use a certain nickname as the inner table of a nested loop join. An index on the join column can be created if none exists.

Consider your needs before issuing CREATE INDEX statements against a nickname for a view. If the view is a simple SELECT on a table with an index, creating indexes on the nickname (locally) that match the indexes on the table at the data source can significantly improve query performance. However, if indexes are created locally over views that are not simple SELECT statements (for example, a view created by joining two tables), query performance may suffer.

Pushdown Analysis and Global Optimization Example

As an example, assume you are using the previously created nickname DB2Sales that points to the table NAMERICA in a DB2 for OS/390 data source. Further, assume that the table has 10,000 rows, that one of the columns contains the last names of employees, and that one of the columns contains salaries. Given the following statement, the optimizer considers several possibilities.

```
"SELECT lastname, COUNT(*) FROM DB2Sales
  WHERE lastname > 'B' AND salary > 50000
  GROUP BY lastname"
```

If the collating sequences at DB2 and DB2 for OS/390 are the same, the query predicate will likely be pushed down to DB2 for OS/390. It is usually more efficient to filter and group results at the data source instead of copying the entire table to DB2 and performing the operations locally. In this case, the predicate and the GROUP BY operation can take place at the data source.

If the collating sequence is not the same, pushdown analysis determines that the entire predicate cannot be evaluated at the data source; however, the optimizer may decide to push down the SALARY > 50000 portion of the predicate. The last name > 'B' portion of the predicate must still be evaluated at DB2.

If the collating sequence is the same and the optimizer knows that the local DB2 server is very fast, the optimizer may decide that performing the GROUP BY operation locally at DB2 is the best (least costly) approach. The predicate will be evaluated at the data source. DB2 considers the available paths and then chooses the most efficient plan.

Analyzing Where a Query Is Evaluated

Two utilities are provided with DB2 that show where queries are evaluated:

- **Visual explain** You can start this utility with the DB2CC or the DB2VEXP command. Use it to view the query access plan graph.

- **SQL explain** You can start this utility with the DB2EXPLN or the DYNEXPLN command. Use it to view the access plan strategy as text.

The Complete Reference

Chapter 19

Data Warehousing

T he systems that contain *operational data*—the data that runs the daily transactions of your business—contain information that is useful to business analysts. However, there are several problems with analysts accessing the operational data directly:

■ They might not have the expertise to query the operational database.

■ Performance is critical for many operational databases, such as databases for a bank. The system cannot handle users making ad hoc queries.

■ The operational data is generally not in a suitable format for use by business analysts. For example, sales data that is summarized by product, region, and season is much more useful to analysts than the raw data.

Data warehousing solves these problems. In *data warehousing,* you create stores of *informational data*—data that is extracted from the operational data and then transformed for end-user decision making. For example, a data warehousing tool might copy all the sales data from the operational database, perform calculations to summarize the data, and write the summarized data to a separate database dedicated to informational data. End users can query the separate database (the data warehouse) without impacting the operational databases.

DB2 Data Warehousing Components

Figure 19-1 depicts the principal components of a DB2 data warehouse and their interrelations. The following sections describe the components and their functions.

The Warehouse Server

The *warehouse server,* installed as a part of DB2 Universal Database (UDB), runs as a Windows service on a Windows NT/2000 server. A warehouse server cannot run on any other platform. This does not mean, however, that a data warehousing system is restricted to using only Windows-based databases as sources or targets. IBM's implementation of data warehousing is based on the client/server model, enabling the warehouse server to access databases on separate machines and on various platforms.

The Warehouse Control Database

To store its technical metadata, the warehouse server uses a DB2 database: the Warehouse Control database. *Technical metadata* is associated with the design, building, and operation of a data warehouse: for example, the names of source and target tables, and security data for the data warehouse.

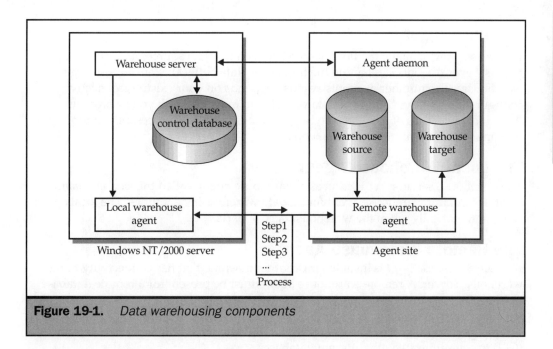

Figure 19-1. *Data warehousing components*

Warehouse Sources

Warehouse sources identify the tables and files that will provide data to your data warehouse. The data sources can be nearly any relational or nonrelational source (table, view, or file) that has connectivity to your warehouse.

It is possible to extract data from DB2, Open Database Connectivity (ODBC), and OLE DB data sources. You can also access several non-DB2 databases as warehouse sources by using ODBC drivers, including Informix, Oracle, Microsoft SQL Server, and Sybase. To avoid errors, do not configure Informix databases with Oracle or Sybase databases on the same workstation.

You can also use federated databases as data sources for your data warehouse. For more information on creating and accessing federated data sources, see Chapter 18.

Warehouse Targets

Warehouse targets are database tables or files that contain data that has been transformed so that it is meaningful for end users. Warehouse targets can also act as warehouse sources and provide other warehouse targets with data.

Warehouse Agents

Warehouse agents manage the flow of data between the data sources and the warehouse targets. Several agents can handle the transfer of data between sources and target warehouses. The number of agents you use depends on your existing connectivity configuration and the volume of data you plan to move through your warehouse. Additional instances of an agent can be generated if multiple processes that require the same agent are running simultaneously.

The Local Warehouse Agent

The warehouse server can function as a warehouse agent, called the *local warehouse agent*: the default warehouse agent for all data warehousing activities. The local agent starts automatically when the warehouse server starts.

The Remote Warehouse Agent

A *remote warehouse agent* is installed on another machine that has connectivity to the warehouse server. A remote warehouse agent must be present for a remote database to be used as a source or a target by a data warehouse.

Agents are available on the Windows NT/2000, AIX, OS/2, OS/390, OS/400, and Solaris operating systems. The agents use ODBC drivers or DB2 Call Level Interface (CLI) to communicate with different databases.

The Agent Site

An *agent site* is the logical name for a workstation where a remote warehouse agent is installed. It is possible to install multiple remote warehouse agents, such as when each is using a different database. It is also possible, therefore, to define multiple agent sites on a single machine. A logical name identifies each agent site.

The *default agent site,* named the Default VW AgentSite, is a local warehouse agent on the Windows NT/2000 server that the warehouse server defines during initialization of the warehouse control database.

The Agent Daemon

An agent daemon starts automatically after a warehouse agent (other than a local warehouse agent) has been installed. The *agent daemon* facilitates communication between the agent site and the warehouse server.

Steps and Processes

A *step* is a logical entity in the data warehouse that defines the following:

- The structure of the output table or file
- The mechanism (either SQL or a program) for populating the output table or file
- The schedule by which the output table or file is populated

Steps move and transform data by using SQL statements or by calling programs. When you run a step, the transfer of data between the warehouse source and the warehouse target—and any transformation of that data—takes place. The steps you define pass through the warehouse server to the warehouse agent, whose source or target warehouse is being called. The targeted warehouse agent then executes the steps it was sent.

A *process* contains a series of steps that perform transformation and movement tasks. In general, a process populates a warehouse target in a warehouse database by extracting data from one or more warehouse sources, which can be database tables or files. However, you can also define a process for launching programs that does not specify any warehouse sources or targets.

You can run steps in the following ways:

■ On demand.

■ According to a schedule: once or repeatedly. For instance, every Friday. If you schedule a process, the first step in the process runs at the scheduled time.

■ In sequence. When one step finishes running, the next step begins.

■ On successful or unsuccessful completion of another step.

When a step or a process runs, it can save data by doing the following:

■ Replacing all the data in the warehouse target with new data

■ Appending the new data to the existing data

■ Appending a separate edition of data

For example, suppose you want to perform the following succession of tasks:

■ Extract data from different databases.

■ Convert the data to a single format.

■ Write the data to a table in a data warehouse.

You would create a process that contained individual steps, and each step would perform a separate task, such as extracting the data from the databases or converting it to the correct format. You would then use another step to populate the target table, which contains the transformed data.

Several types of steps are available for use in the DB2 data warehousing environment:

■ **SQL steps**   SQL steps use an SQL SELECT statement to extract data from a warehouse source and generate an INSERT statement to insert the data into the warehouse target table.

■ **Program steps**   There are several types of program steps: DB2 for AS/400 programs, DB2 for OS/390 programs, DB2 for UDB programs, Visual Warehouse 5.2 DB2 programs, OLAP Server programs, file programs, and replication. These steps run predefined programs and utilities.

■ **Transformer steps**   Transformer steps are stored procedures and user-defined functions that specify statistical or warehouse transformers that you can use to transform data. You can use transformers to clean, invert, and pivot data; generate primary keys and period tables; and calculate various statistics.

In a transformer step, you specify one of the statistical or warehouse transformers. When you run the process, the transformer step writes data to one or more warehouse targets.

■ **User-defined program steps**   User-defined program steps are logical entities that represent an application that you want a warehouse agent to start. A warehouse agent can start a user-defined program step during the population of a warehouse target, after the population of a warehouse target, or by itself.

DB2 Data Warehousing Products

To implement the aforementioned data warehouse model, IBM provides two products: the Data Warehouse Center and the Data Warehouse Manager.

The Data Warehouse Center

The Data Warehouse Center is integrated with DB2 UDB 7.2 and can be accessed from the DB2 Control Center. The Data Warehouse Center simplifies the tasks of warehouse prototyping and development by assuming responsibility for governing queries, analyzing costs, managing resources, and tracking usage. It provides flexible tools and techniques for building, managing, and accessing the warehouse, such as the Process Modeler, Warehouse Schema Modeler, and data extraction functionality.

The Process Modeler

The Process Modeler allows users to graphically link the steps needed to build and maintain data warehouses. Dependency relationships, conditional processing, and notifications can all be included in the model. Processes can be scheduled for one-time or repeated execution, or they can be triggered by internal or external processes.

As a simple example, you can create steps to define the data to be included in the warehouse and then schedule automatic refreshes of the data in the warehouse.

The Warehouse Schema Modeler

Within the Data Warehouse Center, the Warehouse Schema Modeler is a specialized tool for generating and storing star schemas associated with a data warehouse. Any star schemas resulting from this process can be easily passed as metadata to an OLAP tool.

Star schemas are multidimensional arrangements of data. For a detailed description, see Chapter 20.

Data Extraction Functionality

You can define data extract and transform requests in the Data Warehouse Center by using SQL. The SQL Assist facility aids in the development of these requests, with over 100 transformations available. More sophisticated transformation requests can be built by the DB2 Stored Procedure Builder, which allows custom routines to be developed by using languages such as C++, Java, and Visual Basic.

The Data Warehouse Center provides full refresh and incremental update capabilities for data warehouse information.

The DB2 Warehouse Manager

For building global or large departmental data warehouses, use the DB2 Warehouse Manager. It is a separate product that enhances the scalability, manageability, and accessibility of Data Warehouse Center data warehouses. The Data Warehouse Manager provides the Information Catalog Manager, additional data sources, additional warehouse and statistical transformations, the Query Management Facility (QMF) for Windows, and Query Patroller.

The Warehouse Manager product applies only to DB2 Universal Database Enterprise Edition and to DB2 Universal Database Enterprise—Extended Edition.

The Information Catalog Manager

The Information Catalog Manager is an integrated business information catalog that helps users navigate a data warehouse and run associated business intelligence queries, reports, and analyses. The information catalog keeps metadata on data that end users need to access. This tool automates the exchange of metadata with the Data Warehouse Center.

The Information Catalog Manager stores descriptive data about source information. This data can include the type of information, a description of the information, what it contains, who owns and updates it, and where and how to get to it. After you find the information you need, you can start spreadsheet programs, word processors, graphics tools, or other informational applications from the Information Catalog Manager. It remains in the background while you work with the retrieved information in the associated application.

Descriptive data in the information catalog is organized into object types and objects that reflect the business categories and business terminology that your company uses. Objects can be grouped together and contained in a larger object. The object that contains the other objects is called a *grouping object*.

The Information Catalog Manager consists of several components:

- **Information Catalog Manager Tools**   This component includes the Information Catalog Administrator component and the information catalog initialization utility. You must run the information catalog initialization utility to create your information catalogs.

- **Information Catalog Administrator**   You can use this component to enable metadata exchange and to keep your information catalog current with the Warehouse Control database. The Information Catalog Administrator component includes utilities that extract descriptive data from many popular data and information sources, such as Oracle and Microsoft Excel.

- **Information Catalog User**   After you install the Information Catalog Administrator component, you can access functions for both the Information Catalog Administrator component and the Information Catalog User component. The Information Catalog User component helps the business user understand the warehouse data through a browse-and-search interface. Using this interface, business users can launch any program or command file required to display the data or business object.

- **Information Catalog Manager for the Web**   You can use this component to access information catalogs and obtain descriptions of available data, including format, currency, owner, and location. From any Web browser, users can run available helper applications to view data.

Business Metadata   The DB2 Warehouse Manager adds an information catalog to the data warehouse environment, which is used to document and manage business metadata. This information catalog helps business users navigate data warehouse information and business intelligence objects, as well as run associated queries, reports, and analyses. Business users can browse the information catalog by using both graphical and Web-based interfaces.

Business metadata is managed by the DB2 Warehouse Manager information catalog. Metadata in the DB2 Warehouse Manager information catalog is stored in a DB2 database and can be accessed and maintained by using supplied SQL and application APIs and can be imported and exported by using files formatted in a documented tag language.

The Data Warehouse Center is a metadata-driven system. You can create information catalogs that describe business metadata in business terms, organize the metadata into subject areas, and customize it to your workgroup or enterprise's needs. Then you can use the Information Catalog Manager to provide a graphical representation of data relationships and object definitions for warehouse steps.

Warehouse Agent Site Platforms

The DB2 Warehouse Manager provides remote warehouse agents for platforms other than Windows NT/2000, whereas the Data Warehouse Center provides only Windows NT/2000 agents, greatly restricting the platforms from which data can be included in a data warehouse.

The Warehouse Manager supports the following operating systems as remote agent sites:

- Microsoft Windows NT version 4.0 with Service Pack 5 or later
- Microsoft Windows 2000
- IBM AIX version 4.2 or later
- IBM OS/2 Warp version 4 or later
- IBM OS/390 version 2.6 or later
- IBM AS/400 version 4.2 or later
- Solaris Operating Environment version 2.6 or later

Warehouse Transformers

Warehouse transformers are stored procedures and user-defined functions that you can use to transform data. The DB2 Warehouse Manager includes some advanced transformations using Java stored procedures and user-defined functions, including cleaning data, pivoting tables, and generating keys.

The Query Management Facility

The Query Management Facility (QMF) for Windows is a user-friendly query and reporting tool that can publish reports either locally or on the Internet. It is a multipurpose query tool for business reporting, data sharing, server resource protection, and robust application development. Some common applications for QMF include the following:

- Building queries and reports easily using the QMF graphical interface
- Integrating query results with desktop tools, such as spreadsheets
- Rapidly building data access and update applications
- Exploiting DB2 performance and all of its SQL capabilities

The DB2 Query Patroller

The DB2 Query Patroller greatly improves the scalability of a data warehouse by allowing hundreds of users to safely submit queries on multiterabyte class systems. The DB2 Query Patroller acts as an agent on behalf of the end user. It prioritizes and schedules queries so that query completion is more predictable and computer resources are efficiently used.

After an end user submits a query, the DB2 Query Patroller frees up the user's desktop so he or she can perform other work, or even submit additional queries, while waiting for the original query results. The DB2 Query Patroller is integrated with the DB2 optimizer, performs cost analysis on queries, and then schedules and dispatches those queries so that the load is balanced across database partitions.

The DB2 Query Patroller sets individual user and group priorities, as well as user query limits. This enables the data warehouse to deliver the needed results to its most important users as quickly as possible. Large queries are typically put on hold and scheduled for a later time during nonpeak hours. The DB2 Query Patroller also has the ability to limit use of the system by stopping *runaway queries* (queries that result in an infinite loop, for instance) before they even start. If desired, an end user can choose to receive e-mail notification of scheduled query completion or query failure.

Creating a Data Warehouse

The following steps, which are meant to be followed in their presented sequence, explain the tasks involved in creating a data warehouse.

Step 1: Define Warehouse Security

Because the Data Warehouse Center stores user IDs and passwords for various databases and systems, a Data Warehouse Center security structure exists that is separate from the database and operating system security. This structure consists of warehouse groups and warehouse users.

Users gain privileges and access to Data Warehouse Center objects by belonging to a warehouse group. A *warehouse group* is a named grouping of warehouse users and *privileges*, which are the users' authorization to perform functions.

Warehouse users and warehouse groups do not need to match the database users and database groups that are defined for the warehouse control database.

Step 2: Define a Subject Area

A *subject area* identifies and groups the processes that relate to a logical area of your business. For example, if you are building a warehouse of marketing and sales data, you can define a "Sales" subject area and a "Marketing" subject area. You can then add the processes that relate to sales underneath the Sales subject area. Similarly, you can add the definitions that relate to the marketing data underneath the Marketing subject area.

For this step, you simply need to assign a name or a title for the subject area that identifies and groups the processes that you will use in your warehouse.

Step 3: Define Warehouse Sources

In defining warehouse sources, you are choosing the data to be loaded into the data warehouse. You can choose only sources of data that are visible from the warehouse server. *Visible data sources* are those on the same server as the warehouse server, or those on *agent sites* (servers with installed remote warehouse agents). You can choose multiple files, views, and tables.

Step 4: Define Warehouse Targets

Warehouse targets identify the database and tables that the Data Warehouse Center is to use for your data warehouse. Generally, the target tables that are defined in the warehouse target are also used as the dimension and fact tables in the star schema. However, the warehouse target might also include interim target tables that are used for data transformation. See Step 10 for a description of star schemas and how you can define them.

Step 5: Define Data Transformation and Movement

Define how the Data Warehouse Center is to move and transform data from the source warehouse into a format for the target warehouse. First, define a process that contains a series of steps in the data transformation and movement process. Next, specify the source tables that are to be transformed for the warehouse. Finally, define data transformation steps that use two different methods of transformation:

- Load data into the warehouse database with a program.
- Select source data and join tables with SQL statements.

Step 6: Test Warehouse Steps

The Process Model tool in the Data Warehouse Center features a TEST MODE, where you can safely run your steps. Up to this point, the steps you created were in DEVELOPMENT MODE. In development mode, you can change any of the specifications for the step. When you promote the step to test mode, the Data Warehouse Center creates the target table for the step. Therefore, after you promote a step to test mode, you can make only those changes that are not destructive to the target table. For example, you can add columns to a target table when its associated step is in test mode, but you cannot remove columns from the target table.

Step 7: Schedule Warehouse Steps

In the Data Warehouse Center, you can start a step in two ways: you can specify that a step is to start after another step has run, or you can schedule the step to start at a specified date and time. You can combine these methods to run the steps in a process.

Step 8: Perform Warehouse Administration

Before creating the information catalog, configure your data warehouse for optimal performance. The tasks include creating an index, reorganizing a table, and using the performance monitor.

You can create an index to optimize queries for end users of the warehouse. An *index* is a set of keys, each pointing to a row in a table. The index is a separate object from the table data, and the database manager builds the index structure and maintains it automatically. An index gives more efficient access to rows in a table by creating a direct path to the data through the pointers that it creates.

Reorganizing a table rearranges it in physical storage, eliminating fragmentation and making sure that the table is stored efficiently in the database. You can also use reorganization to control the order in which the rows of a table are stored, usually according to an index.

The performance monitor provides information about the state of the DB2 database and the data that it controls, and calls attention to unusual situations. The information is provided in a series of snapshots, each of which represents the state of the system and its databases at a point in time. You can control the frequency of the snapshots and the amount of information collected by each.

Step 9: Create an Information Catalog for the Warehouse

An *information catalog* is a database that contains business metadata. The metadata helps users identify and locate data and information available to them in the organization. End users of the warehouse can search the catalog to determine which tables to query.

Step 10: Define a Star Schema for Warehouse Data

A star schema is a specialized design that consists of multiple *dimension tables* (which describe aspects of a business) and one *fact table* (which contains the facts about the business). For example, if you manufacture soft drinks, some dimension tables are products, markets, and time. The fact table contains transaction information by season about the products that are ordered in each region.

Join the fact table and dimension tables to combine details from the dimension tables with the order information. For example, you could join the product dimension with the fact table to add information about how each product was packaged to the orders.

For a more complete description of star schemas and their components, see Chapter 20.

Chapter 20

Online Analytical Processing

Online analytical processing (OLAP) systems provide decision-support computing environments for business managers who need to analyze consolidated enterprise data in real time. With an OLAP system, decision-support users are able to answer complex questions about their business, and they can create various scenarios to test budgeting, sales, and marketing strategies. For example, a decision-support user might ask the following questions:

- How did a given product sell last month, and how does this figure compare to sales in the same month over the last five years?

- How well did this product sell by branch, region, and territory?

- How will this product sell next month, next quarter, and next year?

- Did commissions and pricing affect how salespeople sold this product?

Provided that the business model and the desired perspectives of business data are accurately depicted to the OLAP system, the user can expect accurate and meaningful answers to such questions.

Introducing OLAP

Relational database products such as DB2 Universal Database (UDB) are not designed for complex decision-support data analysis. DB2 UDB is exceptional in its reliability and performance for storing and retrieving data using relational tables; however, developing DB2 applications to answer the previous questions would be tedious. Where the relational database model—in its use of tables and columns—lends to high performance and maintainability, it does not lend to complex analysis. For this purpose, a multidimensional database is appropriate.

DB2 OLAP Server supports a multidimensional database that can be composed of table data from DB2 UDB, or any online transaction processing (OLTP) database. With an OLAP application, you can access relational database tables and get the results for your analytical queries in spreadsheet format.

Multidimensional Analysis

Tools that employ OLAP technology enable you to ask intuitive and complex ad hoc questions about your business. For example, "What is my profitability for the third quarter across the southeast region for my leading product line?" Such a question requires multiple perspectives of the data, such as time, regions, and products. Each of these perspectives are also known as a *dimension*. The DB2 OLAP Server enables you to organize your data into multiple dimensions for analysis.

Relational data is considered to be two-dimensional because each piece of data—also known as a *fact*—correlates to one row and one column (each of which can be considered a dimension). Dimensions represent the core components of a business plan and often relate to business functions. Accounts, Time, Products, and Regions are typical dimensions. In most databases, dimensions are static, rarely changing over the life of an application.

Each dimension has individual components, known as *members*. For example, the quarters of the year can be members of the Time dimension; individual products can be members of the Products dimension. A dimension can contain an unlimited number of members, but each member must have a unique name. You can have hierarchies of members within dimensions, such as months within the quarters of the Time dimension. Members can simultaneously be parents of some members and children of other members. Unlike dimensions, members and member hierarchies tend to change over time, for instance, as your business grows and new products are added.

The data in a multidimensional database can originate from a variety of sources, such as OLTP databases, text files, and spreadsheet files. The DB2 OLAP Integration Server (described in the section "DB2 OLAP Integration Server") enables you to access data for an OLAP model from a data source that is configured for Open Database Connectivity (ODBC) and that supports SQL 89 or later.

DB2 OLAP Server Components

DB2 OLAP Server is based on the OLAP technology that was developed by Hyperion Solutions Corporation. As a result, you will see references to Hyperion Essbase and Hyperion Integration Server in the product interface and throughout the online documentation.

DB2 OLAP Server includes all of the capabilities of Hyperion Essbase. In addition, it offers the option of storing multidimensional databases as sets of relational tables. Regardless of the storage management option that you choose, you can use the Essbase Application Manager and Essbase commands to create an Essbase application and its associated databases. For further information regarding the Essbase commands, see the online help and the Hyperion documentation.

DB2 OLAP Server supports a variety of platforms: Windows NT/2000, AIX, Solaris, and HP-UX. For best performance, it is recommended that you install the two server components (DB2 OLAP Server and DB2 OLAP Integration Server) on the same machine. Workstation client access to the DB2 OLAP Server is restricted to the Windows NT/2000 platform. However, API access is available for the following platforms: Windows 95/98/ NT/2000, AIX, Solaris, and HP-UX.

Figure 20-1 shows the main components in the DB2 OLAP Server environment. The sections that follow the figure describe each of the depicted components.

DB2 OLAP Server Engine

DB2 OLAP Server uses the Essbase OLAP engine for application design and management, data access and navigation, data load, data calculation, APIs, and the Spreadsheet Add-ins.

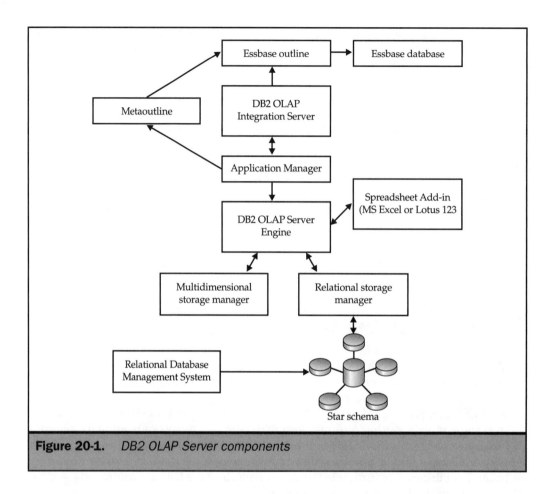

Figure 20-1. *DB2 OLAP Server components*

DB2 OLAP Server operates in a client/server environment as a server to clients such as the Application Manager or DB2 OLAP Integration Server. When the relational storage manager (RSM) is used, it is also a client to a relational database management system (RDBMS).

Relational Storage Manager

In providing improved flexibility, the relational storage manager separates the OLAP engine from the database and provides support for DB2. You can manage the data that is stored by your OLAP applications by using familiar database management, backup, and recovery tools.

Star Schema   When using the RSM, DB2 OLAP Server stores data in a relational database using a star schema data structure. You can access the star schema by using

DB2 OLAP Server clients, and you can access the multidimensional data stored in the star schema by using standard SQL statements. The star schema implementation enables data in relational database tables to be represented in a multidimensional format.

The RSM automatically creates and manages the necessary relational tables, views, and indexes within the star schema. For increased performance, you can specify that the star schema be populated with calculated data. Star schemas, also known as OLAP models, are discussed in greater detail in the later section "Creating an OLAP Application."

Multidimensional Storage Manager

DB2 OLAP Server augments the relational storage manager with a multidimensional data storage manger (MDSM). The MDSM is useful for applications where performance is the critical requirement. This component is also referred to as the storage manager, or the Essbase kernel. The MDSM and the RSM can coexist in the same installation of DB2 OLAP Server.

DB2 OLAP Integration Server

The DB2 OLAP Integration Server is based on the Hyperion Integration Server product. It is accessed with the Application Manager, a graphical interface for easily mapping relational data sources to OLAP structures to create OLAP applications.

In short, an OLAP application developer defines a metaoutline based on a star schema, and from this, the DB2 OLAP Integration Server creates an Essbase outline. DB2 OLAP Integration Server then quickly transfers data from relational tables to an Essbase database through an Essbase outline. OLAP applications access at least one Essbase database. The attributes and functions of the DB2 OLAP Integration Server components are further described in the later section "Creating an OLAP Metaoutline."

DB2 OLAP Starter Kit

The DB2 OLAP Starter Kit provides a subset of the functionality in IBM DB2 OLAP Server and is provided free in DB2 UDB. You can use the desktop interface provided by the DB2 OLAP Integration Server to develop OLAP applications, and analyze the applications by using the Spreadsheet Add-ins in Microsoft Excel or Lotus 1-2-3. The Spreadsheet Add-ins are included with the Starter Kit.

The applications that you can create are OLAP applications with limited users and scope. If you find the DB2 OLAP Starter Kit useful for your business environment and want to expand the use and scope of your OLAP applications, you can purchase the full-function IBM DB2 OLAP Server and the full-function DB2 OLAP Integration Server.

Creating an OLAP Application

The primary tool for creating OLAP applications is the DB2 OLAP Integration Server, which is accessed by the Application Manager. It contains a wizard to guide you through both steps in creating an OLAP application: creating an OLAP model and creating a metaoutline. With a completed OLAP application, decision-support users can analyze business data by using Lotus 1-2-3 or Microsoft Excel Spreadsheet Add-ins.

Creating an OLAP Model

The first step in creating an OLAP application is to establish an *OLAP model*; this is used to represent your business plan to the DB2 OLAP Server. As was discussed previously in the section "DB2 OLAP Server Engine," business database data values are known as facts, and different perspectives of that data are known as dimensions. A star schema is a logical structure that combines facts and dimensions, enabling it to represent a business plan in functioning as an OLAP model.

A star schema is composed of a *fact table* and a set of *dimension tables*. At the center of the star schema, the fact table holds the actual data values for the OLAP database. Radiating from the fact table are the dimension tables, which define the OLAP dimensions and contain data about their members and relationships. Figure 20-2 depicts a star schema (or OLAP model). One or just a few OLAP models can represent most aspects of your business.

You can use DB2 Integration Server Desktop or the Application Manager to create an OLAP model that loads the business data you wish to analyze from a relational database. The following steps are involved in creating an OLAP model:

1. Create a fact table.
2. Create an Accounts dimension, a Time dimension, and other applicable dimensions.
3. Join dimension tables, where appropriate.
4. Establish hierarchies.

Creating a Fact Table

The fact table is composed of one or more relational tables that contain facts (such as units sold or cost of goods), and foreign keys that link the fact table to each dimension table. Information that goes into the fact table must have the following characteristics:

- **Numeric**   The data must be numeric to generate averages or summaries.
- **Additive values**   To summarize a high number of values, data should be additive, or at least semiadditive, so that the DB2 OLAP Server can generate useful, nonmisleading information.
- **Consistently valued**   To effectively evaluate and monitor changes in a business over time, values of data must be weighted on a consistent basis and share the same level of granularity.

Figure 20-3 features a sample fact table, based on the star schema depicted in Figure 20-2.

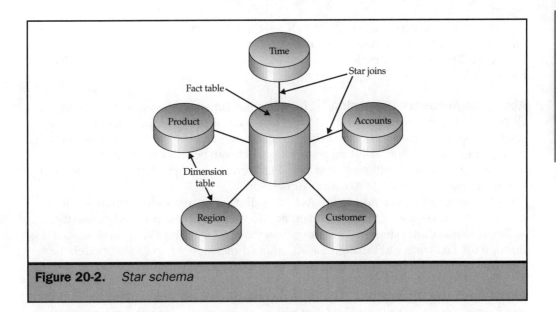

Figure 20-2.   *Star schema*

Creating Dimension Tables

Each dimension table contains data that is related to facts in the fact table. When you join a dimension table to the fact table, the dimension table forms a dimension—a perspective of the business' data.

The structure of the star schema is defined by joins between the dimension tables and the fact table. It is possible to hide columns in the dimension tables so that the columns do not appear as members of the dimensions in the model.

There are three types of dimension tables: Accounts dimension, Time dimension, and Standard dimension. The first two tables are highly specialized, and they serve an important function in the OLAP model. Standard dimension tables are general in their purpose; there is no limit to the number of these tables that you can define.

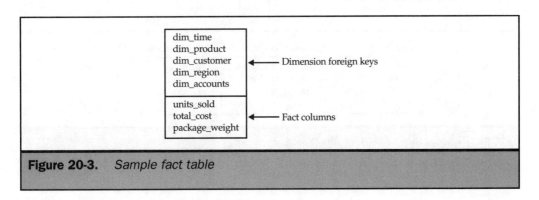

Figure 20-3.   *Sample fact table*

When you create a dimension in an OLAP model, the dimension becomes available for use in creating a dimension in an associated metaoutline.

Figure 20-4 features sample dimension tables based on the star schema depicted in Figure 20-2.

About the Accounts Dimension   The Accounts dimension is mandatory in an OLAP model. It contains numeric data that you want to analyze and track over time, such as sales or inventory. This data is also called *measures data* and enables accounting intelligence during online analytical processing. There can be only one Accounts dimension for a given star schema, although it is possible to create multiple Accounts dimension hierarchies within the single Accounts dimension.

Any columns that you add to the Accounts dimension are added automatically to the fact table. Likewise, columns that you add to the fact table are added automatically to the Accounts dimension. All measures data that you want reported is referenced through the fact table and through the Accounts dimension. In an OLAP model, the fact table and the Accounts dimension are mirror images of each other.

About the Time Dimension   The Time dimension describes how often you collect and update data. You can use Time dimension members, such as year and quarter, to report yearly and quarterly totals for members of other dimensions; for example, total sales of books in Toronto for the first quarter.

It is not mandatory to include a Time dimension in an OLAP model. However, if an application requires analysis to be performed on a time basis, such as examining trends over time or making seasonal sales comparisons, you should include a Time dimension. You can create only one Time dimension in an OLAP model, but you can create many Time dimension hierarchies within that single Time dimension. For example, a time hierarchy can include month, quarter, and year members whereby monthly totals roll up to quarterly totals and quarterly totals roll up to yearly totals.

In an OLAP model, you create a Time dimension to provide a time structure from which to create a Time dimension in an associated metaoutline. You cannot create a Time dimension in a metaoutline if you do not create a dimension that contains a time value in the associated OLAP model.

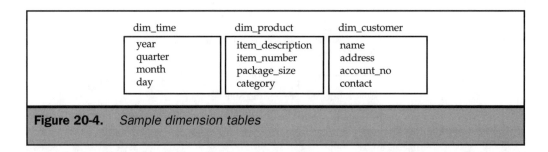

Figure 20-4.   *Sample dimension tables*

Defining Hierarchies

Hierarchies organize parent–child relationships among the columns of a dimension. For example, in the Time dimension, you might define the year member as the top of the hierarchy. The quarter member would be a child of year, and month would be a child of quarter. Creating hierarchies in an OLAP model provides a multilevel structure that you can view when creating dimensions in metaoutlines.

Creating an OLAP Metaoutline

A *metaoutline* describes how information in the OLAP model will be presented to the OLAP application user. Each metaoutline presents a particular portrayal of your business. To create a metaoutline, you need to use the OLAP model that contains the dimensions of the business you want the metaoutline to present. You can create any number of OLAP models for use in building metaoutlines; however, each metaoutline is based on one specific OLAP model. You can tailor the scope of a metaoutline by selecting which dimensions will be visible to OLAP users, and by setting filters that determine which data is retrieved.

Required Metaoutline Components

The following are required components for metaoutlines:

- **Measures data**   Every metaoutline that you use to build an Essbase outline must include at least one measures value. This is because the Essbase database calculates data values, or measures, for each dimension intersection of the associated metaoutline. If you do not define at least one measure in a metaoutline, DB2 OLAP Integration Server cannot validate the metaoutline; consequently, it will not be able to use the metaoutline to build an Essbase outline.

- **Dimensions**   A metaoutline requires at least two dimensions. For every dimension present in a metaoutline, a corresponding dimension is created in the associated Essbase outline.

- **Member Levels**   A metaoutline requires at least one member level. Member levels in metaoutlines and Essbase outlines correspond to member hierarchies in dimension tables. A member level in a metaoutline creates one or more members at the same level in the associated Essbase outline.

While adding member levels to a metaoutline, you can define a set of filters and transformation rules. These determine which members of a member level the DB2 OLAP Integration Server will add to the associated Essbase outline, and which transformations (if any) it will perform on the members of a member level.

You can also arrange member levels into a hierarchy for the metaoutline in the same manner you would in an OLAP model.

Creating an OLAP Application

An OLAP metaoutline is a key component in creating an OLAP application. A metaoutline is based on an OLAP model (a star schema), and it contains the basic structure required to build an Essbase outline. Before the Essbase outline is built, the metaoutline filters the data from the relational data source (according to the metaoutline designer's specifications). The Essbase outline is the component used to load (filtered) data from the appropriate star schemas into an Essbase database. OLAP applications then access one or more Essbase databases to perform an analysis. Figure 20-5 depicts this application creation process.

It is possible to use a metaoutline as the basis for more than one Essbase outline. Furthermore, if you define a metaoutline in a central location, it is possible for it to be used to create various Essbase outlines in multiple locations.

Metaoutlines are created by using the Application Manager interface for the DB2 OLAP Integration Server. In this environment, it is possible to view sample Essbase outlines before you build them.

Accessing OLAP Data with a Spreadsheet

The Spreadsheet Add-ins provide Microsoft Excel and Lotus 1-2-3 with an interface to an OLAP application to enable analysis of multidimensional databases. When you install DB2 OLAP Server, a special menu is added to the spreadsheet program, containing enhanced commands such as Connect, Pivot, Drill-Down, and Calculate. Users can access and analyze data on the DB2 OLAP Server by using simple mouse clicks and drag-and-drop operations. The DB2 OLAP Spreadsheet Add-ins enable multiple users to access and update data on the DB2 OLAP Server simultaneously.

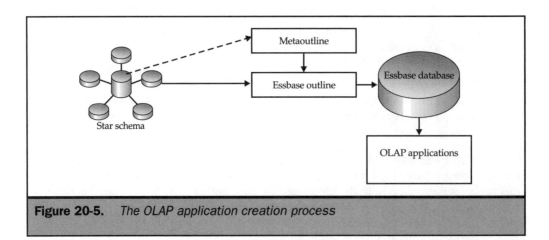

Figure 20-5. *The OLAP application creation process*

The Complete Reference

Part VII

Application Development

Chapter 21

Introduction to Application Development

In most cases, you don't purchase a database management system with the intention of inserting, updating, and retrieving information by manually issuing individual SQL statements. Even if you could afford the time and specialized knowledge needed to design and issue each statement required for different uses of the data, such as generating summary data for business reports or mining data for cluster analysis, you would want to capture that knowledge for reuse in subsequent applications. You really need to develop applications using one or more application programming interfaces (APIs) to efficiently achieve the following goals:

- Automating repetitive and complex tasks
- Achieving platform independence
- Communicating with other applications
- Developing a flexible, usable interface
- Supporting required database functions
- Achieving acceptable performance

This chapter briefly discusses these common goals of application development and then describes many of the popular APIs used to develop DB2 applications using these goals as differentiating criteria.

Automating Repetitive and Complex Tasks

To be the least bit useful, a database application must make your work easier by reducing the need for you to perform similar, repetitive tasks, particularly if those tasks require complex operations involving many database objects. Many database applications are nothing more than scripts that automate administrative tasks like backing up and replicating databases, exporting data, reorganizing tables, and updating statistics for tables.

Any of the APIs discussed in this chapter can achieve the goal of automating repetitive and complex tasks, depending on the functional capabilities of the API. For example, you can write a Java Database Connectivity (JDBC) application that automates data entry and reporting functions, but to perform administrative functions like backing up a database, you need to choose a different language that supports the administrative APIs or administration commands.

Achieving Platform Independence

Choosing an API with the flexibility to run on multiple or most operating systems and hardware combinations might be an important consideration, particularly if scalability has been defined as a requirement in your decision. Scalability implies being able to scale up to take advantage of more powerful hardware such as a mainframe, or scaling down to fit into the footprint of a handheld device. You might want to cut licensing expenses by switching to an operating system like Linux, or to take advantage of commodity hardware prices to create a clustered database environment.

DB2 can operate in all of these situations, but the APIs you use to develop your applications might not. For example, if you choose to develop applications using Microsoft ActiveX Data Objects (ADO), you might be limited to using Microsoft operating systems for both your database clients and servers.

Communicating with Other Applications

An existing development environment in which you install a DB2 database server depends on an existing set of applications. As middleware, DB2 must be able to communicate with other applications as varied as web servers, storage management software, or dynamic front-end tools like Excel. You typically do not have the luxury of replacing the entire infrastructure to suit your preferred database APIs, so your choices depend to some extent on the compatibility of the database APIs with the existing applications in your infrastructure and the role the DB2 database server plays in that infrastructure.

For example, an infrastructure that runs Java clients can easily be extended to include JDBC or Embedded SQL for Java (SQLj) interfaces to the database, and you can use Java servlets on popular web servers like Apache to access the DB2 database. If users currently generate reports with a front-end tool like Excel, your choices might be restricted to the Microsoft Open Database Connectivity (ODBC) or ADO APIs if you want to avoid disrupting current practices.

Of course, it is quite acceptable to use multiple APIs to perform tasks that interoperate with other software, matching the API that best fits the task with the existing software that you need to extend. For example, you can fairly easily create PHP:Hypertext Processor (PHP) applications that run on a web server like Apache to provide a web browser interface to some of your data, write Perl or Python libraries that extend your current set of administrative task automation scripts, and use ADO in developing Microsoft Visual Basic applications to quickly create graphical Windows clients for end users.

Developing a Flexible, Usable Interface

The interface required by your DB2 application is another important criterion for determining which API you will use to develop the application. For developing a graphical user interface (GUI), Java provides the Swing library of GUI elements, while Microsoft Visual Studio offers an integrated development environment for creating a GUI by dragging and dropping elements. Perl and Python also offer a number of libraries that provide access to GUI toolkits, like Tk.

If your target client is a web browser, then obvious candidates for database APIs are PHP and Net.Data. These APIs work in conjunction with a web server to dynamically generate web pages incorporating queries to the underlying database server. Net.Data and PHP can also issue Data Manipulation Language (DML) statements to the database, typically as the result of a submission by Common Gateway Interface (CGI) forms. Other popular choices for web page scripting are the Perl and Python scripting languages, which can run either as CGI applications or, on web servers like Apache, as an interpreter embedded into the web server. Java APIs like JDBC and SQLj can be used in servlets to provide database access.

For command line interfaces, you can choose from almost any of these interfaces. Perl, Python, REXX, and even simple CLP scripts are appropriate choices for straightforward scripting tasks. Embedded SQL, administrative APIs, or the Call Level Interface (CLI) are appropriate for more complex applications; you can even combine all three in a single C program to take advantage of each API's unique strengths. The Java APIs are also relatively easy to develop for command line interfaces, although the decision is subject to the system resources required by the Java runtime environment and, depending on the task, to performance considerations.

Supporting Required Database Functions

An important part of deciding on any database API is determining whether the API will support the database function that you require for your application. For example, embedded SQL might be an attractive API based on its relative simplicity and interoperability across the DB2 family of database servers, but the inability to call stored procedures that return result sets might force you to choose a different API. To perform administrative functions with the database server, an API must provide either strong support for command-line scripting or incorporate the ability to call the administrative APIs—effectively ruling out the Java, Net.Data, SQL procedure, and PHP interfaces.

Achieving Acceptable Performance

The performance required for your application might have some influence on your choice of database APIs or how the APIs are implemented. For example, Perl scripts that run from the command line require the client to initialize a new copy of the Perl interpreter each time the script is run. Perl scripts invoked by a web server as CGI scripts are subject to the same performance penalty unless the Perl interpreter is embedded into the web server environment. You will probably wring the best performance out of your database server by writing your applications in a compiled language such as C with the embedded SQL, CLI, or administrative APIs.

To enhance the performance of almost any application, consider using server-side applications like SQL procedures to perform significant preprocessing of your data on the database server and to avoid passing unnecessary data over the network.

DB2 Application Development APIs and Languages

The following sections provide more details on the capabilities and limitations of the most common application development APIs and languages, along with one or more references for further information.

ActiveX Data Objects

Most ADO applications are written in Microsoft Visual Basic or using Microsoft Visual Studio. It's relatively easy to develop GUI applications that run on Windows workstations and that can access data from both DB2 and non-DB2 data sources that provide an OLE DB provider interface. However, this approach effectively rules out using non-Windows operating systems as clients for your application. You can also serve up web pages to browsers on clients using any operating system by calling ADO functions within Active Server Pages (ASP) processed by the Microsoft Internet Information Server (IIS). The ADO interface enables you to perform typical data access functions like selecting, inserting, and updating data and calling stored procedures.

To connect to a data source like a DB2 database server, ADO requires the services of an OLE DB provider interface. On Windows operating systems, DB2 ships with a native OLE DB provider called the IBM OLE DB Provider for DB2 Servers. To connect to a DB2 database using the native OLE DB provider in a Visual Basic program, set the ADODB.Connection.Provider property to "IBMDADB2":

```
Dim db As ADODB.Connection;
Set db = New ADODB.Connection;
db.Provider = "IBMDADB2";
...
```

If the IBM OLE DB Provider for DB2 Servers does not provide the function required in your application, consider using the OLE DB Provider for ODBC, which uses ODBC as an interface to the DB2 database. To connect to a DB2 database using the OLE DB Provider for ODBC in a Visual Basic program, leave the ADODB.Connection.Provider property unspecified:

```
Dim db As ADODB.Connection;
Set db = New ADODB.Connection;
```

Further information on the following topics is available from these sources:

- If you are writing applications using the IBM OLE DB Provider for DB2 Servers, see http://www.ibm.com/software/data/db2/udb/ad/v7/oledb.html.

- For information on ADO, see http://www.microsoft.com/data/ado/.

Administrative APIs

The DB2 administrative APIs are a set of functions you can easily call from C, C++, COBOL, Fortran, or REXX programs to perform administrative tasks like backing up and restoring databases. The administrative APIs do not provide an interface for selecting or manipulating data, so to combine administrative tasks with data access, you can mix calls to administrative APIs with calls to a data access API like CLI or embedded SQL. For example, you can restart the database in a C program by using an administrative API:

```
db2DatabaseRestart (versionNumber, pParamStruct, pSqlca);
```

You can use other languages to call the administrative APIs if those languages provide an interface to C libraries, and if you take the time to build and test the wrapper code for the administrative APIs you require. Some common languages that offer support for calling functions in other languages are the following: Java, which provides the Java Native Interface (JNI); Perl, which provides the Perl::XS module; and Python, which documents how to extend base Python functions with C or C++ code libraries. A product that supports many languages is the Simplified Wrapper and Interface Generator (SWIG).

Calling any administrative APIs from languages other than those documented as the supported languages in the official IBM documentation is not an officially supported practice.

Chapter 23 provides further information on using administrative APIs, as well as the following IBM publications distributed with DB2 or freely accessible at http://www. ibm.com/software/data/db2/library/:

■ *IBM DB2 Universal Database Administrative API Reference Version 7*

■ *IBM DB2 Universal Database Application Building Guide Version 7*

For information on using administrative APIs with other languages, see these sources:

■ **Java Native Interface**   http://java.sun.com/j2se/1.3/docs/guide/jni/index.html

■ **Perl::XS**   http://www.perldoc.com/perl5.6/pod/perlxs.html

■ **Python**   http://www.python.org/doc/current/ext/ext.html

■ **SWIG**   http://www.swig.org

Call Level Interface

CLI provides the native dynamic SQL interface to DB2 as an implementation of the X/ Open CLI and ISO/IEC Call Level Interface specifications. As a dynamic SQL interface, DB2 applications written in CLI generate the access plan for each SQL statement at run time and therefore can suffer some performance penalties compared to static SQL issued in an embedded SQL application. However, this disadvantage is balanced by the opportunity to take advantage of the latest database statistics to optimize the SQL statement. Also, after a statement has been prepared once, a CLI application can reissue the same statement multiple times in the same session without having to regenerate the access plan.

The CLI API offers a comprehensive set of functions for working with SQL objects. The only drawback to writing CLI applications is the relative complexity of learning an entire library of functions and the lack of good integrated development environment (IDE) support.

A common approach to writing CLI applications is to initially develop the application using the ODBC API, which in most respects is functionally identical to the CLI API. This approach enables programmers to take advantage of IDE support for ODBC, and then make the minor modifications necessary to convert the application to the CLI API and take advantage of the better performance available from using the native dynamic SQL interface to DB2. For example, the following CLI source code could also be compiled as an ODBC application:

```
SQLCHAR * stmt = (SQLCHAR *) "SELECT firstnme, midinit FROM employee";
sqlrc = SQLExecDirect(hstmt, stmt, SQL_NTS);
sqlrc = SQLBindCol(hstmt, 1, SQL_C_CHAR, firstnme, 13, &firstind);
sqlrc = SQLBindCol(hstmt, 2, SQL_C_CHAR, midinit, 2, &midinitind);
sqlrc = SQLFetch(hstmt);
printf("\n    %-12.12s %-1.1s", firstnme, midinit);
```

For further information on CLI, see Chapter 24, as well as the following sources:

- *IBM DB2 Universal Database Application Building Guide Version 7*
- *IBM DB2 Universal Database Call Level Interface Guide and Reference Version 7*
- Official CLI standard: ISO/IEC 9075-3 Database Languages-SQL-Part 3: Call-Level Interface, at http://www.iso.ch

Embedded SQL

An embedded SQL application is a collection of SQL statements embedded within the source files of a standard programming language like C, C++, COBOL, or Fortran. Writing embedded SQL programs is a fast method of developing DB2 applications because you use the standard syntax of your chosen programming language for control structures.

The syntax required for embedding SQL statements is quite simple compared to learning an entirely new set of APIs for an interface like the Call Level Interface. You can use C, C++, COBOL, and Fortran as host languages for embedded SQL on the same platforms on which DB2 supports those languages. The following code demonstrates how a host variable passes data between an SQL statement and regular C statements in an embedded SQL program:

```
EXEC SQL BEGIN DECLARE SECTION;
  char firstname[13];
```

```
EXEC SQL END DECLARE SECTION;
/* Retrieve some data /*
EXEC SQL SELECT FIRSTNME INTO :firstname
        FROM employee
        WHERE LASTNAME = 'JOHNSON';
printf("First name is: %s", firstname);
```

To create an executable application, you precompile the source code to convert the embedded SQL statements to calls to the run-time APIs, and you bind the application against the database to create an access plan for the package of SQL statements issued by the application. The application will use the access plan generated when you bind the package, even if the composition of the database changes dramatically to potentially offer more efficient access plans.

For example, if you add a unique index on a table used by an embedded SQL application, the application will not be able to use that index to access data in the table until you rebind the package for the application. Embedded SQL applications are therefore initially quite efficient, but without regular maintenance, their efficiency can deteriorate as the composition of the database changes. In contrast, dynamic SQL APIs like CLI or JDBC pay a performance penalty the first time they issue an SQL statement because they must create an access plan for the statement. However, subsequent calls to the same statement use the cached version of the access plan.

Embedded SQL might not be the right API to use if your database architecture relies heavily on stored procedures to abstract common SQL queries at the server level. You can call stored procedures using embedded SQL, but you can pass parameters only between the client application and the stored procedure. You cannot return result sets to an embedded SQL application. For example, you can call a stored procedure that returns the total number of accounts that are more than 60 days overdue, but the stored procedure cannot return a list of those accounts to an embedded SQL application.

Further information is available in Chapter 22, as well as in the following sources:

- *IBM DB2 Universal Database Application Building Guide Version 7*
- *IBM DB2 Universal Database Application Development Guide Version 7*

Embedded SQL for Java

The SQLj API enables you to develop DB2 applications in Java by using embedded SQL statements. This is similar to precompiling and binding embedded SQL in other programming languages; you must translate the SQLj source code into JDBC source code, and then customize the profile for the embedded SQL statements into an SQL package on the database server. The SQLj API has been accepted as both an ANSI and an ISO/IEC standard; in addition to DB2, SQLj is also supported by database management systems offered by Informix, Oracle, and Sybase.

The following code demonstrates how a host variable passes data between an SQL statement and regular Java statements in an SQLj program.

```
short activity = 10;
String employee = null;
try {
     #sql { SELECT empno INTO :employee
           FROM emp_act
           WHERE actno = :activity
           AND projno = 'AD3100' };
}
System.out.println("Employee = " + employee);
```

SQLj applications use the JDBC API to establish database connections, and you can mix SQLj statements freely with JDBC methods. This enables you to optimize your application by issuing static SQL statements with SQLj and issuing dynamic SQL statements with JDBC for statements that are likely to benefit from updated database statistics. You must balance the possible performance advantage of SQLj statements against the increased overhead of translating the source code and customizing the profiles of SQLj applications.

For further information, see Chapter 25, as well as the following sources:

- *IBM DB2 Universal Database Application Building Guide Version 7*

- *IBM DB2 Universal Database Application Development Guide Version 7*

- SQLj.org, at http://www.sqlj.org

- Official SQLj standard: Information Technology - Database Languages - SQL - Part 10: Object Language Bindings (SQL/OLB): ANSI X3.135.10-1998, ISO/ IEC 9075-10:2000, at http://www.iso.ch

Java Database Connectivity

JDBC is a Java standard for database access with dynamic SQL; it is based on the X/Open SQL Call Level Interface specification. The JDBC API is distributed with the Java runtime environment in the java.sql.* packages, and it relies on database-specific drivers to implement the API methods. DB2 ships with JDBC drivers that implement both the JDBC 1.20 and JDBC 2.0 specifications.

JDBC applications have the great advantage of running on almost every platform, and drivers are available for almost every database server, so you can easily port your applications between DB2 servers on different platforms without even recompiling. To port a JDBC application from DB2 to a different database server, you simply specify the different database driver within the initialization section of the application.

The JDBC API is well documented as part of the Java API documentation distributed with software development kits for Java. As you would expect of a Java API, JDBC provides an object-oriented interface to the database. A Connection object serves as the basis of all other interactions with the database. For example, the following code returns all of the rows from a SELECT statement as a ResultSet object:

```
Connection con = DriverManager.getConnection("jdbc:db2:sample");
Statement stmt = con.createStatement();
String select = "SELECT firstnme, midinit FROM employee";
ResultSet rs = stmt.executeQuery(select);
// print each row in the ResultSet
while (rs.next()) {
  System.out.println("First name: " + rs.getString("firstnme")
    + " Initial: " + rs.getString("midinit"));
}
```

JDBC is a very good choice for developing highly portable applications that, due to constraints imposed by the Java runtime environment, do not require extremely high performance or a small memory footprint. You can create a GUI database application in Java by using the standard Swing packages, incorporate functions provided by any of the other standard Java packages, compile the application with a freely available Java compiler, and distribute the entire application as a single Java Archive (JAR) file for use on multiple platforms without requiring a recompile of the source code.

The DB2 JDBC net driver provides the unique ability to connect to a DB2 database without installing a DB2 client on your local workstation. However, the performance and stability of this Thin-client approach is significantly poorer than using the DB2 JDBC application driver with a locally installed DB2 client. This architecture is not generally recommended for production use.

See Chapter 25 for further information on using JDBC, as well as the following sources:

- *IBM DB2 Universal Database Application Building Guide Version 7*
- *IBM DB2 Universal Database Application Development Guide Version 7*

The following online sources provide information on the JDBC APIs:

- The JDBC 1.20 API specification can be found at http://java.sun.com/j2se/1.3/docs/guide/jdbc/spec/jdbc-spec.frame.html.
- The JDBC 2.1 API specification can be found at http://java.sun.com/j2se/1.3/docs/guide/jdbc/spec2/jdbc2.1.frame.html.
- The Java 2 Platform API documentation can be found at http://java.sun.com/j2se/1.3/docs/api/index.html.

Net.Data

Net.Data is an IBM proprietary scripting language for producing dynamic web pages that access DB2 databases, Oracle databases, ODBC data sources, and even data stored in flat files. Net.Data ships with most versions of DB2. It supports the CGI and FastCGI web server interfaces, and in conjunction with its own macro language, Net.Data supports programming languages such as Java, Perl, and REXX.

A Net.Data macro for inserting a row into a database can be as simple as the following example:

```
%FUNCTION(DTW_SQL) insertStaff() {
INSERT INTO staff(id, name, dept)
VALUES('$(id)','$(name)','$(dept)')
  %MESSAGE{
    default: "insertStaff: Unexpected Error"
  %}
%}
```

Using Net.Data to serve up DB2 database information on the web is a technically sound approach to creating web applications. Net.Data provides a broad set of functions and it ships with DB2, implying that any necessary service and support should be fairly straightforward. The drawback of choosing Net.Data is that there does not appear to be as much of a development community compared to technologies like PHP or ASP, which fill a similar niche.

You can find further information in the following source:

■ *IBM Net.Data for OS/2, Windows NT, and UNIX Administration and Programming Guide Version 7*

Online information is also available on the Net.Data web site:

■ http://www.ibm.com/software/data/net.data/

Open Database Connectivity

ODBC, a dynamic SQL interface to DB2 and other databases, is an industry-standard database access API developed by Microsoft. The interface is based on the X/Open CLI and ISO/IEC Call Level Interface specifications, and therefore shares much in common with the DB2 CLI API.

ODBC applications for DB2 incur a performance penalty relative to CLI applications because the ODBC support in DB2 is implemented as a layer on top of CLI. You can write your CLI applications to use only those functions supported by ODBC, so that you can compile the application using CLI for the best performance on DB2; then you can recompile the application using ODBC if you need to port the application to another database server.

Many third-party applications use ODBC as a generic data access interface. On Windows operating systems, DB2 ships with an ODBC driver that the Windows ODBC driver manager can use to access DB2 databases. On UNIX platforms, you can use the libdb2.so shared library that ships with DB2 as an ODBC driver. You load this driver by using a third-party ODBC driver manager such as the unixODBC Driver Manager or the iODBC Driver Manager.

Chapter 24 provides further information, as does the following source:

■ *IBM DB2 Universal Database Call Level Interface Guide and Reference Version 7*

The following online sources are also available:

■ Microsoft ODBC documentation is at http://www.microsoft.com/data/odbc.

■ unixODBC Driver Manager code and documentation is at http://www.unixodbc.com.

■ iODBC Driver Manager code and documentation is at http://www.iodbc.org.

Perl

The Perl scripting language, originally intended for system administration tasks, has evolved into a sophisticated language capable of satisfying almost any application requirement. You can write Perl scripts that automate DB2 database administration tasks by issuing DB2 commands through the system() function. To issue SQL statements, you can use the Perl Database Interface (DBI) module through the DB2 database driver (DB2::DBD). To create a GUI for your database application, you can use the Perl/Tk extension to access the Tk 4 widget toolkit. To create dynamic web pages, you can easily write CGI scripts in Perl and enhance the performance of your scripts by embedding a copy of the Perl interpreter in your web server. Perl is freely available on every platform on which DB2 is offered.

The Perl DBI is another database access API that borrows heavily from the X/Open CLI and ISO/IEC Call Level Interface specifications. The architecture is quite similar, but the Perl DBI offers a simplified interface that makes it easy to write database applications. For example, the following Perl code connects to a DB2 database and retrieves a simple result set:

```
use strict;
use DBI;
my ($firstnme, $lastname);
my $dbh = DBI->connect("dbi:DB2:sample", "db2inst1", "ibmdb2");
my $sth = $dbh->prepare("SELECT firstnme, lastname FROM employee");
$sth->execute();
while (($firstnme, $lastname) = $sth->fetchrow()) {
  print "$lastname, $firstnme\n";
```

```
}
$sth->finish();
$dbh->disconnect();
```

Perl is a good all-purpose language for writing DB2 database applications. Its ability to easily incorporate system commands, SQL statements, and GUI widgets without requiring compile and link steps makes it especially good for rapid prototyping or writing quick throwaway scripts. Perl's user community provides plenty of general resources in the form of books, web sites, and newsgroups, and IBM officially supports the DBD::DB2 driver. One of the only drawbacks of using Perl as a language for your database applications is that if you are purely interested in performance, the Perl interpreter will likely be unable to match the performance of embedded SQL or CLI applications.

For further information, refer to this source:

- *IBM DB2 Universal Database Application Development Guide Version 7*

Online sources are also available:

- The Perl DBI web site is at http://dbi.perl.org/.
- The Perl DBI module can be found at http://www.perl.com/CPAN-local/modules/by-module/DBI/.
- The Perl DBD::DB2 driver can be found at http://www.ibm.com/software/data/db2/perl/.

PHP: Hypertext Processor

PHP is a powerful and increasingly popular server-side scripting language for generating dynamic web pages. It is comparable to ASP in that you embed PHP function calls within regular HTML pages, but it offers the advantages that you can compile and run the PHP interpreter on most platforms, and PHP is an open-source, freely available language.

PHP provides a database access API called the Unified ODBC functions. As the name implies, the API resembles a simplified version of the ODBC API. For example, the following PHP code invokes the Unified ODBC functions to generate a web page showing the results of an SQL query:

```
<html>
<head>
  <title>PHP result set</title>
</head>
<body>
  <?php
```

APPLICATION
DEVELOPMENT

```
    $connection = odbc_connect("SAMPLE", "db2inst1", "ibmdb2");
    $stmt = "SELECT firstnme, lastname FROM employee";
    $rs = odbc_exec($connection, $stmt);
    odbc_result_all($rs);
    odbc_close($connection);
  ?>
</body>
</html>
```

PHP's ability to run on most platforms and its portable database access layer for building dynamic web pages is quite comparable to Net.Data. One of the primary differences between Net.Data and PHP is that Net.Data is a proprietary language produced by IBM with a relatively small user community, while PHP is a popular open-source project of the Apache Software Foundation with a large, active, and supportive user community.

Further information can be found online:

■ PHP code and documentation is available at http://www.php.net.

Python

Python is an object-oriented scripting language that offers a range of functions comparable to Perl. A relatively new language, Python is freely available and is gathering an active user community.

To automate database administration tasks, you can issue DB2 commands using the os.popen() function. To issue SQL statements, you can use a driver that implements the Python Database API Specification 2.0 (DB-API) for DB2, such as the mxODBC driver or Man-Yong Lee's Python module for IBM DB2. To create a GUI for your database application, you can use the Tkinter interface to access the Tcl/Tk widget toolkit. To create dynamic web pages, you can easily write CGI scripts in Python, and enhance the performance of your scripts by embedding a copy of the Python interpreter in your web server.

The Python DB-API is another database access API that borrows heavily from the X/Open CLI and ISO/IEC Call Level Interface specifications. The architecture is quite similar, but the DB-API offers an object-oriented interface that simplifies the effort of writing database applications. For example, the following Python code connects to a DB2 database and retrieves a simple result set:

```
import DB2;
con = DB2.connect(dsn='sample', uid='db2inst1', pwd='ibmdb2');
cursor = con.cursor();
cursor.execute('SELECT firstnme, lastname FROM employee');
```

```
allRows = cursor.fetchall();
print allRows;
del cursor;
del con;
```

Python can satisfy most of your application development requirements. Like Perl, it makes an ideal language for rapid prototyping or database administration tasks. However, as an interpreted language, it will not provide the performance offered by C interfaces like embedded SQL or CLI, or by Java interfaces like JDBC or SQLJ. Python is still a relatively new language, and the third-party DB2 drivers for the DB-API are still maturing. For example, mxODBC does not currently offer the ability to call stored procedures, and the Python module for IBM DB2 is not yet threadsafe.

You can find further information online:

- The Python web site is located at http://www.python.org.

- The Python Database API Specification 2.0 can be found at http://www.python.org/topics/database/DatabaseAPI-2.0.html.

- The Python module for IBM DB2 can be found at ftp://people.linuxkorea.co.kr/pub/DB2/.

- The mxODBC Python driver for DB2 can be found at http://www.lemburg.com/files/python/mxODBC.html.

REXX

The REXX (and Object REXX) scripting language is sometimes used to port legacy applications from IBM mainframes. With its unique ability to both issue dynamic SQL statements and invoke administrative APIs, REXX is a good prototyping language for DB2 applications. However, IBM's decision to freeze REXX features at the level of DB2 Universal Database Version 5.2 and not provide further enhancements suggests that REXX is not a good choice for developing production applications.

Further information can be found in the following sources:

- *IBM DB2 Universal Database Administrative API Reference Version 7*
- *IBM DB2 Universal Database Application Development Guide Version 7*

Information is also available online:

- The Object REXX web site is at http://www.ibm.com/software/ad/obj-rexx/.

SQL Procedures

SQL procedures offer a convenient means of abstracting sets of common SQL statements into server-side stored procedures that you can invoke in an application by using a CALL statement. One common reason for calling an SQL procedure rather than performing the equivalent function within a client-side application is that, by performing the database work on the database server, SQL procedures enable you to avoid transferring large amounts of data over the network.

Another common reason for implementing application functions in SQL procedures is that you can quickly develop a set of personalized administration functions for activities like granting and revoking privileges on common sets of SQL objects. You can also quickly recreate those functions on every DB2 database on which you develop applications.

To create an SQL procedure, you must first install and configure a C compiler on your database server. The CREATE PROCEDURE statement contains the metadata about the SQL procedure, such as name, number of result sets, and maximum SQL access level, as well as the set of SQL statements making up the procedure body between the BEGIN and END clauses. For example, the following SQL procedure retrieves a simple result set:

```
CREATE PROCEDURE employees()
DYNAMIC RESULT SETS 1
READS SQL DATA
LANGUAGE SQL
BEGIN
  DECLARE rs1 CURSOR WITH RETURN FOR
    SELECT firstnme, lastname
    FROM employee;

  OPEN rs1;
END
```

The requirement for a C compiler on your development database server is the major drawback of SQL procedures; developers occasionally report difficulty in correctly configuring the C compiler, which causes the CREATE PROCEDURE statement to fail. C compilers are often an entirely separate product from both the database management system and the operating system, possibly requiring DB2 developers to purchase compiler licenses on every platform on which they want to use SQL procedures. DB2 offers the ability to distribute a compiled SQL procedure across multiple servers, but the mechanism is somewhat awkward.

Further information can be found in Chapters 26 and 27, as well as in the following sources:

- *IBM DB2 Universal Database Application Building Guide Version 7*
- *IBM DB2 Universal Database Application Development Guide Version 7*
- *IBM DB2 Universal Database SQL Reference Version 7*

The
Complete
Reference

Chapter 22

Embedded SQL

An *embedded SQL application* is a collection of SQL statements embedded within the source files of a standard programming language like C, C++, COBOL, or Fortran. Writing embedded SQL programs is a fast method of developing DB2 applications because you use the standard syntax of your chosen programming language for control structures. The syntax required for embedding SQL statements is quite simple compared to learning an entirely new set of APIs for an interface like the Call Level Interface (CLI). You can use C, C++, COBOL, and Fortran as host languages for embedded SQL on the same platforms on which DB2 supports those languages.

This chapter focuses on the use of C as a host language for embedded SQL applications. For information on using C++, COBOL, or Fortran as a host language, see the *IBM DB2 Universal Database Application Development Guide* shipped with DB2 or available for download from http://www.ibm.com/software/data/db2/library/.

Creating an Embedded SQL Application

Before attempting to create an embedded SQL application, ensure that your development environment satisfies the following prerequisites:

- A DB2 Application Development Client must be installed on your development workstation.

- A DB2 server, or a database server accessible through a DB2 Connect gateway, must be accessible from your development workstation.

- A supported compiler for the host language of your choice must be installed and configured on your development workstation. The compilers supported for development with DB2 are listed at http://www.ibm.com/software/data/db2/udb/ad.

To create an embedded SQL application, perform the following general steps:

1. Embed the SQL statements within the source file of your chosen host language.

2. Precompile the source files to convert any embedded SQL statements into DB2 run-time APIs. This step creates one or more converted source files and one bind file.

3. Compile and link the converted source files to produce an executable program.

4. On every client from which you will run the program, bind the bind file to the database server to create an access plan package on the server.

Writing an Embedded SQL Source File

You can embed any SQL statement supported by DB2 in a source file for a host language. To tell the DB2 precompiler that a statement within a C source file is an SQL statement, prefix the statement with the keywords EXEC SQL.

Within a typical embedded SQL application source file, you will include statements to do the following:

1. Include the header files provided with the DB2 Application Development Client.

2. Declare an SQLCA structure to hold errors and warnings returned by the SQL statements.

3. Declare any host variables used to pass or receive values within the SQL statements.

4. Connect to the database server.

5. Issue one or more SQL statements.

6. Commit or roll back any transactions.

7. Disconnect from the database server.

Including Header Files

The header files define structures, constants, and functions required by embedded SQL applications:

- sql.h
- sqlca.h
- sqlda.h
- sqlenv.h

Retrieving Errors and Warnings Returned by SQL Statements

To retrieve errors and warnings returned by SQL statements, you must declare an SQLCA structure within the source file for your embedded SQL application. The SQLCA structure holds the SQLCODE and SQLSTATE values returned by the last SQL statement that was issued by the application.

To declare an SQLCA structure, include the following statement within the declaration section of your source file:

```
/* Create an sqlca structure called "sqlca" */
struct sqlca sqlca;
```

After issuing an SQL statement within the application, you can retrieve the SQLCODE and SQLSTATE values from the sqlcode and sqlstate elements of the SQLCA structure as follows:

```
struct sqlca sqlca;
sqlint16 my_sqlcode;
char my_sqlstate[6];
/* SQL statement */
my_sqlcode = sqlca.sqlcode;
strncpy(my_sqlstate, sqlca.sqlstate, 5);
my_sqlstate[5] = '\0';
```

Declaring Host Variables for Embedded SQL Statements

Most of the embedded SQL applications that you write will embed SQL statements that either accept variable values or return variable values. To send and receive values to and from an SQL statement, use host variables to represent the values that will be sent to or received from the SQL statement. A *host variable* is a program variable that the DB2 precompiler recognizes and allows you to use in SQL statements to interact with the database server. To represent an SQL NULL value in an embedded SQL application, you can use a companion variable for each host variable to indicate NULL values being passed to or retrieved from the database server. These variables are called *null indicator variables.*

To declare host variables for embedded SQL statements, follow these steps:

1. Embed the following statement within the declaration area of the source file:

```
EXEC SQL BEGIN DECLARE SECTION;
```

2. Declare host variables that correspond to the SQL data types they will represent in the embedded SQL statements by using the type mappings defined in Table 22-1 (at the end of this chapter). For example, to declare one host variable of type INTEGER and one host variable of type REAL, you would include these statements:

```
sqlint32 my_integer;
float my_real;
```

3. Declare one null indicator variable for each host variable that can send or receive an SQL NULL value. Declare each null indicator variable as follows:

```
sqlint16 null_indicator;
```

4. End the host variable declaration section with the following statement:

```
EXEC SQL END DECLARE SECTION;
```

Connecting to a Database Server

By definition, most database applications require a connection to a database server. The connection enables you to query and update data, manipulate SQL objects, and perform certain administrative tasks on the database server.

To connect to a database server in an embedded SQL application, the database server must already be cataloged on the DB2 client. You can check whether the database server has been successfully cataloged by connecting to the database server from the Command Line Processor (CLP) on the client.

To create a database connection in an embedded SQL application, add the following statements to your application:

1. Declare host variables for the database name, user ID, and password that your application will use to connect to the database server:

```
EXEC SQL BEGIN DECLARE SECTION;
  char database[129];
  char userID[129];
  char password[129];
EXEC SQL END DECLARE SECTION;
```

2. Assign the appropriate values to the connection host variables. The database name might always be the same for every user of the application, but the user ID and password might be supplied in response to a prompt from the application, as arguments from the command line, or as values of environment variables.

```
strcpy(database, "sample");
strcpy(userID, "db2inst1");
strcpy(password, "ibmdb2");
```

3. Embed the CONNECT statement in your embedded SQL application source file by using the host variable names you previously declared:

```
EXEC SQL CONNECT TO :database USER :userID USING :password;
```

Issuing SQL Statements

You can issue many different SQL statements in your embedded SQL applications. When you know the entire SQL statement in advance, and all of the referenced SQL objects exist at the time you precompile the embedded SQL application, then your SQL statement is called a *static* SQL statement. If you do not know the entire SQL statement in advance, or the statement refers to SQL objects that are created within the same application, the statement is called a *dynamic* SQL statement.

Access plans and authorization for static SQL statements are typically determined when the packages are bound, which enables the application to issue static SQL statements immediately based on the database statistics available at the time the package was bound. Typical static SQL statements include the following:

- Issuing SQL statements with a single set of values
- Issuing SQL statements that return multiple sets of values
- Inserting or retrieving LOB values
- Calling stored procedures

Access plans and authorization for dynamic SQL statements are typically determined at run time, preventing the application from issuing the statements immediately but enabling the database to use the most recent statistics to optimize the statements. An overview of embedding dynamic SQL statements in your application is included in the "Issuing Dynamic SQL Statements" section later in the chapter.

Committing or Rolling Back Transactions

You should explicitly commit or roll back transactions in your application. If the application starts a transaction but does not explicitly end the transaction by issuing a COMMIT or ROLLBACK statement before the application exits, the database server automatically rolls back the transaction on every platform except for Windows. To ensure that your application behaves consistently across all platforms, explicitly end all transactions within your application.

To commit a transaction, issue the COMMIT statement:

```
EXEC SQL COMMIT;
return;
```

To roll back a transaction, issue the ROLLBACK statement:

```
EXEC SQL ROLLBACK;
return;
```

Disconnecting from the Database Server

Explicitly disconnecting from a database server ensures that any resources held by the application are released promptly on both the server and the client. To disconnect from a database server, embed the CONNECT RESET statement in your embedded SQL application source file:

```
EXEC SQL CONNECT RESET;
```

Inserting or Retrieving SQL NULL Values

Most host languages do not provide an equivalent representation for the SQL NULL value. An SQL NULL value for an INTEGER column, for example, cannot simply be returned in a host variable with the value of 0 or a negative value, because these are already possible return values for an INTEGER column. An SQL NULL value for a VARCHAR column cannot simply be returned in a host variable as an empty string, because an empty string is an acceptable non-NULL value for a VARCHAR column.

Passing a null indicator variable with a host variable enables the application to send or receive SQL NULL values from the database. To use a null indicator variable, follow these steps:

1. Declare the null indicator as a SMALLINT host variable.

```
EXEC SQL BEGIN DECLARE SECTION;
  char my_midinit[2];
  sqlint16 null_indicator;
EXEC SQL END DECLARE SECTION;
```

2. When passing an SQL NULL value to the database server, set the value of the null indicator variable to –1.

```
/* Pass a NULL value to the database server */
null_indicator = -1;
```

3. Include the null indicator variable in the SQL statement immediately following the host variable representing the nullable field. You can separate the host variable and null indicator variable only with a space.

```
/* Set all middle initials to NULL */
UPDATE employee SET midinit = :my_midinit :null_indicator;
/* Retrieve middle initial of employee */
SELECT firstnme INTO :my_midinit :null_indicator
  FROM employee
  WHERE lastname = 'SCOTT';
```

4. If the value of the null indicator variable for a field returned by the database server is negative, the field represents an SQL NULL value.

```
/* Check for NULL value */
if (null_indicator < 0) {
  printf("Database server returned an SQL NULL value.");
}
```

Issuing SQL Statements with a Single Set of Values

To insert or retrieve a single set of values with an SQL statement, simply issue the SQL statement by using host variables (and null indicator variables, if necessary) in place of the values.

For example, the following sample selects the maximum salary from the set of all employees into the host variable max_salary, then inserts a new row into the employee table by using three host variables:

```c
#include <stdio.h>
#include <stdlib.h>
#include <string.h>
#include <sql.h>
#include <sqlca.h>
#include <sqlda.h>
#include <sqlenv.h>

int   main(int argc, char** args) {
  struct sqlca sqlca;

  EXEC SQL BEGIN DECLARE SECTION;
    double max_salary;
    sqlint16 salary_ind;
    char new_empno[7];
    char new_firstnme[13];
    char new_midinit[2];
    char new_lastname[16];
    sqlint16 new_edlevel;
  EXEC SQL END DECLARE SECTION;

  /* Connect to database server */
EXEC SQL CONNECT TO sample;
  /* Select maximum salary */
  EXEC SQL SELECT MAX(salary) INTO :max_salary :salary_ind FROM employee;
  if (salary_ind < 0) {
    printf("Maximum salary returned an SQL NULL value.");
  }
  else if (sqlca.sqlcode != 0) {
    printf("Maximum salary could not be retrieved. SQLCODE = %d.",
         sqlca.sqlcode);
  }
  else {
    printf("Maximum salary = %9.2f.", max_salary);
  }
```

```
/* Insert new row into employee table */
strcpy(new_empno, "000623");
strcpy(new_firstnme, "Jennifer");
strcpy(new_midinit, "L");
strcpy(new_lastname, "Kabaroff");

EXEC SQL INSERT INTO employee (empno, firstnme,
  midinit, lastname, edlevel) VALUES (:new_empno,
 :new_firstnme, :new_midinit, :new_lastname, :new_edlevel);
if (sqlca.sqlcode != 0) {
  printf("Error inserting row. SQLCODE = %d.", sqlca.sqlcode);
}
else {
  printf("Successfully inserted new row.");
}

/* COMMIT transaction */
EXEC SQL COMMIT;

/* Close connection */
EXEC SQL CONNECT RESET;
return 0;
}
```

Issuing SQL Statements That Return Multiple Sets of Values

A SELECT statement may return a result table composed of multiple rows of data. In an embedded SQL application, you must use a *cursor* to fetch values from the result table one row at a time. A cursor makes rows from the result table available to an application by pointing to a current row of this table. An application can use the cursor to retrieve each row sequentially from the result table using a FETCH statement until a NOT FOUND condition (SQLCODE +100, SQLSTATE '02000') is returned. You cannot retrieve the same row more than once, move backward through a cursor, or access random rows of a cursor in an embedded SQL application.

The steps involved in processing a cursor are as follows:

1. Specify the cursor by using a DECLARE CURSOR statement for the SELECT statement. To enable the application to process multiple cursors at the same time, you must specify a name for the cursor. If you plan to update or delete data in the cursor, specify the FOR UPDATE clause as part of the SELECT statement.

```
EXEC SQL DECLARE CURSOR cursor FOR
  SELECT firstnme, midinit, lastname
  FROM employee
```

```
ORDER BY lastname
FOR UPDATE;
```

2. Perform the query and build the result table by using the OPEN statement.

```
EXEC SQL OPEN cursor;
```

3. Retrieve rows one at a time by using the FETCH statement.

```
EXEC SQL FETCH cursor INTO :my_firstnme, :my_midinit, :my_lastname;
/* Check SQLCA for NOT FOUND condition */
if (sqlca.sqlcode == 100) {
  printf("Cursor has reached the end of data.");
}
```

4. To process the current row in the cursor with the DELETE or UPDATE statement, use the WHERE CURRENT OF *cursor-name* clause.

```
EXEC SQL UPDATE employee SET midinit = NULL
  WHERE CURRENT OF cursor;
```

5. Terminate the cursor by using the CLOSE statement.

```
EXEC SQL CLOSE cursor;
```

Inserting or Retrieving Large Objects

Inserting or retrieving instances of BLOB and CLOB data types can be resource-intensive, particularly if you attempt to read the entire contents of the BLOB or CLOB instance into memory. Rather than forcing you to read up to potentially 2GB of data into memory, embedded SQL applications enable you to specify file reference host variables for large objects. When you specify a file reference host variable for a large object, DB2 automatically reads from or writes to the specified file name, preventing you from having to manipulate the object data directly within your application.

To use file reference host variables to work with large objects, perform the following steps:

1. Declare the file reference host variable by using the SQL TYPE IS BLOB_FILE declaration for BLOBs or the SQL TYPE IS CLOB_FILE declaration for CLOBs.

```
EXEC SQL BEGIN DECLARE SECTION;
  SQL TYPE IS BLOB_FILE picture;
  sqlint16 picture_ind;
EXEC SQL END DECLARE SECTION;
```

2. Specify the file name and file name length for the file that represents the instance of the large object.

```
strcpy(picture.name, "picture.gif");
picture.name_length = 11;
```

3. Set the file options according to your intended purpose. If you plan to retrieve a large object from the database server into the referenced file, set the file option to SQL_FILE_OVERWRITE. If you plan to insert a large object into the database from the referenced file, set the file option to SQL_FILE_READ.

```
/* Retrieve a large object from the database server into the file */
picture.file_options = SQL_FILE_OVERWRITE;
/* Insert a large object into the database server from the file */
picture.file_options = SQL_FILE_READ;
```

4. Issue the SELECT or INSERT statement to complete the operation.

```
/* Retrieve large object from database server */
EXEC SQL SELECT picture INTO :picture :picture_ind
  FROM emp_photo
  WHERE photo_format = 'gif'
  AND empno = '000130';


/* Insert large object into database */
EXEC SQL INSERT INTO employee (picture, photo_format, empno)
  VALUES (:picture, 'gif', '000150');
```

Calling Stored Procedures

To call stored procedures from an embedded SQL application, embed the CALL statement by using host variables for each of the parameters defined for the stored procedure. The following sample code demonstrates a call to a stored procedure named inParameter with one IN parameter of type SMALLINT and two OUT parameters of type INTEGER.

Note *Embedded SQL applications cannot call a stored procedure that passes a DECIMAL parameter or that returns one or more result sets.*

```
EXEC SQL BEGIN DECLARE SECTION;
  sqlint16 in_param;
  sqlint32 out_param1;
  sqlint32 out_param2;
EXEC SQL END DECLARE SECTION;

/* Set value of IN parameter */
in_param = 38;

/* Call stored procedure */
EXEC SQL CALL inParameter(:in_param, :out_param1, :out_param2);
```

APPLICATION
DEVELOPMENT

If the stored procedure was cataloged with the PARAMETER STYLE GENERAL WITH NULLS clause of the CREATE PROCEDURE statement, you can also pass null indicator variables with each of the host variables to send or receive SQL NULL values for any of the parameters.

```
EXEC SQL BEGIN DECLARE SECTION;
   sqlint16 in_param;
   sqlint32 out_param1;
   sqlint32 out_param2;
   sqlint16 in_ind;
   sqlint16 out_ind1;
   sqlint16 out_ind2;
EXEC SQL END DECLARE SECTION;

/* Set value of IN parameter and associated null indicator */
in_param = 38;
in_ind = 0;

/* Set values of OUT parameter null indicators
   to -1 to indicate NULL input to stored procedure */
out_ind1 = -1;
out_ind2 = -1;

/* Call stored procedure with null indicators */
EXEC SQL CALL inParameter(:in_param :in_ind,
   :out_param1 :out_ind1,
   :out_param2 :out_ind2);
```

Issuing Dynamic SQL Statements

When you do not know all or part of an SQL statement that will be issued in your application, or when the objects referenced by an SQL statement do not exist at precompile time, you must use dynamic SQL. If you want an SQL statement to always use the optimal access plan based on current database statistics, consider using dynamic SQL.

To issue a dynamic SQL statement in your application, you must do the following:

1. Create a host variable string containing the dynamic SQL statement. Use parameter markers (?) for any values that might differ each time you execute the statement.

```
EXEC SQL BEGIN DECLARE SECTION;
   char stmt[129];
   char empno[7];
```

```
      char lastname[16];
EXEC SQL END DECLARE SECTION;
/* Contents of stmt could also be generated by user input */
strcpy(stmt, "INSERT INTO employee (empno, lastname) ");
strcat(stmt, "VALUES (?, ?)");
```

2. Generate an access plan for the statement by issuing the PREPARE statement.

```
EXEC SQL PREPARE prep_stmt FROM :stmt;
```

3. Issue the dynamic SQL statement one or more times with the EXECUTE statement. If necessary, include the USING clause to identify the host variables that contain the values of any parameter markers in the statement.

```
strcpy(empno, "000999");
strcpy(lastname, "Spinoza");
EXEC SQL EXECUTE prep_stmt USING :empno, :lastname;
```

Precompiling Embedded SQL Programs

To precompile an embedded SQL source file, you must have the DB2 Application Development Client installed and configured on your development workstation, and you must be able to connect to a DB2 server. The DB2 precompiler uses the connection to the DB2 server to validate the syntax of any SQL statements. To invoke the DB2 precompiler, issue the PRECOMPILE command from the CLP. The syntax for the PRECOMPILE command is as follows:

PRECOMPILE *source-file* [OUTPUT *output-file*] [BINDFILE [USING *bind-file*] [DYNAMICRULES BIND] [OWNER *userID*]

In this command, the parameters are as follows:

- **source-file**   Specifies the file that contains embedded SQL statements.
- **OUTPUT** *output-file*   Specifies the file created by the PRECOMPILE command. In this file, the embedded SQL statements have been replaced by run-time APIs that will call the statements in the package. If this parameter is not specified, the output file name defaults to the prefix of the source filename plus a suffix associated with the host language.
- **BINDFILE USING** *bind-file*   Creates a bind file with the specified name. The bind file contains all of the information about SQL statements for a corresponding application. Including this clause prevents the PRECOMPILE command from automatically creating a package on the server.
- **DYNAMICRULES BIND**   Enables any user to issue dynamic SQL statements using the privileges of your authorization ID.

- **OWNER** *userID*   Designates a user ID from which privileges for dynamic SQL statements are inherited. This is a useful option if you have SYSADM or DBADM authority and you want to provide a standard level of privileges for all users.

To precompile a source file containing embedded SQL statements, perform the following steps:

1. Connect to the database server.
2. Issue the PRECOMPILE command from the CLP. DB2 automatically creates the corresponding SQL package on the server to which the client is connected. To defer the creation of the package until later or to have the option to create the package on other servers, include the BINDFILE clause to create a bind file.

For example, the following CLP script creates a connection to the database server sample, then precompiles the embedded source file embed.sqc to produce the output C source file embed.c, and generates the bind file embed.bnd:

```
CONNECT TO sample;
PRECOMPILE embed.sqc OUTPUT embed.c BINDFILE USING embed.bnd;
```

Binding Embedded SQL Applications

Binding an embedded SQL application creates a package in the database and generates an access plan for the SQL statements in the package. If you do not specify the BINDFILE clause in the PRECOMPILE command, the command automatically creates a package on the server by binding the SQL statements within the embedded SQL source file. Specify the BINDFILE clause in the PRECOMPILE command to create a separate bind file that you can bind later to create a package.

To create a package from a bind file, perform the following steps:

1. Connect to the database server on which you want to create the package.
2. Issue the BIND command from the CLP by using the following basic syntax:

   BIND *filename* [BLOCKING ALL] [COLLECTION *schema-name*] [DEGREE ANY]

   In this command, the parameters are as follows:

   - *filename*   Specifies the name of the bind file.
   - **BLOCKING ALL**   To improve performance, this clause specifies that rows in the result table of a cursor should be returned from the database server in blocks of multiple rows at a time, rather than a single row at a time. To prevent concurrency problems, cursors declared with the FOR UPDATE clause will return only one row at a time.

- **COLLECTION** *schema-name*   Specifies that the package should be created within the identified schema. If this clause is not included in the BIND command, the package is created in the schema of the user ID that issues the BIND command.

- **DEGREE ANY**   To improve performance on massively parallel processing (MPP) and symmetric multiprocessing (SMP) systems, this clause specifies that the database server can use any degree of parallelism to process the SQL statement.

For example, the following CLP script creates a connection to the database server sample, then binds the bind file embed.bnd with blocking enabled for all cursors in the embedded SQL application:

```
CONNECT TO sample;
BIND embed.bnd BLOCKING ALL;
```

Compiling Embedded SQL Applications

To produce an executable application from embedded SQL source files, you must compile the output file generated by the DB2 precompiler to produce an object file, and then link the object file against the applicable DB2 shared library for your platform. On Windows operating systems, link the object file against db2api.lib. On Linux and UNIX operating systems, link the object file against the libdb2.so or libdb2.a shared library.

The DB2 Application Development Client provides batch files on Windows operating systems and build scripts on UNIX operating systems to help you build embedded SQL applications. Check the README files located in the SQLLIB\samples\ *language* subdirectories on Windows operating systems and sqllib/samples/*language* subdirectories on Linux and UNIX operating systems for a description of the batch files and build scripts.

Mapping DB2 Data Types to C Data Types in Embedded SQL

Table 22-1 contains the essential information for working with DB2 data types in embedded SQL applications. The first column contains the names of DB2 types. The second column contains the corresponding platform-independent C type for host variable declarations. The third column describes the DB2 type and indicates size limits for the type.

For information on using C++, COBOL, or Fortran as a host language, see the *IBM DB2 Universal Database Application Development Guide* shipped with DB2 or available for download from http://www.ibm.com/software/data/db2/library/.

DB2 Type	C Type	Description
CHAR(*n*)	char[*n* + 1]	Fixed-length character string. Maximum length is 254 bytes. Strings less than the declared length are padded with spaces.

CHAR FOR BIT DATA	struct tag {
	  sqlint16 length;
	  char[*n*];
	}
		Fixed-length byte array. Maximum length is 254 bytes.

VARCHAR	char[*n* + 1]	Variable-length character string. Maximum length is 32,672 bytes.

VARCHAR FOR BIT DATA	struct tag {
	  sqlint16 length;
	  char[*n*];
	}
		Variable-length byte array. Maximum length is 32,672 bytes.

LONG VARCHAR	struct tag {
	  sqlint16 length;
	  char[*n*];
	}
		Variable-length character string. Maximum length is 32,700 bytes.

LONG VARCHAR FOR BIT DATA	struct tag {
	  sqlint16 length;
	  char[*n*];
	}
		Variable-length byte array. Maximum length is 32,700 bytes.

BLOB	SQL_TYPE IS BLOB_FILE	
CLOB	SQL_TYPE IS CLOB_FILE	Character large object. Maximum length is 2,147,483,647 bytes.
SMALLINT	sqlint16	16-bit signed integer.
INTEGER	sqlint32	32-bit signed integer.
BIGINT	sqlint64	64-bit signed integer.
DOUBLE	double	Single-precision floating point.
DECIMAL	No exact equivalent: use double	Packed decimal.

Table 22-1.   *DB2 Type Mappings to C Types for Embedded SQL*

DB2 Type	C Type	Description
FLOAT	float	Double-precision floating point.
REAL	float	Double-precision floating point.
DATE	char[11]	Holds day, month, and year.
TIME	char[9]	Holds hour, minute, and second.
TIMESTAMP	char[27]	Holds day, month, year, hour, minute, and second.

Table 22-1.   *DB2 Type Mappings to C Types for Embedded SQL* (continued)

APPLICATION
DEVELOPMENT

The Complete Reference

Chapter 23

Administrative
Application
Programming Interfaces

The administrative application programming interfaces (APIs) for DB2 enable you to perform administrative tasks within programs. You can write batch files or shell scripts that include the equivalent administrative commands, but one of the primary advantages of writing programs to perform administrative tasks is that you can use the control structures of the programming language. Writing programs that use administrative APIs also means that you can single-source your administrative tasks so that you can simply compile the program once on each operating system, rather than having to convert shell scripts to batch files if you develop for both UNIX and Windows operating systems.

You can use C, COBOL, Fortran, and REXX as host languages for APIs on the platforms on which DB2 supports those languages. This chapter uses C as a host language for administrative APIs.

Compiling Administrative API Applications

Before compiling an application that includes administrative APIs, ensure that the following prerequisites are installed and configured in your development environment:

- The DB2 Application Development Client, available from http://www. ibm.com/cgi-bin/db2www/data/db2/udb/winos2unix/support/ download.d2w/report
- A compiler supported by DB2, as listed at http://www.ibm.com/software/data/db2/udb/ad

To produce an executable application that includes administrative APIs, you must perform the following general steps:

1. Include the header file or files required by the administrative APIs in the application source code. Table 23-1 (at the end of this chapter) lists the header file each administrative API requires.

2. Link the object file against the applicable DB2 shared library for your platform. On Windows operating systems, link the object file against db2api.lib. On Linux and UNIX operating systems, link the object file against the libdb2.so or libdb2.a shared library.

The DB2 Application Development Client provides batch files on Windows operating systems and build scripts on UNIX operating systems to help you build applications that use administrative APIs. Check the README files located in the SQLLIB\samples\ *language* subdirectories on Windows operating systems and sqllib/samples/*language* subdirectories on Linux and UNIX operating systems for a description of the batch files and build scripts.

Writing Administrative API Applications

To write an application that uses administrative APIs, perform the following steps:

1. Initialize API input structures.
2. Create required database connections or instance attachments.
3. Invoke the API.
4. Check for errors or warnings.
5. Free any allocated resources.
6. Close database connections and instance attachments.

These steps are described in the following sections.

Initializing API Input Structures

To ensure that any input structures for the API are initialized to 0 before setting the values of elements within the structure, call the memset() function for each structure by using the sizeof() function to determine the size of the input structure.

For example, the following code initializes the elements of the input data structure pItemList to 0, then sets the values of the structure elements, and finally invokes the sqlfudb() API:

```
struct sqlca pSqlca;
unsigned short NumItems = 1;
// SQLFUPD structure passes database configuration info to an API
struct sqlfupd pItemList[NumItems];

pItemList[0].ptrvalue = (char *)malloc(sizeof(sqlint16));
memset(&pItemList[0].token, 0, sizeof(sqlint16));
memset(pItemList[0].ptrvalue, 0, sizeof(sqlint16));
// now set the values of structure and call the sqlfudb API
```

Creating Database Connections or Instance Attachments

To perform administrative tasks on the database server with most of the administrative APIs, you must make the right kind of connection to the database server. You can create any required connections either in the environment in which the application is executed, within the application itself using the sqleatin() instance attachment API, or within the application itself using the host application's method of creating a database connection. Table 23-1 (at the end of the chapter) lists the connection levels required for each API.

As a general guide, administrative tasks on the client, such as getting and setting client information using the sqleqryc() and sqlesetc() APIs, require no connection to a database server. Operations at a database instance level such as creating or dropping a database using the sqlecrea() and sqledrpd() APIs generally require an instance attachment either before running the application or within the application using the sqleatin() instance attachment API. Performing operations at a database level, such as backing up or restoring a database using the sqlubkp() and sqlurestore() APIs, generally requires a connection to the database.

Invoking the API

Invoke the API by passing the structures and parameters described in the *IBM DB2 Universal Database Administrative API Reference.*

Checking for Errors or Warnings

Check the SQLCA structure returned by the API to ensure that the operation succeeded; if the return code indicates a failure or warning, you can invoke the sqlaintp() API to retrieve the associated message text.

For example, the following code checks the SQLCA of the sqleatin() API and prints the message text if an error or warning occurs:

```
int rc;
struct sqlca pSqlca;
char errorMsg[1024];
char * pNodeName = "myNode";
char * pUserName = "db2inst1";
char * pPassword = "ibmdb2";

sqleatin(pNodeName, pUserName, pPassword, &pSqlca);
rc = sqlaintp(errorMsg, 1024, 80, &pSqlca);
// return code is the length of the errorMsg string
if( rc > 0) {
  printf("%s\n", errorMsg);
}
```

Freeing Any Allocated Resources

Certain APIs, including db2AutoConfig(), sqlbtcq(), and sqlbmtsq(), automatically allocate resources that are not automatically freed after the API is invoked. Invoke db2AutoConfigFreeMem() or sqlefmem(), as appropriate, to free these resources before the application exits.

Closing Database Connections and Instance Attachments

To prevent resource leaks, you should explicitly close any database connections or instance attachments before the application exits. Close a database connection by using the same method that created the connection. Close instance attachments by invoking the sqledtin() API.

Example: Updating Database Configuration

The following application illustrates how to use the DB2 administrative APIs to create an instance attachment, update the database configuration parameter *locktimeout*, and display any error or warning messages:

```
#include <stdio.h>
#include <stdlib.h>
#include <string.h>
#include <sqlenv.h>
#include <sqlutil.h>

void checkError(int, struct sqlca *);

int main (int args, char **argv) {
  int rc;
  struct sqlca pSqlca;
  char * pNodeName = "fluff";
  char * pUserName = "db2inst1";
  char * pPassword = "ibmdb2";
  char * pDbAlias = "SAMPLE";
  unsigned short NumItems = 1;
  struct sqlfupd pItemList[NumItems];
  sqlint16 locktimeout = 300;

  // 1.Initialize API input structures
  pItemList[0].ptrvalue = (char *)malloc(sizeof(sqlint16));
  memset(&pItemList[0].token, 0, sizeof(sqlint16));
  memset(pItemList[0].ptrvalue, 0, sizeof(sqlint16));
  pItemList[0].token = SQLF_DBTN_LOCKTIMEOUT;
  memcpy((void *) (pItemList[0].ptrvalue),
         (void *) &locktimeout,
         sizeof(sqlint16));
```

```
// 2.Create required database connections or instance attachments
rc = sqleatin(pNodeName, pUserName, pPassword, &pSqlca);
checkError(rc, &pSqlca);

// 3.Invoke the API
rc = sqlfudb (pDbAlias, NumItems, pItemList, &pSqlca);

// 4.Check for errors or warnings
checkError(rc, &pSqlca);

// 5.Free any allocated resources

// 6.Close database connections and instance attachments
rc = sqledtin(&pSqlca);
checkError(rc, &pSqlca);

return 0;
}

void checkError(int rc, struct sqlca * pSqlca) {
  char errorMsg[1024];
  // get error message
  rc = sqlaintp(errorMsg, 1024, 80, pSqlca);
  // return code represents the length of the errorMsg string
  if(rc > 0) {
    printf("%s\n", errorMsg);
  }
}
```

DB2 Administrative APIs

Table 23-1 lists the DB2 administrative APIs with the required include file, connection levels, and authorization level for each API. In the column that describes the required connection levels, "database" indicates that a database connection is required, "instance" indicates that an instance attachment is required, "catalog node" indicates that the API can be issued only on the catalog node of a partitioned database environment, "local node" indicates that the API must be issued on a node of the database server, and "instance (automatic)" means that the API automatically creates an instance attachment.

API Name	Description	Include File	Connection Required	Authorization Required
db2AdminMsgWrite	Write information to log	db2ApiDf.h	None	None
db2ArchiveLog	Archive active log	db2ApiDf.h	None	SYSADM, SYSCTRL, SYSMAINT, DBADM
db2AutoConfig	Access Performance Configuration wizard	db2AuCfg.h	Database	SYSADM
db2AutoConfig FreeMemory	Free memory used by db2AutoConfig	db2AuCfg.h	Database	SYSADM
db2ConvMonStream	Convert monitor information for downlevel clients	db2ApiDf.h	None	None
db2DatabasePing	Ping database	db2ApiDf.h	Database	None
db2DatabaseRestart	Restart database	db2ApiDf.h	Local node	None
db2GetSnapshot	Get snapshot	db2ApiDf.h	Instance	SYSADM, SYSCTRL, SYSMAINT
db2GetSnapshotSize	Estimate size required for db2GetSnapshot()	db2ApiDf.h	Instance	SYSADM, SYSCTRL, SYSMAINT
db2GetSyncSession	Get satellite session identifier	db2ApiDf.h	None	None
db2HistoryCloseScan	Close recovery history file scan	db2ApiDf.h	Instance	(automatic) None
db2HistoryGetEntry	Get next recovery history file entry	db2ApiDf.h	Instance	(automatic) None
db2HistoryOpenScan	Open recovery history file scan	db2ApiDf.h	Instance (automatic)	None
db2HistoryUpdate	Update recovery history file	db2ApiDf.h	Database	SYSADM, SYSCTRL, SYSMAINT, DBADM
db2LdapCatalog Database	Catalog database in LDAP	db2ApiDf.h	None	None
db2LdapCatalogNode	Specify alternate node name or protocol in LDAP	db2ApiDf.h	None	None

Table 23-1.   *DB2 Administrative API Quick Reference*

API Name	Description	Include File	Connection Required	Authorization Required
db2LdapDeregister	Deregister DB2 server from LDAP	db2ApiDf.h	None	None
db2LdapRegister	Register DB2 server from LDAP	db2ApiDf.h	None	None
db2LdapUncatalog Database	Remove database entry from LDAP	db2ApiDf.h	None	None
db2LdapUncatalog Node	Remove node entry from LDAP	db2ApiDf.h	None	None
db2LdapUpdate	Update database communications protocol in LDAP	db2ApiDf.h	None	None
db2LoadQuery	Check status of load operation	db2ApiDf.h	Database	None
db2MonitorSwitches	Get and set monitor switches	db2ApiDf.h	Instance (automatic)	SYSADM, SYSCTRL, SYSMAINT
db2Prune	Prune entries from recovery history or log files	db2ApiDf.h	Database	SYSADM, SYSCTRL, SYSMAINT
db2QuerySatellite Progress	Check status of satellite synchronization	db2ApiDf.h	None	None
db2ResetMonitor	Reset monitor data	db2ApiDf.h	Instance (automatic)	SYSADM, SYSCTRL, SYSMAINT
db2SetSyncSession	Set synchronization session for a satellite	db2ApiDf.h	None	None
db2SyncSatellite	Synchronize a satellite	db2ApiDf.h	None	None
db2SyncSatelliteStop	Pause a satellite synchronization session	db2ApiDf.h	None	None
db2SyncSatelliteTest	Test a satellite's ability to synchronize	db2ApiDf.h	None	None
db2XaGetInfo	Get information for resource manager	sqlxa.h	Database	None
db2XaListIndTrans	List indoubt transactions	db2ApiDf.h	Database	SYSADM, DBADM
sqlabndx	Bind package	sql.h	Database	SYSADM, DBADM

Table 23-1. *DB2 Administrative API Quick Reference* (continued)

API Name	Description	Include File	Connection Required	Authorization Required
sqlaintp	Get error message	sql.h	None	None
sqlaprep	Precompile program	sql.h	Database	SYSADM, DBADM
sqlarbnd	Rebind package	sql.h	Database	SYSADM, DBADM
sqlbctcq	Close tablespace container query	sqlutil.h	Database	SYSADM, SYSCTRL, SYSMAINT, DBADM, LOAD
sqlbctsq	Close tablespace query	sqlutil.h	Database	SYSADM, SYSCTRL, SYSMAINT, DBADM, LOAD
sqlbftcq	Fetch tablespace container query	sqlutil.h	Database	SYSADM, SYSCTRL, SYSMAINT, DBADM, LOAD
sqlbftpq	Fetch tablespace query	sqlutil.h	Database	SYSADM, SYSCTRL, SYSMAINT, DBADM, LOAD
sqlbgtss	Get tablespace statistics	sqlutil.h	Database	SYSADM, SYSCTRL, SYSMAINT, DBADM, LOAD
sqlbmtsq	Query tablespaces	sqlutil.h	Database	SYSADM, SYSCTRL, SYSMAINT, DBADM, LOAD
sqlbotcq	Open tablespace container query	sqlutil.h	Database	SYSADM, SYSCTRL, SYSMAINT, DBADM, LOAD

Table 23-1.   *DB2 Administrative API Quick Reference* (continued)

APPLICATION
DEVELOPMENT

API Name	Description	Include File	Connection Required	Authorization Required
sqlbotsq	Open tablespace query	sqlutil.h	Database	SYSADM, SYSCTRL, SYSMAINT, DBADM, LOAD
sqlbstpq	query single tablespace	sqlutil.h	Database	SYSADM, SYSCTRL, SYSMAINT, DBADM, LOAD
sqlbstsc	Set tablespace containers	sqlutil.h	Database	SYSADM, SYSCTRL
sqlbtcq	Query tablespace container data	sqlutil.h	Database	SYSADM, SYSCTRL, SYSMAINT, DBADM
sqlcspqy	List DRDA indoubt transactions	sqlutil.h	Instance	SYSADM
sqle_activate_db	Activate database	sqlenv.h	None	SYSADM, SYSCTRL, SYSMAINT
sqle_deactivate_db	Deactivate database	sqlenv.h	None	SYSADM, SYSCTRL, SYSMAINT
sqleaddn	Add node	sqlenv.h	Local node	SYSADM, SYSCTRL
sqleatcp	Attach to instance and change password	sqlenv.h	Instance (automatic)	None
sqleatin	Attach to instance	sqlenv.h	Instance (automatic)	None
sqlecadb	Catalog database	sqlenv.h	None	SYSADM, SYSCTRL
sqlecran	Create database at node	sqlenv.h	Instance	SYSADM, SYSCTRL
sqlecrea	Create database	sqlenv.h	Instance	SYSADM, SYSCTRL
sqlectnd	Catalog node	sqlenv.h	None	SYSADM, SYSCTRL

Table 23-1. *DB2 Administrative API Quick Reference* (continued)

API Name	Description	Include File	Connection Required	Authorization Required
sqledcgd	Change database comment	sqlenv.h	None	SYSADM, SYSCTRL
sqledcls	Close database directory scan	sqlenv.h	None	None
sqledgne	Get next database directory entry	sqlenv.h	None	None
sqledosd	Open database directory scan	sqlenv.h	None	None
sqledpan	Drop database at node	sqlenv.h	None	SYSADM, SYSCTRL
sqledreg	Deregister database from network file server	sqlenv.h	None	None
sqledrpd	Drop database	sqlenv.h	Instance (automatic)	SYSADM, SYSCTRL
sqledrpn	Verify node is not in use	sqlenv.h	Local node	SYSADM, SYSCTRL
sqledtin	Detach from instance	sqlenv.h	None	None
sqlefmem	Free memory	sqlenv.h	None	None
sqlefrce	Force applications	sqlenv.h	Instance	SYSADM, SYSCTRL
sqlegdad	Catalog Database Connection Services (DCS) database	sqlenv.h	None	SYSADM, SYSCTRL
sqlegdcl	Close DCS directory scan	sqlenv.h	None	None
sqlegdel	Uncatalog DCS database	sqlenv.h	None	SYSADM, SYSCTRL
sqlegdge	Get DCS directory entry for database	sqlenv.h	None	None
sqlegdgt	Get DCS directory entries	sqlenv.h	None	None
sqlegdsc	Open DCS directory scan	sqlenv.h	None	None
sqlegins	Get INSTANCE environment variable	sqlenv.h	None	None

Table 23-1. *DB2 Administrative API Quick Reference* (continued)

API Name	Description	Include File	Connection Required	Authorization Required
sqleintr	Interrupt request	sqlenv.h	None	None
sqleisig	Install signal handler	sqlenv.h	None	None
sqlemgdb	Migrate database	sqlenv.h	None	SYSADM
sqlencls	Close node directory scan	sqlenv.h	None	None
sqlengne	Get next node directory entry	sqlenv.h	None	None
sqlenops	Open node directory scan	sqlenv.h	None	None
sqlepstart	Start database manager instance	sqlenv.h	Local node	SYSADM, SYSCTRL, SYSMAINT
sqlepstp	Stop database manager	sqlenv.h	Local node	SYSADM, SYSCTRL, SYSMAINT
sqleqryc	Query client connection settings	sqlenv.h	None	None
sqleqryi	Query client information	sqlenv.h	None	None
sqleregs	Register DB2 server with network file server	sqlenv.h	None	None
sqlesact	Set DRDA accounting string	sqlenv.h	None	None
sqlesdeg	Set run-time degree of parallelism	sqlenv.h	Instance	SYSADM, SYSCTRL
sqlesetc	Set client connection attributes	sqlenv.h	None	None
sqleseti	Set client information	sqlenv.h	None	None
sqleuncd	Uncatalog database	sqlenv.h	None	SYSADM, SYSCTRL
sqleuncn	Uncatalog node	sqlenv.h	None	SYSADM, SYSCTRL
sqlfddb	Get database configuration defaults	sqlutil.h	Instance (automatic)	None
sqlfdsys	Get database manager configuration defaults	sqlutil.h	Instance	None

Table 23-1. *DB2 Administrative API Quick Reference* (continued)

API Name	Description	Include File	Connection Required	Authorization Required
sqlfrdb	Reset database configuration	sqlutil.h	Instance (automatic)	SYSADM, SYSCTRL, SYSMAINT
sqlfrsys	Reset database manager configuration	sqlutil.h	Instance	SYSADM
sqlfudb	Update database configuration	sqlutil.h	Instance (automatic)	SYSADM, SYSCTRL, SYSMAINT
sqlfusys	Update database manager configuration	sqlutil.h	Instance	SYSADM
sqlfxdb	Get database configuration	sqlutil.h	Instance (automatic)	None
sqlfxsys	Get database manager configuration	sqlutil.h	Instance	None
sqlogstt	Get SQLSTATE message text	sql.h	None	None
sqluadau	Get authorizations	sqlutil.h	None	None
sqlubkp	Back up database	sqlutil.h	Database	SYSADM, SYSCTRL, SYSMAINT
sqludrdt	Redistribute data across nodes in a nodegroup	sqlutil.h	catalog node	SYSADM, SYSCTRL, SYSMAINT
sqluexpr	Export data	sqlutil.h	Database	SYSADM, SYSCTRL
sqlugrpn	Get row partitioning number	sqlutil.h	Local node	None
sqlugtpi	Get table partitioning information	sqlutil.h	Database	SYSADM, SYSCTRL
sqluimpr	Import data	sqlutil.h	Database	SYSADM, DBADM
sqluload	Load data	sqlutil.h	Database	SYSADM, DBADM
sqlurcon	Reconcile DATALINK entries	sqlutil.h	Database	SYSADM, SYSCTRL, SYSMAINT, DBADM

Table 23-1.   *DB2 Administrative API Quick Reference* (continued)

APPLICATION DEVELOPMENT

API Name	Description	Include File	Connection Required	Authorization Required
sqlureot	Reorganize table	sqlutil.h	Database	SYSADM, SYSCTRL, SYSMAINT, DBADM
sqlurestore	Restore database	sqlutil.h	Database, Instance	SYSADM, SYSCTRL, SYSMAINT
sqlurlog	Read log asynchronously	sqlutil.h	Database	SYSADM, DBADM
sqluroll	Roll forward database	sqlutil.h	None	SYSADM, SYSCTRL, SYSMAINT
sqlustat	Update table statistics	sqlutil.h	Database	SYSADM, SYSCTRL, SYSMAINT, DBADM
sqluvqdp	Quiesce tablespaces for table	sqlutil.h	Database	SYSADM, SYSCTRL, SYSMAINT, DBADM, LOAD

Table 23-1. *DB2 Administrative API Quick Reference* (continued)

The Complete Reference

DB2

Chapter 24

Call Level Interface and Open Database Connectivity

The Call Level Interface (CLI) is a database application programming interface (API) published by X/Open and ISO/IEC. The Open Database Connectivity (ODBC) API developed by Microsoft is based on CLI. The official ODBC specification is available at http://www.microsoft.com/data/odbc/.

The close relationship between the CLI and ODBC specifications means that to write highly portable application source code, you can generally write your application to conform to the ODBC level 3.0 specifications. The *IBM DB2 Universal Database Call Level Interface Guide and Reference* lists the conformance level of each CLI function to the ODBC specification. The primary difference between building a CLI application and building an ODBC application is that to build an ODBC application, you simply include one different header file and link your object code with one additional library.

This chapter explains how to build your application as either a CLI or ODBC application. It provides an overview of the basic structure of CLI and ODBC applications and describes how to write CLI client applications, providing examples of the most common sets of features and functions used in CLI and ODBC.

Building CLI Applications

To build a CLI application, you must have installed the DB2 Application Development Client and one of the C or C++ compilers supported by DB2 as listed at http://www.ibm.com/software/data/db2/udb/ad.

Once you have fulfilled these prerequisites, you just need to perform the following general steps to build a CLI application:

1. Include the sqlcli1.h header file in your application source code.

2. Link your application object code with the DB2 shared library (db2cli.lib on Windows, libdb2.a or libdb2.so on UNIX).

The DB2 Application Development Client provides batch files on Windows operating systems and build scripts on UNIX operating systems to help you build your CLI applications. Check the sqllib/samples/cli/README file for a description of the batch files and build scripts.

Building ODBC Applications

To build an ODBC application, you must have installed the DB2 Application Development Client, one of the C or C++ compilers supported by DB2 as listed at http://www.ibm.com/software/data/db2/udb/ad, and an ODBC driver manager.

The ODBC driver manager used on Windows is the Microsoft Data Access Components Software Development Kit (MDAC SDK), available from http://www.microsoft.com/data/download.htm. A number of different ODBC driver managers are available for UNIX.

Once you have fulfilled these prerequisites, you just need to perform the following general steps to build an ODBC application:

1. Include the sqlcli1.h header file in your application source code.

2. Link your application object code with the ODBC library (odbc32.lib on Windows, varying names on UNIX depending on the ODBC library vendor).

Before running your ODBC application, ensure that you have registered the database to which your application will connect as an ODBC data source on every client from which your application will connect.

Initializing Application Resources

To perform any tasks with a database in a CLI program, you must allocate and initialize one or more CLI application resources, called *handles,* which are required by CLI functions. CLI functions use four different types of handles:

- **Environment handle**   A data object that contains information regarding the global state of the application, such as attributes and connections. An environment handle must be allocated before a connection handle can be allocated.

- **Connection handle**   A data object that contains information associated with a connection to a particular data source (database). This includes connection attributes, general status information, transaction status, and diagnostic information. An application can be connected to several servers at the same time and can establish several distinct connections to the same server. An application requires a connection handle for each concurrent connection to a database server. Call SQLGetInfo() to determine whether a user-imposed limit on the number of connection handles has been set.

- **Statement handle**   A data object that is used to execute—and track the execution of—a single SQL statement. Each statement handle is associated with a connection handle.

- **Descriptor handle**   A data object that contains information about columns in a result set and dynamic parameters in an SQL statement.

The environment handle is the basis of all interactions with the database.

Connecting to a DB2 Database

To create a connection to a DB2 database, start by declaring the following variables:

```
SQLHANDLE henv;
SQLHANDLE hdbc;
SQLCHAR server[9] = "sample";
SQLCHAR user[19] = "db2inst1";
SQLCHAR password[9] = "ibmdb2";
```

Of course, you can assign values to the server, user, and password variables by using input from the command line, the graphic user interface (GUI), or from parameters passed in to a function.

To connect to the database, perform the following steps:

1. Allocate an environment handle:

   ```
   SQLAllocHandle(SQL_HANDLE_ENV, SQL_NULL_HANDLE, &henv);
   ```

2. Allocate a connection handle:

   ```
   SQLAllocHandle(SQL_HANDLE_DBC, henv, &hdbc);
   ```

3. Create the connection:

   ```
   SQLConnect(hdbc, server, SQL_NTS, user, SQL_NTS, password, SQL_NTS);
   ```

4. Disconnect from the database:

   ```
   SQLDisconnect(hdbc);
   ```

   When you disconnect from the database by calling the SQLDisconnect() function, any statement or descriptor handles associated with the connection are automatically freed. To prevent resource leaks, however, you should explicitly free any statement, connection, and environment handles you have allocated in your application:

   ```
   SQLFreeHandle(SQL_HANDLE_STMT, hstmt);
   SQLFreeHandle(SQL_HANDLE_DBC, hdbc);
   SQLFreeHandle(SQL_HANDLE_ENV, henv);
   ```

Controlling SQL Transactions

When you create a connection to a DB2 database in a CLI or ODBC application, the default setting is to automatically commit any changes to the database after each SQL statement is issued. Autocommit normally provides the best performance for your database application because the frequent COMMIT statements prevent the application from acquiring too many locks. DB2 is also able to take advantage of certain optimizations when it knows that autocommit is turned on.

In some situations, however, you might want to explicitly issue ROLLBACK or COMMIT statements, or change the default locking behavior of DB2.

Manually Committing or Rolling Back Transactions

To manually control SQL transactions in your application, you can turn off autocommit for all transactions for a given database connection by calling the SQLSetConnectAttr() function:

```
SQLSetConnectAttr(&hdbc, SQL_ATTR_AUTOCOMMIT, (void *)
SQL_AUTOCOMMIT_OFF, SQL_NTS);
```

After autocommit is turned off for a database connection, the first statement issued against the database begins a transaction. To end a transaction, call the SQLEndTran() function on the associated database connection handle and specify whether you wish to commit or roll back the transaction. To commit a transaction, pass the SQL_COMMIT value as follows:

```
SQLEndTran(SQL_HANDLE_DBC, hdbc, SQL_COMMIT);
```

To roll back a transaction, pass the SQL_ROLLBACK value as follows:

```
SQLEndTran(SQL_HANDLE_DBC, hdbc, SQL_ROLLBACK);
```

For an example of a manually controlled SQL transaction, see the updateResultSet() example in the "Updating or Deleting Data in a Result Set" section later in the chapter.

Changing the Default Locking Behavior of DB2

The locking behavior of a DB2 application is determined by its concurrency level, as described in Chapter 14. The default concurrency level for DB2 is Cursor Stability (CS), which maps to the ODBC transaction isolation level of SQL_TXN_READ_COMMITTED. To change the default locking behavior for DB2 in your CLI or ODBC applications at the database connection level, call the SQLSetConnectAttr() function by using the following syntax:

```
SQLSetConnectAttr(hdbc, SQL_ATTR_TXN_ISOLATION, isolevel, SQL_NTS);
```

Specify the ODBC isolation level that corresponds to the DB2 isolation level of your choice as the third argument to the SQLSetConnectAttr() function. Table 24-1 provides a mapping of ODBC isolation levels to DB2 isolation levels.

APPLICATION
DEVELOPMENT

ODBC Isolation Level	DB2 Isolation Level	Description
No equivalent in ODBC	No Commit	N/A
SQL_TXN_READ_COMMITTED	Cursor Stability (CS)	Locks any row accessed by an application while the cursor is positioned on that row
SQL_TXN_READ_UNCOMMITTED	Uncommitted Read (UR)	The application can access uncommitted changes made by other applications
SQL_TXN_REPEATABLE_READ	Read Stability (RS)	Locks only the rows retrieved by the application within a transaction
SQL_TXN_SERIALIZABLE_READ	Repeatable Read (RR)	Locks all of the rows referenced by the application within a transaction

Table 24-1.   *Mapping DB2 to ODBC Transaction Isolation Levels*

For example, to change the transaction isolation level of your program to the equivalent of the DB2 concurrency level Repeatable Read (RR), you can include the following statement in your application:

```
SQLSetConnectAttr(hdbc, SQL_ATTR_TXN_ISOLATION,
   SQL_TXN_SERIALIZABLE_READ, SQL_NTS);
```

Mapping DB2 Data Types to CLI and ODBC Types

Table 24-2 contains the essential information for working with DB2 data types in CLI and ODBC applications. The first column contains the names of DB2 types. The second column contains the ODBC symbolic names that identify the DB2 data types. The third column contains the names of default C symbolic types; this value tells CLI to which C data type the application will map the corresponding DB2 data type if the application passes SQL_C_DEFAULT to a function instead of an explicit C symbolic name.

Table 24-3 lists the defined C type for each C symbolic data type, along with the base C type from which the defined C type is derived. For maximum portability, we

DB2 Type	CLI/ODBC Symbolic Name	Default C Symbolic Name
BIGINT	SQL_BIGINT	SQL_C_BIGINT
BLOB	SQL_BLOB	SQL_C_BINARY
CHAR	SQL_CHAR	SQL_C_CHAR
CHAR FOR BIT DATA	SQL_BINARY	SQL_C_BINARY
CLOB	SQL_CLOB	SQL_C_CHAR
DATE	SQL_TYPE_DATE	SQL_C_TYPE_DATE
DBCLOB	SQL_DBCLOB	SQL_C_DBCHAR
DECIMAL	SQL_DECIMAL	SQL_C_CHAR
DOUBLE	SQL_DOUBLE	SQL_C_DOUBLE
FLOAT	SQL_FLOAT	SQL_C_DOUBLE
GRAPHIC	SQL_GRAPHIC	SQL_C_DBCHAR
INTEGER	SQL_INTEGER	SQL_C_LONG
LONG VARCHAR	SQL_LONGVARCHAR	SQL_C_CHAR
LONG VARCHAR FOR BIT DATA	SQL_LONGVARBINARY	SQL_C_BINARY
LONG VARGRAPHIC	SQL_LONGVARGRAPHIC	SQL_C_DBCHAR
REAL	SQL_REAL	SQL_C_FLOAT
SMALLINT	SQL_SMALLINT	SQL_C_SHORT
TIME	SQL_TYPE_TIME	SQL_C_TYPE_TIME
TIMESTAMP	SQL_TYPE_TIMESTAMP	SQL_C_TYPE_TIMESTAMP
VARCHAR	SQL_VARCHAR	SQL_C_CHAR
VARCHAR FOR BIT DATA	SQL_VARBINARY	SQL_C_BINARY
VARGRAPHIC	SQL_VARGRAPHIC	SQL_C_DBCHAR

Table 24-2. *DB2 Type Mappings to CLI and ODBC Types*

APPLICATION DEVELOPMENT

strongly recommend that you declare variables in your CLI and ODBC applications by using the defined C type rather than the base C type.

C Symbolic Data Type	Defined C Type	Base C Type
SQL_C_BIGINT	SQLBIGINT	sqlint64
SQL_C_BINARY	SQLCHAR	unsigned char
SQL_C_CHAR	SQLCHAR	unsigned char
SQL_C_DBCHAR	SQLDBCHAR	wchar_t
SQL_C_DECIMAL	SQL_C_CHAR	unsigned char
SQL_C_DOUBLE	SQLDOUBLE	double
SQL_C_FLOAT	SQLREAL	float
SQL_C_LONG	SQLINTEGER	sqlint32
SQL_C_SHORT	SQLSMALLINT	sqlint16
SQL_C_TYPE_DATE	DATE_STRUCT	typedef struct DATE_STRUCT { SQLSMALLINT year; SQLUSMALLINT month; SQLUSMALLINT day; } DATE_STRUCT;
SQL_C_TYPE_TIME	TIME_STRUCT	typedef struct TIME_STRUCT { SQLUSMALLINT hour; SQLUSMALLINT minute; SQLUSMALLINT second; } TIME_STRUCT;
SQL_C_TYPE_ TIMESTAMP	TIMESTAMP_STRUCT	typedef struct TIMESTAMP_STRUCT { SQLUSMALLINT year; SQLUSMALLINT month; SQLUSMALLINT day; SQLUSMALLINT hour; SQLUSMALLINT minute; SQLUSMALLINT second; SQLINTEGER fraction; } TIMESTAMP_STRUCT;

Table 24-3. *Defined C Types for C Symbolic Types*

You can declare variables in your CLI or ODBC application that represent INTEGER, VARCHAR, and TIMESTAMP DB2 data types as follows:

```
SQLSMALLINT integer;
SQLCHAR varchar;
struct TIMESTAMP_STRUCT timestamp;
```

Error Handling

Every function returns a function return code that maps to the following possible states:

- **SQL_SUCCESS**   The function completed successfully, and no additional SQLSTATE information is available.

- **SQL_SUCCESS_WITH_INFO**   The function completed successfully with a warning or other information. Call SQLGetDiagRec() to receive the SQLSTATE and any other informational messages or warnings. The SQLSTATE class is 01.

- **SQL_STILL_EXECUTING**   The function is still running asynchronously and has not yet completed. Control has been returned to the application, but the function has not yet finished executing.

- **SQL_NO_DATA_FOUND**   The function returned successfully, but no data was found. When this is returned after the execution of an SQL statement, additional information may be available and can be obtained by calling SQLGetDiagRec().

- **SQL_NEED_DATA**   The application tried to execute an SQL statement but DB2 lacks parameter data that the application had indicated would be passed at execute time.

- **SQL_ERROR**   The function failed. Call SQLGetDiagRec() to receive the SQLSTATE and any other error information.

- **SQL_INVALID_HANDLE**   The function failed due to an invalid input handle (environment, connection, or statement handle). This is a programming error. No further information is available.

Issuing Simple SELECT Statements

When you issue a SELECT statement, the query can return a result set. A result set consists of one or more rows of data, where the rows are composed of one or more columns of data. The SQLBindCol() and SQLFetch() functions enable you to retrieve data from a result set by specifying the CLI type corresponding to the SQL type returned from the query.

To issue a simple SQL statement (that is, an SQL statement that contains no parameter markers) in a CLI or ODBC application, follow these steps:

1. Create an SQLCHAR string variable containing the SQL statement.
2. Create a statement handle by calling the SQLAllocHandle() function.
3. Issue the SQL statement by calling the SQLExecDirect() function, passing in the variable containing the SQL statement and the statement handle.

If the SQL statement is a query, you must also follow these steps:

4. Bind each column of the result set to a variable of the corresponding type by calling the SQLBindCol() function.
5. Fetch each row into the bound variables by calling the SQLFetch() method until it returns SQL_NO_DATA_FOUND.

In the following example, the SQLFetch() function is used in a while loop to iterate sequentially through the rows of the result set. The cursor is initially positioned before the first row of the result set. SQLFetch() positions the cursor on the next row of the result set, and it returns SQL_NO_DATA_FOUND if no row was found in the result set. Every call to SQLFetch() updates the variables associated with the columns of the result set through the SQLBindCol() function with the values in the new row.

```
int simpleSelect(SQLHANDLE hdbc) {
  SQLHANDLE hstmt;
  SQLRETURN sqlrc = SQL_SUCCESS;
  int rc = 0;
  SQLCHAR * stmt = (SQLCHAR *) "SELECT firstnme, midinit FROM employee";

  SQLCHAR firstnme[13]; // VARCHAR(12) column
  SQLINTEGER firstind;  // null indicator
  SQLCHAR midinit[2];   // CHAR(1) column
  SQLINTEGER midinitind;// null indicator

  printf("\n  Simple SELECT statement");

  sqlrc = SQLAllocHandle(SQL_HANDLE_STMT, hdbc, &hstmt);
  rc = CLICheckHandle(SQL_HANDLE_STMT, hstmt, sqlrc);
  if (rc != 0) {
    printf("\nCould not allocate statement handle. sqlrc = %d", sqlrc);
    return rc;
  }
```

```
sqlrc = SQLExecDirect(hstmt, stmt, SQL_NTS);
rc = CLICheckHandle(SQL_HANDLE_STMT, hstmt, sqlrc);
if (rc != 0) {
  printf("\nCould not execute SQL statement. sqlrc = %d", sqlrc);
  return rc;
}

sqlrc = SQLBindCol(hstmt, 1, SQL_C_CHAR, firstnme, 13, &firstind);
rc = CLICheckHandle(SQL_HANDLE_STMT, hstmt, sqlrc);
if (rc != 0) {
  printf("\nCould not bind column. sqlrc = %d", sqlrc);
  return rc;
}

sqlrc = SQLBindCol(hstmt, 2, SQL_C_CHAR, midinit, 2, &midinitind);
rc = CLICheckHandle(SQL_HANDLE_STMT, hstmt, sqlrc);
if (rc != 0) {
  printf("\nCould not bind column. sqlrc = %d", sqlrc);
  return rc;
}

sqlrc = SQLFetch(hstmt);
rc = CLICheckHandle(SQL_HANDLE_STMT, hstmt, sqlrc);
if (rc != 0) {
  printf("\nCould not fetch result. sqlrc = %d", sqlrc);
  return rc;
}

while (sqlrc != SQL_NO_DATA_FOUND) {
  printf("\n    %-12.12s %-1.1s", firstnme, midinit);
  sqlrc = SQLFetch(hstmt);
  rc = CLICheckHandle(SQL_HANDLE_STMT, hstmt, sqlrc);
  if (rc != 0) {
    printf("\nCould not fetch result. sqlrc = %d", sqlrc);
    return rc;
  }
}

// free the statement handle
sqlrc = SQLFreeHandle(SQL_HANDLE_STMT, hstmt);
rc = CLICheckHandle(SQL_HANDLE_STMT, hstmt, sqlrc);
if (rc != 0) {
```

```
      printf("\nCould not free handle. sqlrc = %d", sqlrc);
      return rc;
  }


  return rc;
}
```

Issuing Prepared Statements with Parameter Markers

Many applications repeatedly issue the same basic SQL statements with parameters that accept variable input. Rather than calling SQLExecDirect() for each variation on the SELECT statement, consider preparing an SQL statement containing parameter markers with the SQLPrepare() function and repeatedly calling SQLExecute().

Parameter markers (question mark (?) characters) represent variable values within an SQL statement. Set the values of the parameter markers by using the SQLBindParameter() function, and then call SQLExecute() to complete the operation.

The following example uses one SQL statement to perform two UPDATE operations.

```
int prepareSQL(SQLHANDLE hdbc) {
  SQLHANDLE hstmt;
  SQLRETURN sqlrc = SQL_SUCCESS;
  int rc = 0;
  SQLCHAR * stmt = (SQLCHAR *) "UPDATE employee SET salary = ? WHERE workdept = ?";

  SQLCHAR salary[10];      // DECIMAL(9,2) column
  SQLCHAR workdept[4];     // CHAR(3) column

  printf("\n  Prepare and execute SQL statement.");

  sqlrc = SQLAllocHandle(SQL_HANDLE_STMT, hdbc, &hstmt);
  rc = CLICheckHandle(SQL_HANDLE_STMT, hstmt, sqlrc);
  if (rc != 0) {
    printf("\nCould not allocate statement handle. sqlrc = %d", sqlrc);
    return rc;
  }

  sqlrc = SQLPrepare(hstmt, stmt, SQL_NTS);
  rc = CLICheckHandle(SQL_HANDLE_STMT, hstmt, sqlrc);
  if (rc != 0) {
    printf("\nCould not prepare SQL statement. sqlrc = %d", sqlrc);
    return rc;
  }
```

```
  sqlrc = SQLBindParameter(hstmt, 1, SQL_PARAM_INPUT, SQL_C_CHAR,
                           SQL_DECIMAL, 9, 2, salary, 10, NULL);
  rc = CLICheckHandle(SQL_HANDLE_STMT, hstmt, sqlrc);
  if (rc != 0) {
    printf("\nCould not prepare SQL statement. sqlrc = %d", sqlrc);
    return rc;
  }


  sqlrc = SQLBindParameter(hstmt, 2, SQL_PARAM_INPUT, SQL_C_CHAR,
                           SQL_CHAR, 4, 0, workdept, 4, NULL);
  rc = CLICheckHandle(SQL_HANDLE_STMT, hstmt, sqlrc);
  if (rc != 0) {
    printf("\nCould not prepare SQL statement. sqlrc = %d", sqlrc);
    return rc;
  }


  // First use of the prepared SQL statement
  strcpy(salary, "35000.75");
  strcpy(workdept, "A00");

  sqlrc = SQLExecute(hstmt);
  rc = CLICheckHandle(SQL_HANDLE_STMT, hstmt, sqlrc);
  if (rc != 0) {
    printf("\nCould not execute SQL statement. sqlrc = %d", sqlrc);
    return rc;
  }


  // Second use of the prepared SQL statement
  strcpy(salary, "37500.57");
  strcpy(workdept, "B01");

  sqlrc = SQLExecute(hstmt);
  rc = CLICheckHandle(SQL_HANDLE_STMT, hstmt, sqlrc);
  if (rc != 0) {
    printf("\nCould not execute SQL statement. sqlrc = %d", sqlrc);
    return rc;
  }


  // free the statement handle
  sqlrc = SQLFreeHandle(SQL_HANDLE_STMT, hstmt) ;
  rc = CLICheckHandle(SQL_HANDLE_STMT, hstmt, sqlrc);
  if (rc != 0) {
    printf("\nCould not fetch result. sqlrc = %d", sqlrc);
    return rc;
  }

  printf("\n  Finished executing prepared statement.");
  return rc;
}
```

APPLICATION
DEVELOPMENT

Updating or Deleting Data in a Result Set

Updating the value of a column in a result set is called a *positioned update*. Deleting the current row in a result set is called a *positioned delete*. To issue a positioned update or positioned delete in a CLI or ODBC result set, perform the following steps:

1. Allocate a statement handle for the SELECT statement that generates the result set.

2. Generate the result set by issuing the SELECT statement.

3. Get the name of the cursor for the result set by calling the SQLGetCursorName() function on the statement handle that generated the result set.

4. Allocate a second statement handle that will be used to execute the positioned update or positioned delete statement.

5. Position the cursor on the row of the result set that contains the data that you want to update.

6. Issue an UPDATE or DELETE statement incorporating the WHERE CURRENT OF clause and specifying the cursor name.

The following example demonstrates how to issue a positioned update statement:

```
int updateResultSet(SQLHANDLE hdbc) {
  SQLHANDLE hstmtSelect;
  SQLHANDLE hstmtUpdate;
  SQLRETURN sqlrc = SQL_SUCCESS;
  int rc = 0;

  SQLCHAR * stmt = (SQLCHAR *) "SELECT firstnme, midinit, edlevel"
                   " FROM employee FOR UPDATE OF firstnme";
  SQLCHAR update[200];
  SQLCHAR cursorName[20];
  SQLSMALLINT cursorLen;

  printf("\n\n  Positioned UPDATE.");

  // turn autocommit off
  sqlrc = SQLSetConnectAttr(hdbc, SQL_ATTR_AUTOCOMMIT,
      (void *) SQL_AUTOCOMMIT_OFF, SQL_NTS);
  rc = CLICheckHandle(SQL_HANDLE_DBC, hdbc, sqlrc);
  if (rc != 0) {
    printf("\nCould not turn autocommit off. sqlrc = %d", sqlrc);
    return rc;
  }
```

```
sqlrc = SQLAllocHandle(SQL_HANDLE_STMT, hdbc, &hstmtSelect);
rc = CLICheckHandle(SQL_HANDLE_STMT, hstmtSelect, sqlrc);
if (rc != 0) {
  printf("\nCould not allocate statement handle. sqlrc = %d", sqlrc);
  return rc;
}

sqlrc = SQLAllocHandle(SQL_HANDLE_STMT, hdbc, &hstmtUpdate);
rc = CLICheckHandle(SQL_HANDLE_STMT, hstmtUpdate, sqlrc);
if (rc != 0) {
  printf("\nCould not allocate statement handle. sqlrc = %d", sqlrc);
  return rc;
}

sqlrc = SQLExecDirect(hstmtSelect, stmt, SQL_NTS);
rc = CLICheckHandle(SQL_HANDLE_STMT, hstmtUpdate, sqlrc);
if (rc != 0) {
  printf("\nCould not execute query. sqlrc = %d", sqlrc);
  return rc;
}

// get the cursor name of the SELECT statement
sqlrc = SQLGetCursorName(hstmtSelect, cursorName, 20, &cursorLen);
rc = CLICheckHandle(SQL_HANDLE_STMT, hstmtUpdate, sqlrc);
if (rc != 0) {
  printf("\nCould not get cursor name. sqlrc = %d", sqlrc);
  return rc;
}

sqlrc = SQLFetch(hstmtSelect);
rc = CLICheckHandle(SQL_HANDLE_STMT, hstmtSelect, sqlrc);
if (rc != 0) {
  printf("\nCould not fetch result. sqlrc = %d", sqlrc);
  return rc;
}

while (sqlrc != SQL_NO_DATA_FOUND) {
  sprintf((char *)update, "UPDATE employee"
      " SET firstnme = 'DRONE' WHERE CURRENT of %s", cursorName);
  sqlrc = SQLExecDirect(hstmtUpdate, update, SQL_NTS);
  rc = CLICheckHandle(SQL_HANDLE_STMT, hstmtUpdate, sqlrc);
```

```
  if (rc != 0) {
    printf("\nCould not update row. sqlrc = %d", sqlrc);
    return rc;
  }

  sqlrc = SQLFetch(hstmtSelect);
  rc = CLICheckHandle(SQL_HANDLE_STMT, hstmtSelect, sqlrc);
  if (rc != 0) {
    printf("\nCould not fetch result. sqlrc = %d", sqlrc);
    return rc;
  }
}

// roll back the transaction
sqlrc = SQLEndTran(SQL_HANDLE_DBC, hdbc, SQL_ROLLBACK);
rc = CLICheckHandle(SQL_HANDLE_STMT, hstmtUpdate, sqlrc);
if (rc != 0) {
  printf("\nCould not issue rollback. sqlrc = %d", sqlrc);
  return rc;
}

// free the statement handles
sqlrc = SQLFreeHandle(SQL_HANDLE_STMT, hstmtSelect);
rc = CLICheckHandle(SQL_HANDLE_STMT, hstmtSelect, sqlrc);
if (rc != 0) {
  printf("\nCould not free handle. sqlrc = %d", sqlrc);
  return rc;
}

sqlrc = SQLFreeHandle(SQL_HANDLE_STMT, hstmtUpdate);
rc = CLICheckHandle(SQL_HANDLE_STMT, hstmtUpdate, sqlrc);
if (rc != 0) {
  printf("\nCould not free handle. sqlrc = %d", sqlrc);
  return rc;
}

// turn autocommit on
sqlrc = SQLSetConnectAttr(hdbc, SQL_ATTR_AUTOCOMMIT,
    (void *) SQL_AUTOCOMMIT_ON, SQL_NTS);
rc = CLICheckHandle(SQL_HANDLE_DBC, hdbc, sqlrc);
if (rc != 0) {
  printf("\nCould not turn autocommit on. sqlrc = %d", sqlrc);
```

```
   return rc;
}

printf("\n  Finished positioned UPDATE.");

return rc;
}
```

Calling Stored Procedures

Stored procedures can accept a combination of input parameters (IN parameters), output parameters (OUT parameters), and parameters that accept input and return a different result (INOUT parameters). A stored procedure can return zero or more result sets. CLI programs call cataloged stored procedures by preparing a CALL statement, binding the IN, OUT, or INOUT parameters for the statement, executing the statement, and retrieving the results.

To call a stored procedure, perform the following steps:

1. Declare the variables that will be used for parameters in the stored procedure.

2. Set the input value of any IN or INOUT parameter variables.

3. Prepare the statement by using the SQLPrepare() function.

4. Bind each parameter of the CALL statement by using the SQLBindParameter() function to specify the call type (IN, OUT, or INOUT), the C data type, the SQL data type, the variable name for the parameter, and associated variable data.

5. Issue the CALL statement by invoking the SQLExecute() function.

6. Retrieve any result sets returned by the stored procedure by calling SQLFetch() on the statement handle.

The simplest example of a stored procedure accepts no parameters and returns no result sets; it might perform some administrative task on the server. The following example calls a simple stored procedure cataloged with the name simpleProc:

```
int callSimpleProcedure (SQLHANDLE hdbc) {
  SQLRETURN sqlrc = SQL_SUCCESS;
  int rc = 0;
  SQLHANDLE hstmt;
  SQLCHAR * stmt = (SQLCHAR *) "CALL simpleProc()";

  printf("\n\n  CALL simple stored procedure.");
```

```
sqlrc = SQLAllocHandle(SQL_HANDLE_STMT, hdbc, &hstmt);
rc = CLICheckHandle(SQL_HANDLE_STMT, hstmt, sqlrc);
if (rc != 0) {
  printf("\nCould not allocate handle. sqlrc = %d", sqlrc);
  return rc;
}

// prepare the CALL statement
sqlrc = SQLPrepare(hstmt, stmt, SQL_NTS);
rc = CLICheckHandle(SQL_HANDLE_STMT, hstmt, sqlrc);
if (rc != 0) {
  printf("\nCould not prepare statement. sqlrc = %d", sqlrc);
  return rc;
}

// issue the CALL statement
sqlrc = SQLExecute(hstmt);
rc = CLICheckHandle(SQL_HANDLE_STMT, hstmt, sqlrc);
if (rc != 0) {
  printf("\nCould not execute statement. sqlrc = %d", sqlrc);
  return rc;
}

// free statement handle
sqlrc = SQLFreeHandle(SQL_HANDLE_STMT, hstmt) ;
rc = CLICheckHandle(SQL_HANDLE_STMT, hstmt, sqlrc);
if (rc != 0) {
  printf("\nCould not free handle. sqlrc = %d", sqlrc);
}

printf("\n  Finished calling simple stored procedure.");

return rc;
}
```

Retrieving OUT Parameters from a Stored Procedure

Many stored procedures return OUT parameters. For error-checking purposes, a stored procedure typically returns an OUT parameter containing a result code. To accept an OUT parameter from a stored procedure, a CLI or ODBC program must perform the following steps:

1. Ensure that the CALL statement represents each parameter with a parameter marker (the question mark (?) character).

2. Prepare the CALL statement by using the SQLPrepare() function.

3. Issue the SQLBindParameter() function for each OUT parameter.

4. Issue the CALL statement by using the SQLExecute() function.

In the following example, the function calls a stored procedure named outParameter that returns two OUT parameters. The first OUT parameter is of type VARCHAR(50) and returns the autocommit state of the stored procedure. The second OUT parameter is of type INTEGER and returns the final SQLCODE value of the stored procedure.

```
int callOutParameter (SQLHANDLE hdbc) {
  SQLRETURN sqlrc = SQL_SUCCESS;
  int rc = 0;
  SQLHANDLE hstmt;
  SQLCHAR * stmt = (SQLCHAR *) "CALL outParameter(?, ?)";
  SQLCHAR autocommit[51];
  SQLINTEGER outrc;

  printf("\n\n  CALL stored procedure with OUT parameters.");

  sqlrc = SQLAllocHandle(SQL_HANDLE_STMT, hdbc, &hstmt);
  rc = CLICheckHandle(SQL_HANDLE_STMT, hstmt, sqlrc);
  if (rc != 0) {
    printf("\nCould not allocate handle. sqlrc = %d", sqlrc);
    return rc;
  }

  // prepare the CALL statement
  sqlrc = SQLPrepare(hstmt, stmt, SQL_NTS);
  rc = CLICheckHandle(SQL_HANDLE_STMT, hstmt, sqlrc);
  if (rc != 0) {
    printf("\nCould not prepare statement. sqlrc = %d", sqlrc);
    return rc;
  }

  // bind parameter 1 to the CALL statement
  sqlrc = SQLBindParameter(hstmt, 1, SQL_PARAM_OUTPUT,
    SQL_C_CHAR, SQL_CHAR,
    51, 0, autocommit,
```

```
      51, NULL);
rc = CLICheckHandle(SQL_HANDLE_STMT, hstmt, sqlrc);
if (rc != 0) {
  printf("\nCould not bind parameter 1. sqlrc = %d", sqlrc);
  return rc;
}

// bind parameter 2 to the CALL statement
sqlrc = SQLBindParameter(hstmt, 2, SQL_PARAM_OUTPUT,
  SQL_C_LONG, SQL_INTEGER,
  0, 0, &outrc,
  0, NULL);
rc = CLICheckHandle(SQL_HANDLE_STMT, hstmt, sqlrc);
if (rc != 0) {
  printf("\nCould not bind parameter 2. sqlrc = %d", sqlrc);
  return rc;
}

// issue the CALL statement
sqlrc = SQLExecute(hstmt);
rc = CLICheckHandle(SQL_HANDLE_STMT, hstmt, sqlrc);
if (rc != 0) {
  printf("\nCould not execute statement. sqlrc = %d", sqlrc);
  return rc;
}

printf("\n   Autocommit state: %s", autocommit);
printf("\n   Returned SQLCODE: %d", (sqlint16) outrc);

// free the statement handle
sqlrc = SQLFreeHandle(SQL_HANDLE_STMT, hstmt) ;
rc = CLICheckHandle(SQL_HANDLE_STMT, hstmt, sqlrc);
if (rc != 0) {
  printf("\nCould not free handle. sqlrc = %d", sqlrc);
}

printf("\n\n  Finished calling simple stored procedure.");

return rc;
}
```

Passing IN Parameters to a Stored Procedure

Stored procedures can accept IN parameters to modify their behavior. For example, you might pass an IN parameter containing a value to be used in a WHERE clause of a SELECT statement issued within the stored procedure.

To pass an IN parameter to a stored procedure, perform the following steps:

1. Ensure that the CALL statement represents each parameter with a parameter marker (the question mark (?) character).

2. Prepare the CALL statement by using the SQLPrepare() function.

3. Set the value of each variable that represents an IN parameter.

4. Issue the SQLBindParameter() function for each IN parameter.

5. Issue the CALL statement by using the SQLExecute() function.

In the following example, the function calls a stored procedure named inParameter that accepts one IN parameter and returns two OUT parameters. The IN parameter is of type SMALLINT and is used within the stored procedure to identify the department number within the WHERE clause of a SELECT statement. The first OUT parameter is of type INTEGER and represents the number of rows returned by the SELECT statement. The second OUT parameter is of type INTEGER and represents the final SQLCODE value within the stored procedure.

```
int callInParameter (SQLHANDLE hdbc) {
  SQLRETURN sqlrc = SQL_SUCCESS;
  int rc = 0;
  SQLHANDLE hstmt;
  SQLCHAR * stmt = (SQLCHAR *) "CALL inParameter(?, ?, ?)";
  SQLSMALLINT inDepartment;
  SQLINTEGER outRows;
  SQLINTEGER outrc;

  printf("\n\n  CALL stored procedure with IN parameter.");

  sqlrc = SQLAllocHandle(SQL_HANDLE_STMT, hdbc, &hstmt);
  rc = CLICheckHandle(SQL_HANDLE_STMT, hstmt, sqlrc);
  if (rc != 0) {
    printf("\nCould not allocate handle. sqlrc = %d", sqlrc);
    return rc;
  }

  // prepare the CALL statement
  sqlrc = SQLPrepare(hstmt, stmt, SQL_NTS);
```

```
rc = CLICheckHandle(SQL_HANDLE_STMT, hstmt, sqlrc);
if (rc != 0) {
  printf("\nCould not prepare statement. sqlrc = %d", sqlrc);
  return rc;
}

// set value of IN parameter
inDepartment = 38;

// bind parameter 1 to the CALL statement
sqlrc = SQLBindParameter(hstmt, 1, SQL_PARAM_INPUT,
  SQL_C_SHORT, SQL_SMALLINT,
  0, 0, &inDepartment,
  0, NULL);
rc = CLICheckHandle(SQL_HANDLE_STMT, hstmt, sqlrc);
if (rc != 0) {
  printf("\nCould not bind parameter 1. sqlrc = %d", sqlrc);
  return rc;
}

// bind parameter 2 to the CALL statement
sqlrc = SQLBindParameter(hstmt, 2, SQL_PARAM_OUTPUT,
  SQL_C_LONG, SQL_INTEGER,
  0, 0, &outRows,
  0, NULL);
rc = CLICheckHandle(SQL_HANDLE_STMT, hstmt, sqlrc);
if (rc != 0) {
  printf("\nCould not bind parameter 2. sqlrc = %d", sqlrc);
  return rc;
}

// bind parameter 3 to the CALL statement
sqlrc = SQLBindParameter(hstmt, 3, SQL_PARAM_OUTPUT,
  SQL_C_LONG, SQL_INTEGER,
  0, 0, &outrc,
  0, NULL);
rc = CLICheckHandle(SQL_HANDLE_STMT, hstmt, sqlrc);
if (rc != 0) {
  printf("\nCould not bind parameter 3. sqlrc = %d", sqlrc);
  return rc;
}
```

```
// issue the CALL statement
sqlrc = SQLExecute(hstmt);
rc = CLICheckHandle(SQL_HANDLE_STMT, hstmt, sqlrc);
if (rc != 0) {
  printf("\nCould not execute statement. sqlrc = %d", sqlrc);
  return rc;
}

printf("\n    Number of rows: %d", (sqlint16) outRows);
printf("\n    Returned SQLCODE: %d", (sqlint16) outrc);

// free the statement handle
sqlrc = SQLFreeHandle(SQL_HANDLE_STMT, hstmt) ;
rc = CLICheckHandle(SQL_HANDLE_STMT, hstmt, sqlrc);
if (rc != 0) {
  printf("\nCould not free handle. sqlrc = %d", sqlrc);
}

printf("\n\n  Finished calling IN stored procedure.");

return rc;
}
```

Passing INOUT Parameters to a Stored Procedure

Stored procedures can accept INOUT parameters. These parameters pass an input value to the stored procedure and return an output value from the stored procedure. For example, you might pass an INOUT parameter containing a value to be used in a WHERE clause of a SELECT statement issued within the stored procedure, and then return the result of the SELECT statement in the same INOUT parameter.

To pass an INOUT parameter to a stored procedure, perform the following steps:

1. Ensure that the CALL statement represents each parameter with a parameter marker (the question mark (?) character).

2. Prepare the CALL statement by using the SQLPrepare() function.

3. Set the value of each variable that represents an INOUT parameter.

4. Issue the SQLBindParameter() function for each INOUT parameter.

5. Issue the CALL statement by using the SQLExecute() function.

In the following example, the function calls a stored procedure named inoutParameter, which accepts one INOUT parameter and returns one OUT parameter. The INOUT parameter is of type SMALLINT and its input value is used within the stored procedure to identify the department number within the WHERE clause of a SELECT statement. The output value of the INOUT parameter represents the number of rows returned by the SELECT statement. The OUT parameter is of type INTEGER and represents the final SQLCODE value within the stored procedure.

```c
int callInoutParameter (SQLHANDLE hdbc) {
  SQLRETURN sqlrc = SQL_SUCCESS;
  int rc = 0;
  SQLHANDLE hstmt;
  SQLCHAR * stmt = (SQLCHAR *) "CALL inoutParameter(?, ?)";
  SQLSMALLINT inout;
  SQLINTEGER outrc;

  printf("\n\n  CALL stored procedure with IN parameter.");

  sqlrc = SQLAllocHandle(SQL_HANDLE_STMT, hdbc, &hstmt);
  rc = CLICheckHandle(SQL_HANDLE_STMT, hstmt, sqlrc);
  if (rc != 0) {
    printf("\nCould not allocate handle. sqlrc = %d", sqlrc);
    return rc;
  }

  // prepare the CALL statement
  sqlrc = SQLPrepare(hstmt, stmt, SQL_NTS);
  rc = CLICheckHandle(SQL_HANDLE_STMT, hstmt, sqlrc);
  if (rc != 0) {
    printf("\nCould not prepare statement. sqlrc = %d", sqlrc);
    return rc;
  }

  // set input value of INOUT parameter
  inout = 38;

  // bind parameter 1 to the CALL statement
  sqlrc = SQLBindParameter(hstmt, 1, SQL_PARAM_INPUT_OUTPUT,
    SQL_C_SHORT, SQL_SMALLINT,
    0, 0, &inout,
    0, NULL);
  rc = CLICheckHandle(SQL_HANDLE_STMT, hstmt, sqlrc);
  if (rc != 0) {
    printf("\nCould not bind parameter 1. sqlrc = %d", sqlrc);
    return rc;
```

```
  }

  // bind parameter 2 to the CALL statement
  sqlrc = SQLBindParameter(hstmt, 2, SQL_PARAM_OUTPUT,
    SQL_C_LONG, SQL_INTEGER,
    0, 0, &outrc,
    0, NULL);
  rc = CLICheckHandle(SQL_HANDLE_STMT, hstmt, sqlrc);
  if (rc != 0) {
    printf("\nCould not bind parameter 2. sqlrc = %d", sqlrc);
    return rc;
  }

  // issue the CALL statement
  sqlrc = SQLExecute(hstmt);
  rc = CLICheckHandle(SQL_HANDLE_STMT, hstmt, sqlrc);
  if (rc != 0) {
    printf("\nCould not execute statement. sqlrc = %d", sqlrc);
    return rc;
  }

  printf("\n    Number of rows: %d", (sqlint16) inout);
  printf("\n    Returned SQLCODE: %d", (sqlint16) outrc);

  // free the statement handle
  sqlrc = SQLFreeHandle(SQL_HANDLE_STMT, hstmt) ;
s  rc = CLICheckHandle(SQL_HANDLE_STMT, hstmt, sqlrc);
  if (rc != 0) {
    printf("\nCould not free handle. sqlrc = %d", sqlrc);
  }

  printf("\n\n  Finished calling INOUT stored procedure.");

  return rc;
}
```

Retrieving Result Sets from Stored Procedures

Stored procedures can have zero, one, or multiple result sets. Working with result
sets returned from a stored procedure is just like working with result sets returned by a
SELECT statement, except that a stored procedure can return multiple result sets.

To work with result sets returned from a stored procedure, perform the following steps:

1. Prepare the CALL statement and bind any parameters as described in the preceding sections.

2. Issue the CALL statement by using the SQLExecute() function.

3. Retrieve rows from the first result set returned from the stored procedure by using the SQLFetch() function until it returns SQL_NO_DATA_FOUND.

4. Get the next result set returned from the stored procedure by calling the SQLMoreResults() function; if it returns SQL_NO_DATA_FOUND, then you have already retrieved all of the result sets.

5. Fetch rows from the new result set by using the SQLFetch() function.

In the following example, the function calls a stored procedure named twoResultSets and iterates through each result set returned by the stored procedure, printing the name and years of service for each row in each of the result sets.

```
int callTwoResultSets (SQLHANDLE hdbc) {
  SQLRETURN sqlrc = SQL_SUCCESS;
  int rc = 0;
  SQLHANDLE hstmt;
  SQLCHAR * stmt = (SQLCHAR *) "CALL twoResultSets(?)";
  SQLSMALLINT inYears;
  SQLCHAR name[10];
  SQLSMALLINT years;

  printf("\n\n  CALL stored procedure with result sets.");

  sqlrc = SQLAllocHandle(SQL_HANDLE_STMT, hdbc, &hstmt);
  rc = CLICheckHandle(SQL_HANDLE_STMT, hstmt, sqlrc);
  if (rc != 0) {
    printf("\nCould not allocate handle. sqlrc = %d", sqlrc);
    return rc;
  }

  // prepare the CALL statement
  sqlrc = SQLPrepare(hstmt, stmt, SQL_NTS);
  rc = CLICheckHandle(SQL_HANDLE_STMT, hstmt, sqlrc);
  if (rc != 0) {
    printf("\nCould not prepare statement. sqlrc = %d", sqlrc);
    return rc;
```

```
  }

  // set input value of INOUT parameter
  inYears = 5;

  // bind parameter 1 to the CALL statement
  sqlrc = SQLBindParameter(hstmt, 1, SQL_PARAM_INPUT,
    SQL_C_SHORT, SQL_SMALLINT,
    0, 0, &inYears,
    0, NULL);
  rc = CLICheckHandle(SQL_HANDLE_STMT, hstmt, sqlrc);
  if (rc != 0) {
    printf("\nCould not bind parameter 1. sqlrc = %d", sqlrc);
    return rc;
  }

  // issue the CALL statement
  sqlrc = SQLExecute(hstmt);
  rc = CLICheckHandle(SQL_HANDLE_STMT, hstmt, sqlrc);
  if (rc != 0) {
    printf("\nCould not execute statement. sqlrc = %d", sqlrc);
    return rc;
  }

  // bind result set columns to variables
  sqlrc = SQLBindCol(hstmt, 1, SQL_C_CHAR, name, 10, NULL);
  rc = CLICheckHandle(SQL_HANDLE_STMT, hstmt, sqlrc);
  if (rc != 0) {
    printf("\nCould not bind column. sqlrc = %d", sqlrc);
    return rc;
  }

  sqlrc = SQLBindCol(hstmt, 2, SQL_C_SHORT, &years, 0, NULL);
  rc = CLICheckHandle(SQL_HANDLE_STMT, hstmt, sqlrc);
  if (rc != 0) {
    printf("\nCould not bind column. sqlrc = %d", sqlrc);
    return rc;
  }

  // fetch from first result set
  sqlrc = SQLFetch(hstmt);
  rc = CLICheckHandle(SQL_HANDLE_STMT, hstmt, sqlrc);
```

```c
  if (rc != 0) {
    printf("\nCould not fetch row. sqlrc = %d", sqlrc);
    return rc;
  }

printf("\n  First result set:");
while (sqlrc != SQL_NO_DATA_FOUND) {
  printf("\n    Name: %s, Years: %d", name, years);
  sqlrc = SQLFetch(hstmt);
  rc = CLICheckHandle(SQL_HANDLE_STMT, hstmt, sqlrc);
  if (rc != 0) {
    printf("\nCould not fetch row. sqlrc = %d", sqlrc);
    return rc;
  }
}

// get second result set
sqlrc = SQLMoreResults(hstmt);
rc = CLICheckHandle(SQL_HANDLE_STMT, hstmt, sqlrc);
if (rc != 0) {
  printf("\nCould not get result set. sqlrc = %d", sqlrc);
  return rc;
}

// fetch from second result set
sqlrc = SQLFetch(hstmt);
rc = CLICheckHandle(SQL_HANDLE_STMT, hstmt, sqlrc);
if (rc != 0) {
  printf("\nCould not fetch row. sqlrc = %d", sqlrc);
  return rc;
}

printf("\n\n  Second result set:");
while (sqlrc != SQL_NO_DATA_FOUND) {
  printf("\n    Name: %s, Years: %d", name, years);
  sqlrc = SQLFetch(hstmt);
  rc = CLICheckHandle(SQL_HANDLE_STMT, hstmt, sqlrc);
  if (rc != 0) {
    printf("\nCould not fetch row. sqlrc = %d", sqlrc);
    return rc;
  }
}
```

```
// free the statement handle
sqlrc = SQLFreeHandle(SQL_HANDLE_STMT, hstmt) ;
rc = CLICheckHandle(SQL_HANDLE_STMT, hstmt, sqlrc);
if (rc != 0) {
  printf("\nCould not free handle. sqlrc = %d", sqlrc);
}

printf("\n\n  Finished calling INOUT stored procedure.");

return rc;
}
```

The Complete Reference

DB2

Chapter 25

Java Support

When you write a DB2 application in Java using the Java Database Connectivity (JDBC) application programming interface (API), you combine the benefits of a strongly typed, object-oriented programming language with a mature, industry-standard API. DB2 has supported JDBC since DB2 version 2 was released, and version 7.2 provides drivers for both the JDBC 1.22 and JDBC 2.0 specifications. Whereas JDBC 1.22 provides a solid foundation for developing database applications, JDBC 2.0 builds on that foundation by offering advanced features like scrollable result sets while maintaining compatibility with JDBC 1.22 applications.

This chapter primarily describes how to write JDBC applications by using the set of features common to both JDBC 1.22 and JDBC 2.0, but it also discusses the features offered by the JDBC 2.0 driver for DB2 in the section called "JDBC 2.0: Scrollable Result Sets, BLOB, and CLOB Data Types." You can find the official JDBC specifications at http://www.javasoft.com/products/jdk/1.2/docs/guide/jdbc. This chapter also discusses how to embed static SQL statements in Java programs by using the SQL for Java (SQLj) support DB2 offers.

Connecting to a DB2 Database Using JDBC

To perform any tasks with a database in a JDBC program, you must create a Connection object. The Connection object is the basis of all interactions with the database. You can create a Connection object with the DB2 JDBC drivers by using either the application driver or the net driver. The application driver offers the best performance, stability, and ease of use, and should be used to connect to the database in all but the most exceptional circumstances. The net driver enables Java programs to connect to a DB2 database without installing a DB2 run-time client, but this convenience comes at the cost of both performance and stability.

Connecting with the Application Driver Using JDBC

To create a Connection object using the DB2 JDBC application driver, include the static initializer in your program:

```
Class.forName("COM.ibm.db2.jdbc.app.DB2Driver");
```

You must also satisfy the following prerequisites:

- Install the DB2 client on every workstation that runs your JDBC program. To roll out a large number of DB2 clients, consider configuring an autoinstallation script as described in the *Quick Beginnings* books shipped with DB2 or available from http://www.ibm.com/software/data/db2/library.

- Catalog the database or databases that your JDBC program connects to on every workstation that runs your JDBC program. Test your connection to the database from the DB2 command line processor (CLP).

- The CLASSPATH environment variable on the client must point to the db2java.zip file provided with the DB2 client. On Windows clients, DB2 sets the CLASSPATH environment variable when you start a DB2 CLP session. On UNIX platforms, DB2 sets the CLASSPATH environment variable when you source the sqllib/db2profile script.

- JDBC applets must make db2java.zip available in the same directory as the applet.

```
public static void main(String argv[]) {
  Connection con = null;
  // URL format for application driver is jdbc:db2:dbname
String url = "jdbc:db2:sample";

  // invoke static initializer for application driver
  try {
    Class.forName("COM.ibm.db2.jdbc.app.DB2Driver");
  }
  catch (ClassNotFoundException e) {
    System.out.println(e);
  }

  try {
    if (argv.length == 0) {
      // connect with the default user ID and password
      con = DriverManager.getConnection(url);
    }
    else if (argv.length == 2) {
      String user = argv[0];
      String password = argv[1];
      // connect with user-provided username and password
      con = DriverManager.getConnection(url, user, password);
    }
  // perform database work here
  con.close();
  }
  catch (SQLException sqle) {
    System.out.println(sqle.toString());
  }
}
```

Connecting with the Net Driver

To create a Connection object using the DB2 JDBC net driver, include the following static initializer in your program:

```
Class.forName("COM.ibm.db2.jdbc.net.DB2Driver");
```

You must also satisfy the following prerequisites:

- Start the DB2 JDBC server on the database server with the db2jstrt <port number> command, where <port number> represents the TCP/IP port on the database server to which JDBC applications connect.

- The client program must use the same version of db2java.zip installed on the DB2 server.

- JDBC applets must make db2java.zip available in the same directory as the applet.

The following sample code creates a connection to the database within the init() method of an applet.

```
public static void init() {
  Connection con = null;
  String server = localhost;
  String port = 6789;
  //  construct the URL
  String url = "jdbc:db2:// " + server + ":" + port + "/" + dbname;
  String userid = getParameter("user");
  String password = getParameter("password");
  try {
    Class.forName("COM.ibm.db2.jdbc.net.DB2Driver");
    // connect to database with userid and password
    con = DriverManager.getConnection(url, user, password );
  // perform database work here
    con.close();
  }
  catch (Exception e) {
    System.out.println(e.toString());
  }
}
```

Controlling SQL Transactions

When you create an instance of a Connection object, the default setting is to automatically commit any changes to the database after each SQL statement is issued. Autocommit normally provides the best performance for your database application because the frequent COMMIT statements prevent the application from acquiring too many locks. DB2 is also able to take advantage of certain optimizations when it knows that autocommit is turned on.

In some situations, however, you might want to explicitly issue ROLLBACK or COMMIT statements or change the default locking behavior of DB2.

Manually Committing or Rolling Back Transactions

To manually control SQL transactions in your application, you can use a combination of the Connection.setAutoCommit(), Connection.commit(), and Connection.rollback() methods, as follows:

1. To start an SQL transaction, turn off autocommit for your database connection by calling the Connection.setAutoCommit(false) method. This setting affects only the database connection on which the method was called; any other instances of database Connection objects in your application are unaffected.

2. Issue data definition language (DDL) statements to drop and create database objects or data manipulation language (DML) statements to delete or update data in the database. These statements comprise the work performed in the transaction. You can also issue SQL statements to retrieve data from the database, but committing or rolling back SQL statements has no effect.

3. Call the Connection.commit() method to commit the work performed by the DDL and DML statements in the transaction. Call the Connection.rollback() method to cancel the work performed by the DDL and DML statements in the transaction.

For an example of a manually controlled SQL transaction, see the simple DDLorDML() method in the "Simple DDL or DML Statements" section later in this chapter.

Changing the Default Locking Behavior of DB2

The locking behavior of a DB2 application is determined by its concurrency level, as described in Chapter 14. The default concurrency level for DB2 is Uncommitted Read, which maps to the JDBC transaction isolation level of Connection.TRANSACTION_READ_COMMITTED.

JDBC Transaction Isolation Level	DB2 Isolation Level	Description
Connection.TRANSACTION_NONE	Not supported on DB2 UDB	N/A
Connection.TRANSACTION_READ_COMMITTED	Cursor Stability (CS)	Locks any row accessed by an application while the cursor is positioned on that row
Connection.TRANSACTION_READ_UNCOMMITED	Uncommitted Read (UR)	The application can access uncommitted changes made by other applications
Connection.TRANSACTION_REPEATABLE_READ	Read Stability (RS)	Locks only the rows retrieved by the application within a transaction
Connection.TRANSACTION_SERIALIZABLE	Repeatable Read (RR)	Locks all of the rows referenced by the application within a transaction

Table 25-1.   *Mapping JDBC Transaction Levels to DB2 Isolation Levels*

To change the default locking behavior for DB2 in your JDBC applications, call the Connection.setTransactionIsolation() method with the JDBC transaction isolation level described in Table 25-1.

For example, to change the transaction isolation level of your program to the equivalent of the DB2 concurrency level Repeatable Read, you can include the following statements in your application:

```
Connection con = new Connection("jdbc:db2:sample", "", "");
con.setTransactionIsolation(Connection.TRANSACTION_SERIALIZABLE);
```

Mapping DB2 Data Types to Java Types

Table 25-2 contains the essential information for working with DB2 data types in JDBC applications. The first and second columns contain the names of the DB2 data types and the corresponding Java types. The third column contains the value that replaces *XXX* in PreparedStatement.setXXX() methods and ResultSet.getXXX() methods using that type. The fourth column contains the parameter type value to use in CallableStatement.registerOutParameter() methods.

DB2 Type	Java Type	Get/Set Method	Java.sql. TYPE	Description
CHAR	java.lang.String	String()	CHAR	Fixed-length character string. Maximum length is 254 bytes. Strings less than the declared length are padded with spaces.
CHAR FOR BIT DATA	byte[]	Bytes()	BINARY	Fixed-length byte array. Maximum length is 254 bytes.
VARCHAR	java.lang.String	String()	VARCHAR	Variable-length character string. Maximum length is 32,672 bytes.
VARCHAR FOR BIT DATA	byte[]	Bytes()	VARBINARY	Variable-length byte array. Maximum length is 32,672 bytes.
LONG VARCHAR	java.lang.String	String()	LONGVARCHAR	Variable-length character string. Maximum length is 32,700 bytes.
LONG VARCHAR FOR BIT DATA	byte[]	Bytes()	LONGVARBINARY	Variable-length byte array. Maximum length is 32,700 bytes.
BLOB (JDBC 2.0)	java.sql.Blob	Blob()	BLOB	Binary large object. Maximum length is 2,147,483,647 bytes.
CLOB (JDBC 2.0)	java.sql.Clob	Clob()	CLOB	Character large object. Maximum length is 2,147,483,647 bytes.

Table 25-2.   *DB2 Type Mappings to Java Types for JDBC*

DB2 Type	Java Type	Get/Set Method	Java.sql. TYPE	Description
SMALLINT	boolean	Boolean	BIT	DB2 does not support a BOOLEAN SQL type; map to a SMALLINT column instead.
SMALLINT	short	Short()	SMALLINT	16-bit signed integer.
INTEGER	int	Int()	INTEGER	32-bit signed integer.
BIGINT	long	Long()	BIGINT	64-bit signed integer.
DOUBLE	float	Double()	DOUBLE	Single-precision floating point.
DECIMAL	java.math. BigDecimal	BigDecimal()	DECIMAL	Packed decimal.
FLOAT	float	Float()	FLOAT	Double-precision floating point.
REAL	float	Float()	REAL	Double-precision floating point.
DATE	java.sql.Date	Date()	DATE	Holds day, month, and year.
TIME	java.sql.Time	Time()	TIME	Holds hour, minute, and second.
TIMESTAMP	java.sql. Timestamp	Timestamp()	TIMESTAMP	Holds day, month, year, hour, minute, and second.

Table 25-2. *DB2 Type Mappings to Java Types for JDBC* (continued)

Note   *The entries for binary large object (BLOB) and character large object (CLOB) data types apply only to applications using the DB2 JDBC 2.0 drivers. For the vendor-specific BLOB and CLOB support offered by the DB2 JDBC 1.22 drivers, refer to the IBM DB2 Universal Database Application Development Guide.*

Error Handling

If a JDBC method results in an SQL error being returned from DB2, the JDBC method throws an instance of an SQLException object. If you enclose your JDBC methods in a try block, your JDBC programs can handle the SQLException in a catch block with the following methods:

- **SQLException.getErrorCode()** Returns the DB2-specific error as an integer
- **SQLException.getSQLState()** Returns the vendor-neutral SQLSTATE string defined by the X/Open SQL specification
- **SQLException.toString()** Returns a text string that briefly describes the reason the SQLException object was thrown

Preventing Resource Leaks

When writing applications using the DB2 JDBC drivers, explicitly invoke the garbage collection routine whenever a database object is no longer needed. This typically means calling the close() method for Connection, Statement, CallableStatement, PreparedStatement, and ResultSet objects before reusing the object or leaving the scope in which the object was created. For example, if you create an instance of a ResultSet object to access the results of a SELECT statement, you should call the close() method on the ResultSet before using that same instance to access the results of a second SELECT statement.

If you do not explicitly invoke the garbage collection routines for your database objects in JDBC applications, your application may crash or leak memory. Even worse, if you reuse an instance of a ResultSet object by assigning the results of a second SQL statement without first calling the close() method on the ResultSet, your application may access some of the remaining data from the first SQL statement. These problems can be particularly troublesome if they occur in a JDBC stored procedure because stored procedures normally stay loaded in memory. After repeated calls to an incorrectly written JDBC stored procedure, the stored procedure may acquire a significant amount of database manager resources due to resource leaks.

To avoid creating resource leaks in JDBC applications, follow this simple rule: every time you encounter a closing brace (}) or the NEW keyword, ask yourself if you need to call the close() method on any database objects.

Issuing Simple SQL Statements in JDBC

To issue a simple SQL statement in a JDBC application, create a Statement object by using the Connection.createStatement() method. Then pass a String object containing the SQL statement to either the Statement.executeQuery() or Statement.executeUpdate() method, depending on the type of SQL statement.

Simple SELECT Statements

Issue simple SELECT statements by using the Statement.executeQuery() method. The Statement.executeQuery() method returns a ResultSet object with which you can access the results of the SELECT statement.

```java
public static void simpleSelect(Connection con) {
  System.out.println("simpleSelect");
  try {
    Statement stmt = con.createStatement();
    String select = "SELECT firstnme, midinit FROM employee";
    ResultSet rs = stmt.executeQuery(select);
    // work with ResultSet
    int i = 0;
    while (rs.next()) {
      i++;
    }
    System.out.println(" Iterated through " + i + " rows.");
    rs.close();
    stmt.close();
  }
  catch (SQLException sqle) {
    System.out.println(sqle.toString());
  }
}
```

Simple DDL or DML Statements

To issue simple DDL or DML statements, you can use the Statement.executeUpdate() method. It returns an int value reflecting the number of rows that were affected by the statement.

```java
public static void simpleDDLorDML(Connection con) {
  System.out.println("simpleDDLorDML");
  try {
    con.setAutoCommit(false);

    Statement stmt = con.createStatement();
    String dml = "DELETE FROM employee WHERE empno = '000010'";
```

```
    int rowsAffected = stmt.executeUpdate(dml);
    System.out.println(rowsAffected +
      " rows were affected by this DML statement");

    String ddl = "CREATE TABLE newTable (serialNumber INTEGER)";
    rowsAffected = stmt.executeUpdate(ddl);
    System.out.println(rowsAffected +
      " rows were affected by the DDL statement");
    stmt.close();

    // roll back the changes made by this method
    con.rollback();
    con.setAutoCommit(true);
  }
  catch (SQLException sqle) {
    System.out.println(sqle.toString());
  }
}
```

Using Prepared Statements with Parameter Markers

Many applications repeatedly issue the same basic SQL statements with parameters that accept variable input. Rather than create a separate Statement object for each variation on the SELECT statement, consider reusing a single PreparedStatement object.

PreparedStatement objects use parameter markers (question mark (?) characters) to represent variable values. Set the values of the parameter markers by using the appropriate setXXX() methods, and then call the PreparedStatement.executeQuery() or PreparedStatement.executeUpdate() method to complete the operation.

The following example uses one PreparedStatement object to perform two UPDATE operations.

```
public static void preparedSQL(Connection con) {
  System.out.println("preparedSQL");
  try {
    String sql= "UPDATE employee SET salary = ? WHERE workdept = ?";
    // Create the prepared statement
    PreparedStatement pStmt = con.prepareStatement(sql);

    // First use of the prepared statement.
```

```
      // Set the value of the first parameter marker
      java.math.BigDecimal dec = new java.math.BigDecimal("35000.75");
      pStmt.setBigDecimal(1, dec);
      // Set the value of the second parameter marker
      pStmt.setString(2, "A00");
      // Execute the prepared statement
      int rowsUpdated = pStmt.executeUpdate();

      System.out.println(" Updated " + rowsUpdated + " rows.");
      // Second use of the prepared statement.
      // Set the value of the first parameter marker
      dec = new java.math.BigDecimal("37500.57");
      pStmt.setBigDecimal(1, dec);
      // Set the value of the second parameter marker
      pStmt.setString(2, "B01");
      // Execute the prepared statement
      rowsUpdated = pStmt.executeUpdate();
      System.out.println(" Updated " + rowsUpdated + " rows.");

      pStmt.close();
   }
   catch (SQLException sqle) {
      System.out.println(sqle.toString());
   }
}
```

Retrieving Data from a Result Set

When you issue a SELECT statement, the Statement or PreparedStatement object
can return a ResultSet object representing a result set. A result set consists of one or
more rows of data, where the rows are composed of one or more columns of data. The
ResultSet.getXXX() methods enable you to retrieve data from a result set, where XXX
represents the Java type corresponding to the SQL type returned from the query. The
ResultSet.getXXX() methods enable you to fetch data by specifying either the index
of the column or the column name.

In the following example, the ResultSet.next() method is used in a while loop to
iterate sequentially through the rows of the result set. The cursor is initially positioned
before the first row of the result set. ResultSet.next() positions the cursor on the next
row of the result set and returns false if there is no row. Within the body of the while
loop, the ResultSet.getXXX() method corresponding to the SQL type returns the data
type for each column of the row.

A common source of confusion with JDBC programs is that JDBC does not directly represent SQL NULL values for primitive types returned by the ResultSet.getXXX() methods. For example, the return value of the ResultSet.getInt() method for an SQL NULL value is 0, not null, as you might expect. The following example calls the ResultSet.wasNull() method after the ResultSet.getInt() method to determine whether the content of the column was an SQL NULL value. Ensure that you check for SQL NULL values in every nullable column of your result set.

```java
public static void readResultSet(Connection con) {
  System.out.println("readResultSet");
  try {
    Statement stmt = con.createStatement();
    String select = "SELECT firstnme, midinit, edlevel FROM employee";
    ResultSet rs = stmt.executeQuery(select);
    // work with ResultSet
    String name, initial;
    int education;
    while (rs.next()) {
      name = rs.getString(1);
      initial = rs.getString("midinit");
      education = rs.getInt(3);
      if (rs.wasNull()) {
        // education was null
      else {
        System.out.print(" Name: " + name + ", " + initial);
        System.out.println(" Education level: " + education);
      }
    }
    rs.close();
    stmt.close();
  }
  catch (SQLException sqle) {
    System.out.println(sqle.toString());
  }
}
```

Note that if your result set contains columns that are the result of an SQL function, DB2 changes the name of the column to reflect the index of the column. For example, for the following SELECT statement, DB2 returns the following column names: 1, MIDINIT, and 3:

```sql
SELECT UCASE(firstnme), midinit, CAST(salary AS DOUBLE) FROM employee
```

Updating or Deleting Data in a Result Set

Updating the value of a column in a result set is called a *positioned update*. Deleting the current row in a result set is called a *positioned delete*. To issue a positioned update or positioned delete in a JDBC result set, perform the following steps:

1. Set the name of the cursor by calling the Statement.setCursorName() method on the Statement object that will return the target result set.

2. Create a new Statement object that will be used to execute the positioned update or positioned delete statements.

3. Position the cursor on the row of the result set that contains the data that you want to update by using the methods described in the preceding section.

4. Issue an UPDATE or DELETE statement incorporating the WHERE CURRENT OF clause and specifying the cursor name.

The following example performs positioned updates on a result set, changing the value of the Firstnme column of the EMPLOYEE table to *Professor* for each row in which the value of the Education column is greater than 20:

```java
public static void updateResultSet(Connection con) {
  System.out.println("updateResultSet");
  try {
    con.setAutoCommit(false);
    // create the Statement object that will return the ResultSet
    Statement stmt = con.createStatement();
    String select = "SELECT firstnme, midinit, edlevel " +
      "FROM employee FOR UPDATE OF firstnme";
    String cursorName = "uniqueCursor";
    stmt.setCursorName(cursorName);
    ResultSet rs = stmt.executeQuery(select);
    // create the Statement object that will issue positioned updates
    Statement updateStmt = con.createStatement();
    String update = "UPDATE employee " +
      "SET firstnme = 'Professor' WHERE CURRENT OF " + cursorName;
    // work with ResultSet
    String name, initial;
    int education;
    while (rs.next()) {
      name = rs.getString(1);
      initial = rs.getString("midinit");
      education = rs.getInt(3);
      if (rs.wasNull()) {
```

```
      // education was null
    }
    else if (education > 20) {
      updateStmt.execute(update);
      System.out.println(" Set " + name + " to Professor");
    }
  }
  rs.close();
  stmt.close();

  // roll back changes made by this method
  con.rollback();
  con.setAutoCommit(true);
}
catch (SQLException sqle) {
  System.out.println(sqle.toString());
}
}
```

Calling Stored Procedures

JDBC programs call cataloged stored procedures by issuing the CALL statement in a CallableStatement.execute() method. Stored procedures can accept a combination of input parameters (IN parameters), output parameters (OUT parameters), and parameters that accept input and return a different result (INOUT parameters). A stored procedure can return zero or more result sets.

The simplest example of a stored procedure accepts no parameters and returns no result sets; it might perform some administrative task on the server. The following example calls a simple stored procedure cataloged with the name *simpleProc*:

```
public static void callSimpleProcedure(Connection con) {
  try {
    String call = "CALL simpleProc()";
    CallableStatement cStmt = con.prepareCall(call);
    cStmt.execute();
    cStmt.close();
  }
  catch (SQLException sqle) {
    System.out.println(sqle.toString());
  }
}
```

Retrieving OUT Parameters from a Stored Procedure

Many stored procedures return OUT parameters. For error-checking purposes, a stored procedure typically returns an OUT parameter containing a result code.

To accept an OUT parameter from a stored procedure, a JDBC program must perform the following steps:

1. Ensure that the CALL statement represents each parameter with a parameter marker (the question mark (?) character).

2. Issue the CallableStatement.registerOutParameter() method for each OUT parameter, passing in the parameter index and the parameter type as arguments to the method.

3. Call the stored procedure.

4. Retrieve the value of the OUT parameter by issuing the CallableStatement.getXXX() method.

In the following example, the stored procedure returns an OUT parameter of type VARCHAR(50) representing the state of the AutoCommit property for the default Connection object, and an OUT parameter of type INTEGER representing the final SQLCODE value within the stored procedure.

```
public static void callOutProcedure(Connection con) {
  System.out.println("callOutProcedure");
  try {
    String call = "CALL outParameter(?, ?)";
    CallableStatement cStmt = con.prepareCall(call);
    cStmt.registerOutParameter(1, java.sql.Types.VARCHAR);
    cStmt.registerOutParameter(2, java.sql.Types.INTEGER);
    cStmt.execute();
    String isAutocommit = cStmt.getString(1);
    int resultCode = cStmt.getInt(2);
    cStmt.close();
    System.out.println("   " + isAutocommit);
    System.out.println("  Result code = " + resultCode);
  }
  catch (SQLException sqle) {
    System.out.println(sqle.toString());
  }
}
```

Passing IN Parameters to a Stored Procedure

Stored procedures can accept IN parameters to modify their behavior. For example, you might pass an IN parameter containing a value to be used in a WHERE clause of a SELECT statement issued within the stored procedure.

To pass an IN parameter to a stored procedure, perform the following steps:

1. Ensure that the CALL statement represents each parameter with a parameter marker (the question mark (?) character).

2. Issue the CallableStatement.setXXX() method for each IN parameter, passing in the parameter index and the parameter value as arguments to the method.

3. Call the stored procedure.

In the following example, the stored procedure accepts an IN parameter of type SMALLINT and returns one OUT parameter of type INTEGER representing the number of rows that matched the IN value and one OUT parameter of type INTEGER representing the final SQLCODE value within the stored procedure.

```java
public static void callInProcedure(Connection con) {
   System.out.println("callInProcedure");
   short inParameterValue = 38;
   try {
      String call = "CALL inParameter(?, ?, ?)";
      CallableStatement cStmt = con.prepareCall(call);
      cStmt.setShort(1, inParameterValue);
      cStmt.registerOutParameter(2, java.sql.Types.INTEGER);
      cStmt.registerOutParameter(3, java.sql.Types.INTEGER);
      cStmt.execute();
      int numRows = cStmt.getInt(2);
      if (cStmt.wasNull()) {
         System.out.println("  IN parameter matched 0 rows");
      }
      else {
         System.out.println("  IN parameter matched " +
            numRows + " rows");
      }
      int resultCode = cStmt.getInt(3);
      System.out.println("  Result code: " + resultCode);
      cStmt.close();
   }
   catch (SQLException sqle) {
      System.out.println(sqle.toString());
   }
}
```

Passing INOUT Parameters to a Stored Procedure

Stored procedures can accept INOUT parameters that both pass in an input value to the stored procedure and return an output value from the stored procedure. For example, you might pass an INOUT parameter containing a value to be used in a WHERE clause of a SELECT statement issued within the stored procedure, and then return the result of the SELECT statement in the same INOUT parameter.

To pass an INOUT parameter to a stored procedure, perform the following steps:

1. Ensure that the CALL statement represents each parameter with a parameter marker (the question mark (?) character).

2. Issue the CallableStatement.setXXX() method for each INOUT parameter, passing in the parameter index and the parameter value as arguments to the method.

3. Issue the CallableStatement.registerOutParameter() method for each INOUT parameter, passing in the parameter index and the parameter type as arguments to the method.

4. Call the stored procedure.

In the following example, the stored procedure accepts an INOUT parameter of type SMALLINT and returns one OUT parameter of type INTEGER. The INOUT parameter passes a value to the stored procedure that limits the scope of a result set and returns a value from the stored procedure representing the number of rows in that result set. The OUT parameter represents the final SQLCODE value within the stored procedure.

```
public static void callInoutProcedure(Connection con) {
  System.out.println("callInoutProcedure");
  short inParameterValue = 38;
  try {
    String call = "CALL inoutParameter(?, ?)";
    CallableStatement cStmt = con.prepareCall(call);
    cStmt.setShort(1, inParameterValue);
    cStmt.registerOutParameter(1, java.sql.Types.INTEGER);
    cStmt.registerOutParameter(2, java.sql.Types.INTEGER);
    cStmt.execute();
    int numRows = cStmt.getInt(1);
    if (cStmt.wasNull()) {
      System.out.println("  IN parameter matched 0 rows");
    }
    else {
      System.out.println("  IN parameter matched " +
```

```
        numRows + " rows");
    }
    int resultCode = cStmt.getShort(2);
    System.out.println("  Result code: " + resultCode);
    cStmt.close();
  }
  catch (SQLException sqle) {
    System.out.println(sqle.toString());
  }
}
```

Retrieving Result Sets from Stored Procedures

Some stored procedures return one or more result sets. The CallableStatement.execute()
method returns a boolean value indicating whether one or more result sets were returned
from the SQL statement. You can then use the CallableStatement.getResultSet() and
CallableStatement.getMoreResults() methods to access the result sets from the
SQL statement.

The following method calls a stored procedure named twoResultSets and iterates
through each result set returned by the stored procedure, printing the name and years
of service for each row in each result set.

```
public static void callTwoResultSets (Connection con) {
  System.out.println("multipleResultSets");
  try {
    short years = 5;
    String name;
    String call = "CALL twoResultSets(?)";
    CallableStatement cStmt = con.prepareCall(call);
    cStmt.setShort(1, years);
    cStmt.execute();

    System.out.println("  First result set");
    ResultSet rs = cStmt.getResultSet();
    rs = cStmt.getResultSet();
    while (rs.next()) {
      name = rs.getString(1);
      years = rs.getShort(2);
      System.out.println("  Name: " + name + ", years: " + years);
    }

    // get next ResultSet until CallableStatement.getMoreResults
```

APPLICATION
DEVELOPMENT

```
      // returns false
      while (cStmt.getMoreResults()) {
        System.out.println("\n  Next result set");
        rs = cStmt.getResultSet();
        while (rs.next()) {
          name = rs.getString(1);
          years = rs.getShort(2);
          System.out.println("  Name: " + name + ", years: " + years);
        }
      }
      rs.close();
      cStmt.close();
    }
  catch (SQLException sqle) {
    System.out.println(sqle.toString());
  }
}
```

Writing Stored Procedures

To write a stored procedure in JDBC, you must create a JDBC method that conforms
to the "SQLj Part 1: SQLj Routines" specification available from http://www.sqlj.org.
To summarize the specification, your JDBC method must follow these rules:

- Declare the JDBC method with a public static void signature.

- Pass IN stored procedure parameters by declaring a variable of the
  corresponding Java type in the method signature.

- Pass OUT and INOUT stored procedure parameters by declaring
  single-element arrays of the corresponding Java type in the method signature.

- Return result sets as single-element ResultSet arrays appended to the method
  signature; do not call the ResultSet.close() method on the ResultSet objects that
  will be returned to the client application.

- Do not call methods that perform operations using System.in, System.out,
  or System.err.

- To perform SQL operations, create a default Connection object in your stored
  procedure method with the following statement:

  ```
  Connection con = DriverManager.getConnection("jdbc:default:connection");
  ```

In addition to writing the stored procedure, you must perform the following steps
on the database server to make the stored procedure available to your client applications:

1. Compile the Java source file into a class file by using the javac command.

2. For Windows operating systems, copy the class file into <path\name>\ SQLLIB\FUNCTION , where <path name> represents the directory in which you installed DB2. For Linux and UNIX operating systems, copy the class file into <pathname>/sqllib/function, where <path name> represents the DB2 instance directory.

3. Set the *Jdk11_path* database manager configuration parameter to the value of the directory in which your Java Development Kit is installed on the server by using the following command:

```
db2 update dbm cfg using JDK11_PATH <path name>
```

4. Catalog the stored procedure by issuing a CREATE PROCEDURE statement using the following basic template:

```
CREATE PROCEDURE <procedure-name> (<procedure-parameters>)
  DYNAMIC RESULT SETS <quantity>
  LANGUAGE JAVA
  PARAMETER STYLE JAVA
  <sql-permissions>
  EXTERNAL NAME '<class-name>.<method.name>'
```

For the exact syntax of the CREATE PROCEDURE statement, see Chapter 27.

Before returning from the method body of a stored procedure, ensure that you have explicitly closed any resources created by the stored procedure, such as Statement, PreparedStatement, ResultSet, or Connection objects.

Simple Stored Procedures

The simplest example of a stored procedure accepts no parameters and returns no result sets; it might perform some administrative task on the server.

The following CREATE PROCEDURE statement catalogs a simple stored procedure called simpleProc contained in a class called SPSample and implemented as a method called simpleProcedure():

```
CREATE PROCEDURE simpleProc ()
  DYNAMIC RESULT SETS 0
  LANGUAGE JAVA
  PARAMETER STYLE JAVA
  NO SQL
  EXTERNAL NAME 'SPSample.simpleProcedure'
```

A Java method stub that implements the stored procedure is as follows:

```
public static void simpleProc() {
  // this stored procedure can't accept any input
  // or return any output; assume that it simply
  // appends an entry to a log file and returns
}
```

Returning OUT Parameters from a Stored Procedure

Many stored procedures return OUT parameters. For error-checking purposes, for example, a stored procedure typically returns an OUT parameter of type INTEGER containing a result code.

The following CREATE PROCEDURE statement catalogs a simple stored procedure called outParameter contained in a class called SPSample and implemented as a method called outParameter():

```
CREATE PROCEDURE outParameter
  (OUT isAutocommit VARCHAR(50), OUT resultCode INTEGER)
  DYNAMIC RESULT SETS 0
  LANGUAGE JAVA
  PARAMETER STYLE JAVA
  READS SQL DATA
  EXTERNAL NAME 'SPSample.outParameter'
```

To return an OUT parameter in a JDBC stored procedure, you must declare the corresponding Java data type for the OUT parameter as a single-element array within the method signature. In the following example, the stored procedure returns an OUT parameter of type VARCHAR(50) to report the autocommit state on the default Connection object. The stored procedure also returns an OUT parameter of type INTEGER to report the SQLCODE in case the stored procedure throws an SQLException.

```
public static void outParameter(String[] outIsAutocommit, int[] outResultCode) {
  // return 0 unless an SQLException occurs
  outResultCode[0] = 0;
  try {
    Connection con = DriverManager.getConnection("jdbc:default:connection");
    if (con.getAutoCommit()) {
      outIsAutocommit[0] = "Autocommit is on";
    }
    else {
      outIsAutocommit[0] = "Autocommit is off";
    }
```

```
    con.close();
  }
  catch (SQLException sqle) {
    outResultCode[0] = sqle.getErrorCode();
  }
}
```

Passing IN Parameters to a Stored Procedure

Stored procedures can accept IN parameters to modify their behavior. For example, you might pass an IN parameter containing a value to be used in a WHERE clause of a SELECT statement issued within the stored procedure. The following CREATE PROCEDURE statement catalogs a simple stored procedure called inParameter contained in a class called SPSample and implemented as a method called inParameter():

```
CREATE PROCEDURE inParameter
  (IN whereValue SMALLINT, OUT numRows INTEGER, OUT resultCode INTEGER)
  DYNAMIC RESULT SETS 0
  LANGUAGE JAVA
  PARAMETER STYLE JAVA
  READS SQL DATA
  EXTERNAL NAME 'SPSample.inParameter'
```

To accept an IN parameter in a JDBC stored procedure, you must declare the corresponding Java data type for the IN parameter as a variable within the method signature. In the following example, the stored procedure accepts an IN parameter of type SMALLINT to use within the WHERE clause of a SELECT statement. The stored procedure also returns an OUT parameter of type INTEGER to report the SQLCODE in case the stored procedure throws an SQLException:

```
public static void inParameter(short inWhere, int[] outNumRows, int[] outResultCode) {
  // return 0 unless an SQLException occurs
  outResultCode[0] = 0;
  try {
    Connection con = DriverManager.getConnection("jdbc:default:connection");
    String sql = "SELECT COUNT(*) FROM staff WHERE dept = ?";
    PreparedStatement pStmt = con.prepareStatement(sql);
    pStmt.setShort(1, inWhere);
    ResultSet rs = pStmt.executeQuery();
    if (rs.next()) {
      outNumRows[0] = rs.getInt(1);
    }
    else {
      outNumRows[0] = -1;
```

```
      }
      rs.close();
      pStmt.close();
      con.close();
    }
  catch (SQLException sqle) {
      outResultCode[0] = sqle.getErrorCode();
    }
}
```

Passing INOUT Parameters to a Stored Procedure

Stored procedures can accept INOUT parameters that both pass in an input value
to the stored procedure and return an output value from the stored procedure. For
example, you might pass an INOUT parameter containing a value to be used in a
WHERE clause of a SELECT statement issued within the stored procedure, and then
return the result of the SELECT statement in the same INOUT parameter.

The following CREATE PROCEDURE statement catalogs a simple stored
procedure called inoutParameter contained in a class called SPSample and
implemented as a method called inoutParameter():

```
CREATE PROCEDURE inoutParameter
  (INOUT whereValue SMALLINT, OUT resultCode INTEGER)
  DYNAMIC RESULT SETS 0
  LANGUAGE JAVA
  PARAMETER STYLE JAVA
  READS SQL DATA
  EXTERNAL NAME 'SPSample.inoutParameter'
```

To accept and return an INOUT parameter in a JDBC stored procedure, you must
declare the corresponding Java data type for the OUT parameter as a single-element
array within the method signature. In the following example, the stored procedure
accepts an INOUT parameter of type SMALLINT to use within the WHERE clause
of a SELECT statement, and it returns the number of rows that matched the query
in the same INOUT parameter. The stored procedure also returns an OUT parameter
of type INTEGER to report the SQLCODE in case the stored procedure throws an
SQLException.

Note *For cleaner code, improved performance, and easier debugging of your stored procedures,
we recommend that you always use separate IN and OUT parameters instead of INOUT
parameters.*

```
public static void inoutParameter(short[] inoutWhere, int[]
outResultCode) {
  // return 0 unless an SQLException occurs
  outResultCode[0] = 0;
  try {
    Connection con =
DriverManager.getConnection("jdbc:default:connection");
    String sql = "SELECT COUNT(*) FROM staff WHERE dept = ?";
    PreparedStatement pStmt = con.prepareStatement(sql);
    pStmt.setShort(1, inoutWhere[0]);
    ResultSet rs = pStmt.executeQuery();
    if (rs.next()) {
      inoutWhere[0] = rs.getShort(1);
    }
    else {
      inoutWhere[0] = -1;
    }
    rs.close();
    pStmt.close();
    con.close();
  }
  catch (SQLException sqle) {
    outResultCode[0] = sqle.getErrorCode();
  }
}
```

Returning Result Sets from Stored Procedures

To return result sets from a stored procedure, catalog the stored procedure with the corresponding value for the DYNAMIC RESULT SETS clause of the CREATE PROCEDURE statement.

The following CREATE PROCEDURE statement catalogs a simple stored procedure called twoResultSets contained in a class called SPSample and implemented as a method called twoResultSets():

```
CREATE PROCEDURE twoResultSets (IN inThreshold SMALLINT)
  DYNAMIC RESULT SETS 2
  LANGUAGE JAVA
  PARAMETER STYLE JAVA
  READS SQL DATA
  EXTERNAL NAME 'SPSample.twoResultSets'
```

To return result sets from a JDBC stored procedure, you must declare each result set as a single-element array of ResultSet objects appended to the method signature. Within the body of the stored procedure, create each ResultSet object from a new Statement or PreparedStatement object. Do not call the ResultSet.close() method on the ResultSet objects that you want to return to the client application, and do not close the Statement or PreparedStatement objects that generated the ResultSet objects. The client is responsible for accepting and closing each ResultSet object returned from the stored procedure.

In the following example, the stored procedure accepts an IN parameter of type SMALLINT to generate two ResultSet objects. The method signature also declares two ResultSet arrays so it can return the result sets to the client:

```
public static void twoResultSets (short inThreshold, ResultSet[] rs1,
  ResultSet[] rs2) throws SQLException {
    Connection con = DriverManager.getConnection("jdbc:default:connection");

    // create first result set
    String sql = "SELECT name, years FROM staff WHERE years < ?";
    PreparedStatement pStmt = con.prepareStatement(sql);
    pStmt.setShort(1, inThreshold);
    rs1[0] = pStmt.executeQuery();

    // create second result set
    sql = "SELECT name, years FROM staff WHERE years > ?";
    PreparedStatement pStmt2 = con.prepareStatement(sql);
    pStmt2.setShort(1, inThreshold);
    rs2[0] = pStmt2.executeQuery();

    con.close();
}
```

JDBC 2.0: Scrollable Result Sets, BLOB, and CLOB Data Types

By default, the JDBC drivers shipped with DB2 support only the JDBC 1.22 specification. However, DB2 also ships with JDBC drivers that support most of the JDBC 2.0 specification. While JDBC 1.22 restricts your applications to processing result sets sequentially with the ResultSet.next() method, JDBC 2.0 adds support for *scrollable result sets*, which enable random access to the rows in a result set. Another important addition to JDBC 2.0 is standardized support for BLOB and CLOB data types.

Using the JDBC 2.0 Drivers: Windows

To use the JDBC 2.0 drivers on Windows, you must install either the IBM or Sun Java Development Kit 1.2.2 or later and run the following command:

```
<path>\SQLLIB\JAVA12\USEJDBC2.BAT
```

where <path> represents the location in which DB2 is installed.

 Setting DB2 to use the JDBC 2.0 drivers is persistent and affects the entire system. Rebooting your system does not affect this setting.

The USEJDBC2.BAT batch file copies the JDBC 2.0 version of db2java.zip into the sqllib\java directory. The change persists until the USEJDBC1.BAT batch file is run on the system.

To use the JDBC 1.22 drivers, run the following command:

```
<path>\SQLLIB\JAVA12\USEJDBC1.BAT
```

where <path> represents the location in which DB2 is installed.

Using the JDBC 2.0 Drivers: Linux and UNIX

To use the JDBC 2.0 drivers on Linux or UNIX, your system must be installed and configured with a Java environment of version 1.2.2 or later. The supported Java environments for each DB2 Universal Database platform are listed at http://www.ibm.com/software/data/db2/java. From within a ksh session, source the usejdbc2 script with the following command:

```
. <home directory>/sqllib/java12/usejdbc2
```

where <home directory> represents the home directory of your DB2 instance.

 In an interactive session, setting DB2 to use the JDBC 2.0 drivers affects only your current shell session. Within a shell script, setting DB2 to use the JDBC 2.0 drivers persists for the duration of the shell script.

The usejdbc2 script file changes the CLASSPATH environment variable to point to the JDBC 2.0 version of db2java.zip in the sqllib/java12 directory. The change persists until either the shell session ends or the usejdbc1 script is sourced within the shell session.

Scrollable Result Sets

The DB2 JDBC 2.0 drivers support the use of scrollable cursors on result sets. To use scrollable cursors, pass the ResultSet type and ResultSet concurrency parameters to the Connection.createStatement() method. You can then use methods like ResultSet.first(), ResultSet.last(), ResultSet.previous(), and ResultSet.absolute() to provide random access to the rows of your result sets.

The following example specifies that ResultSet objects returned by statements executed with the stmt Statement object are insensitive to changes made by other applications (ResultSet.TYPE_SCROLL_INSENSITIVE) and are used only to read data (ResultSet.CONCUR_READ_ONLY).

```
public static void readScrollableResultSet(Connection con) {
  System.out.println("readScrollableResultSet");
  try {
    Statement stmt = con.createStatement(ResultSet.TYPE_SCROLL_INSENSITIVE,
ResultSet.CONCUR_READ_ONLY);
    String select = "SELECT firstnme, midinit, edlevel FROM employee ORDER
BY edlevel";
    ResultSet rs = stmt.executeQuery(select);
    // work with ResultSet
    String name, initial;
    int education;
    rs.afterLast(); // move cursor to position after last row of result set
    while (rs.previous()) { // read rows in reverse order
      name = rs.getString(1);
      initial = rs.getString("midinit");
      education = rs.getInt(3);
      String data = "  " + name + ", " + initial;
      if (rs.wasNull()) {
        // education was null
        System.out.println(data + ", no education on file");
      }
      else {
        System.out.println(data + ", " + education + " years");
      }
    }
    rs.close();
    stmt.close();
  }
  catch (SQLException sqle) {
    System.out.println(sqle.toString());
  }
}
```

Large Objects (BLOB and CLOB Types)

One of the major features of the JDBC 2.0 specification is a standardized means of handling large object types. JDBC 2.0 defines two new Java object types, java.sql.Blob and java.sql.Clob, and associated methods for working with these types. To create an instance of a Blob or Clob object from a result set or a stored procedure, assign the results of the getBlob() or getClob() method to an instance of the appropriate type as follows:

```
Blob blob = rs.getBlob(1);
Clob clob = rs.getClob(2);
```

You can retrieve data from a Blob instance as a java.io.InputStream object by calling the java.sql.Blob.getBinaryStream() method, or you can retrieve a subset of the data from a Blob instance as an array of bytes by using the java.sql.Blob.getBytes() method.

The following example retrieves an entire GIF image from a DB2 table by using the java.sql.Blob.getBinaryStream() method and writes the file to disk:

```
public static void readBinaryLargeObject(Connection con) {
  System.out.println("readBinaryLargeObject");
  java.io.FileOutputStream file;
  java.io.InputStream in;
  java.sql.Blob photo;
  java.sql.ResultSet rs;
  try {
    Statement stmt = con.createStatement();
    String select = "SELECT picture FROM emp_photo " +
     "WHERE empno ='000130' AND photo_format = 'gif'";
    rs = stmt.executeQuery(select);
    while (rs.next()) { // position the cursor on a row
      photo = rs.getBlob(1);
      in = photo.getBinaryStream();
      file = new java.io.FileOutputStream("newblob.gif");
      int i;
      while ((i = in.read()) != -1) {
        file.write(i);
      }
      in.close();
      file.close();
    }
```

```
      rs.close();
      stmt.close();
    }
  catch (Exception e) {
    System.out.println(e.toString());
  }
}
```

Before inserting or retrieving CLOB data types in a DB2 database, you must increase the *udf_mem_sz* database manager configuration parameter beyond the default setting. To enable the following sample code to successfully read the value of a CLOB column, issue the following command, and then restart the database:

```
db2 update dbm cfg using UDF_MEM_SZ 2048
```

To retrieve data from a Clob instance as a java.io.InputStream object, call the java.sql.Clob.getAsciiStream() method. To retrieve a subset of the data from a Clob instance as an array of bytes, call the java.sql.Clob.getBytes() method. The following example searches the value of a CLOB column for a specific substring and displays the substring at the console:

```
public static void readCharacterLargeObject(Connection con) {
  System.out.println("readCharacterLargeObject");
  java.io.InputStream in;
  java.sql.Clob resume;
  java.sql.ResultSet rs;
  try {
    Statement stmt = con.createStatement();
    String select = "SELECT resume FROM emp_resume " +
     "WHERE empno ='000130' AND resume_format = 'ascii'";
    while (rs.next()) { // position the cursor on a row
       resume = rs.getClob(1);
       long workStart = resume.position("Work History", 1);
       long workEnd = resume.position("Interests", 1);
       String workHistory = resume.getSubString(workStart,
(int)(workEnd - workStart));
       System.out.println(workHistory);
    }
    rs.close();
    stmt.close();
  }
  catch (SQLException sqle) {
```

```
      System.out.println(sqle.toString());
   }
}
```

Programming in SQLj

SQLj is the industry standard for embedding static SQL statements within Java programs. It builds on the JDBC framework by using JDBC statements to create database connections and the same mappings between Java data types and DB2 data types, but it offers a simpler interface for operations like working with result sets or calling stored procedures. SQLj programs combine the flexibility of dynamic SQL through JDBC methods with the ease and potential performance increase of embedded static SQL statements. However, the simplified interface of SQLj comes at the cost of a more complex build and deployment process. The official web site of the SQLj consortium is http://www.sqlj.org.

SQLj Syntax

Your SQLj source files must include the following import statements:

```
import java.sql.*; // JDBC support classes
import sqlj.runtime.*; // SQLJ support classes
import sqlj.runtime.ref.*; // SQLJ support classes
```

The complete set of Javadoc API documentation of the DB2 SQLj run-time classes is available at http://www.ibm.com/software/data/db2/java/sqlj/javadoc/packages.html.

To embed an SQL statement within an SQLj source file, use the following syntax:

```
#sql { <SQL statement> };
```

To pass a single value into or retrieve a single value from an SQL statement, you must declare a *host variable* before using it in the SQL statement. Host variables are identified in an SQL statement by prefixing a colon (:) to the name of the Java variable. Ensure that the Java variable type corresponds to the DB2 data type as described in the "Mapping DB2 Data Types to Java Types" section earlier in the chapter.

The following method declares a Java variable of type short to serve as a SMALLINT host variable, and declares a Java variable of type String to serve as a CHAR(6) host variable in the embedded SQL statement:

```
public static void sqljHostVariables(Connection con) {
   System.out.println("sqljHostVariables");
```

```
short activity = 10;
String employee = null;
try {
  #sql { SELECT empno INTO :employee
          FROM emp_act
          WHERE actno = :activity
          AND projno = 'AD3100' };
}
catch (SQLException sqle) {
  System.out.println(sqle);
}
System.out.println("  Employee number is: " + employee);
}
```

Building SQLj Programs

To build an SQLj program, you must first run the sqlj SQLJ command to translate the SQLj statements into regular Java methods, and optionally run the db2profc command to create packages in the database.

Translating SQLj Source Files

Use the sqlj command to translate the source file from its SQLj format into a Java source file. If you provide a database URL, user ID, and password to the sqlj translator, it checks the syntax of your SQL statements, verifies that any database objects referenced in your SQL statements actually exist, and confirms that any Java data types used as host variables in SQL statements map correctly to the corresponding DB2 data types. The sqlj translator also produces one serialized profile per context in the SQLj source file.

To translate an SQLj file into a Java file, issue the sqlj command with the following syntax:

```
sqlj -<options> <SQLJ file>
```

In this command, <options> represents the command line options passed to the sqlj translator, and <SQLJ file> represents the target SQLj file.

To control the properties of the sqlj translator, you can either pass the properties as arguments to the sqlj command or create a file called sqlj.properties in your DB2 instance directory. For example, to perform online checking of the SQL statements against the SAMPLE database with user ID db2inst1 and password ibmdb2, and to generate serialized profiles, include the following entries in sqlj.properties:

```
sqlj.url=jdbc:db2:sample
```

```
sqlj.user=db2inst1
sqlj.password=ibmdb2
sqlj.profile=true
```

For a complete list of SQLj translator properties and options, run the SQLJ-HELP-LONG command.

Customizing Serialized SQLj Profiles

Using the db2profc utility, you can customize serialized SQLj profiles against a specific database. Customizing a serialized profile creates a package of static SQL statements in the database, meaning that when you later run your SQLj program, the embedded static SQL statements have already been prepared and optimized.

To customize a serialized SQLj profile, issue the following command:

```
db2profc -url=jdbc:db2:<database> <file name>
```

In this command, <database> represents the name of the database in which you want to create the package, and <file name> represents the name of the target serialized SQLj profile.

Connecting to a Database

To connect to a database, use the methods described in the "Connecting to a DB2 Database Using JDBC" section earlier in the chapter.

Controlling SQL Transactions

To control transactions in your SQLj programs, turn off autocommit by calling the Connection.setAutoCommit(false) method on your Connection object. You can then issue COMMIT and ROLLBACK statements as regular embedded SQL statements.

The following method disables autocommit, issues a series of SQL statements interspersed with COMMIT or ROLLBACK statements, and then turns autocommit on before returning:

```
public static void sqljTransactions(Connection con) {
  System.out.println("sqljTransactions");
  try {
    con.setAutoCommit(false);
    #sql { DELETE FROM employee };
    #sql { ROLLBACK };
    #sql { UPDATE department SET location = 'Toronto'
```

```
            WHERE deptno = 'B01' };
   #sql { COMMIT };
   String location = null;
   #sql { SELECT location INTO :location
          FROM department
          WHERE deptno = 'B01' };
   System.out.println("  Location of B01 is: " + location);
   con.setAutoCommit(true);
 }
 catch (SQLException sqle) {
   System.out.println(sqle);
 }
}
```

Result Set Iterators

Cursors in SQLj are implemented as forward-only, nonscrollable objects called *result set iterators*. SQLj defines two types of iterators: *named iterators* and *positioned iterators.*

To create a named iterator, you declare both the Java types and variable names for the columns of the iterator, and the sqlj translator then creates methods reflecting the variable names to enable you to access the data in the columns. To create a positioned iterator, you declare only the Java types of the columns and use host variables to access data in the iterator.

Following are the equivalent named iterator and positioned iterator declarations for a SELECT statement that returns a CHAR(6) column and a SMALLINT column:

```
#sql iterator namedIterator (String name, short number) ;
#sql iterator positionedIterator (String, short) ;
```

Declare the iterator, and any special properties for the iterator, after the import statements but before the class definition. The exception is for updatable iterators and iterators with holdability, which must be declared in an entirely separate file.

Retrieving Data from a Named Iterator

To retrieve data from a named iterator within an SQLj program, you must perform the following steps:

1. Declare the iterator.

2. Create an instance of the iterator class.

3. Assign the results of a SELECT statement to the iterator object.

4. Retrieve rows from the iterator by calling NamedIterator.next() until it returns false.

5. Retrieve data from the columns of the iterator by calling the method reflecting the name of the variable you declared for the column in the iterator declaration.

6. When you finish retrieving data from the iterator, explicitly close the iterator by calling its close() method.

The following method demonstrates how to use a named iterator to retrieve data in an SQLj program:

```
#sql iterator NamedIter (String name, short dept ) ;

public static void sqljNamedIter (Connection con) {
  System.out.println("sqljNamedIter");
  String name = null;
  short dept = 0;
  int i = 1;
  try {
    NamedIter nIter;
    #sql nIter = { SELECT name, dept FROM staff WHERE job='Mgr' };
    while (nIter.next()) {
      name = nIter.name();
      dept = nIter.dept();
      System.out.println("  Row " + i + ": " + name + ", " + dept);
      i++;
    }
    nIter.close();
  }
  catch(SQLException sqle) {
    System.out.println(sqle);
  }
}
```

Retrieving Data from a Positioned Iterator

To retrieve data from a positioned iterator within an SQLj program, perform the following steps:

1. Declare the iterator.

2. Create an instance of the iterator class.

3. Assign the results of a SELECT statement to the iterator object.

4. Retrieve rows from the iterator by issuing FETCH ? INTO statements using host variables. When the PositionedIterator.endFetch() method returns true, no rows are left in the result set.

5. Explicitly close the iterator by calling its close() method.

The following method demonstrates how to use a positioned iterator to retrieve data in an SQLj program:

```
#sql iterator PositionedIter (String, short ) ;

public static void sqljPositionedIter (Connection con) {
  System.out.println("sqljPositionedIter");
  String name = null;
  short dept = 0;
  int i = 1;
  try {
    PositionedIter pIter;
    #sql pIter = { SELECT name, dept FROM staff WHERE job='Mgr' };
    while (true) {
      #sql { FETCH :pIter INTO :name, :dept };
      if (pIter.endFetch()) {
        break;
      }
      else {
        System.out.println("  Row " + i + ": " + name + ", " + dept);
        i++;
      }
    }
    pIter.close();
  }
  catch(SQLException sqle) {
    System.out.println(sqle);
  }
}
```

The
Complete
Reference

Chapter 26

SQL Procedures

A n *SQL procedure* is a type of stored procedure that you can create by issuing a CREATE PROCEDURE statement with a procedure body written in SQL statements. Within the procedure body, you can declare and set SQL variables, implement conditional flow-of-control logic, handle exceptions, and insert, update, or delete data. Of course, as with other kinds of stored procedures, you can pass parameters between the client application and the stored procedure, and you can return result sets from the stored procedure to the client application. Client applications written in any supported language can call SQL procedures.

While other database servers implement the equivalent of SQL procedures by using an interpreted language, DB2 converts the SQL procedure statements into an equivalent C application by using embedded SQL. This strategy normally ensures good performance for your stored procedures, but it means that before you create any SQL procedures, you must install and configure a supported C compiler on your database server. Unfortunately, configuring the C compiler can be a difficult task, so general instructions are included in the following section.

DB2 clients on AIX, Solaris, and Windows can use the graphical interface provided by the IBM DB2 Stored Procedure Builder to specify the source statements for the SQL procedure, prepare the procedure for execution, and debug stored procedures.

Configuring the SQL Procedure Environment

To successfully create SQL procedures, you must configure your environment as follows:

- Install the DB2 Application Development Client on the database server.
- Install on the database server one of the C compilers supported by DB2, as listed at http://www.ibm.com/software/data/db2/udb/ad.

If your database server runs on a Windows operating system and the environment variables for the C compiler (%INCLUDE%, %LIB%, %PATH%, etc.) are SYSTEM variables, then you need to take no further action. Otherwise, you must update the DB2_SQLROUTINE _COMPILER_PATH DB2 registry variable on the database server as follows:

- For Microsoft Visual Studio, update the DB2 registry variable with the path of the vcvars32.bat batch file. For example,

  ```
  db2set DB2_SQLROUTINE_COMPILER_PATH="c:\vc98\bin\vcvars32.bat"
  ```

- For IBM VisualAge for C++, update the DB2 registry variable with the path of the setenv.bat batch file. For example,

  ```
  db2set DB2_SQLROUTINE_COMPILER_PATH="c:\ibmcppw40\bin\setenv.bat"
  ```

If your database server runs on a UNIX operating system, DB2 generates an executable script file ($HOME/sqllib/function/routine/sr_cpath) the first time you compile a stored procedure. This script contains the default values for the compiler environment variables for that operating system. Ensure that the default values are appropriate for your environment, and edit the script if necessary.

For more information on setting the environment for SQL procedures, including the default values for each operating system supported by DB2, refer to the *IBM DB2 Universal Database Application Building Guide.*

Deploying SQL Procedures

One method for deploying the same SQL procedure on many DB2 servers is to issue the CREATE PROCEDURE statement on each DB2 server. The drawback of this method is that it requires you to install and configure a C compiler on each DB2 server.

A simpler method is to retrieve the compiled SQL procedure as an SQL archive from your development DB2 server by using the GET ROUTINE command and to deploy the SQL archive on DB2 servers of the same operating system by using the PUT ROUTINE command.

Prerequisites

For each operating system on which you expect to deploy an SQL procedure, you must have one DB2 server with a C compiler installed and configured. Use this server to create the compiled SQL procedure by issuing the CREATE PROCEDURE statement.

Retrieving the Compiled SQL Procedure

From the command line, use the GET ROUTINE command to retrieve the SQL archive from the development server, as follows:

1. Connect to the database.
2. Issue the GET ROUTINE command, specifying the fully qualified or relative path and file name for the SQL archive and the name of the SQL procedure.

For example, to retrieve an SQL procedure named twoResultSets from the database named SAMPLE into an SQL archive named twors.sar, issue the following commands from a DB2 command line:

```
db2 connect to sample
db2 GET ROUTINE INTO twors.sar FROM PROCEDURE twoResultSets
```

Deploying the Compiled SQL Procedure

From the command line, use the PUT ROUTINE command to deploy the SQL procedure from an SQL archive onto a target server, as follows:

1. Connect to the target database.

2. Issue the PUT ROUTINE command, specifying the fully qualified or relative path and file name for the SAR. The SQL procedure is automatically cataloged with the same name and parameters as the original SQL procedure.

For example, to deploy an SQL procedure from the SQL archive named twors.sar to a database named TARGET, issue the following commands from a DB2 command line:

```
db2 connect to target
db2 PUT ROUTINE FROM twors.sar
```

Structure of an SQL Procedure

To create an SQL procedure, issue a CREATE PROCEDURE statement composed of five distinct clauses:

```
CREATE PROCEDURE procedure-name
(parameter-list)
DYNAMIC RESULT SETS number-of-result-sets
allowed-SQL
LANGUAGE SQL
BEGIN
  SQL-procedure-body
END
```

Procedure Name

The *procedure name* identifies the SQL procedure. It must start with a letter followed by zero or more characters, and it can be up to 128 bytes long.

Parameter List

The parameter list defines zero or more parameters that the SQL procedure accepts from and returns to client applications. The parameter list is enclosed in parentheses and commas delimit each parameter. You define a parameter by using the following syntax:

parameter-type name data-type

The different parts of this clause are as follows:

- **Parameter type** There are three types of SQL procedure parameters:
  - **IN (input)** Accept a value from a client application. The value of IN parameters cannot be modified within the body of an SQL procedure.
  - **OUT (output)** Return a value to a client application.
  - **INOUT (input and output)** Accept a value from a client application and return a value to a client application.
- **Name** Parameter names must start with a letter followed by zero or more characters, and they can be up to 64 bytes long.
- **Data type** The SQL data type of the parameter. If appropriate, include precision, scale, and length attributes.

Number of Result Sets

SQL procedures can return zero or more result sets.

Allowed SQL

The value of the allowed-SQL clause indicates whether the stored procedure issues any SQL statements and, if so, what type. The possible values are as follows:

- **NO SQL** Indicates that the stored procedure cannot execute any SQL statements
- **CONTAINS SQL** Indicates that SQL statements that neither read nor modify SQL data can be executed by the stored procedure
- **READS SQL DATA** Indicates that SQL statements that do not modify SQL data can be included in the stored procedure
- **MODIFIES SQL DATA** Indicates that the stored procedure can execute any SQL statement except statements that are not supported in stored procedures

SQL Procedure Body

The SQL *procedure body* contains the logic of the stored procedure, including variable declarations, condition handling, flow-of-control statements, and manipulation of data through SQL statements. The rest of this chapter describes the content of the SQL procedure body.

For example, the following statement defines a simple stored procedure named albert that accepts one IN parameter, returns one OUT parameter, returns no result sets, and has an SQL procedure body consisting of a single SELECT statement:

```
CREATE PROCEDURE albert
(IN deptno SMALLINT, OUT how_many SMALLINT)
```

APPLICATION DEVELOPMENT

```
DYNAMIC RESULT SETS 0
READS SQL DATA
LANGUAGE SQL
BEGIN
  SELECT COUNT(*) INTO how_many
    FROM staff
    WHERE dept = deptno;
END
```

Declaring and Setting Variables

You must declare variables in the first section of the SQL procedure body. To declare a variable, you must assign a unique identifier, declare an SQL data type, and optionally, assign an initial value to the variable. The syntax for a variable declaration follows:

> DECLARE *identifier SQL-data-type* [DEFAULT *initial-value*]

The following example declares an SQL variable of type INTEGER and uses that variable in a simple assignment statement:

```
DECLARE counter INTEGER DEFAULT 0;
SET counter = counter + 1;
```

SQLCODE and SQLSTATE Variables

To handle errors and debug problems in your SQL procedures, consider declaring SQLCODE and SQLSTATE variables. The value of an SQLCODE or SQLSTATE variable represents the return value for the last SQL statement that was issued in the SQL procedure body.

Note that accessing the value of an SQLCODE or SQLSTATE variable immediately alters the subsequent value of the SQLCODE or SQLSTATE variable because the statement in which you access the value of the SQLCODE or SQLSTATE variable is itself an SQL statement. Instead of performing comparisons directly against the SQLCODE or SQLSTATE variables, assign the value of the SQLCODE or SQLSTATE variable to a locally defined variable or parameter to perform conditional processing, or return the locally defined variable to the caller as a diagnostic.

The standard declarations for SQLCODE and SQLSTATE variables are as follows:

```
DECLARE SQLCODE INTEGER DEFAULT 0;
DECLARE SQLSTATE CHAR(5) DEFAULT '00000';
```

Passing Parameters and Returning Result Sets

It is possible to write stored procedures that accept no input parameters and return no output parameters or result sets. However, most useful stored procedures will accept at least one input parameter (to limit the scope of the stored procedure) and return at least one output parameter (to return the result of the stored procedure) to the caller. Many stored procedures will also return one or more result sets of data to the caller. The following sections describe how to write SQL procedures that pass parameters and return result sets.

Returning OUT Parameters

SQL procedures often return OUT parameters to provide summary information or report the success or failure of the stored procedure.

In the following example, the outParameter stored procedure returns two OUT parameters. The first OUT parameter is of type VARCHAR(18) and returns the name of the database on which the stored procedure is running. The second OUT parameter is of type INTEGER and returns the final SQLCODE value of the stored procedure.

```
CREATE PROCEDURE outParameter
(OUT server_name VARCHAR(50), OUT error_code INTEGER)
DYNAMIC RESULT SETS 0
READS SQL DATA
LANGUAGE SQL
BEGIN
  DECLARE SQLCODE INTEGER DEFAULT 0;
  VALUES CURRENT SERVER INTO server_name;
  SET error_code = SQLCODE;
END
```

Accepting IN Parameters

SQL procedures can accept IN parameters to modify their behavior. For example, you might pass an IN parameter containing a value to be used in a WHERE clause of a SELECT statement issued within the stored procedure.

In the following example, the inParameter stored procedure accepts one IN parameter and returns two OUT parameters. The IN parameter is of type SMALLINT and is used within the stored procedure to identify the department number within the WHERE clause of a SELECT statement. The first OUT parameter is of type INTEGER and represents the number of rows returned by the SELECT statement. The second OUT parameter is of type INTEGER and represents the final SQLCODE value within the stored procedure.

APPLICATION DEVELOPMENT

```
CREATE PROCEDURE inParameter
(IN deptno SMALLINT, OUT num_rows INTEGER, OUT error_code INTEGER)
DYNAMIC RESULT SETS 0
READS SQL DATA
LANGUAGE SQL
BEGIN
  DECLARE SQLCODE INTEGER DEFAULT 0;
  SELECT COUNT(*) INTO num_rows
    FROM staff
    WHERE dept = deptno;
  SET error_code = SQLCODE;
END
```

Passing INOUT Parameters

SQL procedures can also accept INOUT parameters. These parameters pass an input value to the stored procedure and return an output value from the stored procedure. For example, you might pass an INOUT parameter containing a value to be used in a WHERE clause of a SELECT statement issued within the stored procedure, and then return the result of the SELECT statement in the same INOUT parameter.

In the following example, the inoutParameter SQL procedure accepts one INOUT parameter and returns one OUT parameter. The INOUT parameter is of type SMALLINT and its input value is used within the stored procedure to identify the department number within the WHERE clause of a SELECT statement. The output value of the INOUT parameter represents the number of rows returned by the SELECT statement. The OUT parameter is of type INTEGER and represents the final SQLCODE value within the stored procedure.

```
CREATE PROCEDURE inoutParameter
(INOUT inout_param SMALLINT, OUT error_code INTEGER)
DYNAMIC RESULT SETS 0
READS SQL DATA
LANGUAGE SQL
BEGIN
  DECLARE SQLCODE INTEGER DEFAULT 0;
  SELECT COUNT(*) INTO inout_param
    FROM staff
    WHERE dept = inout_param;
  SET error_code = SQLCODE;
END
```

Returning Result Sets

SQL procedures can return zero, one, or multiple result sets. To return result sets from a stored procedure, perform the following steps:

1. Declare the number of result sets the SQL procedure will return in the DYNAMIC RESULT SETS clause of the CREATE PROCEDURE statement.

2. Declare the cursors in the SQL procedure body by using the WITH RETURN clause for each result set that will be returned.

3. Open the cursors for the result sets.

4. Leave the cursors open when the stored procedure returns.

In the following example, the twoResultSets SQL procedure accepts one IN parameter and returns two result sets. The IN parameter is of type INTEGER and represents the number of years of service that will be used to generate the result sets. The result sets are composed of the name and years of service of employees in the STAFF table, where the first result set contains those employees with fewer years of service than the value of the IN parameter, and the second result set contains those employees with more years of service than the value of the IN parameter.

```
CREATE PROCEDURE twoResultSets
(IN in_years INTEGER)
DYNAMIC RESULT SETS 2
READS SQL DATA
LANGUAGE SQL
BEGIN
  DECLARE rs1 CURSOR WITH RETURN FOR
    SELECT name, years
      FROM staff
      WHERE years <= in_years;
  DECLARE rs2 CURSOR WITH RETURN FOR
    SELECT name, years
      FROM staff
      WHERE years > in_years;

  OPEN rs1;
  OPEN rs2;
END
```

Issuing Dynamic SQL Statements

Most SQL procedures contain static SQL statements because you know in advance which SQL objects the SQL procedure needs to access. However, DB2 does enable you to issue dynamic SQL statements within the SQL procedure body. If the dynamic SQL statement does not include parameter markers, you can issue the statement by using the EXECUTE IMMEDIATE statement. If the dynamic SQL statement does contain parameter markers or you want to issue the statement multiple times, then you must first prepare the statement as an SQL variable using the PREPARE statement, and then issue the EXECUTE statement.

To issue a dynamic SQL statement in an SQL procedure, perform the following steps:

1. Declare a variable of type VARCHAR that is large enough to hold your dynamic SQL statement by using a DECLARE statement.

2. Assign a statement string to the variable by using a SET statement. You cannot include variables directly in the statement string. Instead, you must use the question mark (?) symbol as a parameter marker for any variables used in the statement.

3. Create a prepared statement from the statement string by using a PREPARE statement.

4. Execute the prepared statement by using an EXECUTE statement. If the statement string includes a parameter marker, use a USING clause to replace it with the value of a variable.

The following SQL procedure executes two dynamic SQL statements. It accepts one IN parameter and returns three OUT parameters. The IN parameter is of type SMALLINT and supplies the dynamic content of the statements.

The first OUT parameter is of type SMALLINT and represents the number of rows in the STAFF table before the dynamic SQL statements insert new rows. The second OUT parameter is of type SMALLINT and represents the number of rows in the STAFF table after the dynamic SQL statements insert new rows. The third OUT parameter is of type INTEGER and represents the final SQLCODE value of the SQL procedure.

The first dynamic SQL statement is simply issued by using the EXECUTE IMMEDIATE statement. The second dynamic SQL statement is converted into a prepared statement by using the PREPARE statement, and it is then executed by using an EXECUTE statement:

```
CREATE PROCEDURE dynamicSQL
(IN in_var INTEGER, OUT count_before SMALLINT,
```

```
    OUT count_after SMALLINT, OUT error_code INTEGER)
DYNAMIC RESULT SETS 0
MODIFIES SQL DATA
LANGUAGE SQL
BEGIN
  DECLARE SQLCODE INTEGER DEFAULT 0;
  DECLARE stmt VARCHAR(1024);

  DECLARE EXIT HANDLER FOR SQLEXCEPTION, SQLWARNING, NOT FOUND
    SET error_code = SQLCODE;

  SELECT COUNT(*) INTO count_before FROM staff;

  SET stmt = 'INSERT INTO staff(id)' ||
    ' VALUES (' || CAST(in_var AS CHAR(8)) ||')';
  EXECUTE IMMEDIATE stmt;

  SET stmt = 'INSERT INTO staff(id)' ||
    ' VALUES (?)';
  PREPARE ps FROM stmt;
  EXECUTE ps USING in_var;

  SELECT COUNT(*) INTO count_after FROM staff;

  SET error_code = SQLCODE;
END
```

Condition Handling

A *condition* within an SQL procedure is raised when a statement within the SQL procedure body returns any SQLSTATE value other than 00000, meaning that an error, data not found, or warning condition has been raised. A *condition handler* is an object declared within an SQL procedure body that determines how an SQL procedure will respond to one or more defined conditions or predefined sets of conditions. Condition handlers must be declared within the SQL procedure body, after variable declarations and cursor declarations.

The syntax for declaring a condition handler is as follows:

DECLARE *handler-type* HANDLER FOR *condition handler-action*

The handler types, conditions, and handler actions are described in the following sections.

Handler Types

There are three types of condition handlers:

- **CONTINUE** After *handler-action* completes, execution continues with the next statement after the statement that raised the condition.
- **EXIT** After *handler-action* completes, the SQL procedure terminates and control is returned to the caller.
- **UNDO** Before *handler-action* executes, DB2 rolls back any SQL operations that have occurred in the SQL procedure. After *handler-action* completes, the SQL procedure terminates and control is returned to the caller.

Conditions

Condition handlers handle either a custom condition based on a specific SQLSTATE value or classes of predefined conditions. The three classes of predefined conditions are the following:

- **NOT FOUND** Identifies any condition that results in an SQLCODE value of +100 or an SQLSTATE value of 02000. This condition typically occurs when a SELECT statement with a restrictive predicate returns zero rows.
- **SQLEXCEPTION** Identifies any condition that results in a negative SQLCODE value.
- **SQLWARNING** Identifies any condition that results in a warning condition (SQLWARN0 is *W*) or that results in a positive SQLCODE value other than +100.

If a NOT FOUND or SQLWARNING condition is raised and a condition handler is not defined for the condition, the condition is ignored and the flow of control passes to the next statement in the SQL procedure body. If an SQLEXCEPTION condition is raised and a condition handler is not defined for the condition, the SQL procedure fails and the flow of control returns to the caller.

The following example declares two condition handlers. The EXIT handler is invoked when either an SQLEXCEPTION or SQLWARNING condition is raised. The EXIT handler sets the value of the variable named stmt to 'aborted' before terminating the SQL procedure and returning the flow of control to the caller. The UNDO handler is invoked when a NOT FOUND condition is raised. Before returning the flow of control to the caller, the UNDO handler rolls back any SQL operations that were completed in the SQL procedure body.

```
DECLARE EXIT HANDLER FOR SQLEXCEPTION, SQLWARNING
  SET stmt = 'aborted';
DECLARE UNDO HANDLER FOR NOT FOUND;
```

If the predefined sets of conditions are too broad for your needs, you can declare a custom condition for a specific SQLSTATE value and then declare a condition handler for the custom condition. The syntax for declaring a custom condition is the following:

DECLARE *unique-name* CONDITION FOR SQLSTATE *'sqlstate'*

The following example from within an SQL procedure body declares a custom condition and a condition handler for that custom condition. The first statement declares a condition named undefined_object for SQLSTATE value '42704', which is raised when reference is made to an undefined object. The second statement declares a CONTINUE condition handler for the custom condition.

```
DECLARE undefined_object CONDITION FOR SQLSTATE '42704';
DECLARE CONTINUE HANDLER FOR undefined_object
   SET stmt = 'undefined';
```

Handler Actions

You can use a single SQL procedure statement to define the behavior of the condition handler. DB2 accepts a compound statement delimited by a BEGIN...END block as a single SQL procedure statement. If you use a compound statement to define the behavior of a condition handler, and you want the handler to retain the value of either the SQLSTATE or SQLCODE variables, you must assign the value of the variable to a local variable or parameter in the first statement of the compound block. If the first statement of a compound block does not assign the value of SQLSTATE or SQLCODE to a local variable or parameter, SQLSTATE and SQLCODE cannot retain the value that caused DB2 to invoke the condition handler.

Labeled Blocks

A *labeled block* within an SQL procedure body is a section of one or more statements identified by a unique SQL name followed by a colon. Labeled blocks help you perform conditional processing within an SQL procedure by providing targets for statements like GOTO and ITERATE, which pass control to a labeled block.

For example, the following SQL procedure body contains two labeled blocks: first_section and second_section:

```
first_section:
   SET counter = counter + 1;
   SET context = "In first_section";
second_section:
   SET counter = counter + 1;
```

APPLICATION
DEVELOPMENT

```
SET context = "In second_section";
IF counter < 5 THEN
  GOTO first_section;
END IF;
```

Flow of Control Structures

You can use the following statements within the SQL procedure body to perform conditional processing within an SQL procedure.

CASE

The CASE structure selects an execution path based on the evaluation of one or more conditions. The WHEN subclause can simply compare a literal value to a variable specified in the CASE expression, as follows:

```
CASE integerValue
  WHEN 1 THEN
    SET wordValue = "one";
  WHEN 2 THEN
    SET wordValue = "two";
  ELSE
    SET wordValue = "I can't count that high!";
END CASE;
```

If no variable is specified for the CASE clause, the WHEN subclause can perform complex comparisons by using comparison operators, as follows:

```
CASE
  WHEN integerValue = 1 THEN
    SET wordValue = "one";
  WHEN wordValue = "two" THEN
    SET integerValue = 2;
  ELSE
    SET wordValue = "I can't count that high!";
END CASE;
```

FOR

The FOR structure executes a block of code for each row of a table. For example, the following code concatenates the first name, middle initial, and last name from each row returned by the SELECT statement within the following FOR structure, and then it inserts that value into a new table:

```
DECLARE fullname VARCHAR(60);
FOR forLoopName AS
    SELECT firstnme, midinit, lastname FROM employee;
  DO
    SET fullname = firstnme || ' ' || midinit || ' ' || lastname;
    INSERT INTO newtable VALUE(fullname);
END FOR;
```

GET DIAGNOSTICS

The GET DIAGNOSTICS statement returns information about the previous SQL statement into an SQL variable. You can retrieve the number of rows updated or potentially affected by the previous SQL statement by using the ROW_COUNT clause, as follows:

```
DECLARE countRows INTEGER DEFAULT 0;
UPDATE employee
  SET firstnme = 'Lynn'
  WHERE firstnme = 'JENNIFER';
GET DIAGNOSTICS countRows = ROW_COUNT;
```

You can retrieve the return value of a CALL statement for an SQL procedure that returns a RETURN integer value, as follows:

```
DECLARE returnValue INTEGER DEFAULT 0;
CALL aStoredProcedure();
GET DIAGNOSTICS returnValue = RETURN_STATUS;
```

GOTO

The GOTO statement transfers control to a labeled block:

```
section:
  SET counter = counter + 1;
  IF counter < 5 THEN
    GOTO section;
  END IF;
```

IF

The IF structure selects an execution path based on the evaluation of conditions. Conditions must be enclosed in parentheses. The ELSEIF and ELSE clauses enable you to branch based on alternative conditions and to specify a default action to perform if the conditions of the IF or ELSEIF clauses were all false:

```
IF counter < 5 THEN
   SET size = "too small";
ELSEIF counter < 10 THEN
   SET size = "just right";
ELSE
   SET size = "too big";
END IF;
```

ITERATE

The ITERATE clause passes the flow of control to the beginning of a labeled loop:

```
section:
  LOOP
    SET counter = counter + 1;
  END LOOP;

  IF counter < 5 THEN
    ITERATE section;
  END IF;
```

LEAVE

The LEAVE clause transfers program control out of a loop or block of code:

```
section:
  LOOP
    SET counter = counter + 1;
    IF counter > 5 THEN
      LEAVE section;
    END IF;
  END LOOP;
```

LOOP

The LOOP clause executes a block of code multiple times until a LEAVE, ITERATE, or GOTO statement transfers control outside of the loop:

```
section:
  LOOP
    SET counter = counter + 1;
    IF counter > 5 THEN
      LEAVE section;
    END IF;
  END LOOP;
```

REPEAT

The REPEAT clause executes a block of code until the search condition specified in the UNTIL clause returns true:

```
REPEAT
  SET counter = counter + 1;
  UNTIL counter > 5;
END REPEAT;
```

RETURN

The RETURN clause returns control from the SQL procedure to the caller. You can also return an integer value to the caller. If the caller is an SQL procedure, the caller can retrieve the return value with the GET DIAGNOSTICS statement:

```
IF test = "success" THEN
  RETURN 0;
ELSE
  RETURN -1;
END IF;
```

SET

The SET clause assigns a value to an output parameter or SQL variable. You cannot assign values to IN parameters:

```
SET counter = counter + 1;
SET outErrorCode = SQLCODE;
```

WHILE

The WHILE clause repeatedly executes a block of code while a specified condition is true:

```
WHILE counter < 5 DO
  SET counter = counter + 1;
END WHILE;
```

Nested SQL Procedures

A *nested SQL procedure* contains a CALL statement within its SQL procedure body. Nested SQL procedures are supported in DB2, but they are subject to the following restrictions:

- **Language** SQL procedures can call stored procedures written only in SQL or C. You cannot call other host language stored procedures from within an SQL procedure.

- **Sixteen levels of nesting** You can include a maximum of only 16 levels of nested calls to SQL procedures. A scenario where SQL procedure A calls SQL procedure B and SQL procedure B calls SQL procedure C is an example of three levels of nested calls.

- **Recursion** You can create an SQL procedure that calls itself recursively. Recursive SQL procedures must comply with the previously described restriction on the maximum levels of nesting. All open cursors must be closed before the end of the SQL procedure body.

- **Security** An SQL procedure cannot call a target SQL procedure that is cataloged with a higher SQL data access level. For example, an SQL procedure created with the CONTAINS SQL clause can call SQL procedures created with either the CONTAINS SQL clause or the NO SQL clause, but it cannot call SQL procedures created with either the READS SQL DATA clause or the MODIFIES SQL DATA clause. An SQL procedure created with the NO SQL clause cannot issue a CALL statement.

Returning Result Sets from Nested SQL Procedures

If you return result sets from nested SQL procedures, you have two options for determining which layer of your application hierarchy will receive each result set:

- **Caller** To indicate that the caller of the SQL procedure will receive the result set, regardless of whether the caller is another SQL procedure or the client application, you must include the WITH RETURN TO CALLER clause in the DECLARE statement for the cursor in the SQL procedure body.

- **Client application** To indicate that the client application that issued the initial CALL statement will receive the result set, even if the result set is issued by a nested SQL procedure 15 levels down in the nested hierarchy, you can include the WITH RETURN TO CLIENT clause in the DECLARE statement for the cursor in the SQL procedure body. This is the default type of result set.

The following SQL procedure named twoResultSetsWithReturn returns two result sets. The first result set, rs1, will always be returned to the client application that issued the initial CALL statement, even if the SQL procedure is called from within another stored procedure. The second result set, rs2, will always be returned to the caller of the SQL procedure.

```
CREATE PROCEDURE twoResultSetsWithReturn
(IN in_years INTEGER)
DYNAMIC RESULT SETS 2
READS SQL DATA
LANGUAGE SQL
BEGIN
  DECLARE rs1 CURSOR WITH RETURN TO CLIENT FOR
    SELECT name, years
      FROM staff
      WHERE years < in_years;
  DECLARE rs2 CURSOR WITH RETURN TO CALLER FOR
    SELECT name, years
      FROM staff
      WHERE years > in_years;

  OPEN rs1;
  OPEN rs2;
END
```

The Complete Reference

Part VIII

Reference

Chapter 27

SQL Statements

This chapter describes the SQL statements used by DB2 Universal Database version 7. Use it as a quick reference for syntax, which is presented in diagrams and accompanying parameter descriptions; examples are also provided for many of the statements. The following explanation of how to read the syntax diagrams applies to the diagrams in Chapter 29 as well.

Read the syntax diagrams from left to right and top to bottom, following the path of the horizontal line (called the *main path*). The >>— symbol indicates the beginning of a statement; the —> symbol indicates that the syntax is continued on the next line; the >— symbol indicates that a statement is continued from the previous line, and the —>< symbol indicates the end of a statement.

Required items appear *on* the horizontal line (the main path):

```
>>-STATEMENT--required item-------------------------------------><
```

Optional items appear *below* the main path:

```
>>-STATEMENT----+---------------+-------------------------------><
                '-optional item--'
```

If an optional item appears *above* the main path, that item has no effect on the execution of the statement, but is included to enhance readability:

```
                .-optional item--.
>>-STATEMENT----+---------------+-------------------------------><
```

If you can choose from two or more items, they appear in a stack. If you *must* choose one of those items, one item in the stack appears on the main path:

```
>>-STATEMENT----+-required choice1-+---------------------------><
                '-required choice2-'
```

If choosing *none* of the items is an option, the entire stack appears below the main path:

```
>>-STATEMENT----+-----------------+---------------------------><
                +-optional choice1-+
                '-optional choice2-'
```

If one of the choices is the default value, it appears above the main path, and the remaining choices are shown below it.

```
                    .-default choice--.
>>-STATEMENT----+-----------------+--------------------------><
                +-optional choice-+
                '-optional choice-'
```

An arrow returning to the left, above the main path, indicates an item that can be repeated. In this case, you must separate repeated items with one or more blank spaces:

```
                  .-------------------.
                  V                   |
>>-STATEMENT-------repeatable item---+------------------------><
```

If the arrow contains a comma, you must separate repeated items with a comma:

```
                  .-,-----------------.
                  V                   |
>>-STATEMENT-------repeatable item---+------------------------><
```

An arrow above a stack indicates that you can make more than one choice from the stacked items, or repeat a single choice.

Keywords appear in uppercase characters (FROM, for example). They must be spelled exactly as shown. Variables (representing user-supplied names or values) appear in lowercase characters (column-name, for example).

If punctuation marks, parentheses, arithmetic operators, or other such symbols are shown, you must enter them as part of the syntax.

Sometimes a single variable represents a set of parameters. For example, in the following diagram, the variable parameter-block represents the syntax fragment called parameter-block, which follows the main part of the diagram. This is usually done to enhance the readability of complex syntax diagrams:

```
>>-STATEMENT----| parameter-block |--------------------------><
parameter-block
|--+-parameter1----------------+----------------------------|
   '-parameter2--+-parameter3-+-'
                 '-parameter4-'
```

Adjacent segments occurring between "large bullets" (*) can be specified in any order. The following example shows that item2 and item3 can be specified in either order:

```
>>-STATEMENT--item1--*--item2--*--item3--*--item4-------------><
```

REFERENCE

In this example, both of the following statements are valid:

```
STATEMENT item1 item2 item3 item4
STATEMENT item1 item3 item2 item4
```

ALTER BUFFERPOOL

The ALTER BUFFERPOOL statement is used to modify the size of the buffer pool on all partitions or on a single partition; turn on or off the use of extended storage; and add the buffer pool definition to a new nodegroup. The authorization ID of the statement must have SYSADM or SYSCTRL authority.

Syntax

```
>>-ALTER--BUFFERPOOL--bufferpool-name-------------------------->

>-----+-+-------------------+--SIZE--number-of-pages--+------->< 
      | '-NODE--node-number--'                              |
      +-+-NOT EXTENDED STORAGE-+---------------------+
      | '-EXTENDED STORAGE-----'                          |
      '-ADD NODEGROUP--nodegroup-name-----------------'
```

The referenced buffer pool must be described in the catalog. The partition (node) must be in one of the nodegroups for the buffer pool. The size of the buffer pool is specified as the number of pages. (The size can be specified with a value of –1, which indicates that the buffer pool size should be taken from the BUFFPAGE database configuration parameter.)

If the extended storage configuration is turned on and EXTENDED STORAGE is specified, pages that are being migrated out of this buffer pool are cached in the extended storage. If NOT EXTENDED STORAGE is specified, pages that are being migrated out of this buffer pool are *not* cached in the extended storage, even if the extended storage configuration is turned on. (Extended storage configuration is turned on by setting the database configuration parameters NUM_ESTORE_SEGS and ESTORE_SEG_SIZE to nonzero values.)

Specifying ADD NODEGROUP *nodegroup-name* adds this nodegroup to the list of nodegroups to which the buffer pool definition is applicable. For any partition in the nodegroup that does not already have the buffer pool defined, the buffer pool is created on the partition using the default size specified for the buffer pool. Table spaces in *nodegroup-name* can specify this buffer pool. The nodegroup must currently exist in the database.

No changes to the actual buffer pool will take effect until the next time the database is started.

ALTER NICKNAME

The ALTER NICKNAME statement modifies a federated database's representation of a data source table or view by changing the local names of the table columns or the view columns; changing the local data types of these columns; or adding, changing, or deleting options for these columns.

The authorization ID of the statement must have at least one of the following: SYSADM or DBADM authority; ALTER privilege on the nickname specified in the statement; CONTROL privilege on the nickname specified in the statement; ALTERIN privilege on the schema, if a schema name for the nickname exists; or definer of the nickname, as recorded in the DEFINER column of the catalog view for the nickname.

Syntax

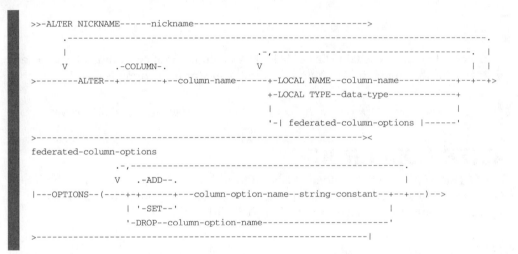

If you need to specify the federated-column-options clause, in addition to the LOCAL NAME parameter, the LOCAL TYPE parameter, or both, you must specify the federated-column-options clause last.

When invoking this statement, specify the *nickname* for the data source table or view that contains the specified *column-name*. It must be a nickname described in the catalog. The *column-name* parameter specifies the column that is to be altered. The value of *column-name* is the federated server's current name for the table or view column at the data source. LOCAL NAME is the new name by which the federated server is to reference the column. LOCAL TYPE maps the specified column's data type to a local data type other than the one that it maps to now. The data type cannot be LONG VARCHAR, LONG VARGRAPHIC, DATALINK, a large object (LOB) data type, or a user-defined type.

The OPTIONS keyword lets you specify which *column options* are to be enabled, reset, or dropped for the specified column. The *numeric_string* 'Y' option specifies that this column contains only strings of numeric data. By setting *numeric_string* to 'Y', you are informing the optimizer that this column contains no blanks that could interfere with the sorting of the column's data. The default setting for the *numeric_string* option is 'N'. The *varchar_no_trailing_blanks* 'Y' option specifies that trailing blanks are absent from this VARCHAR column. If a VARCHAR column has no trailing blanks and you let the optimizer know this, it can develop a more efficient access strategy. The default setting for the *varchar_no_trailing_blanks* option is 'N'.'

Examples

The nickname EMPLOYEE references a DB2 Universal Database for OS/390 table called EMP. SALARY is the local name that references EMP_SAL, a column in the EMP table. The column's data type, FLOAT, maps to the local data type, DOUBLE. Change the mapping so that FLOAT maps to DECIMAL (9, 2):

```
ALTER NICKNAME employee ALTER COLUMN salary LOCAL TYPE DECIMAL(10,5)
```

Specify that an Oracle table has a VARCHAR column with no trailing blanks. The nickname for the table is STAFF2, and the local name for the column is COL1.

```
ALTER NICKNAME staff2 ALTER COLUMN col1 OPTIONS (ADD VARCHAR_NO_TRAILING_BLANKS 'Y')
```

ALTER NODEGROUP

The ALTER NODEGROUP statement is used to add one or more partitions or nodes to a nodegroup, or to drop one or more partitions from a nodegroup. The authorization ID of the statement must have SYSADM or SYSCTRL authority.

Syntax

```
>>-ALTER NODEGROUP--nodegroup-name----------------------------->

     .-,-------------------------------------------------------------.
     V                                                               |
>---------+-ADD--+-NODE--+---| nodes-clause |--+----------------------------+-+--+>
          |      '-NODES-'                     +-LIKE NODE----node-number---+ |
          |                                    '-WITHOUT TABLESPACES--------' |
          '-DROP--+-NODE--+---| nodes-clause |------------------------------'
                  '-NODES-'
>------------------------------------------------------------->< 

nodes-clause

             .-,-------------------------------------.
             V                                       |
|--- (-------node-number1--+--------------------+--+--) ----------|
                           '-TO--node-number2---'
```

The specified nodegroup must be described in the catalog, and it cannot be IBMCATGROUP or IBMTEMPGROUP. The LIKE NODE option specifies that the containers for the existing table spaces in the nodegroup will be the same as the containers on the specified node. The WITHOUT TABLESPACES option specifies that the default table spaces are not to be created on the newly added partition or partitions.

The ALTER TABLESPACE statement, using the FOR NODE clause, must be used to define containers for use with the table spaces that are defined on this nodegroup. If this option is not specified, the default containers are specified on newly added partitions for each table space defined on the nodegroup.

Examples

Assume that you have a six-partition database with the following partitions: 0, 1, 2, 5, 7, and 8. Two partitions (3 and 6) are added to the system. Add both partitions (nodes) to a nodegroup called MAXGROUP. The table space containers are to be like those on partition 2:

```
ALTER NODEGROUP maxgroup ADD NODES (3,6) LIKE NODE 2
```

Drop partition 1 and add partition 6 to nodegroup MEDGROUP. (You will have defined the table space containers for partition 6 separately, using the ALTER TABLESPACE statement.)

```
ALTER NODEGROUP medgroup ADD NODE (6) WITHOUT TABLESPACES DROP NODE (1)
```

ALTER SEQUENCE

The ALTER SEQUENCE statement modifies the attributes of a sequence by doing the following: restarting the sequence; changing the increment between future sequence values; setting new minimum or maximum values; changing the number of cached sequence numbers; changing whether the sequence can cycle; changing whether sequence numbers must be generated in order of request. The authorization ID of the statement must have at least one of the following: definer of the sequence; ALTERIN privilege for the implicitly or explicitly specified schema; SYSADM or DBADM authority.

Syntax

```
>>-ALTER SEQUENCE--sequence-name------------------------------->

    .-------------------------------------------.
    V                                           |
>-------+-RESTART--+-------------------------+-+--+-----------><
        |          '-WITH--numeric-constant--' |
        +-INCREMENT BY--numeric-constant-------+
```

REFERENCE

```
+-+-MINVALUE--numeric-constant--+------+
| '-NO MINVALUE----------------'        |
+-+-MAXVALUE--numeric-constant--+------+
| '-NO MAXVALUE----------------'        |
+-+-CYCLE----+------------------------+
| '-NO CYCLE-'                          |
+-+-CACHE--integer-constant--+---------+
| '-NO CACHE----------------'           |
'-+-ORDER----+------------------------'
'-NO ORDER-'
```

The *sequence-name* parameter specifies the sequence that is to be altered. RESTART restarts the sequence. WITH *numeric-constant* restarts the sequence with the specified value. INCREMENT BY specifies the interval between consecutive values of the sequence. If this value is negative, the sequence of values descends. If this value is positive, the sequence of values ascends.

MINVALUE specifies the minimum value at which a descending sequence either cycles or stops generating values, or the minimum value to which an ascending sequence cycles after reaching the maximum value. NO MINVALUE specifies that for an ascending sequence, the value is the START WITH value, or 1 if the START WITH clause is not specified. For a descending sequence, the value is the minimum value of the data type associated with the sequence.

MAXVALUE specifies the maximum value at which an ascending sequence either cycles or stops generating values, or the maximum value to which a descending sequence cycles after reaching the minimum value.

NO MAXVALUE specifies that for an ascending sequence, the value is the maximum value of the data type associated with the sequence. For a descending sequence, the value is the START WITH value, or –1 if the START WITH clause is not specified.

CYCLE or NOCYCLE specifies whether the sequence should continue to generate values after reaching either its maximum or minimum value. If CYCLE has been specified, duplicate values can be generated for the sequence.

CACHE *integer-constant* specifies the maximum number of sequence values that are to be preallocated and kept in memory. Preallocating and storing values in the cache reduces synchronous I/O to the log when values are generated for the sequence. The minimum value is 2, and the default value is 20.

ORDER or NO ORDER specifies whether the sequence numbers are to be generated in order of request.

ALTER SERVER

The ALTER SERVER statement is used to modify the definition of a specific data source, the definition of a category of data sources, or to make changes in the configuration of a specific data source or the configuration of a category of data sources—changes that will persist over multiple connections to a federated database. The authorization ID of the statement must include either SYSADM or DBADM authority on the federated database.

In this statement, the word *server* and the parameter names that start with *server* refer only to data sources in a federated system.

Syntax

```
>>-ALTER SERVER----------------------------------------------------->
>-----+-server-name--+------------------------------------+-------------------------------------+>
      |                    '-VERSION--| server-version |--'                                      |
      '-TYPE--server-type--+-------------------------------------------------------------+-'
                            '-VERSION--| server-version |--+-----------------------+--'
                                                            '-WRAPPER--wrapper-name--'
          .-,----------------------------------------------------.
          V    .-ADD--.                                          |
>-----OPTIONS--(----+-+------+---server-option-name--string-constant--+--+---)-><
                    | '-SET--'                                       |
                    '-DROP--server-option-name----------------------'

server-version
|---+-version--+--------------------------------+-+-------------------|
    |              '-.--release--+---------+--' |
    |                            '-.--mod--'    |
    '-version-string-constant--------------'
```

The *server-name* parameter identifies the federated server (data source) to which the changes being requested are to apply. The data source must be one that is described in the catalog. After *server-name*, VERSION specifies a new version (version number, an integer; release number, an integer; and modification number, also an integer) of the data source. Alternatively, you can specify a *version-string-constant*, such as 8i or 8.0.3, for example.

TYPE *server-type* specifies the type of data source to which the changes being requested are to apply. The server type must be one that is listed in the catalog. After *server-type*, VERSION specifies the version of the data sources for which server options are to be enabled, reset, or dropped. WRAPPER *wrapper-name* specifies the name of the wrapper that the federated server uses to interact with data sources of the specified type and version. The wrapper must be listed in the catalog.

The OPTIONS parameter indicates which server options are to be enabled, reset, or dropped for the specified data source, or for the specified data source category. *Server options* are used to describe a server, and include the following:

- *collating_sequence* Specifies whether the data source uses the same default collating sequence as the federated database, based on code set and country information. Valid values are: 'Y' (same), 'N' (different), or 'I' (different and case-insensitive).

- *comm_rate* Specifies the communication rate between a federated server and its associated data sources. Expressed in megabytes per second (MBps) (only whole numbers). Valid values are greater than 0 and less than 2,147,483,648.

- *connectstring* Specifies initialization properties needed to connect to an OLE DB provider.

- *cpu_ratio* Indicates how much faster or slower a data source's CPU runs than the federated server's CPU. Valid values are greater than 0 and less than 1×10^{23}. Values may be expressed in any valid double notation, for example 123E10, 123, or 1.21E4.

- *dbname* Name of the data source database that you want the federated server to access.

- *fold_id* Applies to user IDs that the federated server sends to data sources for authentication. Valid values are 'U' (folded to uppercase), 'N' (no action), or 'L' (folded to lowercase). If none of these settings is used, the federated server tries to send the user ID to the data source in uppercase. If the user ID fails, the server tries sending it in lowercase.

- *fold_pw* Applies to passwords that the federated server sends to data sources for authentication. Valid values are 'U' (folded to uppercase), 'N' (no action), or 'L' (folded to lowercase). If none of these settings is used, the federated server tries to send the password to the data source in uppercase. If the password fails, the server tries sending it in lowercase.

- *io_ratio* Indicates how much faster or slower a data source's I/O system runs than the federated server's I/O system. Valid values are greater than 0 and less than 1×10^{23}. Values may be expressed in any valid double notation, for example, 123E10, 123, or 1.21E4.

- *node* Name by which a data source is defined as an instance to its relational database management system (RDBMS). Required for all data sources. For a DB2 family data source, this name is the node specified in the federated database's DB2 node directory. To view this directory, issue the DB2 LIST NODE DIRECTORY command. For an Oracle data source, this name is the server name specified in the Oracle tnsnames.ora file. To access this name on the Windows NT platform, specify the View Configuration Information option of the Oracle SQL Net Easy Configuration tool.

- *password* Specifies whether passwords are sent to a data source. Valid values are 'Y' (always sent and validated), 'N' (neither sent nor validated), or 'ENCRYPTION' (sent in encrypted form and validated; valid only for DB2 family data sources that support encrypted passwords).

- *plan_hints* Specifies whether plan hints are to be enabled. *Plan hints* are statement fragments that provide extra information for data source optimizers. Valid values are 'Y' (if supported) or 'N'.

- *pushdown* Valid values are 'Y' (DB2 will consider letting the data source evaluate operations) or 'N'.

- *varchar_no_trailing_blanks* Specifies whether this data source uses nonblank padded VARCHAR comparison semantics. Valid values are 'Y' or 'N'.

Example

Ensure that the case of authorization IDs that are sent to your Oracle 8.0.3 data sources remains unchanged. Inform the optimizer that these data sources have started to run on an upgraded CPU that is half as fast as your local CPU.

```
ALTER SERVER TYPE oracle VERSION 8.0.3 OPTIONS (ADD FOLD_ID 'N', SET CPU_RATIO '2.0')
```

ALTER TABLE

The ALTER TABLE statement modifies an existing table by adding one or more columns; adding or dropping a primary key; adding or dropping one or more unique or referential constraints; adding or dropping one or more check constraint definitions; altering the length of a VARCHAR column; altering a reference type column to add a scope; altering the generation expression of a generated column; adding or dropping a partitioning key; changing table attributes, such as the data capture option *pctfree*, lock size, or append mode; or setting the table to the not logged initially state.

The authorization ID of the statement must have at least one of the following: SYSADM or DBADM authority; ALTER or CONTROL privilege on the table to be altered; or ALTERIN privilege on the table schema.

Syntax

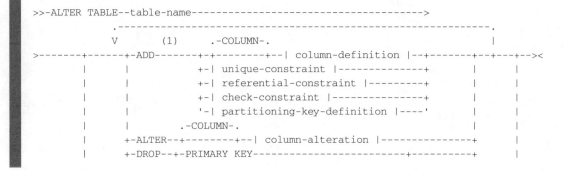

```
>>-ALTER TABLE--table-name------------------------------------->
          .----------------------------------------------------------------.
          V        (1)      .-COLUMN-.                                      |
>-------+------+--ADD-------+-+--------+--| column-definition |--+-------+--+---+-->< 
        |      |                       +-| unique-constraint |--------------+     |      |
        |      |                       +-| referential-constraint |---------+     |      |
        |      |                       +-| check-constraint |---------------+     |      |
        |      |                       '-| partitioning-key-definition |----'     |      |
        |      |          .-COLUMN-.                                              |      |
        |      +-ALTER--+--------+--| column-alteration |---------------+         |
        |      +-DROP--+-PRIMARY KEY--------------------------+---------+         |
```

```
            |       |           +--+-FOREIGN KEY-+---constraint-name--+        |        |
            |       |           |  +-UNIQUE------+                     |        |
            |       |           |  +-CHECK-------+                     |        |
            |       |           |  '-CONSTRAINT--'                     |        |
            |       |           '-PARTITIONING KEY-------------------' |        |
            |       +-DATA CAPTURE--+-NONE----------------------------------+-+  |
            |       |               '-CHANGES--+-----------------------+-' |     |
            |       |                          '-INCLUDE LONGVAR COLUMNS-' |     |
            |       +-ACTIVATE NOT LOGGED INITIALLY--+-------------------+---+   |
            |       |                                '-WITH EMPTY TABLE--'   |   |
            |       +-PCTFREE--integer--------------------------------------+   |
            |       +-LOCKSIZE--+-ROW---+---------------------------------+     |
            |       |           '-TABLE-'                                 |     |
            |       +-APPEND--+-ON--+---------------------------------+         |
            |       |         '-OFF-'                                 |         |
            |       |                        .-CARDINALITY-.          |         |
            |       '--+-VOLATILE-----+--+------------+-------------------'      |
            |          '-NOT VOLATILE-'                                         |
            '-SET SUMMARY AS--+-DEFINITION ONLY-------------+--------------------'
                              '-| summary-table-definition |-'

summary-table-definition
|---(--fullselect--)--| refreshable-table-options |-------------|

refreshable-table-options
|---DATA INITIALLY--DEFERRED------------------------------------->
                                 .-ENABLE QUERY OPTIMIZATION--.
>----REFRESH--+-DEFERRED--+---+-------------------------+----|
              '-IMMEDIATE-'   '-DISABLE QUERY OPTIMIZATION-'

column-alteration
|---column-name------------------------------------------------->
>-----+-SET--+-DATA TYPE--+-VARCHAR-----------+---(--integer--)--+-+--|
      |      |            +-CHARACTER VARYING-+                  | |
      |      |            '-CHAR VARYING------'                  | |
      |      '-EXPRESSION AS--(--generation-expression--)--------' |
      '-ADD SCOPE--+-typed-table-name-+--------------------------'
                   '-typed-view-name--'

column-definition
|--column-name----+-------------------+----------------------->
                  |          (2)      |
                  '-| data-type |-------'
>-----+-------------------+---------------------------------|
      '-| column-options |--'

column-options

.----------------------------------------------------------------------------------.
```

```
      V
   |
   |------+----------------------------------------------------------------------+
--+--|
        +-NOT NULL------------------------------------------------------------------+
        |                    (3)                                                     |
        +-| lob-options |----------------------------------------------------------+
        |                          (4)                                              |
        +-| datalink-options |-----------------------------------------------------+
        |                                    (5)                                    |
        +-SCOPE--+-typed-table-name2-+------------------------------------------------+
        |         '-typed-view-name2--'                                             |
        +-+----------------------------------+---+-+-PRIMARY KEY-+----------------+-+
        | |            (6)                   |   | | '-UNIQUE------'             | |
        | '-CONSTRAINT------constraint-name--'   +-| references-clause |---------+ |
        |                                        '-CHECK--(--check-condition--)--' |
        '-| generated-column-spec |----------------------------------------------'

generated-column-spec
|--+-| default-clause |-------------------------------+--------|
   '-GENERATED ALWAYS AS--(--generation-expression--)--'

default-clause
     .-WITH-.
|---+------+--DEFAULT--+----------------------------------------------------+--|
                       +-constant-----------------------------------------+
                       +-datetime-special-register------------------------+
                       +-USER---------------------------------------------+
                       +-NULL---------------------------------------------+
                       '-cast-function--(--+-constant------------------+---)--'
                                           +-datetime-special-register-+
                                           '-USER--------------------'

lob-options
        .-LOGGED-----.      .-NOT COMPACT--.
|---*--+------------+--*--+--------------+---*-----------------|
        '-NOT LOGGED-'      '-COMPACT------'

datalink-options
|---LINKTYPE URL----------------------------------------------->
     .-NO LINK CONTROL----------------------------.
>----+----------------------------------------------+----------|
     '-FILE LINK CONTROL--+-| file-link-options |-+-'
                          '-MODE DB2OPTIONS-------'

file-link-options
|---*--INTEGRITY----ALL----*--READ PERMISSION--+-FS-+---------->
                                               '-DB-'
>----*--WRITE PERMISSION--+-FS------+--*--RECOVERY--+-NO--+----->
```

```
                             '-BLOCKED-'                    '-YES-'
>----*--ON UNLINK--+-RESTORE-+---*-----------------------------|
                   '-DELETE--'
```

references-clause
```
|---REFERENCES--table-name----+---------------------------+---->
                              |    .-,-------------.      |
                              |    V               |      |
                              '-(-----column-name---+---)--'
>-----| rule-clause |-------------------------------------|
```

rule-clause
```
       .-ON DELETE NO ACTION-----.        .-ON UPDATE NO ACTION--.
|--*--+-----------------------+---*--+--------------------+---*--|
      '-ON DELETE--+-RESTRICT-+-'     '-ON UPDATE RESTRICT---'
                   +-CASCADE--+
                   '-SET NULL-'
```

unique-constraint
```
|--+---------------------------+---+-UNIQUE------+---------->
   '-CONSTRAINT--constraint-name--'   '-PRIMARY KEY-'
         .-,--------------.
         V                |
>----(-----column-name---+---)--------------------------------|
```

referential-constraint
```
|---+--------------------------------+---------------------->
    |                          (7)    |
    '-CONSTRAINT--constraint-name-------'
                      .-,--------------.
                      V                |
>----FOREIGN KEY--(-----column-name---+---)-------------------->
>-----| references-clause |---------------------------------|
```

check-constraint
```
|--+---------------------------+---------------------------->
   '-CONSTRAINT--constraint-name--'
>----CHECK--(--check-condition--)---------------------------|
```

partitioning-key-definition
```
                            .-,--------------.
                            V                |
|---PARTITIONING KEY---(-----column-name---+---)--------------->
     .-USING HASHING-.
>----+--------------+-----------------------------------------|
```

Syntax Notes:

1. For compatibility with version 1, the ADD keyword is optional for unnamed PRIMARY KEY constraints, unnamed referential constraints, or referential constraints whose name follows the FOREIGN KEY phrase.

```
summary-table-definition
|---(--fullselect--)--| refreshable-table-options |------------|
refreshable-table-options
|---DATA INITIALLY--DEFERRED------------------------------------->
                                  .-ENABLE QUERY OPTIMIZATION--.
>----REFRESH--+-DEFERRED--+---+--------------------------+----|
              '-IMMEDIATE-'   '-DISABLE QUERY OPTIMIZATION-'
column-alteration
|---column-name------------------------------------------------->
>-----+-SET--+-DATA TYPE--+-VARCHAR-----------+---(--integer--)--+-+>
      |      |            +-CHARACTER VARYING-+                  | |
      |      |            '-CHAR VARYING------'                  | |
      |      '-EXPRESSION AS--(--generation-expression--)-------' |
      '-ADD SCOPE--+-typed-table-name-+-------------------------'
                   '-typed-view-name--'
      '-+-| identity-alteration
|-------------------------------------+-'
      '-SET
GENERATED--+-ALWAYS-----+---+------------------------+-'
                        '-BY DEFAULT-'    '-| identity-alteration |--'
>------------------------------------------------------------|
identity-alteration
|---+-RESTART--+------------------------+-+-----------------|
    |          '-WITH--numeric-constant---' |
    +-SET INCREMENT BY--numeric-constant----+
    |                   (1)                  |
    +-SET--+-NO MINVALUE----------------+--+
    |      '-MINVALUE--numeric-constant--'  |
    +-SET--+-NO MAXVALUE----------------+--+
    |      '-MAXVALUE--numeric-constant--'  |
    +-SET--+-CYCLE----+-------------------+
    |      '-NO CYCLE-'                   |
    +-SET--+-NO CACHE----------------+-----+
    |      '-CACHE--integer-constant--'    |
    '-SET--+-NO ORDER-+-------------------'
           '-ORDER----'
```

Syntax Notes:

2. These parameters can be specified without spaces: NOMINVALUE, NOMAXVALUE, NOCYCLE, NOCACHE, and NOORDER.

```
column-definition
|--column-name----+--------------------+---------------------->
                  |               (1)   |
                  '-| data-type |-------'
>-----+--------------------+---------------------------------|
      '-| column-options |--'
```

Syntax Notes:

1. If the first column-option chosen is the generated-column-spec, the data type can be omitted and computed by the generation-expression.

```
column-options

   .-------------------------------------------------------------------.
   V                                                                   |
|------+-----------------------------------------------------------+--+->
        +-NOT NULL------------------------------------------------------+
        |                (1)                                            |
        +-| lob-options |-----------------------------------------------+
        |                    (2)                                        |
        +-| datalink-options |------------------------------------------+
        |                            (3)                                |
        +-SCOPE--+-typed-table-name2-+-----------------------------------+
        |        '-typed-view-name2--'                                  |
        +-+-------------------------------+---+-+-PRIMARY KEY-+---------------+-+
        | |              (4)              |   | | '-UNIQUE------'             | |
        | '-CONSTRAINT-------constraint-name--'   +-| references-clause |---------+ |
        |                                         '-CHECK--(--check-condition--)--' |
        '-| generated-column-spec |-----------------------------------------------'
        >-----------------------------------------------------------|
```

Syntax Notes:

1. The lob-options clause applies only to large object types (BLOB, CLOB, and DBCLOB) and distinct types based on large object types.

2. The datalink-options clause applies only to the DATALINK type and distinct types based on the DATALINK type.

3. The SCOPE clause applies only to the REF type.

REFERENCE

4. For compatibility with version 1, the CONSTRAINT keyword may be omitted in a column-definition clause defining a references-clause.

```
generated-column-spec
|--+-| default-clause |-------------------------------+-------|
    '-GENERATED ALWAYS AS--(--generation-expression--)--'
default-clause
     .-WITH-.
|---+------+--DEFAULT--+------------------------------------------------------+->
                       +-constant----------------------------------------------+
                       +-datetime-special-register----------------------------+
                       +-USER-------------------------------------------------+
                       +-NULL-------------------------------------------------+
                       '-cast-function--(--+-constant------------------+---)--'
                                           +-datetime-special-register-+
                                           '-USER--------------------'
>--------------------------------------------------------------|
lob-options
        .-LOGGED-----.      .-NOT COMPACT--.
|---*--+------------+--*--+--------------+---*-----------------|
        '-NOT LOGGED-'      '-COMPACT------'
datalink-options
|---LINKTYPE URL------------------------------------------------>
     .-NO LINK CONTROL----------------------------.
>----+------------------------------------------------+----------|
     '-FILE LINK CONTROL--+-| file-link-options |-+-'
                          '-MODE DB2OPTIONS-------'
file-link-options
|---*--INTEGRITY----ALL----*--READ PERMISSION--+-FS-+----------->
                                               '-DB-'
>----*--WRITE PERMISSION--+-FS------+--*--RECOVERY--+-NO--+----->
                          '-BLOCKED-'               '-YES-'
>----*--ON UNLINK--+-RESTORE-+---*----------------------------|
                   '-DELETE--'
references-clause
|---REFERENCES--table-name----+--------------------------+---->
                             |    .-,--------------.     |
                             |    V                |     |
                             '-(-----column-name---+---)--'
>-----| rule-clause |----------------------------------------|
rule-clause
        .-ON DELETE NO ACTION-----.       .-ON UPDATE NO ACTION--.
|--*--+-------------------------+---*--+--------------------+---*-->
        '-ON DELETE--+-RESTRICT-+-'       '-ON UPDATE RESTRICT---'
```

```
                                +-CASCADE--+
                                '-SET NULL-'
    >------------------------------------------------------------|
    unique-constraint
    |--+---------------------------+---+-UNIQUE------+---------->
        '-CONSTRAINT--constraint-name--'   '-PRIMARY KEY-'
             .-,-------------.
         V                 |
    >----(-----column-name---+---)-------------------------------|
    referential-constraint
    |---+-----------------------------------+--------------------->
        |                             (1)   |
        '-CONSTRAINT--constraint-name-------'
                         .-,-------------.
                     V               |
    >----FOREIGN KEY--(-----column-name---+---)-------------------->
    >-----| references-clause |----------------------------------|
```

Syntax Notes:

1. For compatibility with version 1, *constraint-name* may be specified following FOREIGN KEY (without the CONSTRAINT keyword).

```
check-constraint

    |--+----------------------------+----------------------------->
        '-CONSTRAINT--constraint-name--'

    >----CHECK--(--check-condition--)-----------------------------|
    partitioning-key-definition
                                .-,-------------.
                            V               |
    |---PARTITIONING KEY---(-----column-name---+---)--------------->
            .-USING HASHING-.
    >----+--------------+------------------------------------------|
```

The *table-name* parameter identifies the table to be changed. It must be a table described in the catalog; it cannot be a view or a catalog table, a nickname, or a declared temporary table.

The SET SUMMARY AS parameter allows alteration of the properties of a summary table. DEFINITION ONLY changes a summary table so that it is no longer considered a summary table; it can no longer be used for query optimization. The summary-table-definition clause changes a regular table to a summary table for use during query optimization. The fullselect defines the query on which the table is based.

For information about specifying the fullselect for a summary table, see the description of the CREATE TABLE statement. The refreshable-table-options include the following:

- **DATA INITIALLY DEFERRED** Specifies that the data in the table must be validated by using the REFRESH TABLE or the SET INTEGRITY statement.

- **REFRESH** Indicates how the data in the table is to be maintained. DEFERRED specifies that the data in the table can be refreshed at any time by using the REFRESH TABLE statement. Summary tables defined with this attribute do not allow INSERT, UPDATE, or DELETE statements. IMMEDIATE specifies that changes made to the underlying tables as part of a DELETE, INSERT, or UPDATE operation are to be cascaded to the summary table. Summary tables defined with this attribute do not allow INSERT, UPDATE, or DELETE statements.

- **ENABLE QUERY OPTIMIZATION** Specifies that the summary table can be used for query optimization.

- **DISABLE QUERY OPTIMIZATION** Specifies that the summary table will not be used for query optimization. The table can still be queried directly.

The ADD *column-definition* parameter is used to add a column to the table. The table cannot be a typed table. As part of the column definition, you must specify a column name. You will normally also specify a data type. You can do the following: specify that the column is not to contain NULL values (specify a default-clause); specify options for LOB data types or for DATALINK data types (see the description of the CREATE TABLE statement); specify the scope for a reference type column (the name of a typed table or the name of a typed view); specify a constraint—PRIMARY KEY, UNIQUE, foreign key (references-clause), or CHECK (check-condition); alter the generation expression for a generated column; or specify a default value for the column.

Note *If a specific default value is not given following the DEFAULT keyword, the default value depends on the data type of the column. If the DEFAULT keyword is omitted, the NULL value becomes the default value for the column. The types of values that can be specified with the DEFAULT keyword include a constant, a datetime special register, the USER special register, NULL, and, in certain cases, a cast function.)*

The ADD *unique-constraint* parameter is used to define a unique or primary key constraint. You have the option to name the constraint, but you must specify the names of the columns that make up the key. Only one primary key can be defined on a table. You can also add a referential constraint, add a check constraint, or define a partitioning key. For information about these options, see the description of the CREATE TABLE statement.

ALTER is used to alter the characteristics of a column. SET DATA TYPE VARCHAR *(integer)* can be used to increase the length of an existing VARCHAR column. SET EXPRESSION AS *(generation-expression)* changes the expression for the column; after the column has been altered, the SET INTEGRITY statement must be invoked to update and check all the values in the column against the new expression.

ADD SCOPE adds a scope to an existing reference type column that does not already have a scope defined. If the table being altered is a typed table, the column must not be inherited from a supertable. The parameters *typed-table-name* and *typed-view-name* represent the name of a typed table or a typed view, respectively. The data type of the column must be REF(*S*), where *S* is the type of the typed table or the typed view.

SET GENERATED specifies whether values are to be generated for the column always or only when a default value is needed. ALWAYS specifies that a value will always be generated for the column when a row is inserted or updated in the table. BY DEFAULT specifies that a value will be generated when a row is inserted into the table, unless a value is specified.

RESTART or RESTART WITH *numeric-constant* resets the state of the sequence associated with the identity column. If WITH *numeric-constant* is not specified, the sequence for the identity column is restarted at the value that was specified as the starting value when the identity column was originally created. The numeric constant is used as the next value for the column.

SET INCREMENT BY *numeric-constant* specifies the interval between consecutive values of the identity column. SET MINVALUE *numeric-constant* or NO MINVALUE specifies the minimum value at which a descending identity column either cycles or stops generating values, or the value to which an ascending identity column cycles after reaching the maximum value. MINVALUE *numeric-constant* specifies the minimum numeric constant value. NO MINVALUE specifies that for an ascending sequence, the value is the START WITH value, or 1 if START WITH is not specified.

For a descending sequence, the value is the minimum value for the data type of the column. SET MAXVALUE *numeric-constant* or NO MAXVALUE specifies the maximum value at which an ascending identity column either cycles or stops generating values, or the value to which a descending identity column cycles after reaching the minimum value. MAXVALUE *numeric-constant* specifies the maximum numeric constant value. NO MAXVALUE specifies that for an ascending sequence, the value is the maximum value for the data type of the column. For a descending sequence, the value is the START WITH value, or –1 if START WITH is not specified.

SET CYCLE or NO CYCLE specifies whether this identity column should continue to generate values after generating either the maximum or the minimum value. CYCLE specifies that values are to be generated for the identity column once the maximum or the minimum value has been reached: after an ascending identity column reaches the maximum value, it generates its minimum value, and after a descending sequence reaches the minimum value, it generates its maximum value. The maximum and minimum values for the identity column determine the range that is used for cycling. NO CYCLE specifies that values are not to be generated for the identity column once the maximum or the minimum value has been reached.

SET CACHE *integer-constant* or NO CACHE specifies whether to keep some preallocated values in memory for faster access. This is a performance and tuning option.

CACHE *integer-constant* specifies how many values of the identity sequence are to be preallocated and kept in memory. The minimum value is 2. NO CACHE specifies that values for the identity column are not to be preallocated.

SET ORDER or NO ORDER specifies whether the identity column values must be generated in order of request. ORDER specifies that the identity column values are to be generated in order of request. NO ORDER specifies that the identity column values do not need to be generated in order of request.

DROP PRIMARY KEY specifies that the definition of the primary key, and all referential constraints that depend on this primary key, are to be dropped. DROP FOREIGN KEY *constraint-name* specifies that the named referential constraint is to be dropped. DROP UNIQUE *constraint-name* specifies that the definition of a unique constraint and all referential constraints that depend on this unique constraint, are to be dropped. DROP CONSTRAINT *constraint-name* specifies that the named constraint is to be dropped. The constraint name must identify an existing check constraint, referential constraint, primary key, or unique constraint that is defined on the table. DROP CHECK *constraint-name* specifies that the named check constraint is to be dropped. DROP PARTITIONING KEY specifies that the partitioning key is to be dropped.

DATA CAPTURE specifies whether extra information for data replication is to be written to the log. For information about this option, see the description of the CREATE TABLE statement. INCLUDE LONGVAR COLUMNS specifies that data replication utilities are to be allowed to capture changes made to LONG VARCHAR or LONG VARGRAPHIC columns.

ACTIVATE NOT LOGGED INITIALLY specifies that the NOT LOGGED INITIALLY attribute of the table is to be activated for the current unit of work. The table must have been originally created with the NOT LOGGED INITIALLY attribute. At the completion of the current unit of work, the NOT LOGGED INITIALLY attribute is deactivated, and all operations against the table in subsequent units of work are logged. WITH EMPTY TABLE specifies that all data currently in the table is to be removed. (Any indexes that exist on the table are also emptied.) Once the data has been removed, it cannot be recovered, except through the DB2 RESTORE utility. If the unit of work in which the ALTER TABLE statement was issued is rolled back, the table data is *not* returned to its original state.

PCTFREE *integer* specifies the percentage of each page that is to be left as free space during a load or a reorganization operation. The specified value can range from 0 to 99. If the table is a typed table, this option is supported only on the root table of the typed table hierarchy.

LOCKSIZE specifies the granularity of locks that are to be used when the table is accessed. If the table is a typed table, this option is supported only on the root table of the typed table hierarchy. ROW specifies the use of row locks. This is the default lock size when a table is created. TABLE specifies the use of table locks.

APPEND ON specifies that table data is to be appended, and information about free space on pages is not to be kept. The table must not have a clustered index. APPEND OFF specifies that table data is to be placed where there is available space.

REFERENCE

This is the default option when a table is created. If the table is a typed table, the APPEND option is supported only on the root table of the typed table hierarchy.

VOLATILE specifies to the optimizer that the cardinality of the table can vary significantly at run time, from empty to quite large. The optimizer uses an index scan rather than a table scan to access the table, regardless of the statistics, if all referenced columns are in the index, or that index is able to apply a predicate to the index scan. If the table is a typed table, this option is supported only on the root table of the typed table hierarchy. NOT VOLATILE specifies to the optimizer that the cardinality of the table is not expected to vary significantly at run time. Access plans for this table continue to be based on existing statistics and on the current optimization level. CARDINALITY is an optional key word to indicate that it is the number of rows in the table, and not the table itself, that is volatile.

Examples

Add a referential constraint (called Deptquip) to the Equipment table, so that the owner (Equip_Owner) must be a department number (Deptno) that is present in the Department table. Deptno is the primary key of the Department table. If a department is removed from the Department table, the owner (Equip_Owner) values for all equipment owned by that department are to become unassigned (or set to null):

```
ALTER TABLE EQUIPMENT
  ADD CONSTRAINT DEPTQUIP
    FOREIGN KEY (EQUIP_OWNER)
      REFERENCES DEPARTMENT
      ON DELETE SET NULL
```

An additional column is needed to allow the recording of the quantity associated with this equipment record. Unless specified otherwise, the Equip_Qty column should have a value of 1 and must never be null:

```
ALTER TABLE EQUIPMENT
  ADD COLUMN EQUIP_QTY
  SMALLINT NOT NULL DEFAULT 1
```

Add a check constraint named Revenue to the Employee table, defined so that each employee must receive a total compensation greater than $30,000:

```
ALTER TABLE EMPLOYEE
  ADD CONSTRAINT REVENUE
  CHECK (SALARY + COMM > 30000)
```

Drop the check constraint named Revenue from the Employee table:

```
ALTER TABLE EMPLOYEE
  DROP CONSTRAINT REVENUE
```

Alter the Employee table to add a new column with a default value. Because BIRTHDATE is a distinct type based on DATE, the DATE function is used.

```
ALTER TABLE EMPLOYEE
  ADD COLUMN BIRTHDAY BIRTHDATE DEFAULT DATE('01-01-1950')
```

ALTER TABLESPACE

The ALTER TABLESPACE statement modifies an existing table space by adding a container to a DMS table space; increasing the size of a container in a DMS table space; adding a container to an SMS table space on a partition (or node) that currently has no containers; modifying the PREFETCHSIZE, OVERHEAD, or TRANSFERRATE setting for a table space; or modifying the BUFFERPOOL used for tables in the table space.

The authorization ID of the statement must have SYSADM or SYSCTRL authority.

Syntax

```
>>-ALTER--TABLESPACE--tablespace-name-------------------------->

   .------------------------------------------------------------------------------.
   V                                                                              |
>---------+-ADD--+-| database-container-clause |--+--------------------+-+----------------+--+>
          |      |                                '-| on-nodes-clause |--' |                |
          |      '-| system-container-clause |--| on-nodes-clause |--------'                |
          |          (1)                                                                    |
          +--+-EXTEND-+---------+-| database-container-clause |-+---+--------------------+--+-+
          | '-RESIZE-'          '-| all-containers-clause |-----'   '-| on-nodes-clause |--' |
          +-PREFETCHSIZE--+-number-of-pages-+-----------------------------------------------+
          |               '-integer--+-K-+--'                                               |
          |                          +-M-+                                                  |
          |                          '-G-'                                                  |
          +-BUFFERPOOL--bufferpool-name--------------------------------------------------+
          +-OVERHEAD--number-of-milliseconds---------------------------------------------+
          +-TRANSFERRATE--number-of-milliseconds-----------------------------------------+
          +-DROPPED TABLE RECOVERY--+-ON--+----------------------------------------------+
          |                         '-OFF-'                                              |
          '-SWITCH ONLINE----------------------------------------------------------------'

  >------------------------------------------------------------><
```

```
database-container-clause
      .-,-----------------------------------------------------------.
      V                                                             |
|---(------+-FILE---+--'--container-string--'----+-number-of-pages-+--+---)-->
           '-DEVICE-'                             '-integer--+-K-+--'
                                                             +-M-+
                                                             '-G-'
>-------------------------------------------------------------|
system-container-clause
      .-,-----------------------.
      V                         |
|---(-----'--container-string--'---+---)----------------------|
on-nodes-clause
|---ON----+-NODE--+--(------------------------------------------->
          '-NODES-'
       .-,---------------------------------------.
       V                                         |
>--------node-number1--+--------------------+--+--)-------------|
                       '-TO--node-number2---'
all-containers-clause
           .-CONTAINERS--.
|---(--ALL--+-------------+---+-number-of-pages-+---)-----------|
                             '-integer--+-K-+--'
                                        +-M-+
                                        '-G-'
```

Syntax Notes:

1. The ADD, EXTEND, and RESIZE clauses cannot be specified in the same statement.

ADD specifies that a new container is to be added to the table space. EXTEND specifies that existing containers are to be increased in size. The specified size is the size *by which* an existing container is to be increased. If the all-containers-clause is specified, all containers in the table space are to increase by this size. RESIZE specifies that the size of existing containers is to be increased. The specified size is the *new size* for a container. If the all-containers-clause is specified, all containers in the table space are to increase to this size. The database-container-clause specifies containers for a DMS table space. The system-container-clause specifies containers for an SMS table space on the specified partitions or nodes.

PREFETCHSIZE *number-of-pages* specifies the number of pages that will be read from the table space when data prefetching is being performed. The prefetch size can also be specified as an integer value followed by K (for kilobytes), M (for megabytes), or G (for gigabytes). BUFFERPOOL *bufferpool-name* specifies the name of the buffer pool that is to be used for tables in this table space.

OVERHEAD *number-of-milliseconds* specifies the I/O controller overhead and disk seek and latency time. The value (any numeric literal: integer, decimal, or floating point) is used to determine the cost of I/O during query optimization. If it is not the same for all containers, the number should be the average for all containers that belong to the table space.

TRANSFERRATE *number-of-milliseconds* specifies the time to read one page into memory. The value (any numeric literal: integer, decimal, or floating point) is also used to determine the cost of I/O during query optimization. If it is not the same for all containers, the number should be the average for all containers that belong to the table space.

DROPPED TABLE RECOVERY enables a REGULAR table space for dropped table recovery. Dropped tables in the specified table space can be recovered by using the RECOVER TABLE ON option of the ROLLFORWARD DATABASE command.

SWITCH ONLINE specifies that table spaces that are in offline state are to be brought online if their containers have become accessible.

ALTER TYPE (Structured)

The ALTER TYPE statement is used to add or drop attributes or method specifications for a user-defined structured type. The authorization ID of the statement must have at least one of the following: SYSADM or DBADM authority; ALTERIN privilege on the schema of the type; or definer of the type, as recorded in the DEFINER column of SYSCAT.DATATYPES.

Syntax

```
>>-ALTER TYPE--type-name--------------------------------------->

      .-,-----------------------------------------------------------------------------------------.
      V    (1)                                                                                    |
>---------------+-ADD ATTRIBUTE--| attribute-definition |-----------------------------------+--+>
                |                                    .-RESTRICT-.                            |
                +-DROP ATTRIBUTE--attribute-name-+----------+----------------------------------+
                +-ADD--| method-specification |------------------------------------------------+
                |                                                         .-RESTRICT-.  |
                '-DROP--+-METHOD--method-name-----------------------------+--+----------+--'
                        +-METHOD--method-name--(--+------------------+---)--+
                        |                         |  .-,-----------.  |     |
                        |                         |  V              |  |     |
                        |                         '----data-type---+--'     |
                        '-SPECIFIC METHOD--specific-name--------------------'
      >------------------------------------------------------------><
```

Syntax Note:

1. If both attributes and methods are added or dropped, all attribute specifications must occur before all method specifications.

ADD ATTRIBUTE specifies that an attribute is to be added after the last attribute of the existing structured type. For a description of the attribute-definition clause, see the CREATE TYPE (Structured) statement.

DROP ATTRIBUTE specifies that an attribute of an existing structured type is to be dropped. RESTRICT enforces the rule that no attribute can be dropped if its type is being used as the type of an existing table, view, column, attribute nested inside the type of a column, or an index extension.

ADD *method-specification* specifies that a method specification is to be added to the type identified by *type-name*. The method cannot be used until a separate CREATE METHOD statement is invoked to give the method a body. For more information about the method-specification clause, see the CREATE TYPE (Structured) statement.

DROP METHOD specifies an instance of a method that is to be dropped. The specified method must not have an existing method body. Use the DROP METHOD statement to drop the method body before invoking the ALTER TYPE DROP METHOD statement. METHOD *method-name* specifies a particular method that is to be dropped, and it is valid only if there is exactly one method instance with name *method-name* and subject type *type-name*. METHOD *method-name (data-type,...)* specifies a method signature that uniquely identifies the method that is to be dropped. SPECIFIC METHOD *specific-name* specifies a particular method that is to be dropped, using the name that was specified or defaulted to when the method was defined. RESTRICT specifies that the named method is not to have an existing method body.

ALTER USER MAPPING

The ALTER USER MAPPING statement is used to change the authorization ID or password that is used at a data source for a specified federated server authorization ID. If the authorization ID of the statement is different than the authorization name that is mapped to the data source, the authorization ID of the statement must include SYSADM or DBADM authority; otherwise, if the authorization ID and the authorization name match, no privileges or authorities are required.

Syntax

```
>>-ALTER USER MAPPING FOR----+-authorization-name-+------------->
                             '-USER--------------'
>-----SERVER--server-name----------------------------------------->
```

```
            .-,------------------------------------------------.
            V    .-ADD--.                                      |
>-----OPTIONS--(----+-+------+---user-option-name--string-constant--+--+---->
            | '-SET--'                                        |
            '-DROP--user-option-name-----------------------'
>-------------------------------------------------------------><
```

The *authorization-name* parameter specifies the authorization name under which a user or application is to connect to a federated database. USER specifies the value in the special register USER. SERVER *server-name* specifies the data source that will be accessible under the remote authorization ID that maps to the local authorization ID that is, in turn, denoted by *authorization-name* or referenced by USER.

The OPTIONS parameter indicates which user options are to be enabled, reset, or dropped for the mapping that is being altered. User options include the following:

- *remote_authid*   Specifies the authorization ID (maximum length 255 bytes) that is to be used at the data source.

- *remote_domain*   Specifies the Windows NT domain that is to be used to authenticate users connecting to this data source.

- *remote_password*   Specifies the password (maximum length 32 bytes) that is to be used at the data source.

- *accounting_string*   Specifies a DRDA accounting string (maximum length 255 bytes).

ALTER VIEW

The ALTER VIEW statement modifies an existing view by altering a reference type column to add a scope. The authorization ID of the statement must have at least one of the following: SYSADM or DBADM authority; ALTERIN privilege on the schema of the view; definer of the view to be altered; CONTROL privilege on the view to be altered.

Syntax

```
>>-ALTER VIEW--view-name-------------------------------------->
   .-----------------------------------------------------------.
   V          .-COLUMN-.

>--------ALTER--+--------+----column-name--ADD SCOPE--+-typed-table-name-+-->
                                                      '-typed-view-name--'
>-------------------------------------------------------------><
```

REFERENCE

The *view-name* parameter specifies the view that is to be changed. ALTER COLUMN *column-name* specifies the name of the column that is to be altered. ADD SCOPE specifies that a scope is to be added to an existing reference type column that does not already have a scope defined. The column must not be inherited from a superview. The *typed-table-name* or the *typed-view-name* parameter specifies the name of a typed table or a typed view, respectively. The data type of *column-name* must be REF(*S*), where *S* is the type of *typed-table-name* or *typed-view-name*. No checking is done of any values existing in *column-name* to ensure that the values actually reference existing rows in *typed-table-name* or in *typed-view-name*.

BEGIN DECLARE SECTION

The BEGIN DECLARE SECTION statement marks the beginning of a host variable declaration section; it can be coded in an application wherever declarations are permitted, according to the rules of the host language.

Syntax

```
>>-BEGIN DECLARE SECTION---------------------------------------><
```

CALL

The CALL statement invokes a procedure that is stored at the location of a database (on the server). The stored procedure returns data to the client application. The server procedure at the database runs within the same transaction as the client application. If the client application and stored procedure are on the same partition, the stored procedure is executed locally.

The CALL statement can only be embedded in an application. It is an executable statement that cannot be dynamically prepared. However, the procedure name can be specified through a host variable, and this, coupled with the USING DESCRIPTOR clause, allows both the procedure name and the parameter list to be provided at run time, thus achieving the same effect as a dynamically prepared statement.

The authorization rules vary according to the server on which the procedure is stored. For DB2 Universal Database, for example, the authorization ID of the statement *at run time* must have at least one of the following: EXECUTE or CONTROL privilege for the package associated with the stored procedure; or SYSADM or DBADM authority.

Syntax

```
>>-CALL----+-procedure-name-+---------------------------------->
           '-host-variable--'
```

```
>-----+--------------------------------------------+----------------><
      +-(--+----------------------------+---)--+
      |    |    .-,------------------.   |      |
      |    |    V                    |   |      |
      |    '----host-variable--------+-'        |
      '-USING--DESCRIPTOR--descriptor-name----'
```

The procedure name or the host variable specifies the procedure that is to be called; the procedure must exist at the current server. If *procedure-name* is specified, it must be an ordinary identifier with a maximum length of 254 bytes. It must be left-justified and cannot contain blanks or special characters. Because the value is converted to uppercase characters, if it is necessary to use lowercase names, blanks, or special characters, the name must be specified through a host variable. If *host-variable* is specified, it must be a character-string variable whose length attribute is not greater than 254 bytes, and it must not include an indicator variable.

The form of the procedure name varies according to the server on which the procedure is stored. For DB2 Universal Database, for example, the procedure name can be specified as one of the following:

- *procedure-name*   The name, with no extension, of the procedure to execute. procedure-name is used both as the name of the stored procedure library and the function name within that library.

- *procedure-library!function-name*   The exclamation character acts as a delimiter between the library name and the function name of the stored procedure.

- *absolute-path!function-name*   The absolute path specifies the complete path to the stored procedure library.

Each specification of *host-variable* is a parameter of the CALL statement. The nth parameter of the CALL statement corresponds to the nth parameter of the server's stored procedure.

USING DESCRIPTOR *descriptor-name* specifies an SQLDA that must contain a valid description of host variables.

CLOSE

The CLOSE statement closes a cursor. If a result table was created when the cursor was open, that table is destroyed.

Syntax

```
>>-CLOSE--cursor-name----+--------------+------------------><
                         '-WITH RELEASE--'
```

The cursor-name parameter specifies a declared cursor that is to be closed. When the CLOSE statement is invoked, the cursor must be in the open state. WITH RELEASE specifies that the release of all read locks that have been held for the cursor is to be attempted. Not all of the read locks are necessarily released; some may be held for other operations or activities.

COMMENT ON

The COMMENT ON statement adds or replaces comments in the catalog descriptions of various objects. The authorization ID of the statement must have one of the following: SYSADM or DBADM authority; definer of the object (underlying table for column or constraint), as recorded in the DEFINER column of the catalog view for the object (OWNER column for a schema); ALTERIN privilege on the schema (applicable only to objects allowing more than one-part names); CONTROL privilege on the object (applicable only to index, package, table, and view objects); or ALTER privilege on the object (applicable only to table objects). Note that for table space or nodegroup objects, the authorization ID must have SYSADM or SYSCTRL authority.

Syntax

```
>>-COMMENT ON--------------------------------------------->
>-----+-| objects |--IS--string-constant-----------------------+>
      |                  .-,----------------------------.       |
      |                  V                              |       |
      '--+-table-name-+---(-----column-name--IS--string-constant---+---)--'
         '-view-name--'
>---------------------------------------------------------><
objects
|--------+-ALIAS--alias-name-----------------------------------+---->
         +-COLUMN--+-table-name.column-name-+------------------------+
         |         '-view-name.column-name--'                       |
         +-CONSTRAINT--table-name.constraint-name-------------------+
         +-FUNCTION----function-name--+---------------------------+-+
         |                            '-(--+-----------------+---)--' |
         |                            |    .-,-----------.   |        |
         |                            |    V             |   |        |
```

```
|                                      '----data-type---+--'        |
+-SPECIFIC FUNCTION--specific-name-----------------------------+
+-FUNCTION MAPPING--function-mapping-name---------------------+
|                     (1)                                      |
+-INDEX--index-name------------------------------------------+
+-NICKNAME--nickname-----------------------------------------+
+-NODEGROUP--nodegroup-name----------------------------------+
+-PACKAGE--package-name--------------------------------------+
+-PROCEDURE--procedure-name--+-------------------------------+-+
|                            '-(--+-----------------+---)--' |
|                            |    .-,-----------.   |        |
|                            |    V             |   |        |
|                            '----data-type---+--'          |
+-SPECIFIC PROCEDURE--specific-name--------------------------+
+-SCHEMA--schema-name----------------------------------------+
+-SERVER--server-name----------------------------------------+
+-SERVER OPTION--server-option-name--FOR--| remote-server |----+
+-TABLE--+-table-name-+--------------------------------------+
|        '-view-name--'                                      |
+-TABLESPACE--tablespace-name--------------------------------+
+-TRIGGER--trigger-name--------------------------------------+
+-+----------------+---TYPE--type-name-----------------------+
| |        (2)     |                                         |
| '-DISTINCT------'                                          |
+-TYPE MAPPING--type-mapping-name----------------------------+
'-WRAPPER--wrapper-name-------------------------------------'
>------------------------------------------------------------|

remote-server

|---+-SERVER--server-name-------------------------------------------------------------+->
    '-TYPE--server-type------+-----------------------------------------------------+---'
                             '-VERSION--| server-version |----+-------------------------+--'
                                                              '-WRAPPER--wrapper-name---'
>------------------------------------------------------------|

server-version
|---+-version--+------------------------+-+-----------------|
    |          '-.--release--+---------+--' |
    |                        '-.--mod--'    |
    '-version-string-constant--------------'
```

Syntax Notes:

1. Index-name can be the name of either an index or an index specification.
2. The keyword DATA can be used as a synonym for DISTINCT.

A comment can be added or replaced for the following:

- An alias,
- A column in a table or a view,
- A table constraint,
- A user-defined function (identified by function name, function signature, or specific name) that is not in the SYSIBM schema or the SYSFUN schema,
- A function mapping,
- An index or an index specification,
- A nickname,
- A nodegroup,
- A package,
- A stored procedure (identified by procedure name, procedure signature, or specific name,
- A schema,
- A data source (SERVER *server-name*)
- A server option,
- A table (but not a declared temporary table) or a view,
- A table space,
- A trigger,
- A user-defined type,
- A user-defined data type mapping, or
- A wrapper.

IS *string-constant* specifies the comment that is to be added or replaced. The string can be any character string constant with a maximum size of 254 bytes. (Carriage return and line feed each count as one byte.)

An alternate form of the COMMENT ON statement allows you to specify comments for *several* columns in a table or view: *table-name | view-name (column-name* IS *string-constant,...).*

Examples

Add a comment for the Employee table:

```
COMMENT ON TABLE EMPLOYEE IS 'Reflects first quarter reorganization'
```

Add comments for two different columns of the Employee table:

```
COMMENT ON EMPLOYEE
  (WORKDEPT IS 'see DEPARTMENT table for names',
  EDLEVEL IS 'highest grade level passed in school')
```

COMMIT

The COMMIT statement terminates a unit of work, and it commits the database changes that were made by that unit of work.

Syntax

```
                    .-WORK--.
>>-COMMIT----+-------+-------------------------------------------><
```

All changes made by the following statements during a unit of work are committed: ALTER, COMMENT ON, CREATE, DELETE, DROP, GRANT, INSERT, LOCK TABLE, REVOKE, SET INTEGRITY, SET Variable, and UPDATE. The following statements are *not* under transaction control, and changes made by them are independent of the COMMIT statement:

- SET CONNECTION
- SET CURRENT DEFAULT TRANSFORM GROUP
- SET CURRENT DEGREE
- SET CURRENT EXPLAIN MODE
- SET CURRENT EXPLAIN SNAPSHOT
- SET CURRENT PACKAGESET
- SET CURRENT QUERY OPTIMIZATION
- SET CURRENT REFRESH AGE
- SET EVENT MONITOR STATE
- SET PASSTHRU
- SET PATH
- SET SCHEMA
- SET SERVER OPTION

Compound Statement (Dynamic)

A compound statement groups other statements together into an executable block. You can declare SQL variables within a dynamically prepared atomic compound statement. The authorization ID of the compound statement must have the necessary privileges to invoke the SQL statements that are embedded in the compound statement.

REFERENCE

Syntax

```
dynamic-compound-statement
>>-+--------------+--BEGIN ATOMIC----------------------------->
   |        (1)   |
   '-label:-------'
>-----+----------------------------------------------+-------->
      |  .----------------------------------------.  |
      |  V                                         |  |
      '-----+-| SQL-variable-declaration |-+---;---+--'
            '-| condition-declaration |----'
      .-,--------------------------.
      V                            |
>--------SQL-procedure-statement--;---+---END--+--------+------><
                                              '-label--'
SQL-variable-declaration
              .-,------------------.
              V                    |
|---DECLARE-------SQL-variable-name---+--data-type------------->
     .-DEFAULT NULL-------------.
>-----+-------------------------+----------------------------|
      '-DEFAULT--default-values--'
condition-declaration
|---DECLARE--condition-name--CONDITION--FOR------------------->
                .-VALUE-.
   .-SQLSTATE--+-------+---.
>----+----------------------+---string-constant--------------|
```

Syntax Note:

1. A label can be specified only if the statement is in a function, method, or trigger definition.

If a beginning label is specified, it can be used to qualify SQL variables declared in the dynamic compound statement and can also be specified on a LEAVE statement. If an ending label is specified, it must be the same as the beginning label.

ATOMIC indicates that if an error occurs in the compound statement, all SQL statements in the compound statement will be rolled back, and any remaining SQL statements in the compound statement will not be processed.

SQL-procedure-statement specifies a dynamic compound statement that can contain the following SQL control statements: FOR, GET DIAGNOSTICS, IF, ITERATE, LEAVE, SIGNAL, and WHILE. The following SQL statements can be issued: fullselect, searched UPDATE, searched DELETE, INSERT, and the SET variable statement.

The SQL-variable-declaration clause declares a variable that is local to the dynamic compound statement. The *SQL-variable-name* parameter specifies the name of a local variable. DB2 converts all SQL variable names to uppercase. The name cannot be the same as another SQL variable within the same compound statement, be the same as a parameter name, or be the same as column names. If an SQL statement contains an identifier with the same name as an SQL variable and a column reference, DB2 interprets the identifier as a column.

DEFAULT *default-values* or NULL specifies the default value for the SQL variable. The variable is initialized when the dynamic compound statement is called. The condition-declaration clause declares a condition name and corresponding SQLSTATE value. The condition name must be unique within the procedure body and can be referenced only within the compound statement in which it is declared. FOR SQLSTATE *string-constant* specifies the SQLSTATE associated with the condition. The string constant must be specified as five characters enclosed by single quotation marks, and cannot be '00000'.

Compound SQL (Embedded)

Compound SQL combines one or more SQL statements into an executable block. The individual statements within the block are called *substatements.* The authorization ID of the compound SQL statement must have the appropriate authorization for each statement in the block.

Syntax

```
>>-BEGIN COMPOUND----+-ATOMIC-----+--STATIC--------------------->
                     '-NOT ATOMIC-'
>-----+---------------------------------------------+---------->
      '-STOP AFTER FIRST--host-variable--STATEMENTS--'
      .------------------------.
      V                        |
>--------+------------------+--+--END COMPOUND---------------><
         '-sql-statement--;--'
```

ATOMIC specifies that if any of the substatements within the compound SQL statement fail, all changes made to the database by any of the substatements, including changes made by successful substatements, are to be undone. NOT ATOMIC specifies that regardless of the failure of any substatements, the compound SQL statement is not to undo any changes made to the database by successful substatements. STATIC specifies that input variables for all substatements are to retain their original value.

STOP AFTER FIRST specifies that only a certain number of substatements are to be executed. The host variable is a small integer that specifies the number of substatements that are to be executed. All executable statements except the following can be contained within an embedded static compound SQL statement:

- CALL
- CLOSE
- CONNECT
- Compound SQL
- DESCRIBE
- DISCONNECT
- EXECUTE IMMEDIATE

- FETCH
- OPEN
- PREPARE
- RELEASE (Connection)
- RELEASE SAVEPOINT
- ROLLBACK
- SET CONNECTION

If a COMMIT statement is included, it must be the last substatement. If a COMMIT statement is in this position, it will be issued even if the STOP AFTER FIRST *host-variable* STATEMENTS clause specifies that not all of the substatements are to be executed.

CONNECT (Type 1)

The CONNECT (Type 1) statement connects an application process to the identified application server according to the rules for a remote unit of work. An application process can be connected to only one application server at a time. This is called the current server.

The application process can explicitly connect to a different application server by issuing a CONNECT TO statement. A connection lasts until a CONNECT RESET statement or a DISCONNECT statement is issued, or until another CONNECT TO statement changes the application server. The authorization ID of the statement must be authorized to connect to the identified application server.

Syntax

```
>>-CONNECT--------------------------------------------------->
>-----+--------------------------------------------------------------+>
      +-TO--+-server-name---+---+-----------------+---+------------------+-+
      |     '-host-variable-'   '-| lock-block |--'   '-| authorization |--' |
      +-RESET-------------------------------------------------------+
      |                      (1)                                    |
      '-| authorization |----------------------------------------'
>-------------------------------------------------------------><
authorization
|---USER----+-authorization-name-+--USING----+-password------+-->
            '-host-variable------'            '-host-variable-'
```

```
>-----+-----------------------------------------------+----------|
      '-NEW--+-password------+---CONFIRM--password--'
             '-host-variable-'
lock-block
      .-IN SHARE MODE-------------------------.
|---+-----------------------------------------+-----------------|
      '-IN EXCLUSIVE MODE--+---------------+--'
                           '-ON SINGLE NODE-'
```

Syntax Note:

1. This form is valid only if implicit connect is enabled.

CONNECT (with no operand) returns information about the current server. The information is returned in the SQLERRP field of the SQLCA. If a connection state exists, the authorization ID and database alias are put in the SQLERRMC field of the SQLCA. If no connection exists and implicit connect is possible, an implicit connection is attempted.

TO *server-name* or *host-variable* specifies a database alias that identifies an application server. If a host variable is specified, it must be a character string variable with a maximum length of eight characters, and it must not include an indicator variable. The server name that is contained within the host variable must be left-justified, and it must not be delimited by quotation marks.

IN SHARE MODE specifies that other concurrent connections to the database are to be permitted, and it prevents other users from connecting to the database in exclusive mode. IN EXCLUSIVE MODE specifies that concurrent application processes are not to be permitted to execute any operations at the application server, unless they have the same authorization ID as the user holding the exclusive lock. ON SINGLE NODE specifies that the coordinator partition is to be connected in exclusive mode, and that all other partitions are to be connected in SHARE mode. This option is valid only in a partitioned database environment.

RESET specifies that the application process is to be disconnected from the current server. A commit operation follows. If implicit connect is enabled, the application process remains disconnected until an SQL statement is issued.

USER *authorization-name* or *host-variable* specifies the user ID that is trying to connect to the application server. If a host variable is specified, it must be a character string variable with a maximum length of eight characters, and it must not include an indicator variable. The user ID that is contained within the host variable must be left-justified, and it must not be delimited by quotation marks.

USING *password* or *host-variable* specifies a password for the user ID that is trying to connect to the application server. The password or the host variable has a maximum length of 18 characters. If a host variable is specified, it must be a character string variable with a maximum length of 18, and it must not include an indicator variable.

REFERENCE

NEW *password* or *host-variable* CONFIRM *password* specifies the new password that is to be assigned to the user ID.

CONNECT (Type 2)

The CONNECT (Type 2) statement connects an application process to the identified application server and establishes the rules for application-directed distributed units of work. The server becomes the current server for the process.

This description covers only those elements of Type 2 connections that differ from Type 1 connections.

Syntax

The syntax for CONNECT (Type 2) is the same as the syntax for CONNECT (Type 1). The selection of Type 1 or Type 2 is determined by precompiler options. The rules for coding the name of the server are the same as for Type 1.

If the SQLRULES(STD) option is in effect, the server name must not identify an existing connection of the application process. If the SQLRULES(DB2) option is in effect, and the server name identifies an existing connection of the application process, that connection is made current and the old connection is put into a dormant state; that is, the effect of the CONNECT statement in this situation is the same as that of a SET CONNECTION statement.

If CONNECT with no operand is specified and a connection does not exist, an implicit connection is not attempted; the SQLERRP and SQLERRMC fields of the SQLCA return blanks. Applications can check whether a current connection exists by checking these fields. A CONNECT with no operand that includes USER and USING can still connect an application process to a database using the DB2DBDFT environment variable. This method is equivalent to a Type 2 CONNECT RESET, but it permits the use of a user ID and password.

The RESET option is equivalent to an explicit connect to the default database if it is available. If a default database is not available, the connection state of the application process and the states of its connections remain unchanged.

For detailed information about the differences between Type 1 and Type 2 CONNECT statements, see the *DB2 SQL Reference*.

CREATE ALIAS

The CREATE ALIAS statement defines an alias for a table, view, nickname, or another alias. The authorization ID of the statement must have at least one of the following: SYSADM or DBADM authority; IMPLICIT_SCHEMA privilege on the database if the implicit or explicit schema name of the alias does not exist; CREATEIN privilege on the schema if the schema name of the alias refers to an existing schema.

Syntax

```
>>-CREATE----+-ALIAS--------+--alias-name---FOR---------------->
             |        (1)   |
             '-SYNONYM------'
>-----+-table-name--+----------------------------------------->< 
      +-view-name---+
      +-nickname----+
      '-alias-name2-'
```

Syntax Note:

1. CREATE SYNONYM is accepted as an alternative for CREATE ALIAS.

If a two-part name is specified, the schema name cannot begin with *SYS*. The rules for specifying an alias name are the same as those used for defining a table name. A specified table cannot be a declared temporary table.

CREATE BUFFERPOOL

The CREATE BUFFERPOOL statement creates a new buffer pool. The new buffer pool will not become active until the next time the database is started. The authorization ID of the statement must have SYSADM or SYSCTRL authority.

Syntax

```
>>-CREATE--BUFFERPOOL--bufferpool-name------------------------>
      .-ALL NODES----------------------.
>-----+--------------------------------+--------------------->
      |           .-,--------------. |
      |           V                | |
      '-NODEGROUP-----nodegroup-name---+-'
>----SIZE--number-of-pages----+-----------------------------+--->
                              '-| except-on-nodes-clause |--'
          .-PAGESIZE--4096------------.
>-----*----+-------------------------+--*--------------------->
          '-PAGESIZE--integer--+----+-'
                               '-K--'
      .-NOT EXTENDED STORAGE--.
>----+-----------------------+---*------------------------->< 
      '-EXTENDED STORAGE------'
except-on-nodes-clause
```

```
|---EXCEPT ON----+-NODE--+------------------------------------->
                 '-NODES-'

     .-,-----------------------------------------------------------.
     V                                                             |
>----(-----node-number1--+-------------------+---SIZE--number-of-pages---+---)->
                         '-TO--node-number2---'
 >------------------------------------------------------------|
```

The buffer pool name must not begin with the characters *SYS* or *IBM*. ALL
NODES specifies that the buffer pool is to be created on all partitions in the database.
NODEGROUP *nodegroup-name, ...* specifies one or more nodegroups to which the
buffer pool definition is applicable.

SIZE *number-of-pages* specifies the size of the buffer pool. The size can be specified
with a value of –1 to indicate that the buffer pool size is to be taken from the value of
the *buffpage* database configuration parameter. The except-on-nodes-clause specifies
one or more partitions for which the size of the buffer pool is to be different than the
specified size.

PAGESIZE *integer* [K] specifies the size of pages that are to be used for the buffer
pool. Valid values without the suffix *K* are 4096, 8192, 16384, or 32768; valid values
with the suffix are 4, 8, 16, or 32. The default value is 4096, or 4K.

EXTENDED STORAGE specifies that if the database is configured for extended
storage, pages that are being migrated out of this buffer pool will be cached in extended
storage. A database can be configured for extended storage by setting the database
configuration parameters *num_estore_segs* and *estore_seg_size* to nonzero values. NOT
EXTENDED STORAGE specifies that, even if the database is configured for extended
storage, pages that are being migrated out of this buffer pool will *not* be cached in
extended storage.

CREATE DISTINCT TYPE

The CREATE DISTINCT TYPE statement defines a distinct type. The distinct type is
always sourced on one of the built-in data types. Successful execution of the statement
also generates functions to cast between the distinct type and its source type and,
optionally, generates support for comparison operators (=, <>, <, <=, >, and >=) to
be used with the distinct type.

The authorization ID of the statement must have at least one of the following: SYSADM
or DBADM authority; IMPLICIT_SCHEMA privilege on the database, if the schema name
of the distinct type does not refer to an existing schema; CREATEIN privilege on the schema,
if the schema name of the distinct type refers to an existing schema.

Syntax

```
>>-CREATE DISTINCT TYPE--distinct-type-name--AS---------------->
                                         (1)
>-----| source-data-type |--WITH COMPARISONS-----------------><
source-data-type
|---+-SMALLINT-----------------------------------------------+->
    +-+-INTEGER-+---------------------------------------------+
    | '-INT-----'                                             |
    +-BIGINT-------------------------------------------------+
    +-+-FLOAT--+--------------+-+-----------------------------+
    | |       '-(--integer--)--' |                           |
    | +-REAL---------------------+                            |
    | |          .-PRECISION-.   |                            |
    | '-DOUBLE-+-----------+------'                           |
    +--+-DECIMAL-+---+----------------------------------+--------+
    |  +-DEC-----+   '-(--integer--+-----------+---)--'  |
    |  +-NUMERIC-+                 '-,integer--'         |
    |  '-NUM-----'                                       |
    +--+--+-CHARACTER-+---+-----------+-+---+-------------+--+
    |  |  '-CHAR------'   '-(integer)--' |  '-FOR BIT DATA-'  |
    |  +-VARCHAR(integer)----------------+                    |
    |  '-LONG VARCHAR-------------------'                     |
    +-GRAPHIC--+-----------+---------------------------------+
    |          '-(integer)--'                                |
    +-VARGRAPHIC(integer)------------------------------------+
    +-LONG VARGRAPHIC----------------------------------------+
    +-DATE---------------------------------------------------+
    +-TIME---------------------------------------------------+
    +-TIMESTAMP----------------------------------------------+
    +--+-BLOB---+--(--integer--+---+---)---------------------+
    |  +-CLOB---+              +-K-+                          |
    |  '-DBCLOB-'              +-M-+                          |
    |                         '-G-'                          |
    '-DATALINK--+-----------+--------------------------------'
               '-(integer)--'
>-----------------------------------------------------------|
```

Syntax Note:

1. Required for all source data types, except LOB, LONG VARCHAR, LONG VARGRAPHIC, and DATALINK, which are not supported.

Keywords in predicates (and comparison operators) are reserved for system use, and cannot be used as values for *distinct-type-name*. These reserved names are SOME, ANY, ALL, NOT, AND, OR, BETWEEN, NULL, LIKE, EXISTS, IN, UNIQUE, OVERLAPS, SIMILAR, and MATCH. If a two-part type name is specified, the schema name cannot begin with *SYS*.

The *source-data-type* parameter specifies the built-in data type on which the distinct type is to be based. For a description of the built-in DB2 data types, see Chapter 16. WITH COMPARISONS specifies that system-generated comparison operators are to be created for comparing two instances of a distinct type. This option should not be specified if the source data type is BLOB, CLOB, DBCLOB, LONG VARCHAR, LONG VARGRAPHIC, or DATALINK.

Example

Create a distinct type named SHOESIZE that is based on the INTEGER data type. The statement will also create comparison operators (=, <>, <, <=, >, >=) and the cast functions INTEGER(SHOESIZE) (returning INTEGER) and SHOESIZE(INTEGER) (returning SHOESIZE).

```
CREATE DISTINCT TYPE SHOESIZE AS INTEGER WITH COMPARISONS
```

CREATE EVENT MONITOR

The CREATE EVENT MONITOR statement defines a monitor that will record certain events when the database is being used. The authorization ID of the statement must have SYSADM or DBADM authority.

Syntax

```
>>-CREATE--EVENT--MONITOR--event-monitor-name--FOR------------->

    .-,---------------------------------------------------------.
    V                                                           |
>---------+-+-DATABASE----+-----------------------------------+--+>
          | +-TABLES------+                                    |
          | +-DEADLOCKS---+                                    |
          | +-TABLESPACES-+                                    |
          | '-BUFFERPOOLS-'                                    |
          '--+-CONNECTIONS--+---+------------------------+-'
             +-STATEMENTS---+   '-WHERE--| Event Condition |--'
             '-TRANSACTIONS-'

                                                   .-MANUALSTART--.
>----WRITE--TO--+-PIPE--pipe-name-----------------+---+-------------+>
                '-FILE--path-name--| File Options |--'   '-AUTOSTART----'
```

```
                                   .-LOCAL--.
>-----+---------------------------+---+--------+------------------->< 
      '-ON NODE--node-number--'        '-GLOBAL-'
Event Condition
    .-AND | OR------------------------------------------------------.
    V                                                               |
|------+-----+--+--+--APPL_ID---+---+-=----------+---comparison-string--+--+-
       '-NOT-' | +-AUTH_ID---+   |                |                      |
               | '-APPL_NAME-'   +-<>---------+   |                      |
               |                 +->----------+   |                      |
               |                 |            |   |                      |
               |                 +->=---------+   |                      |
               |                 +-<----------+   |                      |
               |                 |            |   |                      |
               |                 +-<=---------+   |                      |
               |                 +-LIKE-------+   |                      |
               |                 '-NOT--LIKE--'   |                      |
               '-(Event Condition)----------------------------------'
>-----------------------------------------------------------------|
File Options
|---+------------------------------+------------------------->
    |            .-NONE-----------. |
    '-MAXFILES--+-number-of-files-+--'
>-----+------------------------------+---+------------------+----->
      |             .-pages--. |  '-BUFFERSIZE--pages--'
      '-MAXFILESIZE--+-NONE---+--'
      .-BLOCKED----.    .-APPEND--.
>-----+------------+---+---------+---------------------------|
      '-NONBLOCKED-'   '-REPLACE-'
```

FOR specifies the type of event that is to be recorded. DATABASE specifies that the event monitor will record a database event when the last application disconnects from the database. TABLES specifies that the event monitor will record a table event for each active table when the last application disconnects from the database. An *active table* is a table that has changed since the first connection to the database. DEADLOCKS specifies that the event monitor will record a deadlock event whenever a deadlock occurs. TABLESPACES specifies that the event monitor will record a table space event for each table space when the last application disconnects from the database.

BUFFERPOOLS specifies that the event monitor will record a buffer pool event when the last application disconnects from the database. CONNECTIONS specifies that the event monitor will record a connection event when an application disconnects from the database. STATEMENTS specifies that the event monitor will record a statement event when an SQL statement finishes processing. TRANSACTIONS specifies that the event monitor will record a transaction event when a transaction completes, that is, when there is a COMMIT or a ROLLBACK operation.

WHERE defines a filter that determines which connections cause a CONNECTION, STATEMENT, or TRANSACTION event to occur. If no WHERE clause is specified, all events of the specified type are monitored. Filtering can be specified on the application ID, the authorization ID, or the application name of each connection. The application name is the first 20 bytes of the application filename after the last path separator. The *comparison-string* parameter specifies a string that is to be compared with the APPL_ID, AUTH_ID, or APPL_NAME of each application that connects to the database; it must be a string constant. (Host variables and other string expressions are not permitted.)

WRITE TO PIPE *pipe-name* specifies that the target for the event monitor data is a named pipe. WRITE TO FILE specifies that the target for the event monitor data is a file (or a set of files). The event monitor writes out the data stream as a series of eight-character numbered files with the extension *evt* (for example, 00000000.evt, 00000001.evt, 00000002.evt, etc.). The files are written to a directory specified by *path-name*.

MAXFILES NONE specifies that there is to be no limit on the number of event files that the event monitor will create. MAXFILES *number-of-files* specifies a limit on the number of event monitor files that will exist for a particular event monitor at any given time. When this limit is reached, the event monitor turns itself off. MAXFILESIZE *pages* specifies a limit on the size of each event monitor file. MAXFILESIZE NONE specifies that there is to be no set limit on a file's size. If this option is specified, MAXFILES 1 must also be specified, meaning that one file will contain all of the event data for a particular event monitor. In this case, the only event file will be 00000000.evt. BUFFERSIZE *pages* specifies the size of the event monitor buffers (in 4KB pages).

BLOCKED specifies that each agent that generates an event should wait for an event buffer to be written out to disk if the agent determines that the event buffers are full. APPEND specifies that if event data files already exist when the event monitor is turned on, the event monitor will append new event data to the existing stream of data files. REPLACE specifies that if event data files already exist when the event monitor is turned on, the event monitor will erase all of the event files and start writing data to file 00000000.evt.

MANUALSTART specifies that the event monitor is not to be started automatically each time the database is started; it must be activated manually by using the SET EVENT MONITOR STATE statement. AUTOSTART specifies that the event monitor is to be started automatically each time the database is started.

ON NODE *node-number* specifies a partition on which the event monitor is to run. If the monitoring scope is defined as GLOBAL, all partitions report to the specified partition number. GLOBAL specifies that the event monitor is to report from all partitions. With DB2 Universal Database version 7, only deadlock event monitors for a partitioned database can be defined as GLOBAL. LOCAL specifies that the event monitor is to report only from the partition that is running. It gives a partial trace of the database activity.

CREATE FUNCTION (External Scalar)

This statement is used to register a user-defined external scalar function with an application server. A scalar function returns a single value each time it is invoked.

The authorization ID of the statement must have at least one of the following: IMPLICIT_SCHEMA privilege on the database if the schema name of the function does not refer to an existing schema; CREATEIN privilege on the schema if the schema name of the function refers to an existing schema. To create a not-fenced function, the authorization ID of the statement must have SYSADM or DBADM authority; CREATE_NOT_FENCED privilege on the database.

Syntax

```
>>-CREATE FUNCTION--function-name------------------------------->
>----(--+-----------------------------------------------------+---)->
        |   .-,---------------------------------------------.  |  |
        |   V                                               |  |  |
        '----+----------------+---data-type1--+------------+--+--'
             '-parameter-name--'              '-AS LOCATOR--'
>----*--------------------------------------------------------->
>----RETURNS--+-data-type2--+------------+----------------------+>
              |                '-AS LOCATOR--'                  |
              '-data-type3--CAST FROM--data-type4--+------------+-'
                                                   '-AS LOCATOR--'
>----*----+-------------------------+--*-------------------->
          '-SPECIFIC--specific-name--'
>-----EXTERNAL--+---------------------+---*------------------->
               '-NAME--+-'string'---+-'
                       '-identifier-'
                        (1)
>----LANGUAGE--+-C----+---------*------------------------------>
               +-JAVA-+
               '-OLE--'
>----PARAMETER STYLE--+-DB2SQL-----+--*----------------------->
                      +-DB2GENERAL-+
                      '-JAVA-------'
    .-NOT DETERMINISTIC--.        .-FENCED-----.
>-----+-------------------+--*----+------------+---------------->
      |            (2)    |       '-NOT FENCED-'
      '-DETERMINISTIC------'
    .-RETURNS NULL ON NULL INPUT--.  (3)
>-----+---------------------------+---------*---NO SQL--*----->
      '-CALLED ON NULL INPUT--------'
    .-EXTERNAL ACTION----.        .-NO SCRATCHPAD----------.
>-----+-------------------+--*----+-----------------------+--->
```

```
        '-NO EXTERNAL ACTION-'              |                .-100----. |
                                            '-SCRATCHPAD--+--------+-'
                                                          '-length-'
          .-NO FINAL CALL--.          .-ALLOW PARALLEL----.
>----*----+----------------+--*----+-----------------+--*----->
          '-FINAL CALL-----'        '-DISALLOW PARALLEL-'
          .-NO DBINFO--.
>-----+------------+--*----+----------------------------+--*-->
          '-DBINFO-----'          '-TRANSFORM GROUP--group-name--'
>-----+----------------------------------------------+------><
          '-PREDICATES--(--| predicate-specification |--)---'
predicate-specification
|---WHEN--+- = -+---+-constant----------------------+-------->
          +- <> -+    '-EXPRESSION AS--expression-name--'
          +- < -+
          +- > -+
          +- <= -+
          '- >= -'
>-----+-| data-filter |--+-----------------------+-+---------|
      |                     '-| index-exploitation |--' |
      '-| index-exploitation |--+-----------------+-'
                                  '-| data-filter |--'
data-filter
|---FILTER USING--+-function-invocation-+---------------------|
                  '-case-expression-----'
index-exploitation
|---SEARCH BY--+--------+---INDEX EXTENSION--index-extension-name-->
              '-EXACT--'
     .-------------------------.
     V                         |
>-------| exploitation-rule |---+----------------------------|
exploitation-rule
|---WHEN KEY--(--parameter-name1--)-------------------------->
                                 .-,-----------------.
                                 V                   |
>----USE--search-method-name--(-----parameter-name2---+---)-----|
```

Syntax Notes:

1. LANGUAGE SQL is also supported.

2. NOT VARIANT can be specified instead of DETERMINISTIC, and VARIANT can be specified instead of NOT DETERMINISTIC.

3. NULL CALL can be specified instead of CALLED ON NULL INPUT, and NOT NULL CALL can be specified instead of RETURNS NULL ON NULL INPUT.

The unqualified form of *function-name* is an SQL identifier with a maximum length of 18 bytes. If a two-part name is specified, the schema name cannot begin with *SYS*. Keywords in predicates (and comparison operators) are reserved for system use and cannot be used as values for *function-name*. These reserved names are SOME, ANY, ALL, NOT, AND, OR, BETWEEN, NULL, LIKE, EXISTS, IN, UNIQUE, OVERLAPS, SIMILAR, and MATCH.

The *parameter-name* parameter specifies a parameter that can be used in the function definition. The *(data-type1,...)* parameter specifies the data type of each input parameter of the function. One entry in the list must be specified for each parameter that the function is expected to receive. No more than 90 parameters are allowed. A function that has no parameters should be coded with empty parentheses. For LOB types or distinct types that are based on LOB types, the AS LOCATOR clause can be used to specify that a LOB locator (instead of the actual value) is to be passed *to* the UDF. The AS LOCATOR clause cannot be specified if the function is FENCED.

RETURNS specifies the output of the function. The *data-type2* parameter specifies the data type of the output. For LOB types or distinct types that are based on LOB types, the AS LOCATOR clause can be used to specify that a LOB locator (instead of the actual value) is to be passed *from* the UDF. The *data-type3* CAST FROM *data-type4* form of the RETURNS clause is used to return a data type to the invoking statement that is different from the data type that was returned by the function code. For LOB types or distinct types that are based on LOB types, the AS LOCATOR clause can be used to specify that a LOB locator (instead of the actual value) is to be returned from the method.

SPECIFIC *specific-name* specifies a unique name for the instance of the function that is being defined. This specific name can be used when sourcing on the function, dropping the function, or commenting on the function. It cannot be used to invoke the function.

EXTERNAL specifies that the CREATE FUNCTION statement is being used to register a function, based on code written in an external programming language, and adhering to the documented linkage conventions and interface. If the NAME clause is not specified, "NAME *function-name*" is assumed. NAME specifies the name of the user-written code that implements the function being defined. The *'string'* parameter is a string constant with a maximum size of 254 characters. The format for the string depends on the language.

For C, the string specifies a library name and a function within the library, which DB2 invokes to execute the user-defined function. For Java, the string specifies an optional jar file identifier, a class identifier, and a method identifier, which DB2 invokes to execute the user-defined function. For OLE, the string specifies an OLE programmatic identifier or a class identifier, and a method identifier, which DB2 invokes to execute the user-defined function. The *identifier* parameter specifies an SQL identifier that is used as the *library-id* in the string. Unless it is a delimited identifier, the identifier is folded to uppercase. This form of NAME can be used only with LANGUAGE C.

REFERENCE

LANGUAGE specifies the language interface convention to which the user-defined function body is to be written. C specifies that DB2 is to call the user-defined function as if it were a C function. JAVA specifies that DB2 is to call the user-defined function as a method in a Java class. OLE specifies that DB2 is to call the user-defined function as if it were a method exposed by an OLE automation object. LANGUAGE OLE is only supported for user-defined functions that are stored on Windows 32-bit operating systems.

PARAMETER STYLE specifies the conventions that are to be used for passing parameters to and returning a value from functions. DB2SQL specifies conventions that conform to C language calling and linkage conventions, or methods exposed by OLE automation objects. This option must be specified when LANGUAGE C or LANGUAGE OLE is specified. DB2GENERAL specifies conventions that are defined as methods in a Java class. This option can be specified only when LANGUAGE JAVA is specified. JAVA specifies that the function is to use a parameter-passing convention that conforms to the Java language and SQLj Routines specification. This option can be specified only when LANGUAGE JAVA is specified, and there are no structured types as parameter or return types.

NOT DETERMINISTIC or DETERMINISTIC specifies whether the function will always return the same results for given argument values (DETERMINISTIC), or whether the function will depend on some state values that affect the results (NOT DETERMINISTIC).

If a function is registered as FENCED, DB2 insulates its internal resources (for example, data buffers) from access by the function. To change a function from being FENCED to NOT FENCED, the function must be dropped and then re-created.

If RETURNS NULL ON NULL INPUT is specified, and if, at execution time, any one of the function's arguments is null, the user-defined function is not called, and the result is the NULL value. If CALLED ON NULL INPUT is specified, the user-defined function is called even if an argument is null.

NO SQL is a mandatory clause specifying that the function cannot issue any SQL statements. NO EXTERNAL ACTION or EXTERNAL ACTION specifies whether the function is to take some action that changes the state of an object that is not managed by DB2.

If SCRATCHPAD is specified, memory is allocated for a scratchpad to be used by the external function. The *length* parameter specifies the size, in bytes, of the scratchpad; it must be between 1 and 32,767. The default value is 100. The scope of the scratchpad is the SQL statement. There is one scratchpad per reference to the external function in the SQL statement.

NO FINAL CALL or FINAL CALL specifies whether a final call is to be made to an external function. The purpose of such a final call is to enable the external function to free any system resources that it has acquired. It can be useful in conjunction with the SCRATCHPAD keyword if, for example, the external function acquires system resources, such as memory, and anchors them in the scratchpad.

ALLOW PARALLEL or DISALLOW PARALLEL specifies whether, for a single reference to the function, the invocation of the function can be parallelized. The default value is DISALLOW PARALLEL if one or more of the following options is specified in the statement: NOT DETERMINISTIC, EXTERNAL ACTION, SCRATCHPAD, or FINAL CALL.

NO DBINFO or DBINFO specifies whether additional information will be passed to the function in a structure at invocation time. This information includes the following:

- The name of the currently connected database
- Application ID
- Application authorization ID
- Code page
- Schema name
- Table name
- Column name
- Version, release, and modification level of the database server
- Server platform

TRANSFORM GROUP *group-name* specifies the transform group that is to be used for user-defined structured type transformations when invoking the function. A transform is required if the function definition includes a user-defined structured type.

PREDICATES specifies the filtering or index extension exploitation that is to be performed when this function is used in a predicate. If the PREDICATES clause is specified, the function must be defined as DETERMINISTIC with NO EXTERNAL ACTION.

WHEN *comparison-operator* introduces a specific use of the function in a predicate with a comparison operator (=, <, >, >=, <=, <>). A constant or an expression can be specified following the comparison operator.

FILTER USING permits specification of an external function or a case expression to be used for additional filtering of the result table. The index-exploitation clause defines a set of rules (in terms of the search method of an index extension) that can be used to exploit the index.

SEARCH BY INDEX EXTENSION *index-extension-name* specifies the index extension. EXACT specifies that the index lookup is to be exact, in terms of the predicate evaluation. The EXACT predicate is useful if the index lookup returns the same results as the predicate. The exploitation-rule clause describes the search targets and search arguments, and how they can be used to perform the index search through a search method defined in the index extension.

WHEN KEY (*parameter-name1*) specifies the search target. USE *search-method-name(parameter-name2,...)* specifies the search argument. It identifies which search method to use from those defined in the index extension.

CREATE FUNCTION (External Table)

This statement is used to register a user-defined external table function with an application server. A table function can be used in the FROM clause of a SELECT statement, and it returns a table to the SELECT, one row at a time.

The authorization ID of the statement must have at least one of the following: SYSADM or DBADM authority; IMPLICIT_SCHEMA privilege on the database, if the implicit or explicit schema name of the function does not exist; CREATEIN privilege on the schema, if the schema name of the function exists. To create a not-fenced function, the authorization ID of the statement must have at least one of the following: SYSADM or DBADM authority; CREATE_NOT_FENCED privilege on the database.

Syntax

```
>>-CREATE FUNCTION--function-name------------------------------->
>----(--+----------------------------------------------------+---)->
        |   .-,------------------------------------------.   |
        |   V                                            |   |
        '----+---------------+--data-type1--+------------+--+--'
             '-parameter-name-'             '-AS LOCATOR--'
>----*--------------------------------------------------------->
                    .-,------------------------------------------.
                    V                                            |
>----RETURNS TABLE--(-----column-name--data-type2--+------------+--+---)->
                                                   '-AS LOCATOR--'
>----*----+-------------------------+--*----------------------->
          '-SPECIFIC--specific-name--'
>----EXTERNAL--+----------------------+---*------------------->
               '-NAME--+-'string'---+--'
                       '-identifier-'

>----LANGUAGE--+-C----+---------*------------------------------->
               +-JAVA-+
               '-OLE--'
>----PARAMETER STYLE--+-DB2SQL-----+---*----------------------->
                      '-DB2GENERAL-'
    .-NOT DETERMINISTIC--.          .-FENCED-----.
>-----+-------------------+--*----+------------+--*------------>
      |             (1)   |       '-NOT FENCED-'
      '-DETERMINISTIC------'
    .-RETURNS NULL ON NULL INPUT--.
>-----+---------------------------+--*--NO SQL--*------------->
      |                    (2)   |
      '-CALLED ON NULL INPUT--------'
    .-EXTERNAL ACTION----.          .-NO SCRATCHPAD----------.
```

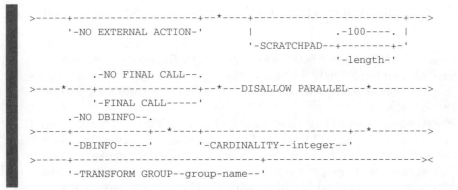

```
>-----+-------------------+--*----+-----------------------+--->
      '-NO EXTERNAL ACTION-'      |             .-100----. |
                                  '-SCRATCHPAD--+--------+-'
                                               '-length-'
             .-NO FINAL CALL--.
>----*----+----------------+--*---DISALLOW PARALLEL---*-------->
          '-FINAL CALL-----'
          .-NO DBINFO--.
>-----+------------+--*----+-----------------------+--*-------->
      '-DBINFO-----'           '-CARDINALITY--integer--'
>-----+--------------------------------+----------------------><
      '-TRANSFORM GROUP--group-name--'
```

Syntax Notes:

1. NOT VARIANT can be specified instead of DETERMINISTIC, and VARIANT can be specified instead of NOT DETERMINISTIC.

2. NULL CALL can be specified instead of CALLED ON NULL INPUT, and NOT NULL CALL can be specified instead of RETURNS NULL ON NULL INPUT.

The unqualified form of *function-name* is an SQL identifier with a maximum length of 18 bytes. If a two-part name is specified, the schema name cannot begin with *SYS*. Keywords in predicates (and comparison operators) are reserved for system use and cannot be used as values for *function-name*. These reserved names are SOME, ANY, ALL, NOT, AND, OR, BETWEEN, NULL, LIKE, EXISTS, IN, UNIQUE, OVERLAPS, SIMILAR, and MATCH.

The *parameter-name* parameter specifies a parameter that can be used in the function definition. The *(data-type1,...)* parameter specifies the data type of each input parameter of the function. One entry in the list must be specified for each parameter that the function is expected to receive. No more than 90 parameters are allowed. A function that has no parameters should be coded with empty parentheses. For LOB types or distinct types that are based on LOB types, the AS LOCATOR clause can be used to specify that a LOB locator (instead of the actual value) is to be passed *to* the UDF. The AS LOCATOR clause cannot be specified if the function is FENCED.

RETURNS TABLE specifies that the output of the function is a table. The name and the data type of each column that is to be included in this table are specified. The data type can be any data type (except a structured type) that is supported for the parameter of a UDF written in the specified language. For LOB types or distinct types that are based on LOB types, the AS LOCATOR clause can be used to specify that a LOB locator (instead of the actual value) is to be passed *from* the UDF.

SPECIFIC *specific-name* specifies a unique name for the instance of the function that is being defined. This specific name can be used when sourcing on the function, dropping the function, or commenting on the function. It cannot be used to invoke the function.

EXTERNAL specifies that the CREATE FUNCTION statement is being used to register a function, based on code written in an external programming language, and adhering to the documented linkage conventions and interface. If the NAME clause is not specified, "NAME *function-name*" is assumed. NAME specifies the name of the user-written code that implements the function being defined. The *'string'* parameter is a string constant with a maximum size of 254 characters. The format for the string depends on the language.

For C, the string specifies a library name and a function within the library, which DB2 invokes to execute the user-defined function. For Java, the string specifies an optional jar file identifier, a class identifier, and a method identifier, which DB2 invokes to execute the user-defined function. For OLE, the string specifies an OLE programmatic identifier or a class identifier, and a method identifier, which DB2 invokes to execute the user-defined function. The *identifier* parameter specifies an SQL identifier that is used as the *library-id* in the string. Unless it is a delimited identifier, the identifier is folded to uppercase. This form of NAME can be used only with LANGUAGE C.

LANGUAGE specifies the language interface convention to which the user-defined function body is to be written. C specifies that DB2 is to call the user-defined function as if it were a C function. JAVA specifies that DB2 is to call the user-defined function as a method in a Java class. OLE specifies that DB2 is to call the user-defined function as if it were a method exposed by an OLE automation object. LANGUAGE OLE is supported only for user-defined functions that are stored on Windows 32-bit operating systems.

PARAMETER STYLE specifies the conventions that are to be used for passing parameters to and returning a value from functions. DB2SQL specifies conventions that conform to C language calling and linkage conventions, or methods exposed by OLE automation objects. This option must be specified when LANGUAGE C or LANGUAGE OLE is specified. DB2GENERAL specifies conventions that are defined as methods in a Java class. This option can be specified only when LANGUAGE JAVA is specified.

NOT DETERMINISTIC or DETERMINISTIC specifies whether the function will always return the same results for given argument values (DETERMINISTIC), or whether the function will depend on some state values that affect the results (NOT DETERMINISTIC).

If a function is registered as FENCED, DB2 insulates its internal resources (for example, data buffers) from access by the function. To change a function from being FENCED to NOT FENCED, the function must be dropped and then re-created.

If RETURNS NULL ON NULL INPUT is specified, and if, at execution time, any one of the function's arguments is null, the user-defined function is not called, and the result is an empty table (a table with no rows). If CALLED ON NULL INPUT is specified, the user-defined function is called even if an argument is null.

NO SQL is a mandatory clause specifying that the function cannot issue any SQL statements.

NO EXTERNAL ACTION or EXTERNAL ACTION specifies whether the function is to take some action that changes the state of an object that is not managed by DB2.

If SCRATCHPAD is specified, memory is allocated for a scratchpad to be used by the external function. The *length* parameter specifies the size, in bytes, of the scratchpad; it must be between 1 and 32,767. The default value is 100. The scope of the scratchpad is the SQL statement. There is one scratchpad per reference to the external function in the SQL statement.

NO FINAL CALL or FINAL CALL specifies whether a final call is to be made to an external function. The purpose of such a final call is to enable the external function to free any system resources that it has acquired. It can be useful in conjunction with the SCRATCHPAD keyword if, for example, the external function acquires system resources, such as memory, and anchors them in the scratchpad. If NO FINAL CALL is specified, DB2 can make only three types of calls to the table function: open, fetch and close. However, if FINAL CALL is specified, a first call and a final call can be made to the table function in addition to open, fetch, and close.

DISALLOW PARALLEL specifies that, for a single reference to the function, the invocation of the function cannot be parallelized. Table functions are always run on a single partition.

NO DBINFO or DBINFO specifies whether additional information will be passed to the function in a structure at invocation time. This information includes the following:

- The name of the currently connected database
- Application ID
- Application authorization ID
- Code page
- Version, release, and modification level of the database server
- Server platform
- An array of numbers identifying the table function result columns that are actually needed for a statement referencing the function

CARDINALITY *integer* specifies an estimate of the expected number of rows to be returned by the function. The value is used for optimization purposes. Valid values for *integer* range from 0 to 2,147,483,647, inclusive.

TRANSFORM GROUP *group-name* specifies the transform group that is to be used for user-defined structured type transformations when invoking the function. A transform is required if the function definition includes a user-defined structured type.

CREATE FUNCTION (OLE DB External Table)

This statement is used to register a user-defined OLE DB external table function to access data from an OLE DB provider. A table function can be used in the FROM clause of a SELECT statement.

The authorization ID of the statement must have at least one of the following: SYSADM or DBADM authority; IMPLICIT_SCHEMA privilege on the database, if the implicit or explicit schema name of the function does not exist; CREATEIN privilege on the schema, if the schema name of the function exists.

Syntax

```
>>-CREATE FUNCTION--function-name-------------------------------->
>----(--+--------------------------------------+---)---*---------->
        '-+----------------+--data-type1---'
          '-parameter-name--'
                          .-,-------------------------.
                          V                           |
>----RETURNS TABLE--(-----column-name--data-type2---+----)---*--->
>-----+----------------------------+--*-------------------------->
      '-SPECIFIC--specific-name--'
>----EXTERNAL--NAME--'string'--*---LANGUAGE----OLEDB-----*------>
     .-NOT DETERMINISTIC--.
>-----+-------------------+--*----------------------------------->
      |             (1)   |
      '-DETERMINISTIC------'
     .-RETURNS NULL ON NULL INPUT--.  (2)
>-----+----------------------------+--------*-------------------->
      '-CALLED ON NULL INPUT--------'
     .-NO EXTERNAL ACTION--.
>-----+--------------------+--*----+---------------------+---->
      '-EXTERNAL ACTION-----'      '-CARDINALITY--integer--'
>----*-------------------------------------------------------><
```

Syntax Notes:

1. NOT VARIANT can be specified instead of DETERMINISTIC, and VARIANT can be specified instead of NOT DETERMINISTIC.
2. NULL CALL can be specified instead of CALLED ON NULL INPUT, and NOT NULL CALL can be specified instead of RETURNS NULL ON NULL INPUT.

The unqualified form of *function-name* is an SQL identifier with a maximum length of 18 bytes. If a two-part name is specified, the schema name cannot begin with *SYS*. Keywords in predicates (and comparison operators) are reserved for system use and cannot be used as values for *function-name*. These reserved names are SOME, ANY, ALL, NOT, AND, OR, BETWEEN, NULL, LIKE, EXISTS, IN, UNIQUE, OVERLAPS, SIMILAR, and MATCH.

The *parameter-name* parameter specifies an optional parameter name. The *data-type1* parameter specifies the data type of the input parameter of the function; the data type can be any character or graphic string data type. A function that has no parameters should be coded with empty parentheses.

RETURNS TABLE specifies that the output of the function is a table. The name and the data type of each column that is to be included in this table is specified.

SPECIFIC *specific-name* specifies a unique name for the instance of the function that is being defined. This specific name can be used when sourcing on the function, dropping the function, or commenting on the function. It cannot be used to invoke the function. EXTERNAL NAME *'string'* specifies the external table and an OLE DB provider. The *'string'* parameter is a string constant with a maximum size of 254 characters. The string is used to establish a connection and a session with an OLE DB provider, and to retrieve data from a rowset (table).

LANGUAGE OLEDB specifies that DB2 will deploy a built-in generic OLE DB consumer to retrieve data from the OLE DB provider. No table function implementation is required by the developer. LANGUAGE OLEDB table functions can be created on any platform, but can be executed only on platforms supported by Microsoft OLE DB.

NOT DETERMINISTIC or DETERMINISTIC specifies whether the function will always return the same results for given argument values (DETERMINISTIC), or whether the function will depend on some state values that affect the results (NOT DETERMINISTIC).

If RETURNS NULL ON NULL INPUT is specified, and if, at execution time, any one of the function's arguments is null, the user-defined function is not called, and the result is an empty table (a table with no rows). If CALLED ON NULL INPUT is specified, the user-defined function is called even if an argument is null.

NO EXTERNAL ACTION or EXTERNAL ACTION specifies whether the function is to take some action that changes the state of an object that is not managed by DB2.

CARDINALITY *integer* specifies an estimate of the expected number of rows to be returned by the function. The value is used for optimization purposes. Valid values for *integer* range from 0 to 2,147,483,647, inclusive.

CREATE FUNCTION (Sourced or Template)

This statement is used to do the following:

- Register a user-defined function, based on another existing scalar or column function, with an application server.

- Register a function template with an application server that is designated as a federated server. A *function template* is a partial function that contains no executable code—it is created for the purpose of mapping it to a data source function. After the mapping is created, the function template can be specified in queries that are submitted to the federated server. When such a query is processed, the federated server invokes the data source function to which the template is mapped and returns values whose data types correspond to those in the RETURNS portion of the template's definition.

The authorization ID of the statement must have at least one of the following: SYSADM or DBADM authority; IMPLICIT_SCHEMA privilege on the database, if the implicit or explicit schema name of the function does not exist; CREATEIN privilege on the schema, if the schema name of the function exists.

Syntax

```
>>-CREATE FUNCTION--function-name------------------------------s->
>-----(--+-----------------------------------------+---)---*---->
         |   .-,----------------------------.  |
         |   V                              |  |
         '----+------------------+---data-type1---+--'
              '-parameter-name--'
>----RETURNS--data-type2---*----+-----------------------------+---->
                                '-SPECIFIC--specific-name--'
>-----*--------------------------------------------------------->
>------+-SOURCE--+-function-name--------------------------------+-+>
       |         +-SPECIFIC--specific-name--------------------+ |
       |         '-function-name--(--+-----------------+---)--' |
       |                             |   .-,----------.  |      |
       |                             |   V            |  |      |
       |                             '----data-type---+--'      |
       |                   .-NOT DETERMINISTIC--.      .-EXTERNAL ACTION----.    |
       '-AS TEMPLATE--*----+--------------------+--*----+--------------------+--*--'
                           '-DETERMINISTIC------'       '-NO EXTERNAL ACTION-'
>----*--------------------------------------------------------><
```

The unqualified form of *function-name* is an SQL identifier with a maximum length of 18 bytes. If a two-part name is specified, the schema name cannot begin with *SYS*. Keywords in predicates (and comparison operators) are reserved for system use and cannot be used as values for *function-name*. These reserved names are SOME, ANY, ALL, NOT, AND, OR, BETWEEN, NULL, LIKE, EXISTS, IN, UNIQUE, OVERLAPS, SIMILAR, and MATCH.

The *parameter-name* parameter specifies a parameter that can be used in the function or function template definition. The *(data-type1,...)* parameter specifies the data type of each input parameter of the function or the function template. One entry in the list must be specified for each parameter that the function or the function template is expected to receive. No more than 90 parameters are allowed. A function or function template that has no parameters should be coded with empty parentheses.

RETURNS specifies the output of the function or the function template. The *data-type2* parameter specifies the data type of the output.

SPECIFIC *specific-name* specifies a unique name for the instance of the function that is being defined. This specific name can be used when sourcing on the function, dropping the function, or commenting on the function. It cannot be used to invoke the function.

SOURCE specifies that the function being created is to be implemented by another function (the source function) already known to DB2. The source function can be a built-in function or a previously created user-defined scalar function. The SOURCE clause can be specified only for scalar or column functions. The *function-name* parameter specifies the particular function that is to be used as the source, and is valid only if there is exactly one specific function in the schema with this function name. This syntax variant is not valid for a built-in source function.

SPECIFIC *specific-name* specifies the particular user-defined function that is to be used as the source, by the name that was specified or defaulted to at function creation time. This syntax variant is also not valid for a built-in source function. The *function-name (data-type,...)* parameter specifies a function signature, which uniquely identifies the source function. This is the only valid syntax variant for a built-in source function.

AS TEMPLATE specifies that this statement is to be used to create a function template, not a function with executable code.

DETERMINISTIC or NOT DETERMINISTIC specifies whether the function always returns the same results for given argument values (DETERMINISTIC) or whether the function depends on some state values that affect the results (NOT DETERMINISTIC).

EXTERNAL ACTION or NO EXTERNAL ACTION specifies whether the function takes some action that changes the state of an object not managed by the database manager.

REFERENCE

CREATE FUNCTION (SQL Scalar, Table, or Row)

This statement is used to define a user-defined SQL scalar, table, or row function. A scalar function returns a single value each time it is invoked, and it is generally valid wherever an SQL expression is valid. A table function can be used in a FROM clause, and returns a table. A row function can be used as a transform function, and returns a row.

The authorization ID of the statement must have at least one of the following: SYSADM or DBADM authority; IMPLICIT_SCHEMA privilege on the database if the schema name of the function does not refer to an existing schema; CREATEIN privilege on the schema if the schema name of the function refers to an existing schema. If the authorization ID of the statement does not have SYSADM or DBADM authority, and the function identifies a table or a view, the authorization ID of the statement (without considering GROUP privileges) must have SELECT WITH GRANT OPTION privilege for each identified table or view.

Syntax

```
>>-CREATE FUNCTION--function-name--------------------------------->
>---- (--+---------------------------------------+---)---*---------->
         |   .-,--------------------------.   |
         | V                              |   |
         '----parameter-name--data-type1---+--'
>----RETURNS--+-data-type2--------------------+--*-------------->
              '--+-ROW---+---| column-list |--'
                 '-TABLE-'
                                              .-LANGUAGE SQL--.
>-----+------------------------+--*----+---------------+--*--->
      '-SPECIFIC--specific-name--'
      .-NOT DETERMINISTIC--.        .-EXTERNAL ACTION----.
>-----+--------------------+--*----+-----------------+--*---->
      '-DETERMINISTIC------'       '-NO EXTERNAL ACTION-'
      .-READS SQL DATA--.       .-STATIC DISPATCH--.
>-----+----------------+--*----+-----------------+--*--------->
      '-CONTAINS SQL----'
                             (1)
      .-CALLED ON NULL INPUT-------.
>-----+-------------------------+--*------------------------->
>-----+----------------------------------------------+--->
      |                                         (2)  |
      '-PREDICATES--(--| predicate-specification |--)-------'
>----| SQL-function-body |-------------------------------->< 
column-list
        .-,-------------------------.
        V                           |
|---(-----column-name--data-type3---+---)---------------------|
SQL-function-body
|---+-RETURN Statement-----------+---------------------------|
    '-dynamic-compound-statement-'
```

Syntax Notes:

1. NULL CALL can be specified instead of CALLED ON NULL INPUT.

2. Valid only if RETURNS specifies a scalar result (*data-type2*).

The unqualified form of *function-name* is an SQL identifier with a maximum length of 18 bytes. If a two-part name is specified, the schema name cannot begin with *SYS*. Keywords in predicates (and comparison operators) are reserved for system use and cannot be used as values for *function-name*. These reserved names are SOME, ANY, ALL, NOT, AND, OR, BETWEEN, NULL, LIKE, EXISTS, IN, UNIQUE, OVERLAPS, SIMILAR, and MATCH.

The *parameter-name* parameter specifies a parameter that can be used in the function. The *(data-type1,...)* parameter specifies the data type of each input parameter of the function.

RETURNS specifies the type of function output. The *data-type2* parameter specifies the data type of the output. ROW *column-list* specifies that the function output is to be a single row. The column list must include at least two columns. A row function can be used as a transform function only for a structured type (having one structured type as its input parameter, and returning only base types). TABLE column-list specifies that the function output is to be a table.

SPECIFIC *specific-name* specifies a unique name for the instance of the function that is being defined. This specific name can be used when sourcing on the function, dropping the function, or commenting on the function. It cannot be used to invoke the function.

LANGUAGE SQL specifies that the function is written using SQL.imited to the RETURN statement.

NOT DETERMINISTIC or DETERMINISTIC specifies whether the function will always return the same results for given argument values (DETERMINISTIC), or whether the function will depend on some state values that affect the results (NOT DETERMINISTIC).

NO EXTERNAL ACTION or EXTERNAL ACTION specifies whether the function is to take some action that changes the state of an object that is not managed by DB2.

READS SQL DATA specifies that some SQL statements that do not modify SQL data can be executed by the function. Nicknames or OLEDB table functions cannot be referenced in the SQL statement. CONTAINS SQL specifies that SQL statements that neither read nor modify SQL data can be executed by the function.

STATIC DISPATCH specifies that at function resolution time, DB2 is to choose a function based on the static types (declared types) of the parameters in the function.

If CALLED ON NULL INPUT is specified, the user-defined function is called even if an argument is null.

For predicates using this function, the PREDICATES clause identifies those that can exploit index extensions, and can use the optional SELECTIVITY clause for the predicate's search condition. If the PREDICATES clause is specified, the function must be defined as DETERMINISTIC with NO EXTERNAL ACTION. For information about predicate specifications, see the CREATE FUNCTION (External Scalar) statement.

The SQL-function-body clause specifies the body of the function. Parameter names can be referenced in the SQL-function-body clause. Parameter names may be qualified with the function name to avoid ambiguous references. If the SQL-function-body clause specifies a dynamic compound statement, it must contain at least one RETURN statement, and a RETURN statement must be executed when the function is called. If the function is a table or row function, it can contain only one RETURN statement, which must be the last statement in the dynamic compound statement.

CREATE FUNCTION MAPPING

The CREATE FUNCTION MAPPING statement is used to do the following:

- Create a mapping between a federated database function or function template and a data source function. The mapping can associate the federated database function or template with a function at a specified data source, or a range of data sources; for example, all data sources of a particular type and version.

- Disable a default mapping between a federated database function and a data source function.

The authorization ID of the statement must have SYSADM or DBADM authority.

Syntax

```
>>-CREATE FUNCTION MAPPING--+---------------------+---FOR----->
                            '-function-mapping-name-'

                          .-,---------------.
                          V                 |
>-----+-function-name--(-----+-----------+--+---)--+----------->
      |                      '-data-type--'        |
      '-SPECIFIC--specific-name-------------------'

>-----+-SERVER--server-name--------------------------------------------------+>
      '-SERVER TYPE--server-type--+----------------------------------------------+-'
                                  '-VERSION--| server-version |--+----------------------+--'
                                                                 '-WRAPPER--wrapper-name--'

>-----+---------------------+--+------------+--------------><
      '-| function-options |--'  '-WITH INFIX-'
server-version
|---+-version--+----------------------------+-+------------------|
    |          '-.--release--+---------+--' |
    |                        '-.--mod--'    |
    '-version-string-constant--------------'
function-options
                .-,------------------------------------------------.
                V  .-ADD--.                                        |
|---OPTIONS--(-----+------+---function-option-name--string-constant---+---)-->
>------------------------------------------------------------|
```

If a value for *function-mapping-name* is not specified, a system-generated unique name is assigned. The *function-name* parameter specifies the qualified or unqualified name of the function or the function template from which a mapping is to be created. For a function or a function template that has input parameters, *data-type* specifies the data type of each parameter. The data type cannot be LONG VARCHAR, LONG VARGRAPHIC, DATALINK, a large object (LOB) type, or a user-defined type.

SPECIFIC *specific-name* specifies the function or the function template from which a mapping is to be created. Specify a value for this parameter if the function or the function template does not have a unique function name in the federated database.

SERVER *server-name* specifies the data source that contains the function to which a mapping is to be created. SERVER TYPE *server-type* specifies the type of data source that contains the function to which a mapping is to be created. VERSION specifies the version (version number, an integer; release number, an integer; and modification number, also an integer) of the specified data source. Alternatively, you can specify a *version-string-constant*, such as 8i or 8.0.3, for example. WRAPPER *wrapper-name* specifies the name of the wrapper that the federated server uses to interact with data sources of the specified type and version.

The OPTIONS parameter indicates which function mapping options are to be enabled. *Function mapping options* provide information about the potential cost of executing a data source function at the data source, and include the following:

- **disable** Disable a default function mapping. Valid values are *Y* and *N*.
- **initial_insts** Estimated number of instructions processed the first and the last time that the data source function is invoked.
- **initial_ios** Estimated number of I/Os performed the first and the last time that the data source function is invoked.
- **ios_per_argbyte** Estimated number of I/Os expended for each byte of the argument set that is passed to the data source function.
- **ios_per_invoc** Estimated number of I/Os per invocation of a data source function.
- **insts_per_argbyte** Estimated number of instructions processed for each byte of the argument set that is passed to the data source function.
- **insts_per_invoc** Estimated number of instructions processed per invocation of the data source function.
- **percent_argbytes** Estimated average percentage of input argument bytes that the data source function will actually read.
- **remote_name** Name of the data source function.

WITH INFIX specifies that the data source function is to be generated in infix format.

CREATE INDEX

The CREATE INDEX statement is used to create an index on a DB2 table, or an *index specification* (metadata that indicates to the optimizer that a data source table has an index). The authorization ID of the statement must have at least one of the following: SYSADM or DBADM authority; CONTROL or INDEX privilege on the table; and

IMPLICIT_SCHEMA authority on the database, if the implicit or explicit schema name of the index does not exist, or CREATEIN privilege on the schema, if the schema name of the index refers to an existing schema.

Syntax

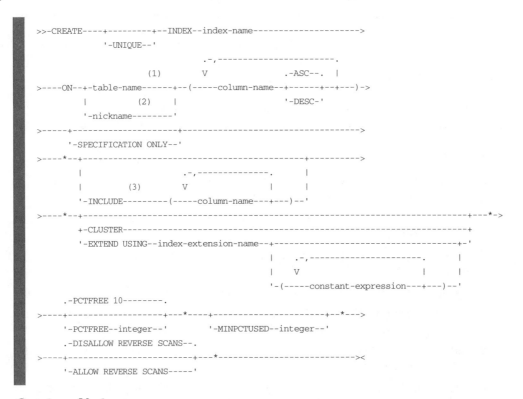

```
>>-CREATE----+---------+--INDEX--index-name-------------------->
             '-UNIQUE--'

                          .-,----------------------.
                 (1)      V            .-ASC--.   |
>----ON--+-table-name------+--(-----column-name--+------+--+---)->
         |         (2)   |                  '-DESC-'
         '-nickname-------'
>-----+------------------+------------------------------------->
      '-SPECIFICATION ONLY--'
>----*--+-----------------------------------------------+---------->
        |                       .-,--------------.       |
        |           (3)         V              |       |
        '-INCLUDE---------(-----column-name---+---)--'
>----*--+----------------------------------------------------------------------+---*->
        +-CLUSTER-----------------------------------------------------------------+
        '-EXTEND USING--index-extension-name--+-----------------------------------+-'
                                   |        .-,----------------------.       |
                                   |        V                      .       |
                                   '-(-----constant-expression---+---)--'
    .-PCTFREE 10--------.
>----+------------------+---*----+---------------------+--*--->
     '-PCTFREE--integer--'      '-MINPCTUSED--integer--'
    .-DISALLOW REVERSE SCANS--.
>----+----------------------------+---*------------------------><
     '-ALLOW REVERSE SCANS-----'
```

Syntax Notes:

1. In a federated system, the table-name must identify a table in the federated database. It cannot identify a data source table.

2. If nickname is specified, the CREATE INDEX statement will create an index specification. INCLUDE, CLUSTER, PCTFREE, MINPCTUSED, DISALLOW REVERSE SCANS, and ALLOW REVERSE SCANS cannot be specified.

3. The INCLUDE clause can be specified only if UNIQUE is specified.

UNIQUE prevents the table from containing two or more rows with the same value of the index key if ON *table-name* is specified. If the table already contains rows with duplicate key values, an index is not created. The table cannot be a declared temporary table.

INDEX *index-name* specifies a name for the index or the index specification. The qualifier cannot be SYSIBM, SYSCAT, SYSFUN, or SYSSTAT.

ON *table-name* specifies a table on which an index is to be created. The table must be a base table (not a view) or a summary table described in the catalog. It must not be a catalog table or a declared temporary table. If UNIQUE is specified and the table is a typed table, it must not be a subtable. If UNIQUE is specified, the table cannot be a summary table. ON *nickname* specifies a data source table whose index is described by the index specification, or a data source view that is based on such a table. The *(column-name, ...)* parameter specifies one or more columns (maximum 16) that are to be part of the index key or, for an index specification, it is the name by which the federated server references a column in a data source table.

ASC specifies that index entries are to be kept in *ascending* order of the column values. DESC specifies that index entries are to be kept in *descending* order of the column values.

SPECIFICATION ONLY specifies that this statement will be used to create an index specification that applies to the data source table referenced by *nickname.* INCLUDE *(column-name, ...)* specifies one or more columns that are to be included in the index for performance reasons, but that are not part of the unique index key.

CLUSTER specifies that the index is the clustering index of the table. EXTEND USING *index-extension-name* specifies the index extension that is to be used to manage this index. If this clause is specified, there must be only one column name specified, and that column must be a structured type or a distinct type. The *(constant-expression, ...)* parameter specifies values for any required arguments for the index extension. Each expression must be a constant value with a data type that exactly matches the defined data type of the corresponding index extension parameters, including length, precision, and scale.

PCTFREE *integer* specifies the percentage of each index page that is to be left as free space when building the index. MINPCTUSED *integer* specifies that indexes are to be reorganized online, and the minimum percentage of each index leaf page that is to be used. If, after a key is deleted from an index leaf page, the percentage of space used on the page is at or below this value, an attempt is made to merge the remaining keys on this page with those of a neighboring page.

DISALLOW REVERSE SCANS specifies that an index is to support only forward scans, or scanning of the index in the order defined when the index was created. ALLOW REVERSE SCANS specifies that an index can support both forward and reverse scans: that is, in the order defined when the index was created, and in the reverse order.

CREATE INDEX EXTENSION

The CREATE INDEX EXTENSION statement creates an extension object for use with indexes on tables that have structured type or distinct type columns. The authorization ID of the statement must have at least one of the following: SYSADM or DBADM authority; IMPLICIT_SCHEMA privilege on the database (if the schema name of the index extension does not refer to an existing schema); CREATEIN privilege on the schema (if the schema name of the index extension refers to an existing schema).

Syntax

```
>>-CREATE INDEX EXTENSION--index-extension-name---------------->
>-----+---------------------------------------------+---------->
      |        .-,----------------------------.      |
      |        V                              |      |
      '-(-----parameter-name1--data-type1---+---)--'
>-----| index-maintenance |--| index-search |------------------><
index-maintenance
|---FROM SOURCE KEY--(--parameter-name2--data-type2--)---------->
>----GENERATE KEY USING--table-function-invocation-------------|
index-search
                      .-,----------------------------.
                      V                              |
|---WITH TARGET KEY--(-----parameter-name3--data-type3---+---)-->
                    .-,----------------------------.
                    V                              |
>----SEARCH METHODS-----| search-method-definition |---+-------|
search-method-definition
                      .-,-----------------------------.
                      V                               |
|---WHEN--method-name--(-----parameter-name4--data-type4---+---)-->
>---RANGE THROUGH--range-producing-function-invocation---------->
>-----+-----------------------------------------------------+-|
      '-FILTER USING--+-index-filtering-function-invocation-+--'
                      '-case-expression--------------------'
```

The *index-extension-name* parameter specifies the name of the new index extension. If a two-part index extension name is specified, the schema name cannot begin with *SYS*.

The *parameter-name1* parameter specifies a parameter that is passed to the index extension when the index is created, and which is used to define the actual behavior of this index extension. This parameter is called an *instance parameter* because the value defines a new instance of an index extension. The *data-type1* parameter specifies the data type of the instance parameter. Valid data types are those that can be used as constants, such as VARCHAR, INTEGER, DECIMAL, DOUBLE, or VARGRAPHIC.

The index-maintenance clause specifies how the index keys of a structured or distinct type column are to be maintained. Index maintenance is the process of transforming the source column to a target key. The transformation process is defined using a table function that has previously been defined in the database.

FROM SOURCE KEY *(parameter-name2 data-type2)* specifies a structured data type or distinct type for the source key column that is supported by this index extension. The *parameter-name2* parameter specifies the parameter that is associated with the source key column. A source key column is the index key column (defined in the CREATE INDEX statement) with the same data type as *data-type2*. The *data-type2* parameter specifies the data type for *parameter-name2*; it must be a user-defined structured type or a distinct type that is not sourced on LOB, DATALINK, LONG VARCHAR, or LONG VARGRAPHIC. When the index extension is associated with the index at CREATE INDEX time, the data type of the index key column must exactly match *data-type2* if it is a distinct type, or be the same type or a subtype of *data-type2* if it is a structured type.

GENERATE KEY USING *table-function-invocation* specifies how the index key is to be generated using a user-defined table function. The output of the GENERATE KEY function must be specified in the TARGET KEY specification.

The index-search clause specifies how searching is to be performed by providing a mapping of the search arguments to search ranges. WITH TARGET KEY specifies the target key parameters that are the output of the key generation function specified on the GENERATE KEY USING clause. The parameter-name3 parameter specifies the parameter associated with a given target key; it corresponds to the columns of the RETURNS table, as specified in the table function of the GENERATE KEY USING clause. The number of parameters specified must match the number of columns returned by that table function. The *data-type3* parameter specifies the data type for *parameter-name3*, and must exactly match the data type of each corresponding output column of the RETURNS table, as specified in the table function of the GENERATE KEY USING clause.

SEARCH METHODS specifies the search methods that are defined for the index. The search-method-definition clause specifies the method details of the index search. It consists of a method name, the search arguments, a range-producing function, and an optional index filter function.

WHEN *method-name* specifies the name of a search method. The *parameter-name4* parameter specifies the parameter of a search argument. The *data-type4* parameter specifies the data type associated with a search parameter.

RANGE THROUGH *range-producing-function-invocation* specifies an external table function that produces search ranges. This function uses *parameter-name1, parameter-name4,* or a constant as arguments, and returns a set of search ranges.

FILTER USING specifies an external function or a case expression to be used for filtering index entries that were returned after applying the range-producing function. The *index-filtering-function-invocation* parameter specifies an external function to be used for filtering index entries. This function uses *parameter-name1, parameter-name3, parameter-name4,* or a constant as arguments, and returns an integer. If the value returned is 1, the row corresponding to the index entry is retrieved from the table; otherwise, the index entry is not considered for further processing. The *case-expression* parameter specifies a case expression for filtering index entries. The case expression must return an integer. A return value of 1 in the result expression means that the index entry is kept; otherwise, the index entry is discarded.

CREATE METHOD

This statement is used to associate a method body with a method specification that is already part of the definition of a user-defined structured type. The authorization ID of the statement must have at least one of the following: SYSADM or DBADM authority; CREATEIN privilege on the schema of the structured type referred to in the CREATE METHOD statement; the DEFINER of the structured type referred to in the CREATE METHOD statement. If the authorization ID of the statement does not have SYSADM or DBADM authority, and the method identifies a table or view in the RETURN statement, the authorization ID of the statement must have SELECT WITH GRANT OPTION for each identified table and view.

Syntax

```
>>-CREATE------------------------------------------------------->
>-----+-METHOD--+-method-name----------+---FOR--type-name--+---->
      |         '-| method-signature |-'                   |
      '-SPECIFIC METHOD--specific-name--------------------'
>-----+-*----EXTERNAL--+----------------------+--*----+-------------------------------+--*--+>
      |                '-NAME--+-'string'---+--'      '-TRANSFORM GROUP--group-name--'     |
      |                        '-identifier-'                                             |
      '-| SQL-method-body |------------------------------------------------------------------'
>------------------------------------------------------------->< 

method-signature
|---method-name--(--+------------------------------------------------------------+---)-->
                    |   .-,------------------------------------------------.    |
                    |   V                                                  |    |
                    '----+-----------------+---data-type1--+-------------+--+-'
                         '-parameter-name--'               '-AS LOCATOR--'
>----+-----------------------------------------------------------------+->
     '-RETURNS--+-data-type2--+-------------+-----------------------+--'
               |              '-AS LOCATOR--'                       |
               '-data-type3--CAST FROM--data-type4--+-------------+-'
                                                    '-AS LOCATOR--'
>-----------------------------------------------------------|

SQL-method-body
|---+-RETURN Statement----------+---------------------------|
    '-dynamic-compound-statement-'
```

METHOD specifies an existing method specification that is associated with a user-defined structured type. The *method-name* parameter specifies the method specification for which a method body is being defined. The implicit schema is the schema of the subject type (*type-name*). The method-signature clause specifies the method signature that uniquely identifies the method to be defined. The method signature must match the method specification that was provided on the CREATE TYPE or the ALTER TYPE statement. The *parameter-name* parameter specifies the parameter name. If parameter names are provided in the method signature, they must be exactly the same as the corresponding parts of the matching method specification. The *data-type1* parameter specifies the data type of each parameter. The AS LOCATOR clause can be added for the LOB types or the distinct types that are based on a LOB type.

The RETURNS clause specifies the output of the method. If a RETURNS clause is provided in the method signature, it must be exactly the same as the corresponding part of the matching method specification on the CREATE TYPE statement. The *data-type2* parameter specifies the data type of the output. The AS LOCATOR clause can be added for LOB types or distinct types that are based on LOB types. This indicates that a LOB locator (instead of the actual value) is to be returned by the method.

The *data-type3* CAST FROM *data-type4* form of the RETURNS clause is used to return a data type to the invoking statement that is different from the data type that was returned by the function code. For LOB types or distinct types that are based on LOB types, the AS LOCATOR clause can be used to specify that a LOB locator (instead of the actual value) is to be returned from the method.

FOR *type-name* specifies the type with which the specified method is to be associated. SPECIFIC METHOD *specific-name* specifies a particular method, using the specific name either specified or defaulted to when the CREATE TYPE statement was invoked.

EXTERNAL specifies that the CREATE METHOD statement is being used to register a method, based on code written in an external programming language, and adhering to the documented linkage conventions and interface. The matching method-specification clause in the CREATE TYPE statement must specify a LANGUAGE other than SQL. When the method is invoked, the subject of the method is passed to the implementation as an implicit first parameter. If the NAME clause is not specified, "NAME *method-name*" is assumed.

NAME specifies the name of the user-written code that implements the method being defined. The *'string'* parameter is a string constant with a maximum size of 254 characters. The *identifier* parameter specifies an SQL identifier that is used as the *library-id* in the string. Unless it is a delimited identifier, the identifier is folded to uppercase. This form of NAME can be used only with LANGUAGE C (as defined in the method-specification clause in the CREATE TYPE statement).

TRANSFORM GROUP *group-name* specifies the transform group that is to be used for user-defined structured type transformations when invoking the method. A transform is required because the method definition includes a user-defined structured type.

The SQL-method-body clause defines how the method is to be implemented if the method specification in CREATE TYPE is LANGUAGE SQL. The SQL-method-body clause must comply with the following parts of the method specification: DETERMINISTIC or NOT DETERMINISTIC; EXTERNAL ACTION or NO EXTERNAL ACTION; CONTAINS SQL or READS SQL DATA. Parameter names can be referenced in the SQL-method-body clause. The subject of the method is passed to the method implementation as an implicit first parameter named SELF.

CREATE NICKNAME

The CREATE NICKNAME statement creates a nickname for a data source table or view. The authorization ID of the statement must have at least one of the following: SYSADM or DBADM authority; IMPLICIT_SCHEMA privilege on the federated database, if the implicit or explicit schema name of the nickname does not exist; CREATEIN privilege on the schema, if the schema name of the nickname exists. In addition, the user's authorization ID at the data source must have the privilege to select from the data source catalog the metadata about the table or view for which the nickname is being created.

Syntax

```
>>-CREATE NICKNAME------nickname-----FOR--remote-object-name---><
```

The *nickname* parameter specifies the federated server's identifier for the table or view that is referenced by *remote-object-name*. The nickname, including the implicit or explicit qualifier, must not identify a table, view, alias, or nickname that is described in the catalog. The schema name must not begin with *SYS*.

The *remote-object-name* parameter specifies a three-part identifier with the format *data-source-name.remote-schema-name.remote-table-name*. The *data-source-name* parameter specifies the data source that contains the table or view for which the nickname is being created. The data source name is the same name that was assigned to the data source in the CREATE SERVER statement. The *remote-schema-name* parameter specifies the schema to which the table or view belongs. The *remote-table-name* parameter specifies the name or an alias of a DB2 table or view, or the name of an Oracle table or view. The table cannot be a declared temporary table.

CREATE NODEGROUP

The CREATE NODEGROUP statement creates a new nodegroup within the database, assigns partitions or nodes to the nodegroup, and records the nodegroup definition in the catalog. The statement creates a partitioning map for the nodegroup. The authorization ID of the statement must have SYSADM or SYSCTRL authority.

Syntax

```
>>-CREATE NODEGROUP--nodegroup-name---------------------------->
       .-ON ALL NODES-----------------------------------------------.
>-----+------------------------------------------------------------+>
       |                     .-,-------------------------------.     |
       |                     V                                       |   |
```

```
'-ON--+-NODES-+--- (-----node-number1--+-------------------+--+---)--'
      '-NODE--'                         '-TO--node-number2---'
>------------------------------------------------------------><
```

The nodegroup name must not begin with the characters *SYS* or *IBM*. ON ALL NODES specifies that the nodegroup is to be defined over all partitions defined on the database when the nodegroup is created. ON NODE *node-number1* specifies a single partition. TO *node-number2* specifies a range of partitions.

Example

```
CREATE NODEGROUP MEDGROUP ON NODES (0 TO 2, 5, 8)
```

CREATE PROCEDURE

The CREATE PROCEDURE statement is used to register a stored procedure with an application server. The authorization ID of the statement must have at least one of the following: SYSADM or DBADM authority; IMPLICIT_SCHEMA privilege on the database, if the implicit or explicit schema name of the procedure does not exist; CREATEIN privilege on the schema, if the schema name of the procedure refers to an existing schema. To create an unfenced stored procedure, the authorization ID of the statement must have at least one of the following: SYSADM or DBADM authority; CREATE_NOT_FENCED privilege on the database.

Syntax

```
>>-CREATE PROCEDURE----------------------------------------->
>----procedure-name-- (--+----------------------------------------+---)->
                         |    .-,-------------------------------------. |
                         |    V .-IN----.                             | |
                         '----+-------+---parameter-name--data-type---+-'
                              +-OUT---+
                              '-INOUT-'
>----*----+------------------------+--*---------------------->
          '-SPECIFIC--specific-name--'
          .- DYNAMIC RESULT SETS 0--------.  (1)
>-----+------------------------------------+---------*--------------->
      '-DYNAMIC RESULT SETS--integer--'
      .-MODIFIES SQL DATA--.         .-NOT DETERMINISTIC--.
>-----+-------------------+--*----+------------------+--*---->
      |          (2)      |         '-DETERMINISTIC------'
      +-NO SQL-------------+
```

```
        +-CONTAINS SQL-------+
        '-READS SQL DATA-----'
                              (3)
        .-CALLED ON NULL INPUT------.
>----+-------------------------+---*------------------------>
>-----+-LANGUAGE--+-C-----+--*----| external-procedure-options |--*--+>
      |           +-JAVA--+                                          |
      |           +-COBOL-+                                          |
      |           '-OLE---'                                          |
      '-LANGUAGE--SQL---*----| SQL-procedure-body |------------------'
>----------------------------------------------------------><
external-procedure-options
                                               .-FENCED-----.
|---*---EXTERNAL--+--------------------+--*----+-----------+->
                 '-NAME--+-'string'---+-'      '-NOT FENCED-'
                         '-identifier-'
>----*---PARAMETER STYLE--+-DB2DARI-----------+--*------------->
                          |             (4)   |
                          +-DB2GENERAL--------+
                          +-GENERAL-----------+
                          +-GENERAL WITH NULLS-+
                          +-DB2SQL------------+
                          '-JAVA--------------'
                                     .-NO DBINFO--.
>-----+-----------------------+--*----+-----------+--*-------|
      '-PROGRAM TYPE--+-SUB--+-'      '-DBINFO-----'
                      '-MAIN-'
SQL-procedure-body
|---SQL-procedure-statement----------------------------------|
```

Syntax Notes:

1. RESULT SETS can be specified instead of DYNAMIC RESULT SETS.

2. NO SQL is not a valid choice for LANGUAGE SQL.

3. NULL CALL can be specified instead of CALLED ON NULL INPUT.

4. DB2GENRL can be specified instead of DB2GENERAL, SIMPLE CALL can be specified instead of GENERAL, and SIMPLE CALL WITH NULLS can be specified instead of GENERAL WITH NULLS.

The unqualified form of *procedure-name* is an SQL identifier with a maximum length of 128 bytes. If a two-part name is specified, the schema name cannot begin with *SYS*.

IN, OUT, and INOUT specify whether the parameter is an input, output, or both input and output parameter, respectively. User-defined data types are not supported.

SPECIFIC *specific-name* specifies a unique name for the procedure instance that is being defined. This specific name can be used when dropping the procedure or when commenting on the procedure. It cannot be used to invoke the procedure. The unqualified form of *specific-name* is an SQL identifier with a maximum length of 18 bytes. The specific name can be the same as an existing procedure name. If no qualifier is specified, the qualifier that was used for the procedure name is used. If a specific name is not specified, DB2 generates a unique name, which is *SQL* followed by a timestamp.

DYNAMIC RESULT SETS *integer* specifies the estimated upper bound of returned result sets for the stored procedure.

NO SQL specifies that the stored procedure cannot execute any SQL statements. CONTAINS SQL specifies that SQL statements that neither read nor modify SQL data can be executed by the stored procedure. READS SQL DATA specifies that some SQL statements that do not modify SQL data can be included in the stored procedure. MODIFIES SQL DATA specifies that the stored procedure can execute any SQL statement, except statements that are not supported in stored procedures.

LANGUAGE is a mandatory clause that is used to specify the language interface convention to which the stored procedure body is written. C specifies that DB2 is to call the stored procedure as if it were a C procedure. JAVA specifies that DB2 is to call the stored procedure as a method in a Java class. COBOL specifies that DB2 is to call the stored procedure as if it were a COBOL procedure. OLE specifies that DB2 is to call the stored procedure as if it were a method exposed by an OLE automation object. LANGUAGE OLE is supported only for procedures that are stored on Windows 32-bit operating systems. SQL specifies that the SQL-procedure-body clause includes the statements that define the processing of the stored procedure.

EXTERNAL specifies that the CREATE PROCEDURE statement is being used to register a new procedure based on code written in an external programming language, and adhering to the documented linkage conventions and interface.

NAME *'string'* specifies the name of the user-written code that implements the procedure that is being defined. The string constant has a maximum length of 254 characters. The string format depends on the specified language. For format details, see the *DB2 SQL Reference*. NAME *identifier* specifies an SQL identifier that is used as the *library-id* in the string. Unless it is a delimited identifier, the identifier is folded to uppercase. If the identifier is qualified with a schema name, the schema name portion is ignored. This NAME form can be used only with LANGUAGE C. If the NAME clause is not specified, NAME *procedure-name* is assumed.

If a stored procedure is registered as FENCED, DB2 insulates its internal resources (for example, data buffers) from access by the procedure. To change a procedure from being FENCED to NOT FENCED, the procedure must be dropped and then re-created.

PARAMETER STYLE specifies the conventions that are to be used for passing parameters to and returning a value from stored procedures. DB2DARI specifies that the stored procedure will use a parameter-passing convention that conforms to C language calling and linkage conventions. DB2GENERAL specifies that the stored procedure will use a parameter-passing convention that is defined for use with Java methods. GENERAL specifies that the stored procedure will use a parameter-passing mechanism in which the stored procedure receives the parameters specified on the

CALL—the parameters are passed directly, as expected by the language; the SQLDA structure is not used. This option can be specified only when LANGUAGE C or COBOL is specified.

GENERAL WITH NULLS specifies that, in addition to the parameters on the CALL statement that are specified with GENERAL, another argument is to be passed to the stored procedure, one that contains a vector of null indicators for each of the parameters on the CALL statement. In C, for example, this would be an array of short integers. This option can be specified only when LANGUAGE C or COBOL is specified. DB2SQL specifies that, in addition to the parameters on the CALL statement, the following arguments are to be passed to the stored procedure: a null indicator for each parameter on the CALL statement; the SQLSTATE that is to be returned to DB2; the qualified name of the stored procedure; the specific name of the stored procedure; and the SQL diagnostic string that is to be returned to DB2.

This option can be specified only when LANGUAGE C, COBOL, or OLE are specified. JAVA specifies that the stored procedure will use a parameter-passing convention that conforms to the Java language and SQLj routines specification. IN/OUT and OUT parameters will be passed as single entry arrays to facilitate returning values. This option can be specified only when LANGUAGE JAVA is specified. PARAMETER STYLE JAVA procedures do not support the DBINFO clause or the PROGRAM TYPE clause.

PROGRAM TYPE specifies whether the stored procedure will expect parameters in the style of a main routine or a subroutine. SUB specifies that the stored procedure will expect the parameters to be passed as separate arguments. MAIN specifies that the stored procedure will expect the parameters to be passed as an argument counter, and a vector of arguments (argc, argv). The name of the stored procedure to be invoked must also be *main*. Stored procedures of this type must be built in the same way that a shared library (rather than a standalone executable) is built.

NOT DETERMINISTIC or DETERMINISTIC specify whether the procedure will always return the same results for given argument values (DETERMINISTIC), or whether the procedure will depend on some state values that affect the results (NOT DETERMINISTIC).

CALLED ON NULL INPUT always applies to stored procedures, and means that the stored procedure is called even if some arguments are null.

NO DBINFO or DBINFO specify whether additional information will be passed to the stored procedure in a structure at invocation time. This information includes the following:

- The name of the currently connected database
- Application ID
- Application authorization ID
- Code page
- Version, release, and modification level of the database server invoking the stored procedure
- Server platform

The SQL-procedure-body clause specifies the SQL statement that is to be the body of the SQL procedure. Multiple SQL procedure statements can be specified within a compound statement.

CREATE SCHEMA

The CREATE SCHEMA statement defines a schema. It is also possible to create some objects and to grant privileges on those objects from within the CREATE SCHEMA statement.

An authorization ID that has SYSADM or DBADM authority can create a schema with any valid schema name or authorization name. An authorization ID that does not have SYSADM or DBADM authority can create a schema only with a schema name or authorization name that matches the authorization ID of the statement. If the statement includes any schema SQL statements, the authorization name (or the authorization ID of the statement) must have at least one of the following: SYSADM or DBADM authority; any privileges required to invoke the schema SQL statements.

Syntax

```
>>-CREATE SCHEMA-----------------------------------------------> 
>-----+-schema-name-------------------------------------+------->
      +-AUTHORIZATION--authorization-name--------------+
      '-schema-name--AUTHORIZATION--authorization-name--'
>-----+--------------------------------+----------------------->< 
      |   .----------------------.   |
      |   V                      |   |
      '----schema-SQL-statement---+--'
```

The specified schema name cannot begin with *SYS*. The owner of the schema is the authorization ID that issued the statement. AUTHORIZATION *authorization-name* specifies the user who owns the schema, and is also used to name the schema. The *schema-name* AUTHORIZATION *authorization-name* parameter specifies a schema called *schema-name*, with the user called *authorization-name* as the schema owner. This schema name also cannot begin with *SYS*.

The *schema-SQL-statement* parameter specifies SQL statements that can be included as part of the CREATE SCHEMA statement. These statements include the following: CREATE TABLE (excluding typed tables and summary tables); CREATE VIEW (excluding typed views); CREATE INDEX; COMMENT ON; and GRANT (Table, View, or Nickname privileges).

CREATE SEQUENCE

The CREATE SEQUENCE statement creates a sequence at the application server. The authorization ID of the statement must have at least one of the following: SYSADM or DBADM authority; CREATEIN privilege for the implicitly or explicitly specified schema.

Syntax

```
                                           .-AS INTEGER-----.
>>-CREATE SEQUENCE--sequence-name---*----+---------------+--*-->
                                           '-AS--data-type--'
>-----+-------------------------------+--*--------------------->
       '-START WITH--numeric-constant--'
       .-INCREMENT BY 1-----------------.
>-----+-------------------------------+--*------------------->
       '-INCREMENT BY--numeric-constant--'
                     (1)
       .-NO MINVALUE----------------.
>-----+-------------------------------+--*--------------------->
       '-MINVALUE--numeric-constant--'
       .-NO MAXVALUE----------------.              .-NO CYCLE--.
>-----+-------------------------------+--*----+-----------+--*---->
       '-MAXVALUE--numeric-constant--'         '-CYCLE-----'
       .-CACHE 20----------------.            .-NO ORDER--.
>-----+-------------------------------+--*----+-----------+--*------><
       +-CACHE--integer-constant--+         '-ORDER-----'
       '-NO CACHE----------------'
```

Syntax Note:

1. These parameters can be specified without spaces: NOMINVALUE, NOMAXVALUE, NOCYCLE, NOCACHE, and NOORDER.

The *sequence-name* parameter specifies the name of the new sequence. If the sequence name is explicitly qualified with a schema name, the schema name cannot begin with *SYS*. AS *data-type* specifies the data type that is to be used for the sequence value. The data type can be any exact numeric type (SMALLINT, INTEGER, BIGINT, or DECIMAL) with a scale of zero, or a user-defined distinct type for which the source type is an exact numeric type with a scale of zero. The default value is INTEGER.

START WITH *numeric-constant* specifies the first value for the sequence. This value can be any positive or negative value that could be assigned to a column of the data type associated with the sequence, without nonzero digits to the right of the decimal point. The default value is MINVALUE for ascending sequences, and MAXVALUE for descending sequences. INCREMENT BY *numeric-constant* specifies the interval between consecutive values of the sequence. If this value is negative, the sequence of values descends. If this value is positive, the sequence of values ascends. The default is 1.

MINVALUE specifies the minimum value at which a descending sequence either cycles or stops generating values, or the minimum value to which an ascending sequence cycles after reaching the maximum value. NO MINVALUE specifies that for an ascending sequence, the value is the START WITH value, or 1 if the START WITH clause is not specified. For a descending sequence, the value is the minimum value of the data type associated with the sequence. MAXVALUE specifies the maximum value at which an ascending sequence either cycles or stops generating values, or the maximum value to which a descending sequence cycles after reaching the minimum value. NO MAXVALUE specifies that for an ascending sequence, the value is the maximum value of the data type associated with the sequence. For a descending sequence, the value is the START WITH value, or –1 if the START WITH clause is not specified.

CYCLE or NOCYCLE specify whether the sequence should continue to generate values after reaching either its maximum or minimum value. If CYCLE has been specified, duplicate values can be generated for the sequence.

CACHE *integer-constant* specifies the maximum number of sequence values that are to be preallocated and kept in memory. Preallocating and storing values in the cache reduces synchronous I/O to the log when values are generated for the sequence. The minimum value is 2, and the default value is 20.

ORDER or NO ORDER specify whether the sequence numbers are to be generated in order of request.

CREATE SERVER

The CREATE SERVER statement defines a data source to a federated database. The term *server* here refers only to data sources in a federated system. It does not refer to the federated server in such a system, or to DRDA application servers.

The authorization ID of the statement must have SYSADM or DBADM authority on the federated database.

Syntax

```
>>-CREATE SERVER--server-name----+-------------------+--------->
                                 '-TYPE--server-type--'
>-----+---------------------------+---WRAPPER--wrapper-name-->
      '-VERSION--| server-version |--'
>-----+-------------------------------------------------------------------+>
      '-AUTHORIZATION--remote-authorization-name----+-------------------+--'
                                                    '-PASSWORD--password--'
```

```
            .-,-------------------------------------------------.
            V   .-ADD--.                                        |
>-----OPTIONS--(-----+------+---server-option-name--string-constant---+---)->
>--------------------------------------------------------------><
server-version
|---+-version--+------------------------+-+-----------------|
    |          '-.--release--+---------+--'  |
    |                        '-.--mod--'     |
    '-version-string-constant--------------'
```

The *server-name* parameter specifies the data source that is being defined to the federated database. TYPE *server-type* specifies a valid data source type. This option is required for the DRDA, SQLNET, and NET8 wrappers. VERSION specifies the version (version number, an integer; release number, an integer; and modification number, also an integer) of the data source. Alternatively, you can specify a *version-string-constant*, such as 8i or 8.0.3, for example. WRAPPER *wrapper-name* specifies the name of the wrapper that the federated server uses to interact with data sources of the specified type and version.

AUTHORIZATION *remote-authorization-name* specifies the authorization ID under which any necessary actions are to be performed at the data source when the CREATE SERVER statement is processed. PASSWORD *password* specifies the password that is associated with the authorization ID. If a password is not specified, the value defaults to the password that is associated with the ID with which the user is connected to the federated database.

The OPTIONS parameter indicates which server options are to be enabled for the specified data source. *Server options* are used to describe a server, and include these:

- *collating_sequence* Specifies whether the data source uses the same default collating sequence as the federated database, based on code set and country information. Valid values are 'Y' (same), 'N' (different), or 'I' (different and case-insensitive).

- *comm_rate* Specifies the communication rate between a federated server and its associated data sources. Expressed in megabytes per second (MBps) (only whole numbers). Valid values are greater than 0 and less than 2,147,483,648.

- *connectstring* Specifies initialization properties needed to connect to an OLE DB provider.

- *cpu_ratio* Indicates how much faster or slower a data source's CPU runs than the federated server's CPU. Valid values are greater than 0 and less than 1×10^{23}. Values may be expressed in any valid double notation, for example, 123E10, 123, or 1.21E4.

- *dbname* Name of the data source database that you want the federated server to access.

■ *fold_id*   Applies to user IDs that the federated server sends to data sources for authentication. Valid values are 'U' (folded to uppercase), 'N' (no action), or 'L' (folded to lowercase). If none of these settings is used, the federated server tries to send the user ID to the data source in uppercase. If the user ID fails, the server tries sending it in lowercase.

■ *fold_pw*   Applies to passwords that the federated server sends to data sources for authentication. Valid values are 'U' (folded to uppercase), 'N' (no action), or 'L' (folded to lowercase). If none of these settings is used, the federated server tries to send the password to the data source in uppercase. If the password fails, the server tries sending it in lowercase.

■ *io_ratio*   Indicates how much faster or slower a data source's I/O system runs than the federated server's I/O system. Valid values are greater than 0 and less than 1×10^{23}. Values may be expressed in any valid double notation, for example, 123E10, 123, or 1.21E4.

■ *node*   Name by which a data source is defined as an instance to its RDBMS. Required for all data sources. For a DB2 family data source, this name is the node specified in the federated database's DB2 node directory. To view this directory, issue the DB2 LIST NODE DIRECTORY command. For an Oracle data source, this name is the server name specified in the Oracle tnsnames.ora file. To access this name on the Windows NT platform, specify the View Configuration Information option of the Oracle SQL Net Easy Configuration tool.

■ *password*   Specifies whether passwords are sent to a data source. Valid values are 'Y' (always sent and validated), 'N' (neither sent nor validated), or 'ENCRYPTION' (sent in encrypted form and validated; valid only for DB2 family data sources that support encrypted passwords).

■ *plan_hints*   Specifies whether plan hints are to be enabled. Plan hints are statement fragments that provide extra information for data source optimizers. Valid values are 'Y' (if supported) or 'N'.

■ *pushdown*   Valid values are 'Y' (DB2 will consider letting the data source evaluate operations) or 'N'.

■ *varchar_no_trailing_blanks*   Specifies whether this data source uses nonblank padded VARCHAR comparison semantics. Valid values are 'Y' or 'N'.

CREATE TABLE

The CREATE TABLE statement defines a table.

The authorization ID of the statement must have at least one of the following: SYSADM or DBADM authority; CREATETAB privilege on the database, and USE privilege on the table space, as well as one of the following: IMPLICIT_SCHEMA privilege on the database, if an implicit or an explicit schema name of the table does not exist; or CREATEIN privilege on the schema, if the schema name of the table refers to an existing schema. If a subtable is being defined, the authorization ID must be the same as the definer of the root table of the table hierarchy.

To define a foreign key, the authorization ID of the statement must have one of the following on the parent table: REFERENCES privilege on the table; REFERENCES privilege on each column of the specified parent key; CONTROL privilege on the table; SYSADM or DBADM authority.

To define a summary table (using a fullselect), the authorization ID of the statement must have at least one of the following on each table or view identified in the fullselect: SELECT privilege on the table or view, and ALTER privilege if REFRESH DEFERRED or REFRESH IMMEDIATE is specified; CONTROL privilege on the table or view; SYSADM or DBADM authority.

Syntax

```
>>-CREATE-+----------+---TABLE-table-name-------------------->
          '-SUMMARY-'
>-----+-| element-list |----------------------------+-------->
      +-OF-type-name1-+------------------------+-+
      |               '-| typed-table-options |-' |
      +-| summary-table-definition |------------------+
      '-LIKE-+-table-name1-+---+------------------+-'
             +-view-name---+   '-| copy-options |-'
             '-nickname----'
         .-DATA CAPTURE NONE----.
>----*-+---------------------+-*---------------------------->
       '-DATA CAPTURE CHANGES-'
>-----+---------------------------------------------+-*------>
      '-IN-tablespace-name1-| tablespace-options |-'
>-----+-----------------------------------------------------+>
      |                     .-,---------.                   |
      |                     V           |     .-USING HASHING-. |
      +-PARTITIONING KEY-(-----column---+---)-+----------------+-+
      '-REPLICATED-----------------------------------------------'
>----*-+---------------------+---*-------------------------><
       '-NOT LOGGED INITIALLY-'


element-list

          .-,--------------------------------.
          V                                  |
|---(------+-| column-definition |------+-+---)---------------|
          +-| unique-constraint |------+
          +-| referential-constraint |-+
          '-| check-constraint |-------'
```

```
typed-table-options
|---+--------------------------+---+----------------------+-|
    +-HIERARCHY—hierarchy-name—+  '-| typed-element-list |-'
    '-| under-clause |-----------'

under-clause
|---UNDER—supertable-name—INHERIT SELECT PRIVILEGES-----------|

typed-element-list
        .-,------------------------------.
        V                                |
|---(------+-| OID-column-definition |-+-+---)-----------------|
          +-| with-options |----------+
          +-| unique-constraint |-----+
          '-| check-constraint |------'

summary-table-definition
|—+--------------------------+---AS—(—fullselect—)-| summary-table-options |—|
  |    .-,--------------.    |
  |    V               |    |
  '-(-----column-name---+---)—'

summary-table-options
|---+-DEFINITION ONLY—+-------------------+-+------------------|
   |                  '-| copy-options |—' |
   '-| refreshable-table-options |----------'

copy-options
|---*----+-------------------------------------------+-*---------->
        |                     .-COLUMN-.            |
        '-+-INCLUDING-+-+--------+—DEFAULTS---'
          '-EXCLUDING-'
                                  .-COLUMN ATTRIBUTES-.
     .-EXCLUDING IDENTITY—+-------------------+—.
>-----+-------------------------------------------+—*---------|
     |                     .-COLUMN ATTRIBUTES-.  |
     '-INCLUDING IDENTITY-+-------------------+---'

refreshable-table-options
|---DATA INITIALLY—DEFERRED—REFRESH—+-DEFERRED—+------------>
                                    '-IMMEDIATE-'
      .-ENABLE QUERY OPTIMIZATION—.
>-------+-----------------------------+-----------------------|
      '-DISABLE QUERY OPTIMIZATION-'

tablespace-options
|—+---------------------------------+---------------------->
```

```
                              (1)    |
        '-INDEX IN─tablespace-name2-------'
>-----+---------------------------+--------------------------|
        '-LONG IN─tablespace-name3─'

column-definition
|---column-name----+-------------------+--------------------->
                   |          (2)   |
                   '-| data-type |-------'
>-----+-------------------+--------------------------------|
        '-| column-options |─'

column-options
.--------------------------------------------------------------------------.
   V
|
|------+----------------------------------------------------------------+-+-|
+-NOT NULL----------------------------------------------------------+
        |           (3)                                             |
        +-| lob-options |--------------------------------------------------+
        |                (4)                                        |
        +-| datalink-options |--------------------------------------+
        |                          (5)                              |
        +-SCOPE─+-typed-table-name-+--------------------------------+
        |        '-typed-view-name─'                                |
        +-+--------------------------------+---+-+-PRIMARY KEY-+---------------+-+
        | |            (6)                 |   | | '-UNIQUE------'          | |
        | '-CONSTRAINT-------constraint-name-'   +-| references-clause |---------+ |
        |                                        '-CHECK─(─check-condition─)─' |
        |                          (7)                              |
        +-| column-default-spec |-----------------------------------+
        |                          (8)                              |
        '-INLINE LENGTH─integer-------------------------------------'

data-type
|─+-SMALLINT---------------------------------------------------------------+-|
  +-+-INTEGER-+-----------------------------------------------------------+
  | '-INT-----'                                                           |
  +-BIGINT----------------------------------------------------------------+
  +-+-FLOAT─+----------------+-+---------------------------------------------+
  | |        '-(─integer─)─' |                                             |
  | +-REAL---------------------+                                           |
  | |            .-PRECISION-.   |                                         |
  | '-DOUBLE-+------------+------'                                         |
  +─+-DECIMAL-+---+---------------------------+-----------------------------+
  | +-DEC-----+   '-(─integer─+-----------+───)─'                          |
```

```
|    +-NUMERIC-+                        '-,integer-'                              |
|    '-NUM-----'                                                                 |
+-+-+-CHARACTER-+---+-------------+---------------+---+---------------------+-+
| |   '-CHAR------'     '-(integer)-'             |   |   (9)             | |
| +-+-VARCHAR------------------+-(-integer-)-+    '-------FOR BIT DATA-' |
| |   '-+-CHARACTER-+---VARYING-'            |                            |
| |     '-CHAR------'                        |                            |
| '-LONG VARCHAR---------------------------'                             |
|                                                                         |
+-+-BLOB---+-(-integer-+---+---)------------------------------------------+
|  +-CLOB---+              +-K-+                                          |
|  '-DBCLOB-'              +-M-+                                          |
|                          '-G-'                                          |
+-GRAPHIC-+------------+--------------------------------------------------+
|          '-(integer)-'                                                   |
+-VARGRAPHIC-(integer)----------------------------------------------------+
+-LONG VARGRAPHIC---------------------------------------------------------+
+-DATE--------------------------------------------------------------------+
+-TIME--------------------------------------------------------------------+
+-TIMESTAMP---------------------------------------------------------------+
+-DATALINK-+----------------+---------------------------------------------+
|           '-(-integer-)-'                                               |
+-distinct-type-name------------------------------------------------------+
+-structured-type-name----------------------------------------------------+
'-REF-(type-name2)--------------------------------------------------------'


default-values
|-+-constant-----------------------------------------+-----|
  +-datetime-special-register-------------------------+
  +-USER----------------------------------------------+
  +-NULL----------------------------------------------+
  '-cast-function-(-+-constant-----------------+---)-'
                    +-datetime-special-register-+
                    '-USER---------------------'


lob-options
      .-LOGGED-----.        .-NOT COMPACT-.
|---*-+------------+---*-+--------------+---*----------------|
      '-NOT LOGGED-'        '-COMPACT------'


datalink-options
|---LINKTYPE URL------------------------------------------------>
     .-NO LINK CONTROL----------------------------.
>----+--------------------------------------------+----------|
     '-FILE LINK CONTROL-+-| file-link-options |-+-'
                          '-MODE DB2OPTIONS-------'
```

```
file-link-options
|---*—INTEGRITY----ALL----*—READ PERMISSION—+-FS-+----------->
                                            '-DB-'
>----*—WRITE PERMISSION—+-FS------+—*—RECOVERY—+-NO—+----->
                        '-BLOCKED-'            '-YES-'
>----*—ON UNLINK—+-RESTORE-+---*----------------------------|
                 '-DELETE—'


column-default-spec
|---+-| default-clause |------------------------------------------+-|
    '-GENERATED—+-ALWAYS-----+---AS-+-| identity-clause |----------+-'
                '-BY DEFAULT-'      '-(—generation-expression—)—'


identity-clause
|---IDENTITY—+-------------------------------------------------+-|
            |    .-,-----------------------------------.      |
            |    V                  .-1---------------. |      |
            '-(------+-START WITH—+-numeric-constant-+---+—+---)—'
                     |               .-1---------------. |
                     +-INCREMENT BY—+-numeric-constant-+-+
                     | .-CACHE—20---------------.        |
                     '-+-NO CACHE---------------+-------'
                       '-CACHE—integer-constant—'


references-clause
|—REFERENCES—table-name----+---------------------------+----->
                          |     .-,-------------.      |
                          |     V               |      |
                          '-(-----column-name---+---)-'
>-----| rule-clause |---------------------------------------|


rule-clause
      .-ON DELETE NO ACTION-----.      .-ON UPDATE NO ACTION—.
|—*—+------------------------+---*—+---------------------+---*—|
    '-ON DELETE—+-RESTRICT-+-'      '-ON UPDATE RESTRICT---'
                +-CASCADE—+
                '-SET NULL-'


default-clause
    .-WITH-.
|---+------+—DEFAULT—+-------------------+-----------------|
                    '-| default-values |—'


unique-constraint
|---+---------------------------+---+-UNIQUE------+---------->
    '-CONSTRAINT—constraint-name-'   '-PRIMARY KEY-'
      .-,-------------.
```

```
        V              |
>----(-----column-name---+---)---------------------------------|

referential-constraint
|---+----------------------------------+—FOREIGN KEY---------->
    |                              (10) |
    '-CONSTRAINT—constraint-name-------'
        .-,--------------.
        V                |
>----(-----column-name---+---)----| references-clause |---------|

check-constraint
|—+---------------------------+----------------------------->
  '-CONSTRAINT—constraint-name-'
>----CHECK—(—check-condition—)-------------------------------|

OID-column-definition
|---REF IS—OID-column-name—USER GENERATED--------------------|

with-options
|---column-name—WITH OPTIONS---| column-options |------------|
```

Syntax Notes:

1. Specifying which table space will contain a table's index can be done only when the table is created.

2. If the first column option chosen is a column-default-spec with a generation-expression, the data type can be omitted. It will be determined from the resulting data type of the generation-expression.

3. The lob-options clause applies only to large object types (BLOB, CLOB, and DBCLOB), and distinct types based on large object types.

4. The datalink-options clause applies only to the DATALINK type and distinct types based on the DATALINK type. The LINKTYPE URL clause is required

5. for these types.

6. The SCOPE clause applies only to the REF type.

7. For compatibility with version 1, the CONSTRAINT keyword can be omitted in a column definition defining a references clause.

8. IDENTITY column attributes are not supported in a DB2 Enterprise—Extended Edition (EEE) database with more than one partition.

9. INLINE LENGTH applies only to columns defined as structured types.

10. The FOR BIT DATA clause can be specified in random order with the other column constraints that follow.

11. For compatibility with version 1, *constraint-name* can be specified following FOREIGN KEY (without the CONSTRAINT keyword).

SUMMARY specifies that a summary table is to be created. If this keyword is specified, the statement must include a summary table definition. The table name must not have a schema name that is SYSIBM, SYSCAT, SYSFUN, or SYSSTAT.

OF *type-name1* specifies that the columns of the table are based on the attributes of a structured type identified by type-name1. If *type-name1* is specified without a schema name, the type name is resolved by searching schemas on the SQL path. The type name must be the name of an existing user-defined type, and it must be an instantiable structured type with at least one attribute.

HIERARCHY *hierarchy-name* specifies the hierarchy table that is associated with the table hierarchy. The data for all subtables in the typed table hierarchy is stored in the hierarchy table.

UNDER *supertable-name* specifies that the table is a subtable of *supertable-name*. The columns of the table include the object identifier column of the supertable with its type modified to be REF*(type-name1)*, followed by columns based on the attributes of *type-name1*. INHERIT SELECT PRIVILEGES specifies that any user or group holding the SELECT privilege on the supertable will be granted an equivalent privilege on the new subtable.

The element-list clause specifies column definitions and constraints on the table. The typed-element-list clause specifies additional elements for a typed table, including additional options for the columns, the addition of an object identifier column (root table only), and constraints on the table.

The summary-table-definition clause is specified if the table definition is based on the result of a query because the table will be a summary table that is based on the query. The column-name parameter specifies the columns in the table. If a list of column names is not specified, the columns of the summary table inherit the names of the columns in the result table of the fullselect. AS *(fullselect)* specifies the query on which the table is based. The summary-table-options clause specifies the attributes of the summary table.

DEFINITION ONLY specifies that the query is to be used only to define the table. The refreshable-table-options clause specifies the refreshable options of the summary table attributes.

DATA INITIALLY DEFERRED specifies that data is not to be inserted into the table as part of the CREATE TABLE operation. REFRESH DEFERRED specifies that the data in the table can be refreshed at any time using the REFRESH TABLE statement. REFRESH IMMEDIATE specifies that the changes made to the underlying tables as part of a DELETE, an INSERT, or an UPDATE operation are cascaded to the summary table.

ENABLE QUERY OPTIMIZATION specifies that the summary table can be used for query optimization under the appropriate circumstances. DISABLE QUERY

OPTIMIZATION specifies that the summary table will not be used for query optimization. The table can still be queried directly.

LIKE *table-name1* or *view-name* or *nickname* specifies that the columns of the table have exactly the same name and description as the columns of the specified table, view, or nickname. A typed table or typed view cannot be specified. The new table does not have any unique constraints, foreign key constraints, triggers, or indexes. Copy options specify whether to copy additional attributes of the source.

INCLUDING COLUMN DEFAULTS specifies that column default values for each updateable column in the source are to be copied. EXCLUDING COLUMN DEFAULTS specifies that column default values are not to be copied. INCLUDING IDENTITY COLUMN ATTRIBUTES specifies that identity column attributes (START WITH, INCREMENT BY, and CACHE values) are to be copied from the source, if possible. EXCLUDING IDENTITY COLUMN ATTRIBUTES specifies that identity column attributes are not to be copied.

The column-definition clause specifies the attributes of a column. The *column-name* parameter specifies the names for a column in the table. The *data-type* parameter specifies a valid data type. For a description of the data types that can be specified, see Chapter 16.

FOR BIT DATA specifies that the contents of the column are to be treated as bit (binary) data. During data exchange with other systems, code-page conversions are not performed. Comparisons are done in binary, regardless of the database collating sequence.

The *distinct-type-name* parameter specifies a user-defined type that is a distinct type. If a distinct type name is specified without a schema name, the distinct type name is resolved by searching schemas on the SQL path.

The *structured-type-name* parameter specifies a user-defined type that is a structured type. If a structured type name is specified without a schema name, the structured type name is also resolved by searching schemas on the SQL path.

REF *(type-name2)* specifies a reference to a typed table. If the type name is specified without a schema name, the type name is also resolved by searching schemas on the SQL path. The underlying data type of the column is based on the representation data type specified in the REF USING clause of the CREATE TYPE statement for *type-name2* or the root type of the data type hierarchy that includes *type-name2*.

The column-options clause specifies additional options related to table columns. NOT NULL specifies that a column cannot contain null values.

The lob-options clause specifies options for the LOB data types. LOGGED specifies that changes to the column are to be written to the recovery log. LOBs that are greater than 1GB cannot be logged. COMPACT specifies that values in the LOB column are to take up minimal disk space. Storing data in this way (without any extra insertion space) may have a performance impact during append operations on the column.

The datalink-options clause specifies options associated with the DATALINK data type. LINKTYPE URL specifies Uniform Resource Locator (URL) as the expected link type. NO LINK CONTROL specifies that there is to be no checking done to determine whether a file exists. Only the syntax of the URL is to be checked. FILE LINK CONTROL specifies that checking is to be done to determine whether a file exists.

REFERENCE

The file-link-options clause specifies the level of DB2 control of the file link. INTEGRITY ALL specifies that any file specified as a DATALINK value is under the control of DB2 and cannot be deleted or renamed using standard file system interfaces. READ PERMISSION FS specifies that read access permission is to be determined by the file system. Such files can be accessed without retrieving the filename from the column. READ PERMISSION DB specifies that read access permission is to be determined by the database. Access to such files will be allowed only after a valid file access token (returned on retrieval of the DATALINK value from the table) has been passed.

WRITE PERMISSION FS specifies that write access permission is to be determined by the file system. Such files can be accessed without retrieving the filename from the column. WRITE PERMISSION BLOCKED specifies that write access is to be blocked. The file will not be directly updateable through any interface. An alternative might be to copy the file, update the copy, and then to update the DATALINK value to point to the updated copy of the file.

RECOVERY YES specifies that DB2 is to support point-in-time recovery of files referenced by values in this column. This option can be specified only if INTEGRITY ALL and WRITE PERMISSION BLOCKED are also specified. RECOVERY NO specifies that point-in-time recovery is not to be supported.

ON UNLINK RESTORE specifies that when a file is unlinked, the DataLink File Manager is to attempt to return the file to its owner, with the permissions that existed when the file was linked. This option can be specified only if INTEGRITY ALL and WRITE PERMISSION BLOCKED are also specified. ON UNLINK DELETE specifies that the file is to be deleted when it is unlinked. This option can be specified only if READ PERMISSION DB and WRITE PERMISSION BLOCKED are also specified. MODE DB2OPTIONS specifies a set of default file link options (INTEGRITY ALL, READ PERMISSION FS, WRITE PERMISSION FS, and RECOVERY NO).

SCOPE specifies the scope of a reference type column. The *typed-table-name* parameter or the *typed-view-name* parameter specify the name of a typed table or a typed view. The data type of column-name must be REF(S), where S is the type of *typed-table-name* or *typed-view-name*.

CONSTRAINT *constraint-name* specifies a constraint. When used with a PRIMARY KEY or a UNIQUE constraint, *constraint-name* can be used to specify the name of an index that was created to support the constraint. PRIMARY KEY specifies a primary key composed of a single column. UNIQUE specifies a unique key composed of a single column. References-clause specifies a foreign key composed of a single column. CHECK (*check-condition*) specifies a check constraint that applies to a single column.

INLINE LENGTH integer specifies the largest structured type instance that can be stored inline with the rest of the column values in a row. Instances of a structured type that are larger than the specified inline length are stored separately from the base table row, in a manner that is similar to the way that LOB values are handled.

The default-clause specifies a default value for the column. DEFAULT specifies a default value that is to be used if a column value is not specified. The types of default values that can be specified include a constant, the value of a datetime special register (CURRENT DATE, CURRENT TIME, or CURRENT TIMESTAMP), the value of the

USER special register, NULL, and a cast function (if the column is defined as a distinct type, a BLOB, or a datetime data type).

GENERATED ALWAYS specifies that DB2 is to generate a value for the column whenever a row is inserted into the table. GENERATED BY DEFAULT specifies that DB2 is to generate a value for the column whenever a row is inserted into the table, *unless a value is specified.*

AS IDENTITY specifies that the column is to be the identity column for this table. START WITH *numeric-constant* specifies the first value for the identity column. The default value is 1. INCREMENT BY *numeric-constant* specifies the interval between consecutive values of the identity column. The default value is 1.

CACHE or NO CACHE specify whether some preallocated identity column values are to be kept in memory for faster access. The *integer-constant* parameter specifies how many values of the identity sequence are to be preallocated and kept in memory. Preallocating and storing values in the cache reduces logging when values are generated for the identity column. The minimum value is 2, and the maximum value is 32,767. The default value is 20.

AS *(generation-expression)* specifies that the definition of the column is to be based on an expression. The data type for the column is based on the result data type of the expression.

REF IS *OID-column-name* USER GENERATED specifies that an object identifier (OID) column is defined as the first column in the table. An OID is required for the root table of a table hierarchy. The table must be a typed table that is not a subtable. The column is defined with type REF(*type-name1*). The keywords USER GENERATED specify that an initial value for the OID column must be provided by the user when inserting a row. Once a row is inserted, the OID column cannot be updated. The with-options clause specifies additional options that apply to the columns of a typed table. WITH OPTIONS *column-options* specifies options for the specified column. If the table is a subtable, primary key or unique constraints cannot be specified.

DATA CAPTURE NONE specifies that no extra information for data replication is to be written to the log. This option is not supported when creating a subtable or a typed table. DATA CAPTURE CHANGES specifies that extra information about SQL changes to the table are to be written to the log. This option is required if the table will be replicated, and the Capture program will be used to capture changes to the table from the log.

IN *tablespace-name1* specifies the table space in which the table will be created. This clause cannot be specified when creating a subtable because the table space is inherited from the root table of the table hierarchy. INDEX IN *tablespace-name2* specifies the table space in which any indexes on the table will be created. This option is valid only for DMS table spaces. LONG IN *tablespace-name3* specifies the table space in which the values will be stored of any long columns (LONG VARCHAR, LONG VARGRAPHIC, LOB data types, distinct types with any of these as source types, or any columns defined with user-defined structured types with values that cannot be stored inline). This option is valid only for DMS table spaces.

PARTITIONING KEY *(column-name,...)* specifies the partitioning key that is to be used when data in the table is partitioned. No column can be used as part of a partitioning key with a data type of LONG VARCHAR, LONG VARGRAPHIC, BLOB, CLOB, DBCLOB, or DATALINK, or a distinct type based on any of these types or a structured type. A partitioning key cannot be specified for a table that is a subtable because the partitioning key is inherited from the root table in the table hierarchy.

USING HASHING specifies that a hashing function is to be used as the partitioning method for data distribution. This is the only supported partitioning method.

REPLICATED specifies that the data stored in the table is to be physically replicated on each database partition of the nodegroup in the table space for which the table is defined. This means that a copy of all the data in the table will exist on each database partition. This option can be specified only for a summary table.

NOT LOGGED INITIALLY specifies that any changes made to the table by an insert, delete, update, create index, drop index, or alter table operation in the same unit of work in which the table is created are not to be logged.

The unique-constraint clause specifies a unique or primary key constraint. If the table has a partitioning key, any unique or primary key must be a superset of the partitioning key. A unique or primary key constraint cannot be specified for a table that is a subtable. If the table is a root table, the constraint applies to the table and all its subtables.

CONSTRAINT *constraint-name* specifies a name for the primary key or the unique constraint. UNIQUE *(column-name,...)* specifies a unique key composed of the identified columns. PRIMARY KEY *(column-name,...)* specifies a primary key composed of the identified columns. No LOB, LONG VARCHAR, LONG VARGRAPHIC, or DATALINK type, or distinct type based on one of these types, or structured type, can be used as part of a unique key or a primary key. A unique constraint or a primary key cannot be specified if the table is a subtable because unique constraints are inherited from the supertable. Only one primary key can be defined on a table.

The referential-constraint clause specifies a referential constraint. CONSTRAINT *constraint-name* specifies a name for the referential constraint. FOREIGN KEY *(column-name,...)* specifies a foreign key composed of the identified columns. The references-clause specifies the parent table and the parent key for the referential constraint. REFERENCES *table-name* specifies a base table that is described in the catalog but is not a catalog table. The *(column-name,...)* parameter specifies the parent key of the referential constraint.

The rule-clause specifies an action that is to be taken against dependent tables. ON DELETE specifies an action that is to be taken when a row of a parent table (a table that has dependents) is deleted. If NO ACTION or RESTRICT is specified, an error is returned, and no rows are deleted. If CASCADE is specified, the delete operation is propagated to the dependents. If SET NULL is specified, each nullable column of the foreign key in each dependent table is set to null. ON UPDATE specifies an action that is to be taken when a row of a parent table is updated. Valid options are NO ACTION or RESTRICT.

The check-constraint clause specifies a check constraint, a search condition that must evaluate to *not false*. CONSTRAINT *constraint-name* specifies a name for the check constraint. CHECK *(check-condition)* specifies a check constraint. Because check constraints are not checked for inconsistencies and duplicate or equivalent conditions, contradictory or redundant check constraints can exist, resulting in possible errors at run time. Check constraints are enforced when rows are inserted or updated. A check constraint that is defined on a table automatically applies to all subtables of that table.

CREATE TABLESPACE

The CREATE TABLESPACE statement creates a new table space within the database, assigns containers to the table space, and records the table space definition and attributes in the catalog. The authorization ID of the statement must have SYSADM or SYSCTRL authority.

Syntax

```
                    .-REGULAR-----------------.
>>-CREATE----+-------------------------------+----------------------->
             +-LONG--------------------+
             | .-SYSTEM--.             |
             '-+---------+---TEMPORARY--'
               '-USER----'
>----TABLESPACE--tablespace-name------------------------------------->
>-----+-------------------------------------+----------------------->
      |       .-NODEGROUP-.                 |
      '-IN-+-----------+--nodegroup-name--'
      .-PAGESIZE--4096------------.
>-----+-------------------------------+----------------------------->
      '-PAGESIZE--integer--+----+-'
                           '-K--'
>----MANAGED BY--+-SYSTEM--| system-containers |------+--------->
                 '-DATABASE--| database-containers |--'
>-----+-------------------------------------+---------------------->
      '-EXTENTSIZE--+-number-of-pages-+--'
                    '-integer--+-K-+--'
                               +-M-+
                               '-G-'
>-----+-------------------------------------+-------------------->
      '-PREFETCHSIZE--+-number-of-pages-+--'
                      '-integer--+-K-+--'
                                 +-M-+
                                 '-G-'
>-----+-------------------------------------+------------------->
      '-BUFFERPOOL--bufferpool-name--'
>-----+-------------------------------------+----------------->
      |              .-24.1-----------------.  |
      '-OVERHEAD--+-number-of-milliseconds-+--'
```

```
>-----+---------------------------------------------+-------------->
      |                   .-0.9-------------------.  |
      '-TRANSFERRATE--+-number-of-milliseconds-+--'
>-----+---------------------------------------------+-------------->< 
      '-DROPPED TABLE RECOVERY--+-ON--+--'
                                '-OFF-'
system-containers
   .---------------------------------------------------------------------.
   |                  .-,-----------------------.                        |
   V                  V                         |                        |
|-----USING--(-----'--container-string--'---+---)----+---------------------+--+-->
                                                     '-| on-nodes-clause |--'
>-----------------------------------------------------------|
database-containers
   .------------------------------------------------------------.
   V                                                            |
|------USING--| container-clause |--+---------------------+--+-|
                                    '-| on-nodes-clause |--'
container-clause
      .-,---------------------------------------------------------.
      V                                                           |
|---(------+-FILE---+--'--container-string--'----+-number-of-pages+--+---)-->
           '-DEVICE-'                            '-integer--+-K-+--'
                                                            +-M-+
                                                            '-G-'
>-----------------------------------------------------------|
on-nodes-clause
|---ON----+-NODE--+--(------------------------------------------->
          '-NODES-'
      .-,------------------------------------.
      V                                      |
>--------node-number1--+-------------------+--+--)------------|
                       '-TO--node-number2---'
```

Use this statement to create table spaces for storing regular data, *long field* (or LOB) data, *system temporary tables* (work areas used by the database manager to perform operations such as sorts or joins), or declared global temporary tables. The table space name must not begin with the characters *SYS*. The only nodegroup that can be specified when creating a SYSTEM TEMPORARY table space is IBMTEMPGROUP. If a nodegroup is not specified, the default nodegroup IBMDEFAULTGROUP is used for REGULAR, LONG, and USER TEMPORARY table spaces; the default nodegroup IBMTEMPGROUP is used for SYSTEM TEMPORARY table spaces.

PAGESIZE *integer* [K] specifies the page size that is to be used for the table space. Valid values for *integer* without the suffix K are 4096, 8192, 16,384, or 32,768; valid values *with* the suffix K are 4, 8, 16, or 32.

MANAGED BY SYSTEM specifies that the table space is to be an SMS table space. USING (*'container-string'*,...) specifies one or more containers that will belong to the SMS table space, and in which the table space data will be stored; the container string cannot be longer than 240 bytes. Each container string can be an absolute or a relative directory name; the directory name, if not absolute, is relative to the database directory. If any component of the directory name does not exist, it is created by the database manager. If a table space is dropped, all components created by the database manager are deleted. If the directory identified by *container-string* exists, it must not contain any files or subdirectories.

The format of *container-string* depends on the operating system. For example, a Windows NT/2000 directory path begins with a drive letter and a colon; on UNIX-based systems, a path begins with a slash (/). In a partitioned database system, the on-nodes-clause specifies one or more partitions on which the containers are to be created.

MANAGED BY DATABASE specifies that the table space is to be a DMS table space. (FILE | DEVICE *'container-string' number-of-pages*,...) specifies one or more containers that will belong to the DMS table space, and in which the table space data will be stored. A mixture of FILE and DEVICE containers can be specified; the container string cannot be longer than 254 bytes. For a FILE container, the container string can be an absolute or a relative filename; the filename, if not absolute, is relative to the database directory. If any component of the directory name does not exist, it is created by the database manager.

If the file does not exist, it is created and initialized to the specified size. If a table space is dropped, all components created by the database manager are deleted. For a DEVICE container, the container string must be the name of an existing device. A container can belong to only one table space. Although containers can differ in size, optimal performance is achieved when all containers are the same size. The format of *container-string* depends on the operating system.

EXTENTSIZE *number-of-pages* specifies the number of pages that will be written to a container before moving to the next container. The default extent size is the value of the *dft_extent_sz* configuration parameter.

PREFETCHSIZE number-of-pages specifies the number of pages that will be read from the table space when data prefetching is being performed. *Prefetching* reads data before it is referenced by a query so that the query is minimally impacted by I/O performance. The default prefetch size is the value of the *dft_prefetch_sz* configuration parameter.

BUFFERPOOL *bufferpool-name* specifies the buffer pool that is to be used for tables in this table space. If not specified, the default buffer pool IBMDEFAULTBP is used. The buffer pool page size must match the table space page size.

OVERHEAD *number-of-milliseconds* specifies the I/O controller overhead and disk seek and latency time. The value (any numeric literal: integer, decimal, or floating point) is used to determine the cost of I/O during query optimization. If it is not the same for all containers, the number should be the average for all containers that belong to the table space.

TRANSFERRATE *number-of-milliseconds* specifies the time to read one page into memory. The value (any numeric literal: integer, decimal, or floating point) is also used to determine the cost of I/O during query optimization. If it is not the same for all containers, the number should be the average for all containers that belong to the table space.

DROPPED TABLE RECOVERY enables a REGULAR table space for dropped table recovery. Dropped tables in the specified table space can be recovered using the RECOVER TABLE ON option of the ROLLFORWARD DATABASE command.

CREATE TRANSFORM

The CREATE TRANSFORM statement defines transformation functions, identified by a group name, that are used to exchange structured type values with host language programs and with external functions and methods. The authorization ID of the statement must have at least one of the following: SYSADM or DBADM authority; definer of the type identified by *type-name*, and definer of every specified function.

Syntax

```
>>-CREATE--+-TRANSFORM--+---FOR--type-name-------------------->
           '-TRANSFORMS-'

       .----------------------------------------------------------------.
       |                .-,------------------------------------------.    |
       V                V                                    (1)  |     |
>---------group-name--(------+-TO SQL---+---WITH--| function-specification |--------+---)---+>
                            '-FROM SQL-'

>------------------------------------------------------------><

function-specification
|---+-FUNCTION--function-name--+--------------------------------+-+->
    |                          '-(--+-------------------+---)--' |
    |                              |  .-,-----------.  |        |
    |                              |  V             |  |        |
    |                              '----data-type---+--'        |
    '-SPECIFIC FUNCTION--specific-name-------------------------'

>------------------------------------------------------------|
```

Syntax Note:

1. The same clause must not be specified more than once.

TRANSFORM or TRANSFORMS specify that one or more transform groups is being defined. FOR *type-name* specifies the user-defined structured type for which the transform group is being defined. In dynamic SQL statements, the CURRENT SCHEMA special register is used as a qualifier for an unqualified type name. In static SQL statements, the QUALIFIER precompile/bind option implicitly specifies the qualifier for an unqualified type name. The *type-name* parameter must specify the name of an existing user-defined type, and it must be a structured type.

The *group-name* parameter specifies the transform group containing the TO SQL and FROM SQL functions. A group name must be an SQL identifier with a maximum length of 18 characters; it cannot begin with the prefix *SYS*. TO SQL specifies the function that is to be used to transform a value to the SQL user-defined structured type format. All of the parameters in the function must be of built-in data types, and the returned type is *type-name*. FROM SQL specifies the function that is to be used to transform a value to a built-in data type value representing the SQL user-defined structured type. The function must have one parameter of data type *type-name*, and return a built-in data type (or a set of built-in data types).

WITH *function-specification* specifies a function instance: If FROM SQL is specified, *function-specification* must identify a function that satisfies the following requirements:

■ There is one parameter of type *type-name*.

■ The return type is a built-in type, or a row whose columns all have built-in types.

■ The signature specifies either LANGUAGE SQL or the use of another FROM SQL transform function that has LANGUAGE SQL.

If TO SQL is specified, *function-specification* must identify a function that satisfies the following requirements:

■ All parameters have built-in types.

■ The return type is *type-name*.

■ The signature specifies either LANGUAGE SQL or the use of another TO SQL transform function that has LANGUAGE SQL.

FUNCTION *function-name* specifies the function. In dynamic SQL statements, the CURRENT SCHEMA special register is used as a qualifier for an unqualified object name. In static SQL statements, the QUALIFIER precompile/bind option implicitly specifies the qualifier for an unqualified object name. The (*data-type*,...) parameter specifies data types that must match the types specified in the CREATE FUNCTION statement. If an unqualified data type is specified, the type name is resolved by searching schemas on the SQL path. It is not necessary to specify length, precision, or scale for parameterized data types; instead, empty parentheses can be coded to indicate that these attributes should be ignored when looking for a data type match.

SPECIFIC FUNCTION *specific-name* specifies a user-defined function, using a specific name defined when the function was created. The specific name must identify a specific function instance in the named or implied schema.

Example

Create two transform groups that associate the user-defined structured type POLYGON with a transform function customized for C, and one specialized for Java.

```
CREATE TRANSFORM FOR POLYGON
   mystruct1 (FROM SQL WITH FUNCTION myxform_sqlstruct,
```

```
                    TO SQL WITH FUNCTION myxform_structsql)
    myjava1     (FROM SQL WITH FUNCTION myxform_sqljava,
                    TO SQL WITH FUNCTION myxform_javasql)
```

CREATE TRIGGER

The CREATE TRIGGER statement defines a trigger in the database.

The authorization ID of the statement that creates the trigger must have at least one of the following: SYSADM or DBADM authority; ALTER privilege on the table on which the trigger is defined, or ALTERIN privilege on the schema of the table on which the trigger is defined, and IMPLICIT_SCHEMA authority on the database, if the implicit or explicit schema name of the trigger does not exist; CREATEIN privilege on the schema, if the schema name of the trigger refers to an existing schema.

If the authorization ID of the statement does not have SYSADM or DBADM authority, the privileges that the authorization ID of the statement holds (without considering PUBLIC or group privileges) must include all of the following, as long as the trigger exists: SELECT privilege on the table on which the trigger is defined, if any transition variables or tables are specified; SELECT privilege on any table or view that is referenced in the triggered action; any privileges that are required to invoke the triggered SQL statements.

Syntax

```
>>-CREATE TRIGGER--trigger-name----+-NO CASCADE BEFORE-+-------->
                                    '-AFTER------------'
>-----+-INSERT---------------------------------+--ON--table-name---->
      +-DELETE----------------------------+
      '-UPDATE--+-----------------------+-'
                |    .-,------------.   |
                |    V              |   |
                '-OF----column-name---+--'
>-----+-----------------------------------------------------------------+>
      |        .----------------------------------------------------.
      |                                                              |
      |           V   (1)   (2)          .-AS-.                      |
      '-REFERENCING------------------+-OLD--+----+--correlation-name--+--+-'
                                     |    .-AS-.                      |
                                     +-NEW-+----+--correlation-name---+
                                     |           .-AS-.               |
                                     +-OLD_TABLE-+----+--identifier---+
                                     |           .-AS-.               |
                                     '-NEW_TABLE-+----+--identifier---'
```

```
>-----+-FOR EACH ROW---------------+--MODE DB2SQL--------------->
      |  (3)                        |
      '--------FOR EACH STATEMENT--'
>-----| triggered-action |------------------------------------><
triggered-action
|--+----------------------------+--SQL-procedure-statement---|
   '-WHEN--(--search-condition--)--'
```

Syntax Notes:

1. OLD and NEW may each be specified only once.

2. OLD_TABLE and NEW_TABLE may each be specified only once, and only for AFTER triggers.

3. FOR EACH STATEMENT may not be specified for BEFORE triggers.

The *trigger-name* parameter specifies a name for the new trigger. The name, including the implicit or explicit schema name, must not identify a trigger that is already described in the catalog. If a two-part name is specified, the schema name cannot begin with *SYS*.

NO CASCADE BEFORE specifies that the triggered action is to be applied *before* any updates to the subject table are applied to the database. It also specifies that the triggered action is not to activate other triggers. AFTER specifies that the triggered action is to be applied *after* any updates to the subject table are applied to the database. INSERT, DELETE, or UPDATE specify that the triggered action is to be executed whenever a corresponding operation is applied to the base table. In the case of UPDATE, if one or more column names is not specified, the trigger is activated whenever *any* column in the table is updated. ON *table-name* must not specify a catalog table, a summary table, a declared temporary table, or a nickname.

REFERENCING specifies correlation names for transition variables and table names for transition tables. Correlation names identify a specific row in the set of rows affected by the triggering SQL operation. Table names identify the complete set of affected rows. Each row affected by the triggering SQL operation is made available to the triggered action by qualifying columns with specified correlation names.

OLD AS *correlation-name* specifies a correlation name that identifies the row state *prior* to the triggering SQL operation. NEW AS *correlation-name* specifies a correlation name that identifies the row state as modified by the triggering SQL operation and by any SET statement in a BEFORE trigger that has already executed.

The complete set of rows affected by the triggering SQL operation is available to the triggered action by specifying a temporary table name. OLD_TABLE AS *identifier* specifies a temporary table that identifies the set of affected rows *prior* to the triggering SQL operation. NEW_TABLE AS identifier specifies a temporary table that identifies the affected rows as modified by the triggering SQL operation and by any SET statement in a BEFORE trigger that has already executed.

FOR EACH ROW specifies that the triggered action is to be applied once for each row of the subject table that is affected by the triggering SQL operation. FOR EACH STATEMENT specifies that the triggered action is to be applied only once for the whole statement. This degree of granularity cannot be specified in a BEFORE trigger. MODE DB2SQL is currently the only supported trigger mode.

The triggered-action clause specifies the action that is to be performed when a trigger is activated. A triggered action is composed of an *SQL-procedure-statement* and an optional condition for the execution of the *SQL-procedure-statement*.

WHEN (*search-condition*) specifies a condition that is true, false, or unknown. The search condition determines whether a certain triggered action should be executed. The associated action is performed only if the specified search condition evaluates as true. If the WHEN clause is omitted, the associated *SQL-procedure statement* is always performed. The *SQL-procedure-statement* can contain a dynamic compound statement or any of the SQL control statements listed in the description of the Compound Statement (Dynamic).

If the trigger is a BEFORE trigger, an *SQL-procedure-statement* can also include a fullselect or a SET variable statement. If the trigger is an AFTER trigger, an *SQL-procedure-statement* can also include one of the following: an INSERT statement, a searched UPDATE statement, a searched DELETE statement, a SET variable statement, or a fullselect.

Example

Create a trigger that ensures that whenever a parts record is updated, the following check and (if necessary) action is taken: If the onhand quantity is less than 10 percent of the maximum stocked quantity, issue a shipping request ordering the number of items for the affected part to be equal to the maximum stocked quantity minus the onhand quantity. ISSUE_SHIP_REQUEST is a user-defined function that sends an order form for additional parts to the appropriate company.

```
CREATE TRIGGER REORDER
    AFTER UPDATE OF ON_HAND, MAX_STOCKED ON PARTS
    REFERENCING NEW AS N
    FOR EACH ROW MODE DB2SQL
    WHEN (N.ON_HAND < 0.10 * N.MAX_STOCKED)
    BEGIN ATOMIC
    VALUES(ISSUE_SHIP_REQUEST(N.MAX_STOCKED - N.ON_HAND, N.PARTNO));
    END
```

CREATE TYPE (Structured)

The CREATE TYPE statement defines a user-defined structured type. A user-defined structured type can include zero or more attributes. A structured type may be a subtype allowing attributes to be inherited from a supertype. Successful execution of the statement generates methods for retrieving and updating values of attributes, and also generates functions for constructing instances of a structured type used in a column, for casting between the reference type and its representation type, and for supporting the comparison operators (=, <>, <, <=, >, and >=) on the reference type. The CREATE TYPE statement also defines any method specifications for user-defined methods to be used with the user-defined structured type.

The authorization ID of the statement must have at least one of the following: SYSADM or DBADM authority; IMPLICIT_SCHEMA authority on the database, if the schema name of the type does not refer to an existing schema; CREATEIN privilege on the schema, if the schema name of the type refers to an existing schema. If UNDER is specified, and the authorization ID of the statement is not the same as the definer of the root type of the type hierarchy, SYSADM or DBADM authority is required.

Syntax

```
>>-CREATE TYPE--type-name----+-------------------------+-------->
                             '-UNDER--supertype-name---'
>-----+-----------------------------------------------+--*-------->
      |          .-,-------------------------.         |
      |          V                           |         |
      '-AS--(-----| attribute-definition |---+---)--'
      .-INSTANTIABLE-----.
>-----+------------------+--*---+-------------------------+--*--->
      '-NOT INSTANTIABLE-'      '-INLINE LENGTH--integer--'
      .-WITHOUT COMPARISONS-.        .-NOT FINAL-.
>----+----------------------+---*---+-----------+---*----------->
>----MODE DB2SQL---*----+----------------------+--*------------->
                        '-WITH FUNCTION ACCESS--'
>-----+-----------------------------------+-------------------->
      '-REF USING--| rep-type |--'
>----*--+----------------------------------------+--*----------->
        '-CAST (SOURCE AS REF) WITH--funcname1--'
>-----+----------------------------------------+--*------------->
      '-CAST (REF AS SOURCE) WITH--funcname2---'
>-----+----------------------------------------+-------------->< 
      |  .-,-----------------------.  |
      |  V                         |  |
      '----| method-specification |---+--'
attribute-definition
|---attribute-name--| data-type |----+-----------------------+---|
                                     +-| lob-options |------+
                                     '-| datalink-options |-'
rep-type
|---+-SMALLINT------------------------------------------------------+->
    +-+-INTEGER-+--------------------------------------------------+
    | '-INT-----'                                                  |
```

```
  +-BIGINT--------------------------------------------------------------------+
  +--+-DECIMAL-+---+------------------------------------+----------------------+
  |  +-DEC-----+   '-(--integer--+------------+---)--'   |
  |  +-NUMERIC-+                  '-,--integer--'        |
  |  '-NUM-----'                                         |
  +--+--+-CHARACTER-+---+------------+---------------+---+----------------------+-+
  |  |  '-CHAR------'   '-(integer)--'               |   |  (1)                 | |
  |  '--+-VARCHAR-------------------+--(--integer--)--'   '-------FOR BIT DATA--' |
  |     '--+-CHARACTER-+---VARYING--'                                            |
  |        '-CHAR------'                                                         |
  |                                                                             |
  +-GRAPHIC--+------------+-----------------------------------------------------+
  |          '-(integer)--'                                                     |
  '-VARGRAPHIC--(--integer--)---------------------------------------------------'
>------------------------------------------------------------------|

method-specification
|---METHOD--method-name----------------------------------->
>----(--+------------------------------------------------------------+---)->
        |  .-,---------------------------------------------.   |   |
        |  V                                               |   |   |
        '----+-----------------+---data-type2--+------------+--+--'
             '-parameter-name--'               '-AS LOCATOR--'
>----*---RETURNS------------------------------------------->
>-----+-data-type3--+------------+----------------------+---->
      |              '-AS LOCATOR--'                     |
      '-data-type4--CAST FROM--data-type5--+------------+-'
                                           '-AS LOCATOR--'
>----*----+-----------------------------+--*---------------------->
          '-SPECIFIC--specific-name--'
>-----+----------------------------+--*-------------------------->
      '-SELF AS RESULT--'
      .-| SQL-routine-characteristics |-------.
>-----+---------------------------------------+--*--------------|
      '-| external-routine-characteristics |--'
SQL-routine-characteristics
        .-LANGUAGE SQL-.          .-NOT DETERMINISTIC--.
|---*---+--------------+---*----+--------------------+--*------->
                               '-DETERMINISTIC------'
     .-NO EXTERNAL ACTION--.       .-READS SQL DATA--.
>-----+--------------------+--*----+-----------------+--*------->
      '-EXTERNAL ACTION-----'       '-CONTAINS SQL----'
     .-CALLED ON NULL INPUT--.
>-----+---------------------+--*--------------------------|
external-routine-characteristics
|---*---LANGUAGE--+-C----+--*---PARAMETER STYLE--+-DB2SQL-----+-->
                  +-JAVA-+                        '-DB2GENERAL-'
                  '-OLE--'
        .-NOT DETERMINISTIC--.        .-FENCED-----.
>----*----+-------------------+--*----+------------+--*-------->
```

```
      |              (2)  |        '-NOT FENCED-'
         '-DETERMINISTIC------'
      .-CALLED ON NULL INPUT-----------.
>-----+-------------------------------+--*---NO SQL---*------->
      |                       (3)  |
      '-RETURNS NULL ON NULL INPUT------'
      .-NO EXTERNAL ACTION--.        .-NO SCRATCHPAD----------.
>-----+--------------------+--*----+----------------------+-->
      '-EXTERNAL ACTION-----'       |            .-100----. |
                                    '-SCRATCHPAD--+--------+-'
                                                  '-length-'
        .-NO FINAL CALL--.        .-ALLOW PARALLEL----.
>----*----+---------------+--*----+-------------------+--*----->
        '-FINAL CALL-----'        '-DISALLOW PARALLEL-'
      .-NO DBINFO--.
>-----+------------+--*-------------------------------------|
      '-DBINFO-----'
```

Syntax Notes:

1. The FOR BIT DATA clause can be specified in random order with the other column constraints that follow.

2. NOT VARIANT can be specified in place of DETERMINISTIC, and VARIANT can be specified in place of NOT DETERMINISTIC.

3. NULL CALL can be specified in place of CALLED ON NULL INPUT, and NOT NULL CALL can be specified in place of RETURNS NULL ON NULL INPUT.

The *type-name* parameter specifies the name of the type that is to be created. The schema name (implicit or explicit) must not be greater than eight bytes. Certain keywords in predicates cannot be used as type names, including SOME, ANY, ALL, NOT, AND, OR, BETWEEN, NULL, LIKE, EXISTS, IN, UNIQUE, OVERLAPS, SIMILAR, or MATCH. Comparison operators cannot be used as type names, and if a two-part type name is specified, the schema name cannot begin with *SYS*. UNDER *supertype-name* specifies that this structured type is a subtype under the specified supertype name. The supertype name must identify an existing structured type. If a supertype name is specified without a schema name, the type is resolved by searching schemas on the SQL path.

The attribute-definition clause defines the attributes of the structured type. The specified attribute name cannot be the same as any other attribute of this structured type or any supertype of this structured type. Certain keywords in predicates cannot be used as attribute names, including SOME, ANY, ALL, NOT, AND, OR, BETWEEN, NULL, LIKE, EXISTS, IN, UNIQUE, OVERLAPS, SIMILAR, or MATCH. Comparison operators cannot be used as attribute names.

The data type of the attribute is one of the data types listed in the description of the CREATE TABLE statement, except for LONG VARCHAR, LONG VARGRAPHIC, and a distinct type based on LONG VARCHAR or LONG VARGRAPHIC. If *data-type* is specified without a schema name, the type is resolved by searching schemas on the SQL path. If the attribute data type is a reference type, the target type of the reference must be a structured type that exists or that is created by this statement.

The lob-options clause specifies the options that are associated with LOB types (or distinct types that are based on LOB types). For a description of lob-options, see the CREATE TABLE statement.

The datalink-options clause specifies the options that are associated with the DATALINK type (or distinct types that are based on the DATALINK type). For a description of datalink-options, see the CREATE TABLE statement.

INSTANTIABLE or NOT INSTANTIABLE specify whether an instance of the structured type can be created.

INLINE LENGTH *integer* specifies the largest structured type instance that can be stored inline with the rest of the column values in a row. Instances of a structured type (or its subtypes) that are larger than the specified inline length are stored separately from the base table row, in a manner that is similar to how LOB values are handled.

WITHOUT COMPARISONS specifies that there is no support for comparison functions for instances of the structured type. NOT FINAL specifies that the structured type can be used as a supertype. MODE DB2SQL is a required clause that allows for direct invocation of the constructor function on this type. WITH FUNCTION ACCESS specifies that all methods of this type and of its subtypes, including methods created in the future, can be accessed using functional notation. This clause can be specified only for the root type of a structured type hierarchy.

REF USING *rep-type* specifies the built-in data type that is to be used as the representation (underlying data type) for the reference type of this structured type and all of its subtypes. This clause can be specified only for the root type of a structured type hierarchy. The *rep-type* cannot be LONG VARCHAR, LONG VARGRAPHIC, BLOB, CLOB, DBCLOB, DATALINK, or a structured type. Its length must be less than or equal to 255 bytes. If this clause is not specified for the root type of a structured type hierarchy, REF USING VARCHAR(16) FOR BIT DATA is assumed.

CAST (SOURCE AS REF) WITH *funcname1* specifies the name of the system-generated function that casts a value with *data type rep-type* to the reference type of this structured type. A schema name must not be specified as part of *funcname1*. The cast function is created in the same schema as the structured type. If the clause is not specified, the default value for *funcname1* is *type-name* (the name of the structured type). A function signature matching *funcname1(rep-type)* must not already exist in the same schema.

CAST (REF AS SOURCE) WITH *funcname2* specifies the name of the system-generated function that casts a reference type value for this structured type to data type *rep-type*. A schema name must not be specified as part of *funcname2*. The cast function is created in the same schema as the structured type. If the clause is not specified, the default value for *funcname2* is *rep-type* (the name of the representation type).

The method-specification clause defines the methods for this type. A method cannot actually be used until it is given a body through the CREATE METHOD statement. The *method-name* parameter must specify an unqualified SQL identifier. The method name is implicitly qualified with the schema used for the CREATE TYPE statement. Certain keywords in predicates cannot be used as method names, including SOME, ANY, ALL, NOT, AND, OR, BETWEEN, NULL, LIKE, EXISTS, IN, UNIQUE, OVERLAPS, SIMILAR, or MATCH. Comparison operators cannot be used as method names. In general, the same name can be used for more than one method if there is some difference in their signatures.

The parameter name cannot be SELF, which is the name for the implicit subject parameter of a method. If the method is an SQL method, all of its parameters must have names. The *data-type2* parameter specifies the data type of each parameter. One entry in the list must be specified for each parameter that the method expects to receive. No more than 90 parameters are allowed, including the implicit SELF parameter.

The AS LOCATOR clause can be used for LOB types or distinct types that are based on a LOB type to specify that a LOB locator is to be passed *to* the method, instead of the actual value. RETURNS is a mandatory clause that identifies the method's result.

The *data-type3* parameter specifies the data type of the method's result. The AS LOCATOR clause can be used for LOB types or distinct types that are based on a LOB type to specify that a LOB locator is to be passed *from* the method, instead of the actual value.

The *data-type4* CAST FROM *data-type5* clause specifies the data type of the method's result, and it is used to return a different data type than the type returned by the method.

SPECIFIC *specific-name* specifies a unique name for the instance of the method that is being defined. This specific name can be used when creating the method body or dropping the method. It can never be used to invoke the method. The unqualified form of *specific-name* is an SQL identifier with a maximum length of 18 bytes. The specific name can be the same as an existing method name. If *specific-name* is not specified, a unique name is generated by the database manager. The unique name is SQL followed by a time stamp: SQL*yymmddhhmmssxxx*.

SELF AS RESULT specifies that this method is a type-preserving method, which means that the declared return type must be the same as the declared subject type.

The SQL-routine-characteristics clause specifies the characteristics of the method body that will be defined for this type, using the CREATE METHOD statement. LANGUAGE SQL specifies that the method is written in SQL, with a single RETURN statement. NOT DETERMINISTIC or DETERMINISTIC specify whether the method will always return the same results for given argument values (DETERMINISTIC), or whether the method will depend on some state values that affect the results (NOT DETERMINISTIC).

NO EXTERNAL ACTION or EXTERNAL ACTION specify whether the method will take some action that changes the state of an object that is not managed by the database manager. READS SQL DATA specifies that SQL statements that do not modify SQL data can be executed by the method. CONTAINS SQL specifies that SQL statements that neither read nor modify SQL data can be executed by the method. CALLED ON NULL INPUT specifies that the user-defined method is called regardless of whether any arguments are null.

LANGUAGE C specifies that the database manager will call the user-defined method as though it were a C function. The user-defined method must conform to the C language calling and linkage convention, as defined by the standard ANSI C prototype. LANGUAGE JAVA specifies that the database manager will call the user-defined method as a method in a Java class. LANGUAGE OLE specifies that the database manager will call the user-defined method as though it were a method exposed by an OLE automation object.

PARAMETER STYLE specifies the conventions that are to be used for passing parameters to (and returning values from) the methods. DB2SQL must be specified when either LANGUAGE C or LANGUAGE OLE is specified. DB2GENERAL can be specified only when LANGUAGE JAVA is specified.

If a method is registered as FENCED, the database manager insulates its internal resources from access by the method. To change a method from FENCED to NOT FENCED, the method must be reregistered by first dropping it and then re-creating it. To register a method as NOT FENCED, SYSADM authority, DBADM authority, or the CREATE_NOT_FENCED privilege is required.

If RETURNS NULL ON NULL INPUT is specified, and if at execution time any one of the method's arguments is null, the method is not called, and the result is the null value. CALLED ON NULL INPUT specifies that the user-defined method is called regardless of whether any arguments are null.

NO SQL is a mandatory clause that specifies that the method cannot issue any SQL statements.

NO EXTERNAL ACTION or EXTERNAL ACTION specify whether the method will take some action that changes the state of an object that is not managed by DB2. If SCRATCHPAD is specified, memory is allocated for a scratchpad to be used by the external method. The *length* parameter specifies the size, in bytes, of the scratchpad; it must be between 1 and 32,767. The default value is 100. The scope of the scratchpad is the SQL statement. There is one scratchpad per reference to the external method in the SQL statement.

NO FINAL CALL or FINAL CALL specify whether a final call is to be made to an external method. The purpose of such a final call is to enable the external method to free any system resources that it has acquired. It can be useful in conjunction with the SCRATCHPAD keyword if, for example, the external method acquires system resources, such as memory, and anchors them in the scratchpad.

ALLOW PARALLEL or DISALLOW PARALLEL specify whether, for a single reference to the method, the invocation of the method can be parallelized. The default value is DISALLOW PARALLEL if one or more of the following options is specified in the statement: NOT DETERMINISTIC, EXTERNAL ACTION, SCRATCHPAD, or FINAL CALL.

NO DBINFO or DBINFO specify whether additional information will be passed to the method in a structure at invocation time. This information includes the following:

- The name of the currently connected database
- Application ID

- Application authorization ID
- Code page
- Schema name
- Table name
- Column name
- Version, release, and modification level of the database server
- Server platform

Example

Create a type hierarchy consisting of a type for employees and a subtype for managers:

```
CREATE TYPE EMP AS
   (NAME       VARCHAR(32),
   SERIALNUM   INT,
   DEPT        REF(DEPT),
   SALARY      DECIMAL(10,2))
   MODE DB2SQL

CREATE TYPE MGR UNDER EMP AS
   (BONUS      DECIMAL(10,2))
   MODE DB2SQL
```

CREATE TYPE MAPPING

The CREATE TYPE MAPPING statement creates a mapping between the data type of a column in a data source table or view that is going to be defined to a federated database and a corresponding data type that is already defined to the federated database. The mapping can associate the federated database data type with a data type at a specified data source, or a range of data sources (for example, all data sources of a particular type and version). A data type mapping must be created only if an existing one is not adequate.

The authorization ID of the statement must have SYSADM or DBADM authority.

Syntax

```
>>-CREATE TYPE MAPPING--+------------------+---FROM--| local-data-type |-->
                        '-type-mapping-name-'
>---TO----| remote-server |--TYPE--data-source-data-type-------->
>-----+------------------------------------------+---------->< 
```

REFERENCE

```
                  +-FOR BIT DATA-----------------------------+
                  '-(--+-p-------+---+--------+---)--+------+-'
                       '-[p..p]--' +-,s------+       +-P=S--+
                                   '-,[s..s]-'       +-P>S--+
                                                     +-P<S--+
                                                     +-P>=S-+
                                                     +-P<=S-+
                                                     '-P<>S-'

local-data-type
|---+-SMALLINT----------------------------------------------------------------+->
    +-+-INTEGER-+----------------------------------------------------------+
    | '-INT-----'                                                          |
    +-BIGINT---------------------------------------------------------------+
    +-+-FLOAT--+--------------+-+------------------------------------------+
    | |        '-(--integer--)--' |                                        |
    | +-REAL---------------------+                                         |
    | |        .-PRECISION-.     |                                        |
    | '-DOUBLE-+-----------+-----'                                         |
    +--+-DECIMAL-+---+--------------------------------+--------------------+
    |  +-DEC-----+   '-(--integer--+-----------+---)--'                    |
    |  +-NUMERIC-+                 '-,integer--'                           |
    |  '-NUM-----'                                                         |
    +--+--+-CHARACTER-+---+-----------+--------------------+---+---------------+--+
    |  |  '-CHAR------'   '-(integer)--'                   |   '-FOR BIT DATA--' |
    |  '--+-VARCHAR------------------+---+--------------+-'                     |
    |     '--+-CHARACTER-+---VARYING--'   '-(--integer--)--'                   |
    |        '-CHAR------'                                                     |
    +-GRAPHIC--+-----------+----------------------------------------------+
    |          '-(integer)--'                                             |
    +-VARGRAPHIC--+-----------+-------------------------------------------+
    |             '-(integer)--'                                          |
    +-DATE----------------------------------------------------------------+
    +-TIME----------------------------------------------------------------+
    '-TIMESTAMP-----------------------------------------------------------'
>----------------------------------------------------------------|

remote-server
|---+-SERVER--server-name---------------------------------------------------------+->
    '-SERVER TYPE--server-type----+-------------------------------------------------+---'
                                  '-VERSION--| server-version |--+---------------------+--'
                                                                 '-WRAPPER--wrapper-name---'
>----------------------------------------------------------------|

server-version
|---+-version--+-------------------------+-+-------------------|
    |          '-.--release--+---------+--' |
    |                        '-.--mod--'    |
    '-version-string-constant---------------'
```

The *type-mapping-name* parameter specifies a name for the data type mapping. A unique name is generated if a value for this parameter is not specified. The local-data-type clause specifies a data type that is defined to a federated database. If specified without a schema name, the type name is resolved by searching schemas on the SQL path. If length or precision (and scale) are not specified, appropriate values are determined from the *data-source-data-type* parameter. The local data type cannot be LONG VARCHAR, LONG VARGRAPHIC, DATALINK, a LOB type, or a user-defined type.

SERVER *server-name* specifies the data source for which *data-source-data-type* is defined. SERVER TYPE *server-type* specifies the type of data source for which *data-source-data-type* is defined.

VERSION specifies the version (version number, an integer; release number, an integer; and modification number, also an integer) of the data source for which *data-source-data-type* is defined. Alternatively, you can specify a *version-string-constant*, such as 8i or 8.0.3, for example.

WRAPPER *wrapper-name* specifies the name of the wrapper that the federated server uses to interact with data sources of the specified type and version.

TYPE *data-source-data-type* specifies the data source data type that is being mapped to local-data-type. The data source data type must be a built-in data type. If the type has a short and a long form (for example, CHAR and CHARACTER), the short form should be specified.

For decimal data:

- *p* Specifies the maximum number of digits that a value can have.

- *[p..p]* Specifies the minimum and the maximum number of digits that a value can have.

- *s* Specifies the maximum number of digits that are allowed to the right of the decimal point.

- *[s..s]* Specifies the minimum and the maximum number of digits that are allowed to the right of the decimal point.

- *P [operand] S* Specifies a comparison between the maximum allowable precision and the maximum number of digits that are allowed to the right of the decimal point. For example, the equal (=) operand indicates that the maximum allowable precision is equal to the maximum number of digits that are allowed to the right of the decimal point.

For character data:

- *p* Specifies the maximum number of characters that a value can have.

- *[p..p]* Specifies the minimum and the maximum number of characters that a value can have.

FOR BIT DATA specifies that the data source data type column contains binary values.

Example

Create a mapping between SYSIBM.DATE and the Oracle data type DATE at all Oracle data sources.

```
CREATE TYPE MAPPING MY_ORACLE_DATE
  FROM SYSIBM.DATE
  TO SERVER TYPE ORACLE
  TYPE DATE
```

CREATE USER MAPPING

The CREATE USER MAPPING statement defines a mapping between an authorization ID that uses a federated database and the authorization ID and password to use at a specified data source. If the authorization ID of the statement is different than the authorization name that is being mapped to the data source, then the authorization ID must include SYSADM or DBADM authority. Otherwise, if the authorization ID and the authorization name match, no privileges or authorities are required.

Syntax

```
>>-CREATE USER MAPPING FOR----+-authorization-name-+------------>
                              '-USER--------------'
>-----SERVER--server-name-------------------------------------->
                 .-,---------------------------------------------.
                 V   .-ADD--.                                     |
>-----OPTIONS--(-----+------+---user-option-name--string-constant---+---)->
>------------------------------------------------------------->< 
```

The *authorization-name* parameter specifies the authorization name under which a user or an application is to connect to a federated database. USER specifies the value in the special register USER. SERVER *server-name* specifies the data source that will be accessible under the mapping authorization ID.

The OPTIONS parameter indicates which user options are to be enabled for the specified data source. *User options* include the following:

- *remote_authid* Specifies the authorization ID (maximum length 255 bytes) that is to be used at the data source
- *remote_domain* Specifies the Windows NT domain that is to be used to authenticate users connecting to this data source
- *remote_password* Specifies the password (maximum length 32 bytes) that is to be used at the data source
- *accounting_string* Specifies a DRDA accounting string (maximum length 255 bytes)

Example

To access a data source called S1, Tallerico must map her authorization name and password on her local database to her user ID and password on S1 (SYSTEM and MANAGER, respectively):

```
CREATE USER MAPPING FOR Tallerico
   SERVER S1
   OPTIONS
   (REMOTE_AUTHID 'SYSTEM',
    REMOTE_PASSWORD 'MANAGER')
```

CREATE VIEW

The CREATE VIEW statement creates a view on one or more tables, views, or nicknames.

The authorization ID of the statement must have at least one of the following: SYSADM or DBADM authority. Or, for each table, view, or nickname identified in any fullselect, it must have CONTROL privilege on the table or view, or SELECT privilege on the table or view, and at least one of the following: IMPLICIT_SCHEMA privilege on the database, if the implicit or the explicit schema name of the view does not exist; CREATEIN privilege on the schema, if the schema name of the view refers to an existing schema.

If creating a subview, the authorization ID of the statement must be the same as the definer of the root table of the table hierarchy; have SELECT WITH GRANT privilege on the underlying table of the subview, or the superview must not have SELECT privilege granted to any user other than the view definer.

Syntax

```
>>-CREATE--+-----------+---VIEW--view-name--------------------->
           '-FEDERATED-'
>-----+----------------------------------------+--AS------->
      |     .-,-------------.                   |
      |     V               |                   |
      +-(-----column-name---+---)---------------+
      '-OF--type-name--+-| root-view-definition |-+-'
                       '-| subview-definition |---'
>----+---------------------------------------+--fullselect------>
     |         .-,-----------------------.    |
     |         V                         |    |
     '-WITH-----common-table-expression---+--'
>-----+---------------------------------------+--------------->< 
      |         .-CASCADED--.                 |
      '-WITH--+-----------+---CHECK OPTION---'
              '-LOCAL-----'
```

```
root-view-definition
|---MODE DB2SQL------------------------------------------------->
>----(--| oid-column |--+--------------------+---)-----------|
                        '-,--| with-options |--'

subview-definition
|---MODE DB2SQL--| under-clause |------------------------------>
>-----+------------------------------+---+--------+---------------|
      '-(--| with-options |--)---'    '-EXTEND--'

oid-column
|---REF IS--oid-column-name--USER GENERATED----+-----------+---|
                                               '-UNCHECKED--'

with-options
       .-,------------------------------------------------------.
       |                         .-,----------------------------. |
       V                         V                              | |
|--------column-name--WITH
OPTIONS----+-SCOPE--+-typed-table-name-+-+--+--+---|
                    |                  |      '-typed-view-name--' |
                    '-READ ONLY------------------'

under-clause
|---UNDER--superview-name--INHERIT SELECT PRIVILEGES-----------|
```

FEDERATED specifies that the view being created references a nickname or an OLEDB table function. VIEW *view-name* specifies a name for the view. The qualifier must not be SYSIBM, SYSCAT, SYSFUN, or SYSSTAT.

The *column-name* parameter specifies the columns in the view. If a list of column names is specified, it must consist of as many names as there are columns in the result table of the fullselect. Each column name must be unique and unqualified. If a list of column names is not specified, the columns of the view inherit the names of the columns in the result table.

OF *type-name* specifies that the columns of the view are based on the attributes of a structured type. If specified without a schema name, the type name is resolved by searching schemas on the SQL path. The type name must be the name of an existing user-defined type, and it must be a structured type that is instantiable.

MODE DB2SQL specifies the mode of the typed view, and it is the only mode that is currently supported.

UNDER *superview-name* specifies that the view is a subview of *superview-name*. The columns of the view include the object identifier column of the superview with its type modified to be REF(*type-name*), followed by columns based on the attributes of *type-name* (the type includes the attributes of its supertype).

INHERIT SELECT PRIVILEGES specifies that any user or group holding a SELECT privilege on the superview will be granted an equivalent privilege on the newly created subview. The subview definer is considered to be the grantor of this privilege.

REF IS *OID-column-name* USER GENERATED specifies that an object identifier (OID) column is defined as the first column in the view. An OID is required for the root view of a view hierarchy. The view must be a typed view that is not a subview.

UNCHECKED specifies that the object identifier column of the typed view definition is assumed to be unique. This option is mandatory for view hierarchies that range over multiple hierarchies, legacy tables, or views. By specifying UNCHECKED, the user takes responsibility for ensuring that each row of the view has a unique OID.

WITH OPTIONS SCOPE *typed-table-name* or *typed-view-name* specify the scope of the reference type column. A scope must be specified for any column that is to be used as the left operand of a dereference operator, or as the argument of the DEREF function. READ ONLY is used to force a column to be read-only, so that subview definitions can specify an expression for the same column that is implicitly read-only.

WITH *common-table-expression* specifies a common table expression for use with a fullselect. A common table expression cannot be specified when defining a typed view. A *fullselect* defines the view, which consists of the rows that would be returned if the SELECT statement were invoked. The fullselect must not reference host variables, parameter markers, or declared temporary tables.

WITH CHECK OPTION specifies the constraint that every row that is inserted or updated through the view must satisfy. CASCADED specifies that the view is to inherit the search conditions as constraints from any updateable view on which it depends. Every updateable view that depends on the view is also subject to these constraints. LOCAL specifies that the search condition for the view is to be applied as a constraint for any insert or update operations on the view, or on any view that depends on the view.

Example

Create a view named PRJ_LEADER that contains the first four columns (PROJNO, PROJNAME, DEPTNO, RESPEMP) from the PROJECT table, together with the last name (LASTNAME) and total pay (SALARY + BONUS + COMM) of the person who is responsible for the project (RESPEMP). Obtain the name from the EMPLOYEE table by matching EMPNO in EMPLOYEE to RESPEMP in PROJECT. Select only those projects with mean staffing (PRSTAFF) greater than 1:

```
CREATE VIEW PRJ_LEADER
  (PROJNO, PROJNAME, DEPTNO, RESPEMP, LASTNAME, TOTAL_PAY)
  AS SELECT PROJNO, PROJNAME, DEPTNO, RESPEMP, LASTNAME, SALARY+BONUS+COMM
    FROM PROJECT, EMPLOYEE
    WHERE RESPEMP = EMPNO
    AND PRSTAFF > 1
```

Specifying the column name list can be avoided by naming the expression SALARY+BONUS+COMM as TOTAL_PAY in the fullselect:

```
CREATE VIEW PRJ_LEADER
  AS SELECT PROJNO, PROJNAME, DEPTNO, RESPEMP, LASTNAME, SALARY+BONUS+COMM
```

REFERENCE

```
    AS TOTAL_PAY
  FROM PROJECT, EMPLOYEE
  WHERE RESPEMP = EMPNO AND PRSTAFF > 1
```

CREATE WRAPPER

The CREATE WRAPPER statement registers a *wrapper* (a mechanism by which a federated server can interact with a certain category of data sources) to a federated database. The authorization ID of the statement must have SYSADM or DBADM authority.

Syntax

```
>>-CREATE WRAPPER----wrapper-name------------------------------->
>-----+---------------------------+---------------------------><
      '-LIBRARY--'library-name'--'
```

The wrapper name can be a predefined name or a user-supplied name. If a predefined name is specified, the federated server automatically assigns a default value to *'library-name'*. The predefined names are DRDA (for all DB2 family data sources), NET8 (for all Oracle data sources that are supported by Oracle's Net8 client software), OLEDB (for all OLE DB providers supported by Microsoft OLE DB), and SQLNET (for all Oracle data sources that are supported by Oracle's SQL*Net client software).

LIBRARY *'library-name'* specifies the file that contains the wrapper module.

DECLARE CURSOR

The DECLARE CURSOR statement defines a cursor. The authorization ID of the statement must have at least one of the following: SYSADM or DBADM authority; SELECT or CONTROL privilege on the table or view.

Syntax

```
>>-DECLARE--cursor-name--CURSOR----+-----------+--------------->
                                   '-WITH HOLD--'
>-----+---------------------------+--------------------------->
      |                .-TO CALLER--.  |
      '-WITH RETURN--+-----------+--'
                     '-TO CLIENT--'
```

```
>----FOR--+-select-statement-+------------------------------><
          '-statement-name---'
```

The *cursor-name* parameter specifies the name of the cursor that is to be created when the source program is run.

WITH HOLD specifies that resources are to be maintained across multiple units of work. For units of work ending with COMMIT, open cursors defined WITH HOLD remain open, and the cursor is positioned before the next logical row of the results table; all locks are released, except locks protecting the current cursor position of open WITH HOLD cursors; UPDATE and DELETE CURRENT OF CURSOR are valid only for rows that are fetched within the same unit of work; and LOB locators are freed. For units of work ending with ROLLBACK, all open cursors are closed; all locks acquired during the unit of work are released; and LOB locators are freed.

WITH RETURN specifies that the cursor is to be used as a result set from a stored procedure.

TO CALLER specifies that the cursor can return a result set to the caller. For example, if the caller is another stored procedure, the result set is returned to that stored procedure. If the caller is a client application, the result set is returned to the client application.

TO CLIENT specifies that the cursor can return a result set to the client application. This cursor is invisible to any intermediate nested procedures.

The *select-statement* parameter specifies the SELECT statement of the cursor. The *select-statement* must not include parameter markers, but it can include references to host variables. The declarations of host variables must precede the DECLARE CURSOR statement in the source program. The SELECT statement of the cursor is the *prepared* SELECT statement, identified by *statement-name*, when the cursor is opened.

Example

The DECLARE CURSOR statement associates the cursor name C1 with the result set that is returned by the SELECT statement:

```
EXEC SQL DECLARE C1 CURSOR FOR
    SELECT DEPTNO, DEPTNAME, MGRNO FROM DEPARTMENT WHERE ADMRDEPT = 'A00';
```

DECLARE GLOBAL TEMPORARY TABLE

The DECLARE GLOBAL TEMPORARY TABLE statement defines a temporary table for the current session. When the session ends, the rows of the table are deleted, and the description of the temporary table is dropped.

The authorization ID of the statement must include at least one of the following: SYSADM or DBADM authority; USE privilege on the USER TEMPORARY table space. When defining a table using LIKE or a fullselect, the authorization ID of the statement must also include SELECT or CONTROL privilege on the table or view.

Syntax

```
>>-DECLARE GLOBAL TEMPORARY TABLE--table-name------------------>

                .-,----------------------.
                V                        |
>-----+-(-----| column-definition |---+---)------------------------+>
      +-LIKE--+-table-name2-+---+------------------+--------------+
      |       '-view-name---'   '-| copy-options |--'            |
      '-AS--(--fullselect--)--DEFINITION ONLY--+------------------+-'
                                               '-| copy-options |--'
                          .-ON COMMIT DELETE ROWS---.
>----*--+--------------+---*--+------------------------+----*--NOT LOGGED--*->
        '-WITH REPLACE-'     '-ON COMMIT PRESERVE ROWS-'
>----+----------------------+---*------------------------------>
     '-IN--tablespace-name--'
>----+--------------------------------------------------------------+---*->
     |                      .-,--------------.                       |
     |                      V                |     .-USING HASHING-. |
     '-PARTITIONING KEY--(-----column-name---+---)--+---------------+--'
>-------------------------------------------------------------><
column-definition
|---column-name---| data-type |----+--------------------+------|
                                   '-| column-options |--'
column-options
|---*--+----------+---*--+----------------------------------------------+---*-->
       '-NOT NULL--'     +-| default-clause |-----------------------------------+
                         '-GENERATED--+-ALWAYS-----+---AS--| identity-clause |--'
                                      '-BY DEFAULT-'
>-----------------------------------------------------------|
copy-options
                                                    .-COLUMN ATTRIBUTES-.
                                   .-EXCLUDING IDENTITY-+-------------------+--.
|---*--+------------------------------------+---*--+-------------------------------------+---*-->
       |                .-COLUMN-.          |     |          .-COLUMN ATTRIBUTES-.       |
       '--+-INCLUDING-+--+--------+--DEFAULTS--'   '-INCLUDING IDENTITY-+-------------------+---'
          '-EXCLUDING-'
>-----------------------------------------------------------|
```

The specified table name is qualified by the schema name SESSION. Each session that defines a declared global temporary table with the same table name has its own unique description of that declared global temporary table. It is possible that a table, view, alias, or nickname with the same name and schema name already exists in the catalog, and in this case, a declared global temporary table may still be defined, and any references to SESSION.*table-name* will resolve to the declared global temporary table, rather than the SESSION.*table-name* that is already defined in the catalog.

The column-definition clause is used to define the attributes of a column in the temporary table. Specify a column name, a data type, and one or more column options, if appropriate. BLOB, CLOB, DBCLOB, LONG VARCHAR, LONG VARGRAPHIC, DATALINK, reference, and structured types cannot be used with declared global temporary tables. For more information about allowable types and options, see the description of the CREATE TABLE statement.

LIKE specifies that the columns of the table are to have exactly the same name and description as the columns of the identified table, view, or nickname. The name specified after LIKE must identify a table, view, or nickname that exists in the catalog, or a declared temporary table. A typed table or typed view cannot be specified.

AS *(fullselect)* DEFINITION ONLY specifies that the table definition is to be based on the column definitions from the result of a query expression.

The copy-options clause specifies whether additional attributes of the source are to be copied. INCLUDING COLUMN DEFAULTS specifies that column default values for each updateable column of the source result table definition are to be copied. EXCLUDING COLUMN DEFAULTS specifies that column default values are not to be copied.

INCLUDING IDENTITY COLUMN ATTRIBUTES specifies that identity column attributes (START WITH, INCREMENT BY, and CACHE values), if available, are to be copied from the source result table definition. EXCLUDING IDENTITY COLUMN ATTRIBUTES specifies that identity column attributes are not to be copied from the source result table definition.

ON COMMIT specifies the action that is to be taken against the global temporary table when a COMMIT operation is performed: DELETE ROWS specifies that all rows are to be deleted if no WITH HOLD cursor is open on the table (default behavior); and PRESERVE ROWS specifies that rows are not to be deleted. NOT LOGGED specifies that changes to the table (including creation of the table itself) are not to be logged. WITH REPLACE specifies that, if a declared global temporary table with the same name already exists, the existing table is to be replaced.

IN *tablespace-name* specifies the table space in which the global temporary table will be instantiated. The table space must exist and be a USER TEMPORARY table space over which the authorization ID of the statement has the USE privilege.

PARTITIONING KEY *(column-name,...)* specifies the partitioning key that is to be used when data in the table is partitioned. If this clause is not specified and the table resides in a multiple partition nodegroup, the partitioning key is defined as the first column of the declared temporary table. USING HASHING specifies that the hashing function is to be used as the partitioning method for data distribution. This is the only supported partitioning method.

DELETE

The DELETE statement deletes rows from a table or a view. Deleting a row from a view deletes the row from the table on which the view is based. A *searched delete* is used to delete one or more rows (optionally determined by a search condition). A *positioned delete* is used to delete exactly one row (determined by the current position of a cursor).

The authorization ID of the statement must have at least one of the following: SYSADM or DBADM authority; DELETE or CONTROL privilege on the table or the view from which rows are to be deleted. To perform a *searched delete*, the authorization ID of the statement must also have SELECT or CONTROL privilege on each table or view referenced by a subquery. If the specified table or view is preceded by the ONLY keyword, the authorization ID of the statement must also have the SELECT privilege on every subtable or subview of the specified table or view.

Syntax

Searched DELETE:

```
>>-DELETE FROM----+-table-name-------------------+-------------->
                  +-view-name-------------------+
                  '-ONLY--(--+-table-name-+---)--'
                            '-view-name--'
>-----+-------------------------------+--------------------------->
      | .-AS-.                         |
      '-+----+--correlation-name--'
>-----+-------------------------------+-------------------------><
      '-WHERE--search-condition--'   '-WITH--+-RR-+--'
                                             +-RS-+
                                             +-CS-+
                                             '-UR-'
```

Positioned DELETE:

```
>>-DELETE FROM----+-table-name-------------------+-------------->
        +-view-name-------------------+
        '-ONLY—(—+-table-name-+---)—'
                 '-view-name—'
>----WHERE CURRENT OF—cursor-name----------------------------><
```

FROM *table-name* or *view-name* specifies the table or the view from which rows are to be deleted. The name must identify a table or a view that exists in the catalog, but it must not identify a catalog table, a catalog view, a summary table, or a read-only view. The ONLY keyword specifies that the statement is to apply only to data from the specified *typed* table or view, and that rows from proper subtables or subviews are not to be deleted.

A correlation name can be used within the search condition to designate the table or view. WHERE specifies the condition under which the rows that are to be deleted are selected. If the clause is omitted, all rows in the table or view are deleted.

WITH specifies the isolation level used when locating the rows to be deleted. Valid values are RR (Repeatable Read); RS (Read Stability); CS (Cursor Stability); and UR (Uncommitted Read). The default isolation level of the statement is the isolation level of the package in which the statement is bound.

CURRENT OF *cursor-name* specifies a cursor that is defined by a DECLARE CURSOR statement in the program. The DECLARE CURSOR statement must precede the DELETE statement. The specified table or view must also be named in the FROM clause of the SELECT statement for the cursor, and the result table for the cursor must not be read-only.

Examples

Delete department 'D11' from the DEPARTMENT table:

```
DELETE FROM DEPARTMENT WHERE DEPTNO = 'D11'
```

Delete all the departments from the DEPARTMENT table (that is, empty the table):

```
DELETE FROM DEPARTMENT
```

DESCRIBE

The DESCRIBE statement returns information about a prepared statement.

Syntax

```
>>-DESCRIBE--statement-name--INTO--descriptor-name------------><
```

The *statement-name* parameter specifies a prepared statement about which information is required. INTO *descriptor-name* specifies an SQL descriptor area (SQLDA).

DISCONNECT

The DISCONNECT statement destroys one or more connections when there is no active unit of work (that is, after a *commit* or a rollback operation). If a single connection is the target of the DISCONNECT statement, the connection is destroyed only if the database has participated in any existing unit of work. For example, if several other databases have done work but the target in question has not, it can still be disconnected without destroying the connection.

Syntax

```
                                      (1)
>>-DISCONNECT----+-server-name------+-------------------------><
                 +-host-variable----+
                 +-CURRENT----------+
                 |       .-SQL-.       |
                 '-ALL-+-----+------'
```

Syntax Note:

1. An application server named CURRENT or ALL can be identified only by a host variable.

The application server is specified by a server name or a host variable that contains the server name. If a host variable is specified, it must be a character string variable with a maximum length of eight bytes, and it must not include an indicator variable. The server name that is contained within the host variable must be left-justified and must not be delimited by quotation marks. The server name is a database alias identifying the application server; it must be listed in the application requester's local directory. The specified database alias, or the database alias contained in the host variable, must identify an existing connection of the application process.

CURRENT specifies the current connection of the application process. The application process must be in the connected state. ALL specifies that all existing connections of the application process are to be destroyed.

The optional keyword SQL is included to be consistent with the syntax of the RELEASE statement.

DROP

The DROP statement deletes an object. Any objects that directly or indirectly depend on that object are either deleted or made inoperative. When an object is deleted, its description is removed from the catalog and any packages that reference the object are invalidated.

The authorization ID required of the statement depends on the type of object that is being dropped:

- For objects that allow two-part names, the authorization ID of the statement must have at least one of the following: SYSADM or DBADM authority; DROPIN privilege on the schema for the object; definer of the object, as recorded in the DEFINER column of the catalog view for the object; CONTROL privilege on the object (applicable only to indexes, index specifications, nicknames, packages, tables, and views); definer of the user-defined type, as recorded in the DEFINER column of the catalog view SYSCAT.DATATYPES (applicable only when dropping a method associated with a user-defined type).

- For a table or view hierarchy, the authorization ID of the statement must have one of the privileges described previously for each table or view in the hierarchy.
- For a schema, the authorization ID of the statement must have SYSADM or DBADM authority, or be the schema owner, as recorded in the OWNER column of SYSCAT.SCHEMATA.
- For a buffer pool, a nodegroup, or a table space, the authorization ID of the statement must have SYSADM or SYSCTRL authority.
- For an event monitor, a server definition, a data type mapping, a function mapping, or a wrapper, the authorization ID of the statement must have SYSADM or DBADM authority.
- For a user mapping, the authorization ID of the statement must have SYSADM or DBADM authority if this authorization ID is different from the federated database authorization name within the mapping; otherwise, if the authorization ID and the authorization name match, no authorities or privileges are required.
- For a transform, the authorization ID of the statement must have SYSADM or DBADM authority, or it must be the DEFINER of the type name.

Syntax

```
>>-DROP--------------------------------------------------------->
            (1)
>-----+-ALIAS-------alias-name---------------------------------------+>
      +-BUFFERPOOL--bufferpool-name-----------------------------------+
      +-EVENT--MONITOR--event-monitor-name----------------------------+
      +-FUNCTION----function-name--+----------------------------------+---------+
      |                            '-(--+------------------+---)--'    |
      |                            |    .-,----------.     |          |
      |                            |    V            |     |          |
      |                            '----data-type---+--'          |
      +-SPECIFIC FUNCTION--specific-name------------------------------+
      +-FUNCTION MAPPING--function-mapping-name-----------------------+
      |                   (2)                                         |
      +-INDEX--index-name---------------------------------------------+
      +-INDEX EXTENSION--index-extension-name--RESTRICT---------------+
      +-METHOD--method-name--+-----------------------------+---FOR--type-name--+
      |                      '-(--+------------------+---)--'               |
      |                      |    .-,----------.     |                   |
      |                      |    V            |     |                   |
      |                      '----datatype---+--'                    |
      +-SPECIFIC METHOD--specific-name--------------------------------+
      +-NICKNAME--nickname--------------------------------------------+
      +-NODEGROUP--nodegroup-name-------------------------------------+
      |          (3)                                                  |
      +-PACKAGE-------package-name------------------------------------+
```

```
+-PROCEDURE--procedure-name--+------------------------------+-----------+
|                            '-(--+-------------------+---)--'          |
|                                 |  .-,----------.   |                 |
|                                 |  V            |   |                 |
|                                 '----data-type---+--'                 |
+-SPECIFIC PROCEDURE--specific-name-------------------------------------+
+-SCHEMA--schema-name--RESTRICT----------------------------------------+
+-SEQUENCE--sequence-name--RESTRICT------------------------------------+
+-SERVER--server-name--------------------------------------------------+
+-TABLE--table-name---------------------------------------------------+
+-TABLE HIERARCHY--root-table-name------------------------------------+
|                        .-,----------------.                         |
|                        V                  |                         |
+--+-TABLESPACE--+------tablespace-name---+---------------------------+
|  '-TABLESPACES-'                                                    |
+--+-TRANSFORM--+---+-ALL--------+---FOR--type-name-------------------+
|  '-TRANSFORMS-'   '-group-name-'                                    |
+-TRIGGER--trigger-name-----------------------------------------------+
+-+---------------+---TYPE--type-name---------------------------------+
| |        (4)    |                                                   |
| '-DISTINCT------'                                                   |
+-TYPE MAPPING--type-mapping-name-------------------------------------+
+-USER MAPPING FOR--+-authorization-name-+---SERVER--server-name------+
|                   '-USER-------------'                              |
+-VIEW--view-name----------------------------------------------------+
+-VIEW HIERARCHY--root-view-name-------------------------------------+
'-WRAPPER--wrapper-name----------------------------------------------'
>---------------------------------------------------------------><
```

Syntax Notes:

1. SYNONYM can be used as a synonym for ALIAS.

2. *Index-name* can be the name of either an index or an index specification.

3. PROGRAM can be used as a synonym for PACKAGE.

4. DATA can also be used when dropping any user-defined type.

ALIAS *alias-name* specifies the alias that is to be dropped. All tables, views, and triggers that reference the alias are made inoperative. This includes both the table referenced in the ON clause of the CREATE TRIGGER statement, and all tables referenced within the triggered SQL statements.

BUFFERPOOL *bufferpool-name* specifies the buffer pool that is to be dropped. There can be no table spaces assigned to the buffer pool. The IBMDEFAULTBP buffer pool cannot be dropped. The storage for the buffer pool will not be released until the database is stopped.

EVENT MONITOR *event-monitor-name* specifies the event monitor that is to be dropped. If event files are in the target path of the event monitor when the event monitor is dropped, the event files are not deleted. If a new event monitor specifies the same target path, the event files are deleted.

FUNCTION specifies an instance of a user-defined function that is to be dropped. Functions that are implicitly generated by the CREATE DISTINCT TYPE statement cannot be dropped. FUNCTION *function-name* specifies a particular function, and it is valid only if there is exactly one function instance with that function name. FUNCTION *function-name (data-type,....)* specifies the function signature that uniquely identifies the function that is to be dropped. The specified data types must match the data types that were specified for the CREATE FUNCTION statement.

If data-type is unqualified, the type name is resolved by searching schemas on the SQL path. It is not necessary to specify the length, precision, or scale for parameterized data types; instead, an empty set of parentheses can be coded to specify that these attributes are to be ignored when looking for a data type match. FLOAT() cannot be used because this parameter value specifies different data types (REAL or DOUBLE).

SPECIFIC FUNCTION *specific-name* specifies the particular user-defined function that is to be dropped. The specified name must identify a specific function instance in the named or implied schema. It is not possible to drop a function that is in the SYSIBM schema or the SYSFUN schema. All dependencies must be removed before a function can be dropped, except for packages that will be marked inoperative.

FUNCTION MAPPING *function-mapping-name* specifies a function mapping that is to be deleted from the database. Packages that have a dependency on a dropped function mapping are invalidated.

INDEX *index-name* specifies an index or an index specification that is to be dropped. It cannot be an index that is required by the system for a primary key constraint, a unique constraint, or a replicated summary table. The index or index specification is deleted, and packages that have a dependency on the dropped index or index specification are invalidated.

INDEX EXTENSION *index-extension-name* specifies an index extension that is to be dropped. RESTRICT specifies that no index that depends on this index extension definition is to be defined.

METHOD specifies a method body that is to be dropped. Method bodies that are implicitly generated by the CREATE TYPE statement cannot be dropped. The method specification (signature) remains as part of the definition of the subject type. After the method body is dropped, the method specification can be removed from the subject type definition through the ALTER TYPE DROP METHOD statement. METHOD *method-name* specifies a particular method, and it is valid only if there is exactly one method instance with that method name and subject type.

METHOD *method-name (data-type,....)* specifies the method signature that uniquely identifies the method that is to be dropped. The specified data types must match the data types that were specified for the CREATE TYPE or the ALTER TYPE statement. If *data-type* is unqualified, the type name is resolved by searching schemas on the SQL path. It is not necessary to specify the length, precision, or scale for parameterized data types; instead, an empty set of parentheses can be coded to specify that these attributes are to be ignored when looking for a data type match. FLOAT() cannot be used because this parameter value specifies different data types (REAL or DOUBLE). FOR *type-name* specifies the type for which the specified method is to be dropped.

SPECIFIC METHOD *specific-name* specifies the particular method that is to be dropped, using a name either specified or defaulted to during invocation of the CREATE TYPE or the ALTER TYPE statement. All dependencies must be removed before a method can be dropped, except for packages that will be marked inoperative.

NICKNAME *nickname* specifies a nickname that is to be deleted from the database. All information about columns and indexes that are associated with the nickname is deleted from the catalog. Any index specifications that depend on the nickname are dropped. Any views that depend on the nickname are marked inoperative.

NODEGROUP *nodegroup-name* specifies a nodegroup that is to be dropped. Dropping a nodegroup drops all table spaces defined in the nodegroup. All existing database objects with dependencies on the tables in the table spaces (such as packages, referential constraints, and so on) are dropped or invalidated, and dependent views and triggers are made inoperative. System-defined nodegroups cannot be dropped.

PACKAGE *package-name* specifies a package that is to be deleted. All privileges on the package are also deleted.

PROCEDURE specifies an instance of a stored procedure that is to be dropped. PROCEDURE *procedure-name* specifies a particular procedure, and it is valid only if there is exactly one procedure instance with that procedure name in the schema. PROCEDURE *procedure-name (data-type,....)* specifies the procedure signature that uniquely identifies the procedure that is to be dropped. The specified data types must match the data types that were specified for the CREATE PROCEDURE statement. If *data-type* is unqualified, the type name is resolved by searching schemas on the SQL path. It is not necessary to specify the length, precision, or scale for parameterized data types; instead, an empty set of parentheses can be coded to specify that these attributes are to be ignored when looking for a data type match. FLOAT() cannot be used because this parameter value specifies different data types (REAL or DOUBLE).

SPECIFIC PROCEDURE *specific-name* specifies the particular stored procedure that is to be dropped, using a name either specified or defaulted to during invocation of the CREATE PROCEDURE statement.

SCHEMA *schema-name* specifies a schema that is to be dropped. RESTRICT specifies that no objects are to be defined in the schema that is being deleted from the database.

SEQUENCE *sequence-name* RESTRICT specifies the particular sequence that is to be dropped. The sequence name, along with the implicit or explicit schema name, must identify an existing sequence at the current server. The RESTRICT keyword enforces the rule that the sequence is not dropped if the definition of a table column refers to the sequence (through an IDENTITY column).

SERVER *server-name* specifies a data source whose definition is to be deleted from the catalog. All nicknames for tables and views residing at the data source are dropped.

Any index specifications that depend on these nicknames are dropped. Any user-defined function mappings, user-defined type mappings, and user mappings that depend on the dropped server definition are also dropped. All packages that depend on the dropped server definition, function mappings, nicknames, and index specifications are invalidated.

TABLE *table-name* specifies a base table, a declared temporary table, or a summary table that is to be deleted from the database. All subtables must be dropped before a supertable can be dropped. All indexes, primary keys, foreign keys, check constraints, and summary tables referencing the specified table are dropped. All views and triggers that reference the table are made inoperative. (This includes both the table referenced in the ON clause of the CREATE TRIGGER statement and all tables referenced within the triggered SQL statements.)

All packages that depend on any object that is dropped or marked inoperative will be invalidated. This includes packages that depend on any supertables above the subtable in the hierarchy. Any reference columns for which the dropped table is defined as the scope of the reference become unscoped. Packages do not depend on declared temporary tables; therefore, they are not invalidated when such a table is dropped. All files that are linked through any DATALINK columns are unlinked. (The *unlink* operation is performed asynchronously, so the files may not be immediately available for other operations.) When a subtable is dropped from a table hierarchy, the columns associated with the subtable are no longer accessible. Dropping a subtable has the effect of deleting all the rows in the subtable from the supertables. This may result in activation of triggers or referential integrity constraints defined on the supertables.

TABLE HIERARCHY *root-table-name* specifies a typed table hierarchy that is to be dropped. The specified typed table and all of its subtables are deleted from the database. All indexes, summary tables, primary keys, foreign keys, and check constraints referencing the dropped tables are dropped. All views and triggers that reference the dropped tables are made inoperative. All packages that depend on any object that is dropped or marked inoperative are invalidated. Any reference columns for which one of the dropped tables is defined as the scope of the reference become unscoped. All files that are linked through any DATALINK columns are unlinked. (The unlink operation is performed asynchronously so the files may not be immediately available for other operations.)

TABLESPACE *tablespace-name* specifies one or more table spaces that are to be dropped. The table spaces will not be dropped if there is any table that stores at least one of its parts in a table space being dropped, and has one or more of its parts in another table space that is not being dropped. (These tables must be dropped first.) System table spaces cannot be dropped, and SYSTEM TEMPORARY table space cannot be dropped if it is the only temporary table space that exists in the database. A USER TEMPORARY table space cannot be dropped if it contains a declared temporary table. Even if a declared temporary table has been dropped, the USER TEMPORARY table space is considered to be in use until the unit of work containing the DROP TABLE statement has been committed.

Dropping a table space drops all objects that are defined in the table space. All existing database objects with dependencies on the table space, such as packages, referential constraints, and so on, are dropped or invalidated, and dependent views and triggers are made inoperative. Containers created by the user are not deleted; directories in the container path that were created by DB2 *are* deleted. All containers under the database directory are deleted. For SMS table spaces, the deletions occur after all connections are disconnected or the DEACTIVATE DATABASE command has been issued.

TRANSFORM ALL FOR *type-name* specifies that all transform groups defined for the user-defined data type *type-name* are to be dropped. The transform functions referenced in these groups are not dropped. Packages that depend on a transform function associated with the named transform group are marked inoperative. TRANSFORMS *group-name* FOR *type-name* specifies that a transform group for the user-defined data type *type-name* is to be dropped. The transform functions referenced in this group are not dropped.

TRIGGER *trigger-name* specifies a trigger that is to be deleted. Dropping triggers causes certain packages to be marked invalid.

TYPE *type-name* specifies a user-defined type that is to be dropped. The associated reference type for a structured type is also dropped.

TYPE MAPPING *type-mapping-name* specifies a user-defined data type mapping that is to be deleted from the database.

USER MAPPING FOR *authorization-name* | USER SERVER *server-name* specifies a user mapping that is to be deleted. This mapping associates an authorization name that is used to access a federated database with an authorization name that is used to access a data source. The first of these two authorization names is either identified by *authorization-name* or referenced by the special register USER.

VIEW *view-name* specifies a view that is to be deleted. All dependent subviews must be dropped before a superview can be dropped. The definition of any view or trigger that directly or indirectly depends on the specified view is marked inoperative. Any summary table that depends on any view that is marked inoperative is dropped. Any packages that depend on a view that is dropped or marked inoperative are invalidated; this includes packages that depend on any superviews above the subview in the hierarchy. Any reference columns for which the dropped view is defined as the scope of the reference become unscoped.

VIEW HIERARCHY *root-view-name* specifies a typed view hierarchy that is to be dropped. The specified typed view and all of its subviews are deleted from the database. The definition of any view or trigger that directly or indirectly depends on any of the dropped views is marked inoperative. Any packages that depend on any view or trigger that is dropped or marked inoperative are invalidated. Any reference columns for which a dropped view (or a view marked inoperative) is defined as the scope of the reference become unscoped.

WRAPPER *wrapper-name* specifies a wrapper that is to be deleted. All server definitions, user-defined function mappings, and user-defined data type mappings that depend on the wrapper are dropped. All user-defined function mappings, nicknames, user-defined data type mappings, and user mappings that depend on the dropped server definitions are also dropped. Any index specifications that depend on the dropped nicknames are dropped, and any views that depend on these nicknames are marked inoperative. All packages that depend on the dropped objects and inoperative views are invalidated.

Example

Drop the BUSINESS_OPS nodegroup. To drop the nodegroup, the two table spaces (ACCOUNTING and PLANS) in the nodegroup must first be dropped:

```
DROP TABLESPACE ACCOUNTING
DROP TABLESPACE PLANS
DROP NODEGROUP BUSINESS_OPS
```

END DECLARE SECTION

The END DECLARE SECTION statement marks the end of a host variable declare section; it can be coded in an application wherever declarations are permitted, according to the rules of the host language.

Syntax

```
>>-END DECLARE SECTION--------------------------------------><
```

EXECUTE

The EXECUTE statement executes a prepared SQL statement. For statements where authorization checking is performed at statement execution time (data definition language; GRANT and REVOKE statements), the privileges held by the authorization ID of the statement must include those required to execute the SQL statement specified by the PREPARE statement. For statements where authorization checking is performed at statement preparation time (data manipulation language), no authorization is required to use this statement.

Syntax

```
>>-EXECUTE--statement-name----------------------------------->
>-----+-------------------------------------+---------------><
      |          .-,--------------.         |
```

```
|        V                    |         |
+-USING-----host-variable---+--------+
'-USING DESCRIPTOR--descriptor-name--'
```

The *statement-name* parameter identifies the prepared statement (not a SELECT statement) that is to be executed.

USING introduces a list of host variables whose parameter markers (question marks) are to be substituted with values. Locator variables and file reference variables, where appropriate, can be provided as the source of values for parameter markers.

DESCRIPTOR identifies an input SQLDA that must contain a valid description of host variables.

Examples

In this C example, an INSERT statement with parameter markers is prepared and executed; h1–h4 are host variables that correspond to the format of TDEPT:

```
strcpy (s,"INSERT INTO TDEPT VALUES(?,?,?,?)");
EXEC SQL PREPARE DEPT_INSERT FROM :s;
   .
   .
(Check for successful execution and put values into :h1, :h2, :h3, :h4)
   .
   .
EXEC SQL EXECUTE DEPT_INSERT USING :h1, :h2, :h3, :h4;
```

This EXECUTE statement uses an SQLDA:

```
EXECUTE S3 USING DESCRIPTOR :sqlda3
```

EXECUTE IMMEDIATE

The EXECUTE IMMEDIATE statement prepares an executable form of an SQL statement from a character string form of the statement and then executes the statement. EXECUTE IMMEDIATE combines the basic functions of the PREPARE and the EXECUTE statements. It can be used to prepare and execute SQL statements that contain neither host variables nor parameter markers.

The authorization rules are those defined for the SQL statement specified in the EXECUTE IMMEDIATE statement.

Syntax

```
>>-EXECUTE IMMEDIATE--host-variable---------------------------><
```

The specified host variable must identify a host variable (character string variable) that is described in the program. The value of the identified host variable is called the statement string. The statement string must be one of the following SQL statements:

- ALTER
- COMMENT ON
- COMMIT
- CREATE
- DELETE
- DECLARE GLOBAL TEMPORARY TABLE
- DROP
- GRANT
- INSERT
- LOCK TABLE
- REFRESH TABLE
- RELEASE SAVEPOINT
- RENAME TABLE
- RENAME TABLESPACE
- REVOKE

- ROLLBACK
- SAVEPOINT
- SET CURRENT DEGREE
- SET CURRENT EXPLAIN MODE
- SET CURRENT EXPLAIN SNAPSHOT
- SET CURRENT QUERY OPTIMIZATION
- SET CURRENT REFRESH AGE
- SET CURRENT TRANSFORM GROUP
- SET EVENT MONITOR STATE
- SET INTEGRITY
- SET PASSTHRU
- SET PATH
- SET SCHEMA
- SET SERVER OPTION
- UPDATE

The statement string must not contain a statement terminator, except for the CREATE TRIGGER statement, which can contain a semicolon (;) to separate triggered SQL statements, or the CREATE PROCEDURE statement to separate SQL statements in the SQL procedure body.

Example

Use C program statements to move an SQL statement to the host variable *qstring* (char[80]). Prepare and execute whatever SQL statement is in the host variable.

```
if ( strcmp(accounts,"BIG") == 0 )
   strcpy (qstring,"INSERT INTO WORK_TABLE SELECT *
```

```
    FROM EMP_ACT WHERE ACTNO < 100");
else
  strcpy (qstring,"INSERT INTO WORK_TABLE SELECT *
    FROM EMP_ACT WHERE ACTNO >= 100");

  .

  .

EXEC SQL  EXECUTE IMMEDIATE :qstring;
```

EXPLAIN

The EXPLAIN statement captures information about the access plan chosen for a specified explainable statement and puts this information into the Explain tables. Explainable statements include DELETE, INSERT, SELECT, SELECT INTO, UPDATE, VALUES, and VALUES INTO. The authorization rules are those defined for the SQL statement specified in the EXPLAIN statement. The authorization ID of the statement must have the INSERT privilege on the Explain tables.

Syntax

```
>>-EXPLAIN--+-PLAN SELECTION-+---+----------------------+------>
            +-ALL-----------+   '--+-FOR--+---SNAPSHOT--'
            |               |      '-WITH-'
            '-PLAN----------'
>-----+----------------------------------+---------------------->
      '-SET QUERYNO =---integer--'
>-----+----------------------------------------+---------------->
      '-SET QUERYTAG =---string-constant--'
>----FOR--explainable-sql-statement--------------------------><
```

PLAN SELECTION specifies that the information from the plan selection phase of SQL compilation is to be inserted into the Explain tables. Specifying ALL or PLAN is equivalent to specifying PLAN SELECTION. (PLAN provides syntax toleration for existing database applications from other systems.)

The FOR SNAPSHOT clause specifies that only an Explain Snapshot is to be taken and placed into the SNAPSHOT column of the EXPLAIN_STATEMENT table. Explain Snapshot information is intended for use with Visual Explain. The WITH SNAPSHOT clause specifies that an Explain Snapshot is to be taken in addition to regular Explain information.

The SET QUERYNO parameter associates a specified positive integer value with the specified explainable statement (through the QUERYNO column in the EXPLAIN_STATEMENT table).

The SET QUERYTAG parameter associates a specified string constant (maximum length: 20 bytes) with the specified explainable statement (through the QUERYTAG column in the EXPLAIN_STATEMENT table).

Examples

Explain a simple SELECT statement and tag with QUERYNO = 13:

```
EXPLAIN PLAN SET QUERYNO = 13 FOR SELECT C1 FROM T1;
```

Explain a simple SELECT statement and tag with QUERYTAG = 'TEST13':

```
EXPLAIN PLAN SELECTION SET QUERYTAG = 'TEST13' FOR SELECT C1 FROM T1;
```

Explain a simple SELECT statement and tag with QUERYNO = 13 and QUERYTAG ='TEST13':

```
EXPLAIN PLAN SELECTION SET QUERYNO = 13 SET QUERYTAG = 'TEST13' FOR SELECT C1 FROM T1;
```

Attempt to get Explain information when Explain tables do not exist:

```
EXPLAIN ALL FOR SELECT C1 FROM T1;
```

This statement fails because Explain tables have not been defined.

FETCH

The FETCH statement positions a cursor on the next row of its result table and assigns the values of that row to host variables. See the description of the DECLARE CURSOR statement for an explanation of the authorization required to use a cursor.

Syntax

```
>>-FETCH--+-------+---cursor-name------------------------------->
          '-FROM--'
                     .-,---------------.
                     V                 |
>-----+-INTO-----host-variable---+---------+------------------><
      '-USING DESCRIPTOR--descriptor-name--'
```

The *cursor-name* parameter identifies the cursor that is to be used in the fetch operation. The cursor must be open.

INTO specifies one or more host variables. The first value in the result row is assigned to the first host variable in the list, and so on.

USING DESCRIPTOR specifies an SQLDA that contains a valid description of host variables.

Examples

In this C example, the FETCH statement fetches the results of the SELECT statement into the program variables *dnum, dname,* and *mnum:*

```
EXEC SQL DECLARE C1 CURSOR FOR SELECT DEPTNO, DEPTNAME, MGRNO FROM TDEPT WHERE ADMRDEPT = 'A00';
EXEC SQL OPEN C1;
   while (SQLCODE==0) {
      EXEC SQL FETCH C1 INTO :dnum, :dname, :mnum;
   }
 EXEC SQL CLOSE C1;
```

This FETCH statement uses an SQLDA:

```
FETCH CURS USING DESCRIPTOR :sqlda3
```

FLUSH EVENT MONITOR

The FLUSH EVENT MONITOR statement writes current database monitor values for all active monitor types associated with a specified event monitor to the event monitor input/output (I/O) target. When an event monitor is flushed, its active internal buffers are written to the event monitor output object. Flushing out an event monitor does not cause its values to be reset.

The authorization ID of the statement must have either SYSADM or DBADM authority.

Syntax

```
>>-FLUSH--EVENT--MONITOR--event-monitor-name--+---------+------><
                                              '-BUFFER--'
```

The event-monitor-name parameter specifies the one-part name of an event monitor. BUFFER specifies that the event monitor buffers are to be written out.

FREE LOCATOR

The FREE LOCATOR statement removes the association between a locator variable and its value.

Syntax

```
                                .-,--------------.
                                V                |
>>-FREE--LOCATOR-------variable-name---+---------------------><
```

The *variable-name* parameter specifies one or more locator variables that must be declared in accordance with the rules for declaring locator variables. The *locator-variable* must currently have a locator assigned to it. That is, a locator must have been assigned during this unit of work (by a FETCH statement or a SELECT INTO statement) and must not subsequently have been freed (by a FREE LOCATOR statement). If more than one locator is specified, all locators that can be freed will be freed, regardless of errors detected in other locators in the list.

Example

In a COBOL program, free the BLOB locator variables TKN-VIDEO and TKN-BUF, and the CLOB locator variable LIFE-STORY-LOCATOR:

```
EXEC SQL
FREE LOCATOR :TKN-VIDEO, :TKN-BUF, :LIFE-STORY-LOCATOR
END-EXEC.
```

GRANT (Database Authorities)

This form of the GRANT statement grants authorities that apply to the entire database (rather than privileges that apply to specific objects within the database).

SYSADM authority is required to grant DBADM authority. SYSADM or DBADM authority is required to grant other authorities.

Syntax

```
                      .-,----------------------.
                      V                        |
>>-GRANT--------+-BINDADD-----------+--+--ON DATABASE----------->
                +-CONNECT----------+
```

```
                    +-CREATETAB---------+
                    +-CREATE_NOT_FENCED-+
                    +-IMPLICIT_SCHEMA---+
                    +-DBADM-------------+
                    '-LOAD-------------'
           .-,-------------------------------------.
           V                                       |
>----TO----+-+-------+---authorization-name--+--+-------------><
           | +-USER--+                       |
           | '-GROUP-'                       |
           '-PUBLIC-----------------------'
```

BINDADD grants the authority to create packages. The creator of a package automatically has the CONTROL privilege on that package and retains this privilege even if the BINDADD authority is subsequently revoked.

CONNECT grants the authority to access the database.

CREATETAB grants the authority to create base tables. The creator of a base table automatically has the CONTROL privilege on that table. The creator retains this privilege even if the CREATETAB authority is subsequently revoked. There is no explicit authority required for view creation. A view can be created at any time if the authorization ID of the statement used to create the view has either the CONTROL or SELECT privilege on each base table of the view.

CREATE_NOT_FENCED grants the authority to register functions that execute in the database manager's process. Once a function has been registered as *not fenced,* it continues to run in this manner even if CREATE_NOT_FENCED is subsequently revoked.

IMPLICIT_SCHEMA grants the authority to implicitly create a schema.

DBADM grants database administrator authority. A database administrator has all privileges against all objects in the database and can grant these privileges to others. DBADM cannot be granted to PUBLIC.

LOAD grants the authority to use the DB2 load utility with this database.

Example

Give users TALLERICO and CERNY the privilege to connect to the database:

```
GRANT CONNECT ON DATABASE TO USER TALLERICO, USER CERNY
```

GRANT (Index Privileges)

This form of the GRANT statement grants the CONTROL privilege on indexes. The authorization ID of the statement must have SYSADM or DBADM authority.

Syntax

```
>>-GRANT--CONTROL--ON INDEX--index-name------------------------->
           .-,-----------------------------------.
           V                                     |
>----TO----+-+-------+---authorization-name--+--+-------------><
           | +-USER--+                        |
           | '-GROUP-'                        |
           '-PUBLIC------------------------'
```

CONTROL grants the privilege to drop the index. This privilege is automatically granted to creators of indexes.

Example

Give user TALLERICO the privilege to drop the Deptidx index:

```
GRANT CONTROL ON INDEX DEPTIDX TO USER TALLERICO
```

GRANT (Package Privileges)

This form of the GRANT statement grants privileges on a package.

The authorization ID of the statement must have at least one of the following: CONTROL privilege on the referenced package; SYSADM or DBADM authority.

Syntax

```
                .-,------------------.
                V                    |
>>-GRANT--------+-BIND---------+--+------------------------------>
                +-CONTROL------+
                |       (1)    |
                '-EXECUTE------'
                   (2)
>----ON--PACKAGE-------package-name----------------------------->
      .-,-----------------------------------.
      V                                     |
>----TO----+-+-------+---authorization-name--+--+-------------><
           | +-USER--+                        |
           | '-GROUP-'                        |
           '-PUBLIC------------------------'
```

Syntax Notes:

1. RUN can be used as a synonym for EXECUTE.

2. PROGRAM can be used as a synonym for PACKAGE.

BIND grants the privilege to bind a package. The BIND privilege is really a rebind privilege; because the package exists, it must have been bound previously.

CONTROL grants the privilege to rebind, drop, or execute the package, and extend package privileges to other users.

EXECUTE grants the privilege to execute the package.

ON PACKAGE specifies the name of the package on which privileges are to be granted.

Example

Give all users the privilege to execute the Corpdata.pkga package:

```
GRANT EXECUTE ON PACKAGE CORPDATA.PKGA TO PUBLIC
```

GRANT (Schema Privileges)

This form of the GRANT statement grants privileges on a schema. Privileges cannot be granted on schema names SYSIBM, SYSCAT, SYSFUN, or SYSSTAT.

The authorization ID of the statement must have at least one of the following: WITH GRANT OPTION for each identified privilege on *schema-name*; SYSADM or DBADM authority.

Syntax

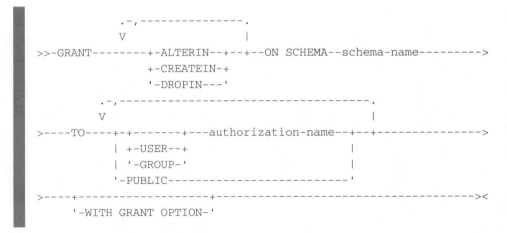

```
              .-,--------------.
              V                |
>>-GRANT--------+-ALTERIN--+--+--ON SCHEMA--schema-name--------->
               +-CREATEIN-+
               '-DROPIN---'

           .-,---------------------------------.
           V                                   |
>----TO----+-+-------+---authorization-name--+--+-------------->
           | +-USER--+                        |
           | '-GROUP-'                        |
           '-PUBLIC-----------------------'

>----+-----------------+------------------------------------><
     '-WITH GRANT OPTION-'
```

ALTERIN grants the privilege to alter or comment on all objects in the schema. The owner of an explicitly created schema automatically receives the ALTERIN privilege.

CREATEIN grants the privilege to create objects in the schema. Other authorities or privileges required to create the object (such as CREATETAB) are still required. The owner of an explicitly created schema automatically receives the CREATEIN privilege. An implicitly created schema has the CREATEIN privilege automatically granted to PUBLIC.

DROPIN grants the privilege to drop all objects in the schema. The owner of an explicitly created schema automatically receives the DROPIN privilege.

ON SCHEMA specifies the schema on which the privileges are to be granted.

WITH GRANT OPTION allows the specified authorization names to grant the privileges to others. If this option is omitted, the specified authorization names can grant the privileges to others only if they have DBADM authority or they received the ability to grant privileges from some other source.

Examples

Give user TALLERICO the privilege to create objects in the CORPDATA schema:

```
GRANT CREATEIN ON SCHEMA CORPDATA TO TALLERICO
```

GRANT (Sequence Privileges)

This form of the GRANT statement grants privileges on a user-defined sequence. The authorization ID of the statement must have at least one of the following: SYSADM or DBADM authority; owner of the sequence.

Syntax

```
>>-GRANT--USAGE--ON SEQUENCE--sequence-name--TO PUBLIC--------><
```

USAGE grants the USAGE privilege for a sequence. ON SEQUENCE *sequence-name* specifies the sequence on which the USAGE privilege is to be granted. TO PUBLIC grants the USAGE privilege to all users.

GRANT (Server Privileges)

This form of the GRANT statement grants the privilege to access and use a specified data source in passthrough mode. The authorization ID of the statement must have either SYSADM or DBADM authority.

Syntax

```
>>-GRANT PASSTHRU ON SERVER--server-name----TO----------------->

          .-,----------------------------------.
          V                                    |
>-------+-+-------+---authorization-name--+--+---------------><
        | +-USER--+                       |
        | '-GROUP-'                       |
        '-PUBLIC------------------------'
```

The *server-name* parameter specifies the data source for which the privilege to use in passthrough mode is being granted. This parameter must identify a data source that is described in the catalog.

Example

Give users TALLERICO and CERNY the privilege to access and use the SERVALL data source in passthrough mode:

```
GRANT PASSTHRU ON SERVER SERVALL TO USER TALLERICO, USER CERNY
```

GRANT (Table, View, or Nickname Privileges)

This form of the GRANT statement grants privileges on a table, view, or nickname. The authorization ID of the statement must have at least one of the following: CONTROL privilege on the referenced table, view, or nickname; the WITH GRANT OPTION for each identified privilege. If ALL is specified, the authorization ID must have some grantable privilege on the identified table, view, or nickname; SYSADM or DBADM authority.

Syntax

```
>>-GRANT------------------------------------------------------->
                .-PRIVILEGES--.
>-----+-ALL--+------------+----------------------------------+>
      |   .-,----------------------------------------.    |
      |   V                                          |    |
      '----+-ALTER-----------------------------------+--+-'
           +-CONTROL----------------------------------+
           +-DELETE-----------------------------------+
           +-INDEX------------------------------------+
           +-INSERT-----------------------------------+
           +-REFERENCES----+-------------------------+-+
```

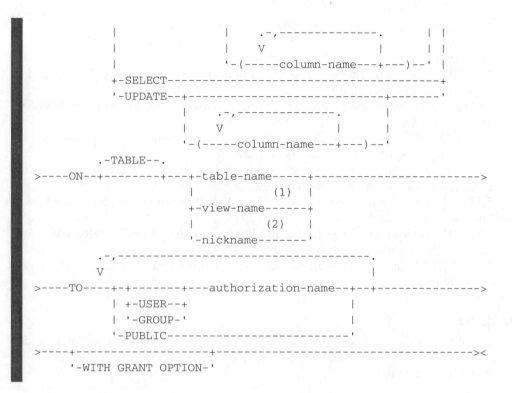

```
                  |              |        .-,--------------.      | |
                  |              |        V                |      | |
                  |              |        '-(-----column-name---+---)--' |
              +-SELECT------------------------------------------------+
              '-UPDATE--+---------------------------------+-------'
                        |          .-,--------------.      |
                        |          V                |      |
                        '-(-----column-name---+---)--'
          .-TABLE--.
    >----ON--+--------+---+-table-name-----+----------------------->
                         |            (1)  |
                         +-view-name------+
                         |            (2)  |
                         '-nickname-------'
       .-,-------------------------------------.
       V                                       |
    >----TO----+-+-------+---authorization-name--+---+--------------->
             | +-USER--+                       |
             | '-GROUP-'                       |
             '-PUBLIC-------------------------'
    >----+----------------+--------------------------------------><
         '-WITH GRANT OPTION-'
```

Syntax Notes:

1. ALTER, INDEX, or REFERENCES privileges are not applicable to views.
2. DELETE, INSERT, SELECT, or UPDATE privileges are not applicable to nicknames.

ALL or ALL PRIVILEGES grant all the appropriate privileges, except CONTROL, on the specified base table, view, or nickname.

ALTER grants the privilege to add columns to a base table definition; create or drop a primary key or a unique constraint on a base table; create or drop a foreign key on a base table (the REFERENCES privilege on each column of the parent table is also required); create or drop a check constraint on a base table; create a trigger on a base table; add, reset, or drop a column option for a nickname; change a nickname, column name, or data type; and add or change a comment on a base table, a view, or a nickname.

CONTROL grants all appropriate privileges, and the ability to grant them (except for CONTROL) to others; the ability to drop a base table, view, or nickname; the ability to invoke the *runstats* utility on a table and indexes; and the ability to issue the SET INTEGRITY statement against a base table or a summary table.

DELETE grants the privilege to delete rows from a table or updateable view.

INDEX grants the privilege to create an index on a table or an index specification on a nickname. The creator of an index or index specification automatically has the

CONTROL privilege on the index or index specification (authorizing the creator to drop the index or index specification). In addition, the creator retains the CONTROL privilege even if the INDEX privilege is revoked.

INSERT grants the privilege to insert rows into a table or an updateable view and to invoke the DB2 import utility.

REFERENCES grants the privilege to create or to drop a foreign key that references the table as the parent.

REFERENCES (*column-name,...*) grants the privilege to create or to drop a foreign key using only the specified columns as the parent key.

SELECT grants the privilege to retrieve rows from a table or a view, create views on a table, and invoke the DB2 export utility against a table or a view.

UPDATE grants the privilege to use the UPDATE statement on a table or an updateable view.

UPDATE (*column-name,...*) grants the privilege to use the UPDATE statement to update only the specified columns.

The WITH GRANT OPTION allows the specified authorization names to grant the privileges to others.

Examples

Grant the appropriate privileges on the EMPLOYEE table so that users Rosemary and Joanna can read it and insert new entries into it. Do not allow them to change or remove any existing entries:

```
GRANT SELECT, INSERT ON employee TO USER  Rosemary, USER Joanna
```

Grant INSERT, SELECT, and CONTROL privileges on the EMPLOYEE table to user Teresa. Teresa must be able to pass the privileges on to others:

```
GRANT CONTROL ON TABLE employee TO Teresa WITH GRANT OPTION
```

The result of this statement includes a warning that CONTROL was not given the WITH GRANT OPTION. Teresa now has the ability to grant any privilege on the EMPLOYEE table, including INSERT and SELECT, as requested, but Teresa cannot grant CONTROL on the EMPLOYEE table to other users unless she has SYSADM or DBADM authority.

User John created a nickname for an Oracle table that had no index. The nickname is ORAREM1. Later, the Oracle DBA defined an index for this table. User Shawn now wants DB2 to know that this index exists so that the optimizer can devise strategies to access the table more efficiently. Shawn can do this by creating an index specification for ORAREM1. Give Shawn the index privilege on this nickname so that he can create the index specification:

```
GRANT INDEX ON NICKNAME ORAREM1 TO USER Shawn
```

GRANT (Table Space Privileges)

This form of the GRANT statement grants privileges on a table space.

The authorization ID of the statement must have at least one of the following: the WITH GRANT OPTION for use of the table space; or SYSADM, SYSCTRL, or DBADM authority.

Syntax

```
>>-GRANT--USE--OF TABLESPACE--tablespace-name----TO------------->
      .-,-----------------------------------.
      V                                     |
>-------+-+-------+---authorization-name--+--+----------------->
        | +-USER--+                       |
        | '-GROUP-'                       |
        '-PUBLIC------------------------'
>-----+-------------------+--------------------------------><
        '-WITH GRANT OPTION--'
```

USE grants the privilege to specify a table space when creating a table.

OF TABLESPACE *tablespace-name* specifies the table space on which the USE privilege is to be granted. The table space cannot be SYSCATSPACE or a system temporary table space.

WITH GRANT OPTION allows the specified authorization names to grant the USE privilege to others. If this option is omitted, the specified authorization names can grant the USE privilege to others only if they have SYSADM or DBADM authority, or they received the ability to grant the USE privilege from some other source.

Example

Grant user Teresa the ability to create tables in table space PLANS, and to grant this privilege to others:

```
GRANT USE OF TABLESPACE plans TO Teresa WITH GRANT OPTION
```

INCLUDE

The INCLUDE statement inserts declarations into a source program. When a program is precompiled, the INCLUDE statement is replaced by source statements. The INCLUDE statement should therefore be specified at a point in the program where the resulting source statements are acceptable to the compiler.

Syntax

```
>>-INCLUDE----+-SQLCA-+----------------------------------------><
              +-SQLDA-+
              '-name--'
```

SQLCA specifies that the description of an SQL Communications Area (SQLCA) is
to be included.

SQLDA specifies that the description of an SQL Descriptor Area (SQLDA) is to be
included.

The *name* parameter specifies an external file containing text that is to be included
in the source program being precompiled. It can be an SQL identifier without a file
name extension, or a literal enclosed by single quotation marks. An SQL identifier
assumes the file name extension of the source file being precompiled. If a file name
extension is not provided by a literal that is enclosed by single quotation marks, none
is assumed.

INSERT

The INSERT statement inserts rows into a table or a view. Inserting a row into a view
also inserts the row into the table on which the view is based.

The authorization ID of the statement must have at least one of the following:
INSERT privilege on the table or the view; CONTROL privilege on the table or the
view; SYSADM or DBADM authority. In addition, for each table or view referenced in
any fullselect used in the INSERT statement, the authorization ID of the statement must
have at least one of the following: SELECT privilege, CONTROL privilege, SYSADM,
or DBADM authority.

Syntax

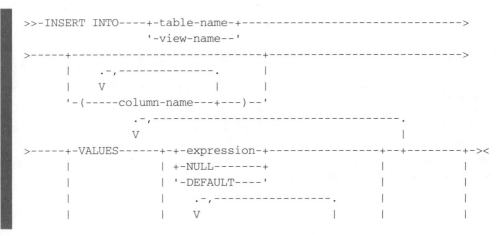

```
>>-INSERT INTO----+-table-name-+------------------------------->
                  '-view-name--'
>-----+----------------------------+-------------------------->
      |      .-,--------------.     |
      |      V                |     |
      '-(-----column-name---+---)--'
                    .-,------------------------------------.
                    V                                      |
>-----+-VALUES------+-+-expression-+----------------+--+--------+-><
      |               | +-NULL-------+              |        |
      |               | '-DEFAULT----'              |        |
      |               |     .-,----------------.    |        |
      |               |     V                  |    |        |
```

```
        |                    '-(------+-expression-+--+---)--'            |
        |                           +-NULL-------+                        |
        |                           '-DEFAULT----'                        |
        '-+----------------------------------------+---fullselect--'
          |           .-,-------------------------.  |
          |           V                           |  |
          '-WITH-----common-table-expression---+--'
 >-----+--------------+------------------------------------------------><
       '-WITH--+-RR-+--'
               +-RS-+
               +-CS-+
               '-UR-'
```

INTO specifies the object of the *insert* operation. The name must identify a table or a view that exists at the application server, but it must not identify a catalog table, a summary table, a view of a catalog table, or a read-only view. A value cannot be inserted into a view column that is derived from a constant, expression, or scalar function; the same base table column as some other column of the view; or a column derived from a nickname.

The *column-name* parameter specifies the table or view columns for which insert values are provided. Omission of the column list is an implicit specification of a list in which every column of a table or a view is identified in left-to-right order. This list is established when the statement is prepared, and therefore does not include columns that were added to a table after the statement was prepared.

VALUES specifies one or more rows of values to be inserted. A value can be an expression, the NULL value (only for nullable columns), or a default value. The number of values for each row must equal the number of names in the column list. The first value is inserted in the first column in the list, the second value in the second column, and so on.

The first WITH clause specifies a common table expression for use with the fullselect that follows.

The *fullselect* parameter specifies a set of new rows in the form of the result table of a fullselect. The number of columns in the result table must equal the number of names in the column list. The value of the first column of the result table is inserted into the first column in the list, the second value is inserted into the second column, and so on.

The second WITH clause specifies the isolation level at which the fullselect is executed. Valid values are RR, RS, CS, and UR. The default isolation level of the statement is the isolation level of the package in which the statement is bound.

Examples

Insert a new record into the Department table. Specify a department number (E31), department name (ARCHITECTURE), manager number (00390), and the number of the department to which this department reports (E01):

```
INSERT INTO DEPARTMENT VALUES ('E31', 'ARCHITECTURE', '00390', 'E01')
```

Insert a new record into the Department table. Specify a department number (E31), department name (ARCHITECTURE), and the number of the department to which this department reports (E01):

```
INSERT INTO DEPARTMENT (DEPTNO, DEPTNAME, ADMRDEPT) VALUES ('E31', 'ARCHITECTURE', 'E01')
```

Insert two new records into the Department table:

```
INSERT INTO DEPARTMENT (DEPTNO, DEPTNAME, ADMRDEPT) VALUES ('B11',
'PURCHASING', 'B01'), ('E41', 'DATABASE ADMINISTRATION', 'E01')
```

After creating a temporary table called Ma_Emp_Act with the same columns as the Emp_Act table, insert rows from the Emp_Act table into the Ma_Emp_Act table. Insert only those rows that have a project number starting with MA:

```
INSERT INTO MA_EMP_ACT SELECT * FROM EMP_ACT WHERE SUBSTR(PROJNO, 1, 2) = 'MA'
```

Use a C program statement to add a skeleton project to the PROJECT table. Obtain the project number (PROJNO), project name (PROJNAME), department number (DEPTNO), and responsible employee (RESPEMP) from host variables. Use the current date as the project start date (PRSTDATE). Assign a NULL value to the remaining columns in the table (by not specifying a non-null value for them):

```
EXEC SQL INSERT INTO PROJECT (PROJNO, PROJNAME, DEPTNO, RESPEMP, PRSTDATE)
VALUES (:PRJNO, :PRJNM, :DPTNO, :REMP, CURRENT DATE);
```

LOCK TABLE

The LOCK TABLE statement prevents concurrent application processes from using or changing a table.

The authorization ID of the statement must have at least one of the following: SELECT privilege on the table; CONTROL privilege on the table; SYSADM or DBADM authority.

Syntax

```
>>-LOCK TABLE--table-name--IN----+-SHARE-----+--MODE----------><
                                 '-EXCLUSIVE-'
```

The *table-name* parameter must identify a table that exists at the application server, but it must not identify a catalog table. It cannot be a nickname or a declared temporary table. If it is a typed table, it must be the root table of the table hierarchy.

IN SHARE MODE prevents concurrent application processes from executing any but read-only operations on the table.

IN EXCLUSIVE MODE prevents concurrent application processes from executing any operations on the table. (IN EXCLUSIVE MODE does *not* prevent concurrent application processes that are running at isolation level UR from executing read-only operations on the table.)

OPEN

The OPEN statement opens a cursor so that it can be used to fetch rows from its result table. See the description of the DECLARE CURSOR statement for the authorization required to use a cursor.

Syntax

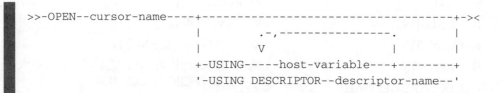

```
>>-OPEN--cursor-name----+----------------------------------+-><
                        |          .-,---------------.      |
                        |          V                 |      |
                        +-USING-----host-variable---+-------+
                        '-USING DESCRIPTOR--descriptor-name--'
```

The specified cursor must have been defined in a DECLARE CURSOR statement earlier in the program.

USING specifies a list of host variables whose values are substituted for the parameter markers (question marks) of a prepared statement.

DESCRIPTOR specifies an SQLDA that must contain a valid description of host variables.

PREPARE

The PREPARE statement is used by applications to dynamically prepare an SQL statement for execution. The PREPARE statement creates an executable SQL statement, called a *prepared statement*, from a character string form of the statement, called a *statement string*.

For statements where authorization checking is performed at statement preparation time (data manipulation language), the privileges held by the authorization ID of the statement must include those required to execute the SQL statement specified by the PREPARE statement. For statements where authorization checking is performed at statement execution (data definition language, GRANT and REVOKE statements), no authorization is required to use the statement; however, the authorization is checked when the prepared statement is executed.

Syntax

```
>>-PREPARE--statement-name----+----------------------+-------->
                              '-INTO--descriptor-name--'
>----FROM--host-variable-------------------------------------><
```

The *statement-name* parameter names the prepared statement. If the name identifies an existing prepared statement, that statement is destroyed. The name must not identify a prepared statement that is the SELECT statement of an open cursor.

INTO places information about the successfully prepared statement into the SQLDA specified by *descriptor-name*.

FROM specifies the statement string, the value of the specified host variable. The statement string must be an executable statement that can be dynamically prepared. It must be one of the following SQL statements:

- ALTER
- COMMENT ON
- COMMIT
- CREATE
- DECLARE GLOBAL TEMPORARY TABLE
- DELETE
- DROP
- EXPLAIN
- FLUSH EVENT MONITOR
- GRANT
- INSERT
- LOCK TABLE
- REFRESH TABLE
- RELEASE SAVEPOINT
- RENAME TABLE
- RENAME TABLESPACE
- REVOKE
- ROLLBACK
- SAVEPOINT
- SELECT-STATEMENT
- SET CURRENT DEFAULT TRANSFORM GROUP
- SET CURRENT DEGREE
- SET CURRENT EXPLAIN MODE
- SET CURRENT EXPLAIN SNAPSHOT
- SET CURRENT QUERY OPTIMIZATION
- SET CURRENT REFRESH AGE
- SET EVENT MONITOR STATE
- SET INTEGRITY
- SET PASSTHRU
- SET PATH
- SET SCHEMA
- SET SERVER OPTION
- UPDATE

Example

Prepare and execute a statement from within a C program. Assume that the statement can contain any number of parameter markers:

```
EXEC SQL PREPARE STMT_NAME FROM :holder;
EXEC SQL EXECUTE STMT_NAME USING DESCRIPTOR :insert_da;
```

Assume that the following statement is to be prepared:

```
INSERT INTO DEPT VALUES(?, ?, ?, ?)
```

The columns in the DEPT table are defined as follows:

```
DEPT_NO    CHAR(3) NOT NULL, -- department number
DEPTNAME   VARCHAR(29), -- department name
MGRNO      CHAR(6), -- manager number
ADMRDEPT   CHAR(3)  -- admin department number
```

Before issuing the EXECUTE statement to insert a new department record, ensure that the structure INSERT_DA contains the necessary values.

REFRESH TABLE

The REFRESH TABLE statement refreshes the data in a summary table. The authorization ID of the statement must have at least one of the following: CONTROL privilege on the table; SYSADM or DBADM authority.

Syntax

```
                   .-,-------------.
                   V               |
>>-REFRESH--TABLE-----table-name---+-------------------------><
```

The table name, including the implicit or explicit schema, must identify a table that already exists at the current server. The table must allow table refresh operations. This type of table includes summary tables defined with REFRESH IMMEDIATE or REFRESH DEFERRED.

RELEASE (Connection)

The RELEASE statement puts one or more connections in release pending state.

Syntax

```
                   (1)
>>-RELEASE----+-server-name------+----------------------------><
              +-host-variable----+
              +-CURRENT----------+
              |       .-SQL-.     |
              '-ALL-+-----+------'
```

Syntax Note:

1. An application server named CURRENT or ALL can be identified only by a host variable.

   The application server is identified by the specified server name or by the specified host variable that contains the server name. If a host variable is specified, it must be a character string variable with a length attribute that is not greater than eight, and it must not include an indicator variable. The server name that is contained within the host variable must be left-justified and must not be delimited by quotation marks. The server name is a database alias identifying the application server. It must be listed in the application requester's local directory. The specified database alias, or the database alias contained in the host variable must identify an existing connection of the application process.

   CURRENT specifies the current connection of the application process, which must be in the connected state.

   ALL specifies all existing connections of the application process. This form of the RELEASE statement puts all existing connections of the application process in release pending state. All connections are destroyed during the next commit operation. The optional keyword SQL is included to be compatible with DB2/MVS SQL syntax.

RELEASE SAVEPOINT

The RELEASE SAVEPOINT statement is used to specify that the named savepoint is no longer to be maintained. After this statement has been invoked, roll back to the savepoint is no longer possible. The name of the savepoint that was released can be reused in another SAVEPOINT statement.

Syntax

```
              .-TO-.
>>-RELEASE--+----+--SAVEPOINT--savepoint-name------------------><
```

RENAME TABLE

The RENAME TABLE statement renames an existing table. The authorization ID of the statement must have at least one of the following: CONTROL privilege on the table; SYSADM or DBADM authority.

Syntax

```
                .-TABLE-.
>>-RENAME--+-------+--source-table-name--TO--target-identifier--><
```

The specified source table name must not be the name or alias of a catalog table, a summary table, or a typed table; it must also not be a nickname or the name of an object that is not a table. The schema name associated with the source table name is used to qualify the new name for the table. The qualified name must not identify a table, view, or alias that already exists in the database.

If a table is to be renamed, it must not be referenced in any existing view definitions or summary table definitions; be referenced in any triggered SQL statements in existing triggers, or be the subject table of an existing trigger; be referenced in an SQL function; have any check constraints; have any generated columns other than the identity column; be a parent or dependent table in any referential integrity constraints; or be the scope of any existing reference column.

RENAME TABLESPACE

The RENAME TABLESPACE statement renames an existing table space. (The SYSCATSPACE table space cannot be renamed, nor can a table space that is in roll-forward pending state or in roll-forward in progress state be renamed.)

The authorization ID of the statement must have either SYSADM or SYSCTRL authority.

Syntax

```
>>-RENAME--TABLESPACE--source-tablespace-name--TO--target-tablespace-name-->>
```

The source table space name must identify a table space that already exists in the catalog. The target table space name must *not* identify a table space that already exists in the catalog, and it cannot start with *SYS*. The new table space name must be used when restoring a table space from a backup image that was created *before* the table space was renamed.

REVOKE (Database Authorities)

This form of the REVOKE statement revokes authorities that apply to the entire database. The authorization ID of the statement must have SYSADM or DBADM authority. SYSADM authority is required to revoke DBADM authority.

Syntax

```
                       .-,--------------------.
                       V                      |
>>-REVOKE------+-BINDADD-----------+--+--ON DATABASE------------>
              +-CONNECT-----------+
              +-CREATETAB---------+
              +-CREATE_NOT_FENCED-+
              +-IMPLICIT_SCHEMA---+
              +-DBADM-------------+
              '-LOAD-------------'
            .-,---------------------------------.
            V                                   |
>----FROM----+-+-------+---authorization-name--+--+----------->< 
             | +-USER--+                        |
             | '-GROUP-'                        |
             '-PUBLIC-------------------------'
```

For a description of the privileges that can be revoked by this statement, see the description of the GRANT (Database Authorities) statement.

REVOKE (Index Privileges)

This form of the REVOKE statement revokes the CONTROL privilege on an index. The authorization ID of the statement must have SYSADM or DBADM authority.

Syntax

```
>>-REVOKE--CONTROL--ON INDEX--index-name---------------------->
            .-,---------------------------------.
            V                                   |
>----FROM----+-+-------+---authorization-name--+--+----------->< 
             | +-USER--+                        |
             | '-GROUP-'                        |
             '-PUBLIC-------------------------'
```

For a description of the privileges that can be revoked by this statement, see the description of the GRANT (Index Privileges) statement.

REVOKE (Package Privileges)

This form of the REVOKE statement revokes CONTROL, BIND, or EXECUTE privileges against a package.

The authorization ID of the statement must have at least one of the following: CONTROL privilege on the referenced package; SYSADM or DBADM authority. SYSADM or DBADM authority is required to revoke the CONTROL privilege.

Syntax

```
                    .-,----------------.
                    V                  |
>>-REVOKE------+-BIND---------+--+------------------------------->
              +-CONTROL------+
              |        (1)   |
              '-EXECUTE------'
                   (2)
>----ON--PACKAGE-------package-name----------------------------->
          .-,----------------------------------.
          V                                    |
>----FROM----+-+-------+---authorization-name--+--+------------><
             | +-USER--+                       |
             | '-GROUP-'                       |
             '-PUBLIC-------------------------'
```

Syntax Notes:

1. RUN can be used as a synonym for EXECUTE.
2. PROGRAM can be used as a synonym for PACKAGE.

For a description of the privileges that can be revoked by this statement, see the description of the GRANT (Package Privileges) statement.

REVOKE (Schema Privileges)

This form of the REVOKE statement revokes the privileges on a schema. The authorization ID of the statement must have SYSADM or DBADM authority.

Syntax

```
                .-,-------------.
                V               |
>>-REVOKE------+-ALTERIN--+--+--ON SCHEMA--schema-name---------->
               +-CREATEIN-+
               '-DROPIN---'
           .-,-----------------------------------.
           V                                     |
>----FROM----+-+-------+---authorization-name--+--+------------><
             | +-USER--+                        |
             | '-GROUP-'                        |
             '-PUBLIC------------------------'
```

For a description of the privileges that can be revoked by this statement, see the description of the GRANT (Schema Privileges) statement.

REVOKE (Server Privileges)

This form of the REVOKE statement revokes the privilege to access and use a specified data source in *passthrough* mode. The authorization ID of the statement must have SYSADM or DBADM authority.

Syntax

```
>>-REVOKE PASSTHRU ON SERVER--server-name----FROM-------------->
        .-,-----------------------------------.
        V                                     |
>-------+-+-------+---authorization-name--+--+---------------><
          | +-USER--+                      |
          | '-GROUP-'                      |
          '-PUBLIC------------------------'
```

For a description of the privileges that can be revoked by this statement, see the description of the GRANT (Server Privileges) statement.

REVOKE (Table, View, or Nickname Privileges)

This form of the REVOKE statement revokes privileges on a table, view, or nickname. The authorization ID of the statement must have at least one of the following: CONTROL privilege on the referenced table, view, or nickname; SYSADM or DBADM authority. SYSADM or DBADM authority is required to revoke the CONTROL privilege or the privileges on catalog tables and views.

Syntax

```
                        .-PRIVILEGES--.              .-TABLE--.
>>-REVOKE----+-ALL--+-------------+-+--ON----+--------+--------->
             |  .-,--------------. |
             |  V                | |
             '----+-ALTER------+--+-'
                  +-CONTROL----+
                  +-DELETE-----+
                  +-INDEX------+
                  +-INSERT-----+
                  +-REFERENCES-+
                  +-SELECT-----+
                  '-UPDATE-----'
>-----+-table-name+------------------------------------------->
      +-view-name--+
      '-nickname---'
             .-,------------------------------------.
             V                                      |
>----FROM----+-+-------+---authorization-name--+--+------------><
             | +-USER--+                       |
             | '-GROUP-'                       |
             '-PUBLIC--------------------------'
```

For a description of the privileges that can be revoked by this statement, see the description of the GRANT (Table, View, or Nickname Privileges) statement.

REVOKE (Table Space Privileges)

This form of the REVOKE statement revokes the USE privilege on a table space. The authorization ID of the statement must have SYSADM, SYSCTRL, or DBADM authority.

Syntax

```
>>-REVOKE--USE--OF TABLESPACE--tablespace-name---FROM----------->
      .-,----------------------------------.
      V                                    |
>-------+-+-------+---authorization-name--+--+----------------><
```

```
| +-USER--+                          |
| '-GROUP-'                          |
'-PUBLIC-------------------------'
```

For a description of the privileges that can be revoked by this statement, see the description of the GRANT (Table Space Privileges) statement.

ROLLBACK

The ROLLBACK statement is used to back out of the database changes that were made within a unit of work or a savepoint.

Syntax

```
                    .-WORK--.
>>-ROLLBACK----+-------+-------------------------------------->
>-----+-------------------------------------+-----------------><
      '-TO SAVEPOINT--+---------------+--'
                      '-savepoint-name--'
```

The unit of work in which the ROLLBACK statement is executed is terminated, and a new unit of work is initiated. All changes made to the database during the unit of work are backed out. The following statements, however, are not under transaction control, and changes made by them are unaffected by a ROLLBACK statement:

- SET CONNECTION
- SET CURRENT DEGREE
- SET CURRENT DEFAULT TRANSFORM GROUP
- SET CURRENT EXPLAIN MODE
- SET CURRENT EXPLAIN SNAPSHOT
- SET CURRENT PACKAGESET
- SET CURRENT QUERY OPTIMIZATION
- SET CURRENT REFRESH AGE
- SET EVENT MONITOR STATE
- SET PASSTHRU
- SET PATH
- SET SCHEMA
- SET SERVER OPTION

TO SAVEPOINT specifies that a partial rollback operation is to be performed. If no savepoint is active, an error is returned. After a successful ROLLBACK operation, the savepoint continues to exist. If a value for the *savepoint-name* parameter is not provided, transactions are rolled back to the most recently set savepoint. If this clause is omitted, the entire transaction is rolled back, and savepoints within the transaction are released.

SAVEPOINT

The SAVEPOINT statement is used to set a savepoint within a transaction.

Syntax

```
>>-SAVEPOINT--savepoint-name----+---------+-------------------->
                                '-UNIQUE--'
                                         .-ON ROLLBACK RETAIN LOCKS--.
>----ON ROLLBACK RETAIN CURSORS--+--------------------------+--><
```

Requesting a UNIQUE savepoint specifies that the application does not intend to reuse this savepoint name while the savepoint is active.

The RETAIN CURSORS clause specifies that, whenever possible, open cursors are to be left unchanged by a roll back to savepoint operation.

The RETAIN LOCKS clause specifies that locks acquired after the savepoint will not be rolled back (released) during a roll back to savepoint operation.

SELECT

The SELECT statement is a form of query. For detailed information, see the descriptions of "select-statement" and "subselect" in Chapter 16.

SELECT INTO

The SELECT INTO statement produces a result table consisting of at most, one row, and assigns the values in that row to host variables. If the table is empty, the statement does not assign values to the host variables. If more than one row satisfies the search condition, an error is returned.

The authorization ID of the statement must have, for each table or view referenced in the statement, at least one of the following: SELECT privilege; CONTROL privilege; SYSADM or DBADM authority.

Syntax

```
                              .-,----------------.
                              V                  |
>>-select-clause--INTO-------host-variable---+--from-clause----->
>----+--------------+--+-----------------+--+----------------+--->
     '-where-clause-'  '-group-by-clause-'  '-having-clause-'
>-----+--------------+------------------------------------------><
      '-WITH-+-RR-+-'
            +-RS-+
            +-CS-+
            '-UR-'
```

For a description of the *select-clause, from-clause, where-clause, group-by-clause,* and *having-clause,* see Chapter 16.

WITH specifies the isolation level at which the SELECT INTO statement is executed. Valid values are RR, RS, CS, and UR. The default isolation level of the statement is the isolation level of the package in which the statement is bound.

The first value in the result row is assigned to the first host variable in the list, the second value is assigned to the second host variable, and so on. If an error occurs, no value is assigned to any host variable.

Examples

This C example puts the maximum salary in the Emp table into the host variable named MAXSALARY:

```
EXEC SQL SELECT MAX(SALARY) INTO :MAXSALARY FROM EMP;
```

This C example puts the row corresponding to employee 528671 in the Emp table into host variables:

```
EXEC SQL SELECT * INTO :h1, :h2, :h3, :h4 FROM EMP WHERE EMPNO = '528671';
```

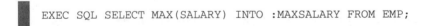

SET CONNECTION

The SET CONNECTION statement changes the state of a connection from dormant to current, making the specified location the current server. It is not under transaction control.

Syntax

```
>>-SET CONNECTION---+-server-name---+------------------------><
                    '-host-variable-'
```

The application server is identified by the specified server name or by the specified host variable that contains the server name. If a host variable is specified, it must be a character string variable with a length attribute that is not greater than eight, and it must not include an indicator variable. The server name that is contained within the host variable must be left-justified and must not be delimited by quotation marks. The server name is a database alias identifying the application server. It must be listed in the application requester's local directory. The specified database alias or the database alias contained in the host variable must identify an existing connection of the application process.

Example

Execute SQL statements at DB1, execute SQL statements at DB2, and then execute more SQL statements at DB1:

```
EXEC SQL CONNECT TO DB1; /* Execute stmts referencing objects at DB1 */
EXEC SQL CONNECT TO DB2; /* Execute stmts referencing objects at DB2 */
EXEC SQL SET CONNECTION DB1; /* Execute stmts referencing objects at DB1 */
```

The first CONNECT statement creates the DB1 connection, the second CONNECT statement puts it in a dormant state, and the SET CONNECTION statement returns it to the current state.

SET CURRENT DEFAULT TRANSFORM GROUP

The SET CURRENT DEFAULT TRANSFORM GROUP statement changes the value of the CURRENT DEFAULT TRANSFORM GROUP special register. This statement is not under transaction control.

Syntax

```
         .-CURRENT-.
>>-SET--+---------+--DEFAULT TRANSFORM GROUP------------------->
     .- = --.
>----+------+---group-name----------------------------------><
```

The *group-name* parameter specifies a one-part name that identifies a transform group defined for all structured types. This name can be referenced in subsequent statements (or until the special register value is changed again). The name must be an SQL identifier, up to 18 characters long. The definition of the named transform group is checked for validity only when a structured type is specifically referenced.

Example

Set the default transform group to MYSTRUCT1. The TO SQL and FROM SQL functions defined in the MYSTRUCT1 transform group will be used for exchanging user-defined structured type variables with the current host program.

```
SET CURRENT DEFAULT TRANSFORM GROUP = MYSTRUCT1
```

SET CURRENT DEGREE

The SET CURRENT DEGREE statement assigns a value to the CURRENT DEGREE special register. This statement is not under transaction control.

Syntax

```
                           .-=-.
>>-SET--CURRENT--DEGREE--+---+----+-string-constant-+---------><
                               '-host-variable---'
```

The value of CURRENT DEGREE is replaced by the value of a string constant or a host variable. The value must be a character string that is not longer than five bytes; it must be the character string representation of an integer between 1 and 32,767 inclusive, or 'ANY'.

If the value of CURRENT DEGREE is '1' when an SQL statement is dynamically prepared, the execution of that statement will not use intrapartition parallelism. If the value is greater than '1', the execution of that statement can involve intrapartition parallelism with the specified degree. If the value of CURRENT DEGREE is 'ANY' when an SQL statement is dynamically prepared, the execution of that statement can involve intrapartition parallelism, using a degree that is determined by the database manager.

The specified host variable must be of data type CHAR or VARCHAR, with a maximum length of five bytes.

SET CURRENT EXPLAIN MODE

The SET CURRENT EXPLAIN MODE statement changes the value of the CURRENT EXPLAIN MODE special register. It is not under transaction control.

If the Explain facility is activated, the current authorization ID must have the INSERT privilege on the Explain tables.

Syntax

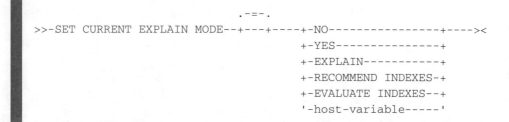

```
                            .-=-.
>>-SET CURRENT EXPLAIN MODE--+---+----+-NO--------------+---><
                                 +-YES-------------+
                                 +-EXPLAIN---------+
                                 +-RECOMMEND INDEXES-+
                                 +-EVALUATE INDEXES--+
                                 '-host-variable-----'
```

NO disables the Explain facility. No explain information is captured. NO is the initial value of the special register.

YES enables the Explain facility and causes explain information to be inserted into the Explain tables for eligible dynamic SQL statements. All dynamic SQL statements are compiled and executed normally.

EXPLAIN enables the Explain facility and causes Explain information to be captured for any eligible dynamic SQL statement that is prepared; however, dynamic statements are not executed.

RECOMMEND INDEXES enables the SQL compiler to recommend indexes. All queries that are executed under this Explain mode populate the ADVISE_INDEX table with recommended indexes. Although Explain information is captured in the Explain tables to reveal how the recommended indexes are used, the statements are neither compiled nor executed.

EVALUATE INDEXES enables the SQL compiler to evaluate indexes. The indexes to be evaluated are read from the ADVISE_INDEX table and must be marked with EVALUATE = Y. The optimizer generates virtual indexes based on the values from the catalogs. All queries that are executed in this Explain mode will be compiled and optimized using estimated statistics based on the virtual indexes. The statements are not executed.

The host variable must be of data type CHAR or VARCHAR, with a maximum length of 254 bytes. The specified value must be one of NO, YES, EXPLAIN, RECOMMEND INDEXES, or EVALUATE INDEXES.

SET CURRENT EXPLAIN SNAPSHOT

The SET CURRENT EXPLAIN SNAPSHOT statement changes the value of the CURRENT EXPLAIN SNAPSHOT special register. It is not under transaction control.

If the explain snapshot facility is activated, the current authorization ID must have the INSERT privilege on the explain tables. The explain snapshot facility is intended for use with Visual Explain.

Syntax

```
                                               .-=-.
>>-SET--CURRENT--EXPLAIN--SNAPSHOT--+---+----+-NO-----------+->< 
                                             +-YES----------+
                                             +-EXPLAIN------+
                                             '-host-variable-'
```

NO disables the Explain snapshot facility. No snapshot is taken. NO is the initial value of the special register.

YES enables the Explain snapshot facility, creating a snapshot of the internal representation for each eligible dynamic SQL statement. This information is inserted into the SNAPSHOT column of the EXPLAIN_STATEMENT table.

EXPLAIN enables the explain snapshot facility, creating a snapshot of the internal representation of each eligible dynamic SQL statement that is prepared; however, dynamic statements are not executed.

The host variable must be of data type CHAR or VARCHAR, with a maximum length of eight bytes. The specified value must be one of NO, YES, or EXPLAIN.

Example

Retrieve the current value of the CURRENT EXPLAIN SNAPSHOT special register into a host variable called SNAP:

```
EXEC SQL VALUES (CURRENT EXPLAIN SNAPSHOT) INTO :SNAP;
```

SET CURRENT PACKAGESET

The SET CURRENT PACKAGESET statement sets the schema name (collection identifier) that will be used to select the package for subsequent SQL statements. This statement is not under transaction control.

Syntax

```
                                  .-=-.
>>-SET--CURRENT PACKAGESET--+---+----+-string-constant-+------->< 
                                   '-host-variable---'
```

The specified character string constant has a maximum length of 30 bytes.

The host variable must be of data type CHAR or VARCHAR, with a maximum length of 30 bytes. It cannot be set to null.

SET CURRENT QUERY OPTIMIZATION

The SET CURRENT QUERY OPTIMIZATION statement assigns a value to the CURRENT QUERY OPTIMIZATION special register. This value specifies the current class of optimization techniques enabled when preparing dynamic SQL statements. This statement is not under transaction control.

Syntax

```
                                         .-=-.
>>-SET--CURRENT--QUERY--OPTIMIZATION--+---+-------------------->
>-----+-0------------+------------------------------------------><
      +-1------------+
      +-2------------+
      +-3------------+
      +-5------------+
      +-7------------+
      +-9------------+
      '-host-variable-'
```

The optimization class can be specified as an integer constant or the name of a host variable that will contain an appropriate value at run time:

- **0** Specifies that a minimal amount of optimization be performed to generate an access plan. This class is appropriate for simple dynamic SQL access to well-indexed tables.

- **1** Specifies that optimization roughly comparable to DB2 version 1 be performed to generate an access plan.

- **2** Specifies a level of optimization higher than that of DB2 version 1, but at significantly less cost than levels 3 and above, especially for very complex queries.

- **3** Specifies that a moderate amount of optimization be performed to generate an access plan.

- **5** Specifies that a significant amount of optimization be performed to generate an access plan. For complex dynamic SQL queries, heuristic rules are used to limit the amount of time spent selecting an access plan. Where possible, queries will use summary tables instead of the underlying base tables.

REFERENCE

- **7** Specifies that a significant amount of optimization be performed to generate an access plan. Similar to 5, but without the heuristic rules.

- **9** Specifies that a maximal amount of optimization be performed to generate an access plan. This class can greatly expand the number of possible access plans that are evaluated, and it should be used to determine if a better access plan can be generated for very complex and long-running queries that use large tables.

The host variable is of data type INTEGER. The value must be one of 0, 1, 2, 3, 5, 7, or 9. If the host variable has an associated indicator variable, the value of that indicator variable must not indicate a NULL value.

SET CURRENT REFRESH AGE

The SET CURRENT REFRESH AGE statement changes the value of the CURRENT REFRESH AGE special register. This statement is not under transaction control.

Syntax

```
                                    .-=-.
>>-SET--CURRENT REFRESH AGE--+---+----+-numeric-constant-+------><
                                 +-ANY-------------+
                                 '-host-variable----'
```

The numeric constant is a DECIMAL(20,6) value representing a timestamp duration. The value must be 0 or 99999999999999. (The microseconds portion of the value is ignored.) Zero specifies that only summary tables defined with REFRESH IMMEDIATE can be used to optimize the processing of a query. 99999999999999 or ANY specifies that any summary tables defined with REFRESH DEFERRED or REFRESH IMMEDIATE can be used to optimize the processing of a query.

The host variable is of type DECIMAL(20,6), or another type that is assignable to DECIMAL(20,6). It cannot be set to null. If the host variable has an associated indicator variable, the value of that indicator variable must not indicate a NULL value. The value of the host variable must be 0 or 99999999999999.000000.

SET ENCRYPTION PASSWORD

The SET ENCRYPTION PASSWORD statement sets the password that will be used by the encryption and decryption functions. The password is not tied to DB2 authentication, and it is used only for data encryption. This statement is not under transaction control.

Syntax

```
                              .-=-.
>>-SET--ENCRYPTION PASSWORD--+---+--+-host-variable---+-------->< 
                                    '-string-constant-'
```

This statement can be used by the ENCRYPT, DECRYPT_BIN, and DECRYPT_CHAR built-in functions for password-based encryption. The length of the password must be between 6 and 127 characters, inclusive. All characters must be specified in the exact case intended because there is no conversion to uppercase characters. The host variable is a variable of type CHAR or VARCHAR; it cannot be set to null.

SET EVENT MONITOR STATE

The SET EVENT MONITOR STATE statement activates or deactivates an event monitor. This statement is not under transaction control.

The authorization ID of the statement must have either SYSADM or DBADM authority.

Syntax

```
>>-SET--EVENT--MONITOR--event-monitor-name--STATE-------------->
      .-=-.
>----+---+--+-0------------+--------------------------------->< 
             +-1------------+
             '-host-variable-'
```

The *event-monitor-name* parameter specifies the event monitor that is to be activated or deactivated. The name must identify an event monitor that exists in the catalog.

The new state can be specified as an integer constant or the name of a host variable that contains an appropriate value at run time. A value of 0 specifies that the event monitor should be deactivated; a value of 1 specifies that the event monitor should be activated.

The host variable is of type INTEGER, with a value of 0 or 1. If the host variable has an associated indicator variable, the value of that indicator variable must not indicate a NULL value.

SET INTEGRITY

The SET INTEGRITY statement is used to turn off integrity checking for one or more tables (primary key and unique constraints continue to be checked); or turn integrity checking back on, with or without deferred checking being carried out. If the statement is used to check the integrity of a table after a DB2 load operation, the system will, by default, check only the appended portion for constraints violations. The SET INTEGRITY statement is under transaction control.

To turn integrity checking *off*, the authorization ID of the statement must have at least one of the following: CONTROL privilege on the tables and all of their dependents; SYSADM or DBADM authority; LOAD authority.

To turn integrity checking *on* and carry out deferred checking, the authorization ID of the statement must have at least one of the following: CONTROL privilege on the tables and, if exceptions are being posted, INSERT privilege on the exception tables; SYSADM or DBADM authority; LOAD authority and, if exceptions are being posted, SELECT and DELETE privilege on each table being checked, and INSERT privilege on the exception tables.

To turn integrity checking on without first carrying out deferred checking, the authorization ID of the statement must have at least one of the following: CONTROL privilege on the tables; SYSADM or DBADM authority; LOAD authority.

Syntax

```
>>-SET--INTEGRITY---------------------------------------------->

              .-,-------------.
              V               |
>-----+-FOR-----table-name---+---+-OFF-----------------------------------------+--+>
      |                          +-TO DATALINK RECONCILE PENDING-------------+  |
      |                          '-IMMEDIATE CHECKED--+-------------------+-'   |
      |                                               '-| check-options |--'    |
      |        .-,------------------------------------.                         |
      |        V                                      |                         |
      '-FOR-----table-name--| integrity-options |---+--IMMEDIATE UNCHECKED-- ---'
>------------------------------------------------------------------->< 

check-options
|--*---+-------------+---*---+-----------------+---*------------>
       '-INCREMENTAL-'       '-FORCE GENERATED-'
>-----+-------------------------+-----------------------------|
      '-| exception-clause |-'
exception-clause
                     .-,----------------------------------.
                     V                                    |
|---FOR--EXCEPTION-------IN--table-name--USE--table-name---+----|
integrity-options
|---+-ALL----------------------------------+------------------|
    |  .-,----------------------------. |
    |  V                              | |
    '----+-FOREIGN KEY----------------+--+-'
```

```
+-CHECK--------------------+
+-DATALINK RECONCILE PENDING-+
+-SUMMARY-------------------+
'-GENERATED COLUMN----------'
```

The *table-name* parameter specifies one or more tables for integrity processing. The tables must be described in the catalog, and must not be views, catalog tables, or typed tables.

OFF specifies that the tables are to have their foreign key constraints, check constraints, and column generation turned off and are to be put in check pending state. If a specified table is a summary table, immediate refreshing (if applicable) is turned off, and the summary table is put in check pending state.

TO DATALINK RECONCILE PENDING specifies that the tables are to have DATALINK integrity constraint checking turned off, and the tables are to be put in check pending state. If a table is already in DataLink Reconcile Not Possible (DRNP) state, it remains in this state, and it is also in check pending state. Otherwise, the table is put in DataLink Reconcile Pending (DRP) state.

IMMEDIATE CHECKED specifies that the table is to have its integrity checking turned on, and that the integrity checking that was deferred is to be carried out. This is done according to information in the STATUS and CONST_CHECKED columns of the SYSCAT.TABLES catalog; that is, the value in STATUS must be C (the table is in check pending state), and the value in CONST_CHECKED indicates which integrity options are to be checked. If it is a summary table, the data is checked against the query and refreshed as necessary. DATALINK values are not checked, even if the table is in DRP or DRNP state. The reconcile utility should be used to reconcile DATALINK values. The table will be taken out of check pending state, but it will continue to have the DRP or DRNP flag set. This makes the table usable, and the reconciliation of DATALINK values can be deferred.

The INCREMENTAL check option specifies the application of deferred integrity checking on the appended portion (if any) of the table. If such a request cannot be satisfied (that is, the system detects that the whole table needs to be checked for data integrity), an error is returned. If this clause is not specified, the system determines whether incremental processing is possible; if it is not, the whole table is checked.

The FORCE GENERATED check option specifies that if the table includes generated columns, the values are to be computed on the basis of the expression and stored in the column. If this clause is not specified, the current values are compared to the computed value of the expression, as though an equality check constraint were in effect.

FOR EXCEPTION specifies that any row that is in violation of a foreign key constraint or a check constraint is to be copied to an exception table *and deleted from the original table.* Even if errors are detected, the constraints are turned back on again, and the table is taken out of check pending state. A warning is returned to indicate that one or more rows have been moved to the exception table. If the FOR EXCEPTION clause is not specified and any constraints are violated, only the first violation is returned. This clause cannot be specified if the table is a summary table.

IN *table-name* specifies the table from which rows that violate constraints are to be copied. USE *table-name* specifies the corresponding exception table into which the rows are to be copied.

The integrity-options clause is used to specify the integrity options that are to be set to IMMEDIATE UNCHECKED. ALL specifies that all integrity options are to be turned on. Individual integrity options that can be turned on include foreign key constraints, check constraints, DATALINK integrity constraints, and generated columns. SUMMARY specifies that immediate refreshing should be turned on for a summary table that has the REFRESH IMMEDIATE attribute.

IMMEDIATE UNCHECKED specifies one of the following: the table is to have integrity checking turned on (and is to be taken out of check pending state) without being checked for integrity violations; the summary table is to have immediate refreshing turned on, and be taken out of check pending state; the table is to have one type of integrity checking turned on, but is to be left in check pending state.

Examples

Following is a query that gives information about the check pending state of tables. The SUBSTR function is used to extract the first two bytes of the CONST_CHECKED column in SYSCAT.TABLES. The first byte represents foreign key constraints, and the second byte represents check constraints:

```
SELECT TABNAME, SUBSTR(CONST_CHECKED, 1, 1) AS FK_CHECKED, SUBSTR(CONST_CHECKED,
2, 1) AS CC_CHECKED FROM SYSCAT.TABLES WHERE STATUS = 'C'
```

Check integrity for TABLE1 and TABLE2, and put the violating rows into exception tables EXCEPT1 and EXCEPT2:

```
SET INTEGRITY FOR TABLE1, TABLE2 IMMEDIATE CHECKED FOR EXCEPTION IN TABLE1
USE EXCEPT1, IN TABLE2 USE EXCEPT2
```

Add a check constraint and a foreign key to the EMP_ACT table, using two ALTER TABLE statements. To perform constraints checking in a single pass, turn integrity checking off before invoking the ALTER TABLE statements, and on after they have completed successfully:

```
SET INTEGRITY FOR EMP_ACT OFF;
ALTER TABLE EMP_ACT ADD CHECK (EMSTDATE <= EMENDATE);
ALTER TABLE EMP_ACT ADD FOREIGN KEY (EMPNO) REFERENCES EMPLOYEE;
SET INTEGRITY FOR EMP_ACT IMMEDIATE CHECKED;
```

REFERENCE

SET PASSTHRU

The SET PASSTHRU statement opens and closes a session for submitting a data source's native SQL directly to that data source. This statement is not under transaction control.

The authorization ID of the statement must have the authority to pass through to the data source and to satisfy security measures at the data source.

Syntax

```
>>-SET PASSTHRU----+-server-name-+--------------------------><
                   '-RESET-------'
```

The *server-name* parameter specifies the data source for which a passthrough session is to be opened. The data source must be described in the catalog.

RESET closes a passthrough session.

SET PATH

The SET PATH statement changes the value of the CURRENT PATH special register. The CURRENT PATH special register specifies the SQL path used to resolve user-defined data types, procedures, and functions in dynamic SQL statements. This statement is not under transaction control.

Syntax

```
                            .-FUNCTION-.
          .-CURRENT--+---------+---.                  .-=-.
>>-SET--+-------------------------+---PATH---+---+-------------->
        .-,---------------------------------.
        V                                   |
>-------+-schema-name-------------------+--+---------------><
        +-SYSTEM PATH-------------------+
        +-USER--------------------------+
        |              .-FUNCTION--.     |
        +-CURRENT--+-----------+---PATH--+
        +-host-variable-----------------+
        '-string-constant---------------'
```

The *schema-name* parameter specifies a schema that exists at the application server. Specifying SYSTEM PATH is equivalent to specifying the schema names "SYSIBM","SYSFUN".

USER specifies the value of the USER special register.

CURRENT PATH specifies the value of the CURRENT PATH special register before the execution of this statement.

The host variable is of type CHAR or VARCHAR, with a maximum length of 30 bytes. It cannot be set to null. If the host variable has an associated indicator variable, the value of that indicator variable must not indicate a NULL value. The characters must be left-justified. When specifying the schema name with a host variable, all characters must be specified in the exact case intended because there is no conversion to uppercase characters. The character string constant has a maximum length of eight bytes.

SET SCHEMA

The SET SCHEMA statement changes the value of the CURRENT SCHEMA special register. The value of the CURRENT SCHEMA special register is used as the schema name in all dynamic SQL statements, except for the CREATE SCHEMA statement, where an unqualified reference to a database object exists. If a package is bound with the DYNAMICRULES BIND option, the statement has no effect. This statement is not under transaction control.

Syntax

```
           .-CURRENT-.              .-=-.
>>-SET--+---------+--SCHEMA--+---+----+-schema-name-----+------><
                                  +-USER-----------+
                                  +-host-variable---+
                                  '-string-constant-'
```

The *schema-name* parameter specifies a schema that exists at the application server. The length must not exceed 30 bytes.

USER specifies the value of the USER special register.

The host variable is of type CHAR or VARCHAR, with a maximum length of 30 bytes. It cannot be set to null. If the host variable has an associated indicator variable, the value of that indicator variable must not indicate a NULL value. The characters must be left-justified. When specifying the schema name with a host variable, all characters must be specified in the exact case intended because there is no conversion to uppercase characters. The character string constant has a maximum length of 30 bytes.

SET SERVER OPTION

The SET SERVER OPTION statement specifies a server option setting that is to remain in effect while a user or application is connected to a federated database. This statement must be invoked at the start of the first unit of work that is processed after the connection has been established. When the connection ends, this server option's previous setting is reinstated. This statement is not under transaction control.

The authorization ID of the statement must have either SYSADM or DBADM authority on the federated database.

Syntax

```
>>-SET SERVER OPTION--server-option-name---TO--string-constant-->

>----FOR--SERVER--server-name----------------------------------><
```

The *server-option-name* parameter specifies the server option that is to be set.

TO specifies the server option setting as a character string constant.

SERVER specifies the data source to which *server-option-name* applies. It must be a server that is described in the catalog.

SET Variable

The SET Variable statement assigns values to local variables or to new transition variables. It is under transaction control. To reference a transition variable, the authorization ID of the trigger creator must have at least one of the following: SYSADM or DBADM authority; UPDATE privilege on the columns referenced on the left side of the assignment, and SELECT privilege on any columns referenced on the right side; CONTROL privilege on the subject table of the trigger. To execute this statement with a row fullselect as the right side of the assignment, the authorization ID of either the trigger definer or the dynamic compound statement owner must also have at least one of the following for each referenced table or view: SYSADM or DBADM authority; SELECT privilege; CONTROL privilege.

Syntax

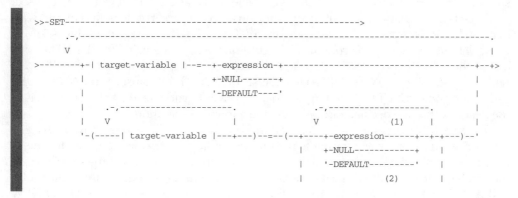

```
                                             '-row-fullselect------------'
>-------------------------------------------------------------><
target-variable
|---+-SQL-variable-name--------+---+-------------------------+-|
     '-transition-variable-name-'   |   .-------------------.   |
                                    |   V                   |   |
                                    '----..attribute-name---+--'
```

SYNTAX NOTES:

1. The number of expressions, NULLs, and DEFAULTs must match the number of target variables.

2. The number of columns in the select list must match the number of target variables.

The target-variable clause specifies the target variable of the assignment. The *SQL-variable-name* parameter specifies the SQL variable that is the assignment target. SQL variables must be declared before they are used. SQL variables can be defined in a dynamic compound statement. The *transition-variable-name* parameter specifies the column that is to be updated. A transition variable name must identify a column in the subject table of a trigger. The *..attribute-name* parameter specifies the attribute of a structured type that is set. (This is referred to as an *attribute assignment*.)

The specified SQL variable name or the transition variable name must be defined with a user-defined structured type. The specified attribute must be an attribute of the structured type. An assignment that does not involve the *..attribute-name* parameter is referred to as a *conventional assignment*.

The *expression* parameter specifies the new value of the target variable. The expression cannot include a column function, except when it occurs within a scalar fullselect. In the context of a CREATE TRIGGER statement, an expression can contain references to OLD and NEW transition variables and must be qualified by the correlation name that specifies the transition variable. NULL specifies the NULL value and can be specified only for nullable columns. DEFAULT specifies that the default value is to be used.

If the target variable is a column, the value inserted depends on how the column was defined. If the column was defined using the WITH DEFAULT clause, the value is set to the default defined for the column. If the column was defined using the IDENTITY clause, the value is generated by the database manager. If the column was defined without specifying the WITH DEFAULT clause, the IDENTITY clause, or the NOT NULL clause, the value is NULL. If the target variable is an SQL variable, the value inserted is the default value, as specified or implied in the variable declaration.

The *row-fullselect* parameter specifies a fullselect that returns a single row with a number of columns corresponding to the number of target variables specified for the *assignment* parameter. The values are assigned to each corresponding target variable. If the result of the row fullselect is no rows, NULL values are assigned. In the context of a CREATE TRIGGER statement, a row fullselect can contain references to OLD and NEW transition variables, which must be qualified by their correlation name that specifies the transition variable.

Example

Set the salary and the commission column of the row on which a trigger action is currently executing to the average salary and commission of the corresponding department.

```
SET (NEW_VAR.SALARY, NEW_VAR.COMM) = (SELECT AVG(SALARY), AVG(COMM) FROM
EMPLOYEE E WHERE E.WORKDEPT = NEW_VAR.WORKDEPT);
```

SIGNAL SQLSTATE

The SIGNAL SQLSTATE statement is used to signal an error. It can be used as a triggered SQL statement only within a trigger.

Syntax

```
>>-SIGNAL--SQLSTATE--string-constant---(--diagnostic-string--)--><
```

The specified string constant represents an SQLSTATE. It must be a character string constant with exactly five characters: each character must be from the set of digits ('0' through '9') or nonaccented uppercase letters ('A' through 'Z'); the SQLSTATE class (first two characters) cannot be '00', '01' or '02'; if the SQLSTATE class starts with the character '0' through '6', or 'A' through 'H', the subclass (last three characters) must start with a letter in the range of 'I' through 'Z'; if the SQLSTATE class starts with the character '7' through '9', or 'I' through 'Z', the subclass can be any of '0' through '9', or 'A' through 'Z'.

The specified diagnostic string describes the error condition. It is an expression of type CHAR or VARCHAR that returns a character string up to 70 bytes long; if the string is longer than 70 bytes, it is truncated.

Example

An order system records orders in an ORDERS table only if there is sufficient stock in the PARTS table:

```
CREATE TRIGGER check_avail
  NO CASCADE BEFORE INSERT ON orders
  REFERENCING NEW AS new_order
  FOR EACH ROW MODE DB2SQL
  WHEN (new_order.quantity >
```

```
        (SELECT on_hand FROM parts
          WHERE new_order.partno = parts.partno))
     BEGIN ATOMIC
       SIGNAL SQLSTATE '75001' ('Insufficient stock for order');
     END
```

UPDATE

The UPDATE statement updates the values of specified columns in rows of a table or
view. Updating a row in a view updates a row in its base table.

A *searched update* is used to update one or more rows (optionally identified by a
specified search condition). A *positioned update* is used to update exactly one row
(determined by the current position of a cursor).

The authorization ID of the statement must have at least one of the following:
UPDATE privilege on the table or view; UPDATE privilege on each column to be
updated; CONTROL privilege on the table or view; SYSADM or DBADM authority.

If a row fullselect is included in the assignment, the authorization ID of the
statement must have at least one of the following (for each referenced table or view):
SELECT privilege; CONTROL privilege; SYSADM or DBADM authority.

For each table or view referenced by a subquery, the authorization ID of the
statement must have at least one of the following: SELECT privilege; CONTROL
privilege; SYSADM or DBADM authority.

If a package is precompiled with SQL92 rules (that is, precompiled with
LANGLEVEL SQL92E or MIA), and a searched update includes a reference to a table
or view column on the right side of the assignment clause or anywhere in the search
condition, the authorization ID of the statement must have at least one of the following:
SELECT privilege; CONTROL privilege; SYSADM or DBADM authority.

If the ONLY keyword is specified, the authorization ID of the statement must have
the SELECT privilege for every subtable or subview of the specified table or view.

Syntax

Searched UPDATE:

```
>>-UPDATE--+-table-name----------------+---------------------->
           +-view-name-----------------+
           '-ONLY--(--+-table-name-+--)-'
                      '-view-name--'
--+--------------------------+--SET--| assignment-clause |----->
  | .-AS-.                 |
  '-+----+--correlation-name-'
--+--------------------------+--+--------------+--------------><
  '-WHERE--search-condition-'  '-WITH--+-RR-+-'
```

```
                                    +-RS-+
                                    +-CS-+
                                    '-UR-'
```

Positioned UPDATE:

```
>>-UPDATE--+-table-name----------------+---------------------->
           +-view-name-----------------+
           '-ONLY--(--+-table-name-+--)-'
                      '-view-name--'
--+-------------------------+--SET--| assignment-clause |----->
  | .-AS-.                  |
  '-+----+--correlation-name-'
--WHERE CURRENT OF--cursor-name------------------------------><

assignment-clause
    .-,---------------------------------------------------------------------------------.
    V                                                                                   |
|----+-column-name--+------------------------+--=--+-expression-+------------------------+-+--|
     |              | .-----------------.    |     +-NULL-------+                        |
     |              | V                 |    |     '-DEFAULT----'                        |
     |              '---..attribute-name-+-'                                             |
     |    .-,----------------------------------.        .-,------------------.           |
     |    V                                    |        V             (1)  |           |
     '-(----column-name--+--------------------+-+--)--=--(--+----+-expression-+------+-+--)-'
                         | .-----------------. |           |  +-NULL-------+          |
                         | V                 | |           |  '-DEFAULT----'          |
                         '---..attribute-name-+-'          |            (2)           |
                                                           '-row-fullselect----------'
```

Syntax Notes:

1. The number of expressions, NULLs, and DEFAULTs must match the number of column names.

2. The number of columns in the select list must match the number of column names.

The *table-name* or the *view-name* parameter specifies the table or the view that is to be updated. The name must identify a table or a view that is described in the catalog, but not a catalog table, a view of a catalog table (unless it is one of the updateable SYSSTAT views), a summary table, a read-only view, or a nickname. If the table is a typed table, its rows, or the rows of its proper subtables, may get updated by the statement. Only the columns of the specified table can be set or referenced in the WHERE clause. For a positioned update, the associated cursor must also have specified the same table or view in the FROM clause without specifying the ONLY keyword.

Applicable to typed tables, the ONLY (*table-name*) parameter specifies that the statement applies only to data from the specified table, and that rows from proper subtables cannot be updated by the statement. For a positioned update, the associated cursor must also have specified the table in the FROM clause, specifying the ONLY keyword. If the table is not a typed table, the ONLY keyword is ignored.

Applicable to typed views, the ONLY (*view-name*) parameter specifies that the statement applies only to data from the specified view, and that rows from proper subviews cannot be updated by the statement. For a positioned update, the associated cursor must also have specified the view in the FROM clause, specifying the ONLY keyword. If the view is not a typed view, the ONLY keyword is ignored.

A correlation name can be used to specify the table or view in a search condition.

SET introduces the assignment of values to column names.

The *column-name* parameter specifies a column to be updated; it must be an updateable column of the specified table or view.

The *..attribute-name* parameter specifies the attribute of a structured type that is to be set. This is referred to as an *attribute assignment*. The specified column name must be defined with a user-defined structured type, and the attribute must be of that structured type. An assignment that does not involve the *..attribute-name* parameter is referred to as a *conventional assignment*.

The *expression* parameter specifies a new value for the column. The expression cannot include a column function, except when it occurs within a scalar fullselect. An expression can contain references to columns in the target table.

NULL specifies the NULL value, and can be specified only for nullable columns. NULL cannot be the value in an attribute assignment unless it was specifically cast to the data type of the attribute.

DEFAULT specifies that a default value should be used, based on how the corresponding column was defined.

The *row-fullselect* parameter specifies a fullselect that returns a single row with a number of columns that corresponds to the number of column names specified. Values are assigned to each corresponding column name. If the fullselect returns no rows, NULL values are assigned. A row fullselect can contain references to columns in the target table.

WHERE *search-condition* specifies which rows are to be updated. If the clause is omitted, all rows in the table or view are updated. Each specified column in the search condition, other than in a subquery, must be a column in the table or the view. If the search condition includes a subquery in which the same table is the base object of both the UPDATE statement and the subquery, the subquery is completely evaluated before any rows are updated.

WHERE CURRENT OF *cursor-name* specifies the cursor that is to be used in the update operation. In this case, the DECLARE CURSOR statement must precede the UPDATE statement in the program. The specified table or view must also be named in the FROM clause of the SELECT statement for the cursor, and the result table for the cursor must not be read-only. When the UPDATE statement is executed, the row on which the cursor is positioned is the row that is updated.

WITH specifies the isolation level at which the UPDATE statement is executed. Valid values are RR, RS, CS, and UR. The default isolation level of the statement is the isolation level of the package in which the statement is bound.

Examples

Change the job title of employee number 000290 in the Employee table to LABORER:

```
UPDATE EMPLOYEE SET JOB = 'LABORER' WHERE EMPNO = '000290'
```

All of the employees (except the manager) of department E21 have been reassigned. Change their job titles to NULL and their compensation values to zero in the Employee table:

```
UPDATE EMPLOYEE SET JOB = NULL, SALARY = 0, BONUS = 0, COMM = 0 WHERE
WORKDEPT = 'E21' AND JOB <> 'MANAGER'
```

Following is an alternate form of the previous statement:

```
UPDATE EMPLOYEE SET (JOB, SALARY, BONUS, COMM) = (NULL, 0, 0, 0) WHERE
WORKDEPT = 'E21' AND JOB <> 'MANAGER'
```

Update the salary and the commission of employee number 000120 to the average salary and commission of this employee's department:

```
UPDATE EMPLOYEE EU SET (EU.SALARY, EU.COMM) = (SELECT AVG(ES.SALARY), AVG(ES.COMM)
FROM EMPLOYEE ES WHERE ES.WORKDEPT = EU.WORKDEPT) WHERE EU.EMPNO = '000120'
```

VALUES

The VALUES statement is a form of query. For detailed information, see the description of fullselect in Chapter 16.

VALUES INTO

The VALUES INTO statement produces a result table consisting of at most, one row, and assigns the values in that row to host variables.

Syntax

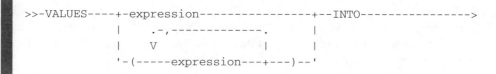

```
>>-VALUES----+-expression----------------+--INTO--------------->
             |      .-,-------------.      |
             |      V               |      |
             '-(-----expression---+---)--'
```

```
    .-,----------------.
    V                  |
>--------host-variable---+--------------------------------------><
```

The *expression* parameter defines the value of a single column in a result table consisting of at most, one row. The first value in the result row is assigned to the first host variable in the list, the second value in the result row is assigned to the second host variable in the list, and so on.

Example

This C example retrieves the value of the CURRENT PATH special register into a host variable:

```
EXEC SQL VALUES(CURRENT PATH) INTO :hvl;
```

WHENEVER

The WHENEVER statement specifies the action that is to be taken when a specified exception condition occurs.

Syntax

```
>>-WHENEVER----+-NOT FOUND--+------------------------------------->
               +-SQLERROR---+
               '-SQLWARNING-'
>-----+-CONTINUE-------------------------------+------------------><
      '--+-GOTO--+---+----+---host-label--'
         '-GO TO-'   '-:--'
```

NOT FOUND specifies any condition that results in an SQLCODE of +100, or an SQLSTATE of '02000'.

SQLERROR specifies any condition that results in a negative SQLCODE.

SQLWARNING specifies any condition that returns a warning or that results in a positive SQLCODE other than +100.

CONTINUE specifies that the next sequential instruction in the source program is to be executed.

GOTO or GO TO *host-label* specifies that control is to pass to the statement identified by *host-label*. Substitute a single token for *host-label*, optionally preceded by a colon. The form of the token depends on the host language.

The Complete Reference

DB2

Chapter 28

Environment and Registry Variables

nvironment and registry variables are used to establish certain conditions within your working environment either at the instance or the database level. Some of the environment and registry variables specify conditions that are specific to a particular operating environment, such as DB2DOMAINLIST, which defines one or more Windows NT domains. Some of the variables specify conditions that are specific to the use of hardware, such as DB2_STRIPED_CONTAINERS, which can be used when your system is using redundant array of independent disks (RAID) devices for your table space containers.

Furthermore, some variables are specific to the communications your system is using, such as DB2COMM, which specifies the communications managers that are started when the database manager is started. Some variables affect the performance of the database manager or databases in your working environment, such as DB2_AWE, which allows the database manager on Windows 2000 to allocate buffer pools that use up to 64GB of memory. Still others specify how related products like Distributed Computing Environment (DCE) and Data Links are used, how built-in facilities like the command line processor (CLP) and SQL compiler are used, and how aspects of a partitioned database environment are defined and controlled. Finally, some variables do not fit into a specific category.

Users with system administration (SYSADM) authority for a given instance can update registry values for that instance. You can use the DB2SET command to update registry variables without rebooting. The changes are stored immediately in the profile registries. The DB2 registry applies the updated values to the DB2 server instances and DB2 applications started after the changes are made. (Changes do not affect the currently running DB2 applications or users. Applications started following the update use the new values.)

To view a list of all supported registry variables, use the DB2SET –LR command. To list all defined registry variables for the current or default instance, use the DB2SET command. To list all defined registry variables in the profile registry, use the DB2SET –ALL command.

The generalized form of the DB2SET command to change the value of a registry variable in the current or default instance is the following:

```
db2set <registry variable>=<new value>
```

To change the registry variable default for all databases in the instance, use this command:

```
db2set <registry variable>=<new value> -i instance name
```

The values used in the descriptions of the binary registry variables have equivalent values. *Binary registry variables* are those that have only two states: ON or OFF. Each of the values YES, 1, and ON, is equivalent. In the same way, the values NO, 0, and OFF are equivalent.

In each of the following sections, the variables are presented in the same way. The name of the variable is the heading, and it is followed by the operating system where the variable is applicable (shown as *OS:*). Then the default value is given, followed by the allowed values that may be used with this registry variable. Finally, some information about the variable and its use is provided.

Note   *Users can override registry variable settings for their session by changing session environment variable settings using the SET command (or the EXPORT command on UNIX platforms). In addition, the DB2 environment variables DB2INSTANCE, DB2NODE, DB2PATH, and DB2INSTPROF may not be stored in the DB2 profile registries, depending on the operating system. The SET command must be used. These changes are in effect until the next time the system is rebooted.*

Installation Considerations and Variables

During the installation process, the following variables are set:

- The DB2INSTANCE environment variable is set to DB2.
- The DB2INSTDEF registry variable is set to DB2.

To change the location of the instance directory from DB2PATH by using the DB2INSTPROF environment variable, you need write access for the instance directory. If you want the directories created in a path other than DB2PATH, you have to set DB2INSTPROF *before* entering the DB2ICRT command.

The database manager determines the current instance based on the following:

- If the DB2INSTANCE environment variable is set for the current session, its value is the current instance. To set the DB2INSTANCE environment variable, enter **set db2instance=<new instance name>**.
- If the DB2INSTANCE environment variable is not set for the current session, the database manager uses the setting for the DB2INSTANCE environment variable from the system environment variables. On Windows NT, system environment variables are set in the system environment. On Windows 95, they are set in the autoexec.bat file. On OS/2, they are set in the config.sys file.
- If the DB2INSTANCE environment variable is not set at all, the database manager uses the DB2INSTDEF registry variable. To set the DB2INSTDEF registry variable at the global level of the registry, enter **db2set DB2INSTDEF=<new instance name> -g** .

Performance Variables

The performance variables affect how your instance and the contained databases will perform. You use these variables in conjunction with the important performance configuration parameters presented in Chapter 14.

DB2_AVOID_PREFETCH

OS: All; Default: OFF; Values: ON or OFF

This variable specifies whether prefetch will be used during crash recovery. When the value is ON, prefetch is not used.

DB2_AWE

OS: Windows 2000; Default: Null; Values: <entry>[, <entry>,...]

The <entry> is equivalent to <buffer pool ID>, <number of physical pages>, and <number of address windows>.

When values are present, you can allocate buffer pools that use up to 64GB of memory. Windows 2000 must be configured correctly to support Address Windowing Extensions (AWE) buffer pools. For more information, see Chapter 14.

DB2_BINSORT

OS: All; Default: YES; Values: YES and NO

Once enabled, this variable allows the use of a new sort algorithm that reduces CPU time and the elapsed time of sort operations.

DB2BPVARS

OS: Windows NT; Default: <path>; Values: Any valid path

This variable specifies a path to a file containing parameters used to tune buffer pools. The currently supported parameters are NT_SCATTER_DMSFILE, NT_SCATTER_DMSDEVICE, and NT_ SCATTER_SMS.

Each of these parameters has a default of OFF. The acceptable values are OFF and ON. They work in conjunction with the DB2NTNOCACHE variable. When this variable is turned on, then each of the parameters in the DB2BPVARS file is used to turn scatter read on for the respective types of containers, as indicated by the names of the parameters. For more information on scatter read and sequential prefetching, see Chapter 14 and the *IBM DB2 Universal Database Administration Guide: Performance* volume.

DB2CHKPTR

OS: All; Default: OFF; Values: ON or OFF

This variable specifies whether pointer checking is required for input values.

DB2_ENABLE_BUFFPD

OS: All; Default: OFF; Values: ON or OFF

This variable specifies whether DB2 will use intermediate buffering to improve query performance. There is no guarantee that this type of buffering will improve performance in all environments. You should test in your environment to see if there is any performance improvement to individual queries that you run.

DB2_EXTENDED_OPTIMIZATION

OS: All; Default: OFF; Values: ON or OFF

This variable specifies whether the query optimizer uses optimization extensions to improve query performance. The extensions may not improve query performance in all environments. Testing should be done to determine individual query performance improvements.

DB2MAXFSCRSEARCH

OS: All; Default: 5; Values: –1, 1 to 33,554

This variable specifies how many free space control records should be searched when adding a record to a table. After searching the specified number, the database manager places the new record at the bottom of the table. Modifying this value allows you to balance insert speed with space reuse. A large value maximizes space reuse; a smaller value increases insert speed. Using –1 forces the database manager to search all free space control records when inserting.

DB2MEMDISCLAIM

OS: AIX; Default: YES; Values: YES or NO

Do you want DB2 agents to explicitly request that the AIX operating system disassociate the reserved paging space from the freed memory? If you set this variable to YES, there will be fewer paging space requirements and possibly less disk activity from paging. The opposite will occur when you set it to NO. In some situations, when paging space is plentiful and sufficient memory exists such that paging never occurs, setting this variable to NO provides a minor performance improvement.

DB2MEMMAXFREE

OS: All; Default: 8,388,608 bytes; Values: 0 to (2 to the 32) –1 bytes

This variable specifies the maximum amount of unused memory in bytes retained by DB2 processes. The default value is recommended for most environments.

DB2_MMAP_READ

OS: AIX; Default: ON; Values: ON or OFF

You use this variable in conjunction with DB2_MMAP_WRITE. Together, they allow DB2 to use a multifunction, multiservice access platform (MMAP) as an alternative method of I/O. Use MMAP to avoid operating system locks when multiple processes are writing to different sections of the same file.

DB2_MMAP_WRITE

OS: AIX; Default: ON; Values: ON or OFF

You use this variable in conjunction with DB2_MMAP_READ. Together, they allow DB2 to use a multifunction, multiservice access platform (MMAP) as an alternative method of I/O. Use MMAP to avoid operating system locks when multiple processes are writing to different sections of the same file.

DB2_NO_PKG_LOCK

OS: All; Default: OFF; Values: ON or OFF

This variable allows the global SQL cache to operate without the use of package locks (internal system locks) to protect cached package entries. Performance is improved when you choose to work without allowing package locks. Without package locking, certain database operations are not allowed, such as operations that invalidate packages, operations that cause packages not to work or function, and operations that directly change a package.

DB2NTMEMSIZE

OS: Windows NT; Default: Varies by memory segment; Values: A valid number of bytes

Windows NT requires that all shared memory segments be reserved at database link library (DLL) initialization time to guarantee matching addresses across processes. This variable allows you to override the DB2 defaults on Windows NT if necessary.

- **Database Kernel**   Default size is 16,777,216 bytes (16MB); override option is DBMS: <number of bytes>
- **Parallel FCM Buffers**   Default size is 22,020,096 bytes (21MB); override option is FCM: <number of bytes>
- **Database Admin GUI**   Default size is 33,554,432 bytes (32MB); override option is DBAT: <number of bytes>
- **Fenced Stored Procedures**   Default size is 16,777,216 bytes (16MB); override option is APLD: <number of bytes>

You can override more than one segment by separating the override options with a semicolon (;).

DB2NTNOCACHE

OS: Windows NT; Default: OFF; Values: ON or OFF

This variable specifies whether DB2 will open database files with a NOCACHE option. When this variable is set to ON, file system caching is eliminated. When set to OFF, file system caching works with DB2 files except for those files containing long fields or large objects (LOBs). Eliminating system caching allows more memory to be available to the database so that the buffer pool or sortheap can be increased.

DB2NTPRICLASS

OS: Windows NT; Default: Null; Values: R, H (any other value)

This variable sets the priority class for the DB2 instance (program DB2SYSCS.EXE). The classes are the following:

- NORMAL_PRIORITY_CLASS (the default)
- REALTIME_PRIORITY_CLASS (set by using *R*)
- HIGH_PRIORITY_CLASS (set by using *H*)

Individual process and thread priorities are set using DB2PRIORITIES. The DB2NTPRICLASS variable is used in conjunction with DB2PRIORITIES to determine the absolute priority of DB2 processes and threads relative to other processes and threads in the system.

 Misusing this variable could adversely affect overall system performance. For more information, see the SetPriorityClass() API in the Win32 documentation.

DB2NTWORKSET

OS: Windows NT; Default: 1,1; Values: Minimum and maximum megabytes for the working set size

The default behavior when Windows NT is not in a paging situation is that the process' working set can grow as large as needed. When Windows NT is in a paging situation, the process' working set can have approximately 1MB. This variable allows you to override the default when in a paging situation.

DB2_OVERRIDE_BPF

OS: All; Default: Not set; Values: A positive numeric number of pages

This variable specifies the size of the buffer pool in pages to be created at database activation or first connection time. It tends to be used following receipt of memory constraint failures at the time of database activation or first connection.

When the minimum buffer pool size of 16 pages is too large, the value for this variable will be used to start the database. Memory constraints may occur because of a real memory shortage (which is rare); or constraints may occur because the database manager attempts to allocate large, inaccurately configured buffer pools.

DB2_PARALLEL_IO

OS: All; Default: Null; Values: A list of comma-separated table space IDs, or an asterisk (*)

When data is placed on RAID devices, you can use this variable to use a parallelism value based on the prefetch size and the extent size. For example, if the prefetch size was 4 times the extent size, then regardless of the number of containers, DB2 will create 4 prefetch requests, each an extent in size. This allows 4 prefetchers to work in parallel. The default behavior (when the variable is not enabled) is to create prefetch requests based on the number of containers in the table space.

Setting the value of this variable to an asterisk (*) means that parallel I/O is turned on for every table space. Setting the value of this variable to a list of table space IDs separated by commas means that parallel I/O is turned on for only those table spaces specified.

DB2_PINNED_BP

OS: AIX, HP-UX; Default: NO; Values: YES or NO

This variable is used to hold the database global memory (including buffer pools) associated with the database in the main memory. This allows database performance to be more efficient.

When working with HP-UX in a 64-bit environment, in addition to modifying this variable, the DB2 instance group must also be given the MLOCK privilege. This privilege is given by having a user with root access rights do the following:

- Add the DB2 instance group to the /etc/privgroup file.
- Issue the following command:

```
setprivgrp -f /etc/privgroup
```

DB2PRIORITIES

OS: All; Default: Platform dependent; Values: Established by platform-dependent means

This variable controls the priorities of DB2 processes and threads. (See also the "DB2NTPRICLASS" section earlier in this chapter for Windows NT specifics on the DB2 instance.) See the operating system documentation showing how to set and control priorities.

DB2_RR_TO_RS

OS: All; Default: NO; Values: YES or NO

Next key locking guarantees the Repeatable Read (RR) isolation level by automatically locking the next key for all INSERT and DELETE statements and the next higher key value above the result set for SELECT statements. For UPDATE statements that alter key parts of an index, the original index key is deleted and the new key value is inserted. Next key locking is done on both the key insertion and key detection. Next key locking is required to guarantee ANSI and SQL92 standard RR, and it is the DB2 default.

If your application appears to stop or hang, you should examine snapshot information for your application. If the problem appears to be with next key locking, you can set this variable to YES if both of these conditions are true:

- None of your applications rely on RR behavior.
- It is acceptable for scans to skip over uncommitted deletes.

The skipping behavior affects the RR, Read Stability (RS), and Cursor Stability (CS) isolation levels. (There is no row locking for the Uncommitted Read (UR) isolation level.)

When this variable is on, RR behavior cannot be guaranteed for scans on user tables because next key locking is not done during index key insertion and deletion. Catalog tables are not affected by this option. The other change in behavior when this variable is set to YES is that scans will skip over rows that have been deleted but not committed, even though the row may have qualified for the scan.

DB2_SORT_AFTER_TQ

OS: All; Default: NO; Values: YES or NO

This variable is applicable only to a partitioned database environment. It specifies how the optimizer works with directed table queues when the receiving end requires the data to be sorted, and the number of receiving partitions or nodes is equal to the number of sending partitions or nodes. When this variable is set to NO, the optimizer tends to sort at the sending end and merge rows at the receiving end. When this variable is set to YES, the optimizer tends to transmit the rows unsorted, no merge occurs, and after all the rows are received, they are then sorted at the receiving end.

DB2_STPROC_LOOKUP_FIRST

OS: All; Default: OFF; Values: ON or OFF

This variable was formerly called DB2_DARI_LOOKUP_ALL. The variable specifies whether the database manager will perform a catalog lookup for every database application remote interface (DARI) and stored procedure before looking in the function subdirectory of the sqllib subdirectory; and in the unfenced subdirectory, in the function subdirectory of the sqllib subdirectory.

Note *For stored procedures of PARAMETER TYPE DB2DARI that are located in the directories just mentioned, setting this variable to ON causes performance to degrade. The catalog lookup required may occur on another partition or node in a partitioned database environment before these directories are searched.*

To enhance the performance of stored procedures that are not cataloged as PARAMETER TYPE DB2DARI, set this variable to ON. This setting forces the database manager to look up the name of the shared library for the stored procedures in the system catalog before searching these directories.

DB2_STRIPED_CONTAINERS

OS: All; Default: OFF; Values: ON or OFF

When using RAID devices for table space containers, the recommendation is that the table space be created with an extent size that is equal to or a multiple of the RAID stripe size. However, because there is a one-page container tag, the extents will not line up with the RAID stripes. As a result, during an I/O request, it may be necessary to access more physical disks than would be optimal.

You can create database-managed space (DMS) table space containers so that the one-page container tag is placed in its own extent. This avoids the access problem just mentioned, but it requires an extra extent of overhead within the container.

Setting this variable to ON allows the creation of table spaces where the one-page container tag is placed in its own extent. Existing containers will remain unchanged.

To verify that a container was created as a striped container, use the /DTSF option of DB2DART to dump table space and container information. The type field for the container will give you the information.

System Environment Variables

The following are the system environment variables that you can modify. These variables control some aspects of the interaction of the database manager with the operating system.

DB2CONNECT_IN_APP_PROCESS

OS: All; Default: YES; Values: YES or NO

When the value of this variable is NO, local DB2 Connect clients on a DB2 Connect Enterprise Edition machine are forced to run within an agent. Advantages to running within an agent are that local clients can be monitored and they can use system complex (SYSPLEX) support. A SYSPLEX is a set of MVS or OS/390 systems communicating and cooperating with each other through certain multisystem hardware components and software services to process work on those systems.

DB2DOMAINLIST

OS: Only Windows NT server; Default: Null; Values: A list of Windows NT domain names separated by commas (,)

Should be used only under a pure Windows NT domain environment with DB2 servers and clients running DB2 Universal Database version 7.1 (or later). The variable defines one or more Windows NT domains. Only users belonging to these domains will have their connection or attachment requests accepted.

DB2ENVLIST

OS: UNIX; Default: Null; Values: A valid list of system variable names

This variable allows you to explicitly list specific variable names for use by either stored procedures or user-defined functions. By default, the DB2START command filters out all user environment variables except those prefixed with DB2 or db2.

> **Note** *You will notice that all variables in this chapter are prefixed with DB2. This identifies them as being specific to the DB2 Universal Database system. There may be other environment variables specific to the operating system or other installed products that you want the database manager to be able to use. These variables are not prefixed by DB2.*

If special registry variables must be passed to either stored procedures or user-defined functions, you can list the variable names in this variable. Each name in the list should be separated by one or more spaces. The database manager constructs its own PATH and LIBPATH, so if PATH or LIBPATH is specified in this variable list, the actual value of the variable name is appended to the end of the DB2-constructed value.

DB2INSTANCE

OS: All; Default: DB2INSTDEF on OS/2 and Windows 32-bit operating systems

Use this variable to specify the instance that is active by default. On UNIX, users must specify a value for this variable.

DB2INSTPROF

OS: OS/2, Windows 3.*x*, and Windows 32-bit operating systems; Default: Null

This variable is used to specify the location of the instance directory on the given operating systems if the location is different from DB2PATH.

DB2LIBPATH

OS: UNIX; Default: Null

This variable specifies the value of LIBPATH in the DB2LIBPATH variable.

The value of LIBPATH cannot be inherited between parent and child processes if the user ID has changed. Because the DB2START executable is owned by root, the database manager cannot inherit the LIBPATH settings of end users.

REFERENCE

If you list the variable name, LIBPATH, in the DB2ENVLIST registry variable, you must also specify the value of LIBPATH in the DB2LIBPATH registry variable. The DB2START executable then reads the value of DB2LIBPATH and appends this value to the end of the database manager–constructed LIBPATH.

DB2NODE

OS: All; Default: Null; Values: 1 to 999

This variable is used to specify the target logical partition/node of a DB2 Enterprise—Extended Edition (EEE) database partition server that you want to attach to or connect to. If this variable is not set, the target logical partition/node defaults to the logical partition/node that is defined with port 0 on this machine.

DB2_PARALLEL_IO

OS: All; Default: Null; Values: An asterisk (*) (meaning every table space) or a comma-separated list of more than one defined table space

While reading or writing data to and from table space containers, the database manager may use parallel I/O operations if the number of containers in the database is greater than 1. To force parallel I/O for a single container, use this registry variable.

DB2PATH

OS: OS/2, Windows 3.x, and Windows 32-bit operating systems; Default: Varies by operating system; Values: A valid path to a directory

This variable is used to specify the directory where the product is installed on the operating system.

DB2_STRIPED_CONTAINERS

OS: All; Default: Null; Values: ON, NULL

When using RAID devices for table space containers, we suggest that you create the table space with an extent size that is equal to or a multiple of the RAID stripe size. However, because of the one-page container tag, the extents will not line up with the RAID stripes, and during an I/O request, it may be necessary to access more physical disks than would be optimal.

When using DMS table space containers, you can avoid this problem by allocating the tag its own (full) extent. This solution still requires an extra extent of overhead within the container. Setting this variable to ON removes this problem. However, you would set the variable to ON only if you needed optimal performance when using RAID devices for table space containers.

Communication Variables

The following communication variables allow for communication between machines.

DB2CHECKCLIENTINTERVAL

OS: AIX, server only; Default: 0; Values: A numeric value greater than zero

This variable is used to verify the status of APPC client connections. It permits early detection of client termination, rather than waiting until after the completion of the query.

When set to 0, no verification check is made. When set to a numerical value greater than zero, the value represents DB2 internal work units. For guidance, the following check frequency values are given: low frequency, use 300; medium frequency, use 100; high frequency, use 50. Checking more frequently for client status while executing a database request lengthens the time to complete the queries.

If the DB2 workload is heavy (that is, it involves many internal requests), then setting this variable to a low value has a greater impact on performance than in a situation in which the workload is light and the database manager is waiting most of the time.

DB2COMM

OS: All, server only; Default: Null; Values: Any combination of APPC, IPXSPX, NETBIOS, NPIPE, and TCPIP

This variable specifies the types of communications managers that are started when the database manager is started. If this is not set, no database manager communications managers are started on the server.

DB2_FORCE_NLS_CACHE

OS: AIX, HP-UX, Sun Solaris; Default: FALSE; Values: TRUE or FALSE

You use this variable to eliminate the chance of lock contention in multithreaded applications. When set to TRUE, the code page and country code information is saved the first time a thread accesses it. From that point, the cached information is used for any other thread that requests this information. This eliminates lock contention and results in a performance benefit in certain situations.

Don't use this setting if the application changes locale settings between connections. It is probably not needed in this type of situation because multithreaded applications typically do not change their locale settings; it is not "thread-safe" to do so.

DB2NBADAPTERS

OS: OS/2 and Windows NT; Default: 0; Values: 0 to 15; multiple values separated by commas

This variable is used to specify which local adapters to use for DB2 NetBIOS LAN communications. You specify each local adapter by using its logical adapter number.

DB2NBCHECKUPTIME

OS: OS/2 and Windows NT, server only; Default: 1 minute; Values: 1 to 720 minutes

This variable specifies the time interval between each invocation of the NetBIOS protocol checkup procedure. Checkup time is specified in minutes. Using lower values ensures that the NetBIOS protocol checkup runs more often, freeing up memory and other system resources left when unexpected agent or session termination occurs.

DB2NBINTRLISTENS

OS: OS/2 and Windows NT, server only; Default: 1; Values: 1 to 10; multiple values separated by commas

This variable specifies the numbers of NetBIOS listen and send commands called network control blocks (NCBs) that will be asynchronously issued in readiness for remote client interrupts. It is for use in interrupt-active environments to ensure that interrupt calls from remote clients are able to establish connections when servers are busy servicing other remote interrupts.

Using a lower value for this variable conserves NetBIOS sessions and NCBs at the server. However, in an environment in which client interrupts are common, you may need to set this variable to a higher value to be responsive to interrupting clients.

 Values specified are position-sensitive. Each position corresponds to the values found in the same positions for DB2NBADAPTERS.

DB2NBRECVBUFSIZE

OS: OS/2 and Windows NT, server only; Default: 4096 bytes; Values: 4096 to 65,536 bytes

This variable specifies the size of the DB2 NetBIOS protocol receive buffers. These buffers are assigned to the NetBIOS receive NCBs. Lower values conserve server memory. Higher values may be required when client data transfers are larger.

DB2NBBRECVNCBS

OS: OS/2 and Windows NT, server only; Default: 10; Values: 1 to 99

This variable specifies the number of NetBIOS receive_any commands (NCBs) that the server issues and maintains during its operation. The value should be adjusted based on the number of remote clients connecting to your server. Lower values conserve server resources.

 Each adapter in use can have its own unique receive NCB value specified by this variable. Each position corresponds to the values found in the same positions for DB2NBADAPTERS.

DB2NBRESOURCES

OS: OS/2 and Windows NT, server only; Default: Null

This variable specifies the number of NetBIOS resources to allocate for database manager use in a multicontext environment. This variable is restricted to multicontext client operation.

DB2NBSENDNCBS

OS: OS/2 and Windows NT, server only; Default: 6; Values: 1 to 720

This variable specifies the number of send NetBIOS commands (NCBs) that the server will reserve for use. The value should be adjusted based on the number of remote clients to which your server is connected. Lower values conserve server resources. However, a higher value may be needed to prevent the server from waiting to send to a remote client when all the other send commands are in use.

DB2NBSESSIONS

OS: OS/2 and Windows NT, server only; Default: Null; Values: 5 to 254

This variable specifies the number of sessions that the database manager should reserve for its own use. The value for this variable can be set to request a specific session for each adapter specified using DB2NBADAPTERS.

 Each position corresponds to the values found in the same positions for DB2NBADAPTERS.

DB2NBXTRANCBS

OS: OS/2 and Windows NT, server only; Default: 5 per adapter; Values: 5 to 254

This variable specifies the number of "extra" NetBIOS commands (NCBs) the server reserves when the DB2START command is issued. The value of this variable can be set to request a specific session for each adapter specified using DB2NBADAPTERS.

DB2NETREQ

OS: Windows 3.x; Default: 3; Values: 0 to 25

This variable specifies the number of NetBIOS requests that can be run concurrently on Windows 3.x clients. The higher you set this variable, the more memory below the 1MB level will be used. When the concurrent number of requests to use NetBIOS services reaches the number you have set, subsequent incoming requests for NetBIOS services are held in a queue. The requests in the queue become active once the current requests complete.

Setting the value of this variable to 0 causes the Windows database client to issue NetBIOS calls in synchronous mode using the NetBIOS wait option. In this mode, only one NetBIOS request is active at a time. This affects the performance of other applications. The 0 value is provided only for backwards compatibility. We strongly recommend not using 0 as a value for this variable.

DB2RETRY

OS: OS/2 and Windows NT; Default: 0; Values: 0 to 20,000

This variable specifies how many times the database manager attempts to restart the advanced program-to-program communication (APPC) listener. If the systems network architecture (SNA) subsystem at the server or gateway is down, this variable, along with DB2RETRYTIME, can be used to automatically restart the APPC listener without disrupting client communications using the other protocols. In this case, it is not necessary to stop and restart the APPC client communications.

DB2RETRYTIME

OS: OS/2 and Windows NT; Default: 1 minute; Values: 0 to 7200 minutes

This variable specifies, in increments of one minute, the number of minutes that the database manager allows between performing successive retries to start the APPC listener. If the SNA subsystem at the server or gateway is down, you can use this variable, along with DB2RETRY, to automatically restart the APPC listener without disrupting client communications using the other protocols. In this case, it is not necessary to stop and restart the APPC client communications.

DB2SERVICETPINSTANCE

OS: OS/2, Windows NT, AIX, Sun Solaris; Default: Null

This variable is used to solve the problem caused by more than one instance running on the same machine, and by a version 6 instance or version 7 instance running on the same machine attempting to register the same TP names. When the DB2START command is invoked, the instance specified starts the APPC listeners for the following TP names: DB2DRDA and x'07'6DB.

DB2SOSNDBUF

OS: Windows 95/NT; Default: 32,767

This variable specifies the value of the TCP/IP send buffers on Windows 95 and Windows NT operating systems.

DB2SYSPLEX_SERVER

OS: OS/2, Windows NT, and UNIX; Default: Null

This variable specifies whether SYSPLEX exploitation is enabled when connected to DB2 for OS/390. If this variable is not set (which is the default) or is set to a nonzero value, exploitation is enabled. If the variable is set to 0, exploitation is disabled. In the latter case, SYSPLEX exploitation is disabled for the gateway regardless of how the DCS database catalog entry has been specified. For more information, see Chapter 6.

DB2TCPCONNMGRS

OS: All; Defaults: 1 on serial machines; square root of the number of processors rounded up to a maximum of eight connection managers on symmetric multiprocessor machines; Values: 1 to 8

The default number of connection managers is created if this variable is not set. If this variable is set, the value assigned overrides the default value.

The number of TCP/IP connection managers specified is created, up to a maximum of eight. If a value of less than one is given, the value of 1 is used and a warning message is logged. If a value of greater than eight is given, the value of 8 is used and a warning message is logged. Values between 1 and 8 are used as given.

When more than one connection manager is created, connection throughput should improve when multiple client connections are received simultaneously. There may be additional TCP/IP connection manager processes (on UNIX operating systems) or threads (on OS/2 and Windows operating systems) if the user is running on an SMP machine or has modified this variable. Additional processes or threads require additional storage.

Having the number of connection managers set to 1 can cause both a drop in performance on remote connections in systems with a lot of users and/or frequent connections and disconnections.

DB2_VI_ENABLE

OS: Windows NT; Default: OFF; Values: ON or OFF

This variable specifies whether to use the Virtual Interface (VI) Architecture communications protocol. When this variable is set to ON, Fast Communications Manager (FCM) uses VI for interpartition communication. When this variable is set to OFF, FCM uses TCP/IP for interpartition communication.

The value of this variable must be the same across all the database partitions in the instance.

DB2_VI_VIPL

OS: Windows NT; Default: vipl.dll

This variable specifies the name of the Virtual Interface Provider Library (VIPL) that the database manager will use. To load the library successfully, the library name used in this variable must be in the PATH user environment variable. The currently supported implementations all use the same library name.

DB2_VI_DEVICE

OS: Windows NT; Default: Null; Values: nic0 or VINIC

This variable specifies the symbolic name of the device or Virtual Interface Provider Instance associated with the network interface card (NIC). Independent hardware vendors each produce their own NIC. Only one NIC is allowed per Windows NT machine. Multiple logical nodes on the same physical machine will share the same NIC.

The symbolic name *VINIC* must be in upper case and can be used only with Synfinity Interconnect. All other currently supported implementations use nic0 as the symbolic device name.

SQL Compiler Variables

When you are working with applications and you want specific aspects of the SQL compiler and the optimizer to work in specific ways, consider using the following SQL compiler variables.

DB2_ANTIJOIN

OS: All; Default: NO in an EEE environment, and YES in a non-EEE environment; Values: YES or NO

In a DB2 Universal Database EEE environment, when YES is specified, the optimizer searches for opportunities to transform NOT EXISTS subqueries into antijoins that can be processed more efficiently by the database manager. In a non-EEE environment, when NO is specified, the optimizer limits the opportunities to transform NOT EXISTS subqueries into antijoins.

DB2_CORRELATED_PREDICATES

OS: All; Default: YES; Values: YES or NO

When this variable is set to YES, the optimizer uses the KEYCARD information of unique index statistics to detect cases of correlation and dynamically adjusts the combined cardinality estimates of the correlated predicates. As a result, a more accurate estimate of the join size and cost can be obtained.

DB2_HASH_JOIN

OS: All; Default: NO; Values: YES or NO

This variable specifies that a hash join is a possible join method when compiling an access plan.

DB2_LIKE_VARCHAR

OS: All; Default: Y, N; Values: Y, N, S, or a floating-point constant between 0 and 6.2

This variable controls the collection and use of *subelement statistics*: statistics about the content of data in columns when the data has a structure in the form of a series of subfields or subelements delimited by blanks.

This registry variable affects how the optimizer deals with a predicate of this form:

```
COLUMN LIKE '%xxxxxx%'
```

The *xxxxxx* is any string of characters.

The following is the syntax showing how this registry variable is used:

```
db2set DB2_LIKE_VARCHAR=[Y|N|S|num1] [,Y|N|S|num2]
```

The term preceding the comma, or the only term to the right of the predicate, means the following, but only for columns that do not have positive subelement statistics:

- **S**   The optimizer estimates the length of each element in a series of elements concatenated together to form a column based on the length of the string enclosed in the percent (%) characters.
- **Y**   The default. Use a default value of 1.9 for the algorithm parameter. Use a variable-length subelement algorithm with the algorithm parameter.
- **N**   Use a fixed-length subelement algorithm.
- **num1**   Use the value of num1 as the algorithm parameter with the variable-length subelement algorithm.

The term after the comma means the following:

- **N**   The default. Do not collect or use subelement statistics.
- **Y**   Collect subelement statistics. Use a variable-length subelement algorithm that uses the collected statistics together with the 1.9 default value for the algorithm parameter in the case of columns with positive subelement statistics.
- **num2**   Collect subelement statistics. Use a variable-length subelement algorithm that uses the collected statistics together with the value of num2 as the algorithm parameter in the case of columns with positive subelement statistics.

DB2_NEW_CORR_SQ_FF

OS: All; Default: OFF; Values: ON or OFF

This variable affects the selectivity value computed by the SQL optimizer for certain subquery predicates when it is set to ON. Use it to improve the accuracy of the selectivity value of equality subquery predicates that use the MIN or MAX aggregate function in the SELECT list of the subquery.

DB2_PRED_FACTORIZE

OS: All; Default: NO; Value: YES or NO

This variable specifies whether the optimizer will search for opportunities to extract additional predicates from disjunctive predicates. In some circumstances, the additional predicates can alter the estimated cardinality of the intermediate and final result sets.

DB2_SELECTIVITY

OS: All; Default: NO; Values: YES or NO

This variable specifies where the SELECTIVITY clause can be used. See Chapter 3 in the *IBM DB2 Universal Database SQL Reference* for complete details on the SELECTIVITY clause. When the value for this variable is YES, the clause can be specified when the predicate is a basic predicate where at least one expression contains host variables.

Command Line Processor Variables

The following variables can affect the operation of the command line processor (CLP).

DB2BQTIME

OS: All; Default: 1 second; Maximum value: 1 second

This variable specifies how long the command line front-end process will sleep before checking if the back-end process is active and establishing a connection to it.

DB2BQTRY

OS: All; Default: 60 retries; Minimum value: 0 retries

This variable specifies how many times the command line processor front-end process tries to determine whether the back-end process is already active. It works in conjunction with DB2BQTIME.

DB2IQTIME

OS: All; Default: 5 seconds; Minimum value: 1 second

This variable specifies how long the command line processor back-end process waits on the input queue for the front-end process to pass commands.

DB2OPTIONS

OS: All except Windows 3.1 and Macintosh; Default: Null

This variable is used to set the command line processor options.

DB2RQTIME

OS: All; Default: 5 seconds; Minimum value: 1 second

This variable specifies how long the command line processor back-end process waits for a request from the front-end process.

Miscellaneous Variables

The following variables do not clearly fit into one of the other categories. They may fit in two or more categories or in none of the mentioned categories. You may find some of these miscellaneous variables useful depending on your environment and needs.

DB2ADMINSERVER

OS: OS/2, Windows 95/NT, and UNIX; Default: Null

This variable specifies which DB2 instance is set up as the DB2 Administration Server (DAS).

DB2CLIINIPATH

OS: All; Default: Null; Values: A valid path

You use this variable to override the default path of the DB2 CLI/ODBC configuration file (db2cli.ini) and specify a different location on the client. The value specified must be a valid path on the client system.

DB2DEFPREP

OS: All; Default: No; Values: ALL, YES, NO

This variable simulates the run-time behavior of the DEFERRED_PREPARE precompiler option for applications that were precompiled prior to this option becoming available. For example, if a DB2 version 2.1.1 or earlier application were run in a DB2 version 2.1.2 or later environment, DB2DEFPREP could be used to indicate the desired *deferred prepare* behavior.

DB2_DJ_COMM

OS: All; Default: Null; Values: Include libdrda.a, libsqulnet.a, libnet8.a, libdrda.dll, libsqlnet.dll, libnet8.dll, and so on

This variable is not available unless the *federated* database manager configuration parameter is set to YES. It specifies the wrapper libraries that are loaded when the database manager is started. Once specified, this variable reduces the run-time cost of loading frequently used wrappers.

Values for other operating systems are supported. For example, the .dll extension is for the Windows NT operating system; the .a extension is for the AIX operating system. Library names vary by protocol and operating system.

DB2DMNBCKCTLR

OS: Windows NT; Default: Null; Values: A question mark (?) character or a domain name

If you know it, enter the name of the domain for which your local DB2 server is the backup domain controller by setting this variable equal to the domain name. The domain name must be in uppercase. If you want DB2 to determine the domain for which your local DB2 server is the backup domain controller, set this variable equal to the question mark (?) character. If this variable is not set or it is set to blank, the database manager performs authentication at the primary domain controller.

The database manager does not use the existing domain controller as the default because a backup domain controller can get out of synchronization with the primary domain controller. When they are not synchronized, there is a possible security exposure. Getting out of synchronization can occur when the primary domain controller's security database is updated but the changes are not propagated to the backup domain controller. This situation is possible if there are network latencies or if the computer browser service is not operational.

DB2_ENABLE_LDAP

OS: All; Default: NO; Values: YES or NO

This variable specifies whether the Lightweight Directory Access Protocol (LDAP) is used. LDAP is an access method to directory services.

DB2_FALLBACK

OS: Windows NT; Default: OFF; Values: ON or OFF

Use this variable to force off all database connections during fallback processing. This variable is used in conjunction with the failover support in the Windows NT environment with Microsoft Cluster Server (MSCS). If this variable is not set or is set to OFF, and a database connection exists during the fallback, the DB2 resource cannot be brought offline, and fallback processing will fail.

DB2_FORCE_TRUNCATION

OS: All; Default: NO; Values: YES or NO

Use this variable only under the direction of IBM Service and Support personnel. This variable is used during restart recovery. If the variable is set to NO, restart recovery is halted when it is determined that a bad page is stopping the restart recovery too soon. This problem could occur when all active logs have not been read. A bad page is typically found in one of the logs. This variable can be set to YES to indicate to restart recovery to continue processing as if the end of logs were reached. After setting the variable to YES, logs not read during restart recovery are overwritten when the database becomes active again.

DB2_GRP_LOOKUP

OS: Windows NT; Default: Null; Values: LOCAL, DOMAIN

You use this variable to tell the database manager where to validate user accounts and perform group member lookup. When set to LOCAL, the database manager must always enumerate groups and validate user accounts on the DB2 server. When set to DOMAIN, the database manager must always enumerate groups and validate user accounts on the Windows NT domain to which the user account belongs.

DB2_INDEX_2BYTEVARLEN

OS: All; Default: NO; Values: YES or NO

This variable allows columns longer than 255 bytes to be specified as part of an index key. Indexes created before setting this variable to YES will continue to be restricted to the 255-byte key limit restriction. Indexes created after setting this variable to YES will behave as a 2-byte index (even when this variable is set to NO some time later).

 Several SQL statements are affected by this change to index operations. They include CREATE TABLE, CREATE INDEX, and ALTER TABLE. For more information, see these statements in Chapter 27.

DB2LDAP_BASEDN

OS: All; Default: Null; Values: Any valid base domain name

This variable specifies the base domain name for the LDAP directory.

DB2LDAPCACHE

OS: All; Default: YES; Values: YES or NO

This variable specifies whether the LDAP cache should be enabled. This cache is used to catalog the database, node/partition, and DCS directories on the local machine. To ensure that you have the latest entries in the cache, enter the following commands:

```
REFRESH LDAP DB DIR
REFRESH LDAP NODE DIR
```

These commands update and remove incorrect entries from the database directory and the node/partition directory.

DB2LDAP_CLIENT_PROVIDER

OS: Windows 9*x*/NT/2000; Default: Null (If available, Microsoft is used; otherwise, IBM is used); Values: IBM or Microsoft

The database manager supports only LDAP clients or IBM LDAP clients to access the LDAP directory.

 To display the current value of this variable, use this command:
`db2set DB2LDAP_CLIENT_PROVIDER`

DB2LDAPHOST

OS: All; Default: Null; Values: Any valid hostname

This variable specifies the hostname of the location for the LDAP directory.

DB2LDAP_SEARCH_SCOPE

OS: All; Default: DOMAIN; Values: LOCAL, DOMAIN, GLOBAL

This variable specifies the search scope for information found in partitions or domains in the LDAP directory. Using the value of LOCAL disables searching in the LDAP directory. Using the value of DOMAIN searches in LDAP only for the current directory partition. Using the value of GLOBAL searches in LDAP in all directory partitions until the object is found.

DB2LOADREC

OS: All; Default: Null; Values: Any valid path

You use this variable to override the location of the load copy during a roll-forward recovery action. If a user has changed the location of the load copy, you must set DB2LOADREC before issuing the roll forward.

DB2LOCK_TO_RB

OS: All; Default: Null; Values: STATEMENT

This variable specifies whether lock timeouts cause the entire transaction to be rolled back or only the current statement. When set to STATEMENT, locked timeouts cause only the current statement to be rolled back. Any other setting results in transaction rollback.

DB2NOEXITLIST

OS: All; Default: OFF; Values: ON or OFF

This variable tells the database manger whether to install an EXIT LIST handler in applications and whether to perform a COMMIT. Normally, the database manager does both if the application ends normally. By setting the value of this variable to ON, the database manager will not install an EXIT LIST handler in applications and will not perform a COMMIT.

For applications that dynamically load the DB2 library and unload it before the application terminates, the invocation of the EXIT LIST handler fails because the handler routine is no longer loaded in the application. If your application operates in this way, you should set this variable to ON and ensure that your application explicitly invokes all required COMMITs.

DB2REMOTEPREG

OS: Windows 95/NT; Default: Null; Value: Any valid Windows 95/NT machine name

This variable specifies the remote machine name that contains the Win32 registry list of DB2 instance profiles and instances. After the DB2 product is installed, you should set the value for this variable only once. It should not be modified from that point.

Use this variable with extreme caution. If incorrectly modified, when the database manager is started, it may not be able to find the environment and registry variables that are part of the DB2 instance profiles or the location of the instances themselves. This will prevent the database manager from working. No instance will be running and no databases can be accessed and used.

DB2ROUTINE_DEBUG

OS: AIX and Windows NT; Default: OFF; Values: ON or OFF

Do you want to enable the debug capability for Java stored procedures? If not, leave the value for this variable set to OFF. If you want this capability, be aware that there is a performance impact. See the *IBM DB2 Universal Database Application Development Guide* for more information about debugging Java stored procedures.

DB2SORCVBUF

OS: Windows 95/NT; Default: 32,767

This variable specifies the value of TCP/IP receive buffers on Windows 95/NT operating systems.

DB2SORT

OS: All, server only; Default: Null; Values: Any valid path

This variable identifies the location of a library to be loaded at run time by the load utility. The library contains the entry point for functions used in sorting indexing data. Use this variable to exploit vendor-supplied sorting products for use with the load utility in generating system indexes. The path supplied must be relative to the database server.

DB2SYSTEM

OS: Windows 95/NT, OS/2, and UNIX; Default: Null; Values: Varies by operating system

This variable identifies the name of the DB2 server system used by your users and database administrators. If possible, this name should be unique within your network. To aid administrators in identifying server systems that can be administered from the Control Center, this name is displayed in the system level of the Control Center's object tree.

When using the Search the Network function of the Client Configuration Assistant, DB2 discovery returns this name and it is displayed at the system level in the resulting object tree. This name aids users in identifying the system that contains the database they wish to access. A value for this variable is set at installation time as follows:

- On Windows 95/NT, the setup program sets it equal to the computer name specified for the system.

- On OS/2, the user is prompted to enter the name during the installation process.

- On UNIX systems, it is set equal to the UNIX system's TCP/IP hostname.

DB2UPMPR

OS: OS/2; Default: ON; Values: ON or OFF

This variable applies only to OS/2. It specifies whether the user profile manager (UPM) logon screen will be displayed when the user enters the wrong user ID or password.

DB2_VENDOR_INI

OS: AIX, HP-UX, Sun Solaris, and Windows NT; Default: Null; Values: Any valid path and file

This variable gives the path and filename containing all vendor-specific environment settings. The value is picked up when the database manager starts.

DB2_XBSA_LIBRARY

OS: AIX, HP-UX, Sun Solaris, and Windows NT; Default: Null; Values: Any valid path and file

This variable gives the path and filename of the vendor-supplied X/Open Backup Services API (XBSA) library. On AIX, the setting must include the shared object if it is not named shr.o. HP-UX, Sun Solaris, and Windows NT do not require the shared object name.

The XBSA interface can be invoked through the BACKUP DATABASE or the RESTORE DATABASE commands.

NEWLOGPATH2

OS: UNIX; Default: 0; Values: 0 or 1

This variable specifies whether a secondary path should be used to implement dual logging. Appending a 2 to the current value of the logpath database configuration parameter generates the path used.

General Variables

The following general registry variables are either appropriate to all operating systems or are needed for informational purposes within the system.

DB2ACCOUNT

OS: All; Default: Null

This is the accounting string that is sent to the remote host. See the *IBM DB2 Connect User's Guide* for more information.

DB2BIDI

OS: All; Default: NO; Values: YES or NO

This variable enables bidirectional support, and the DB2CODEPAGE variable (described shortly) is used to declare the code page to be used. For more details on bidirectional support, see the *IBM DB2 Universal Database Administration Guide: Planning* in appendix D.

DB2_BLOCK_ON_LOG_DISK_FULL

OS: All; Default: NO; Values: YES or NO

This variable is used to prevent "disk full" errors from being generated when the database manager cannot create a new log file in the active log path. Instead of an error, the database manager attempts to create the log file every five minutes until it succeeds. After each attempt, the database manager writes a message to the db2diag.log file. If you want to confirm that your application is hanging because of a log disk full condition, you should monitor the contents of the db2diag.log file.

Until the log file is successfully created, any user application that attempts to update table data will not be able to commit transactions. Read-only queries may not be directly affected; however, if a query needs to access data that is locked by an update request or by a data page that is fixed in the buffer pool by the updating application, read-only queries will also appear to hang.

DB2CODEPAGE

OS: All; Default: Derived from the language ID as specified by the operating system

This variable specifies the code page of the data presented to the database manager from the application on the database client. The user should *not* set this variable unless explicitly stated in the DB2 product library, or when asked to by DB2

Service representatives. Setting this variable to a value not supported by the operating system can produce unexpected and unwanted results. In most cases, you will not need to set this variable because the database manager automatically derives the code-page information from the operating system.

DB2COUNTRY

OS: All; Default: Derived from the language ID as specified by the operating system

This variable specifies the country, region, or territory code of the client application, which influences date and time formats.

DB2DBDFT

OS: All; Default: Null; Values: Any valid database alias name

This variable specifies the database alias name of the database to be used for implicit connections. If an application has no database connection but SQL statements are issued, an implicit connection attempt will be made provided this variable has been given a default database alias name.

DB2DBMSADDR

OS: Windows 32-bit operating systems; Default: 0x20000000 for Windows NT, 0x20000000 for Windows 95; Values: 0x20000000 to 0xB0000000 in increments of 0x10000

This variable specifies the default database manager shared memory address in hexadecimal format. If DB2START fails due to a shared memory address collision, this registry variable can be modified to force the database manager instance to allocate its shared memory at a different address.

DB2_DISABLE_FLUSH_LOG

OS: All; Default: OFF; Values: ON or OFF

This variable specifies whether to disable or allow the closing of the active log file when the online backup is completed. The default is to allow the closing of the active log file. Set the value of this variable to ON to disable closing the active log file.

When an online backup completes, the last active log file is truncated, closed, and made available to be archived. This ensures that your online backup has a complete set of archived logs available for recovery.

You may wish to disable closing the last active log if you are concerned that you are wasting portions of the log sequence number (LSN) space. Each time an active log file is truncated, the LSN is incremented by an amount proportional to the space truncated. If you perform a large number of online backups each day, then you may wish to disable closing the last active log file.

You may also wish to disable closing the last active log file if you find you are receiving log full messages a short time after the online backup completes. When a log file is truncated, the reserved active log space is incremented by the amount proportional to the size of the truncated log. The active log space is freed once the truncated log file is reclaimed. The reclamation occurs shortly after the log file becomes inactive. In the short interval between that, you may receive log full messages.

DB2DISCOVERYTIME

OS: OS/2 and Windows 32-bit operating systems; Default: 40 seconds; Minimum: 20 seconds

This variable specifies how long you would like SEARCH discovery to search for DB2 systems. The default is probably sufficient for your environment unless it is particularly complex with many other systems or you know that communications are slow between systems.

DB2INCLUDE

OS: All; Default: The current directory; Values: Any valid directory or list of directories

This variable specifies the path used during the processing of the SQL INCLUDE text-file statement during DB2 precompiler processing. It provides a list of directories where the INCLUDE file might be found. See the *IBM DB2 Universal Database Application Development Guide* for descriptions of how this variable is used in the different precompiled languages.

DB2INSTDEF

OS: OS/2 and Windows 32-bit operating systems; Default: DB2; Values: A valid name for your DB2 instance

This variable sets the value to be used if DB2INSTANCE is not defined.

DB2INSTOWNER

OS: Windows NT; Default: Null; Values: A valid name for the instance-owning machine

This variable is created in the DB2 profile registry when the instance is first created. It is set to the name of the instance-owning machine.

DB2_LIC_STAT_SIZE

OS: All; Default: Null; Range: 0 to 32,767

This variable is used to determine the maximum size in megabytes of the file containing the license statistics for the system. A value of 0 turns the license statistics gathering off. If the variable is not recognized or not defined, the variable defaults to unlimited. The statistics are displayed using the License Center.

DB2NBDISCOVERRCVBUFS

OS: All; Default: 16 buffers; Minimum: 16 buffers; Values: A valid number of buffers

This variable is used for NetBIOS SEARCH discovery. The variable specifies the number of concurrent discovery responses that a client can receive. If more than the specified concurrent discovery responses are received, then the excess responses are discarded by the NetBIOS layer. If a number less than 16 is chosen, the default value is used.

DB2SLOGON

OS: Windows 3.*x*; Default: Null; Values: YES or NO

This variable enables a secure logon in DB2 for Windows 3.*x* operating systems. If DB2SLOGON is YES, the database manager does not write user IDs and passwords to a file, but instead uses a segment of memory to maintain them. When this variable is enabled, the user must log on each time Windows 3.*x* is started.

DB2TIMEOUT

OS: Windows 3.*x* and Macintosh; Default: Not set; Values: Minimum of 30 seconds; 0 or a negative value disables this feature

You use this variable to control the timeout period for Windows 3.*x* and Macintosh clients during long SQL queries. After the timeout period has expired, a dialog box appears asking if the query should be interrupted or allowed to continue. The default is that this feature is disabled.

DB2TRACENAME

OS: Windows 3.*x* and Macintosh; Default: DB2WIN.TRC (on Windows 3.*x*) and DB2MAC.TRC (on Macintosh)

This variable specifies the name of the file where the trace information is stored. The default for each system is saved in your current instance directory (for example, \sqllib\db2). It is strongly recommended that you specify the full pathname.

DB2TRACEON

OS: Windows 3.*x* and Macintosh; Default: NO; Values: YES or NO

This variable turns the trace on to provide information to IBM in case there is a problem. (Turn trace on only when you encounter a problem you cannot resolve.) See the *IBM DB2 Universal Database Troubleshooting Guide* for information on using the trace facility with clients.

DB2TRCFLUSH

OS: Windows 3.*x* and Macintosh; Default: NO; Values: YES or NO

You can use this variable in conjunction with DB2TRACEON=YES. When both variables are enabled, each trace record is written immediately to the trace file. This causes performance degradation, so you should use this variable only in serious cases, such as when an application hangs the system and the system needs to be rebooted. Setting this variable guarantees that the trace file and trace entries are not lost by the reboot.

DB2TRCSYSERR

OS: Windows 3.*x* and Macintosh; Default: 1; Values: 1 to 32,767

This variable specifies the number of system errors to trace before turning off tracing.

DB2YIELD

OS: Windows 3.*x*; Default: NO; Values: YES or NO

This variable specifies the client behavior while communicating with a remote server. When the value is NO, the client does not yield the CPU to other applications, and the Windows environment is halted while the client application is communicating with the remote server. The communications operation must complete before any other tasks can resume. When the value is YES, the system operates as normal.

We recommend that you run with the value as YES. If the system crashes, you will need to set the value to NO. When writing applications, ensure that the application is written to accept and handle Windows messages while waiting for a communications operation to complete.

DCE Directory Variables

The following sections present the DCE directory variables. DCE is another way of controlling the communications between your local server and other servers in your network. For more information on DCE, see the *IBM DB2 Universal Database Administration Guide: Implementation* volume.

DB2DIRPATHNAME

OS: OS/2, UNIX, and Windows 32-bit operating systems; Default: Null

This variable specifies a temporary override of the DIR_PATH_NAME parameter value in the database manger configuration file. If a directory server is used and the target of a CONNECT statement or ATTACH command is not explicitly cataloged, then the target is concatenated with the contents of this variable (if specified) to form the fully qualified DCE name.

The content of this variable doesn't affect the instance's global name, which is always identified by the database manager configuration parameters DIR_PATH_NAME and DIR_OBJ_NAME.

DB2CLIENTADPT

OS: OS/2 and Windows 32-bit operating systems; Default: Null; Values: 0 to 15

This variable specifies the client adapter number for the NetBIOS protocol on OS/2 and Windows 32-bit operating systems. The value for this variable overrides the DFT_CLIENT_ADPT parameter value in the database manager configuration file.

DB2CLIENTCOMM

OS: OS/2, UNIX, and Windows 32-bit operating systems; Default: Null

This variable specifies a temporary override of the DFT_CLIENT_COMM parameter value in the database manager configuration file. If neither DFT_CLIENT_COMM nor this variable is specified, then the first protocol found in the object is used. If either one or both of them are specified, then only the first matching protocol is used. In either case, no retry is attempted if the first connect fails.

DB2ROUTE

OS: OS/2, UNIX, and Windows 32-bit operating systems; Default: Null

This variable specifies the name of the routing information object the client uses when it connects to a database with a different database protocol. The value of this variable overrides the ROUTE_OBJ_NAME parameter value in the database manager configuration file.

Data Links Variables

The following sections show the registry variables associated with a data links environment. When creating or altering tables, you can specify that certain columns are to link to outside data sources. Typically, you use this strategy with preexisting legacy data found on other nonrelational database systems. For more information on linking to data found outside of relational databases, see the *IBM DB2 Universal Database SQL Reference*.

DLFM_BACKUP_DIR_NAME

OS: AIX, Windows NT; Default: Null; Values: TSM or any valid path

This variable specifies the backup device to use. Changing this variable will not affect the placement of the archived files. If you change the setting of this variable between TSM and a path at run time, the archived files are not moved. Only new backups are placed in the new location. TSM refers to the Tivoli Storage Manager (TSM) user exit option that may be available on your system.

DLFM_BACKUP_LOCAL_MP

OS: AIX, Windows NT; Default: Null; Values: Any valid path to the local mount point in the distributed file system (DFS)

This variable specifies the fully qualified path to a mount point in the DFS system. When a path is given, it is used instead of the path given with DLFM_BACKUP_DIR_NAME.

DLFM_BACKUP_TARGET

OS: AIX, Windows NT; Default: Null; Values: LOCAL, TSM, XBSA

This variable specifies the type of backup used.

DLFM_BACKUP_TARGET_LIBRARY

OS: AIX, Windows NT; Default: Null; Values: Any valid and fully qualified path to the DLL or shared library name

The DLL or shared library is loaded by using the libdfmxbsa.a library.

DLFM_ENABLE_STPROC

OS: AIX, Windows NT; Default: NO; Values: YES or NO

This variable specifies whether a stored procedure is used to link groups of files. When the value of this variable is set to YES, a stored procedure is used to link groups of files.

DLFM_FS_ENVIRONMENT

OS: AIX, Windows NT; Default: NATIVE; Values: NATIVE or DFS

This variable specifies the environment in which Data Links servers operate. NATIVE indicates that the Data Links server is in a single machine where the server can take over files on its own machine. DFS indicates that the Data Links server is in a DFS where the server can take over files throughout the file system.

Note   *You are not allowed to mix these two environments.*

DLFM_GC_MODE

OS: AIX, Windows NT; Default: PASSIVE; Values: SLEEP, PASSIVE, or ACTIVE

This variable specifies the garbage file collection on the Data Links server. When set to SLEEP, no garbage collection occurs. When set to PASSIVE, garbage collection runs

REFERENCE

only if no other transactions are running. When set to ACTIVE, garbage collection runs even if other transactions are running.

DLFM_INSTALL_PATH

OS: AIX, Windows NT; Default: On AIX: /usr/lpp/db2_07_00/adm, on Windows NT: DB2PATH/bin

This variable specifies the path where the Data Links executables are installed.

DLFM_LOG_LEVEL

OS: AIX, Windows NT; Default: LOG_INFO; Values: LOG_CRIT, LOG_DEBUG, LOG_ERR, LOG_INFO, LOG_NOTICE, LOG_WARNING

This variable specifies the level of diagnostic information to be recorded. Each of the values that are used with this variable represent the different types of log messages that may be generated, from critical messages (LOG_CRIT) to informational messages (LOG_INFO).

DLFM_PORT

OS: All, except Windows 3.x; Default: 5100; Values: Any valid port number

This variable specifies the port number used to communicate with the Data Links servers running the DB2 Data Links Manager. This variable is used only when a table contains a DATALINKS column.

DLFM_TSM_MGMTCLASS

OS: AIX, Windows NT, Sun Solaris; Default: The default TSM management class; Values: Any valid TSM management class

This variable specifies the TSM management class to use to archive and retrieve linked files. The default TSM management class is used if there is no explicit value for this variable.

Partitioned Database Variables

The following variables are concerned with a partitioned database environment. If you do not work in such an environment, you will not need any of these variables.

DB2ATLD_PORTS

OS: DB2 UDB EEE on AIX, Sun Solaris, and Windows NT; Default: 6000:6063; Values: num1:num2, where both are between 1 and 65535, and num1 <= num2

This variable specifies the range of port numbers used for the AutoLoader utility's internal TCP/IP communication. If not set, AutoLoader uses the internal default port range 6000:6063. When you have other applications using the AutoLoader default port range, you can use this variable to select an alternate port range.

DB2ATLD_PWFILE

OS: DB2 UDB EEE on AIX, Sun Solaris, and Windows NT; Default: Null; Values: A file path expression

This variable specifies a path to a file that contains a password used during AutoLoader authentication. If not set, AutoLoader either extracts the password from its configuration file or prompts you interactively. Using this variable addresses password security concerns. It also allows the separation of AutoLoader configuration information from authentication information.

DB2CHGPWD_EEE

OS: DB2 UDB EEE on AIX and Windows NT; Default: Null; Values: YES or NO

This variable specifies whether you are allowing other users to change passwords on AIX or Windows NT EEE systems. Setting the variable to YES allows other users to change passwords.

Passwords for all partitions must be maintained centrally by using a Windows NT domain controller, or network information service (NIS) (on AIX). If not maintained centrally, passwords may not be consistent across all partitions. This could result in a password being changed only at the database partition to which the user connects to make the change. To modify this global registry variable, you must be at the root directory and on the DAS instance.

DB2_FORCE_FCM_BP

OS: AIX; Default; NO; Values: YES or NO

This variable specifies from where the FCM resources are allocated when you have multiple logical partitions. The resources may be allocated from either the database global memory or a separate shared memory segment. Setting the variable to YES has the FCM resources allocated from a separate shared memory segment.

When the FCM buffers are created in a separate memory segment, the communication between FCM daemons of different logical partitions on the same physical node occurs through shared memory. Otherwise, FCM daemons on the same node communicate through UNIX sockets. The advantage of communicating through shared memory in this way is that it is faster. The disadvantage is that fewer shared memory segments are available for other uses, most notably, database buffer pools. This reduces the maximum size of database buffer pools.

DB2_NUM_FAILOVER_NODES

OS: All; Default: 2; Values: 0 to the number of logical nodes

This variable specifies the number of partitions or nodes that can be used as failover nodes in a high availability environment. *High availability* means that if a partition fails, it can be restarted as a logical partition on a different host machine. The number you use with this variable determines how much memory is reserved for FCM resources for failover partitions.

DB2PORTRANGE

OS: Windows NT; Values: nnnn:nnnn

This variable specifies the TCP/IP port range used by FCM so that any additional partitions created on another machine will also have the same port range.

DB2_UPDATE_PART_KEY

OS: All; Default: YES; Values: YES or NO

This variable specifies whether updating the partitioning key is permitted. For FixPak 3 or later, the default value is YES.

The Complete Reference

DB2

Chapter 29

Introduction to DB2 Commands, Utilities, and Tools

The decision of IBM and Oracle to go with SQL is one of the reasons that their relational database products have been so durable, while other relational pioneers like Ingres and DBase have suffered for their late adoption of SQL. SQL is great: the statements fall into familiar computer science file system concepts (select/insert/update/delete), almost every statement begins with a verb and ends with a noun, and the language is readily accessible to people who can read English but who can't read C or Assembler. SQL is probably the most successful 4GL (Fourth Generation Language) ever, although seldom recognized as such.

This chapter is not about SQL. While all successful relational database products share SQL as a common way to get at data, they differ in the utilities. They all have tools called LOAD, IMPORT, EXPORT, and SORT (LIES), but the syntax differs by product (and even platform). DB2 on UNIX and Windows does not have an UNLOAD utility, BACKUP has different meanings depending on the product, and key utilities like REORGANIZATION, RUNSTATS (or "GATHER STATISTICS"), and ROLLFORWARD differ both syntactically and semantically.

This chapter shows you the *utilities*: the command line directives and programs that are your tools as the DB2 "orchestra conductor." They are variously called commands, utilities, and even executables (for the commands that start with *DB2...* like DB2START) in the DB2 documentation. *Commands* is the best generic name, and it helps distinguish them from SQL statements. Every one of them begins with DB2 and ends with a set of initials or a verb that describes what the command does.

In this chapter, each command is explained, the authority or authorities needed to run it are listed, the syntax is provided, and command parameters are listed and described. For complex commands, examples are provided.

DB2ADMIN

DB2ADMIN manages the DB2 Administration Server—a special DB2 instance on each machine that manages the database instances with commands typically run by SYSADM.

Authorization

Local administrator on Windows or OS/2, or SYSADM on UNIX and OS/2.

Syntax

```
>>-db2admin-------------------------------------------------------->

>-----+----------------------------------------------------------------+>
      +-START---------------------------------------------------------+
      +-STOP----------------------------------------------------------+
      +-CREATE--+-----------------------------+---+----------------------+-+
```

```
|              '-/USER:--user-account--'   '-/PASSWORD:--user-password--' |
+-DROP---------------------------------------------------------------+
+-SETID--user-account--user-password--------------------------------+
'--?----------------------------------------------------------------'

>---------------------------------------------------------------><
```

Description

The DB2 Administration Server is a special DB2 instance that contains no databases. It manages all other DB2 instances on the same machine. This command allows you to create, drop, start, and stop the DB2 Administrator instance. (Type **db2admin** with no parameters to learn the name of the DB2 Administrator instance.) The ability to link the Administrator instance with the user account is supported on Windows and OS/2. This is done with the SETID parameter or on the DB2ADMIN CREATE command.

Example

Link the DB2ADMIN ID to a user account on Windows:

```
db2admin SETID userid password
```

Create a DB2ADMIN instance, specifying a user ID and password:

```
db2admin CREATE /USER:adamache /PASSWORD:password
```

DB2ADUTL

DB2ADUTL manages backup images and log files saved with IBM Tivoli Storage Manager (TSM).

Authorization

None.

Syntax

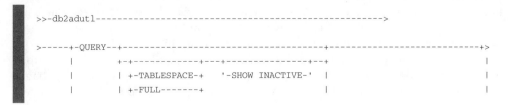

```
>>-db2adutl------------------------------------------------------>

>-----+-QUERY--+-------------------------------------------+-------------------------+>
      |        +-+-----------+---+-------------+--+         |                         |
      |        | +-TABLESPACE-+   '-SHOW INACTIVE-'  |      |                         |
      |        | +-FULL-------+                       |      |                         |
```

```
     |          | '-LOADCOPY---'                               |                    |
     |          '-LOGS--+---------------------+-------'                              |
     |                  '-BETWEEN sn1 AND sn2-'                                      |
     +-EXTRACT--+-------------------------------------------------------------+--+
     |          +-+-----------+---+---------------+----+--------------------+-+ |
     |          | +-TABLESPACE-+  '-SHOW INACTIVE-'    '-TAKEN AT-timestamp--' | |
     |          | +-FULL-------+                                             | |
     |          | '-LOADCOPY---'                                             | |
     |          '-LOGS--+---------------------+----------------------------' |
     |                  '-BETWEEN sn1 AND sn2--'                               |
     +-DELETE--+-----------------------------------------------------------+----------+
     |         +-+-----------+---+-------------------------------------+-+            |
     |         | +-TABLESPACE-+   +-KEEP--n-----------------------+ |            |
     |         | +-FULL-------+   +-OLDER--+-------+---+-timestamp-+-+ |            |
     |         | '-LOADCOPY---'   |        '-THAN--'  '-n--days---' | |            |
     |         |                  '-TAKEN AT--timestamp-------------' |            |
     |         '-LOGS--+---------------------+--------------------'              |
     |                 '-BETWEEN--sn1--AND--sn2--'                                |
     '-VERIFY--+-------------------------------------------------------------+-'
               +-+-----------+---+---------------+---+--------------------+-+
               | +-TABLESPACE-+  '-SHOW INACTIVE--'  '-TAKEN AT--timestamp--' |
               | '-FULL-------'                                              |
               '-LOGS--+-------------------+----------------------------'
                       '-BETWEEN sn1 AND sn2--'


>-----+-----------------------------+---------------------->
      '--+-DATABASE-+--database_name---'
         '-DB------'


>-----+-------------------+---+-------------------+--------->
      '-NODE--node_number--'  '-PASSWORD--password--'


>-----+-------------------+---+-------------------+--------->
      '-NODENAME--node_name--'  '-WITHOUT PROMPTING--'


>-----+--------------+------------------------------------><
      '-OWNER--owner--'
```

Description

Storage managers like those made by IBM (Tivoli Storage Manager), Legato, and Veritas automate the storage of the pieces of DB2 needed to restore in disaster recovery: database backup images and the logs that roll forward to the point in time before the disaster. Storage managers seek to combine the speed of backing up to disk with the low cost of backing up to tape by directing backups to a remote server, and then handling multiple archives and the deletion of old backup images when they become useless (garbage collection). LOAD, which is not logged, can also have a copy directed to TSM for quicker recovery if the disaster occurs during the LOAD.

As you can see from the syntax, this command operates on a FULL backup image, a LOAD copy, the backup image of a tablespace (useful for subset restore, which is invoked with RESTORE TABLESPACE), and can also be used to handle archived logs.

Use QUERY to see that you have archived, EXTRACT to pull an image off the storage manager server, DELETE to do manual garbage collection, and VERIFY to validate that an archive operation was successful.

Using a storage manager will make you a more effective DBA if you plan it correctly: you can optimize storage space, speed up backup operations, and use one backup server to provide a disaster recovery option for several DB2 servers. You can also help your users answer questions like "What was our accounts payable before the embezzler in Purchasing began deleting suppliers to cover his tracks?" TSM can provide a contingency for a variety of disasters.

If you try to use DB2 and a storage manager without learning either properly, you'll find yourself learning two complex software products in the middle of a disaster. If you choose TSM, do yourself a favor and fake a disaster: measure the time to get the correct backup image and logs off the TSM server, restore the database and roll forward, and verify the consistency of the database with a SELECT COUNT(*) from the tables you care most about. You'll then know what your recovery window is. When you've completed this fire drill successfully, put your coworkers through this process so they know what to do if you're incommunicado when the real disaster hits. You should also read the "Recovery" section in the *DB2 Administration Guide*.

DB2ADUTL requires the TSM/ADSM client to be installed on the DB2 server. Because the data TSM cares about is on the DB2 server, the TSM client runs on the DB2 server, and the TSM server is a superserver (perhaps on a mainframe) running in the background. (See Figure 29-1.)

Example

Ask Tivoli Storage manager what it has stored, assuming defaults for all values:

```
db2adutl query
```

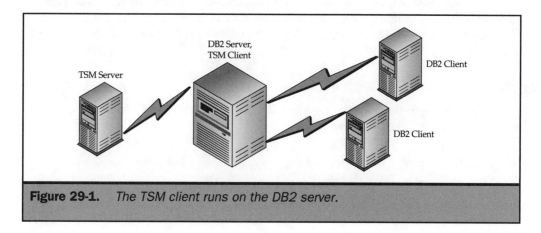

Figure 29-1.   *The TSM client runs on the DB2 server.*

DB2ADVIS

DB2ADVIS is the command line version of the index advisor: a DB2 wizard that will ask you questions about the database design, users, and typical queries, and then advise you on which indexes to create.

Authorization

Read access to the database, and read/write to the Explain tables.

Syntax

```
>>-db2advis----d--database-name----+-------------------+------->
                                    +--w--workLOAD-name--+
                                    +--s--"statement"----+
                                    '--i--filename-------'

>-----+------------------------+---+----------------+------->
       '--a--userid--+---------+--'   '--l--disk-limit--'
                     '-/passwd--'

>-----+--------------------+---+-----+--------------------->< 
       '--t--max-advise-time--'   '--h--'
```

Description

This command is generally easier to use from the graphical user interface in the Control Center. (Choose the system name, the instance, the database name, and then right-click Indexes to invoke the Create Indexes Wizard.)

If you run DB2ADVIS with a particular statement, and that SQL statement really represents the most critical access to the database, consider turning the results of the SQL statement into a summary table (that is, a materialized view) by using the CREATE SUMMARY TABLE... SQL statement. This essentially stores the results of the statement as a report.

Example

Ask for index suggestions for the sample database using a SELECT * from a user table with the predicate "like 'Adamache%'":

```
db2advis -d sample -s select * from address where name like 'Adamache%'
```

DB2AUDIT

You can audit insert/update/delete activity with triggers. If your audit requirements are broader, or you do not wish to define three triggers for each table in your database, consider DB2AUDIT.

Authorization

SYSADM.

Syntax

```
|>- db2audit --- configure --- reset ----------------------------->< |
              |                     |-( Audit Configuration )-|          |
              |- describe ----------------------------------------------|
              |- extract -( Audit Extraction )--------------------------|
              |- flush -------------------------------------------------|
              |- prune --- all -----------------------------------------|
              |          |- date YYYYMMDDHH -|  |- pathname PATH -|
              |- start -------------------------------------------------|
              |- stop --------------------------------------------------|


Audit Configuration:
|--------------------------------------------------------->
   |- scope --- all ---------|  |- status --- both ----|
              |  V- , ----|  |                |- success -|
              |--- audit -----|                |- failure -|
              |--- checking --|
              |--- objmaint --|
              |--- secmaint --|
              |--- sysadmin --|
              |--- validate --|
              |--- context   -|


>--------------------------|
   |- errortype --- audit --|
                |- normal -|


Audit Extraction:
|------------------------------------------------------------------------->
   |- file FILE NAME -------------------|  |                 V- , ------|  |
   |- delasc ---------------------------|  |- category --- audit -----|
              |- delimiter LOAD DELIMITER-|                |- checking --|
                                                           |- objmaint --|
```

```
                                                   |- secmaint --|
                                                   |- sysadmin --|
                                                   |- validate --|
                                                   |- context   -|

>---------------------------------------------------------|
   |- database DATABASE NAME -|   |- status --- success -|
                                              |- failure -|
```

Description

This command warrants an entire chapter in the *DB2 Administration Guide.* DB2AUDIT records are written to an audit log: db2audit.log. This file is located in the instance's security subdirectory (x:\SQLLIB\DB2\SECURITY by default on Windows, for example). Running DB2AUDIT can make DB2 run slightly slower.

DB2AUDIT runs at the database manager instance level, recording all instance-level activities and database-level activities. You can use it to do the following:

- Start recording auditable events within the DB2 instance.
- Stop DB2AUDIT.
- Configure DB2AUDIT.
- Select the categories of the auditable events to be recorded.
- Request the current audit configuration.
- Flush any pending audit records from the instance and write them to db2audit.log.
- Extract audit records by formatting and copying them from the audit log to a flat file or ASCII-delimited files. Extraction is done for one of two reasons: preparation for analysis of log records, or preparation for pruning log records. ASCII-delimited files can be IMPORTed into DB2 tables so you can use SQL to do analysis.
- Prune audit records from the current audit log.

Example

Extract audit records in ASCII-delimited format:

```
db2audit extract delasc
```

DB2ATLD

AutoLOADer (DB2ATLD) is run only on DB2 Enterprise—Extended Edition (EEE), and is used to LOAD tables spread across multiple machines (nodes) or multiple logical nodes. By running several LOAD commands in parallel, DB2ATLD fully exploits the scalability of EEE. DB2ATLD can also call DB2SPLIT, splitting a large file into the input files required by each LOAD command to be run on each node.

Authorization

One of the following:

- SYSADM authority
- DBADM authority
- LOAD authority on the database and the following:
    - INSERT privilege on the table when the LOAD utility is invoked in INSERT mode, TERMINATE mode (to terminate a previous LOADLOAD INSERT operation), or RESTART mode (to restart a previous LOAD LOADINSERT operation)
    - INSERT and DELETE privilege on the table when the LOAD utility is invoked in REPLACE mode, TERMINATE mode (to terminate a previous LOADLOAD REPLACE operation), or RESTART mode (to restart a previous LOADLOAD REPLACE operation)
    - INSERT privilege on the exception table, if such a table is used as part of the LOADLOAD operation.

Syntax

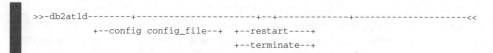

```
>>-db2atld--------+--------------------+--+------------+--------------------<<
                  +--config config_file--+  +--restart----+
                                            +--terminate--+
```

Config identifies the configuration file (the default is "autoLOADer.cfg"). Restart tells DB2 to attempt to restart any interrupted AutoLOADer operation. Terminate allows you to stop an AutoLOADer operation that was interrupted.

Description

LOADLOAD is run with one input file and one DB2 instance as the target to receive the data. DB2ATLD is a meta-LOAD, allowing LOADLOAD to run over the multiple DB2 instances required for an EEE database. It also handles taking one input file and splitting it with DB2SPLIT to create an input file for each partition of a table spread over multiple DB2 instances.

While LOAD supports three flat file formats (nondelimited ASCII [*ASC*], delimited ASCII [*DEL*], and PC/IXF), DB2ATLD can be used only to split ASC and DEL files. PC/IXF files cannot be split, but DB2ATLD can be used to LOAD them into a single database partition by using the noheader modifier for the LOAD.

If you want to LOAD an IXF file into a multiple-partition table, you must first LOAD it into a single-partition table, and then insert the data into the multiple-partition table by using a SELECT from the single-partition table. If you're using LOAD to get data into DB2 quickly, running a SELECT with INSERT after a LOAD defeats the goal of speed.

The exception is where the target table of the LOAD is a staging table, when you want to get the data into DB2 fast, and the target of the SELECT with INSERT is a table that must stay online because of constant access.

AutoLOADer can be run in one of four modes (see the line "# running mode" in the code example that follows):

- ■ **SPLIT_AND_LOAD** Data is partitioned (ideally in parallel) and LOADed simultaneously on the corresponding database partitions.

- ■ **SPLIT_ONLY** Data is partitioned (ideally in parallel), and the output is written to files in a specified location, or in the AutoLOADer current working directory.

- ■ **LOAD_ONLY** Data is already partitioned; the split process is skipped, and the data is LOADed simultaneously on the corresponding database partitions.

- ■ **ANALYZE** This mode generates an optimal partitioning map with even distribution across all database partitions. It is used in planning for the eventual implementation of one of the preceding options (or an enormous number of INSERTs to populate the table).

In a *partitioned database*, a large amount of data is located across many partitions. *Partition keys* are used to determine the target database partition for each row of the table. The rows must be split before they can be LOADed on the correct database partition. The AutoLOADer utility can perform each of split and LOAD on their own, or combine the two steps, first splitting the data and then LOADing it.

AutoLOADer uses the same hashing algorithm as DB2: inserting or updating rows to partition the data into as many output sockets as there are database partitions in the nodegroup in which the table was defined. AutoLOADer LOADs from these output sockets concurrently across the set of database partitions in the nodegroup. AutoLOADer can also use multiple database partitions for the splitting phase, making this a faster operation through parallelism as well.

Example

The DB2ATLD syntax looks simple, but only because the IMPORTant choices are made in the AutoLOADer configuration file. Here is a sample configuration file for UNIX. The lines starting with the pound symbol (#) are comments:

```
###############
# release level
###############
RELEASE=V7.00
##################
# command line processor LOAD command
##################
```

```
db2 LOAD from /home/user/atld_work/test.dat of del replace into user.test
###############
# database name
###############
database=SAMPLE
#################
# split partition list - lists the nodes used to split the input file
#################
SPLIT_NODES=(0,2)
##############
# running mode
##############
mode=split_and_LOAD
###############
# log file token
###############
logfile=mylog
######################################
# frequency of progressive information
#
# print out progressive info every 10
# megabytes of data
######################################
STATUS_INTERVAL=10
```

You would call the preceding file with this command:

```
db2atld -config sample.atld.cfg
```

DB2BATCH

DB2BATCH is used to measure performance of SQL statements. It is better at this than the command line processor (CLP) because it eliminates certain overhead that the CLP uses to be a well-behaved DB2 application. This overhead is necessary for production use of DB2 (stuff like error checking), but it is not required if you want to isolate only the time an SQL statement takes to execute when you're prototyping. Consider a design that will eventually be implemented in an application that does not use the CLP: for this, DB2BATCH is more accurate than the CLP for measuring the time required for each SQL statement. For this reason, DB2BATCH is the best way to estimate performance of SQL statements that you are prototyping for use in programs.

Authorization

Determined by the authorization required for the SQL statements issued.

Syntax

```
>>-db2batch----d--dbname----+---------------+------------------>
                            '--f--file_name--'

>-----+-------------------------+---+------------+--------------->
      '--a--userid/password--'   '--t--delcol--'

>-----+-------------------------------+---+--------------+-------->
      '--r--outfile--+-----------+--'   |       .-on--.  |
                     '-,outfile2-'      '--c--+-off-+--'

>-----+----------------+---+--------------+------------------>
      |    .-short----. |  '--o--options--'
      '--i--+-long-----+--'
            '-complete-'

>-----+--------------+---+-------------+---+--------------+-->
      |   .-off--.  |  |     .-on--.  |  |     .-off--.  |
      '--v--+-on---+--'  '--s--+-off-+--'  '--q--+-on---+--'
                                                 '-del--'

>-----+--------+---+------------------+----------------------->
      '--l--x--'   '--p--+-s---------+--'
                         +-t--table--+
                         '-d---------'

>-----+--------------------------+---+-----+----------------->< 
      '--cli--+------------+--'   '--h--'
              '-cache-size--'
```

Description

The following are the descriptions for each DB2BATCH parameter:

-d dbname

This option specifies the name of the database you're running the SQL against. The default is the value of the DB2DBDFT environment variable.

-f file_name

This option specifies the input file containing the SQL statements. The default is standard input. Comments in the file start with two hyphens (—).

Text you want in the output should be marked as follows:

```
--#COMMENT <comment>
```

A *block* is two or more SQL statements measured together: information is collected for all of those statements at once, instead of one at a time. Identify the beginning of a block of queries with the following:

```
--#BGBLK.
```

Identify the end of a block of queries with the following:

```
--#EOBLK
```

Specify one or more control options as follows:

```
--#SET <control option>  <value>
```

Valid control options are as follows:

- **ROWS_FETCH** Number of rows to be fetched from the answer set. Choices are –1 to *n*. The default value, –1, will fetch all rows.
- **ROWS_OUT** Number of fetched rows to be sent to output. Choices are –1 to *n*. The default value, –1, will send all fetched rows to output.
- **PERF_DETAIL** The level of performance information to be returned. Choices for DB2 version 5 and later are as follows:
  - **0** No timing
  - **1** Return only elapsed time
- **DELIMITER** A one- or two-character end-of-statement delimiter. The default is a semicolon (;).
- **SLEEP** Number of seconds to sleep from 1 to *n*.
- **PAUSE** The user will be prompted to continue at this point—similar to using the |more command from the operating system command line.
- **TIMESTAMP** Generates a timestamp.

-a userid/password

This option specifies the user name and password used to connect to the database. The slash (/) must be included.

-t delcol

This option specifies a single-character column separator. To include a tab column delimiter, use

```
-t TAB
```

-r outfile

This option specifies an output file that will contain the query results.

, outfile2

This option can be used only if *–r outfile* is specified. *outfile2* contains the results summary. The default is standard output.

-c

DB2 automatically commits changes resulting from each SQL statement when this option is set to on; off sets autocommit off.

-i

This option specifies an elapsed time interval (in seconds). The value must be one of:

- **short** The time taken to open the cursor, complete the fetch, and close the cursor.
- **long** The elapsed time from the start of one query to the start of the next query, including pause and sleep times, and command overhead.
- **complete** The time to prepare, execute, and fetch, expressed separately.

-o options

This option allows you to specify control options. Valid options are described in the following sections.

f rows_fetch   This option specifies the number of rows to be fetched from the answer set. Choices are –1 to *n*. The default value is –1. (All rows are fetched.)

r rows_out   This specifies the number of fetched rows sent to output. Choices are –1 to *n*. The default value is –1. (All fetched rows are to be sent to output.)

p perf_detail   This option specifies the level of performance information to be returned. Choices are as follows:

- No timing
- Return only elapsed time

query_optimization_class   This option sets the query optimization class. The choices are as follows:

- ■ **0** Perform minimal optimization. Query rewrite not active. This choice is most suitable for simple dynamic SQL access to well-indexed tables.

- ■ **1** Optimization roughly comparable to DB2/UNIX version 1. No query rewrite.

- ■ **2** A level of optimization higher than that of DB2 version 1, but at significantly less optimization cost than levels 3 and above, especially for very complex queries.

- ■ **3** A moderate amount of optimization to generate an access plan.

- ■ **5** A significant amount of optimization to generate an access plan. For complex dynamic SQL queries, heuristic rules are used to limit the amount of time spent selecting an access plan. Where possible, queries will use summary tables instead of the underlying base tables.

- ■ **7** A significant amount of optimization to generate an access plan. Similar to 5, but without the heuristic rules.

- ■ **9** A maximal amount of optimization to generate an access plan. This can greatly expand the number of possible access plans that are evaluated. This class should be used to determine whether a better access plan can be generated for very complex and very long-running queries using large tables. Explain and performance measurements can be used to verify that a better plan has been generated.

e explain_mode

This option sets the EXPLAIN mode under which DB2BATCH runs. The Explain tables must be created prior to using this option (use x:\sqllib\misc\explain.ddl). The choices are as follows:

- ■ Run query only (default).

- ■ Populate Explain tables only. This option populates the explain tables and causes explain snapshots to be taken.

- ■ Populate explain tables and run query. This option populates the Explain tables and causes explain snapshots to be taken.

-v

-v stands for *Verbose* and takes no value. This option sends information to standard error during query processing. The default value is off.

-s

-s stands for *Summarization* and takes no value. This option provides a summary for each query or block of queries, containing elapsed time (if selected), CPU times (if selected), the rows fetched, and the rows printed. The arithmetic and geometric means for elapsed time and CPU times are provided if collected.

REFERENCE

-q

Query output. The choices are as follows:

- **on** Print only the nondelimited output of the query.
- **off** Print the output of the query and all associated information. This is the default.
- **del** Print only the delimited output of the query.

-l x

x stands for the termination character, specified by –1.

-p

-p selects parallel (and is allowed only if you are running EEE). Only SELECT statements are supported in this mode. Output names must have a fully qualified path. The choices for this option are the following:

- **s** Single table or collocated join query. SELECT statements cannot contain only column functions.
- **t** Use an existing table as the staging table to populate with the EXPORT data. If the query contains multiple tables in the FROM clause and the tables are not collocated, the result set is inserted into the specified table and a SELECT is issued in parallel on all partitions to generate the files with the EXPORT data.
- **d** Creates a system table in IBMDEFAULTGROUP to be used for an INSERT INTO statement. If the query contains multiple tables in the FROM clause and the tables are not collocated, the result set is inserted into the specified table and a SELECT is issued in parallel on all partitions to generate the files with the EXPORT data. If a local output file is specified (using the *-r* option), the output from each node will go into a separate file with the same name on each node. If a file that is on an NFS-mounted file system is specified, all of the output will go into this file.

-cli

This option runs DB2BATCH in CLI mode (dynamically against DB2's Call Level Interface). The default is to use embedded dynamic SQL. The statement memory can be set manually by using the cache-size parameter.

The cache-size parameter specifies the size of the statement memory, expressed as a number of statements. The default value is 25. If the utility encounters an SQL statement that has already been prepared, it will reuse the old plans. This parameter can be set only when DB2BATCH is run in CLI mode.

-h

When this option is specified, help information is displayed and all other options are ignored—only the help information is displayed.

Example

Run DB2BATCH interactively against the sample database:

```
db2batch -d sample
```

DB2BFD

DB2BFD interrogates the contents of a bind file during problem determination. It can display the host variables and SQL statements associated with a bind file.

Authorization

None.

Syntax

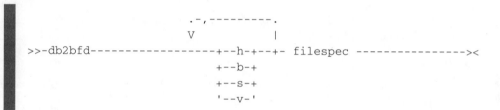

```
                          .-,---------.
                          V           |
>>-db2bfd------------------+--h-+--+- filespec ----------------><
                          +--b-+
                          +--s-+
                          '--v-'
```

Description

These are the parameters supported by DB2BFD:

- **filespec** Name of the bind file.
- **-h** Displays help information. When this option is specified, all other options are ignored, and only the help information is displayed.
- **-b** Displays the bind file header.
- **-s** Displays the SQL statements.
- **-v** Displays the host variable declarations.

Example

Display the SQL statements in the DB2LOOK bind file:

```
db2bfd -s db2look.bnd
```

 DB2CAP

DB2CAP profiles statements normally submitted through the CLI, such as those from ODBC applications, so they can gain the performance advantages of static SQL.

Authorization

One of the following is required:

- Access privileges to any database objects referenced by SQL statements recorded in the capture file.

- Sufficient authority to set bind options such as OWNER and QUALIFIER if they are different from the connect ID used to invoke the DB2CAP command.

- BINDADD authority if the package is being bound for the first time; otherwise, BIND authority is required.

Syntax

```
>>-db2cap----+----+--bind----capture-file----database_alias---->
            +--h-+
            '--?-'


>-----+-------------------------------+----------------------><
 '--u--userid--+--------------+--'
               '--p--password--'
```

Description

This command processes the capture file generated during the static profiling session of a CLI/ODBC/JDBC application so that it can be used by the DB2 CLI driver to execute static SQL statements.

The following are the descriptions for each DB2CAP parameter:

- **-h/-?** Displays help text for the command syntax.

- **bind capture-file** Binds the statements from the capture file and creates one or more packages.

- **-d database_alias** The database alias for the database that will contain one or more packages.

- **-u userid** The user ID to be used to connect to the data source. If a user ID is not specified, a trusted authorization ID is obtained from the system.

- **-p password** The password used to connect to the data source.

When using this utility to create a package, static profiling must be disabled. The number of packages created depends on the isolation levels used for the SQL statements that are recorded in the capture file. The package name consists of up to a maximum of the first seven characters of the package keyword from the capture file, and one of the following two-character suffixes:

- Uncommitted Read (UR)
- Cursor Stability (CS)
- Read Stability (RS)
- Repeatable Read (RR)
- No Commit (NC)

DB2CC

Most users start the Control Center from an icon, or it's automatically started with their desktop. The only reason to use DB2CC to start the Control Center is to gather diagnostic information when you're having problems.

Authorization

SYSADM.

Syntax

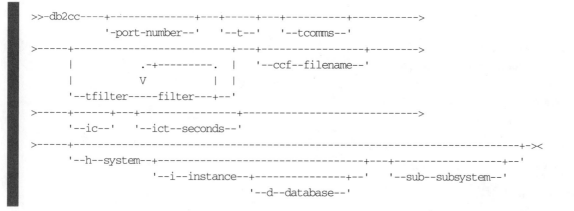

```
>>-db2cc----+-------------+---+-----+---+----------+-----------><
            '-port-number--'   '--t--'   '--tcomms--'
>-----+-------------------------+---+-----------------+--------><
      |              .-+---------.  |   '--ccf--filename--'
      |              V          | |
      '--tfilter-----filter---+--'
>-----+------+---+---------------+---------------------------><
      '--ic--'   '--ict--seconds--'
>-----+------------------------------------------------------+-><
      '--h--system--+------------------------------------+---+-----------------+--'
                    '--i--instance--+---------------+--'   '--sub--subsystem--'
                                    '--d--database--'
```

Description

These are the parameters for DB2CC:

- **port-number** The reserved DB2JD port number. For example, 6790. The default value is 6789.

- **-t** Turns on NavTrace for an initialization code.

- **-tcomms** Limits tracing to communications events.

- **-tfilter filter** Limits tracing to entries containing the specified filter or filters.

- **-ccf filename** Opens the Command Center initialized with the specified filename. The Command Center can be started from an icon or with DB2CCTR.

- **-ic** Opens the Information Center.

- **-ict seconds Idle Connection Timer** Closes any idle connections in the pools maintained by the Control Center after the number of seconds specified. The default is 30 minutes.

- **-h system** Opens the Control Center in the context of a system.

- **-i instance** Opens the Control Center in the context of an instance.

- **-d database** Opens the Control Center in the context of a database.

- **-sub subsystem** Opens the Control Center in the context of a subsystem.

DB2CDBCR

The DB2CDBCR command creates a control database in the current instance. The control database stores the metadata about the defined database objects. This command is used when running Data Warehouse Center.

Authorization

Must be run by the instance owner.

Syntax

```
>>-db2cdbcr----+-----+----n--CDB_name------------------------><
               '--d--'
```

Description

These are the parameters for DB2CDBCR:

- **-d** Gathers diagnostic information.

- **-n CDB_name** Specifies the name of the database to be used for the control database. If the database name specified does not exist, DB2CDBCR will create it.

DB2CFEXP

This command exports connectivity configuration information, creating an EXPORT profile with information for use at another workstation with the same type of instance.

Authorization

SYSADM or SYSCTRL.

Syntax

```
                              .-TEMPLATE--.
>>-db2cfexp--filename--+-BACKUP----+-------------------------><
                       '-MAINTAIN--'
```

Description

The following are the descriptions for each DBCFEXP parameter:

- **-filename** Specifies the fully qualified name of the target EXPORT file. This file is the configuration profile.

- **TEMPLATE** Creates a configuration profile for use as a template for other instances of the same instance type. The profile includes information about the following:

  - All databases, including related ODBC and DCS information

  - All nodes associated with the EXPORTed databases

  - Common ODBC/CLI settings

  - Common client settings in the database manager configuration

  - Common client settings in the UDB registry

- **BACKUP** Creates a configuration profile of the UDB instance for local backup purposes. This profile contains the entire instance configuration, including information of a specific nature relevant only to this local instance. The profile includes information about protocols in addition to what's gathered for a template.

- **MAINTAIN** Creates a configuration profile containing only database- and node-related information for maintaining or updating other instances.

DB2CFIMP

This command imports connectivity configuration information from a file known as a *configuration profile*. This is used to duplicate the connectivity information from another similar instance that was configured previously. It is especially useful when multiple similar remote UDB clients will be installed, configured, and maintained.

Authorization

SYSADM or SYSCTRL.

Syntax

```
>>-db2cfimp--filename------------------------------------><
```

Description

The filename is the fully qualified name of the configuration profile to be IMPORTed. Valid IMPORT configuration profiles are created by any DB2 UDB or DB2 Connect connectivity configuration EXPORT method, or server access profiles.

DB2CIDMG

Remote Database Migration is intended for remote unattended migration in the configuration installation distribution (CID) architecture environment.

Authorization

SYSADM or DBADM.

Syntax

```
>>-db2cidmg----+-database----+---+-------------+---+-----+----><
               +-/r=respfile-+   '-/l1=logfile--'   '-/b--'
               '-/e---------'
```

Description

The following are the descriptions for each DB2CIDMG parameter:

- **database** An alias for the database to be migrated. If this is not specified, a response file or /e must be provided. The database alias must be cataloged on the target workstation. However, it can be a local or remote database.

- **/r** The response file to use. The response file is an ASCII file containing a list of databases to be migrated. If this is not specified, a database alias or /e must be provided for program invocation.

- ◼ **/e** Indicates that every single database cataloged in the system database directory should be migrated.

- ◼ **/l1** The pathname of the file for error log information from remote workstations can be written after the migration is complete. If more than one database is specified in the response file, the log information for each database migration is appended to the file. Regardless of whether /l1 is specified, a log file with the name db2cidmg.log is generated and kept in the workstation's file system where the database has been migrated.

- ◼ **/b** Indicates that all packages in the database are to be rebound once migration is complete.

DB2CKBKP

Check Backup tests whether a backup image can be restored. It can also display the metadata stored in the backup header.

Authorization

Read permission on the backup file.

Syntax

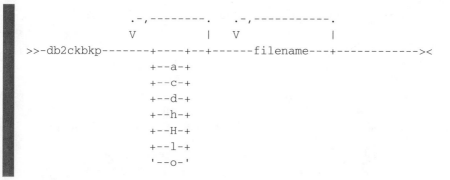

```
                  .-,--------.     .-,-----------.
                  V          |     V             |
>>-db2ckbkp-------+----+--+------filename---+------------><
                  +--a-+
                  +--c-+
                  +--d-+
                  +--h-+
                  +--H-+
                  +--l-+
                  '--o-'
```

Description

The following are the descriptions for each DB2CKBKP parameter:

- ◼ **-a** Displays all available information.
- ◼ **-c** Displays results of checkbits and checksums.
- ◼ **-d** Displays information from the headers of database-managed storage (DMS) table space data pages.
- ◼ **-h** Displays media header information, including the name or path of the image expected by the RESTORE utility.

- **-H** Displays only the media header information. This option does not validate the image. Validation is performed on the entire image if *–H* is not specified. *-H* not valid in combination with any other option.

- **-l** Displays Log File Header data.

- **-o** Displays detailed information from the object headers.

- **filename** Specifies the name of the backup image file. One or more files can be checked at a time. If the complete backup consists of multiple objects, the validation will succeed only if DB2CKBKP is used to validate all of the objects at the same time. When checking multiple parts of an image, the first backup image object (.001) must be specified first.

Example

This example checks the backup image of the sample database taken on August 17, 1999, at 3:07 P.M.:

```
db2ckbkp SAMPLE.0.krodger.NODE0000.CATN0000.19990817150714.*
 [1] Buffers processed:   ##
 [2] Buffers processed:   ##
 [3] Buffers processed:   ##
Image Verification Complete - successful.


db2ckbkp -h SAMPLE2.0.krodger.NODE0000.CATN0000.19990818122909.001
=====================
MEDIA HEADER REACHED:
=====================
         Server Database Name           -- SAMPLE2
         Server Database Alias          -- SAMPLE2
         Client Database Alias          -- SAMPLE2
         Timestamp                      -- 19990818122909
         Node                           -- 0
         Instance                       -- krodger
         Sequence Number                -- 1
         Release ID                     -- 900
         Database Seed                  -- 65E0B395
         DB Comment's Codepage (Volume) -- 0
         DB Comment (Volume)            --
         DB Comment's Codepage (System) -- 0
         DB Comment (System)            --
         Authentication Value           -- 255
         Backup Mode                    -- 0
         Backup Type                    -- 0
         Backup Gran.                   -- 0
```

```
Status Flags                    -- 11
System Cats inc                 -- 1
Catalog Node Number             -- 0
DB Codeset                      -- ISO8859-
DB Territory                    --
Backup Buffer Size              -- 4194304
Number of Sessions              -- 1
Platform                        -- 0
```

The proper image filename would be the following:

```
SAMPLE2.0.krodger.NODE0000.CATN0000.19990818122909.001
  [1] Buffers processed:  ####
  Image Verification Complete - successful.
```

DB2CKBKP cannot check images created with a variable block size. However, if a backup was created using multiple sessions, DB2CKBKP can examine all of the files at the same time. (Users are responsible for ensuring that the session with sequence number 001 is the first file specified.) DB2CKBKP can also verify backup images on tape, prepare the tape for a restore operation, and then invoke the utility, specifying the tape device name. For example, on UNIX:

```
db2ckbkp -h /dev/rmt0
```

On Windows NT:

```
db2ckbkp -d \\.\tape1
```

If the backup image resides on TSM, see DB2ADUTL.

DB2CKMIG

DB2CKMIG verifies that a database can be migrated. DB2CKMIG is not normally installed with DB2. It is supplied on the installation media.

Authorization

SYSADM.

Syntax

```
>>-db2ckmig----+-database-+---l filename----+------------+------>
               '--e-------'                  '--u userid--'
```

```
>-----+-------------+---------------------------------------><
      '--p password--'
```

Description

To verify that a database is ready to be migrated,

- Logon as the instance owner.
- Issue the DB2CKMIG command.
- Check the log file. If it shows errors, see the *Quick Beginnings* manual for corrective actions. The log file displays the errors that occur when the DB2CKMIG command is run. Check that the log is empty before continuing with the migration process.

DB2CKMIG has these parameters:

- **database** Indicates an alias name of a database to be checked.
- **-e** Indicates that all local cataloged databases are to be scanned.
- **-l** Specifies the name for a log file to keep a list of errors and warnings generated for the scanned database.
- **-u** Specifies the user ID of the system administrator.
- **-p** Specifies the password of the system administrator's user ID.

DB2CLI

DB2CLI launches the interactive CLI environment for design and prototyping in CLI. The db2cli.exe file is located in the sqllib\samples\cli\ subdirectory of the home directory of the database instance owner (for example, x:\sqllib\samples\cli on Windows).

Authorization

None.

Syntax

```
>--db2cli-------------------------------------------------><
```

Description

DB2CLI is a programmers' testing tool; it is not intended for end users. Two types of commands are supported:

- **CLI commands** Commands that correspond to (and have the same name as) each of the function calls that is supported by the DB2 CLI.
- **Support commands** Commands that do not have an equivalent CLI function.

For more information about DB2CLI, see the file intcli.doc, located in the same directory as DB2CLI.

DB2CMD

DB2CMD is used to open a DB2 command window in Windows. It is not needed on UNIX and OS/2, where an operating system command prompt can function as a DB2 command window. This command is equivalent to clicking the DB2 command window icon.

Authorization

None.

Syntax

```
>>-db2cmd----+----+--------------------------------------------><
             +--c-+
             +--w-+
             +--i-+
             '--t-'
```

Description

The following are the descriptions for each DB2CMD parameter:

- **-c** Executes the command and then terminates. For example, "db2cmd /c dir" causes the DIR command to be invoked in a command window, and then the command window closes.
- **-w** Waits until the cmd.exe process ends. For example, "db2cmd /c /w dir" invokes the DIR command, and db2cmd.exe does not end until the command window closes.
- **-i** Runs the command window, sharing the same console and inheriting file handles. For example, "db2cmd /c /w /i db2 get database manager configuration > myoutput" invokes cmd.exe to run the DB2 command and to wait for its completion. A new console is not assigned, and stdout is piped to the myoutput file .
- **-t** Instead of using "DB2 CLP" as the title of the command window, *-t* has the new window inherit the title from the window where DB2CMD is run. This is useful if , for example, you want to set up an icon with a different title that invokes DB2CMD /t.

REFERENCE

Example

All switches must appear before any commands to be executed. For example,

```
db2cmd /t db2
```

Run the script ld.txt ECHO command text to standard output and write it to tLOAD.out:

```
db2cmd.exe db2 -tvf c:\ixf\ld.txt -r tLOAD.out -o
```

DB2DCLGN

DBDCLGN generates declarations for a specified database table, eliminating the need to look up those declarations in the catalogs or documentation, much like %type and %rowtype do in Oracle. The generated declarations can be modified as necessary. The supported host languages are C/C++, COBOL, Java, and Fortran.

Authorization

None.

Syntax

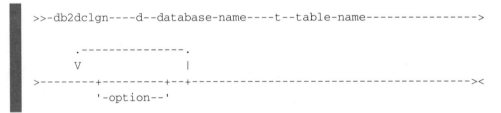

```
>>-db2dclgn----d--database-name----t--table-name--------------->

          .---------------.
          V               |
>--------+---------+--+--+------------------------------------><
         '-option--'
```

Description

The following are the descriptions for each DB2DCLGN parameter:

- **-d database-name** The name of the database.
- **-t table-name** The name of the table for which column information is to be retrieved to generate declarations.
- **Option** One or more of the following:
    - **-a action** Specifies whether declarations are to be added or replaced. Valid values are ADD and REPLACE. The default value is ADD.
    - **-b lob-var-type** The type of variable to be generated for a LOB column. Valid values are the following:

- **LOB (default)** For example, in C, SQL TYPE is CLOB(5K) x.
- **LOCATOR** For example, in C, SQL TYPE is CLOB_LOCATOR x.
- **FILE** For example, in C, SQL TYPE is CLOB_FILE x.

- **–c** Specifies whether the column name is to be used as a suffix in the field name when a prefix (-*n*) is specified. If no prefix is specified, this option is ignored. The default behavior is to not use the column name as a suffix, but instead to use the column number, which starts at 1.

- **–i** Specifies whether indicator variables are to be generated. Because host structures are supported in C and COBOL, an indicator table is generated of size equal to the number of columns, whereas for Java and Fortran, individual indicator variables are generated for each column. The names of the indicator table and the variable are the same as the table name and the column name, respectively, prefixed by *IND-* (for COBOL) or *ind_* (for the other languages). The default behavior is to not generate indicator variables.

- **-l language** Specifies the host language in which the declarations are to be generated. Valid values are C, COBOL, JAVA, and FORTRAN. The default behavior is to generate C declarations, which are also valid for C++.

- **-n name** Specifies a prefix for each of the field names. A prefix must be specified if the -*c* option is used. If it is not specified, the column name is used as the field name.

- **-o output-file** Specifies the name of the output file for the declarations. The default behavior is to use the table name as the base filename, with an extension that reflects the generated host language:

  - .h for C and C++
  - .cbl for COBOL
  - .java for Java
  - .f for Fortran (UNIX)
  - .for for Fortran (Windows and OS/2)

- **-p password** Specifies the password to be used to connect to the database. It must be specified if a user ID is specified. The default behavior is to provide no password when establishing a connection.

- **-r remarks** Specifies whether column remarks, if available, are to be used as comments in the declarations, to provide more detailed descriptions of the fields. Remarks are added with the SQL statement COMMENT ON.

- **-s structure-name** Specifies the structure name that is to be generated to group all the fields in the declarations. The default behavior is to use the unqualified table name.

REFERENCE

- **-u userid** Specifies the user ID used to connect to the database. It must be specified if a password is specified. The default behavior is to provide no user ID when establishing a connection.
- **-v** Specifies whether the status (for example, the connection status) of the utility is to be displayed. The default behavior is to display only error messages.
- **-w DBCS-var-type** Specifies whether sqldbchar or wchar_t is to be used for a GRAPHIC/VARGRAPHIC/DBCLOB column in C.
- **-y DBCS-symbol** Specifies whether *G* or *N* is to be used as the DBCS symbol in COBOL.

Example

Generate declarations for the employee table (of the current user) and adamache.org from the sample database:

```
db2dclgn -d sample -t employee
db2dclgn -d sample -t adamache.org
```

DB2DRDAT

DB2DRDAT is used to capture the DRDA data stream between a DRDA Application Requestor (AR) and the Application Server (AS). This can help with problem determination and performance tuning in a client/server environment.

Authorization

None.

Syntax

```
                          .---------.
              .-on-.  V            |
>>-db2drdat----+-+----+----+--r-+--+---+-----------+--+--------><
              |              +--s-+         '--l=length-'  |
              |              +--c-+                        |
              |              '--i-'                        |
              '-off--+-------------+--+--------+----'
                      '--t=tracefile-'  '--p=pid-'
```

Description

The following are the descriptions for each DB2DRDAT parameter:

- **on** Turns on AS trace events (all if none specified).
- **off** Turns off AS trace events.
- **-r** Traces DRDA requests received from the DRDA AR.
- **-s** Traces DRDA replies sent to the DRDA AR.
- **-c** Traces the SQLCA received from the DRDA server on the host system. This is a formatted, easy-to-read version of SQLCA (SQL Communications Area) that is not null.
- **-i** Timestamps are included in the trace information when you specify *-i*.
- **-l** The size of the buffer used to store the trace information. Defaults to 1MB.
- **-p** Traces events only for this process. If *-p* is not specified, all agents with incoming DRDA connections on the server are traced. The process id (pid) traced can be found in the agent field returned by LIST APPLICATIONS.
- **-t** The destination for the trace. If a filename is specified without a complete path, the current path is assumed. If tracefile is not specified, messages are directed to db2drdat.dmp in the current directory.

| Caution | *Do not issue* DB2TRC *while* DB2DRDAT *is active.*

DB2DRDAT writes the following information to tracefile:

- -r
  - Type of DRDA request
  - Receive buffer
- -s
  - Type of DRDA reply/object
  - Send buffer
- CPI-C error information
  - Severity
  - Protocol used
  - API used
  - Local LU name
  - Failed CPI-C function
  - CPI-C return code

The command returns an exit code. A zero value indicates that the command completed successfully, and a nonzero value indicates that the command was unsuccessful.

If DB2DRDAT sends the output to a file that already exists, the old file will be erased unless the permissions on the file do not allow it to be erased, in which case, the operating system will return an error.

DB2EVA

DB2EVA starts the event analyzer, allowing the user to trace performance data produced by DB2 event monitors that have their data directed to files.

Authorization

None, unless connecting to the database and selecting from the catalogs (*-evm, -db,* and *-conn*); then one of the following is required: SYSADM, SYSCTRL, SYSMAINT, or DBADM.

Syntax

```
>>-db2eva-------------------------------------------------------->

>-----+--path--evmon-target--+-----------------------------------+-+>
      |                       '--conn--+---------------------+--' |
      |                                '--db---database-alias--'  |
      '--evm--evmon-name---db--database-alias--+--------+---------'
                                               '--conn--'

>-------------------------------------------------------------->< 
```

Description

The following are the descriptions for each DB2EVA parameter:

- **-path evmon-target** Use *-path* to specify the directory for writing the event monitor trace files.

- **-conn** Requests that DB2EVA maintain a connection to the database specified with *-db,* or if *-db* is not used, then to the database specified in the event monitor trace header. Maintaining a connection allows the event analyzer to obtain information not contained in the trace files (for example, the text for static SQL). A statement event record contains the package creator, package, and section number; when *-conn* is specified, DB2EVA can retrieve the text from the database system catalog view (syscat.statements).

- **-db database-alias** The name of the database defined for the event monitor. If *-path* is specified, the database name in the event monitor trace header is overwritten.

- **-evm evmon-name** The name of the event monitor whose traces are to be analyzed.

Although there is no required connection, DB2EVA attempts to connect to the database if *-conn* or *-evm* and *-db* are used. If the user can access the database and has the appropriate authorization, the SQL text for static statements can be displayed. Without the required access or authority, only the text for dynamic statements is available.

There are two methods of reading event monitor traces:

- Specifying the directory where the trace files are located (using the *-path* option). This allows users to move trace files from a server and analyze them locally. This can be done even if the event monitor has been dropped.

- Specifying the database and event monitor names allows automatic location of the trace files. The event analyzer connects to the database and issues a select target from sysibm.syseventmonitors to locate the directory where the event monitor writes its trace files. The connection is then released unless *-conn* was specified. This method cannot be used if the event monitor has been dropped.

The event analyzer can be used to analyze the data produced by an active event monitor. However, event monitors buffer their data before writing it to disk; therefore, some information may be missing. Turn off the event monitor, thereby forcing it to flush its buffers.

DB2EVMON

DB2EVMON formats event monitor file and named pipe output, and writes it to standard output.

Authorization

None, unless connecting to the database (*-evm, -db*); then, one of the following is required: SYSADM, SYSCTRL, SYSMAINT, or DBADM.

Syntax

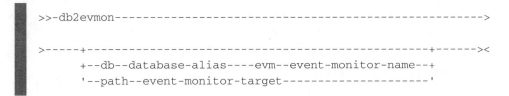

```
>>-db2evmon------------------------------------------------------>

>-----+------------------------------------------------+------><
      +--db--database-alias----evm--event-monitor-name--+
      '--path--event-monitor-target--------------------'
```

Description

The following are the descriptions for each DB2EVMON parameter:

- **-db database-alias** Uses -db to specify the database whose data is to be displayed. This parameter is case-sensitive.

■ **-evm event-monitor-name** Specifies the one-part name of the event monitor, an ordinary or delimited SQL identifier. This parameter is case-sensitive.

■ **-path event-monitor-target** Uses -path to specify the directory to contain the event monitor trace files.

If the data is being written to files, DB2EVMON formats the files for display using standard output. In this case, the monitor is turned on first, and any event data in the files is displayed. To view any data written to files after the tool has been run, reissue DB2EVMON.

If the data is being written to a pipe, the tool formats the output for display using standard output as events occur. In this case, the tool is started before the monitor is turned on.

DB2FLSN

Find log sequence number (FLSN), or DB2FLSN, returns the name of the file that contains the log record identified by a specified log sequence number (LSN).

Authorization

None.

Syntax

```
>>-db2flsn----+-----+--input_LSN------------------------------><
              '--q--'
```

Description

The following are the descriptions for each DB2FLSN parameter:

■ **-q** Specifies that only the log filename be printed. No error or warning messages will be printed, and status can be determined only through the return code. These are the valid error codes:

■ **-100** Invalid input

■ **-101** Cannot open LFH file

■ **-102** Failed to read LFH file

■ **-103** Invalid LFH

■ **-104** Database is not recoverable

■ **-105** LSN too big

■ **-500** Logical error

Other valid return codes are the following:

- **0** Successful execution
- **99 Warning** Result is based on the last known log file size
- **input_LSN** A 12-byte string that represents the internal (6-byte) hexadecimal value with leading zeros

Example

Name the log file containing log sequence number 000000BF0030:

```
db2flsn 000000BF0030
 Given LSN is contained in log file S0000002.LOG
```

Provide the name of only the log containing log sequence number 000000BF0030:

```
db2flsn -q 000000BF0030
 S0000002.LOG
```

Provide the name of the log when the log sequence number is in active logs (somewhere before the value of the database configuration parameter logfilsz):

```
db2flsn 000000BE0030
Warning: the result is based on the last known log file size.
The last known log file size is 23 4K pages starting from log extent 2.
Given LSN is contained in log file S0000001.LOG


C:\DB2\NODE0000\SQL00002>db2flsn 000000000001
Warning: the result is based on the last known log file size (250
4K pages starting from log extent 0).  The input_LSN might be before
the database becomes recoverable.
Given LSN is contained in log file S9999936.LOG
```

The log header control file sqlogctl.lfh must reside in the current directory. Because this file is located in the database directory, DB2FLSN can be run from the database directory, or the control file can be copied to the directory from which DB2FLSN is run.

DB2FLSN uses the logfilsiz database configuration parameter. DB2 records the three most recent values for this parameter and the first log file that is created with each logfilsiz value; this enables the tool to work correctly when *logfilsiz* changes. If the specified LSN predates the earliest recorded value of *logfilsiz*, the tool uses this value and returns a warning.

This tool can be used only with recoverable databases. A database is recoverable if it has either of the database configuration parameters *logretain* or *userexit* turned on.

REFERENCE

DB2GOV

The DB2 Governor monitors and changes the behavior of applications that run against a database. By default, a daemon is started on every logical node. The Governor can also be used to start a single daemon at a specific node to monitor the activity against the database partition at that node. For a graphical equivalent, see the *DB2 Query Patroller Administration Guide*.

Authorization

SYSADM or SYSCTRL.

Syntax

```
>>-db2gov-------------------------------------------------------->

>------+-START--datadase--+-------------------+---config-file--log-file--+>
       |                  '-NODENUM--node-num--'                         |
       '-STOP--database--+-------------------+--------------------------'
                         '-NODENUM--node-num--'

>------------------------------------------------------------------><
```

Description

The following are the descriptions for each DB2GOV parameter:

- **START database** Starts the governor daemon to monitor the specified database. Either the database name or the database alias can be specified. The name specified must be the same as the one specified in the governor configuration file. One daemon runs for each database that is being monitored. In a partitioned database environment, one daemon runs for each database partition. If the governor is running for more than one database, there will be more than one daemon running at that database server.

- **NODENUM node-num** Specifies the database partition on which to start or stop the governor daemon. The number specified must be the same as the one specified in the node configuration file.

- **config-file** Specifies the configuration file to use when monitoring the database. The default location for the configuration file is the sqllib directory. If the specified file is not there, the front end assumes that the specified name is the full name of the file.

- **log-file** Supported only on Windows, this is the base name of the file where the governor writes log records. The log file is stored in the log subdirectory of the sqllib directory. The number of database partitions on which the governor runs is automatically appended to the log filename. For example, mylog.0, mylog.1, mylog.2.

- **STOP database** Stops the governor daemon that is monitoring the specified database. In a partitioned database environment, the FRONT-END utility stops the Governor on all database partitions by reading the node file.

DB2GOVLG

DB2GOVLG extracts records of specified type from the Governor log files.

Authorization

None.

Syntax

```
>>-db2govlg--log-file----+-----------------+----------------->
                         '-nodenum--node-num--'

>-----+--------------------+----------------------------><
      '-rectype--record-type--'
```

Description

The following are the descriptions for each DB2GOVLG parameter:

- **log-file** Specifies the base name of one or more log files to be queried.
- **nodenum node-num** Indicates the number of the node on which the governor is running (applies only to EEE).
- **rectype record-type** Specifies the type of record to be queried. Valid record types are as follows:
  - START
  - FORC
  - NICE
  - ERROR
  - WARNING
  - READCFG
  - STOP
  - ACCOUNT

DB2ICRT

DB2ICRT is used to create DB2 instances. On UNIX, you must create a DB2 instance after you install. The default instance on Windows and OS/2 is called DB2. On UNIX, this utility is located in the DB2DIR/instance directory, where DB2DIR represents /usr/lpp/ db2_07_nn on AIX, /usr/IBMdb2/V7.n on Linux, and /opt/IBMdb2/V7.n on all other UNIX systems. On Windows or OS/2, it is located in the \sqllib\bin subdirectory.

Authorization

Root access on UNIX or Local Administrator on Windows or OS/2.

Syntax

The syntax differs depending on the platform. This is the syntax for UNIX:

```
>>-db2icrt----+----+---+-----+---+-------------+-------------->
              +--h-+   '--d--'   '--a--AuthType--'
              '--?-'   '--w--'


>-----+--------------+---+--------------+---+--------------+->
      '--p--PortName--'   '--s--InstType--'   '--u--FencedID--'

>----InstName-------------------------------------------------><
```

This is the syntax for Windows and OS/2:

```
>>-db2icrt----+--------------+---+-----------------------+--->
              '--s--InstType--'   '--u--UserName, Password--'

>-----+----------------+---+---------------+-------------->
      '--p--InstProfPath--'   '--c--ClusterName--'

>-----+--------------+---+--------------+--InstName--------><
      '--h--HostName--'   '--r--PortRange--'
```

Description

These are the parameters for DB2ICRT on UNIX:

- **-h or -?** Displays help.
- **-d** Turns DEBUG mode on.
- **-w** Creates a 64-bit instance (only AIX, HP-UX, and Solaris).

- **-a AuthType** Specifies the authentication type (SERVER, CLIENT or DCS) for the instance. The default is SERVER.
- **-p PortName** Specifies the port name or number used by the instance.
- **-s InstType** Specifies the type of instance to create (EEE, EE, or CLIENT). Specify EE for DB2 Workgroup Edition.
- **-u Fenced ID** Specifies the user ID under which fenced user-defined functions and fenced stored procedures will run.
- **InstName** Specifies the name of the instance.

These are the parameters for Windows and OS/2:

- **-s InstType** The type of instance to create. Valid values are these:
  - **Client** Creates a client instance
  - **Standalone** Creates an instance DB2 Personal Edition
  - **EE** Creates an instance for a database server with local and remote clients, such as Workgroup or Enterprise Edition
  - **EEE** Creates an instance for a partitioned database server
- **-u Username, Password** Specifies the account name and password for the DB2 service. Required when creating a partitioned database instance.
- **-p InstProfPath** Specifies the instance profile path. Required when creating a partitioned database instance.
- **-h HostName** Overrides the default TCP/IP hostname if there is more than one for the current machine. The TCP/IP hostname is used when creating the default node (node 0). This option is valid only for EEE.
- **-c ClusterName** Sets the Microsoft Cluster Server (MSCS) cluster name on Windows. Specified to create a DB2 instance that supports MSCS.
- **-r PortRange** Specifies the range of TCP/IP ports used by the partitioned database instance when running in MPP mode. The services file of the local machine will be updated with the following entries if specified:

```
DB2_InstName          baseport/tcp
DB2_InstName_END      endport/tcp
```

- **InstName** Specifies the name of the instance.

Example

Create an instance called DB2X:

```
db2icrt DB2X
```

Create a 64-instance called db2inst1 (AIX, HP-UX, or Solaris) using db2fenc1 as the user ID for fenced user-defined functions and fenced stored procedures:

```
db2icrt -w 64 -u db2fenc1 db2inst1
```

DB2IDROP

DB2IDROP removes a DB2 instance that was created by DB2ICRT. It also removes the instance entry from the list of instances (also called the instance directory). See DB2ICRT for the location of DB2IDROP.

Authorization

Root access on UNIX or Local Administrator on Windows or OS/2.

Syntax

The syntax differs depending on the platform. This is the syntax for UNIX:

```
>>-db2idrop----+----+--InstName------------------------------><
               +--h-+
               '--?-'
```

This is the syntax for Windows and OS/2:

```
>>-db2idrop----+-----+--InstName------------------------------><
               '--f--'
```

Description

The following are the parameters for UNIX:

■ **-h or -?** Displays help

■ **InstName** Specifies the name of the instance

These are the parameters for Windows and OS/2:

■ **-f** Supported only on Windows, *-f* is the force applications flag. If this flag is specified, all the applications using the instance are forced to terminate.

■ **InstName** Specifies the name of the instance.

Example

Drop the instance DB2X:

```
db2idrop DB2X
```

DB2ILIST

DB2ILIST lists all the instances that are available on a system. See DB2ICRT for the location of this utility.

Authorization

Root access on UNIX. On Windows and OS/2, no authorization is required.

Syntax

```
>>-db2ilist--------------------------------------------------><
```

DB2IMIGR

DB2IMIGR migrates an existing instance following installation of the database manager. (This normally occurs automatically during installation on Windows and OS/2.) See DB2ICRT for the location of this utility on UNIX.

DB2IUPDT

On UNIX, DB2IUPDT updates a specified DB2 instance to enable a new system configuration or function associated with the installation or removal of certain product options. It is used in version 7 to create instances that can address 64-bit memory.

On Windows NT and Windows 2000, this command updates single-partition instances for use in a partitioned database. It is installed only with EEE.

See DB2ICRT for the location of this utility.

Authorization

Root access on UNIX or Local Administrator on Windows NT and Windows 2000.

Syntax

The syntax differs depending on the platform. This is the syntax for UNIX:

```
>>-db2iupdt----+-----+---+-----+---+-----+---+-----+---+-----+---->
               +--h-+    '--d--'   '--k--'   '--s--'   '--w--'
               '--?-'

>-----+--------------+---+--------------+---+-InstName-+------><
      '--a--AuthType--'   '--u--FencedID--'   '--e-------'
```

REFERENCE

This is the syntax for Windows NT and Windows 2000:

```
>>-db2iupdt---InstName---/u:--username,password----------------->

>-----+------------------------------+------------------------->
      '-/p:--instance profile path--'

>-----+------------------------+---+---------------+---------><
      '-/r:--baseport,endport--'   '-/h:--hostname--'
```

Description

These are the parameters for UNIX:

- **-h or -?** Displays help.
- **-d** Turns on DEBUG mode.
- **-k** Keeps the current instance type during the update.
- **-s** Ignores the existing Syncpoint Manager (SPM) log directory. (The SPM is used for two-phase commit applications and has its own log files.)
- **-w** Converts instance to 64-bit memory addressability (only AIX, HP-UX, and Solaris).
- **-a** AuthType: Windows the authentication type (SERVER, CLIENT, or DCS) for the instance. The default is SERVER.
- **-u Fenced ID** Specifies the user ID under which fenced user-defined functions and fenced stored procedures will run.
- **InstName** Specifies the name of the instance.
- **-e** Updates every instance.

These are the parameters for Windows NT and Windows 2000:

- **InstName** Specifies the name of the instance.
- **/u:username,password** Specifies the account name and password for the DB2 service.
- **/p:instance profile path** Specifies the new instance profile path for the updated instance.
- **/r:baseport,endport** Sets the range of TCP/IP ports used by the partitioned database instance when running in MPP mode. When specified, the services file on the local machine will be updated with the following entries:

```
DB2_InstName          baseport/tcp
DB2_InstName_END      endport/tcp
```

■ **/h:hostname** Overrides the default TCP/IP hostname if there is more than one TCP/IP hostname for the current machine.

Example

Update instance db2inst1 (on AIX, HP-UX, or Solaris) to support 64-bit memory addressing:

```
db2iupdt -w 64 db2inst1
```

 # DB2LDCFG

DB2LDCFG configures the Lightweight Directory Access Protocol (LDAP) user distinguished name (DN) and password for the current logon user in an LDAP environment.

Authorization

None.

Syntax

```
>>-db2ldcfg----+--u--user's Distinguished Name---w--password--+-><
               '--r-------------------------------------------'
```

Description

■ **-u user's Distinguished** Specifies the LDAP user's DN when accessing the LDAP directory

■ **-w password** Specifies the password

■ **-r** Removes the user's DN and password from the machine environment

In an LDAP environment using an IBM LDAP client, the default LDAP user's DN and password can be configured for the current logon user. Once configured, the LDAP user's DN and password are saved in the user's environment and used whenever DB2 accesses the LDAP directory. This eliminates the need to specify the LDAP user's DN and password when issuing the LDAP command or API. However, if the LDAP user's DN and password are specified when the command or API is issued, the default settings will be overridden.

On a Microsoft LDAP client, the current logon user's credentials will be used.

DB2LEVEL

DB2LEVEL returns information about the FixPak level of DB2. This command is used by the IBM service. Do not build programming dependencies on DB2LEVEL because its output is subject to change with any DB2 maintenance. With DB2 version 7.1, DB2LEVEL returns the following:

- The current instance name
- The code release level (similar to the signature returned from a CONNECT statement)
- The date that IBM compiled the installed level of DB2
- The FixPak number (such as WR21198)

Syntax

```
>>-db2level----------------------------------------><
```

Example

Run DB2LEVEL to see the installed FixPak:

```
db2level
DB21085I  Instance "DB2" uses DB2 code release "SQL07020" with level
identifier "03010105" and informational tokens "DB2 v7.1.0.40",
"n010415" and "WR21254".
```

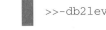

DB2LOOK

DB2LOOK extracts the required DDL statements to reproduce the database objects of a production database on a test database. It is also used to generate the required UPDATE statements used to replicate the statistics on the objects in a test database, as well as the database configuration, database manager configuration parameters, registry, and environment variables so that these match on the test database. This allows the test system to contain a subset of the production system's data and have similar access plans. Both the catalog statistics and the configuration parameters for the test system must be updated to match those of the production system. DB2LOOK makes it possible to create a test database where access plans are similar to those that would be used on the production system.

DB2LOOK's -e option to extract DDL is also powerful when DB2LOOK is used in combination with DB2MOVE (discussed next) to move schemas and data from one database to another. Apart from moving databases between HP-UX and Solaris, DB2 does not support cross-platform backup and restore, so DB2LOOK and DB2MOVE provide this function.

Authorization

SELECT privilege on the system catalogs.

Syntax

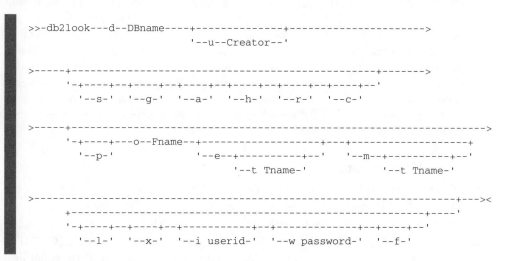

```
>>-db2look---d--DBname----+-------------+--------------------->
                          '--u--Creator--'

>-----+-------------------------------------------------+------->
      '-+----+--+----+--+----+--+----+--+----+--+----+--'
        '--s-'    '--g-'    '--a-'    '--h-'    '--r-'    '--c-'

>-----+--------------------------------------------------------->
      '-+----+---o--Fname--+------------------+---+------------------+
        '--p-'             '--e-+----------+--'   '--m--+----------+--'
                                '--t Tname-'            '--t Tname-'

>--------------------------------------------------------+--->< 
      +------------------------------------------------+----'
      '-+----+--+----+--+----+-----------+--+------------+--+----+--'
        '--l-'    '--x-'    '--i userid-'    '--w password-'    '--f-'
```

Description

The following are the descriptions for each DB2LOOK parameter:

- **-d DBname** Specifies name of the database to be queried. DB2 databases can be queried on any of the following databases: UNIX, Windows, OS/2, or OS/390. If the DBname is a DB2 UDB for OS/390 database, the DB2LOOK utility will extract the DDL and UPDATE statistics statements for OS/390 objects. These DDL and UPDATE statistics statements will have syntax that can be used only on UNIX, Windows, and OS/2. This is for users who want to extract OS/390 objects and re-create them on UNIX, Windows, or OS/2. If DBname is an OS/390 database, then the DB2LOOK output is limited to the following:
  - Generated DDL for tables, indexes, and views
  - Generated UPDATE statistics statements for tables, columns, column distributions, and indexes
- **-u Creator** Limits output to objects with this creator ID. If option *-a* is specified, this parameter is ignored. If neither *-u* nor *-a* is specified, the environment variable USER is used.
- **-s** Generates a PostScript file.
  - This option removes all LaTeX and .tmp PostScript files.

- ■ Required: LaTeX, dvips.
- ■ The psfig.tex file must be in the LaTeX input path.
- ■ **-g** Uses a graph to show fetch page pairs for indexes.
- ■ **-a** When specified, the output is not limited to the objects created under a particular creator ID. All objects created by all users are considered. For example, if this option is specified with the *-e* option, DDL statements are extracted for all objects in the database. If this option is specified with the *-m* option, UPDATE statistics statements are extracted for all user-created tables and indexes in the database. If neither *-u* nor *-a* is specified, the environment variable USER is used. On UNIX, this variable does not have to be explicitly set; on Windows, however, there is no default value for the USER environment variable. On Windows, a user variable in the SYSTEM variables must be set, or a set USER=<username> must be issued for the session.
- ■ **-h** Displays help information. When specified, all other options are ignored, and only help is displayed.
- ■ **-r** When specified in conjunction with *-m*, DB2LOOK does not generate the RUNSTATS command. The default action is to generate the RUNSTATS command. The *-r* option is ignored if the *-m* option is not specified.
- ■ **-c** When specified in conjunction with *-m*, DB2LOOK does not generate COMMIT, CONNECT, and CONNECT RESET statements. The default action is to generate these statements. The *-c* option is ignored if the *-m* option is not specified.
- ■ **-t Tname** Specifies the table name. Limits the output to a particular table.
- ■ **-p** Uses plain text format.
- ■ **-o Fname** If using LaTeX format, writes the output to filename.tex. If using plain text format, writes the output to filename.txt. If not specified, output is written to standard output.
- ■ **-e** Extracts DDL statements for database objects. Can be used in conjunction with *-m*. DDL for the following database objects are extracted when using *-e*:
  - ■ Tables
  - ■ Views
  - ■ Automatic summary tables (ASTs)
  - ■ Aliases
  - ■ Indexes
  - ■ Triggers
  - ■ User-defined distinct types
  - ■ Primary key, RI, and CHECK constraints
  - ■ User-defined structured types
  - ■ User-defined functions

- User-defined methods
- User-defined transforms

The DDL generated by DB2LOOK can be used to re-create user-defined functions successfully. However, the user source code that a particular user-defined function references (the EXTERNAL NAME clause, for example) must be available for the user-defined function to be usable.

- **-m** Generates the required UPDATE statements to replicate the statistics on tables, columns, and indexes. The *-p, -g,* and *-s* options are ignored when *-m* is specified.

- **-l** Generates DDL for user-defined table spaces, nodegroups, and buffer pools. DDL is extracted for the following database objects when using –l:
  - User-defined table spaces
  - User-defined nodegroups
  - User-defined buffer pools

- **-x** If specified, DB2LOOK generates a data control language (DCL) such as GRANT and REVOKE statements.

- **-i userid** Used to identify the user when working with a remote database.

- **-w password** Used with *–i*; this option allows the user to run DB2LOOK against a database that resides on a remote system. The user ID and the password are sent by DB2LOOK to log on to the remote system.

- **-f** Used to extract configuration parameters and registry variables.

Only configuration parameters and registry variables that affect the DB2 query optimizer are extracted.

Example

Show the DDL for the ADDRESS table created by the current user in the SAMPLE database, and send the output to the screen:

```
db2look -d sample -e -t address
```

Generate the DDL statements for objects created by user walid in database DEPARTMENT, and send the output to file db2look.sql:

```
db2look -d department -u walid -e -o db2look.sql
```

Generate the UPDATE statements to replicate the statistics for the tables and indexes created by user walid in database DEPARTMENT, and send the output to file db2look.sql:

```
db2look -d department -u walid -m -o db2look.sql
```

Generate both the DDL statements for the objects created by user walid and the UPDATE statements to replicate the statistics on the tables and indexes created by the same user, and send the output to file db2look.sql:

```
db2look -d department -u walid -e -m -o db2look.sql
```

Generate the DDL statements for objects created by all users in the database DEPARTMENT, and send the output to file db2look.sql:

```
db2look -d department -a -e -o db2look.sql
```

Generate the DDL statements for all user-defined nodegroups, buffer pools, and table spaces, and send the output to file db2look.sql:

```
db2look -d department -l -o db2look.sql
```

Generate the UPDATE statements for the database and database manager configuration parameters, as well as the DB2SET statements for the registry variables in database DEPARTMENT, and send the output to file db2look.sql:

```
db2look -d department -f -o db2look.sql
```

DB2MOVE

DB2MOVE allows you to automate EXPORTing many tables. IMPORTing or LOADing these tables into a target database is also automated. This is ideal for moving databases between operating systems where DB2 backup/restore cannot be used (for example, moving tables from Windows to Linux). DB2 backup/restore can be used between HP-UX and Solaris. Any other operating system change for a database can benefit from DB2MOVE. See also DB2LOOK (previously) and the -e option for extracting DDL and DCL.

DB2MOVE queries the catalog tables and compiles a list of all user tables. It then EXPORTs these tables in PC/IXF format. The files can be IMPORTed or LOADed to another local DB2 database on the same system, or they can be transferred to another workstation platform and IMPORTed. Tables with structured type columns are not moved when this tool is used.

Authorization

DB2MOVE calls the DB2 EXPORTIMPORTLOADEXPORT, IMPORT, and LOAD APIs, depending on the action requested by the user. Therefore, the requesting user ID must have the correct authorization required by those APIs, or the request will fail.

Syntax

```
                               .----------------------------.
                               V                            |
>>-db2move--dbname--action-------+--------------------+--+---><
                               +--tc--table-creators--+
                               +--tn--table-names-----+
                               +--io--IMPORT-option---+
                               +--lo--LOAD-option-----+
                               +--l--lobpaths---------+
                               +--u--userid-----------+
                               '--p--password---------'
```

Description

DB2MOVE EXPORTs, IMPORTs, or LOADs only user-created tables. If a database is to be duplicated from one operating system to another operating system, you also need to move other objects. DB2LOOK (see previously) can help with triggers, views, distinct types (user-defined data types), user-defined functions, and indexes. DDL is also typically recorded in a column called TEXT for metaobject catalogs like SYSCAT.TRIGGERS and SYSCAT.VIEWS.

When EXPORT, IMPORT, or LOAD APIs are called by DB2MOVE, the FileTypeMod parameter is set to lobsinfile, so LOB data is kept in separate files from the PC/IXF files. There are 26,000 filenames available for LOB files. The table space where the LOADed tables reside is placed in backup pending state and is not accessible. A full database backup, or a table space backup, is required to take the table space out of backup pending state.

The following are the descriptions for each DB2MOVE parameter:

- **dbname** Specifies the name of the database.
- **action** Sets one of EXPORT, IMPORT, or LOAD. EXPORT creates the IXF files. IMPORT or LOAD puts them into the target database.
- **-tc** Specifies the table creators, and the default is all creators. This is only an EXPORT action. If specified, only those tables created by the creators listed with this option are EXPORTed. If not specified, the default is to use all creators. When specifying multiple creators, separate each by a comma; no blanks are allowed between creator IDs. The maximum number of creators that can be specified is ten. This option can be used with the *-tn* table-names option to select the tables for EXPORT. An asterisk (*) can be used as a wildcard character that can be placed anywhere in the string. For example, USA* captures all tables created by users who start with USA.

- **-tn** Specifies the table names; the default is all user tables. This only is an EXPORT action. If specified, only those tables whose names match exactly those in the specified string are EXPORTed. If not specified, the default is to use all user tables. When specifying multiple table names, separate each by a comma. No blanks are allowed between table names. The maximum number of table names that can be specified is ten. This option can be used with the *-tc* table-creators option to select the tables for EXPORT. DB2MOVE only EXPORTs those tables whose names are matched with specified table names and whose creators are matched with specified table creators. An asterisk (*) can be used as a wildcard character that can be placed anywhere in the string.

- **-io** Specifies the IMPORT option; the default is REPLACE_CREATE. Valid options are INSERT, INSERT_UPDATE, REPLACE, CREATE, and REPLACE_CREATE.

- **-lo** Specifies the LOAD option; the default is INSERT. Valid options are INSERT and REPLACE.

- **-l** Specifies the LOB paths; the default is the current directory. This option specifies the absolute pathnames where LOB files are created (as part of EXPORT) or searched for (as part of IMPORT or LOAD). When specifying multiple LOB paths, separate each by a comma; no blanks are allowed between LOB paths. If the first path runs out of space (during EXPORT), or the files are not found in the path (during IMPORT or LOAD), the second path will be used, and so on. If the action is EXPORT and LOB paths are specified, all files in the LOB path directories are deleted, the directories are removed, and new directories are created. If not specified, the current directory is used for the LOB path.

- **-u** Specifies the user ID; the default is the logged on user ID. Both user ID and password are optional. However, if one is specified, the other must be specified. If the command is run on a client connecting to a remote server, user ID and password should be specified.

- **-p** Specifies the password; the default is the logged on password. Both user ID and password are optional. However, if one is specified, the other must be specified.

The following files are required and generated when using EXPORT:

- **EXPORT.out** The summarized result of the EXPORT action.

- **db2move.lst** The list of original table names, their corresponding PC/IXF filenames (tabnnn.ixf), and message filenames (tabnnn.msg). This list, the EXPORTed PC/IXF files, and LOB files (tabnnnc.yyy) are used as input to the DB2MOVE IMPORT or LOAD action.

- **tabnnn.ixf** The EXPORTed PC/IXF file of a specific table.

- **tabnnn.msg** The EXPORT message file of the corresponding table.

- **tabnnnc.yyy** The EXPORTed LOB files of a specific table. *nnn* is the table number. *c* is a letter of the alphabet. *yyy* is a number ranging from 001 to 999. These files are created only if the table being EXPORTed contains LOB data.

If created, these LOB files are placed in the lobpath directories. There are a total of 26,000 possible names for the LOB files.

- **system.msg** The message file containing system messages for creating or deleting file or directory commands. This is used only if the action is EXPORT, and a LOB path is specified.

The following files are required and generated when using IMPORT:

- Input:
  - **db2move.lst** An output file from the EXPORT action.
  - **tabnnn.ixf** An output file from the EXPORT action.
  - **tabnnnc.yyy** An output file from the EXPORT action.
- Output:
  - **IMPORT.out** The summarized result of the IMPORT action.
  - **tabnnn.msg** The IMPORT message file of the corresponding table.

The following files are required and generated when using LOAD:

- Input:
  - **db2move.lst** An output file from the EXPORT action.
  - **tabnnn.ixf** An output file from the EXPORT action.
  - **tabnnnc.yyy** An output file from the EXPORT action.
- Output:
  - **LOAD.out** The summarized result of the LOAD action.
  - **tabnnn.msg** The LOAD message file of the corresponding table.

Example

EXPORT the tables EMPLOYEE, EMP_ACT, EMP_PHOTO, and EMP_RESUME from the sample database:

```
db2move sample EXPORT -tn emp*
```

EXPORT all tables in the SAMPLE database; default values are used for all options:

```
db2move sample EXPORT
```

EXPORT all tables created by userid1 or user IDs LIKE us%rid2, and with the name tbname1 or table names LIKE %tbname2:

```
db2move sample EXPORT -tc userid1,us*rid2 -tn tbname1,*tbname2
```

IMPORT all tables in the SAMPLE database on Windows using LOB paths D:\LOBPATH1 and C:\LOBPATH2 to search for LOB files:

```
db2move sample IMPORT -l D:\LOBPATH1,C:\LOBPATH2
```

On UNIX, LOAD all tables in the SAMPLE database; both the /home/userid/lobpath subdirectory and the tmp subdirectory are searched for LOB files:

```
db2move sample LOAD -l /home/userid/lobpath,/tmp
```

DB2MSCS

DB2MSCS creates the infrastructure for DB2 to support failover on the Windows environment using MSCS. This command can be used to enable failover in both single-partition and partitioned database environments. Failover is described in the *Data Recovery and High Availability Guide and Reference.*

Authorization

The user must be logged on to a domain user account that belongs to the Administrators group of each machine in the MSCS cluster.

Syntax

```
>>-db2mscs----+-----------------+-----------------------------><
              '--f:--input_file--'
```

Description

The -f:input_file parameter specifies the DB2MSCS.CFG input file used by the MSCS utility. If not specified, the DB2MSCS command reads the DB2MSCS.CFG file in the current directory.

DB2PERFC

DB2PERFC resets the database performance values in the Windows performance monitor. While DB2 has its own event analyzer and event monitor for performance monitoring in the Control Center, you may choose to use the performance monitor if large Windows applications like a web server are on the same machine as DB2, or if you're comfortable with the performance monitor.

DB2PERFC resets the performance values for one or more databases. When an application calls the DB2 monitor APIs, the information returned is normally the cumulative values since the DB2 server was started. DB2PERFC allows you to reset the performance values, run a test, reset the values again, and then rerun the test.

Syntax

```
>--db2perfc---------------------------------------------------><
```

DB2PERFI

DB2PERFI registers the DB2 for Windows performance counters. This must be done to make DB2 and DB2 Connect performance information accessible to the performance monitor. It also enables any other Windows application using the Win32 performance APIs to get performance data.

Syntax

```
>--db2perfi----+-----i-------------+----------------------------><
               '-----u-------------'
```

Description

The following are the descriptions for the two DB2PERFI parameters:

- **-i** Installs the performance monitor counters.
- **-u** Removes (uninstalls) the performance monitor counters.

DB2PERFR

DB2PERFR registers a Windows administrator user to see objects from another DB2 Windows machine. (You cannot use the default performance monitor user because SYSTEM is a DB2 reserved word.)

Syntax

```
>--db2perfr----+--r <UserId> <Password> --+----------------------------><
               '--u----------------------'
```

Description

The following are the descriptions for the two DB2PERFR parameters:

- **DB2PerfR -r <UserId> <Password>** Registers a user to view performance information from a remote DB2 Windows machine
- **DB2PerfR –u** Removes the user

REFERENCE

Example

Register the Windows Administrator adamache with the password blairpassw:

```
db2perfr -r adamache blairpassw
```

 # DB2RBIND

Run DB2RBIND to rebind all packages for a database. This is useful if you have installed a new FixPak or level of DB2. If DB2RBIND is not run, each package gets implicitly rebound the first time it is run on the new level of DB2, which can take a little time. If you don't have time to run DB2RBIND, you can avoid implicit rebinding by explicitly using BIND or REBIND for particular packages.

Authorization

SYSADM or DBADM.

Syntax

```
>>-db2rbind--database--/l logfile----+------+----------------->
                                     '-all--'

                                              .-conservative--.
>-----+------------------------+--/r--+-any-----------+------><
       '-/u userid--/p password--'
```

Description

The following are the descriptions for the DB2RBIND parameters:

■ **database** Specifies the database in which packages are revalidated.

■ **/l** Specifies the optional path and mandatory filename used for recording errors that result from running DB2RBIND.

■ **all** Rebinds all valid and invalid packages. If *all* is not specified, all packages in the database are checked, but only those packages marked invalid are rebound. This removes the need for rebinding the next time the application runs.

■ **/u** Specifies the user ID; this must be specified if a password is specified.

■ **/p** Specifies the password; required if a user ID is specified.

■ **/r Resolve** Specifies whether rebinding of the package is to be performed with conservative binding semantics. This affects whether new functions and data types are considered during function resolution and type resolution on static DML statements in the package. Valid values are as follows:

- **conservative** Functions and types only in the SQL path that were defined before the last explicit bind timestamp are considered for function and type resolution. This is the default.

- **any** Any of the functions and types in the SQL path are considered for function and type resolution.

DB2SAMPL

DB2SAMPL creates the SAMPLE database. Its tables are described in Appendix G of the *SQL Reference*.

Authorization

SYSADM or SYSCTRL.

Syntax

```
>>-db2sampl--+------+--+----+-------------------------------><
             '-path-'  '--k-'
```

Description

The following are the descriptions for the two DB2SAMPL parameters:

- **path** The path on which to create the SAMPLE database. A single drive letter for OS/2 and Windows. If not specified, SAMPLE is created on the default database path (the *dftdbpath* parameter in the database manager configuration). On UNIX, the default is the home directory of the instance owner. On OS/2 or Windows, it is the root directory (where DB2 is installed).

- **-k** create primary keys on the following SAMPLE tables. For example,

```
Table           Primary Key
-----           -----------
DEPARTMENT      DEPTNO
EMPLOYEE        EMPNO
ORG             DEPTNUMB
PROJECT         PROJNO
STAFF           ID
```

On Windows, see also db2sampk.bat in the \samples\db2sampl directory, which can add primary keys to the sample database if *-k* was not specified. db2sampk.bat runs these statements:

```
ALTER TABLE department ADD PRIMARY KEY (deptno)
ALTER TABLE employee ADD PRIMARY KEY (empno)
ALTER TABLE org ADD PRIMARY KEY (deptnumb)
ALTER TABLE project ADD PRIMARY KEY (projno)
ALTER TABLE staff ADD PRIMARY KEY (id)
ALTER TABLE staffg ADD PRIMARY KEY (id)
```

The user ID issuing the command is used as the qualifier for the tables in SAMPLE. If SAMPLE already exists, DB2SAMPL creates the tables for the user ID issuing the command and grants the appropriate privileges.

DB2SET

Registry and environment variables are set in DB2 using DB2SET. See also UPDATE DATABASE MANAGER CONFIGURATION for instance configuration parameters (applicable to all databases managed by the instance) and UPDATE DATABASE CONFIGURATION.

Authorization

SYSADM.

Syntax

```
>>-db2set----+------------------+------------------------------->
             '-variable=--value--'

>-----+------------------------------------------+---+-------+------>
      +--g-----------------------------------+    '--all--'
      '-+----------------------------------+-'
        '--i--instance--+-------------+--'
                        '-node-number--'

>-----+--------+---+-------------------------------+---------->
      '--null--'   '--r--instance--+-------------+--'
                                   '-node-number--'

>-----+--------------------------------------------------+------>
```

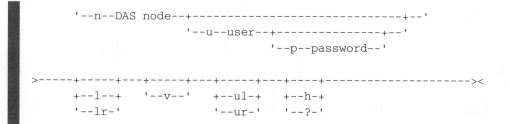

```
        '--n--DAS node--+----------------------------+--'
                        '--u--user--+--------------+--'
                                    '--p--password--'

>-----+-----+---+-----+---+-----+---+----+-------------------->< 
      +--l--+   '--v--'   +--ul-+   +--h-+
      '--lr-'             '--ur-'   '--?-'
```

Description

The following are the descriptions for the DB2SET parameters:

- **variable= value** Sets a variable to the value.

- **-g** Accesses the global profile variables (for example, DB2SYSTEM, DB2PATH, DB2INSTDEF, DB2COMM, DB2ADMINSERVER).

- **-i** Specifies the instance profile to use instead of the current or default.

- **node-number** Used only with EEE, a node number from 0–999 that must match a node number listed in the db2nodes.cfg file.

- **-all** Displays all occurrences of the local environment variables as defined in the following:

  - The environment, denoted by [e]

  - The node level registry, denoted by [n]

  - The instance level registry, denoted by [i]

  - The global level registry, denoted by [g]

- **-null** Sets the value of the variable at the specified registry level to NULL. This avoids having to look up the value in the next registry level.

- **-r instance** Resets the profile registry for the instance.

- **-n DAS node** Specifies the remote DB2 Administration Server node name.

- **-u user** Specifies the user ID for the Administration Server attachment.

- **-p password** Specifies the password for the Administration Server attachment.

- **-l** Lists all instance profiles.

- **-lr** Lists all supported registry variables.

- **-v** Specifies VERBOSE mode, providing more information.

- **-ul** Accesses the user profile variables (supported only on Windows).

- **-ur** Refreshes the user profile variables (supported only on Windows).

- **-h/-?** Displays help. All other options are ignored, and only the help is shown.

Changes to settings take effect after the instance has been restarted. To delete a variable, specify variable=, followed by no value.

Example

Display all defined profiles (DB2 instances):

```
db2set -l
```

Display all supported registry variables:

```
db2set -lr
```

Display all defined global variables:

```
db2set -g
```

Display all defined variables for the current instance:

```
db2set
```

Display all defined values for the current instance:

```
db2set -all
```

Turn off the binary sort algorithm (db2_binsort can improve sort performance):

```
db2set db2_binsort=NO
```

Allow the optimizer to use hash joins in addition to other join methods (merge and nested loop):

```
db2set db2_hash_join=YES
```

Display all defined values for DB2COMM for the current instance:

```
db2set -all DB2COMM
```

Reset all defined variables for the instance INST on node 3:

```
db2set -r -i INST 3
```

Set the variable DB2COMM to be TCP/IP globally:

```
db2set -g DB2COMM=TCPIP
```

Set the variable DB2COMM to null at the given instance level:

```
db2set -null DB2COMM
```

DB2START

DB2START starts the current database manager instance background processes on a single node or on all the nodes defined in a multinode environment. You need to start the DB2 server before connecting to a database, precompiling an application, or binding a package to a database. DB2START calls START DATABASE MANAGER.

DB2STOP

DB2STOP stops the current database manager. DB2STOP calls STOP DATABASE MANAGER.

DB2TBST

DB2TBST translates hex values from LIST TABLESPACES to tell you the state of the table space in English.

Authorization

None.

Syntax

```
>>-db2tbst--tablespace-state---------------------------------><
```

Description

These are the possible states (also available in SQLLIB\INCLUDE\sqlutil.h):

Hex Value	State of Table Space
0x0	Normal
0x1	Quiesced: SHARE
0x2	Quiesced: UPDATE

Hex Value	State of Table Space
0x4	Quiesced: EXCLUSIVE
0x8	LOAD pending
0x10	Delete pending
0x20	Backup pending
0x40	Roll forward in progress
0x80	Roll forward pending
0x100	Restore pending
0x100	Recovery pending (not used)
0x200	Disable pending
0x400	Reorg in progress
0x800	Backup in progress
0x1000	Storage must be defined
0x2000	Restore in progress
0x4000	Offline and not accessible
0x8000	Drop pending
0x2000000	Storage may be defined
0x4000000	StorDef is in 'final' state
0x8000000	StorDef was changed prior to rollforward
0x10000000	DMS rebalancer is active
0x20000000	TBS deletion in progress
0x40000000	TBS creation in progress
0x8	For IBM service use only

Example

```
Determine the values of states 0x2000 and 0x0000:db2tbst 0x2000
State = Restore in Progress
db2tbst 0x0000
State = Normal
```

DB2TRC

DB2TRC activates DB2 tracing of events, dumps trace data to a file, and formats trace data into a readable form.

Authorization

On UNIX: SYSADM, SYSCTRL, or SYSMAINT. On OS/2 or Windows: No authorization required.

Syntax

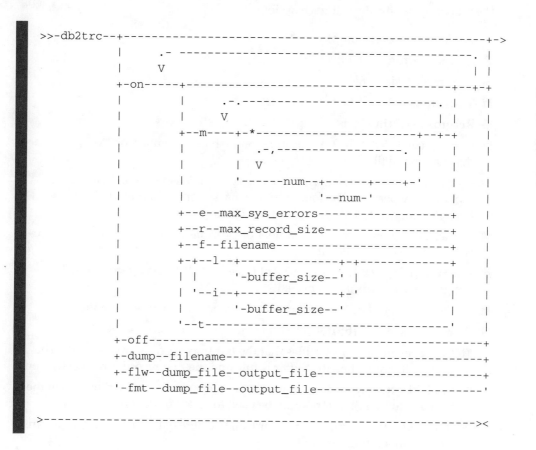

```
>>-db2trc--+------------------------------------------------+->
           |         .- -------------------------------------. |
           |         V                                      | |
           +-on-----+----------------------------------+--+-+
           |        |           .-.------------------.  |   |
           |        |           V                  |  |   |
           |        +--m----+--*--------------------+--+-+  |
           |        |       |     .-,-------------.  |   |  |
           |        |       |     V             |  |   |  |
           |        |       '------num--+------+----+-'  |   |  |
           |        |                   '--num-'        |   |  |
           |        +--e--max_sys_errors----------------+   |
           |        +--r--max_record_size---------------+   |
           |        +--f--filename----------------------+   |
           |        +-+--l--+-------------+-+-----------+   |
           |        | |     '-buffer_size--' |          |   |
           |        | '--i--+-------------+-'           |   |
           |        |       '-buffer_size--'            |   |
           |        '--t-------------------------------'   |
           +-off------------------------------------------+
           +-dump--filename-------------------------------+
           +-flw--dump_file--output_file------------------+
           '-fmt--dump_file--output_file------------------'

   >----------------------------------------------------------><
```

Description

The following are the descriptions for the DB2TRC parameters:

- **on** Starts DB2 trace.
- **dump** Sends trace information to a file. The file is saved in the current directory unless the path is specified.
- **off** Turns trace off.
- **flw | fmt flw** Sorts by DB2 process (UNIX) or thread (Windows and OS/2). fmt shows events chronologically. For either option, specify the name of the dump file and the name of the output file that will be generated.

The following are the default trace options:

- **mask** * (trace everything)
- **max_sys_errors** -1 (collect all)
- **max_record_size** 16KB
- **Trace destination** -s (shared memory)
- **Records to retain** - l (last)
- **buffer_size** 64KB if the trace destination is shared memory, or 1MB if the trace destination is a file.
- **-m mask** Traces specific events. The mask variable is four one-byte masks separated by periods. The four one-byte masks correspond to products, event types, components, and functions, respectively.
- **-e max_sys_errors** Limits the number of DB2 internal system errors the trace will hold to max_sys_errors.
- **-r max_record_size** Limits the size of trace records to max_record_size bytes. Longer trace records are truncated.
- **-f filename** Specifies trace buffer location in shared memory or a file.
- **-l [buffer_size] | -i [buffer_size]** specifies the buffer size as one of:
  - **'-l' ("l" as in "last")** Specifies that the last trace records are retained. (The trace will wrap when the buffer is full, and the first records are overwritten.)
  - **'-i'** Initial trace records are retained (no more records are written when the buffer is full). Either option can be used to pick a buffer size.
  - **-t** Includes timestamps. (Valid for UNIX, where gathering timestamps can slow the operating system.)

By convention, unformatted traces should use the file extension .dmp. Traces formatted with flw should have the extension .flw. Traces formatted with fmt should have the extension .fmt.

Example

Write the current trace buffer contents to db2trc.dmp:

```
db2trc dump db2trc.dmp
```

Turn off the trace:

```
db2trc off
```

Format the trace in db2trc.dmp, order by process or thread, and write it to db2trc.flw:

```
db2trc flw db2trc.dmp db2trc.flw
```

DB2UNTAG

DB2UNTAG removes the DB2 tag on a table space container. The tag prevents data loss by stopping DB2 from reusing a container in more than one table space (like the "do not record" tab on the bottom of an audio or video cassette). DB2UNTAG also displays information about the container tag, identifying the database with which the container is associated. Use this to release a container owned by a database that has since been deleted.

 Pay attention to what you're doing when using DB2UNTAG—you can lose data and even destroy the database if you make a mistake. Removing the tag from a table space with active production data will likely cause users to lose all access to the data.

Authorization

Requires read/write access to the container for a table space that is owned by the ID that created the database.

Syntax

```
>>-db2untag---f--filename-------------------------------------><
```

Description

For DB2UNTAG, -f filename specifies the fully qualified name of the table space container from which the DB2 tag is to be removed. A container can be used by only one table space at a time.

An SQLCODE -294 (Container in Use error) is typically returned from any command (CREATE DATABASE, CREATE TABLESPACE, ALTER TABLESPACE) if the container is already owned by another table space. If the database that used the container has been dropped, you can use the DB2UNTAG command to make the container reusable. For SMS containers, remove the directory and its contents by using the appropriate delete commands. For DMS raw containers, either delete the file or device, or let DB2UNTAG remove the container tag. DB2UNTAG leaves such a DMS container otherwise unmodified.

DB2UPDV7

DB2UPDV7 is used after installing a new DB2 FixPak or released to enable new functions or column types (such as generated sequence columns introduced in DB2 version 7.1, FixPak 3).

Syntax

```
>>-db2updv7---d--dbname--+-------------------------+---->
                         '--u--userid---p--password-'

--+----+---+----+------------------------------------><
   '--h-'    '--n-'
```

Description

The following are the descriptions for the DB2UPDV7 parameters:

- **-d <dbname>** Specifies the database to be updated
- **-u <userid>** Specifies the user ID for database connection; must be used with -p.
- **-p <password>** Specifies the password for database connection; must be used with –u.
- **-h** Shows help.
- **-n** Disables the warning prompt. Specifying this option indicates that you accept this risk: "Warning: Processing of this command will change the database to run with this level (or higher) of the database manager. You will not be able to run this database with any previous FixPak level. A full offline backup of the database should be performed prior to running DB2UPDV7 to restore to the previous FixPak level."

Index

D

E

M

U

INTERNATIONAL CONTACT INFORMATION

AUSTRALIA
McGraw-Hill Book Company Australia Pty. Ltd.
TEL +61-2-9417-9899
FAX +61-2-9417-5687
http://www.mcgraw-hill.com.au
books-it_sydney@mcgraw-hill.com

CANADA
McGraw-Hill Ryerson Ltd.
TEL +905-430-5000
FAX +905-430-5020
http://www.mcgrawhill.ca

**GREECE, MIDDLE EAST,
NORTHERN AFRICA**
McGraw-Hill Hellas
TEL +30-1-656-0990-3-4
FAX +30-1-654-5525

MEXICO (Also serving Latin America)
McGraw-Hill Interamericana Editores S.A. de C.V.
TEL +525-117-1583
FAX +525-117-1589
http://www.mcgraw-hill.com.mx
fernando_castellanos@mcgraw-hill.com

SINGAPORE (Serving Asia)
McGraw-Hill Book Company
TEL +65-863-1580
FAX +65-862-3354
http://www.mcgraw-hill.com.sg
mghasia@mcgraw-hill.com

SOUTH AFRICA
McGraw-Hill South Africa
TEL +27-11-622-7512
FAX +27-11-622-9045
robyn_swanepoel@mcgraw-hill.com

**UNITED KINGDOM & EUROPE
(Excluding Southern Europe)**
McGraw-Hill Education Europe
TEL +44-1-628-502500
FAX +44-1-628-770224
http://www.mcgraw-hill.co.uk
computing_neurope@mcgraw-hill.com

ALL OTHER INQUIRIES Contact:
Osborne/McGraw-Hill
TEL +1-510-549-6600
FAX +1-510-883-7600
http://www.osborne.com
omg_international@mcgraw-hill.com